Collaborative and Social Information Retrieval and Access:
Techniques for Improved User Modeling

Max Chevalier
University of Toulouse, IRIT (UMR 5505), France

Christine Julien
University of Toulouse, IRIT (UMR 5505), France

Chantal Soulé-Dupuy
University of Toulouse, IRIT (UMR 5505), France

T0344281

INFORMATION SCIENCE REFERENCE

Hershey · New York

Director of Editorial Content:	Kristin Klinger
Director of Production:	Jennifer Neidig
Managing Editor:	Jamie Snavely
Assistant Managing Editor:	Carole Coulson
Typesetter:	Jeff Ash
Cover Design:	Lisa Tosheff
Printed at:	Yurchak Printing Inc.

Published in the United States of America by
Information Science Reference (an imprint of IGI Global)
701 E. Chocolate Avenue, Suite 200
Hershey PA 17033
Tel: 717-533-8845
Fax: 717-533-8661
E-mail: cust@igi-global.com
Web site: http://www.igi-global.com

and in the United Kingdom by
Information Science Reference (an imprint of IGI Global)
3 Henrietta Street
Covent Garden
London WC2E 8LU
Tel: 44 20 7240 0856
Fax: 44 20 7379 0609
Web site: http://www.eurospanbookstore.com

Library of Congress Cataloging-in-Publication Data

Collaborative and social information retrieval and access : techniques for improved user modeling / Max Chevalier, Christine Julien, and Chantal Soule-Dupuy, editors.

    p. cm.

Includes bibliographical references and index.

Summary: "This book deals with the improvement of user modeling in the context of Collaborative and Social Information Access and Retrieval (CSIRA) techniques"--Provided by publisher.

ISBN 978-1-60566-306-7 (hardcover) -- ISBN 978-1-60566-307-4 (ebook)

1. User interfaces (Computer systems) 2. Recommender systems (Information filtering) 3. Information storage and retrieval systems--Social aspects. 4. Cognitive science. I. Chevalier, Max, 1975- II. Julien, Christine. III. Soule-Dupuy, Chantal.

QA76.9.U83C62 2009

005.4'37--dc22

                    2008040202

British Cataloguing in Publication Data
A Cataloguing in Publication record for this book is available from the British Library.

Table of Contents

Section I
User Modeling in Collaborative and Social
Information Retrieval and Access (CSIRA)

Section II
Advances in User Modeling in CSIRA

Section III
Improved User Modeling:
Application of CSIRA

Section IV
Selected Readings

Detailed Table of Contents

Section I
User Modeling in Collaborative and Social
Information Retrieval and Access (CSIRA)

Chapter I

> *Laurent Candillier, Orange Labs Lannion, France*
> *Kris Jack, Orange Labs Lannion, France*
> *Françoise Fessant, Orange Labs Lannion, France*
> *Frank Meyer, Orange Labs Lannion, France*

This chapter describes the state of the art related to recommender systems. It deals with the three main types of filtering techniques and the way such techniques can be evaluated.

Chapter II

> *Neal Lathia, University College London, UK*

This chapter is focused on Collaborative Filtering techniques underlying different issues and system vulnerabilities. The chapter also presents a discussion related to when such techniques should be used, and how recommendations are generated or evaluated.

Section II
Advances in User Modeling in CSIRA

Chapter III

Edwin Simpson, HP Labs, UK
Mark H. Butler, HP Labs, UK

This chapter investigates methods for enabling improved navigation, user modeling, and personalization using collaboratively generated tags. The authors discuss the advantages and limitations of tags, and describe how relationships between tags can be used to discover latent structures that can automatically organize a collection of tags owned by a community.

Chapter IV

Steve Cayzer, Hewlett-Packard Laboratories, UK
Elke Michlmayr, Vienna University of Technology, Austria

This chapter shows how a user profile can be built without any explicit input. Based on implicit behavior on social information networks, the profiles which are created are both adaptive (up to date) and socially connective. The proposed approach relies on the use of a Collaborative Tagging System like Delicious.

Chapter V

Eugene Santos, Jr., Dartmouth College, USA
Hien Nguyen, University of Wisconsin - Whitewater, USA

The authors of this chapter study and present their results on the problem of employing a cognitive user model for Information Retrieval (IR) in which a user's intent is captured and used for improving his/her effectiveness in an information seeking task. The user intent is captured by analyzing the commonality of the retrieved relevant documents.

Chapter VI

Mihaela Brut, Alexandru Ioan Cuza University of Iasi, Romania
Florence Sedes, Institut de Recherche en Informatique de Toulouse, France
Corinne Zayani, Institut de Recherche en Informatique de Toulouse, France

This chapter explores a Semantic Web-based modeling approach for document annotations and user competencies profile development. This approach is based on a same domain ontology set, which constitutes the binder between materials and users. A variant of the nearest neighbor algorithm is applied to recommend concepts of interest and then document contents according to competencies profiles.

Section III
Improved User Modeling:
Application of CSIRA

Chapter VII

Colum Foley, Dublin City University, Ireland
Alan F. Smeaton, Dublin City University, Ireland
Gareth J. F. Jones, Dublin City University, Ireland

This chapter explores the effectiveness of a sharing of knowledge policy on a collaborating group in order to satisfy a shared information need. The search engine exploits user relevance judgments to propose a new ranked list.

Chapter VIII

Charles Delalonde, EDF R&D, France
Eddie Soulier, Université de Technologie de Troyes, France

This chapter suggests a social search engine that identifies documents, but more specifically, users relevant to a query. It relies on a transparent profile construction based upon user activity, community participation, and shared documents.

Chapter IX

Hager Karoui, Université Paris XIII, France

This chapter proposes a Peer-to-Peer bibliographical reference recommender system. It consists in finding relevant documents and interesting people related to the interests and preferences of a single person belonging to a like-minded.

Chapter X

Zehra Cataltepe, Istanbul Technical University, Turkey
Berna Altinel, Istanbul Technical University, Turkey

Collaborative, content-based, and case-based recommendation systems and their hybrids have been used for music recommendation. This chapter shows how specific user information can be used to improve user model for ameliorate music recommendation accuracy.

This chapter is dedicated to a novel machine learning (based on reinforcement learning) perspective toward the Web recommendation problem. A hybrid Web recommendation method is proposed by making use of the conceptual relationships among Web resources to derive a novel model of the problem, enriched with semantic knowledge about the usage behavior. The method is evaluated under different settings and it is shown how this method can improve the overall quality of recommendations.

This chapter presents a twofold approach for adapting content information delivered to a group of mobile users. It is based on a filtering process which considers both the user's current context and her/his preferences for this context.

Section IV
Selected Readings

This chapter describes the user-centered design approach we adopted in the development and evaluation of an adaptive Web site. The development of usable Web sites, offering easy and efficient services to heterogeneous users, is a hot topic and a challenging issue for Adaptive Hypermedia and Human-Computer Interaction. User-centered design promises to facilitate this task by guiding system designers in making decisions, which take the user's needs in serious account. Within a recent project funded by the Italian Public Administration, we developed a prototype information system supporting the on-line search of data about water resources. As the system was targeted to different types of users, including generic citizens and specialized technicians, we adopted a user-centered approach to identify their information needs and interaction requirements. Moreover, we applied query analysis techniques to identify further information needs and speed up the data retrieval activity. In this chapter we describe the requirements analysis, the system design and its evaluation.

Chapter XIV

Antonella Carbonaro, University of Bologna, Italy
Rodolfo Ferrini, University of Bologna, Italy

Active learning is the ability of learners to carry out learning activities in such a way that they will be able to effectively and efficiently construct knowledge from information sources. Personalized and customizable access on digital materials collected from the Web according to one's own personal requirements and interests is an example of active learning. Moreover, it is also necessary to provide techniques to locate suitable materials. In this paper, we introduce a personalized learning environment providing intelligent support to achieve the expectations of active learning. The system exploits collaborative and semantic approaches to extract concepts from documents and maintaining user and resources profiles based on domain ontologies. In such a way, the retrieval phase takes advantage from the common knowledge base used to extract useful knowledge and produces personalized views of the learning system.

Chapter XV

Hanh Huu Hoang, Vienna University of Technology, Austria
Tho Manh Nguyen, Vienna University of Technology, Austria
A Min Tjoa, Vienna University of Technology, Austria

Formulating unambiguous queries in the Semantic Web applications is a challenging task for users. This article presents a new approach in guiding users to formulate clear requests based on their common nature of querying for information. The approach known as the front-end approach gives users an overview about the system data through a virtual data component which stores the extracted metadata of the data storage sources in the form of an ontology. This approach reduces the ambiguities in users' requests at very early stage; and allows the query process effectively performs to fulfill users' demands in a context-aware manner. Furthermore, the approach provides a powerful query engine, called context-aware querying, that recommends the appropriate query patterns according to the user's querying context.

Foreword

New and complex modes of interaction in today's Web-based applications have resulted in ever increasing amounts of online information that is rich, dynamic, and interconnected. Although the proliferation of the new media and a variety of collaborative frameworks is continuing to impact the way we communicate, shop, entertain ourselves, conduct business, or develop relationships; it also exacerbates the age-old problem of information overload. More than ever, intelligent Web applications must be able to decipher the true intent of a user, to adapt to the user's changing preferences, to compare or connect that user to other users within a community or with similar interests, and to, finally, provide that user with pertinent and useful information.

Adaptive and personalized systems, such as recommender systems, have emerged as an important part of the solution to the information overload problem facing today's Web users. Combining ideas and techniques from information retrieval and filtering, user modeling, artificial intelligence, user interface design, and human-computer interaction, these systems provide users with proactive suggestions that are tailored to meet their particular information needs and preferences. Such systems typically accomplish tasks such as individualized information filtering, personalized search result re-ranking, or intelligent navigation support by relying on different sources of knowledge from implicit or explicit user feedback to encoded domain knowledge. As a result, personalized adaptive applications have enjoyed considerable commercial success and continue to play an increasingly important role in many online services, from Amazon and Yahoo!, to iTunes and Last.fm.

The ability of a personalization system to tailor content and recommend items implies that it must be able to infer what a user requires based on previous or current interactions with that user, and possibly other users. This, in turn, requires the collection and modeling of the data that accurately reflect the interests of a user or a community of users, as well as their interactions with other users and with available resources. The problem of user modeling, therefore, is the fundamental problem of the adaptive Web.

With the emergence of the "social Web" applications, in which users can collaboratively create, annotate, and share resources, the problem of user modeling has become even more challenging. Users connected (implicitly or explicitly) with their peers within online communities which are, themselves, interconnected. Furthermore, users' interests and preferences can be manifested in a variety of ways including free text annotation given to resources, the properties of communities to which they belong, the usage of available online resources, and the content of the accessed information.

User modeling for the adaptive social information access will require building on traditional techniques in order to harness the rich and complex underlying user data in order to create models of users' information needs, relationships, behavior or context, and use these models to improve the relevance of information offered to users. This edited volume, Collaborative and Social Information Retrieval and Access: Techniques for Improved User Modeling, is precisely intended to explore state-of-the-art and recent developments in this area, including foundational issues and advances in user modeling, as well as new applications in collaborative and social information retrieval and access.

The book begins with two survey-oriented chapters of recommender systems in general and collaborative filtering recommenders in particular, setting the stage for the exploration of more advanced and emerging concepts in user modeling. The second part of the book, focusing on advances in user modeling, provides a comprehensive view of the important problems and techniques in user modeling, as well as emerging challenges. The fundamental and emerging topics covered in this part include the use of social annotations (such as that used in collaborative tagging environments) to support navigation; the use of cognitive models to decipher users' information search intent; and the use of ontology-based domain knowledge in learning richer user models and using them for more effective recommendations.

An important aspect of the book is the collection of chapters in the third part, providing as a whole, a survey of the state-of-the-art in emerging trends, techniques, and applications in collaborative and social information retrieval and access. These chapters cover novel approaches to recommendation and adaptation from cooperative case-based reasoning to reinforcement learning to collaborative agents. The application covered in these chapters span a variety of typical domains involving new media or emerging collaborative frameworks, including collaborative information retrieval environments, music recommendation systems, content-based Web recommender systems, peer-to-peer bibliographic recommendation system, and mobile information management systems.

Overall, this volume represents a laudable effort by Max Chevalier, Christine Julien, and Chantal Soulé-Dupuy, to deal with some of the most challenging problems in adaptive and social Web domain the resolution of which will pave the way for a new generation of more useful and intelligent online information systems and services. The comprehensive set of topics, techniques and applications covered in the volume should provide an excellent guide for Web technology developers and an indispensible resource for researches interested in user modeling, personalization, and recommender systems.

Bamshad Mobasher
School of Computing, DePaul University, Chicago

Bamshad Mobasher is a professor of Computer Science and the director of the Center for Web Intelligence at the School of Computing of DePaul University in Chicago. His research areas include Web mining, Web personalization, predictive user modeling, agent-based systems, and information retrieval. He has published more than 100 scientific articles, numerous book chapters, and several edited books in these areas. Dr. Mobasher received his PhD at Iowa State University in 1994. Prior to DePaul he was an assistant professor of Computer Science at the University of Minnesota, Twin Cities, where he did some seminal work on Web mining and started some of the first research groups focusing on Web Usage Mining. Dr. Mobasher is considered one of the leading authorities in the areas of Web mining, Web personalization, and recommender systems, and has served as an organizer and on the program committees of numerous related conferences. Some of his original articles on Web usage mining have citations indexes of 1000 or more. His work in these areas has been used by a variety of companies, including Amazon.com, as part of their analytics and personalization systems. As the director of the Center for Web Intelligence, Dr. Mobasher is directing research in Web mining, Web analytics, and personalization, as well as overseeing several related joint projects with the industry. His most recent activities include an edited volume, "Intelligent Techniques for Web Personalization", published by Springer, culminating from a series of successful workshops at IJCAI and AAAI on the same topic; and a special issue of ACM Transactions on Internet Technologies on Web personalization. He has also been one of the founding organizers of the highly successful WebKDD workshops on Knowledge discovery on the Web which have been held at ACM SIGKDD conference for the past 10 years. He is currently editing a special issue of User Modeling and User Adapted Interaction on Data Mining for Personalization, and he is the program co-chair of the 2008 ACM International Conference on Recommender Systems. He serves on the editorial boards of several prominent computing journals, including User Modeling and User-Adapted Interaction, and the Journal of Web Semantics.

Preface

This book deals with the improvement of user modeling in the context of Collaborative and Social Information Retrieval and Access (CSIRA) techniques. Information retrieval and access techniques are aimed at helping users to find information relevant to their needs. Today, in order to improve their effectiveness, some specific techniques have to take into account external characteristics such as those related to the user (and his context) which are most of the time little or not known by the system. Nevertheless we can observe that the applications related to the Web 2.0 which integrate users' characteristics bring rather best results and at least personalized results.

It thus seems acquired that the collaborative and social aspects characterizing the users' social context can be used to improve the way the information access and retrieval systems "know" each user through user modeling approaches.

Consequently improving user modeling taking into account social and collaborative aspects for information retrieval and access is a vast domain in which several disciplines intervene (computer science, cognitive science, information science, etc.). This is a recent research trend that integrates recommender systems, social networks analysis (Wasserman et al., 1994), adaptive information retrieval, user modeling, and social information retrieval (Kirsh, 2003) techniques and so on.

The objective of this book is to draw up a panorama of the concepts, techniques. and applications linked to CSIRA. This book is aimed at readers of any disciplines (information science or information technology, cognitive science, computer science, etc.) and contributes to the diffusion of the concepts to any public (graduate and post-graduate students, information system designers, information retrieval system designers, scientists, etc.).

ORGANIZATION

This book presents operational and innovative ideas to integrate user modeling in order to improve CSIRA effectiveness. This book includes twelve chapters gathered in three sections. Section I covers generalities related to user modeling in the context. Section II deals with advances in user modeling and Section III presents some applications of such improved user modeling.

As it can be seen in the following description of the chapters, the contributions cover a large scope of techniques to improve user modeling in such a context. The reference section in each chapter includes numerous reference sources to help interested readers to find comprehensive sources and additional information.

Section I

User Modeling in CSIRA

This section introduces one of the classical techniques of CSIRA and the way users are taken into account in these techniques. The two chapters are focused on recommender systems that are tools aiming at helping users to find items/information that they should consider as relevant from huge catalogues.

Chapter I describes the state of the art related to recommender systems. It deals with the three main types of filtering techniques and the way such techniques can be evaluated.

Chapter II is focused on Collaborative Filtering techniques underlying different issues and system vulnerabilities. This chapter also presents a discussion related to when such techniques should be used, how recommendations are generated / evaluated.

Section II

Advances in User Modeling in CSIRA

Through four chapters, this section is dedicated to the introduction of some advances in user modeling. Those advances are based on novel approaches taking into account communal tags, ontology-based semantic features, user intents and competencies.

Chapter III investigates methods for enabling improved navigation, user modeling and personalization using collaboratively generated tags. The authors discuss the advantages and limitations of tags, and describe how relationships between tags can be used to discover latent structures that can automatically organize a collection of tags owned by a community.

Chapter IV shows how a user profile can be built without any explicit input. Based on implicit behavior on social information networks, the profiles which are created are both adaptive (up to date) and socially connective. The proposed approach relies on the use of a Collaborative Tagging System like *Delicious*.

The authors of **Chapter V** study and present their results on the problem of employing a cognitive user model for Information Retrieval (IR) in which a user's intent is captured and used for improving his/her effectiveness in an information seeking task. The user intent is captured by analyzing the commonality of the retrieved relevant documents.

Chapter VI explores a Semantic Web-based modeling approach for document annotations and user competencies profile development. This approach is based on a same domain ontology set which constitutes the binder between materials and users. A variant of the nearest neighbor algorithm is applied to recommend concepts of interest and then document contents according to competencies profiles.

Section III

Improved User Modeling: Application of CSIRA

This section supplies six chapters describing applications for which a specific user modeling is used to improve information retrieval and access techniques in a collaborative and social context. Such improved techniques are aimed at recommending more adapted bibliographical references, Web pages or music for instance and at adapting the information content to mobile users.

Chapter VII explores the effectiveness of a sharing of knowledge policy on a collaborating group in order to satisfy a shared information need. The search engine exploits user relevance judgments to propose a new ranked list.

Chapter VIII suggests a social search engine that identifies documents but more specifically users relevant to a query. It relies on a transparent profile construction based upon user activity, community participation, and shared documents.

Chapter IX proposes a Peer-to-Peer bibliographical reference recommender system. It consists in finding relevant documents and interesting people related to the interests and preferences of a single person belonging to a like-minded.

Collaborative, content-based, and case-based recommendation systems and their hybrids have been used for music recommendation. **Chapter X** shows how specific user information can be used to improve user model for ameliorate music recommendation accuracy.

Chapter XI is dedicated to a novel machine learning (based on reinforcement learning) perspective toward the Web recommendation problem. A hybrid Web recommendation method is proposed by making use of the conceptual relationships among Web resources to derive a novel model of the problem, enriched with semantic knowledge about the usage behavior. The method is evaluated under different settings and it is shown how this method can improve the overall quality of recommendations.

Chapter XII presents a twofold approach for adapting content information delivered to a group of mobile users. It is based on a filtering process which considers both the user's current context and her/his preferences for this context.

CONCLUSION

The variety of the approaches developed to improve CSIRA effectiveness, as the richness of the various work undertaken on this subject tend to show that user modeling is in the center of the current concerns. In this way this book constitutes a real survey of advances and applications in user modeling for CSIRA.

Selected Readings

A User-Centered Approach to the Retrieval of Information in an Adaptive Web Site

This chapter describes the user-centered design approach we adopted in the development and evaluation of an adaptive Web site. The development of usable Web sites, offering easy and efficient services to heterogeneous users, is a hot topic and a challenging issue for Adaptive Hypermedia and Human-Computer Interaction. User-centered design promises to facilitate this task by guiding system designers in making decisions, which take the user's needs in serious account.

Within a recent project funded by the Italian Public Administration, we developed a prototype information system supporting the on-line search of data about water resources. As the system was targeted to different types of users, including generic citizens and specialized technicians, we adopted a user-centered approach to identify their information needs and interaction requirements. Moreover, we applied query analysis techniques to identify further information needs and speed up the data retrieval activity. In this chapter we describe the requirements analysis, the system design and its evaluation.

Personalized Information Retrieval in a Semantic-based Learning Environment

Active learning is the ability of learners to carry out learning activities in such a way that they will be able to effectively and efficiently construct knowledge from information sources. Personalized and customizable access on digital materials collected from the Web according to one's own personal requirements and interests is an example of active learning. Moreover, it is also necessary to provide techniques to locate suitable materials. In this paper, we introduce a personalized learning environment providing intelligent support to achieve the expectations of active learning. The system exploits collaborative and semantic approaches to extract concepts from documents and maintaining user and resources profiles based on domain ontologies. In such a way, the retrieval phase takes advantage from the common knowledge base used to extract useful knowledge and produces personalized views of the learning system.

A Semantic Web based Approach for Context-Aware User Query Formulation and Information Retrieval

Formulating unambiguous queries in the Semantic Web applications is a challenging task for users. This article presents a new approach in guiding users to formulate clear requests based on their common nature of querying for information. The approach known as the front-end approach gives users an overview about the system data through a virtual data component which stores the extracted metadata of the data storage sources in the form of an ontology. This approach reduces the ambiguities in users' requests at very early stage; and allows the query process effectively performs to fulfill users' demands in a context-aware manner. Furthermore, the approach provides a powerful query engine, called context-aware querying, that recommends the appropriate query patterns according to the user's querying context.

REFERENCES

Kirsh S. M. (2003). *Social Information Retrieval*, PhD Thesis in Computer Science, Friedrich-Wilhelms-Universität, Bonn, Germany, March 14th 2003.

Wasserman, S., & Faust, K. (1994). Ganovetter M., *Social Network Analysis: Methods and Applications*, Cambridge University Press, ISBN 978-0521387071.

Acknowledgment

Such a project remains time and perseverance. We started the story of this book in June 2007. More than one year later it is now published and available. We would like to thank all the people who participate to this project and make it possible.

First of all we would like to thank all authors who submitted chapters even if they not have been selected for publishing. Their motivation, the considerable effort provided and their investment help us to improve the quality of this book. Finally, 12 chapters have been selected for publication among the 23 proposed submissions. The authors of selected chapters are located in several countries in the world (Belgium, Colombia, France, Iran, Ireland, Romania, Turkey, UK and USA).

To select these chapters each one has been blind reviewed by at least 2 reviewers. The review committee is composed of authors and of additional reviewers (external experts). Thank all of them for the time they spent in reading, proofing, writing their complete remarks. Their remarks have been really relevant and accurate to authors who improved the quality of their chapter. This is the reason why we would like to thank each of them personally: *Alan Smeaton, Alexander Felfering, Angela Carrillo-Ramos, Catherine Berrut, Charles Delalonde, Colum Foley, David Vallet, Désiré Kompaoré, Françoise Fessant, Gareth J. F. Jones, Gilles Hubert, Guillaume Cabanac, Hager Karoui, Hien Nguyen, Josiane Mothe, Manuele Kirsch Pinheiro, Mark Butler, Mark van Setten, Marlène Villanova-Oliver, Melanie Gnasa, Mihaela Brut, Nathalie Denos, Neal Lathia, Nima Taghipour, Patrick Brézillon, Philippe Lopisteguy, Phivos Mylonas, Steve Cayzer, Susan Gauch, Sylvie Calabretto, Victor Odumuyiwa, Zehra Cataltepe, Zeina Jrad.*

We would like to sincerely thank *Pr. Bamshad Mobasher* who accepted to participate to this project in writing the Foreword.

A special thank must go to IGI Global team and particularly Ms. *Deborah Yahnke*, and Ms. *Rebecca Beistline*, assistant development editor, for their intensive support and their help allowing us to achieve this project.

Max Chevalier
Christine Julien
Chantal Soulé-Dupuy
Editors

Section I
User Modeling in Collaborative and Social Information Retrieval and Access (CSIRA)

Chapter I
State–of–the–Art
Recommender Systems

Laurent Candillier
Orange Labs Lannion, France

Kris Jack
Orange Labs Lannion, France

Françoise Fessant
Orange Labs Lannion, France

Frank Meyer
Orange Labs Lannion, France

ABSTRACT

The aim of Recommender Systems is to help users to find items that they should appreciate from huge catalogues. In that field, collaborative filtering approaches can be distinguished from content-based ones. The former is based on a set of user ratings on items, while the latter uses item content descriptions and user thematic profiles. While collaborative filtering systems often result in better predictive performance, content-based filtering offers solutions to the limitations of collaborative filtering, as well as a natural way to interact with users. These complementary approaches thus motivate the design of hybrid systems. In this chapter, the main algorithmic methods used for recommender systems are presented in a state of the art. The evaluation of recommender systems is currently an important issue. The authors focus on two kinds of evaluations. The first one concerns the performance accuracy: several approaches are compared through experiments on two real movies rating datasets MovieLens and Netflix. The second concerns user satisfaction and for this a hybrid system is implemented and tested with real users.

INTRODUCTION

There has been a growth in interest in *Recommender Systems* in the last two decades (Adomavicius & Tuzhilin, 2005), since the appearance of the first papers on this subject in the mid-1990s (Resnick et al., 1994). The aim of such systems is to help *users* to find *items* that they should appreciate from huge catalogues.

Items can be of any type, such as films, music, books, web pages, online news, jokes, restaurants and even lifestyles. Recommender systems help users to find such items of interest based on some information about their historical preferences. (Nageswara Rao & Talwar, 2008) inventory a varied list of existing recommender systems and their application domain that have been developed in the academia and in the industry.

Three types of recommender systems are commonly implemented:

- collaborative filtering;
- content-based filtering;
- and hybrid filtering.

These systems have, however, their inherent strengths and weaknesses. The recommendation system designer must select which strategy is most appropriate given a particular problem. For example, if little item appreciation data is available then a collaborative filtering approach is unlikely to be well suited to the problem. Likewise, if item descriptions are not available then content-based filtering approaches will have trouble. The choice of approach can also have important effects upon user satisfaction. The designer must take all of these factors into account in the early conception of the system.

This chapter gives an overview of the state-of-the-art in recommender systems, considering both motivations behind them and their underlying strategies. The three previously mentioned recommendation approaches are then described

in detail, providing a practical basis for going on to create such systems. The results from a number of experiments, carried out in the field of film recommendation, are then presented and discussed, making two novel contributions to the field. First, a number of baseline tests are carried out in which numerous recommendation strategy approaches are compared, allowing the reader to see their strengths and weaknesses in detail and on a level playing field. Second, a novel hybrid recommendation system is introduced that is tested with real users. The results of the testing demonstrate the importance of user satisfaction in recommendation system design.

RECOMMENDER SYSTEM APPROACHES

As previously introduced, recommender systems are usually classified into three categories: *collaborative, content-based* and *hybrid filtering*, based on how recommendations are made. We review in this section the main algorithmic approaches.

Collaborative Filtering

In collaborative filtering, the input to the system is a set of user ratings on items. Users can be compared based upon their shared appreciation of items, creating the notion of user neighbourhoods. Similarly, items can be compared based upon the shared appreciation of users, rendering the notion of item neighbourhoods. The item rating for a given user can then be predicted based upon the ratings given in her user neighbourhood and the item neighbourhood. We can distinguish three main approaches: *user-based*, *item-based* and *model-based* approaches. These approaches are formalized and compared in this section.

Let U be a set of N users, I a set of M items, and R a set of ratings r_{ui} of users $u \in U$ on item

$i \in I$. $S_u \subseteq I$ stands for the set of items that user u has rated.

The goal of collaborative filtering approaches is then to be able to predict the rating p_{ai} of a user a on an item i. User a is presumed to be *active*, meaning that she has already rated some items, so $S_a \neq \varnothing$. The item to be predicted is not yet known to the user, making $i \notin S_a$.

User-based Approaches

For user-based approaches (Resnick et al., 1994; Shardanand & Maes, 1995), the prediction of a user rating on an item is based on the ratings, on that item, of the nearest neighbours. So a similarity measure between users needs to be defined before a set of nearest neighbours is selected. Also, a method for combining the ratings of those neighbours on the target item needs to be chosen.

The way in which the similarity between users is computed is discussed below. For now, let $sim(a,u)$ be the similarity between users a and u. The number of neighbours considered is often set by a system parameter, denoted by K. So the set of neighbours of a given user a, denoted by T_a, is made up of the K users that maximise their similarity to user a.

A possible way to predict the rating of user a on item i is then to use the weighted sum of the ratings of the nearest neighbours $u \in T_a$ that have already rated item i:

$$p_{ai} = \frac{\sum_{\{u \in T_a | i \in S_u\}} sim(a,u) \times r_{ui}}{\sum_{\{u \in T_a | i \in S_u\}} |sim(a,u)|} \quad (1)$$

In order to take into account the difference in use of the rating scale by different users, predictions based on deviations from the mean ratings have been proposed. p_{ai} can be computed from the sum of the user's mean rating and the weighted sum of deviations from their mean rating of the neighbours that have rated item i:

$$p_{ai} = \overline{r_a} + \frac{\sum_{\{u \in T_a | i \in S_u\}} sim(a,u) \times (r_{ui} - \overline{r_u})}{\sum_{\{u \in T_a | i \in S_u\}} |sim(a,u)|} \quad (2)$$

$\overline{r_u}$ represents the mean rating of user u:

$$\overline{r_u} = \frac{\sum_{\{i \in S_u\}} r_{ui}}{|S_u|} \quad (3)$$

Indeed, supposing that items are rated between 1 and 5. One user may rate an item that he likes at 4 and an item that he dislikes at 1. Another user, however, may rate an item that he likes at 5 and an item that he dislikes at 2. By using deviations from the mean rating, the individual user's semantics, with respect to his appreciation of the items, is better accounted for.

The time complexity of user-based approaches is $O(N^2 \times M \times K)$ for the neighbourhood model construction and $O(K)$ for one rating prediction. The space complexity is $O(N \times K)$.

Item-based Approaches

Recently, there has been a rising interest in the use of item-based approaches (Sarwar et al., 2001; Karypis, 2001; Linden et al., 2003; Deshpande & Karypis, 2004). Given a similarity measure between items, such approaches first define item neighbourhoods. The predicted rating for a user on an item is then derived by using the ratings of the user on the neighbours of the target item.

The possible choices of the similarity measure $sim(i,j)$ defined between items i and j are discussed later. Then, as for user-based approaches, the item neighbourhood size K is a system parameter that needs to be defined. Given T_i, the neighbourhood of item i, two ways for predicting new user ratings can be considered:

1.   using a weighted sum:

$$p_{ai} = \frac{\sum_{\{j \in S_a \cap T_i\}} sim(i,j) \times r_{aj}}{\sum_{\{j \in S_a \cap T_i\}} |sim(i,j)|} \quad (4)$$

2. using a weighted sum of deviations from the mean item ratings:

$$p_{ai} = \overline{r_i} + \frac{\sum_{\{j \in S_a \cap T_i\}} sim(i,j) \times (r_{aj} - \overline{r_j})}{\sum_{\{j \in S_a \cap T_i\}} |sim(i,j)|} \quad (5)$$

$\overline{r_i}$ is the mean rating on item *i*:

$$\overline{r_j} = \frac{\sum_{\{u \in U | i \in S_u\}} r_{ui}}{|\{u \in U | i \in S_u\}|} \quad (6)$$

The time complexity of item-based approaches is $O(M^2 \times N \times K)$ for the neighbourhood model construction and $O(K)$ for one rating prediction. The space complexity is $O(M \times K)$.

Model-based Approaches

A quadratic complexity is too high for huge datasets and many real applications need predictions that can be made very quickly. These considerations are the starting points of model-based approaches (Breese et al., 1998). The general idea is to derive a model of the data off-line in order to predict on-line ratings as fast as possible.

The first type of models that have been proposed consist of grouping users using clustering and then predicting a user rating on an item using only the ratings of the users that belong to the same cluster.

Bayesian models have also been proposed to model dependencies between items. The clustering of items has been studied extensively (e.g. Ungar & Foster, 1998; O'Conner & Herlocker, 1999). Also, models based on association rules have been studied by (Sarwar et al., 2000) and (Lin et al., 2002).

Probabilistic clustering algorithms have also been used in order to allow users to belong, at some level, to different groups (Pennock et al., 2000; Kleinberg & Sandler, 2004). And hierarchies of clusters have been proposed, so that if a given cluster of users does not have an opinion on a particular item, then the super-cluster can be considered (Kelleher & Bridge, 2003).

In such approaches, the number of clusters considered is of key importance. In many cases, different numbers of clusters are tested, and the one that leads to the lowest error rate in cross-validation is kept. Clusters are generally represented by their centroid, and then the predicted rating of a user for an item can be directly derived from the rating of its nearest centroid. If both user and item clustering are used, the predicted rating is the mean rating, on the item's group members, of the user's group members. This kind of algorithm needs to be run many times with random initial solutions in order to avoid local minima. A parameter *L* that represents the required number of runs must be introduced.

The time complexity of cluster-based approaches is then $O(N \times M \times K \times L)$ for the learning phase and $O(1)$ for one rating prediction. The space complexity, when both user and item clustering are considered, is $O((N+M) \times K)$.

Similarity Measures

The similarity defined between users or items is crucial in collaborative filtering. The first one proposed in (Resnick et al., 1994) is the *Pearson* correlation. It corresponds to the *Cosine* of deviations from the mean. Simple *Cosine* or *Manhattan* similarities are also traditional ones.

For these similarity measures, only the set of attributes in common between two vectors are considered. Thus two vectors may be completely similar even if they only share one appreciation on one attribute.

Such measures have drawbacks. For example, in the context of film recommendation, consider the case when one user is a fan of science fiction while another only watches comedies. Furthermore, these users haven't rated any film in common so their similarity is null. Now they both say that they like *"Men In Black"*, a science fiction comedy. These users thus become completely similar according to the previously presented measures, given that their only common reference point was equally rated.

The *Jaccard* similarity, however, doesn't suffer from this limitation since it measures the overlap that two vectors share with their attributes. On the other hand, such a measure doesn't take into account the difference of ratings between the vectors. In this case, if two users watch the same films but have completely opposite opinions on them, then they are considered to be similar anyway according to Jaccard similarity.

When Jaccard is combined with the other similarity measures, a system can benefit from their complementarily. For example, the product of Jaccard with another similarity measure produces a new result. In this case, Jaccard serves as a weight. *wPearson* can thus represent a weighted Pearson measure, produced by the product of Pearson and Jaccard. Similarly, *wCosine* and *wManhattan* denote the combination of Jaccard with Cosine and Manhattan respectively. The values of Cosine-based similarity measures lie between −1 and 1 while the other similarity values lie between 0 and 1. Experimental results based on this weighted similarity measure are presented later. We will show that this similarity which is tailored to the type of data that is typically available (i.e. very sparse), tends to lead to better results.

Among the main drawbacks of collaborative filtering systems we can mention the *cold start* problem occurring when a new user has not provided any ratings yet or a new item has not yet received any rating from the users. The system lacks data to produce appropriate recommendations (for instance, the MovieLens recommender system requires at least 15 ratings before it is able to provide recommendations). For the new user problem (Nguyen et al., 2007) propose to exploit demographic data about the user such as their age, location and occupation to improve the first recommendations provided to a new user, without her having to rate any items. The new-item and new-user problems can also be addressed using hybrid recommendation approaches (these approaches will be described below).

Content-Based Filtering

Content-based recommendation systems recommend an item to a user based upon a description of the item and a *profile* of the user's interests. Content-based recommendation systems share in common a means for describing the items that may be recommended, a means for creating a profile of the user that describes the types of items the user likes, and a means of comparing items to the user profile to determine what to recommend. Item descriptors can be the genre of a film or the location of a restaurant, depending upon the type of item being recommended. Finally, items that have a high degree of proximity to a given user's preferences would be recommended.

A *User profile* may be built *implicitly* from the user's preferences for items, by searching for commonalities in liked and disliked item descriptions, based upon her past actions or *explicitly* through questionnaires about her preferences for the item descriptions.

A *User model* may be learned *implicitly* by an automatic learning method, using item descriptions as input to a supervised learning algorithm, and producing user appreciations of items as output.

User profiles are often represented as vectors of weights on item descriptions. Any other user model may be considered if an automatic learning method is used. If a rule induction algorithm was to be used in a film recommender, then user models could contain information such as "IF genre IS action AND actor IS Stallone THEN film IS liked". (Pazzani & Billsus, 2007) discuss the different ways to represent item contents and user profiles as well as the ways to learn user models.

Preferences indicate a relationship between a given user and data. In recommender system research, a preference must be both machine codable and carry useful information for making recommendations. For example, in the field of cinematography, the monadic preference *"I like Jackie Chan as an actor"* can be coded as a high score for films with this actor. In turn, films with this higher score will be more recommended than films that are not promoted in this way. In addition, dyadic preferences can be asserted such as *"I like comedies more than dramas"*, allowing a wide number of films to be compared.

While these preferences can be used to improve recommendations, they suffer from certain drawbacks, the most important of these being their limited *coverage*. The coverage of a preference is directly related to the coverage of the attribute(s) to which it is applied. An attribute has a high coverage when it appears in many items and a low coverage when it appears in few items. The coverage of the preference *"I like Jackie Chan as an actor"* is extremely low in most film databases. As such, recommenders that rely solely upon content-based preferences often require a large amount of user details before good recommendations can be made.

It is possible, however, to extend the coverage of a preference by employing the notion of similarity to attributes. A preference for one attribute can also be inferred for all other attributes that are very similar. For example, if *Jackie Chan* and *Bruce Lee* are considered to be very similar, then the preference *"I like Jackie Chan as an actor"* can be extended to include *"I like Bruce Lee as an actor"*. This extension, assuming that it does not contradict other given preferences, extends the coverage of the preference.

Several approaches are commonly followed to determine the similarity between attributes. Most traditionally, this falls within the remit of a domain expert who can construct, by hand, a rich ontology of the domain. While this approach remains popular within smaller domains, recom-

mendation systems are often employed in large domains where instantiation by hand is impractical. Alternatively, measures of similarity can be used that exploit the wealth of information present on the internet. One such similarity metric, the *Normalised Google Distance* (Cilibrasi & Vitanyi, 2007), infers similarities between textual terms using their co-occurrence on websites, as found by *Google*. This metric tends to perform well under diverse conditions and, since it employs the internet, is not domain specific.

The Normalised Google Distance metric has proved useful in finding the similarity between attributes such as actors (Jack & Duclaye, 2008) in the domain of movies. Unfortunately, it is difficult to determine complete similarity matrices for large scale databases due to restrictions on the use of the Google API.

To evade such restrictions, similarity metrics that directly analyse the available recommendation system database are often preferred. For example, given two actors in a film database, a vector can be constructed for each one that describes their film history. The vector can contain information such as the genre of films in which they have played, the directors with whom they have worked and the actors with whom they have co-starred. A similarity measure such as wCosine can then be used to compare the two actor vectors.

As introduced above, another set of possible approaches for content-based filtering consists of using a classifier, like *Naive Bayes*, having as input the item descriptions and as output the tastes of a user for a subset of items. The classifier is trained over a set of items already considered by the user. It is then able to predict if a new item will be liked or not by the user, according to its content description (Adomavicius & Tuzhilin, 2005).

These content-based methods are thus able to tackle some limitations of collaborative ones. They are able to provide recommendations for new items even when no rating is available. They can also handle situations where users do not consider the same items but consider similar items.

However, to be efficient, content-based approaches need rich and complete descriptions of items and well-constructed user profiles. This is the main limitation of such systems. Since well-structured item descriptions are hard to come by in many domains, such approaches have mainly been applied in those where items are described by textual information that can be parsed automatically, such as documents, web sites and Usenet news messages (Pazzani & Billsus, 1997; Mooney & Roy, 1999).

Besides, content-based approaches can also suffer from *overspecialisation* (Zhang et al., 2002). That is, they often recommend items with similar content to that of the items already considered, which can lead to a lack of originality. On the other hand, privacy issues (Lam et al., 2006), such as users who do not want to share their preferences with others, are avoided.

A user's appreciation of an item is often based on more information than can be practically stored in an item's description. Even rich databases can omit information that may be crucial to a user when deciding if they like an item or not. In the case of films for instance, viewers generally select a film to watch based upon more elements than only its genre, director and actors.

Collaborative methods do not require such difficult to come by, well-structured item descriptions. Instead, they are based on users' preferences for items, which can carry a more general meaning than is contained in an item description. They have the advantage of providing a *meta* view on the interest and quality of the items. These complementary approaches thus motivate the design of hybrid systems.

Hybrid Filtering

In the case of hybrid filtering, both types of information, collaborative and content-based, are exploited. These technologies can be combined in various ways that make use of both user appreciations of items and their descriptor-based preferences. Other sources of data like social and demographic data about users can also be used.

The first direct way to design a hybrid recommender system is to independently run a collaborative and a content-based one, and then combine their predictions using a voting scheme.

In (Balabanovic & Shoham, 1997), the combination is performed by forcing items to be, at the same time, close to the user thematic profile, and highly rated by her neighbours. In (Pazzani, 1999), users are compared according to their content profiles, and the generated similarity measures are then used in a collaborative filtering system.

In (Polcicova et al., 2000; Melville et al., 2002), the rating matrix is enriched with predictions based on the content, and then collaborative filtering is run. In (Vozalis & Margaritis, 2004), the similarity between items is computed by using their content descriptions as well as their associated rating vectors. An item-based collaborative filtering algorithm is them launched. In this paper the authors also explore how several existing collaborative filtering algorithms can be enhanced by the use of demographic data about users. Two users could be considered similar not only if they rated the same items similarly, but also if they belong to the same demographic segment.

In (Han & Karypis, 2005), it is proposed to extend the prediction list of a collaborative filtering method to the items whose content are close to the recommended items. Based on the same idea, the content-based similarity between items is used in (Wang et al., 2006) in order to compare users not only according to their shared appreciations for some items, but by considering also their shared appreciations for items whose contents are similar.

A hybrid system can also be designed that follows a content-based filtering strategy and uses the data produced from collaborative filtering to enrich item similarity descriptions. At its core, it is a content-based filtering system that makes use of attribute similarities, similar to a personalised information retrieval system where requests are null (Jack & Duclaye, 2007). Items are recommended that are similar to the user's likes but not to his dislikes. The similarities between genres, nationalities and language attributes are defined by hand, while the wCosine measure is used to calculate director and actor similarities. Each film also contains a unique identification attribute. This identifier is compared to the films that have been previously noted by the user. The notion of similarity, for attributes of this type, is that embodied in the collaborative filtering algorithms. The more that a strictly collaborative filtering algorithm recommends a film, the closer the film is to the user's profile. This type of hybrid system thus treats social data (found through collaborative filtering) as an attribute of an item, like any other. By weighing the importance of each characteristic, the system can vary from being purely content-based through to purely collaborative.

Collaborative filtering techniques are more often implemented than the other two and often result in better predictive performance. Collaborative filtering seems to be more suitable as the core method of the recommender system while content-based filtering offers solutions to the limits of collaborative filtering, as well as a natural way to interact with the users. Indeed, users should be allowed to exert control over the system, thus building a meaningful relationship, and leading to psychological benefits such as the increase of trust in recommendations. This naturally leads to the issue of evaluating the performance of a recommender system.

RECOMMENDER SYSTEM EVALUATION

The evaluation of a recommender system is an important issue. In most recommender system literature, algorithms are evaluated by performance in terms of accuracy. The estimated ratings are compared against the actual rating. In these approaches many measures can be used. The most widely used ones are:

1. *Mean Absolute Error* (MAE);
2. *Root Mean Squared Error* (RMSE);
3. *Precision* measures.

The first two measures evaluate the capability of a method to predict if a user will like or dislike an item, whereas the third measure evaluates its capacity to order a list of items based on user tastes. These measures thus carry different meanings (McNee et al., 2006). In the first two cases, the method needs to be able to predict dislike, but there is no need to order items. In the last case, however, the method only focuses on items that users will like and the order in which these items are ranked is important.

(Herlocker et al., 2004) have noticed that beyond the importance of the predictive performance of recommender systems, other crucial criteria that try to capture the quality and usefulness of recommendations may be taken into consideration in their evaluation. The *scalability* of the proposed system is for example an important characteristic that needs to be taken into account. The *coverage* of a method, that is the proportion of recommendations it can provide, can also be considered. Finally, the system's ability to provide a level of *confidence* in a recommendation (Basu et al., 1998) and to *explain* why a recommendation was made (Herlocker et al., 2000; Bilgic, 2004) can be used to define its potential interest to the user.

The actual studies about recommender system evaluation investigate the factors that affect user satisfaction. Evaluating a recommender system based on real users' opinions is important because, in many cases, recommending the set of items that maximise their predicted ratings does not necessarily lead to user satisfaction. For instance, users may estimate that such recommendations lack originality, or they may think that the proposed list of recommendations is not varied enough (Ziegler et al., 2005). Users may also want to have some control over the system, rather than having little or no direct influence on the results.

The quality of recommendations is ultimately judged by the user of the recommendation system. Many recommendation systems suffer from the 'one-visit' problem where users login, use the system once and then never return. Even users who receive good recommendations can quit using a recommendation system because they become frustrated that they cannot express particular preferences or find that the system lacks flexibility and is not user friendly.

One of the most important aspects of user interaction is that of control. Users must feel like they are in control of their recommendations and that they can navigate themselves out of awkward situations. For example, when a system incorrectly learns a user's preferences, the user should be able to correct the error. While algorithms like collaborative filtering can predict a user's tastes well, they cannot take into account attribute-based preferences, for example, the possibility for the users to express that they do not like some genre of films and that they no longer want them to be recommended. Giving such control to the user not only improves the recommendations but also improves the users' interaction experience.

Explicit preference entry (EPE) interfaces are designed to allow users to explicitly indicate a preference to the system. There are many examples of EPE interfaces, from questionnaire-based entry forms (Miller et al., 2003) to dialogue systems (Krulwich, 1997). Blog recommenders, such as MineKey (www.minekey.com), and website recommenders, such as StumbleUpon (www.stumbleupon.com), often ask users to indicate their preferences with respect to general topic (e.g. sports, hobbies and arts). Similarly, MovieLens asks users to rate films that are presented in a list format. Unfortunately such interfaces are often boring to use. Many systems use interactive data visualisation techniques in order to provide a fun and engaging setting for the user. For ex-

ample, both Music Plasma (www.musicplasma. com) and Amaznode (amaznode.fladdict.net) have shown how recommendations can be attractively visualised to the user. EPE interfaces can make use of data visualisation techniques in order to guide users into finding attributes that they know and hence help them to find familiar points at which express their preferences (Jack & Duclaye, 2008).

Another important issue regarding user interaction concerns the necessary diversification of the recommendations. One possible way proposed in (Ziegler et al., 2005) for recommendation diversification consists of selecting, among the list of items considered as the most appropriate to a user, a subset as diverse as possible. To do that, the item with the highest predicted interest is first selected. The system then chooses the item that optimises a criterion mixing its predicted interest and its difference with the first selected item. This process is iterated until the desired number of items is reached.

Explaining why a recommendation is given can also be useful for a user (Billsus & Pazzani, 1999). Explanations can be based on the neighbours used for the recommendation, in the case of collaborative filtering or based on the elements in the user profile that match those found in a film's attributes when a content-based filtering is used. In (Bilgic, 2004), this second type of information has been shown to be more expressive to the users. Explanation is useful for increasing user confidence in a recommendation. It also helps the user to understand how the system works, so that she is then able to provide more relevant information when constructing her profile and interacting with the system.

EXPERIMENTS

The experiments presented in this chapter use two real rating datasets that are publicly available in the movies domain: *MovieLens* (www.grouplens.

org) and *Netflix* (www.netflixprize.com). The first dataset contains 1,000,209 film ratings collected from 6,040 users on 3,706 films and the second contains 100,480,507 film ratings collected from 480,189 users on 17,770 films. These datasets are independent of one another. Ratings are integers ranging from 1 (meaning dislike) to 5 (meaning like).

Two complementary ways for evaluating recommender systems are proposed. The first one consists of evaluating the prediction performance of the system using the two movies datasets and cross-validation. The second focuses upon user satisfaction.

Performance Comparison

The MovieLens and Netflix datasets are divided into two parts in order to perform cross-validation, training the chosen model using 90% of the data and testing it on the last 10%. In reality, recommendation system designers would use all 100% of the data to train their systems but a portion is omitted here for testing purposes.

Given $T = \{(u, i, r)\}$ the set of (user, item, rating) triplets used for test, the Mean Absolute Error Rate (MAE) and Root Mean Squared Error (RMSE) are used to evaluate the performance of the algorithms:

$$MAE = \frac{1}{|T|} \sum_{(u,i,r) \in T} |p_{ui} - r| \qquad (7)$$

$$RMSE = \sqrt{\frac{1}{|T|} \sum_{(u,i,r) \in T} (p_{ui} - r)^2} \qquad (8)$$

The predicted ratings are rounded when the MAE is reported. First of all, this improves the results. Besides, rounding ratings is natural in practice, since real users generally prefer rating scales based on natural numbers than on real numbers.

We report the precision of the system that is the proportion of truly high ratings among those that were predicted to be high by the recommender system. Some precision measures specifically designed for the current context are used. *Precision*$_5$ concerns the proportion of maximum ratings in the test dataset, with a value for the maximum rating fixed to 5, which are retrieved as the best predicted ratings. Similarly, *precision*$_4$ stands for the proportion of test ratings higher than the maximum value minus one (i.e. 4) that are considered as the best ratings by the given recommender system.

Finally, the time spent learning the models and making predictions are also reported. The computer used for these experiments has 32GB RAM and 64 bits 3.40GHz 2-cores CPU.

Considering only the principal collaborative filtering approaches already leads to a lot of choices and parameters. When implementing a user- or item-based approach, one may choose:

1. a similarity measure: Pearson, Cosine, Manhattan, Jaccard, or the proposed combinations of Jaccard with the others;
2. a neighbourhood size K;
3. how to compute predictions: using a weighted sum of rating values (equations (1) and (4)), or using a weighted sum of deviations from the mean (2) and (5).

For model-based approaches, the following parameters need to be defined:

1. clustering users and/or items;
2. the number of clusters.

The clustering algorithm considered in this section is *Bisecting K-means* using *Euclidian* distance. *K-means* is the well-known full-space clustering algorithm based on the evolution of K centroids that represent the K clusters to be found, while Bisecting K-means is based on the recursive use of (*K=2*)-means. At each step, the cluster that maximises its inertia is split.

A prediction scheme that is based on deviations from the mean has been shown to be more effective in (Candillier et al., 2007). So in the following, only the results using this scheme are reported.

One important aspect of collaborative filtering is the choice of the similarity measure used. Figures 1 to 3 show the Mean Absolute Error Rate obtained using the presented measures, varying the neighbourhood size K from 10 to the maximum number of possible neighbours, for both user- and item-based approaches, and on both MovieLens and Netflix datasets.

Figure 1 first shows the error rates of item-based approaches depending on the similarity measure used and the neighbourhood size. The optimum is reached with the weighted Pearson similarity and 100 neighbours. All similarity measures are improved when they are weighted with Jaccard, at least when few neighbours are considered. All these weighted similarity measures reach their

optimum when 100 neighbours are selected. On the contrary, non-weighted similarity measures need much more neighbours to reach their optimum. 700 neighbours shall be selected when using simple Manhattan similarity, and 1500 when using simple Cosine or simple Pearson.

Figures 2 and 3 show that the same conclusions hold when using user-based approaches, as well as when the Netflix dataset is used instead of MovieLens. Weighted Pearson similarity always leads to the best results. Weighting the similarity measures with Jaccard always improves the results. 300 neighbours shall be considered for a user-based approach on MovieLens, and 70 for an item-based approach on Netflix. On the contrary, 2000 to 4000 neighbours need to be selected to reach the minimum error rate with non-weighted similarity measures.

The results have been presented for the MAE. They are highly similar to the other performance measures: RMSE and precisions. Beyond the improvement of predictive performance when the proposed weighting scheme is used, another

Figure 1. Comparing MAE on MovieLens when using item-based approaches with different similarity measures and neighbourhood sizes (K)

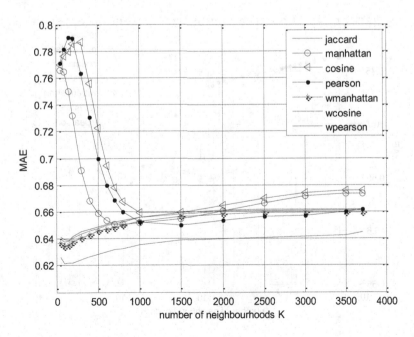

Figure 2. Comparing MAE on MovieLens when using user-based approaches with different similarity measures and neighbourhood sizes (K)

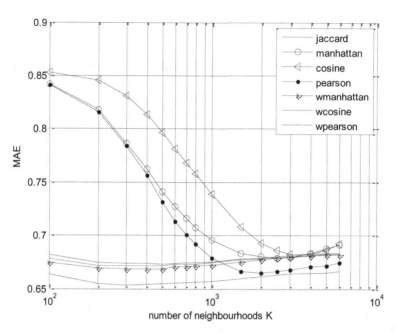

Figure 3. Comparing MAE on Netflix when using item-based approaches with different similarity measures and neighbourhood sizes (K)

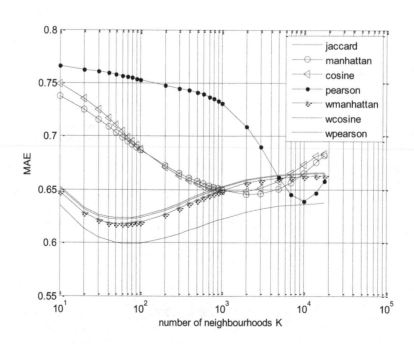

important advantage is that fewer neighbours need to be selected, so that the algorithms also gain in scalability.

In fact, when a non-weighted similarity measure is used, the nearest neighbours do not share many attributes. They often have only one attribute in common. On the contrary, by using Jaccard similarity, the selected neighbours are those that share a maximum number of attributes. Jaccard searches to optimise the number of common attributes between vectors, but this may not be the best solution for nearest neighbour selection since the values of the vectors on the shared attributes may differ. So weighted similarity measures offer an interesting compromise between Jaccard and the other non-weighted measures.

Figures 4 and 5 then show the results obtained by using model-based approaches on both MovieLens and Netflix datasets. The three possible approaches are compared: user clustering, item clustering and double clustering. On MovieLens, user and item clustering behave the same and both outperform the double clustering. Optimal results are reached by using 4 item clusters. On Netflix however, using 70 user clusters leads to the best results.

Tables 1 and 2 summarise the results of the best of each approach, including learning and prediction times, and precisions. Both user- and item-based approaches reach optimal results when the weighted Pearson similarity is used. On MovieLens, 300 neighbours are selected for the best user-based approach, and 100 for the best item-based one. On Netflix, considering 70 neighbours leads to the lowest error rate. User-based approaches, however, face scalability issues. It is too expensive to compute the entire user-user matrix. So instead, a clustering is first run, and then only the users that belong to the same cluster are considered as potential neighbours. Considering

Figure 4. Comparing MAE on MovieLens when using model-based approaches with different options and numbers of clusters (K)

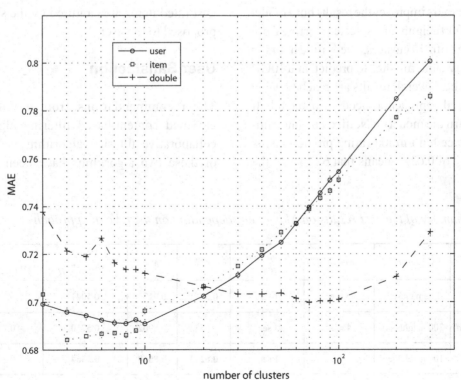

Figure 5. Comparing MAE on Netflix when using model-based approaches with different options and numbers of clusters (K)

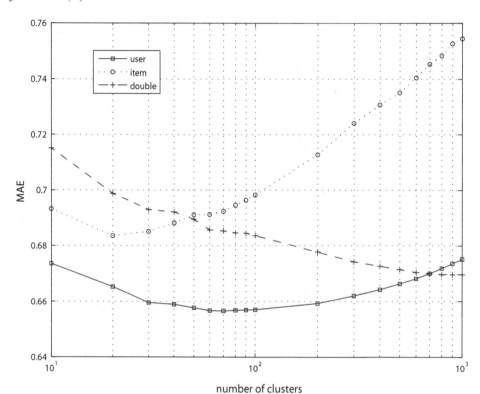

many neighbours improves the results but a model based on 1,000 neighbours, selected starting from a clustering with 90 clusters, needs nine hours to learn, twenty eight minutes to predict, and 10GB RAM. The best overall results are reached using an item-based approach. It needs two and a half hours to learn the model on Netflix, and one minute to produce ten million rating predictions. A *precision*$_5$ of 0.6216 means that 62.16% of the best rated items are captured by the system and proposed to the users.

User Satisfaction

The recommendations from a semantically enriched content-based filtering algorithm, a collaborative filtering algorithm and a hybrid of these two algorithms have been compared

Table 1. Summary of the best results on MovieLens depending on the type of approach

	Parameter	*Learning time*	*prediction time*	*MAE*	*RMSE*	*precision*$_5$	*precision*$_4$
model-based	4 item clusters	**5 sec.**	**1 sec.**	0.6841	0.9172	0.5041	0.7550
user-based	300 neighbours	4 min.	3 sec.	0.6533	0.8902	0.5710	0.7810
item-based	100 neighbours	2 min.	1 sec.	**0.6213**	**0.8550**	**0.5864**	**0.7915**

Table 2. Summary of the best results on Netflix depending on the type of approach

	Parameter	Learning time	prediction time	MAE	RMSE	$precision_5$	$precision_4$
model-based	70 user clusters	**24 min.**	**3 sec.**	0.6566	0.8879	0.5777	0.7608
user-based	1,000 neighbours	9 h	28 min.	0.6440	0.8811	0.5902	0.7655
item-based	70 neighbours	2 h 30	1 min.	**0.5990**	**0.8436**	**0.6216**	**0.7827**

in a study with human participants. As well as considering the quality of the recommendations produced by the different algorithms, as judged by the participants, the participants' actions and comments are also analysed. In doing so, a number of conclusions can be drawn as to how user needs can be accounted for to produce more natural and satisfying interactions with recommendation systems.

The film database was generated from two sources. Film details (used for content-based filtering) came from an in-house Orange database while user ratings (used for collaborative filtering) came from Netflix. A database of 3,626 films was produced by taking the intersection of films from both data sources. Each film was described by five characteristics: actors; directors; genres; languages; and nationalities.

A recommendation system interface was constructed with three primary screens: a login screen, a profile manager and a recommendation screen. The login screen allowed the participant to enter their username and be identified by the system. On first identification, a user profile is created. The participant could manage their profile using the profile manager, which allowed for both monadic and dyadic preferences to be expressed. Monadic preferences could be expressed for any of the five characteristics and films themselves (e.g. *"I like Charlie Chaplin as an actor"* and *"I dislike Scary Movie"*) on a 3-point scale (like, neutral, dislike). Dyadic preferences could be expressed for the relative importance of each of the five characteristics and films themselves (e.g. *"the genre is more important than the director"* and *"the actor is less important than the film"*).

The first recommendation algorithm was a content-based algorithm that interpreted monadic and dyadic preferences with respect to the five film characteristics. Item attributes were also semantically enriched with the notion of similarity. The similarities among directors and actors were derived using the wCosine measure and the complete in-house database. Genre, language and nationality similarities were constructed by hand, since there were a manageable number, by ontology experts. The second algorithm was an item-based collaborative filtering algorithm that used the wPearson similarity. Finally, a hybrid algorithm that acted as a content-based algorithm, where collaborative filtering data appeared as a single film attribute, was put in place.

Thirty participants were recruited. All were experienced computer users who had received a university level education. Six participants had already used a recommendation of some sort while the rest had not. Participants were given an instruction sheet that explained the how the interface could be operated. The study took around thirty minutes to complete per participant.

Participants were asked to enter some of their film preferences and then to request some recommendations. It was stressed that they should only enter as many or as few preferences as they would normally do so in the comfort of their own home. There was no pressure to enter any particular type of preference (film or film attribute).

The system showed a single list of recommendations produced by the three algorithms within. Each algorithm produced five recommendations. Recommendations for films that were the direct subject of preferences were not produced (i.e. if a user noted that they liked Titanic then it would not be recommended to them). The fifteen total recommendations were randomly ordered in a list with duplicate recommendations being removed. Such duplicates could be produced by different the different algorithms recommending the same film. The participant was then asked to score each of the recommendations. If they had already seen the film then they were asked to give a score as to how much they liked it, on a scale from 1-5 (1 being the least and 5 being the most). If they had not already seen the film, then they were asked how much they would like to see it, on the same scale from 1-5. As the semantics of the scale may differ depending upon the question, it is important to analyse the results separately.

After scoring all films, the participant was asked to return to the profile manager to enter more preferences and to ask for recommendations once more. The scores given for recommendations were not used to influence neither the user's profile nor future recommendations and were for study use alone. On requesting a second list of recommendations, the participant was asked to score them. Once all films were scored, the participant then had the choice to quit the system or to repeat the preference entry followed by recommendation scoring process. On choosing to quit the system, the participant was given a short questionnaire to complete.

The participants scored at least two recommendation lists. The difference between the average scores given to seen films in their first list of recommendations is compared with the average scores given to seen films in their last list of recommendations (Figure 6). On receiving the first recommendations, the collaborative filtering algorithm produces significantly better results (mean = 4.00; standard deviation SD = 0.91) than the content-based filtering algorithm (mean = 3.35; SD = 1.13). Given the final recommenda-

Figure 6. Average scores given by the participants to the recommended films that they had already seen before

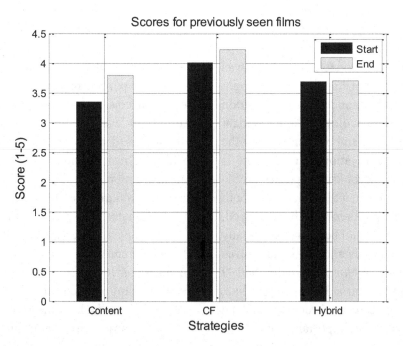

tion, the collaborative filtering algorithm (mean = 4.23; SD = 0.66) produces significantly better results than both the content-based filtering (mean = 3.79; SD = 0.89) and hybrid (mean = 3.70; SD = 0.88) algorithms. The content-based filtering algorithm is the only algorithm that significantly improves between the first and last recommendations given. The content-based and collaborative filtering algorithms tend to improve when more preferences are available while the hybrid filtering algorithm remains stable.

Similarly, the same average scores can be found for unseen films. In this case, no significant differences were found between the scores produced by the three algorithms although there was a trend for each algorithm to produce better results when more preferences were available. Participants have reported a strong desire to watch the unseen films that were recommended (mean score of 4 out of 5 for the statements *"I found new films that I want to watch"*, 5 being equivalent to strongly agree).

Participants were asked to enter as many preferences into their profile as they felt comfortable with. They were not encouraged to enter any particular type of preference. In comparing the profiles created by users in the first round of the study, with those at the end of the study, the average constitution tends to change in quantity alone (Figure 7). The number of preferences that are given for films is comparable to the number of preferences that are given for film attributes (the five characteristics). Out of the film attributes, participants tended to give their preferences for genres.

In the questionnaire, participants were also asked to indicate which type of characteristics they were comfortable in giving preferences for or against (Table 3). The majority of participants were comfortable giving preferences for films and many indicated that they were comfortable giving preferences for actors, genres and directors. Only a few participants were comfortable giving preferences for nationalities or languages. In addition, a number of participants indicated that they would like to express preferences for the release dates of films, a characteristic that was not present in their profile.

Participants also commented in the questionnaires that they would have preferred a preference

Figure 7. Evolution of the profile information given by the participants

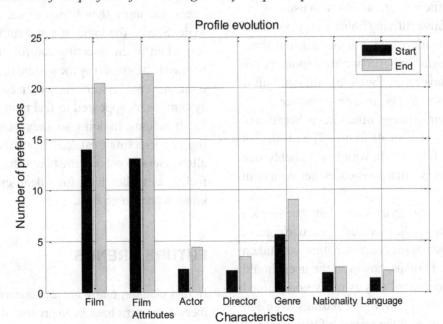

Table 3. Film characteristics declared as important by the participants

Characteristic	% of Participants
Films	75
Actors	58
Genres	54
Directors	42
Language	17
Nationality	12

rating scale that was richer, such as a 5-point scale that begins at "hate", rising through "dislike", "neutral" and "like" and finishing at "love". As well as enriching the scale, they also expressed an interest in declaring complex preferences that were interdependent or contextual. For example, they would have liked to have expressed a preference for *"Charlie Chaplin"* but only in some of his films and not in all of them.

To summarise, these experiments with real users confirm that collaborative filtering systems have better predictive performance than content-based and hybrid systems. On the other hand, content data have been shown to be important to provide an efficient interaction with users.

Collaborative filtering holds a very powerful kind of information that is not found in item data. It allows tastes to be aligned with one another even when items have no attributes in common. This is the main reason for its good performance.

The content strategy offers items because of the proximity of item attributes. The results for this strategy faired well, which is probably due to the semantic similarity encoded between item attributes.

The hybrid strategy appears to have been pulled between the two. The user was allowed to control how much each of the characteristics were taken into account. Perhaps, however, the user should not be able to control this as many complained that they did not know which settings to select. Also, it appears that the mixed information was not best handled by the current system. Further research into hybrid systems is necessary in order to understand the best way in which they can be integrated.

Participants were also asked how they thought that the system operated after receiving all of their recommendations. It is interesting to note that no participants were conscious of the working of the collaborative filtering algorithm. All participants who offered an explanation of the system's logic focused upon the correspondence between individual characteristics of films, such as actors and directors and the preferences that they had indicated. This shows that users are conscious of attribute-based decisions. The use of content data in interacting with the users seems to be a good technique for gaining the user's trust. It also encouraged them to try and influence the system by making profile modifications.

The participants entered as much information about film attributes as they did about films. Although the suitable algorithms were not yet in place in this study in order to exploit the both of them effectively, it is important to note that users want to express both types of information. An interesting effect was also witnessed. The more that users added their film attribute preferences, the more they began to see the system's logic. Seeing the logic of a system is extremely important when asserting control. In fact, users wanted to be guided by the system in order to give it the most useful information. In controlling the system, users appeared to feel more responsible for its actions. In doing so, they were more willing to correct its mistakes. Systems that do not allow users to correct mistake often leave users feeling as if they have hit a dead-end and don't know where to go next.

FUTURE TRENDS

In this chapter, many issues concerning recommender systems have been presented. At the core of these systems is the concept of item appreciation predictions. Current research for improving such is largely focussed on the combination of different approaches. In that field, many *ensemble methods* can be considered (Paterek, 2007), (Takacs et al., 2007). Specific combinations of different recommender systems are also proposed (Bell et al., 2007). Algorithms that are able to learn the similarity metric instead of using predefined ones are also in development (Bell et al., 2007). Taking the temporal evolution of ratings in account, where more recent ones are counted more than older ones, is also proving useful.

The accuracy performances of the current best recommender algorithms are now very similar and can't really be distinguished (for example the best results of the NetFlix Prize http://www.netflixprize.com/leaderboard differentiate only on the third decimal place). In practice, users can't see these differences so it is therefore useful to consider factors other than accuracy, that try to capture quality and usefulness (e.g. coverage, algorithmic complexity, scalability, novelty, confidence and trust, and user satisfaction) (Herlocker et al., 2004).

Experiments with real users suggest that systems should guide them in constructing their profiles. This issue is encouraging new research that is related to the field of *Active Learning* (Cohn et al., 1996). Indeed, which items should be rated to optimise the accuracy of collaborative filtering systems, and which item attributes are more critical for optimal content-based recommendations, are issues that are worth exploring. This naturally raises the parallel issue of how to design an efficient user interface for such an interaction.

CONCLUSION

In the field of recommender systems, collaborative filtering methods often result in better predictive performance than content-based ones, at least

when enough rating data are available. Recommending items based on a set of users' preferences for items carries more meaning than item content information alone. This is especially true with films, since viewers generally choose a film to watch based upon more factors than its genre, director and actors.

On the other hand, content-based filtering offers solutions to the limits of collaborative filtering and provides for a more natural way to interact with users. This issue of designing user-friendly interfaces should not be underestimated. Users must feel like they are in control of their recommendations and that they can navigate themselves out of awkward situations. Otherwise, even if the recommender system is accurate in its predictions, it can suffer from the 'one-visit' problem, if users become frustrated that they cannot express particular preferences or find that the system lacks flexibility. Creating a fun and enduring interaction experience is as essential as making good recommendations.

Focusing on collaborative filtering approaches, item-based ones have been shown to outperform user-based ones. Besides their very good results, item-based approaches also have faster learning and prediction times, at least for datasets that contain more users than items and they are able to produce relevant predictions as soon as a user has rated their first item. Moreover, such models are also appropriate for navigating in item catalogues even when no information about the current user is available, since they can also present a user with the nearest neighbours of an item that she is currently interested in. Finally, the learned neighbourhood matrix can be exported to systems that can exploit items similarities without compromising user privacy.

An important issue in recommender system now is to explore criteria that try to capture quality and usefulness of recommendations from the user's satisfaction perspective like coverage, algorithmic complexity, scalability, novelty, confidence and trust, user interaction.

REFERENCES

Adomavicius, G., & Tuzhilin, A. (2005). Toward the next generation of recommender systems: A survey of the state-of-the-art and possible extensions. *IEEE Transactions on Knowledge and Data Engineering, 17*(6), 734–749.

Balabanovic, M., & Shoham, Y. (1997). Fab: Content-based, collaborative recommendation. *Communications of the ACM, 40*(3), 66-72.

Basu, C., Hirsh, H., & Cohen, W. W. (1998). Recommendation as classification: Using social and content-based information in recommendation. In *15th National Conference on Artificial Intelligence* (pp. 714–720).

Bell, R., Koren, Y., & Volinsky, C. (2007). Modeling relationships at multiple scales to improve accuracy of large recommender systems. In *13th ACM SIGKDD International Conference on Knowledge Discovery and Data Mining* (pp. 95–104). New York, NY, USA. ACM.

Bilgic, M. (2004). *Explanation for Recommender Systems: Satisfaction vs. Promotion*. PhD thesis, University of Texas at Austin, Department of Computer Sciences.

Billsus, D., & Pazzani, M J. (1999). A personal news agent that talks, learns and explains. In Etzioni, O., Müller, J.P., & Bradshaw, J.M. (Ed.), *3rd International Conference on Autonomous Agents* (pp. 268-275). ACM Press.

Breese, J., Heckerman, D., & Kadie, C. (1998). Empirical analysis of predictive algorithms for collaborative filtering. In *14th Conference on Uncertainty in Artificial Intelligence* (pp. 43–52). Morgan Kaufman.

Candillier, L., Meyer, F., & Boullé, M. (2007). Comparing state-of-the-art collaborative filtering systems. In Perner, P. (Ed.), *5th International Conference on Machine Learning and Data Mining in Pattern Recognition* (pp. 548–562), Leipzig, Germany. Springer Verlag.

Cilibrasi, R., & Vitanyi, P.M.B. (2007). The Google similarity distance. *IEEE Transactions on Knowledge and Data Engineering, 19*(3), 370-383.

Cohn, D. A., Ghahramani, Z., & Jordan M. I. (1996). Active Learning with Statistical Models. In *Journal of Artificial Intelligence Research, 4*, 129-145.

Deshpande, M., & Karypis, G. (2004). Item-based top-N recommendation algorithms. In *ACM Transactions on Information Systems, 22*(1), 143–177.

Han, E.-H. S., & Karypis, G. (2005). Feature-based recommendation system. In *14th Conference of Information and Knowledge Management* (pp. 446-452).

Herlocker, J., Konstan, J., & Riedl, J. (2000). Explaining collaborative filtering recommendations. In *ACM Conference on Computer Supported Cooperative Work*.

Herlocker, J., Konstan, J., Terveen, L., & Riedl, J. (2004). Evaluating collaborative filtering recommender systems. In *ACM Transactions on Information Systems, 22*(1), 5–53.

Jack, K., & Duclaye, F. (2007). Etude de la pertinence de critères de recherche en recherche d'informations sur des données structurées. In *PeCUSI, INFORSID* (pp. 285-297). Perros-Guirec, France.

Jack, K., & Duclayee, F. (2008). Improving Explicit Preference Entry by Visualising Data Similarities. In *Intelligent User Interfaces, International Workshop on Recommendation and Collaboration (ReColl)*. Spain.

Karypis, G. (2001). Evaluation of item-based top-N recommendation algorithms. In *10th International Conference on Information and Knowledge Management* (pp. 247–254).

Kelleher, J., & Bridge, D. (2003). Rectree centroid: An accurate, scalable collaborative recommender. In Cunningham, P., Fernando, T., & Vogel, C. (Ed.), *14th Irish Conference on Artificial Intelligence and Cognitive Science* (pp. 89–94).

Kleinberg, J., & Sandler, M. (2004). Using mixture models for collaborative filtering. In *36th ACM Symposium on Theory of Computing* (pp. 569–578). ACM Press.

Krulwich, B. (1997). LIFESTYLE FINDER: Intelligent User Profiling Using Large-Scale Demographic Data. *AI Magazine* (pp. 37-45).

Lam, S. K., Frankowski, D., & Riedl, J. (2006). Do you trust your recommendations? An exploration of security and privacy issues in recommender systems. In *International Conference on Emerging Trends in Information and Communication Security*.

Lin, W., Alvarez, S., & Ruiz, C. (2002). Efficient adaptive-support association rule mining for recommender systems. In *Data Mining and Knowledge Discovery*, 6, 83–105.

Linden, G., Smith, B., & York, J. (2003). Amazon.com recommendations: Item-to-item collaborative filtering. In *IEEE Internet Computing, 7*(1), 76–80.

McNee, S., Riedl, J., & Konstan, J. (2006). Being accurate is not enough: How accuracy metrics have hurt recommender systems. In *Extended Abstracts of the 2006 ACM Conference on Human Factors in Computing Systems*.

Melville, P., Mooney, R., & Nagarajan, R. (2002). Content-boosted collaborative filtering for improved recommendations. In *18th National Conference on Artificial Intelligence* (pp. 187-192).

Miller, B., Albert, I., Lam, S., Konstan, J., & Riedl, J. (2003). MovieLens unplugged: experiences with an occasionally connected recommender system. In *8th international conference on Intelligent User Interfaces* (pp. 263-266). ACM.

Mooney, R., & Roy, L. (1999). Content-based book recommending using learning for text categorization. In *ACM SIGIR'99, Workshop on Recommender Systems: Algorithms and Evaluation*.

Nageswara Rao, K., & Talwar, V.G. (2008). Application domain and functional classification of recommender systems a survey. In *Desidoc journal of library and information technology*, vol 28, n°3, 17-36.

Nguyen, A., Denos, N., & Berrut, C. (2007). Improving new user recommendations with rule-based induction on cold user data. In *RecSys2007* (pp. 121-128).

O'Conner, M., & Herlocker, J. (1999). Clustering items for collaborative filtering. In *ACM SIGIR Workshop on Recommender Systems*.

Paterek A. (2007). Improving regularized singular value decomposition for collaborative filtering. In *KDD cup Workshop at SIGKDD*.

Pazzani, M., & Billsus, D. (1997). Learning and revising user profiles: The identification of interesting web sites. In *Machine Learning, 27*, 313–331.

Pazzani, M., & Billsus, D. (2007). Content-Based Recommendation Systems. In *The Adaptive Web*, 325-341.

Pazzani, M. J. (1999). A framework for collaborative, content-based and demographic filtering. In *Artificial Intelligence Review, 13*(5-6), 393–408.

Pennock, D., Horvitz, E., Lawrence, S., & Giles, C. L. (2000). Collaborative filtering by personality diagnosis: A hybrid memory-and model-based approach. In *16th Conference on Uncertainty in Artificial Intelligence* (pp. 473–480).

Polcicova, G., Slovak, R., & Navrat, P. (2000). Combining content-based and collaborative filtering. In *ADBIS-DASFAA Symposium* (pp. 118-127).

Resnick, P., Iacovou, N., Suchak, M., Bergstrom, P., & Riedl, J. (1994). Grouplens: An open architecture for collaborative filtering of netnews. In *Conference on Computer Supported Cooperative Work* (pp. 175–186). ACM.

Sarwar, B. M., Karypis, G., Konstan, J. A., & Riedl, J. (2000). Analysis of recommendation algorithms for e-commerce. In *ACM Conference on Electronic Commerce* (pp. 158–167).

Sarwar, B. M., Karypis, G., Konstan, J., & Riedl, J. (2001). Item-based collaborative filtering recommendation algorithms. In *10th International World Wide Web Conference*.

Shardanand, U., & Maes, P. (1995). Social information filtering: Algorithms for automating "word of mouth". In *ACM Conference on Human Factors in Computing Systems*, *1*, 210–217.

Takacs, G., Pilaszy, I., Nemeth, B., & Tikk, D. (2007). On the gravity recommendation system. In *KDD cup Workshop at SIGKDD*.

Ungar, L., & Foster, D. (1998). Clustering methods for collaborative filtering. In *Workshop on Recommendation Systems*. AAAI Press.

Vozalis, M., & Margaritis, K. G. (2004). Enhancing collaborative filtering with demographic data: The case of item-based filtering. In *4th International Conference on Intelligent Systems Design and Applications* (pp. 361–366).

Wang, J., de Vries, A. P., & Reinders, M. J. (2006). Unifying user-based and item-based collaborative filtering approaches by similarity fusion. In *29th International ACM SIGIR Conference on Research and Development in Information Retrieval* (pp. 501-508).

Zhang, Y., Callan, J., & Minka, T. (2002). Novelty and redundancy detection in adaptive filtering. In *ACM SIGIR '02*.

Ziegler, C.-N., McNee, S., Konstan, J., & Lausen, G. (2005). Improving recommendation lists through topic diversification. In *14th International World Wide Web Conference* (pp. 22–32).

Chapter II
Computing Recommendations with Collaborative Filtering

Neal Lathia
University College London, UK

ABSTRACT

Recommender systems generate personalized content for each of its users, by relying on an assumption reflected in the interaction between people: those who have had similar opinions in the past will continue sharing the same tastes in the future. Collaborative filtering, the dominant algorithm underlying recommender systems, uses a model of its users, contained within profiles, in order to guide what interactions should be allowed, and how these interactions translate first into predicted ratings, and then into recommendations. In this chapter, the authors introduce the various approaches that have been adopted when designing collaborative filtering algorithms, and how they differ from one another in the way they make use of the available user information. They then explore how these systems are evaluated, and highlight a number of problems that prevent recommendations from being suitably computed, before looking at the how current trends in recommender system research are projecting towards future developments.

INTRODUCTION

Recommender systems are experiencing a growing presence on the Internet; they have evolved from being interesting additions of e-commerce web sites into essential components and, in some cases, the core of online businesses. The success of these systems stems from the underlying algorithm, based on collaborative filtering, which re-enacts the way humans exchange recommendations in a way that can be scaled to communities of millions of online users. Users of these systems will thus see personalized, unique, and interest-based recommendations presented to them computed according to the opinions of the other users in the system, and can actively contribute to other's recommendations by inputting their own ratings.

This chapter introduces recommender systems and the algorithms, based on collaborative filtering, that fuel the success these systems are experiencing in current online applications. There are a number of methods that have been applied when designing filtering algorithms, but they all share a common assumption: the users, and the interactions between them, can be modeled in such a way that it is possible to filter content based on the responses they input.

In particular, the objectives of this chapter can be decomposed into a number of questions:

- Why do we need recommender systems; what problem do they address?
- How are recommendations generated? This question explores collaborative filtering: what it is, how it works, and how different fields of research have led collaborative filtering to be categorized into memory- and model-based approaches.
- How are recommender systems evaluated? In particular, what problems do these systems face, and how does research address these problems? Lastly,
- What are the current future directions of recommender system research?

We explore these questions by considering the participants of a recommender system as members of a community of users. This method highlights the importance of user models within recommender systems, both as a means of reasoning about the underlying operations on the data and building a system that end-users will respond positively to. However, we begin by looking at the motivating problems and history of these systems.

BACKGROUND

As the Internet grows, forever broadening both the range and diversity of information that it makes accessible to its users, a new problem arises: the amount of information available, and the rate at which new information is produced, becomes too great for individuals to sift through it all and find relevant resources. Resources may include, but are not limited to, movies, music, products of e-commerce catalogues, blogs, news articles and documents. Users, unable to dedicate the time to browse all that is available, are thus confronted with the problem of *information overload*, and the sheer abundance of information diminishes users' ability to identify what would be most useful and valuable to each of their needs.

Recommender systems, based on the principles of collaborative filtering, have been developed in response to information overload, by acting as a decision-aiding tool. However, recommender systems break away from merely helping users search for content towards providing interest-based, personalized content without requiring any search query. Recommender systems diverge from traditional information retrieval by building long term models of each user's preferences, and selectively combining different users' opinions in order to provide each user with unique recommendations.

Research into the field of collaborative filtering began in the early 1990s, with the first filtering system, Tapestry, being developed at the Xerox Palo Alto Research Center (Goldberg et al, 1992). This system, recognizing that simply using mailing lists would not ensure that all users interested in an e-mail's content would receive the message, allowed users to annotate e-mail messages so that others could filter them by building complex queries. This was the first system to capture the power of combining human judgments, expressed in message annotations, with automated filtering, in order to benefit all of the system's users. Similar concepts were later applied to Usenet news by the GroupLens research project, which extended previous work by applying the same principles to the Internet discussion forum, which had become too big for any single user to manage (Konstan et al, 1997). In doing so, they created the first *virtual community of recommenders*, which we will explore further below. The GroupLens project continues contributing to recommender system research, and has also implemented the MovieLens movie recommender system, providing the research community with valuable data of user ratings.

The initial success that recommender systems experienced reflected the surge of web sites dedicated to e-commerce; Schafer et al (2001) review and describe a number of mainstream examples that implement these systems. The cited sites, like Amazon.com and CDNow.com, implement recommenders to build customer loyalty, increase profits, and boost item-cross selling. In fact, it has been reported that 35% of Amazon.com's product sales come from recommendations, recommendations generate 38% more click-through on Google news, and over two thirds of movies rented by online movie-renting site Netflix were recommended (Celma & Lamere, 2007). The same technologies can also be used to address a wide range of different needs. These include ad targeting and one-to-one marketing. However, Schafer et al also describe the relationship between recommender systems and users rating buyers and sellers on sites like eBay.com; in fact, they touch upon the overlap between recommendation and reputation systems. More recently, web sites like Last.fm have reaped the benefits of collecting user-music listening habits, in order to provide customized radio stations and music recommendations to their subscribers. The influence, presence, and importance of the recommender system is not only well established, but also grows over time, as we address the evermore important problem of filtering never ending content.

Before introducing the underlying algorithms of recommender systems, it is useful to define the terms that will be used throughout this chapter.

- **User:** the end-user of the system, or the person we wish to provide with recommendations. This is often referred to as the *active user*; however, in this chapter we differentiate between the current users we are generating recommendations for and the users contributing to the recommendation by referring to the latter users as *recommenders*. The entire set of users is referred to as the *community.*

- **Rating:** The problem of generating recommendations is often described as a problem of *predicting* how much a user will like, or the exact rating that the user will give to, a particular item. Ratings can be explicit or implicit, as detailed in the next section.

- **Profile:** Users in a recommender system can be modeled according to a wide variety of information, but the most important information is the set of ratings that users have provided the system with, which corresponds to each user's profile. These are considered in more depth below.

RATINGS AND USER PROFILES

The focal point of recommender systems is the set of user profiles; by containing a collection of judgments, or ratings, of the available content, this set provides an invaluable source of information that can be used to provide each user with recommendations.

Human judgments, however, can come from two separate sources. These are related to the broader category of *relevance feedback* from the information retrieval community (Ruthven & Lalmas, 2003); a comprehensive review of information retrieval techniques can be found Faloutsos & Oar, 1995. On the one hand, the judgments could be in the form of *explicit* ratings. For example, a user who liked a movie could give it a 4-star rating, or can give a faulty product a 1-star rating; the judgment is a numeric value that is input directly by the user. On the other hand, judgments can be extracted from the *implicit* behavior of the user. These include time spent reading a web page, number of times a particular song or artist was listened to, or the items viewed when browsing an online catalogue. Measuring these qualities is an attempt to capture taste by measuring how users interact with the content, and thus will often depend on the specific context that the recommender system is operating upon. For example, movie-recommender systems often prefer to let users explicitly rate movies, since it might often be the case that users disliked a particular movie. Music recommender systems, on the other hand, tend to construct user profiles based on listening habits, by collecting meta-data of the songs each user has listened to; these systems favor implicit ratings by assuming that users will only listen to music they like. Implicit ratings can be converted to a numeric value with an appropriate transpose function, and therefore the algorithms we describe below are equally applicable to both types of data. They also both share a common characteristic: the set of available judgments for each user, compared to the total number of items that can be rated, will be very small. This stems from the very nature of the information overload problem, and without it, recommender systems would no longer be needed. The lack of information is often referred to the problem of data *sparsity*, and has a strong effect on the predictive power of any algorithms that base their recommendations on this data. A small example of a set of user profiles, often called

a user-rating matrix, for a movie recommender system, is shown in Table 1.

The problem of data sparsity reveals itself in this example; not all users have rated all the content. It also paves the way for the algorithms we describe in the following sections, which aim at predicting ratings for each user. It is important to note, however, that the techniques described here can be equally applied to both user profiles, which contain a vector of content (or item) ratings, and item profiles, which contain a vector of user ratings (Sarwar et al, 2001; Linden et al, 2003). For example, a user-centered approach would refer to "Alice's" profile as containing "Citizen Kane" and "Hannibal," with 4 and 3 star ratings, respectively. An item-centered approach, instead, would consider "The Matrix's" profile as "Bob" and "David," who assigned 5 and 2 stars to the item. Both methods produce comparable results, and differ only in their perspective of the system; one considers the rows of the user-rating matrix, and the other uses the columns. In this chapter, we focus on the user-centered approach. Furthermore, a rating give by user u for item i will be referred to as r_{ui}, and the set of ratings that correspond to user u's profile is R_u.

Although above we have differentiated between the explicit and implicit collection of user preferences, the two methods need not be separate. In fact, Basu et al (2001) discuss how technical papers can be recommended to reviewers by combining information from multiple sources; not limiting the sources of information can improve recommendation by increasing the knowledge we have of each user's profile. However, Herlocker et al (2004) identified that user profiles are created

Table 1.

	The Matrix	Citizen Kane	Hannibal	Snow White	...
Alice		4	3		...
Bob	5		4	1	...
David	2	4		4	...
...	...	...	...	...	...

for different reasons, including self-expression, and helping or influencing others' decisions. Similarly, the tasks that are requested of recommender systems can vary, from finding good items, finding all items, recommending a sequence of items, or as a browsing aide. However, the main goal of recommender systems remains the same: we aim at filtering content in order to provide relevant and useful suggestions to each user of the system. The particular task, or context, will influence the approaches that can be used, which we discuss below. Filters are often classified into one of two categories; *content*-based filters, or *collaborative*-filters.

CONTENT-BASED FILTERS

Content-based recommender system algorithms disregard the *collaborative* component, which we will explore further below, and base their recommendation generative power on matching descriptions of the content in the system to individual user profiles (Pazzani & Billsus, 2007). The key to these recommendations lies in decomposing the content in the system into a number of attributes, which may be based on enumerable, well-defined descriptive variables, such as those found in an explicit taxonomy. The attributes can also be extracted features, such as word frequency in news articles, or user-input tags. The user profile, on the other hand, contains a model of the items that are of interest to that user. These may include a history of purchases, or explicitly defined areas of interest; for example, a user may input the sort of qualities desired when looking for a product (e.g. "price is less than," "album artist is," and so on).

Recommendations can then be generated by applying one of a wide variety of methods to the user model of preferences. These include rule induction methods and decision trees; a comprehensive review can be found in Pazzani & Billsus (2007). However, an interesting consequence of

building recommender systems this way is that they can quickly adapt to and change recommendations based on the user's immediate feedback. This leads to the idea of *conversational* recommenders, which allows users to revise the preferences they input by critiquing the obtained results (Viappiani et al, 2007). In doing so, user models themselves are highly dynamic and specific to the current recommendation that is sought, and allow users to understand the effect of their preferences on the recommendations they are given.

Content-based systems, however, are not appropriately or readily applied to the entire range of scenarios where users may benefit from recommendations. On the one hand, these systems require content that favors analysis, and can be described in terms of a number of attributes, which may not always be the case. Eliciting preferences is a valid data collection technique in a limited number of contexts and more suitable for environments where content attributes play a significant role in each user's ultimate decision, such as selecting an apartment, a restaurant, or a laptop computer. In other cases, it may be too much work to impose on the user, and the collaborative filtering alternative is a more appropriate solution.

COLLABORATIVE FILTERING

Unlike content-based systems, collaborative filtering algorithms take a "black-box" approach to content that is being filtered (Herlocker et al, 1999). In other words, they completely disregard any descriptions or attributes of the data, or what the data actually is, in favor of human judgments, and focuses on generating recommendations based on the opinions that have been expressed by a community of users. In doing so, they augment the power of filtering algorithms towards pure quality-based filtering, and have been widely applied to a variety of Internet web sites, such as the ones explored above.

The problem of generating recommendations, and the use of the data that is available to tackle this task, has been approached from a very wide range of perspectives. Each perspective applies different heuristics and methodologies in order to create recommendations. In the following sections, we review the two broadest categories of filters: memory- and model-based collaborative filtering followed by a brief look at other methods and hybrid approaches.

Memory-Based Collaborative Filtering

Memory-based collaborative filtering is often referred to as the dominant method of generating recommendations; its clear structure, paired with the successful results it produces, makes it an easy choice for system developers. It is called memory-based filtering since it relies on the assumption that users who have been historically like-minded in the past will continue sharing their interests in the future (Herlocker et al, 1999). Therefore, recommendations can be produced for a user by generating predicted ratings of unrated content, based on an aggregate of the ratings given by the most similar (or "nearest") users from within the community. This is why the process is often referred to as *k*NN, or *k* nearest-neighbor filtering, and can be decomposed into three stages; neighborhood formation, opinion aggregation, and recommendation.

Neighborhood Formation

This first step aims at finding a unique subset of the community for each user, by identifying others with similar interests to act as recommenders. To do so, every pair of user profiles is compared, in order to measure the degree of similarity $w_{a,b}$ shared between all user pairs a and b. In general, similarity values range from 1 (perfect similarity) to -1 (perfect dissimilarity), although different measures may only return values on a limited

amount of this range. If a pair of users has no profile overlap, there is no means of comparing how similar they are, and thus the similarity is set to 0.

Similarity can be measured in a number of ways, but the main goal of this measure remains that of modeling the potential relationship between users with a numeric value. The simplest means of measuring the strength of this relationship is to count the proportion of co-rated items shared by the pair of users (Charikar 2002):

$$w_{a,b} = \frac{|R_a \cap R_b|}{|R_a \cup R_b|} \tag{1}$$

This similarity measure disregards the values of the ratings input by each user, and instead opts to only consider *what* each user has rated; it is the size of the intersection of the two users' profiles over the size of the union. The underlying assumption is that two users who continuously rate the same items share a common characteristic: their choice to rate those items.

However, the most cited method of measuring similarity is the Pearson Correlation Coefficient, which aims at measuring the degree of linearity that exists on the intersection of the pair of users' profiles (Breese et al, 1998; Herlocker et al, 1999): this is a measure of linearity between two user's profiles.

$$w_{a,b} = \frac{\sum_{i=1}^{N} (r_{a,i} - \overline{r_a})(r_{b,i} - \overline{r_b})}{\sqrt{\sum_{i=1}^{N} (r_{a,i} - \overline{r_a})^2 \sum_{i=1}^{N} (r_{b,i} - \overline{r_b})^2}} \tag{2}$$

Each rating above is normalized by subtracting the user's mean rating; this value is the average of all the ratings in the user profile. The Pearson Correlation similarity measure has been subject to a number of improvements. For example, if the intersection between the pair of user's profiles is very small, the resulting similarity measure is highly unreliable, as it may indicate a very strong relationship between the two users (who, on the other hand, have only co-rated very few items). To address this, Herlocker et al (1999) introduced *significance weighting*: if the number of co-rated items n is less than a threshold value x, the similarity measure is multiplied by n/x. This modification reflects the fact that similarity measures become more reliable as the number of co-rated items increases, and has positive effects on the predictive power of the filtering algorithm. The same researchers also cite the *constrained* Pearson correlation coefficient, which replaces the user means in the above equation with the rating scale midpoint.

There are a number of other ways of measuring similarity that have been applied in the past. These include the Spearman Rank correlation, the Vector Similarity (or cosine angle between the two user profiles), Euclidean and Manhattan distance, and other methods aimed at capturing the proportion of agreement between users, such as the methods explored by Agresti and Winner (1997). Each method differs in the operations it applies in order to derive similarity, and may have a strong effect on the power the algorithm has to generate predicted ratings.

Similarity measures are also often coupled with other heuristics that aim at improving the reliability and power of the derived measures. For example, Yu et al (2001) introduced *variance weighting*; when comparing user profiles, items that have been rated by the community with greater variance receive a higher weight. The aim here is to capture the content that, by being a measurably high point of disagreement amongst community members, is a better descriptor of taste. Measuring similarity, however, remains an open issue; to date, there is little that can be done other than comparing prediction accuracy in order to demonstrate that one similarity measure outperforms another on a particular dataset.

Opinion Aggregation

Once comparisons between the user and the rest of the community of recommenders (regardless of the method applied) are complete, we have a set of recommender weights, and predicted ratings of unrated content can be computed. As above, there are a number of means of computing these predictions. Here we present two (Herlocker et al, 1999; Bell & Koren, 2007):

$$p_{a,i} = \overline{r_a} + \frac{\sum \left(r_{b,i} - \overline{r_b} \right) w_{a,b}}{\sum w_{a,b}} \qquad (3)$$

$$p_{a,i} = \frac{\sum \left(r_{b,i} \times w_{a,b} \right)}{\sum w_{a,b}} \qquad (4)$$

Both equations share a common characteristic: a predicted rating $p_{a,i}$ of item i for user a is computed as a weighted average of neighbor ratings $r_{b,i}$. The weights $w_{a,b}$ are the similarity measures we found in the first step, and therefore neighbors who are more similar will have greater influence on the prediction. The main difference between the two methods is that Equation 3 subtracts each recommender's mean from the relative rating. The aim of this method is to minimize the differences between different recommender's rating style, by considering how much ratings deviate from each recommender's mean rather than the rating itself.

The natural question to ask at this step is: which recommender ratings are chosen to contribute to the predicted rating? A variety of choices is once again available, and has a direct impact on the performance that can be achieved. In some cases, only the top-k most similar neighbors are allowed to contribute ratings, thus guaranteeing that only the closest ratings create the prediction. However, it is often the case that none of the top-k neighbors have rated the item in question, and thus the prediction *coverage*, or the number of items that can be successfully predicted, is negatively impacted. A straightforward alternative, therefore, is to consider the top-k recommenders who *can* give rating information about the item in question. On the one hand, this method guarantees that all predictions will be made; on the other hand, predictions may now be made according to ratings provided by only modestly-similar users, and may thus be less accurate.

A last alternative is to only select users above a pre-determined similarity threshold. Given that different similarity measures will produce different similarity values, generating predictions this way may also prevent predictions from being covered. All methods, however, share a common decision: what should the threshold value, or value of k, be? This question remains unanswered and dependent on the available dataset; however, research in the area tends to publish results for a wide range of values.

Recommendation

Once predicted ratings have been generated for the items, and sorted according to predicted value, the top-n items can be proposed to the end user as recommendations. This step completes the process followed by recommender systems, which can now elicit feedback from the user. User profiles will grow, and the recommender system can begin cycling through the above process: re-computing user similarity measures, predicting ratings, and offering recommendations.

It is important to note that the user interface of the system plays a vital role in this last step. The interface does not only determine the ability the system has to present generated recommendations to the end user in a clear, transparent way, but will also have an effect on the response that the user gives to received recommendations. Wu & Huberman (2007) conducted a study investigating the temporal evolution of opinions of products posted on the web. They concluded that if the aggregate rating of an item is visible to users and the cost

of expressing opinions for users is low (e.g. one click of a mouse), users will tend to express either neutral ratings or reinforce the view set by previous ratings. On the other hand, if the cost is high (such as requiring users to write a full review), users tended to offer opinions when they felt they could offset the current trend. Changing the visibility of information and the cost imposed on users to express their opinions, both determined by the interface provided to end users, will thus change the rating trend of the content, and the data that feeds into the filtering algorithm.

Up to this point, we have considered the process of generating recommendations strictly from the memory-based, nearest-neighbor approach. However, tackling the problem of information overload has been approached from a wide range of research fields and backgrounds. In the following section we review some of the contributions made by the field of machine learning, often referred to as model-based collaborative filtering.

Model-Based Collaborative Filtering

Model-based approaches to collaborative filtering, stemming from the field of machine learning, aim to apply the broad set of solutions developed by that field of research to the problem of information filtering. A complete introduction to machine learning is beyond the scope of this chapter, although there are many sources available for background reading, such as Alpaydin (2004).

The applicability of machine-learning techniques is founded in our original description of the aim of filtering: we would like to predict how much users will like, or rate, the content they have not rated already, and rank these items in order to provide the top-n as recommendations. In other words, collaborative filtering falls between the broader categories of *classification*, or deciding what rating group unrated items belong to, and *regression*, the process of modeling the relationship a variable (such as a user rating) has with other variables (the set of user profiles).

An example that highlights the applicability of these techniques to recommender systems is the use of a p-rank algorithm (Crammer & Singer, 2001). The items that a user has rated, in this case, are considered as a set of training *instances*. Each instance can be described by a vector of features x; in our case, the features correspond to the ratings given to the item by the community of users. The goal of the algorithm is to learn a *ranking rule*, or mapping from an instance to the correct rank (or, equivalently, a mapping from a user-item to the correct rating). To do so, the algorithm needs to learn how to weight the individual features, and will attempt to do so by iterating over the training instances. It begins with a vector of weights w (set to an initial value), and a set of b *thresholds*, one for each rank possible. Therefore, for example, if a 5-star rating scale is implemented, $b = 5$. At each step, it will make a prediction based on the current set of weights, by multiplying the feature vector x with the weight vector w. The predicted rank is then computed as the index r of the smallest threshold such that $w \times x < b_r$. When the user inputs the actual rating, the algorithm can check to see if it made a mistake, and, if it did, it will update its weights w and thresholds b. Over time, this algorithm aims to minimize the loss between predicted and actual ranks, by learning how to make accurate predictions using a set of instance features. This algorithm approaches the problem of filtering as an instance of a linear classification problem, and thus its inception is based on perceptron classifiers.

The p-rank algorithm is just one of the solutions proposed by the machine learning community. Other quoted examples include the use of singular value decomposition, neural net classifiers, Bayesian networks, support vector machines, induction rule learning, and latent semantic analysis (Breese et al, 1998; Yu et al, 2004). Each differs in the method applied to learn how to generate recommendations, but they all share a similar high-level solution: they are based on inferring rules and patterns from the available rating data.

Model-based approaches are attractive solutions since, once trained, they compute predicted ratings extremely efficiently. However, they have had limited success, since (the simpler) memory-based approaches have been shown to be just as accurate (Grcar et al, 2005). The two categories of solutions also differ in their interpretation of the users operating within the system. Memory-based methods model all user interactions based on measurable similarity-values, and thus leads to the notion of a community of recommenders. Model-based approaches, instead, train a *separate* model for each user in the system, and are thus characterized by a stronger subjective view of the recommender system's end users.

Hybrid Methods

As we have seen, filtering algorithms have been designed from a number of different backgrounds, leading to the categorization of these algorithms into memory- and model-based groups. Each method provides a number of advantages, and faces a number of weaknesses. Hybrid methods, combining a series of techniques from both groups, aim at achieving the best of both worlds: the advantages of each method stripped of the weaknesses that it faces when operating alone.

For example, Rashid et al (2006) proposed a filtering algorithm suitable for extremely large datasets that combines a clustering algorithm with the nearest-neighbor prediction method. The aim was to cluster similar users together first, in order to overcome the incredibly costly operation of measuring the similarity between all of the community user pairs in the system, and then apply a nearest-neighbor technique to make predictions in order to reap the high accuracy it tends to achieve. Much like the work presented by Li & Kim (2003), clustering methods can be implemented to replace the "neighborhood formation" step of memory-based approach described above. The Yoda system, designed by Shahabi et al (2001), is an example system that performs similar functions: clustering is implemented to address the scalability issues that arise as the community of users and available items grows. A full overview of the performance of memory- and model-based approaches is available in Breese et al (1998).

Other means of modeling a community of users in order to successfully filter information for each member have been proposed; for example, Cayzer & Aickelin (2002) drew parallels between information filtering and the operation of the human immune system, in order to construct a novel means of filtering. Another example moves into the domain of recommending a *coherent* ordering of songs by applying case-based reasoning (Baccigalupo & Plaza, 2007). Case-based reasoning looks at a set of previous experiences in order to derive information that can be applied to a new problem. Solving the new problem follows similar steps to that described for general machine learning procedures, and entails retrieving the correct sub-set of experiences, applying them to the current problem, and then revising the solution based on any received feedback. This technique was applied successfully to a domain where simply predicting good songs was not enough, but predicting a good sequence of songs was desired.

Up to now, we have had a high-level overview of the multiple approaches applied to recommender systems. However, as we will discuss in the next section, none of the above methods is perfect; moreover, they all share common weaknesses and problems that hinder the generation of useful recommendations.

RECOMMENDER SYSTEMS: PROBLEMS AND EVALUATIONS

The issues that recommender systems face can be grouped into three generic categories: problems arising from within the algorithm, user issues, and

system vulnerabilities. A good part of research into collaborative filtering has thus centered on solving these problems, or minimizing the effect that they have on the system and the end user experience. In doing so, the primary metrics used to evaluate these systems emerge, and further questions regarding the suitability of these evaluation methods arise. In this section we will take a look at how experiments on filtering algorithms are conducted, what error measures can be extracted, and the problems that these measures highlight in the operation of recommender systems.

Algorithm

The first set of issues stem from the filtering algorithms applied to generate recommendations. As we have seen above, the common goal of the many algorithms is to *predict* how much users will like different items on offer to them.

Missing Data

Predictions are based on the rating information that has been input by the community of users, and the breadth and number of ratings available is generally much smaller than the full possible set of ratings. In other words, as we have seen, the user-rating matrix is very *sparse*. This characteristic of the data prevents user profiles from being compared to one another, as there will often not be an overlap between the two profiles, and therefore the incomparable pair of users will never be able to contribute to each other's predictions. In other words, the amount of information that can be propagated around the community by means of similarity becomes limited. Solutions to this problem have been proposed; these include dimensionality reduction techniques, such as singular value decomposition (Paterek, 2007), and missing data prediction algorithms (Ma et al, 2007).

Accuracy Error Metrics

Regardless of whether a method is applied to tackle data sparsity, the main task remains that of predicting items users will like. To evaluate how well an algorithm is accomplishing this task, experiments are performed on one of the available user-rating datasets. The dataset is first partitioned into two subsets; the first acts as a *training* set, and will be used to set any values required by the algorithm. These may include, in the case of nearest-neighbor filtering, user-similarity values and determining each user's top-*k* recommenders. In the case of model-based approaches, the training set would determine what instances are available for the algorithm to learn from. The second subset is the *test* set, and remains hidden to the algorithm. An evaluation will feed the training set into the algorithm, and then ask the algorithm to make predictions on all the items in the test set. Predictions can thus be compared to the actual, hidden values held in the test set, and measures of accuracy and coverage can be extracted.

Accuracy metrics aim to evaluate how well the system is making predictions. Available measures of statistical accuracy include the mean absolute error (MAE) and the root mean squared error (RMSE):

$$MAE = \frac{\sum_N |r_{a,i} - p_{a,i}|}{N} \tag{5}$$

$$RMSE = \sqrt{\frac{\sum_N (r_{a,i} - p_{a,i})^2}{N}} \tag{6}$$

Both of the above measures focus on the difference between a rating of item *i* by user *a*, $r_{a,i}$, and the prediction for the same user and item, $p_{a,i}$. In general, both metrics measure the same thing and will thus behave similarly; if an experiment outputs a reduced MAE, the RMSE will also reduce. The difference lies in the degree to which different mistakes are penalized.

The traditional focus on accuracy in recommender research continues to be disputed. On the one hand, the above accuracy metrics focus on the predictions that have been output by the algorithm, regardless of whether the prediction was at all possible or not. Massa & Avesani (2007) have shown that, in terms of prediction accuracy, these systems seem to perform well when pre-defined values are returned. For example, if each prediction simply returned the current user mean (thus not allowing content to be ranked and converted into recommendations), accuracy metrics would still not reflect such poor behavior. McLaughlin & Herlocker (2004) further this argument, by arguing that striving for low mean errors biases recommender systems towards good predictors rather than recommenders. In other words, a error in a prediction affects the mean error the same way, regardless of whether the prediction enabled the entry to qualify as a top-*n* recommendation or not. Furthermore, as shown in the work by Yu et al (2001), many items will have a low rating variance. A natural consequence of this is that an evaluation method that only makes predictions on items in the test set, items that the user has rated, will tend to show good performance. Real systems, that have to provide recommendations based on making predictions on *all* unrated items may have much worse performance. Mean errors will therefore not tend to reflect the end-user experience. Concerns over accuracy-centric research continues; McNee et al (2006) even argued that striving for accuracy is detrimental to recommender system research, and propose that evaluations should revert to user-centric methods.

Accuracy metrics persist, however, due to the need for empirical evaluations of filtering algorithms which can compare the relative performance of different techniques without including the subjective views of a limited (and, more often than not, inaccessible) group of test subjects. Some fixes have been proposed; for example, Lathia et al (2008) limit the measurement of error to predictions that were possible. In this case, it is imperative to report both accuracy and coverage metrics (as described below) to provide a clear picture of an algorithm's performance; however, this fix does not address the issue of whether a prediction excludes an item from a top-*n* list, and the effect this will have on the end user.

Coverage metrics aim to explore the breadth of predictions that were possible using the given method. Looking back on Equations 3 and 4, it is possible to conceive of a scenario where no neighbor rating information can be found, and thus no prediction can be made. In these cases a default value is returned instead; often this value is the user's rating mean, and these predictions will be labeled uncovered. Coverage metrics compare the proportion of the dataset that is uncovered to the size of the test set, in order to measure the extent that predictions were made possible using the current algorithm and parameters.

Other error measures have been applied when analyzing the accuracy of a filtering algorithm, including receiver-operating characteristic (ROC) sensitivity (Herlocker et al, 1999). This measure draws from work done in Information Retrieval, and aims at measuring how effectively predicted ratings helped a user select high-quality items. Recommendations are therefore reduced to a binary decision: either the user "consumed" the content (i.e. watched the movie, listened to the song, read the article) and rated it, or did not. By comparing the number of false-positives, or items that should have been recommended that were not, and false-negatives, or not recommending an item that should have been, this metric aims at measuring the extent to which the recommender system is helping users making good decisions. However, this method relies on a prediction score threshold that determines whether the item was recommended or not, which is often not translate to the way that users are presented with recommendations.

User-Related Problems

Although poor accuracy and coverage will have a great influence on the user response to the recommender system, the second set of problems is tied much closer to the immediate user experience with the system.

The first of these issues is referred to as the *cold-start* problem; this problem can affect users, items, and new recommender systems equally. On the one hand, users with no historical ratings, which include any new-entrants into the system, will not be able to receive any personalized recommendations. No historical profile implies that no neighbors can be computed, recommender weights will all be zero, and no predictions will be possible. On the other hand, items that have not been rated by any member of the community can not be recommended to any users. This highlights the dependence of filtering algorithms on the altruism of the community of users making use of the recommender system; if users do not rate items, or contribute to their profile then the cycling process of generating recommendations can not be completed.

A number of solutions have been proposed to confront the cold-start problem. In the case of recommender systems based on explicit ratings, the system could require users to rate a number of items as part of the sign-up procedure (Rashid et al, 2002). This method imposes an additional burden on users, but guarantees that there will be a limited amount of profile information to generate the first recommendations. Other researchers proposed to counter the cold-start problem by making inferences from non-profile information which may be included in the sign-up process, such as simple demographic values like age, gender, and location (Nguyen et al, 2007). In this case, a rule-based induction process is applied in order to identify, for each user, a sub-set of the community that will most likely include good recommenders. However, not all recommender systems require users to input demographic data; this solution is dependent on the details of the sign-up procedure. Other solutions to the user cold-start problem diverge away from similarity, and lean towards the broader notion of trust (Massa & Avesani, 2007). Trust is defined as a user-input measure of how relevant and interesting other recommender's ratings (or reviews) seem to be; it thus has a strong overlap with similarity, but is received from the end-users rather than being computed, and can successfully be propagated over an entire community. However, as described above, the cold-start problem does not only affect users: it can also plague a new system, or prevent new items from being recommended. In this case, Park et al (2006) proposed the use of *filter-bots*, or automated surrogate users who rate items purely based on their content or attributes. Although these bots do not equal the ability a community of users has to find high quality content, they ensure that new items will not be excluded from the recommendation process.

The second set of issues regards the effect that recommendations, when they can be generated, have on the user. On the one hand, there is an issue of *transparency*; in other words, do users understand how their recommendations were generated? This issue will be of primary concern to those developing the user interface with the system, who will aim to present recommendations in a clear, understandable way (Tintarev & Masthoff, 2007). On the other hand, users look to recommender systems for new, interesting, and surprising (or *serendipitous*) information. If a user rates an item (for example, rating an album by The Beatles), loading the user's recommendations with extremely similar items (i.e. all of the other albums by The Beatles) is often not helpful at all; the user has not been pointed towards new information, and is only inundated with recommendations towards content that is probably known already. The question therefore becomes: to what extent do filtering algorithms

generate serendipitous recommendations? This is a very difficult characteristic to measure, and remains an open research question.

The last user-issue that we consider here is also tied with the algorithm chosen to generate recommendations. Whether the algorithms are learning over training instances or computing relationships between the user pairs of the community, these algorithms suffer from very high latency. Computing user similarity or feeding data into a learning algorithm is a very expensive operation, often requiring exponential space or time, and can not be continuously updated. Recommender systems therefore tend to perform iterative, regular updates. Users will not be continuously offered new recommendations, and will have to wait for a system update to see their recommendations change. Constant time algorithms have been proposed (Goldberg et al, 2000), but have yet to be widely applied.

System Vulnerabilities

The last set of problems faced by recommender systems are system vulnerabilities; these are the set of problems that are caused by malicious users attempting to game or modify the system. Why would users want to exploit a recommender system? Attempting to modify or control the recommendations that are output by a system aims at harvesting the success of recommender systems for the attacker's selfish purposes. This may be done in order to artificially promote a piece of content, to demote content (perhaps since it competes with the attacker's content), or to target a specific target audience of users. These attacks are aided by the near-anonymity of users in the recommender system community. In some cases, signing up to an e-service that uses recommender system technology only requires an email address. Creating a number of fake accounts is thus not beyond the realms of possibility; furthermore, if each of these fake accounts has an equal contribution to predicted ratings that honest user profiles do, it becomes possible to direct the output of recommender systems at will.

Malicious users can therefore build a number of fake profiles in order to influence the underlying collaborative filtering algorithm. These attacks have often been referred to as shilling, profile-injection, or Sybil attacks (Mobasher et al, 2007). All of these share the common method of inserting multiple entities into the system in order to change the resulting predicted ratings for the target item, user, or set of users. In other words, they take advantage of the way that users are modeled by the algorithm in order to achieve a desired outcome. The fake profiles that are being inserted can be engineered to be highly correlated to the target user (or item), with the small exception of the rating for the item under attack. This way, nearest-neighbor methods, as described in previous sections, will select the fake profile when generating a predicted rating, and thus will return a prediction that will deviate a lot from the experience the user will have. For example, a movie may be predicted to have a five star rating, while the user would in fact input only two stars; the injected profiles have managed to change the outcome of the recommendations and favor the disliked movie.

Profile-injection attacks are often classified according to the amount of information attackers require in order to successfully construct fake profiles. Lam & Riedl (2004) explored the effectiveness of introducing profiles based on random-valued ratings against profiles based on ratings centered on the global mean of the dataset. Attacks are more effective if they are based on full knowledge of the underlying dataset distribution; however, many filtering datasets share similar distributions, and thus most malicious users will be able to perform more than a simple, naïve attack.

Research in the field of recommender system vulnerabilities can be broken into two categories. On the one hand, system administrators require

a means of *identifying* attacks, by being able to recognize when an attack is occurring and which users are malicious profiles. To do so, Chirita et al (2005) propose to identify attackers by measuring characteristics of the injected profiles. A malicious profile can be identified if it shares high similarity with a large subset of users, has a strong effect on the predictive accuracy of the system, and includes ratings that have a strong deviation from the mean agreement amongst the community members. Although this technique can be used to successfully eliminate injected profiles, the difficulty of the problem is also highlighted: what if an honest user's profile is identified as a malicious one?

On the other hand, the vulnerabilities themselves are addressed; how can these attacks be prevented? How can the cost or effect be minimized? General solutions often involve minimizing the number of recommenders that users can interact with, mimicking the social behavior of not trusting unknown people. Model-based approaches have also been shown to be more resilient to manipulation. Resnick & Sami (2007) propose a manipulation-resistant recommender system that protects its user community by applying a reputation score to recommenders. A more comprehensive review of the vulnerabilities of collaborative recommender systems and their robustness to attack can be found in Mobasher et al (2007).

FUTURE TRENDS

Recommender system research is by no means waning. In fact, it has recently been encouraged by the announcement of the Netflix competition, which has contributed to research by releasing one of the largest user-rating datasets available to date[1]. The competition aims at reducing the error in the Netflix movie recommender. It has therefore given way to a surge in research aiming at mere accuracy, and, as we discussed above, there is much more to recommender systems than solving the prediction problem.

Research to date has widely ignored the temporal characteristic of recommender systems. The only exception lies in the definition of the cold-start problem, which recognizes that new entrants into the system will not receive suitable recommendations until their profile has grown. Exploring the temporal characteristic of these systems would shed light on how they grow, evolve over time and the influence that varying amounts of available rating information has on the accuracy of a system. In other words, a temporal view of the system would shed light on the effect of filtering algorithms applied to a community of users. One method of approaching this problem is to consider a recommender system as a graph. Nodes in this graph correspond to users, and a link between a pair of users is weighted with the similarity shared between the two (Lathia et al, 2008). This paves the way for the techniques described by graph-theory research to be applied to recommender systems.

As we have seen, both the user and community model is essential to collaborative filtering algorithms. These models are based on measurable similarity in order to allow opinion information to be propagated around the community. Understanding how similarity evolves over time, therefore, would also highlight how interactions between recommenders can be designed, and what properties of the system emerge when different filtering algorithms are applied.

Majority of the focus of recommender system research has been context-specific. The datasets available reinforce this focus; the publicly available datasets do not cross between different types of content. However, performing cross-context recommendations remains an open question. Given a user profile of movie preferences, can the user be recommended music successfully? If a user's music has been profiled, can the user be recommended live music events or concerts of interest? This issue is of particular interest

to e-commerce portals, which tend to provide a wide range of items and are not limited to a specific type. Many services also only profile a user in a given context, and thus users tend to build multiple profiles over a wide range of locations. Finding means of porting profiles from one place to another, and successfully using them for cross-contextual recommendations has yet to be explored.

Recommender systems also hold the potential to be applied in non-centralized domains: including peer to peer file sharing networks and mobile telephones. There has been a wide range of work done addressing peer to peer network recommendations (Ziegler, 2005), but little work addressing how collaborative filtering would operate in a mobile environment. Mobile collaborative filtering would allow users to benefit as they have when using online services. It would allow them to, for example, share content when on the move, and receiving recommendations relating to their immediate surroundings. Porting collaborative filtering to distributed environments brings to light a new set of obstacles. How will recommendations be computed? Where will profiles be stored, and who will they be shared with? Data *privacy* and *security* gain renewed importance (Lathia et al, 2007).

CONCLUSION

In this chapter, we have introduced the underlying algorithms of recommender systems, based on collaborative filtering. Recommender systems were conceived in response to information overload, a natural consequence of the ever-expanding breadth of online content; it has become impossible to sift through or browse online content without recommendations. Collaborative filtering automates the process of generating recommendations by building on the common assumption of like-mindedness. In other words, people who have displayed a degree of similarity in the past will continue sharing the same tastes in the future. The model of users held by these systems therefore focuses on the set of preferences that each individual has expressed, and interactions between users can be determined according to values derived by operating on the information available in user's profiles.

The approaches themselves, however, originate from a wide variety of backgrounds, and thus have been separated into content-based methods, which infer recommendations from item attributes, model-based solutions, which draw on the success of machine learning techniques, and the dominant memory-based, nearest neighbor technique. Nearest neighbor algorithms follow a three-stage process: finding a set of recommenders for each user, based on a pre-defined measure of similarity, computing predicted ratings based on the input of these recommenders, and serving recommendations to the user, hoping that they will be accurate and useful suggestions. The choice of what method to implement relies on a fine balance between accuracy, performance, and is also dependent on specific context that recommendations need to be made for. Each method has its own strengths and weaknesses, and hybrid methods attempt to reap the best of both worlds by combining a variety of methods.

The most general problems faced by recommender systems remain the same, regardless of the approach used to build the filtering algorithm. These problems were grouped into three categories: problems originating from the algorithm, including accuracy, coverage, and whether they actually help the user's decision making process, problems centered on the users, including the cold-start problem and displaying serendipitous, transparent recommendations, and lastly, system-wide vulnerabilities and their susceptibility to attack. However, the exciting on-going research promises to not only solve, but clarify the effects of these algorithms on end-users and boost their potential to help users in a wide range of contexts.

REFERENCES

Agresti, A., & Winner, L. (1997). Evaluating Agreement and Disagreement Among Movie Reviewers. *Chance, 10*, 10-14.

Alpaydin, E. (2004). *Introduction to Machine Learning. Massachusetts*, USA. MIT Press.

Basu, C., Hirsh, H., & Cohen, W. (2001). Technical Paper Recommendation: A Study in Combining Multiple Information Sources. *Journal of Artificial Intelligence Research, 14*, 213-252.

Baccigalupo, C., & Plaza, E. (2007). A Case-Based Song Scheduler For Group Customized Radio. In *Proceedings of the International Conference on Case Based Reasoning (ICCBR)*. Belfast, Ireland: Springer.

Breese, J. S., Heckerman, D., & Kadie, C. (1998). Empirical Analysis of Predictive Algorithms for Collaborative Filtering (Tech Rep. No. MSR-TR-98-12). Redmond, WA: Microsoft Research.

Borchers A., Herlocker J., Konstan J., & Riedl J. (1998). Ganging up on Information Overload. *IEEE Computer, 31*, 106-108.

Cayzer, S., & Aickelin, U. (2002). A Recommender System based on the Immune Network. In *Proceedings of the Fourth Congress on Evolutionary Computation (CEC-2002)*, Honolulu, USA: IEEE.

Celma O., & Lamere, P. (2007, September). Music Recommendation Tutorial. *Presented at the 8th International Conference on Music Information Retrieval*, Vienna, Austria.

Charikar, M. (2002). Similarity Estimation Techniques From Rounding Algorithms. In *Annual ACM Symposium on Theory of Computing*, Montreal, Canada: ACM Press.

Chirita, P-A., Nejdl, W., & Zamfir, C. Preventing Shilling Attacks in Online Recommender Systems. In *Proceedings of the 7th Annual ACM*

International Workshop on Web Information and Data Management. Bremen, Germany: ACM Press.

Faloutsos, C., & Oard, D. (1995). *A Survey of Information Retrieval and Filtering Methods* (Tech. Rep. No. CS-TR-3514). Maryland, USA: University of Maryland, Department of Computer Science.

Goldberg, D., Nichols, D., Oki, B. M., & Terry, D. (1992). Using Collaborative Filtering to Weave an Information Tapestry. *Communications of the ACM, 35*, 61-70. ACM Press.

Goldberg, K., Roeder T., Gupta, D., & Perkins, C. (2000). *Eigentaste: A Constant Time Collaborative Filtering* Algorithm (Tech Rep. No. UCB/ERL M00/41). Berkeley, California: University of California, EECS Department.

Grcar, M., Fortuna, B., & Mladenic, D. (2005, August). KNN versus SVM in the Collaborative Filtering Framework. In *Workshop on Knowledge Discovery on the Web*.

Herlocker, J. L., Konstan, J. A., Borchers, A., & Riedl, J. (1999). An Algorithmic Framework for Performing Collaborative Filtering. In *Proceedings of the 22nd Annual International ACM SIGIR Conference on Research and Development in Information Retrieval*, Berkley, CA: ACM Press.

Herlocker J., Konstan J., Terveen, L., & Riedl, J. (2004). Evaluating Collaborative Filtering Recommender Systems. *ACM Transactions on Information Systems, 22*, 5-53.

Konstan, J., Miller, B., Maltz, D., Herlocker, J., Gordon, L., & Riedl, J. (1997) GroupLens: Applying Collaborative Filtering to Usenet News. *Communications of the ACM, 40*, 77-87. ACM Press.

Lam, S. K., & Riedl, J. (2004). Shilling recommender systems for fun and profit. In *Proceedings of the 13th international conference on World Wide Web*, New York, NY, USA: ACM Press.

Lathia, N., Hailes, S., & Capra, L (2007). Private Distributed Collaborative Filtering Using Estimated Concordance Measures. In *Proceedings of the 2007 ACM Conference on Recommender Systems (RecSys)*. Minneapolis, USA: ACM Press.

Lathia, N., Hailes, S., & Capra, L. (2008). The Effect of Correlation Coefficients on Communities of Recommenders. In *23rd Annual ACM Symposium on Applied Computing, Trust, Recommendations, Evidence and other Collaboration Know-how (TRECK) Track*. Fortaleza, Ceara, Brazil: ACM Press.

Li, Q., & Kim, B. M. (2003). Clustering Approach for Hybrid Recommender System. In *Proceedings of the 2003 IEEE/WIC International Conference on Web Intelligence*. Beijing, China: IEEE Press.

Linden, G., Smith, B., & York, J. (2003). Amazon.com Recommendations: Item-to-Item Collaborative Filtering. *IEE Internet Computing, 7*, 76-80.

Ma, H., King, I., Lyu, M. R. (2007). Effective Missing Data Prediction for Collaborative Filtering. In *Proceedings of the 30th Annual International ACM SIGIR Conference on Research and Development in Information Retrieval*. Amsterdam, Holland: ACM Press.

Massa, P., & Avesani, P. (2007). Trust-aware Recommender Systems. In *Proceedings of the 2007 ACM Conference on Recommender Systems (RecSys)*. Minneapolis, USA: ACM Press.

McLaughlin, M. R., & Herlocker, J. L. (2004). A Collaborative Filtering Algorithm and Evaluation Metric that Accurately Model the User Experience. In *Proceedings of the 27th Annual International ACM SIGIR Conference on Research and Development in Information Retrieval*. Sheffield, United Kingdom: ACM Press.

McNee, S. M., Riedl, J., & Konstan, J. A. (2006, April). Being Accurate is Not Enough: How Accuracy Metrics have hurt Recommender Systems. In *Extended Abstracts of the 2006 ACM Conference on Human Factors in Computing Systems (CHI 2006)*. Montreal, Canada: ACM Press.

Mobasher, B., Burke, R., Bhaumik, R., & Williams, C. (2007). Towards Trustworthy Recommender Systems: An Analysis of Attack Models and Algorithm Robustness. *Transations on Internet Technology (TOIT)*. 7, 4.

Nguyen, A., Denos, N., & Berrut, C. (2007). Improving new user recommendations

with rule-based induction on cold user data. In *Proceedings of the 2007ACM Conference on Recommender Systems (RecSys)*. Minneapolis, USA: ACM Press.

Park, S., Pennock, D., Madani, O., Good, N., & DeCoste, D. (2006). Naïve filterbots for Robust Cold-start Recommendations. In *Proceedings of the ACM Conference on Knowledge Discovery and Data Mining*. Philadelphia, USA: ACM Press.

Paterek, A. (2007). Improving Regularized Singular Value Decomposition For Collaborative Filtering. In *Proceedings of the ACM Conference on Knowledge Discovery and Data Mining*. Philadelphia, USA: ACM Press.

Pazzani, M. J., & Billsus, D. (2007) Content-Based Recommendation Systems. *The Adaptive Web, 4321*, 325-341.

Rashid, A. M., Albert, I., Cosley, D., Lam, S. K., McNee, S. M., Konstan, J. A., & Riedl, J. (2002). Getting to Know You: Learning New User Preferences in Recommender Systems. In *International Conference on Intelligent User Interfaces (IUI 2002)*. Miami, Florida: ACM Press.

Rashid, A. M., Lam, S. K., Karypis G., & Riedl, J. (2006, August). ClustKNN: A Highly Scalable Hybrid Model- & Memory-Based CF Algorithm. In *The 12th ACM Conference on Knowledge Discovery and Data Mining* Philadelphia, Pennsylvania, USA: ACM Press.

Resnick, P., & Sami, R. The Influence Limiter: Provably Manipulation Resistant Recommender Systems. In *Proceedings of the 2007ACM Conference on Recommender Systems (RecSys)*. Minneapolis, USA: ACM Press.

Ruthven, I., & Lalmas, M. (2003). A Survey on the Use of Relevance Feedback for Information Access Systems. *The Knowledge Engineering Review, 18*, 95-145.

Sarwar, B., Karypis, G., Konstan, J., & Riedl, J. (2001). Item-based collaborative filtering recommendation algorithms. In *Proceedings of the 10th International World Wide Web Conference (WWW10)*, Hong Kong, China: ACM Press.

Sarwar, B., Konstan, J., Borchers, A., Herlocker, J., Miller, B., & Riedl, J. (1998). Using Filtering Agents to Improve Prediction Quality in the GroupLens Research Collaborative Filtering System. *Proceedings of the 1998 Conference on Computer Supported Cooperative Work*. New Orleans, USA: ACM Press.

Schafer, J., Konstan, J., & Riedl, J. (2001) E-Commerce Recommendation Applications. In *Data Mining and Knowledge Discovery, 5*(1), 115-153.

Shahabi, C., Banaei-Kashani, F., Chen Y.-S., & McLeod, D. (2001). Yoda: An Accurate and ScalableWeb-based Recommendation System. In *Proceedings of Sixth International*

Conference on Cooperative Information Systems. Trento, Italy: Springer.

Tintarev, N., & Masthoff, J. (2007). Effective Explanantions of Recommendations: User-Centered Design. In *Proceedings of the 2007 ACM Conference on Recommender Systems (RecSys)*. Minneapolis, USA: ACM Press.

Viappiani, P., Pu, P., & Faltings, B. (2007). Conversational Recommenders with Adaptive Suggestions. In *Proceedings of Recommender Systems (RecSys)*. Minneapolis, USA: ACM Press

Yu, K., Schwaighofer, A., Tresp, V., Xu, X., & Kriegel, H. (2004). Probabilistic memory-based collaborative filtering. *IEEE Transactions on Knowledge and Data Engineering, 16,* 56–69.

Yu, K., Wen, Z., Xu, X., & Ester, M. (2001). Feature Weighting and Instance Selection for Collaborative Filtering. In *Proceedings of the 12th International Workshop on Database and Expert Systems Applications.* Munich, Germany: IEEE Press.

Wu, F., & Huberman, B. A. (2007). *Public Discourse in the Web Does Not Exhibit Group Polarization* (Technical Report). Palo Alto, CA: HP Labs Research.

Ziegler, C. (2005). *Towards Decentralised Recommender Systems.* (PhD Thesis), Freiburg, Germany: Freiburg University, Department of Computer Science.

ENDNOTE

[1] http://www.netflixprize.com

Section II
Advances in User Modeling in CSIRA

.

Chapter III
Analyzing Communal Tag Relationships for Enhanced Navigation and User Modeling

Edwin Simpson
HP Labs, UK

Mark H. Butler
HP Labs, UK

ABSTRACT

The increasing amount of available information has created a demand for better, more automated methods of finding and organizing different types of information resources. This chapter investigates methods for enabling improved navigation, user modeling, and personalization using collaboratively generated tags. The authors discuss the advantages and limitations of tags, and describe how relationships between tags can be used to discover latent structures that can automatically organize a collection of tags owned by a community. They give a hierarchical clustering algorithm for extracting latent structure and explain methods for determining tag specificity, then use visualization to examine latent structures. Finally the authors discuss future trends including using latent tag structures to create user models.

INTRODUCTION

Most current methods of accessing information do not incorporate a user's personal perspective or current task, even though such context significantly affects their information needs. As a result, users are often overwhelmed by the number of information resources that potentially match their requirements. This problem can be reduced by giving users a clearer overview of the available resources, or by the system making better use of data about the user. Specifically, if a system is able to model a user's perspective, current tasks and diverse information resources, it can push relevant information to users and improve navigation by automatically filtering and organizing resources for the user (Belkin, 1992).

In order to do this, a system requires a model that describes information resources, users and their context. An ideal model should be applicable across heterogeneous information sources, capture the user's interests, their interactions with information, and describe their current tasks.

One starting point for such a model could come from the simple and flexible descriptors used in information retrieval systems called *tags*. Tags are in widespread use by systems such as photo, bookmark and video management applications on the Web, and a collection of tags used by a particular system is known as a *folksonomy*. However, because these folksonomies lack the explicit structure of taxonomies, they suffer from problems with synonyms, polysemy, depth of specificity and scalability. Research has shown that there are various hidden structures in folksonomies that can help overcome these problems (Mika, 2005; Diederich & Iofciu, 2006). This chapter explores how we can find relationships between tags, and hence expose the latent structure in folksonomies by extracting topic clusters and hierarchies. We then describe how these structures could be used to improve navigational interfaces and model user interests.

This chapter aims to inform the reader of various techniques that use tags to automatically organize resources and model the interests of users in a community. Readers will be able to apply this set of techniques to help derive greater value from large communities and repositories of information, by improving the way users explore and access resources.

In the second section, *Background*, we explain current uses of tagging and alternative methods for organizing information. We also define some key terms and concepts.

Then, in the third section, *Extracting Latent Structure from Folksonomies*, we describe the latent structure present in folksonomies and ex-

plain tag similarity methods that may be used to detect this structure. We present some different methods of representing latent structure, focusing on one method, clustering, in more detail. We then consider how we can use latent structure to represent general concepts in the folksonomy.

In the fourth section, *Visualization of Latent Structures*, we describe how to visualize the resulting latent structure and analyze the results of applying our clustering method to two datasets.

In the fifth section, *Future Trends*, we suggest the development of dynamic and hierarchical visualizations and discuss the possibility of modeling user interests and current tasks using information derived from folksonomies.

BACKGROUND

The Web is notable for its increasing abundance of information and the freedom it allows for new innovation, particularly the development of new methods to connect users with information and allow them to organize resources. These methods augment more established approaches such as free-text search (Gudivada et al., 1997; Page et al., 1998), directories and taxonomies (Garshol, 2004), explicit communication between users and subscriptions to news feeds or mailing lists. In this section we describe folksonomies and consider both the advantages and limitations of this approach. We then compare tagging with thesauri and controlled vocabularies, and consider how these techniques can be combined with tagging.

Tagging

As already mentioned, one idea for improving information access which is now in widespread use is *tagging*. Tagging is a process where users add arbitrary labels, known as *tags,* to information resources.

An example system using tagging is Delicious (http://delicious.com), a web-based URL bookmarking service, which allows users to attach tags to bookmarks so that they or others with similar interests can find content without relying on typical search engines. Another example is the photo-sharing website Flickr (http://www.flickr.com), which allows users to tag their own images. This helps retrieval as the images do not necessarily have associated text content that can be searched in the same way as text documents, a common problem when dealing with audio, video or images. Hence both these sites use tags to store information useful for retrieval that is not already present in the contents of the resources. The widespread use of tags suggests they are a popular and useful means of organizing and finding resources.

Tagging systems can therefore vary greatly in style, but the way they are used to browse documents is similar from system to system. Like most tagging systems, both Delicious and Flickr allow users to search through their own tags or all tags in the system, or click on a tag in a list of tags. These methods of browsing give little guidance about related tags and become difficult to use when the number of tags increases. In the following subsections we will discuss these problems in greater depth, and then in the remainder of the chapter we will explain solutions that enable more sophisticated interfaces.

Advantages of Tagging Systems

One of the advantages of tagging is that a user's choice of tags is not restricted by a predefined taxonomy or controlled vocabulary (Morville & Rosenfeld, 2007). Users can add new terms and choose the vocabulary they use, making tagging flexible to personal needs. For example, a user might add workflow-oriented tags such as "to read" to a set of resources they wish to return to. Such classifications are not normally supported in a formal taxonomy, which only describes re-

sources. The classification system that emerges as a community of users adds tags to a system is known as a *folksonomy* (Mathes, 2004; Vanderwal, 2007). This term is derived from the words *taxonomy* and *folk*, as tags are an alternative to using a *taxonomy* for classification and are developed by the community or *folk* rather than system designers. Folksonomies can therefore match the community's vocabulary and their usage of the system better than a predefined taxonomy.

Another reason for using tagging is the low cost to users. The cognitive processes involved in adding tags are simpler than those required for classifying resources in a taxonomy (Sinha, 2005). This is because the user does not have to refer to or interpret the taxonomy to select a label. Hence users can be persuaded to add tag data relatively easily, thus providing information necessary for retrieval and sharing as they use the system.

As users add tags or use them to search for resources, they also provide information about their interests or information needs. Tagging could therefore be an extremely useful way to capture profile information for automatic recommendation and personalization, as discussed in the section *Future Trends*.

Limitations of Tagging Systems

The flexibility of tagging described in the previous section can introduce problems when trying to use tags added by other users. Specifically, folksonomies often suffer from problems with synonymy, polysemy and depth of specificity (Noruzi, 2006; Golder & Huberman, 2006; Speller, 2007).

The problem of *synonyms*, such as alternative words for the same concept, alternative spellings, abbreviations and plurals, primarily affects search recall. For example, when searching using the tag "www", the result set will not include other relevant resources tagged with "worldwide web".

Polysemy refers to ambiguous tags, such as "Paris" which could refer to a number of different locations or people. These primarily affect search precision by introducing unwanted resources into search results.

Depth of specificity refers to the fact that some tags are more general than others. More general tags could apply to a larger number of resources than specific tags. General tags are less useful in determining the relevance of a resource to a specific query. For example, the tag "animal" could be applied to an image of a cat or an elephant. Taxonomies, by contrast, are designed explicitly to avoid this problem by picking the most specific category for a resource. This relies on professional categorizers, however, and general users may not have the same discipline when choosing tags. An additional problem is that using only highly-specific tags could reduce search recall: a resource with an overly specific tag would not be found using a more general query. Taxonomies overcome this problem by using a definition of relationships between general and specific terms in search.

The issue of specificity also limits the power of tags to describe user interests: a user with the tags "Paris" and "France" in their profile may not be interested in all resources relating to the city. A more specific tag, such as "parisian art" or "architecture paris" might provide more insight into their interests; being able to differentiate specific and general tags is therefore important for tag-based user modeling.

The tools provided by folksonomies for structuring tags are limited compared to other organization systems. For example, in Delicious it is possible to combine tags into *bundles* but this is much less sophisticated than a taxonomy. Taxonomies structure categories hierarchically, making it possible to hide irrelevant information from users, a key strategy when creating efficient, usable interfaces. Without hierarchical organization, users must browse large folksonomies using long lists of tags. Consequently, users cannot gain a good overview of how tags have been used or what types of resource exist in the system, and must revert to using search. Unlike taxonomies,

tags lack the structure to guide users effectively from a very broad query to a specific resource.

It is important to distinguish between resource focused, task focused and context dependent tagging. Resource focused tags may be *factual* or *subjective*. For example, consider the tags "interesting" and "paris" applied to an image of the Eiffel Tower. These are *resource focused tags* as they describe the resource, but "interesting" is subjective whereas "paris" is factual. However, if the "paris" tag is applied to details of a power adapter because the user requires it for a trip to Paris, France, it is an example of *task focused tagging*. The "toread" tag, often used to track whether a user intends to read a resource, is another task focused tag. Tags such as "me" or "dad" are *context dependent tags* because their meaning depends on the user who assigned them. An alternative classification of tags is presented by Melenhorst & van Setten (2007).

Despite these problems, tags provide much of the information vital to searching, browsing and profiling of users. A mechanism for resolving vocabulary issues and adding the kind of structure provided by taxonomies could improve information retrieval and significantly increase the value of tags for user modeling.

Thesauri and Controlled Vocabularies

One method of resolving differences in the usage of tags by different users is to look up tags in a thesaurus or controlled vocabulary (Laniado et al., 2007; Morville & Rosenfeld, 2007). We could use a controlled vocabulary to resolve the problem of synonyms, as a controlled vocabulary specifies a set of synonyms for a concept and its preferred terms. For example, imagine a user wishes to see all documents related to the tag "car". The system could look up "car" in a controlled vocabulary to discover that it is a synonym of "automobile", then display all resources tagged either "car" or "automobile". Thesauri contain additional information on relationships between terms, including more specific, more general or otherwise related terms. By looking up tags in a thesaurus, applications could use this relationship information to determine the specificity of tags.

Wordnet (Miller et al., 1990) is a semantic lexicon for English that goes beyond a thesaurus by providing extensive term relationship information and word definitions. Wordnet could be used to identify ambiguous tags and therefore resolve the problem of polysemy (Laniado et al., 2007). For example, the system could look up the tag "Paris" to find multiple definitions, then use additional information attached to the resource to disambiguate the definition. For instance, if a resource was also tagged "France" and "city" we would know which definition of Paris applied.

Unfortunately, this would require defining every meaning of every tag used in a folksonomy. This is a major obstacle to this approach because definitions may be missing, even if reusing an existing source such as Wordnet. Additionally, even if a number of definitions are present, one particular alternative may be missing. In the latter case it is not so obvious that data is missing from the thesauri, leading to confusing errors. For example, the term "Paris" has four definitions on Wordnet, but they do not include Paris Hilton, who at the time of writing is a well known celebrity often referred to as "Paris". A recent investigation of data from Delicious found that only 8% of tags appear in Wordnet (Laniado et al., 2007).

Causes of missing definitions include: terminology that develops over time; is highly specific to a particular domain; tags created by composing or abbreviating words; misspellings that cannot be corrected automatically; alternative forms; unknown proper nouns such as people, projects and events. These problems considerably increase the work required to construct a domain-specific lexicon and make the effort required to create and maintain a general purpose dictionary immense.

A fundamental problem with taking an approach similar to a taxonomy – for example, predefining categories of related tags - is that folksonomies change over time. Definitions should reflect the way a community uses tags: in company X, a tag "software" might refer to company X's software development division, but may also refer to useful software downloads that employees have tagged. Using a thesaurus to differentiate between the two meanings is unlikely to be successful. In the section *Extracting Latent Structure from Folksonomies,* we attempt to overcome these problems by proposing a solution that analyses the way tags are used in practice, so remains more complete and up-to-date.

Alternative Organization Techniques

Document clustering, term clustering and classification are alternative information organization techniques that rely on resource contents rather than tags added by users. *Document clustering* involves placing documents into clusters based on the similarity of their contents (Jain et al., 1999). *Term clustering* is an alternative way to produce topic clusters by clustering keywords extracted from resources using a measure such as TF-IDF (Salton & Buckley, 1988). *Classification* involves assigning class labels to resources based on prior knowledge of available classes (Sebastiani, 2002). Table 1 compares the use of tags to organize resources with classification and clustering techniques.

Combining these techniques can enable us to organize resources in different ways or overcome the problems of a single technique. For example, we could associate tags with document clusters to disambiguate tags (Yeung, 2007). The next section explains how to create topic clusters by combining clustering and tags.

Table 1. Comparing tagging, classification and clustering

	Tagging	Classification	Clustering	
			Term	**Document**
Advantages	Classification scheme can evolve over time	Creating training data or rules is less work than large scale annotation	No annotations or training data required Categorization scheme adapts to new data	
	Can classify a resource into multiple categories	Can classify a resource into multiple categories	Can classify a resource into multiple categories	
Dis-advantages	Depends on quality of annotation	Depends on quality of training data or rules; writing rules is hard for naive users Normally decide on classification scheme in advance		Can only classify a resource in a single category

EXTRACTING LATENT STRUCTURE FROM FOLKSONOMIES

This section discusses the latent structure present in folksonomies. It describes four similarity methods that can be used to identify this structure: *lexical, vector-space, textual* and *co-occurrence similarity.* Then, using these similarity measures, we outline how to extract three types of latent structure: tag graphs, topic clusters and cluster hierarchies. We contrast partitional and hierarchical clustering approaches and detail an approach for applying hierarchical clustering to tags, later refining this approach using betweenness centrality. The initial experimental results are shown for applying the hierarchical clustering algorithm to obtain topic clusters. Finally, this section considers different ways latent structure can reflect general concepts in the folksonomy: using general tags identified from subsumption relationships or node betweenness; or using clusters, which require appropriate labels.

Latent Structure in Folksonomies

Relationships emerge between tags in folksonomies, creating a latent structure. Extracting this structure has the potential to improve tagging systems, and is an alternative to the predefined thesauri and taxonomies described previously. Unlike thesaurus-based approaches, the latent structure more accurately reflects the way the community uses tags, so could resolve issues with synonymy and polysemy.

Extracting latent structure involves finding pairs of similar tags and general-specific relationships between tags. The resulting information can overcome problems with depth of specificity, and thus be used to enhance browsing and generate better models of user interests. For example, instead of long, flat lists of tags or search boxes, an interface can list related tags, highlighting more general and more specific tags to guide the user. Additionally, a system could find related resources by comparing tags, even when the tags are not identical.

Many approaches to latent structure in folksonomies are based on the assumption that more similar objects are more closely related. In this chapter we also consider similarity as a measure of relatedness when comparing resources to user interests, or user interests to other users' interests.

Tag Similarity Methods

Four relevant methods of determining tag similarity are lexical, vector-space, textual and co-occurrence similarity. These similarity methods all apply thresholding so that values below a certain threshold value are discarded as insignificant.

Lexical Similarity is the similarity between two words as defined by a thesaurus or semantic lexicon such as Wordnet, typically by their distance in the taxonomy graph (Banerjee & Pedersen, 2003; Budanitsky & Hirst, 2001). If we apply this approach to tags, we encounter the problems of combining a thesaurus with a folksonomy explained in the section *Thesauri and Controlled Vocabularies*.

Vector-Space Similarity involves creating a feature vector for each tag: each feature in the vector corresponds to a resource in the system; the feature vector stores the number of users who applied the tag to the corresponding resource. Cosine similarity or Euclidean distance can be used to compare these vectors (Frakes & Baeza-Yates, 1992; Salton, 1989). Using this approach, tags are considered similar if they have been used with similar sets of resources.

Textual Similarity can be calculated by comparing the contents of tagged documents. We extract and concatenate the text from all resources with a given tag. Then we remove stop-words, perform stemming and select significant terms using TF-IDF values (Salton and Buckley, 1988), which we use to create a term frequency vector. Similarity is calculated by comparing the term-frequency vectors using a vector-space similarity measure such as cosine similarity, which can be used when the term frequency vectors are sparse (Salton, 1989). Ambiguous tags are likely to have disproportionately low similarity to other related tags, as the term-frequency vector represents a combination of all possible meanings.

Co-occurrence Similarity is derived from the frequency of *tag co-occurrence*, which is when two tags are used to annotate the same resource. Tag co-occurrence may be valid between tags added at different times or by different users. Alternatively we may derive co-occurrence similarity from the co-occurrence between a tag and a term in the contents of a resource. Using raw frequency of co-occurrence as similarity is problematic: extremely popular tags are used many times with many other tags, so their co-occurrence values would suggest high similarity to many other tags. Therefore to avoid biasing similarity toward popular tags, we calculate *Normalized Tag Co-Occurrence (NTCO)*. Co-occurrence could be normalized using a number of different calculations. In this chapter we use the Jaccard Index, $J(A,B)$ (Begelman et al., 2006). Here A is the set of resources with tag a, B the set of resources with tag b, and $|A|$ refers to the cardinality of A:

Figure 1. Normalized tag co-occurrence using the Jaccard Index

$$NTCO(a,b) = J(A,B) = \frac{|A \cap B|}{|A \cup B|}$$

In this chapter we use this definition of NTCO for our examples, as similarity based on co-occurrence has a number of advantages over other methods. Textual and vector-space similarity require the system to compare many tags to find strong tag relationships represented by high similarity. NTCO avoids this because we assume that tags with few or no co-occurrences have a similarity of zero. Unlike textual similarity, NTCO does not require text extraction or preprocessing so can be used with resources that do not have associated content, or for which content extraction is expensive. In addition to these advantages, the

NTCO approach captures the associations that users and communities make when adding tags, so is more likely to reflect their intentions.

Types of Latent Structure

Using similarity methods described above we can extract several different types of latent structure, including tag graphs, topic clusters, and cluster hierarchies.

A *tag graph* is a useful, generic structure that represents different relationships between tags. In the tag graph, tags are represented by nodes, and the edges usually indicate related tags by connecting tags with high similarity. Alternatively, it is possible to add nodes representing resources or users, in which case edges represent relationships between resources and tags or users and tags. By visualizing the tag graph it is possible to observe some of the latent structure present in the folksonomy.

Topic clusters are created by grouping synonymous and closely related tags into a unified topic (Begelman et al., 2006; Hassan-Montero & Herrero-Solana, 2006). They are potentially more inclusive than tags alone as all resources that cover a given topic can be associated with the same topic cluster, even if they use different tags. Unlike normal document clustering, resources can be associated with several topic clusters. Users can browse topic clusters to gain an overview of resources rather than browsing a long, flat list of tags. Clusters can also help identify ambiguous tags and tags that lack specificity, as such tags will be members of multiple clusters. The topic clusters associated with a user can also be used to form a profile, as described in the section *Enhancing User Models using Latent Structures*.

Cluster Hierarchies are formed by joining or splitting topic clusters using a hierarchical clustering algorithm (Cimiano et al., 2004; Van Damme et al., 2007). Tags are placed in the leaves at the bottom of the hierarchy, with specialized topics immediately above and general topics higher up.

An alternative to cluster hierarchies is to generate a hierarchy of tags from general-specific relationships between tags, which we explain in the section *Representing General Concepts*. Hierarchies are an intuitive way to indicate relationships between tags and their specificity, and hence how closely related two resources are. If a user is interested in the tags "Paris" and "Paris Sightseeing", for example, we can use a hierarchy to determine that "Paris Sightseeing" is more specific, so resources with this tag are more likely to be relevant.

Clustering Tag Graphs

Clustering Algorithms

Topic clusters and hierarchical clusters both require a clustering algorithm to group tags based on similarity. There are various suitable clustering algorithms which may produce different sizes and numbers of clusters (Jain et al., 1999). Two major categories of clustering algorithms are partitional and hierarchical clustering. These algorithms can produce many different outputs for a single data set, which we refer to as *clusterings*.

Partitional clustering algorithms, such as the K-means algorithm, divide the data directly into a single set of clusters (Jain et al., 1999). These algorithms typically detect clusters by identifying groups with maximal similarity between tags, or by iteratively optimizing an estimated set of clusters. In some cases, partitional clustering may be quicker to compute than hierarchical clustering. However, many classical partitional clustering algorithms, such as K-means, require a prior estimate of the number or size of clusters required.

Hierarchical clustering algorithms produce clusterings that can be arranged hierarchically in a tree-like diagram called a *dendrogram*, with individual items (in this case tags) in the leaves, small clusters immediately above them and fewer but increasingly large clusters above them. The most appropriate clustering could be selected by specifying the number of clusters, the mean size of clusters, or the mean similarity between tags in a cluster. A variant of this last measure is *modularity*, which is the relative similarity between items in a cluster compared to items in different clusters.

Hierarchical clustering algorithms are commonly classed as agglomerative or divisive. Agglomerative algorithms start with individual items, merging them to form clusters, then merging clusters together (Brooks & Montanez, 2006). Conversely, divisive algorithms produce the same kind of dendrogram, but start from a single cluster containing all items, which they divide until they obtain individual items. Hierarchical clustering dendrograms can be mapped to taxonomies (Cimiano et al., 2004; Van Damme et al., 2007) and provide a way of comparing clusters as well as individuals to one another using their tree distance. This is useful if we wish to evaluate the similarity between tags in related clusters without reverting to re-calculating cluster or tag similarities from the original graph.

Hierarchical Clustering of Tags

A divisive hierarchical clustering algorithm could partition a tag graph into separate sub-graphs by removing edges likely to fall between clusters. One method of finding these edges is to select those representing the lowest tag similarity. For example, we can remove the edges with the lowest NTCO as they connect tags with weak co-occurrence that should be placed in different clusters.

When using NTCO as a similarity measure for clustering, we refer to the algorithm as *NTCO divisive clustering*. In this algorithm we select edges to remove from the whole graph. Begelman et al. (2006) investigated an alternative in which edges are selected for removal from within a cluster we wish to divide.

NTCO divisive clustering partitions a graph based on its structure rather than on estimates of desired cluster size or number of clusters. There-

fore, large clusters containing many very similar tags are possible and tags that are rarely used for the same topics are less likely to be placed in the same cluster. This approach seems appropriate for folksonomies where groups of users tend to concentrate on certain topics, meaning we expect to see large, dense clusters around the main interests, with smaller, less dense clusters for minor topics where fewer tags have been used.

Hierarchical clustering produces a potentially very large and complex hierarchy of clusters. We could simplify the hierarchy by selecting only the most intuitive clusterings that best reflect the way the community used the tags. To select these clusterings we can calculate the *modularity,* a measure of how well a given clustering fits the original graph structure (Newman & Girvan, 2004):

$$Modularity = Tr\mathbf{e} - \|\mathbf{e}^2\|$$

$Tr\mathbf{e}$ is the fraction of edges in the original graph that connect nodes in the same cluster. $\|\mathbf{e}^2\|$ is the expected fraction of edges that would connect nodes in the same cluster if the clusters had been marked randomly in the graph (Begelman et al., 2006). If the clustering reflects the original graph structure, more edges are expected to connect nodes in the same cluster, meaning that $Tr\mathbf{e}$ is high.

As edges are removed to produce different clusterings, we expect the modularity to rise and fall, reaching an overall peak at the set of clusters most fitting to the graph. If the original graph contains a truly hierarchical set of clusters, where individual tags are strongly related to those in the same topic, and similar topics are strongly related to one another, we expect the modularity to have several local maxima where the graph is divided intuitively into topics and sub-topics. Thus we can select the clusterings which possess local maxima for modularity as levels in a simplified hierarchy.

The *NTCO divisive clustering* algorithm is given below, where input is a set of tags and NTCO similarities for pairs of tags, and output is a hierarchical set of clusterings.

Figure 2. NTCO Divisive Clustering Algorithm

1. Create tag graph:
2. Add all tags as nodes
3. Add edges between pairs of tags with *NTCO > edge_threshold*
4. Create an empty list of clusterings *local_max_clusterings*
5. *previous_modularity* = modularity of the initial graph
6. *local_maximum = previous_modularity*
7. **Repeat while *previous_modularity > min_modularity_threshold* {**
   8. Find x edges with lowest NTCO, remove them from the graph
   9. *modularity* = calculate modularity of the clustering
   10. If *modularity >= previous_modularity*:
       11. *local_maximum = modularity*
   12. Else if *modularity < previous_modularity* AND *previous_modularity == local_maximum*:
       13. Add previous clustering to *local_max_clusterings*
   14. *previous_modularity = modularity*
   }
15. Return *local_max_clusterings*

The algorithm described produces a hierarchical set of clusterings, `local _ max _ clus-terings`. From these we can obtain a set of topic clusters by selecting one clustering according to criteria such as desired cluster size or number of clusters. We can avoid the need for setting such criteria by selecting the clustering with the highest value of modularity. In the section *Example Visualization of Latent Structures,* we describe

the application of this algorithm to two real-world datasets and examine the results visually.

Betweenness Centrality

An alternative approach to clustering is to use betweenness (Brandes, 2001) to divide the graph into clusters, instead of removing edges representing the lowest similarity (Newman & Girvan, 2004). *Betweenness* is a measure of *centrality,* the relative importance of a node or edge in a graph. To calculate betweenness, we must first calculate all shortest paths between nodes in the graph. The betweenness of an edge *e* is the number of shortest paths that include *e*. Edges with high betweenness lie in sparse parts of the graph between more densely connected areas, so high betweenness indicates that an edge lies between two clusters and should be removed to divide the graph. We can therefore modify line 8 in Figure 2 to remove x edges with the highest betweenness rather than lowest NTCO. We call the resulting modified algorithm the *betweenness divisive clustering* algorithm.

After removing x edges in line 8, we need to re-calculate the betweenness centrality of the remaining edges. In the original graph, some edges that lie between clusters may also lie on paths slightly longer than the shortest paths, and therefore have low betweenness. In one iteration we may remove edges from the shortest path, causing the slightly longer path to become the shortest remaining path. We then re-calculate betweenness, so edges on the remaining path that lie between clusters now have high betweenness and can be removed in the next iteration.

This algorithm runs in $O(m^2n)$ time, where m is the number of edges in the graph and n is the number of nodes (Newman & Girvan, 2004). This is due to the betweenness calculation, which is $O(mn)$ being repeated for each iteration. However, Newman (2004) suggests there are a number of modifications that would reduce this cost, potentially by approximating betweenness.

A possible advantage of the betweenness divisive clustering algorithm is that outlying nodes whose edges have low similarity are less likely to be placed in separate clusters, as the algorithm will often place them in their nearest cluster. This may be desirable if the outlying tags are genuinely related to popular tags but a relatively low number of occurrences causes a low co-occurrence similarity. We discuss results using betweenness divisive clustering in *Example Visualization of Latent Structures*, showing example visualizations of topic clusters.

Representing General Concepts

General Tags versus Clusters

To organize a folksonomy, we need to find general concepts (e.g. "France") and specific concepts (e.g. "Paris Sightseeing"), either using general tags already in the folksonomy or using clusters to group tags. In hierarchical clustering, clusters represent general concepts, as all tags remain at the lowest level in the hierarchy, so user interfaces require human readable labels for the clusters.

Alternatively we could try to identify general tags and related specific tags. In a tag graph, a general tag such as "Spain" would be a connecting node between a many other tags, so the NTCO values for its edges may be low. As a result the clustering algorithm may separate "Spain" into its own cluster containing no other tags. Rather than placing more general tags in separate clusters, or placing an instance of them into every corresponding cluster, we can place these tags at the corresponding higher level in the hierarchy to aid us in labeling the clusters for user browsing. It is also important to position these tags correctly when performing similarity calculations using the hierarchy because less specific tags do not tell us if a resource is closely related to a user's specific interests, so are less useful for finding relevant resources. Two methods for calculating

tag generality are betweenness centrality and subsumption relationships.

Using Betweenness Centrality to Find General Tags

The betweenness calculation described earlier for discovering edges that lie between clusters can also be applied to nodes. If the "Spain" tag is a connecting node between more specific tags in the graph, it is likely that it will have high betweenness. Nodes with high betweenness are important connectors between other groups of nodes, and as such are likely to be general tags. Tags with lower betweenness but high similarity to a more general tag can be considered more specific but related to the general term. Such general-specific relationships can be used to construct a hierarchy of tags (Heymann & Garcia-Molina, 2006).

If using hierarchical clustering, we can identify the most general terms in a given cluster by calculating betweenness considering only shortest paths between cluster members. Tags with high betweenness inside a high-level cluster in a hierarchy could be reasonable descriptors of that cluster as they are typically associated with multiple lower-level clusters.

Using Subsumption Relationships to Find General Tags

We can also detect general tags from subsumption relationships. These could be used as an alternative to hierarchical clustering to construct a tag hierarchy. A subsumption relationship *(a Subsumes b)* exists when the concept of *a* contains, subsumes or includes the concept of *b* (Lawrie & Croft, 2000). We define this relationship using conditional probability:

if $p(a|b) = 1$ then **(a subsumes b)**

We can determine $p(a|b)$ by comparing co-occurrences of the terms to the overall number of occurrences of *b*, using the following equation, where *A* is the set of resources tagged with *a* and *B* is the set of resources tagged with *b*.

$$p(a \mid b) = \frac{p(a \cap b)}{p(b)} = \frac{|A \cap B|}{|B|}$$

In a folksonomy we do not expect $p(a|b) = 1$ in many cases, as users often omit more general tags when they feel they are not useful, so we use:

if $p(a|b) >$ *subsumption_threshold* then **(a subsumes b)**

From a set of subsumption relationships we can form a directed graph. The graph is a rough hierarchy of tags in which nodes may have multiple parents. This measure can produce symmetrical relationships, however, if both $p(a|b)$ and $p(b|a)$ are greater than *subsumption_threshold*, which could occur if the terms are used together most of the time. To construct a hierarchy using subsumption we would need to remove this cyclical relationship: if $p(a|b)$ and $p(b|a)$ are identical, we could merge *a* and *b* so they both simply have the same parents and children; *if* $p(a|b) > p(b|a)$ we could discard the relation *(b subsumes a)*. Subsumption can therefore produce a hierarchy where tags represent general concepts.

Cluster Labeling

In user interfaces, labels identify the concept represented by a cluster. A simple way of labeling a cluster is to concatenate the tags in the cluster into a single string. The tags are ordered by number of uses, and the string is truncated if too long.

The most popular tags are not necessarily the best descriptors, however. Clusters may contain several sub-topics. If one sub-topic is more popular, its tags will be used as a label, thus omitting to describe the other sub-clusters. For example, a cluster containing articles about Paris may contain a large number of articles with the tag "art", and a smaller number with the tag "architecture" and

"food". If the label for the cluster was derived from the most popular tags it may be "Paris Art", which would exclude the other topics. Therefore, selecting higher level tags using subsumption or betweenness may represent the cluster better than selecting the most popular tags. Various other cluster labeling methods are also possible (Winter & Rijke, 2007).

To use subsumption relationships to label clusters we could find the subsumption relations within a cluster and construct a directed graph. We then select tags at the roots of the directed graph, and possibly their immediate children. The selected tags are used as labels for the cluster.

Example Visualization of Latent Structures

An effective way to identify structural patterns in a folksonomy is to visualize the tag similarity graph. These visualizations can highlight patterns such as clusters by placing similar tags close together, allowing us to compare extracted clusters with patterns in the graph. Visualizations can also help identify general tags, ambiguous tags and find synonym tags by revealing their associations. Here we use visualization to examine the clusters produced from two different datasets using the NTCO divisive clustering algorithm.

We collected the first dataset from *Labbies,* an internal bookmarking service used by a group of researchers at HPLabs to anonymously record and tag interesting URLs. The second dataset is a subset of Delicious bookmarks, obtained by selecting all tags from all users who have used the tag "dspace" during a 16 week period. The use of a common tag ensures there are relationships between tags in the dataset, so the graph is not already separated into clusters before applying the algorithm. Statistics are given in Table 2.

The visualizations (Figure 3 to Figure 6) show tag graphs, where nodes represent tags, size of nodes corresponds to tag popularity and edges show co-occurrence relationships. To position

Table 2. Dataset statistics

Dataset	Labbies	Delicious
Number of Users	20	136
Number of Bookmarks	1935	95155
Number of Tags	2092	8012
No. Tag Co-occurrences	9526	61453

the nodes we used a Spring Layout (Eades, 1984), which places nodes closer together if they have strong connecting edges. Topic clusters are also shown by filling all nodes of the same cluster with the same color or pattern. The topic clusters in Figure 3 and Figure 4 were produced by running the NTCO divisive clustering algorithm (Figure 2), then selecting the clustering with the highest modularity. Figure 5 and Figure 6 show the clusters with the highest modularity produced by the betweenness divisive clustering algorithm.

Graph visualizations can be complex even for small datasets, so we can clarify them by selecting and filtering the tag graph. To focus on an area of interest, we can visualize a sub-graph defined by specifying a root node and including only tags within a given *tag distance*, which is the number of edges between this tag and the root tag. Alternatively we can select a sub-graph by specifying a root cluster and selecting all clusters within a given *cluster distance,* which is the shortest number of edges between a tag in the root cluster and a tag in another cluster. The resulting graph displays tags in the selected clusters only. Where further clarification is required we also filter out edges with NTCO below a threshold, and remove tags where the number of uses is below a threshold.

Figure 3 shows tags from the Labbies dataset. The structure of the graph shows a dense cluster around the tags "policies" and "rules". These tags are strongly related concepts that we would expect to find in the same topic cluster and have been identified successfully as a topic cluster by

the algorithm. A range of topic clusters are related to "mit": knowledge of the related topics suggests that this tag refers to the Massachusetts Institute of Technology (MIT), which could be considered a high-level tag as it is associated with a number of projects and topics. This tag has been placed in its own *singleton* cluster, as have "dspace" and "rdf", which are also related to several projects or topics. This separation would occur when the NTCO values of edges connecting these tags are lower than NTCO values for edges connecting tags in a cluster. According to the definition of NTCO in Figure 1, an edge could have a low NTCO value either if the number of co-occurrences is low or if one of the tags was used many times with other tags. If popular high-level tags are used with many specific tags, their connecting edges could all have low NTCO, and the high-level tag would be separated into a singleton cluster. Further investigation may therefore show that separation of popular, high-level tags is a characteristic of this algorithm.

When we applied the betweenness divisive clustering algorithm to the Labbies dataset we obtained very different clusters: using NTCO divisive clustering produced 674 clusters with modularity=0.75, while betweenness divisive clustering produced 275 clusters with modularity=0.41.

Table 3 shows that the betweenness-based algorithm produced different cluster sizes, with far fewer singleton clusters and more large clusters.

Figure 3. NTCO Clustering on Labbies, root="mit"; cluster distance < 2; tag use threshold=3; NTCO threshold=0.06

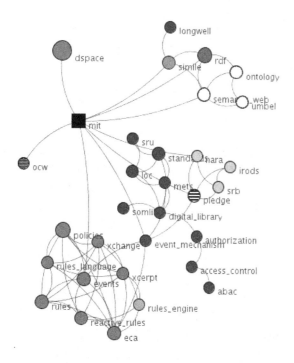

Figure 4 shows a similar graph to *Figure 3*, with clusters produced using betweenness divisive clustering. Many clusters here are larger, so tags are included that were not present in *Figure 3*, such as "tagging", which has been clustered with "semantic_web" in this case. It is interesting to see that while "mit" remains a singleton cluster, "dspace" has been associated with a relatively large cluster containing tags such as "digital_li-

braries". DSpace is a large digital library project, so it may be intuitive to place the "dspace" tag inside a digital libraries topic cluster or mark it out as a separate, high level topic relating to various other topics. As a result, the NTCO and betweenness divisive clusterings may be suitable in different applications and user studies may be necessary to determine the most applicable algorithm for a given use case.

Figure 5 shows how some of the clusters in the Delicious dataset compare to the graph structure. Here potential high-level tags such as "visualization" and "web2.0" are associated with many different topics and have been placed into singleton clusters. Small, well connected clusters are also visible around topics such as "mapping" and "graphics", while a larger, less specific cluster has also been produced including the tags "collaboration", "webmaster" and "ui". This dataset produced different cluster sizes (for example the largest cluster was 716 tags) so different types of folksonomy may have different latent structures and require different modifications to the clustering algorithms.

Figure 6 shows a sub-graph of the delicious dataset showing distinctive clusters around "news", "biking", "marathon" and "handlebar". The largest cluster produced in this dataset contained the tag "dspace", so as with the Labbies dataset the betweenness divisive algorithm has behaved differently to the NTCO divisive algorithm and has not separated this potentially high level tag into

Table 3. Cluster sizes

Dataset	Clustering Algorithm	No. Clusters				No. Tags in clusters with > 40 tags
		1 tag	2-4 tags	5-40 tags	> 40 tags	
Labbies	NTCO	338	596	74	3	426
Labbies	Betweenness	133	211	47	16	1041
Delicious	NTCO	2074	3079	244	8	1293
Delicious	Betweenness	1678	2386	60	1	4863

Figure 4. Betweenness Divisive Clustering on Labbies dataset; root="dspace"; cluster distance < 3; tag use threshold = 12; NTCO threshold = 0.06

a singleton cluster. The largest cluster had 4863 tags, which is difficult to visualize. This very large cluster could be due to the dataset being selected using the "dspace" tag, so it may have a large, dense network of co-occurrences. If this situation poses a problem, the clustering algorithm could be modified to recursively split large clusters, for example, using the algorithm tested by Begelman et al. (2006). An alternative solution may be removing or *pre-filtering* infrequently used tags prior to clustering (Simpson, 2007).

The different results using betweenness and NTCO suggest that each algorithm may have different advantages and that further study is required to determine the best algorithm for a given situation. When assessing the quality of topic clusters it may also be important to note that the clusters reflect the way topics are used together in this particular folksonomy, so a community may develop associations between topics that are not found in other data sources. This could make an

Figure 5. NTCO Divisive Clustering on Delicious dataset; root="visualization"; tag distance < 3; tag use threshold=50; NTCO threshold=0.06

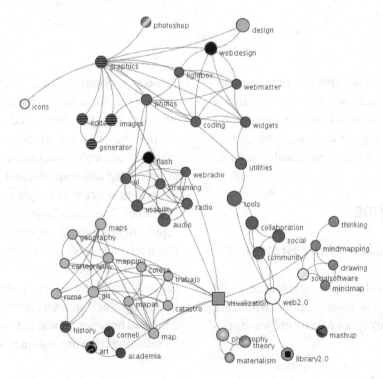

Figure 6. Betweenness Divisive Clustering on Delicious dataset; root="biking"; tag distance < 5; tag use threshold=25; NTCO threshold=0.075

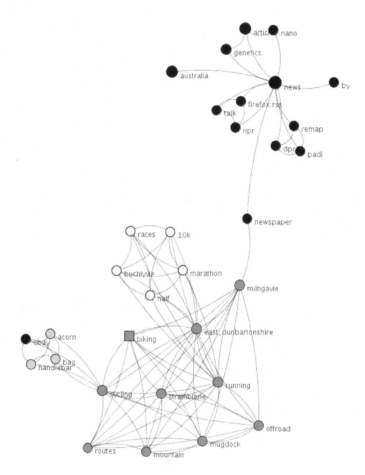

objective assessment of cluster quality more difficult, as the clusters cannot easily be compared to most existing taxonomies. However, the patterns in these examples suggest that visualizations are a useful tool for understanding latent structure.

FUTURE TRENDS

Tag Graph and Hierarchy Browsing

Novel user interfaces for exploring resources could be based on tag graph visualizations, which are able to convey many types of information simul-

taneously. Visualizations could also represent user interests by including users as nodes with edges drawn to tags they have used.

In situations where graphs are too complex, we could visualize an extracted hierarchy. Hierarchies simplify tag relationships and guide users from general to specific concepts to identify relevant resources. Tags and clusters in the hierarchy may represent orthogonal properties of a resource that the user may wish to combine, such as topic, related project or author. Users could therefore refine a search by selecting multiple nodes in a hierarchy. Such an interface would be similar to a faceted browser, in which users filter resources by selecting from pre-assigned values of different properties (Yee et al., 2003). This approach is often better than conventional search when the user is not yet clear about what they want, or when there are insufficient numbers of resources to overcome potentially poor search recall. Faceted interfaces could therefore motivate further research in latent structure extraction.

Enhancing User Models Using Latent Structures

Another important focus for future research could be developing user models based on folksonomies and latent structures. These models would enable applications to adapt to user interests, providing them with recommended resources or personalized interfaces.

One model is a *user profile* that consists of a frequency vector containing tags the user has added and the numbers of resources they were added to. The utility of user profiles may be limited by the issues described in *Limitations of Tagging*, but could be overcome by matching user profiles to latent structures.

User profiles could be mapped to cluster hierarchies to create a *hierarchical user profile*, $H_{user\_profile}$. The following algorithm outlines how we may produce $H_{user\_profile}$ from a hierarchy of a complete folksonomy.

1. Extract a latent hierarchy H from the complete folksonomy
2. For each tag t in the user profile P:
3.   Add t to the simplified hierarchy, $H_{user\_profile}$
4.   For each parent node n of t in H:
5.   If n is not already added to $H_{user\_profile}$:
6.   Add n to $H_{user\_profile}$

As $H_{user\_profile}$ contains the parent nodes of tags in the user profile, it allows us to generalize from the user's tags, enabling us to compare $H_{user\_profile}$ with related but non-identical tags or profiles. This model is also promising because users can

visualize $H_{user\_profile}$ to browse their current interests. Users could also switch from viewing a tag in $H_{user\_profile}$ to viewing the same tag in H to navigate from their current interests to explore related topics in the hierarchy.

A *clustered user profile* simplifies and generalizes tags in a user profile by assigning them to topic clusters. Applications could present the user with *shortcuts* to clusters in their profile, providing a simpler interface than the hierarchical view. Shortcuts could be links on a web page or buttons in a user interface, which display relevant resources or re-focus a graph visualization when selected.

Similarity calculations between clustered user profiles would be inaccurate, however, if clusters are too general or too specific. Using a hierarchical user profile may be more robust because it enables a more continuous measure of similarity: the more closely a resource matches a user's specific interests, the higher its similarity (Kim & Chan, 2003).

While the user profile records recent and long term activities, future browsing applications may take into account the user's *current task*. If the user is currently working with a tagged document, these tags could describe the current task's topic, although this would be a very simplistic model of current task context, as described by Suchman (1987). Applications can adapt automatically using the current task's tags, for example, by altering the user interface. Figure 7 illustrates this with a customized web browser: the left-hand side of the screen shows a webpage; the right-hand side of the screen shows additional links and a tag graph visualization. Latent structures could be used to map the page's tags to related user profiles and other resources, which are shown as links. They could also be used recommend other relevant tags and to produce a simple tag graph visualization focused on the current task's topic. Incorporating contextual shortcuts in the manner described enables serendipitous discovery, and

Figure 7. Possible interface for displaying resources related to current task in a web browser

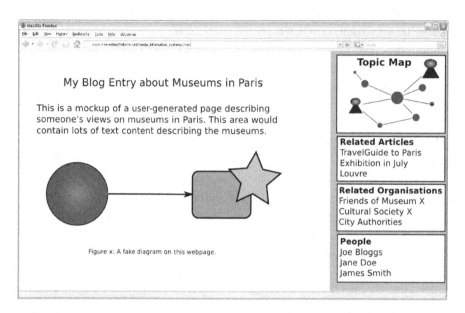

enables interfaces to adapt to individuals.

Tags added by users are particularly valuable for building a user model because they record the features of a resource a user is interested in or their reasons for liking it (Nakamoto et al., 2007), so the system can take into account users who like the same resource for different reasons. When generating user models from tags, latent structures enable more robust similarity calculations. For example, hierarchical user profiles enable a more continuous calculation of similarity between resources and potentially interested users. Future research is likely to involve testing and refining similarity measures and tag-based profile design. Techniques for updating latent structures could also prove important (Michlmayr et al., 2007), as could novel visualization techniques and recommender systems based around these ideas.

CONCLUSION

This chapter described methods for extracting latent structures from tagging systems. User-generated tags capture a user's perspective of resources they use, so could be valuable for user modeling and navigation. However, tags are limited because users use different vocabulary and the specificity of tags is unknown. Solutions using thesauri or controlled vocabularies are of limited success due to the dynamic nature of tagging.

In the third section, *Extracting Latent Structure from Folksonomies*, we explained how tag similarity relationships form latent structures that could help overcome these limitations, and suggested various tag similarity methods. The clustering algorithm presented here can be used to extract topic clusters. Additionally, several methods exist for differentiating general and specific tags and constructing hierarchies. Further research may attempt to clairfy the strengths and suitable applications of each clustering algorithm and tag specificity technique, potentially through prototyping applications and user testing.

As described in *Visualization of Latent Structures,* visual representations of latent structures could enhance the exploration of information resources. *Future Trends* proposed that research may now focus on utilizing latent structures to contextualize applications. We expect to see continuing experimentation with user profiles and current task models across various application domains, which will result in greater use and refinement of latent structure extraction. We believe that tags are an important data source for user modeling, and that latent structures are an important way to exploit their value.

ACKNOWLEDGMENT

Many thanks to Steve Cayzer, Michael Rhodes and Desmond Elliott for their valuable input.

REFERENCES

Banerjee, S., & Pedersen, T. (2003). Extended Gloss Overlaps as a Measure of Semantic Relatedness. *Eighteenth International Joint Conference on Artificial Intelligence* (pp 805-810). Retrieved February 15, 2008, from http://citeseer.ist.psu.edu/banerjee03extended.html

Begelman, G., Keller, P., & Smadja, F. (2006). Automated Tag Clustering: Improving Search and Exploration in the Tag Space. In *Proceedings of the 15th International Conference on World Wide Web* (pp. 33-42). New York: ACM Press. Retrieved February 15, 2008, from http://www.pui.ch/phred/automated_tag_clustering/

Belkin, N. J., & Croft, B. (1992). Information filtering and information retrieval: Two sides of the same coin? *Communications of the ACM, 34* (12), 29-39. Retrieved January 25, 2008, from http://www.ischool.utexas.edu/~i385d/readings/Belkin_Information_92.pdf

Brooks, C. H., & Montanez, N. (2006). Improved annotation of the blogosphere via autotagging and hierarchical clustering. In *Proceedings of the 15th World Wide Web Conference* (pp. 625-632). New York: ACM Press. Retrieved February 17, 2008, from http://www.cs.usfca.edu/~brooks/papers/brooks-montanez-www06.pdf

Brandes, U. (2001). A faster algorithm for betweenness centrality, *Journal of Mathematical Sociology, 25*(2), 163-177. Retrieved February 15, 2008, from http://citeseer.ist.psu.edu/brandes-01faster.html

Budanitsky, A., & Hirst, G. (2001, June). *Semantic Distance in WordNet: An Experimental Application-oriented Evaluation of Five Measures.* Paper presented at Workshop on WordNet and Other Lexical Resources (NAACL), Pittsburgh, PA. Retrieved February 15, 2008, from http://citeseer.ist.psu.edu/budanitsky01semantic.html

Cimiano, P., Hotho, A., & Staab, S. (2004, May). *Clustering Concept Hierarchies from Text by Agglomerative Clustering.* Paper presented at the Fourth International Conference On Language Resources And Evaluation. Lisbon, Portugal. Retrieved February 15, 2008, from http://www.aifb.uni-karlsruhe.de/WBS/pci/lrec04.pdf

Diederich, J., & Iofciu, T. (2006). Finding Communities of Practice from User Profiles Based on Folksonomies. In E. Tomadaki and P. Scott (Eds.), *EC-TEL 2006 Workshops Proceedings* (pp. 288-297). Aachen, Germany: Redaktion Sun SITE. Retrieved January 25, 2008, from http://www.l3s.de/~diederich/Papers/TBProfile-telcops.pdf

Eades, P. A. (1984). A Heuristic for Graph Drawing. In Ralph G. (Ed.), *Congressus Numerantium* (pp. 149-160). Winnipeg: Utilitas Mathematica.

Frakes, W., & Baeza-Yates, R. (1992). *Information Retrieval: Data Structures and Algorithms.* Englewood Cliffs, New Jersey: Prentice Hall.

Garshol, L. M. (2004). Metadata? Thesauri? Taxonomies? Topic Maps! Making sense of it all. *Journal of Information Science, 30*(4), 378-391. Retrieved February 14, 2008, from http://www.ontopia.net/topicmaps/materials/tm-vs-thesauri.html

Golder, S., & Huberman, B. A. (2006). Usage patterns of Collaborative Tagging Systems. *Journal of Information Science, 32*(2), 198-208. Retrieved January 25, 2007, from http://www.hpl.hp.com/research/idl/papers/tags/tags.pdf

Gudivada, V. N., Raghavan, V. V., Grosky, W. I., & Kasanagottu, R. (1997). Information retrieval on the World Wide Web. *IEEE Internet Computing, 1*(5), 56-68.

Hassan-Montero, Y., & Herrero-Solana, V. (2006, October). *Improving Tag-Clouds as Visual Information Retrieval Interfaces.* Paper presented at International Conference on Multidisciplinary Information Sciences and Technologies, Merida, Spain. Retrieved February 15, 2008, from http://www.nosolousabilidad.com/hassan/improving_tagclouds.pdf

Heymann, P., & Garcia-Molina, H. (2006). Collaborative Creation of Communal Hierarchical Taxonomies in Social Tagging Systems, *Stanford InfoLab Technical Report (2006-10).* Retrieved February 17, 2008, from http://dbpubs.stanford.edu:8090/pub/2006-10

Hotho, A., Jäschke, R., Schmitz, C., & Stumme, G. (2006). Information Retrieval in Folksonomies: Search and Ranking. In Y. Sure & J. Domingue (Eds.), *The Semantic Web: Research and Applications* (pp. 411-426). Heidelberg: Springer. Retrieved January 25, 2008, from http://www.kde.cs.uni-kassel.de/stumme/papers/2006/hotho2006information.pdf

Jain, A. K., Murty, M. N., & Flynn, P. J. (1999). Data Clustering: A Review. *ACM Computing Surveys, 31*(3), 264-323. Retrieved May 22, 2008, from http://www.cs.rutgers.edu/~mlittman/courses/lightai03/jain99data.pdf

Kim, H., & Chan, P. (2003). Learning Implicit User Interest Hierarchy for Context in Personalization. In *Proceedings of the 8th International Conference on Intelligent User Interfaces* (pp. 101-108). New York: ACM Press. Retrieved February 15, 2008, from http://cs.fit.edu/~pkc/papers/iui03.pdf

Laniado, D., Eynard, D., & Colombetti, M. (2007, December). *Using WordNet to turn a folksonomy into a hierarchy of concepts.* Paper presented at the Fourth Italian Semantic Web Workshop, Bari, Italy. Retrieved February 14, 2008, from http://ftp.informatik.rwth-aachen.de/Publications/CEUR-WS/Vol-314/51.pdf

Lawrie, D., & Croft, W. B. (2000, April). *Discovering and Comparing Topic Hierarchies.* Paper presented at RIAO 2000, Paris, France. Retrieved February 15, 2008, from http://www.cs.loyola.edu/~lawrie/papers/lawrieRIOA2000.pdf

Mathes, A. (2004). *Folksonomies: Cooperative Classification and Communication Through Shared Metadata.* Urbana-Champaign, Illinois: Graduate School of Library and Information Science, University of Illinois Urbana-Champaign. Retrieved January 21, 2008, from http://www.adammathes.com/academic/computer-mediated-communication/folksonomies.html

Melenhorst, M., & van Setten, M. (2007, September). *Usefulness of Tags in Providing Access to Large Information Systems.* Paper presented at IEEE Professional Communication Society Conference. Retrieved May 13, 2008, from http://www.x-cd.com/ipcc07CD/pdfs/55.pdf

Michlmayr, E., Cayzer, S., & Shabajee, P. (2007). Adaptive User Profiles for Enterprise Information Access, *HP Labs Technical Report HPL-2007-7.* Retrieved January 24, 2008, from http://www.hpl.hp.com/techreports/2007/HPL-2007-72.pdf

Miller, G. A, Beckwith, R., Fellbaum, C., Gross, D., & Miller, K. J. (1990). Introduction to Word-Net: an on-line lexical database. *International Journal of Lexicography, 3*(4), 235-244. Retrieved February 7, 2008, from ftp://ftp.cogsci.princeton.edu/pub/wordnet/5papers.ps

Mika, P. (2005). Ontologies are us: A unified model of social networks and semantics. In Y. Gil, E. Motta, R. V. Benjamins & M. Musen (Eds.), *The Semantic Web – ISWC 2005* (pp. 522-536).

Heidelberg, Germany: Springer. Retrieved January 25, 2008, from http://www.cs.vu.nl/~pmika/research/papers/ISWC-folksonomy.pdf

Morville, P., & Rosenfeld, L. (2007). *Information Architecture for the Worldwide Web.* Sebastopol, California: O'Reilly.

Nakamoto, R., Nakajima, S., Miyazaki, J., Uemura, S. (2007, February). Tag-Based Contextual Collaborative Filtering. Paper presented at the 18th IEICE Data Engineering Workshop, Hiroshima, Japan. Retrieved February 15, 2008, from http://www.ieice.org/~de/DEWS/DEWS2007/pdf/m5-6.p*df*

Newman, M. E. J. (2004). Detecting Community Structure in Networks. *The European Physical Journal B, 38*(2), 321-330. Retrieved May 27, 2008, from http://www-personal.umich.edu/~mejn/papers/epjb.pdf

Newman, M. E. J., & Girvan, M. (2004). Finding and evaluating community structure in networks. *Physical Review E, 69*(2), 6113. Retrieved February 15, 2008, from http://arxiv.org/abs/cond-mat/0308217

Noruzi, A. (2006). Folksonomies: (Un)Controlled Vocabulary. *Knowledge Organization, 33*(4), 199-203. Retrieved January 25, 2008, from http://eprints.rclis.org/archive/00011286/01/Folksonomy%2C_UnControled_Vocabulary.pdf

Page, L., & Brin, S. (1998). The Anatomy of a Large-Scale Hypertextual Web Search Engine. *Computer Networks and ISDN Systems, 30*(1-7), 108-118. Retrieved January 25, 2008, from http://infolab.stanford.edu/~backrub/google.html

Salton, G., & Buckley, C. (1988). Term-weighting approaches in automatic text retrieval. *Information Processing & Management, 24*(5), 513-523. Retrieved May 22, 2008, from http://www.doc.ic.ac.uk/~jmag/classic/1988.Term-weighting%20approaches%20in%20automatic%20text%20retrieval.pdf

Salton, G. (1989). *Automatic Text Processing; The Transformation, Analysis and Retrieval of Information by Computer.* Boston, Massachusetts: Addison-Wesley.

Sebastiani, F. (2002) Machine Learning in Automated Text Categorization. *ACM Computing Surveys, 34*(1), 1-47. Retrieved February 14, 2008, from http://dienst.isti.cnr.it/Dienst/UI/2.0/Describe/ercim.cnr.iei/1999-B4-31-12?tiposearch=cnr

Simpson, E. (2007). Clustering Tags in Enterprise and Web Folksonomies. *HP Labs Technical Report HPL-2007-190.* Retrieved January 24, 2008, from http://library.hp.com/techpubs/2007/HPL-2007-190.html

Sinha, R. (2005). *A cognitive analysis of tagging (or how the lower cognitive cost of tagging makes it popular).* Retrieved January 25, 2007, from http://www.rashmisinha.com/2005/09/a-cognitive-analysis-of-tagging

Speller, E. (2007). Collaborative tagging, folksonomies, distributed classification or ethnoclassification: a literature review. *Library Student Journal 2007, University of Buffalo.* Retrieved January 25, 2008, from http://informatics.buffalo.edu/org/lsj/articles/speller_2007_2_collaborative.pdf

Suchman, L. A. (1987). *Plans and Situated Actions – The Problem of Human-Machine Communciation.* Cambridge, UK: Cambridge University Press.

Vanderwal, T. (2007). *Folksonomy Coinage and Definition.* Retrieved January 21, 2008, from http://www.vanderwal.net/folksonomy.html

Van Damme, C., Hepp, M., & Siorpaes, K. (2007, June). *FolksOntology: An Integrated Approach for Turning Folksonomies into Ontologies.* Paper presented at the European Semantic Web Conference, Innsbruck, Austria. Retrieved February 15, 2008, from http://www.kde.cs.uni-kassel.de/ws/eswc2007/proc/ProceedingsSemnet07.pdf

Winter, W. de, & Rijke, M. de (2007, March). *Iden-tifying Facets in Query-Biased Sets of Blog Posts.* Paper presented at the International Conference on Weblogs and Social Media, Boulder, Colorado. Retrieved February 17, 2008, from http://icwsm. org/papers/3--Winter-Rijke.pdf

Yee, K. P., Swearingen, K., & Hearst, M. (2003). Faceted Metadata for Image Search and Brows-ing. In *Proceedings of the Conference on Human Factors in Computing Systems* (pp. 401-408). New York: ACM Press. Retrieved January 25, 2008, from http://flamenco.berkeley.edu/papers/ flamenco-chi03.pdf

Yeung, C. A., Gibbins, N., & Shadbolt, N. (2007). Tag Meaning Disambiguation through Analysis of Tripartite Structure of Folksonomies. In *Proceed-ings of the 2007 IEEE/WIC/ACM International Conferences on Web Intelligence and Intelligent Agent Technology - Workshops* (pp. 3-6). New York: ACM Press. Retrieved February 14, 2008, from http://eprints.ecs.soton.ac.uk/14762/1/tag_ disambiguation.pdf

Chapter IV
Adaptive User Profiles

Steve Cayzer
Hewlett-Packard Laboratories, UK

Elke Michlmayr
Vienna University of Technology, Austria

ABSTRACT

A major opportunity for collaborative knowledge management is the construction of user models which can be exploited to provide relevant, personalized, and context-sensitive information delivery. Yet traditional approaches to user profiles rely on explicit, brittle models that go out of date very quickly, lack relevance, and have few natural connections to related models. In this chapter the authors show how it is possible to create adaptive user profiles without any explicit input at all. Rather, leveraging implicit behaviour on social information networks, the authors can create profiles that are both adaptive and socially connective. Such profiles can help provide personalized access to enterprise resources and help identify other people with related interests.

INTRODUCTION

There are many ways to deal with the challenges of collaborative knowledge management and discovery within enterprises. This chapter focuses on personalized, adaptive approaches, leveraging user behaviour on social information systems.

A major challenge for enterprise information systems is presenting the information that us-

ers want in a way that makes sense to them. In traditional approaches to information filtering, the user has to explicitly create his or her profile, and manually keep the profile up to date. Can we take advantage of the popularity of collaborative tagging systems, such as delicious.com or flickr. com, and use the recorded tagging behaviour to construct implicit, yet realistic and dynamic user profiles?

The use of profiles for personalization is not new, but such systems typically rely on an explicit, manually entered user profile. This imposes a burden on the user, both at initial creation time, and more importantly over time as the user's skills and interests change, so the profile has to be updated. Typically, the created user profiles go out of date, fast.

Of course, this problem has been well understood for decades and much research has focused on the possibility of creating implicit user profiles. Put simply, such approaches attempt to 'look over the user's shoulder' so to speak, and create a profile out of normal behaviour. The advantage with these approaches is that the mined profile should evolve simply and naturally with ongoing changes in user behaviour patterns.

There are some drawbacks with these approaches. It is, for example, difficult to mine accurate user profiles from observed behaviour. Another problem is dealing with the changing nature of user interests. How can one distinguish between long term characteristics (as for example defined by a user's profession), medium term interests (such as ruby or agile_management for software engineers), and transient foci of attention (this year's holiday planning, news articles)? How does one choose the right level of 'forgetfulness' in the user's profile? A more subtle problem is that implicit user profiles are not examinable, or *scrutable*. Without some control over their profiles, users are likely to become distrustful of systems that use these profiles, particularly if they make egregious errors. While users do not want to spend excessive time doing 'profile gardening', they would like the facility to examine and tweak the profiles to correct errors or to proactively direct the system. A related issue is that of privacy: certainly on the public Internet, users are increasingly wary of the amount of information that is being gathered without their explicit consent

So we are in a situation where we would like to generate realistic, dynamic user profiles which are scrutable and privacy preserving. Where can we find such profiles? This chapter is primarily concerned with collaborative tagging systems, but this is just one possibility. Many of the principles discussed in this chapter are equally applicable to any system that a user interacts with on a regular basis. The use of folders in email, web browsing and document management is one possibility. User queries, both on the intra/internet and to enterprise systems, are another. Communities of interest, such as forums and mailing lists, provide yet another rich source of user behaviour to observe and to mine.

The basic operation of collaborative tagging systems is very simple. Users annotate a resource of interest, often a web page, with an arbitrary number of free text tags. These tags, personal or communal, can be used to browse a community's resources, both documents and people. The popularity of such systems provides a useful store of personally identifiable user behaviour which can be used to create implicit user profiles. In this chapter we will survey related work on user profiles. Then, taking collaborative tagging systems as an exemplar of a source from which we can construct user profiles, we will present

1. algorithms for creating such profiles
2. approaches to profile analysis and evaluation
3. methods for dynamic visualization of the generated profiles
4. a discussion of the potentials of using such profiles for personalized access to enterprise data sources.

User Profiles

Both academia (Gauch et al, 2007) and enterprises (Karat et al, 2003) have experimented with user profiles for personalization. Indeed, user profiling is a prominent feature of many modern content management systems like Microsoft Office Sharepoint Server[1]. The trouble with such systems, as we mentioned above, is that they rely on an explicit, static, manually entered user profile. In this section, we explain the need for user profiles to be implicit, dynamic and scrutable.

Implicit user profiles are created by looking over the shoulder of a user performing their usual tasks (Goecks & Shavlik, 2000). Such tasks can include email, document management or web browsing (Middleton et al, 2001). By removing the obligation of a user to manually create a profile, data collection is easier and the risk of 'data entry fatigue', or inaccurate profiling, is reduced. Most work to date has focused on collecting terms from visited web pages (Godoy & Amandi, 2005; Kim & Chan, 2008) rather than tags applied by a user. Algorithmically, both sources of data can be treated similarly but the effect may be rather different, as one is author-supplied metadata and the other annotations from the reader.

Even gathered implicitly, a user profile is prone to go out of date as users' interests change over time. **Dynamic** user profiles are those which update as the user task is changed. Godoy & Amandi (2005) present such an approach using a hierarchical organization of users' interests, while Nanas et al (2004) use a more graph-like representation. In both works an artificial change of task context is employed: we show in this chapter how this approach can be applied to real life user behaviour over time.

It is possible to use sophisticated machine learning techniques to produce 'black box' profiles (Pazzani & Billsus, 1997). However, such profiles can be frustrating for the users, who are unable to examine, let alone control, the profile. The term **scrutable** has been proposed to describe profiles that can be examined and understood by a user (Kay, 2006). Such profiles allow a user to nominate an area of interest that may not have yet shown up in his/her profile (a new area of research perhaps). Profile errors can be corrected, and parts of the profile can be hidden so that user privacy is respected.

Collaborative Tagging Systems

Collaborative tagging systems provide interfaces for annotating bookmarks with free-text keywords. The basic operation of such systems is very simple. Users annotate a resource of interest (often a web page) with an arbitrary number of free text tags. Usually there is some browser button (bookmarklet) utility to make this process very lightweight. Often the bookmarklet will provide tag suggestions based on your previous tags and others' tags for this resource. Once this is done, one can browse the user community's bookmarked resources by an arbitrary combination of tags and/or users. Usually, these queries can be persisted and published as an RSS/Atom[2] feed. Often, users are allowed to mark bookmarks as private so that they are not visible to such queries.

Perhaps the best well known collaborative tagging system is delicious.com (formerly known as del.icio.us). It has proved extremely popular, quickly growing to 1 million users in 2006[3] and then 3 million in 2007[4]. Alternatives abound, both on the public Internet and on corporate intranets. Within Hewlett-Packard there are at least three such systems, each exhibiting different characteristics and capabilities. The first, 'bookmarks', shares most of the characteristics above but also ties bookmarks into an organisation structure (so one can ask, for example, 'show me all bookmarks for Jim's work group'). The second, 'Labbies', provides 'tiny' URLs (drastically shortened but still unique URL aliases) which can be used to identify that bookmark in other resources about that bookmark, such as email discussions. It is also privacy preserving in that bookmarks are anonymous. The third, me@hp.com, is an experimental KM system. Every person in HP has a me@hp page, which is populated by default with basic data from the LDAP directory. However, users may enrich this profile with free text descriptions, photos and tags which describe their interests. Thus rather than tagging documents or web pages, tags are applied to people and hence represent communities of interest.

The simplicity and the immediate usefulness of collaborative tagging systems have attracted a high number of users. As increasingly bookmark collections have lifespans of years, these data sources contain fine-grained information about a user's changing interests over time; a valuable resource that we should be able to leverage. Unlike many other profile learning mechanisms, which rely on relevance feed-back from the user, using tagging metadata does not require any additional user input. Moreover, since tagging data is time-based, it allows us to create user profiles that dynamically adapt to drifts in users' interests.

We should note in passing that the community dynamics of collaborative tagging systems are fascinating and have been well studied (Golder & Huberman, 2006). However such dynamics are not the primary focus of discussion here, as instead we focus on the changes in an individual's tagging behaviour over time.

CREATING IMPLICIT USER PROFILES FROM COLLABORATIVE TAGGING SYSTEMS

How can we take advantage of the popularity of collaborative tagging systems, and use the recorded tagging behaviour to construct implicit, yet realistic and dynamic user profiles? Here we take a user-centric perspective, focusing on those tags which have been employed by a single user. Tagging data can be treated as a continuous stream of information about a user's interests which can be used for creating a rich user profile.

In fact, there is a fascinating interplay between community and individual effects. Individuals are free to choose their own tags; however many choose tags that are popular in the community. Indeed, systems like flickr and delicious positively encourage this behaviour by recommending tags to their users. Some tags will nevertheless be unique to a particular user. In a small sample taken by (Byde et al, 2007) about one third of all tagged URLs had completely unique tags. We believe it would be inappropriate for a user profile to treat such tags, or indeed atypical uses of existing tags, as outliers.

Figure 1. Sample data. A user stores a collection of 15 bookmarks. These bookmarks are annotated with the tags shown as space-separated lists. The lists are ordered according to the time the corresponding bookmarks were added to the bookmark collection. The oldest one is shown first (line 1). Note that this is a very small data sample, for explanatory purposes. However the data are drawn from a real user's bookmark collection.

```
 1   datamining rdf tools web
 2   algorithms design geo java library programming
 3   danger security pc tools web
 4   ais security research article
 5   bbc media rss social syndication
 6   blog flickr fun geo metadata social uk web
 7   ai turing teaching
 8   ajax eclipse programming jsp spring tools uml web
 9   geo google gps javascript tools web web2.0
10   owl rdf semanticweb web2.0
11   ai teaching
12   ai teaching
13   teaching ai
14   ontology opensource research security
15   design research robot ai teaching
```

There are more subtle dynamics at work when considering connections between tags. Co-tagging behaviour can be guided by tag recommendation mechanisms, but frequent and repeated co-tagging, particularly in the absence of recommendation clues, indicates a connection between those tags in the user's mind. To an individual user, these deviations from community norms may be tremendously important in defining their particular niche interest and perspective. It is these personal, perhaps idiosyncratic choices that we seek to exploit in this chapter, while acknowledging that such choices will depend at least in part on social cues (Golder & Huberman, 2006; Mika, 2005).

What is it, then, that we want to extract from a user's tagging activity? Clearly the tags themselves are important, and their relative importance to the user. We also want to capture the relationships that exist between tags. Finally we need to make use of the temporal dynamics implicit in tagging activity over a sustained period.

We present a 'toy' example for illustrative purposes. Consider a user's bookmark collection consisting of a user defined number of bookmarks. Each bookmark in the collection is composed of a title, a description, a URL, a date, and a set of tags. Some sample data is shown in Figure 1.

For creating the profile, we focus on the tags and their temporal ordering by increasing date.

We will use the sample data to illustrate three different methods for profile construction: a naive approach; an approach based on co-occurrence; and an adaptive approach.

Naive Approach

Perhaps the simplest method of analysis is to count the occurrence of tags. The result of this computation is a list of tags which is ranked according to tag popularity. For the sample data in Figure 1, the ranked tag list is shown in Table 1. It reveals that most tags have been used only once, and that there are only a few tags which were used most frequently. The user profile can then be created by selecting the top k most popular tags from the ranked list. If we select the top 3 tags, for example, the resulting user profile consists of the tags: web, ai, teaching.

The benefit of this method is that it is very simple, and hence fast. However, it has some drawbacks. One major problem is that those tags which are used most often tend not to be very specific (e.g., the tag web is a very general one). Moreover, although the tagging data includes information about the relationships between those tags, these relationships are not included in the user profile.

Despite its simplicity and limitations, this naïve method is commonly and popularly employed in

Table 1. List of tags ranked by their number of occurrence

#Occ.	Tag
5	web, ai, teaching
4	tools
3	security, research, geo
2	web2.0, rdf, social, programming, design
1	semanticweb, danger, rss, turing, metadata, jsp, fun, library, owl, article, ontology, google, eclipse, ajax, syndication, ais, javascript, bbc, robot, media, pc, uml, flickr, blog, java, spring, datamining, gps, opensource, uk, algorithms

the form of a *tag cloud*. This is a visualization method in which all tags a user has employed so far are listed alphabetically and the font size of a tag is set according to how often it has been used so far.

Co-Occurrence Approach

The resulting profile is more specific if we focus not only on which tags have been used, but rather on which tags have been used in combination. This can be achieved by relying on the co-occurrence technique known from Social Network Analysis (Wasserman & Faust, 1994). If two tags are used in combination (*co-occur*) by a certain user for annotating a certain bookmark, there is some kind of semantic relationship between them. The more often two tags are used in combination, the more intense this relationship is. This can be represented by a graph with labeled nodes and undirected weighted edges in which nodes correspond to tags and edges correspond to the relationship between tags. Each time a new tag is used, a new node for this tag is added to the graph. Each time a new combination of tags is used, a new edge with weight 1 between the corresponding nodes is created in the graph. If

two tags co-occur again, the weight for the corresponding edge is increased by 1.

Co-occurrence techniques have been employed for diverse purposes. First and foremost, the folksonomy providers often use it for computing related tags. Moreover, co-occurrence is also used in knowledge discovery from databases (Chen & Lynch, 1992), for extracting light-weight ontologies from tagging data (Mika, 2005), or for tag recommendation (Byde et al., 2007; Xu et al, 2006). The approach described in this section is different in that it uses co-occurrence at a smaller scale; for a single bookmark collection. Therefore the relationships between the tags are not the result of a community-driven process, but are created by a single user. Hence, the relationships between the tags might not make sense to anyone except the user who created them. However, in the case of user profile creation this is acceptable and even desirable, because for this task we need to find out about how the interests of a user are connected to each other, no matter how unorthodox these connections might be.

The co-occurrence graph is created by parsing the tags for all items in the bookmark collection and applying the technique described above. In the second step, a user profile is derived from

Figure 2. Co-occurrence network for the sample data. Two nodes are linked with an edge if the corresponding tags have been used in combination for annotating a bookmark. Edge weights are not shown

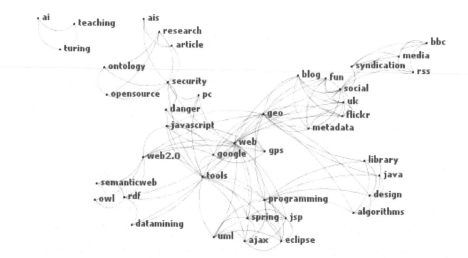

Table 2. Top 4 tag combinations ranked by their number of occurrences. Note that only those combinations with weights higher than 1 are shown.

Weight	Tag combination
4	ai - teaching, tools - web
2	geo - web, security - research

the graph by selecting the top *k* edges with the highest weights and their incident nodes. Figure 2 shows the resulting graph when applying the co-occurrence approach to the sample data. Note that although the amount of sample data is rather small, the resulting network is quite big. A ranked list of the weights of the resulting graph's edges for the sample data is shown in Table 2. Selecting the top 3 edges and their incident nodes for the user profile returns a graph with 5 nodes and the following edges:

ai-teaching tools-web geo-web

One drawback of the co-occurrence approach is that it does not include bookmarks that are annotated with a single tag. In order to overcome this issue, it would be necessary to combine it with the naive approach. The result would be a graph with weighted nodes and weighted edges. However, it may be the case that the average percentage of bookmarks annotated with only one tag is rather low; typically less than 10% (Michlmayr et al, 2007). So the loss of these data must be balanced against the advantages of a simpler method.

Another drawback of this approach is that the age of bookmarks and their temporal ordering is not considered. This issue is addressed by the adaptive approach presented in the next section.

Adaptive Approach

Since social bookmarking systems are now a mature technology, many users manage rather large bookmark collections to which they have been adding items for several months or even

years (Michlmayr et al, 2007). Hence, the age information of the tagging data is important. It makes a difference if a user has used a certain tag and, therefore, specified a certain interest, one day or one year ago. In the co-occurrence approach, this information is not considered. To include the age of the bookmarks in the user profile it is possible to extend the co-occurrence approach with the evaporation technique known from ant algorithms (Dorigo & Caro, 1999).

Evaporation is a simple method to add time-based information to the weights of the edges in the graph. Each time the profile graph is updated with tags from a newly added bookmark, the weights of the edges that already exist in the graph are decreased slightly by removing a small percentage of the current value of the weight. Obviously, when creating the profile graph for the adaptive approach by parsing the tags for all items in the bookmark collection, it is necessary to start parsing from the oldest item and to process the items in the same temporal order as they were added to the bookmark collection.

Applying the adaptive approach to the sample data apparently returns the same profile graph as before (Figure 2). However the weights of the links in this graph are different. Table 3 lists the highest weighted edges in this graph. Selecting the top 3 edges and their incident nodes for the user profile returns a graph with 6 nodes and the following edges:

ai-teaching tools-web security-research

The difference between this user profile and the one returned by the co-occurrence approach shows the effect of using evaporation for profile creation. The combinations geo-web and security-research co-occur the same number of times in the sample data. In the co-occurrence approach, a random selection of one of them was made for inclusion in the profile. With the adaptive approach it is possible to detect that the latter combination has been used at a later point in time and can therefore be considered as currently more important to the user.

In summary, the naïve approach just looks at tags which it treats as weighted nodes in a edgeless graph; the co-occurrence approach includes weighted edges whose weight monotonically increases; and the adaptive approach uses evaporation to increase the contrast of more recently used connections. The differences are summarized in Table 4.

The Add-A-Tag Algorithm

Now we formally define a possible implementation of the adaptive algorithm described above. The high level pseudocode is followed by formal mathematical descriptions of each step. The algo-

rithm includes both creation of the profile graph, and extraction of a user profile from it.

```
initialize profile to an empty graph
                                    (a)
for each bookmark in collection
    perform evaporation
                                    (b)
    apply reinforcement
                                    (c)
extract user profile from graph
                                    (d)
```

(a) Initialize the profile graph

The profile graph is $G = (V, E)$ where $V = \{v_1 \ldots v_n\}$ is the set of vertices (which correspond to tags) and $E = \{e_1 \ldots e_m\}$ is the set of edges, each of which connects two vertices with a certain weight:

$$e_x = \{v_i, v_j, w_x\} \tag{1}$$

We initialize G to an empty graph and V and E to empty sets.

Table 3. Top 4 tag combinations for the adaptive approach with parameters $\alpha = 1.0$, $\beta = 1.0$, $\rho = 0.01$ (see text for details). Again only those combinations with weights higher than 1 are shown

Weight	Tag combination
3.83	ai - teaching
3.63	tools - web
1.89	security - research
1.85	geo - web

Table 4. Comparison of naïve, co-occurrence and adaptive approaches, showing how each creates a graph (nodes connected by edges) with different characteristics

Method	Naïve	Co-occurrence	Adaptive
Weighted Nodes	Yes	No	No
Weighted Edges	No	Yes	Yes
Evaporation	No	No	Yes

(b) Perform evaporation

In this step, the existing information in the graph is changed by applying the evaporation formula shown in equation 2 to every edge $e_x \in E$

$$e_x(t+1) = \{v_i, v_j, w_x(t+1)\} \qquad (2)$$

where

$$e_x(t) = \{v_i, v_j, w_x(t)\} \qquad (3)$$

and

$$w_x(t+1) = w_x(t) - \rho\, w_x(t) \qquad (4)$$

where $\rho \in [0, 1]$ is a constant and $w_x(t)$ is the weight of edge e_x at time t

Thus, each edge weight is decreased by the evaporation coefficient ρ.

(c) Apply reinforcement

In the next step, the tags from the bookmarked item are added to the graph. Let the tags to be added form a set $T = \{t_1 \ldots t_k\}$ For every combination $t_i t_j : t_i \in T, t_j \in T, i < j$, the following procedure is executed:

1. If $t_i \notin V$ then t_i is added to V
2. If $t_j \notin V$ then t_j is added to V
3. If $e_x = \{t_i, t_j, w_x\} \in E$ then e_x is updated according to the following equation:

$$e_x(t+1) = \{t_i, t_j, w_x(t+1)\} \qquad (5)$$

where $w_x(t+1) = w_x(t) + \beta \qquad (6)$

and $0 < \beta \ and \ \beta \in \mathfrak{R} \qquad (7)$

4. If $e_x = \{t_i, t_j, w_x\} \notin E$ then e_x is added to E with $w_x = \alpha$ where

$$0 < \alpha \ and \ \alpha \in \mathfrak{R} \qquad (8)$$

So each possible tag combination in the current bookmark's tags either causes a new edge to be added to the graph (with weight a) or increases the weight of an existing edge (by weight b).

The procedure described above (steps (b) and (c): evaporation followed by reinforcement) is executed each time the user adds a bookmark item to the bookmark collection.

(d) Extract the user profile from the graph

Once the graph contains all the required bookmarks, extraction of the user profile from the profile graph can proceed as follows:

1. Create a ordered set E_s from E where E_s contains all edges $e_x = \{v_i, v_j, w_x\}$ in E in decreasing order of weight w_x.
2. Create set E_k by extracting the top k elements from set E_s, where $0 < k \ and \ k$ is a natural number.
3. Create graph G_k which is defined thus:

$$G_k = (V_k, E_k)$$
$$s.t. \ \forall e_x = \{v_i, v_j, w_x\} \in E_k,$$
$$v_i \in V_k, and$$
$$v_j \in V_k$$

Thus the user profile contains the top k tag combinations from the graph; more formally, G_k contains all the edges from E_k and all the vertices which are incident to one of these edges.

The size of the user profile G_k is determined by the value chosen for parameter k.

Evaluation of Profile Algorithms

Many statistical analyses use large bookmark data sets scraped or otherwise collected from systems like delicious.com. Since we deal with user-related data, privacy concerns arise. Therefore, permission should be sought before collecting this data and using it for analysis. Although this is likely to result in a small test set, useful information can nevertheless be gleaned, as explained in the case study below.

Evaluating the adaptive aspects of the user profile creation mechanism can be achieved by computing the user profile of user u at two different times, and measuring the difference (distance) between these two user profiles. If we use the graph based profile approach detailed in the last section, we are hampered by the fact that measuring the distance between two graphs is a difficult and only partly solved issue (Buckley & Harary, 1990). However, we can simplify the problem by mapping the graphs onto a simpler structure which only contains the information we need for the comparison. Using a set of edges in decreasing weight order would be a good approach, because several methods for comparing ordered sets exist. Therefore, we suggest the Kendall τ coefficient (Abdi, 2007). It is a standard measure for comparing ordered sets that includes rank correlation.

We define a metric dist(S1, S2) for the distance between two sets S1 and S2 based on the Kendall τ coefficient as shown in Equations 2a to 2c in such a way that it obeys the rules for metrics: positiveness, reflexivity, symmetry, and triangle inequality. The result values for dist(S1, S2) are in the range of 0 (if S1 and S2 are ranked in exactly the same order) to +1 (if the ranking of S1 can be obtained by reversing S2).

$$dist(s_1, s_2) = \frac{2*t(s_1, s_2)}{n*(n-1)}, \qquad (2a)$$

where

$$\tau(s_1, s_2) = \sum_{i,j \in P, i < j} \bar{\tau}_{i,j}(s_1, s_2) \qquad (2b)$$

and

$$\bar{\tau}_{i,j}(s_1, s_2) = \begin{cases} 0 \text{ if } i.j \text{ are in the same order in } s_1 \text{ and } s \\ 1 \text{ otherwise} \end{cases}$$

$$(2c)$$

In Equation 2a, variable n is the size of the sets. Equation 2b compares pairs of distinct elements in S1 and S2. Equation 2c counts *discordant pairs*. We need to make one pre processing modification to our tag lists, since Kendall τ is applicable only for sets which have the same members and are consequently of the same size. Thus new tags (which appear in S2 but not S1) and discarded tags (tags in S1 which don't appear in S2) could be problematic. We can deal with such tags in one of two ways. We could simply discard tags used in only one of the compared profiles (an intersection-based approach). Or we could take a union-based approach by appending new tags to the end of S1 and discarded tags to the end of S2.

Case Study

This section is drawn from work described in (Michlmayr et al 2007). The authors used a test set consisting of six users' bookmark collections for both evaluation experiments and a user study (see next section). It consists of three small (user 1, 2 and 3), two medium (user 4 and 6) and one large bookmark collection (user 5). The owners of the bookmark collections included in the test set were personally known to at least one of the authors of this paper, and were explicitly asked for permission to retrieve and evaluate their personal tagging data.

Table 5 shows the basic properties of the six bookmark collections in the test set. It can be seen that the bookmark collections varied in number of days of use, number of items, number of tags, number of unique tags, and average number of tags per item. No proportional relationship between any of these figures could be found. In addition, as shown in Figure 3, the users' activity patterns were unpredictable. Some users maintained a reasonably constant level of activity, whereas others exhibited a bursty pattern.

Table 5. Properties of the test set

User	1	2	3	4	5	6
Number of days in use	531	887	435	386	681	726
Number of bookmarked items	368	897	448	1112	2823	1362
Number of tags overall	937	1331	2234	4703	16334	6343
Number of unique tags overall	189	217	488	817	3451	1648
Average number of tags per item	2.3	3.8	4.3	4.3	5.8	4.3
Percentage of tags used only once	20%	13%	8%	1%	1%	2%

Figure 3. Average number of items added per month for the 6 sample users. It can be seen that each user's tagging activity is variable (perhaps dependent on mood and workload) and does not follow any predictable patterns.

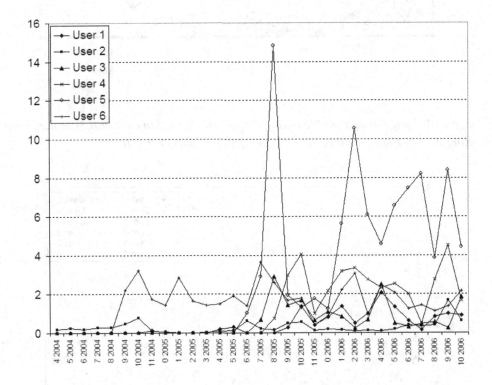

Results

For each user, every user profile G_k for week $t+1$ was compared to the user profile G_k for the previous week t using Kendall τ as described above.

Figure 4 shows the results of this computation for the co-occurrence approach (parameter k set to 20) and Figure 5 shows the results for the Add-A-Tag algorithm outlined above (parameter k set to 20, $\alpha = 1.0$, $\beta = 1.0$, $\rho = 0.01$). In both figures,

Figure 4. Degree of change in user profile plotted against week of activity using co-occurrence approach ($\rho = 0$, $k = 20$)

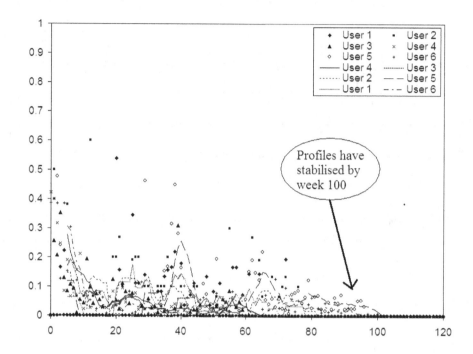

Figure 5. Degree of change in user profile (using dist metric defined in equation 2) plotted against week of activity using Add-A-Tag algorithm ($\alpha = 1.0$, $\beta = 1.0$, $\rho = 0.01$, $k = 20$)

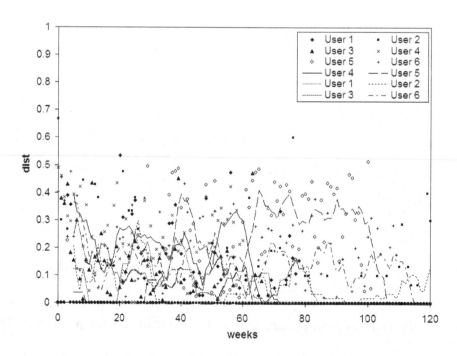

the data points show the metric values, and trend lines of type moving average with period 6 show the performance of the metric values over time for the different users.

Figure 4 shows the co-occurence approach, and it can be seen that in general the degree of change in the user profiles decreases over time. The profiles gradually stabilize (`dist` tends to zero) so that by week 100 there is little change. Although the users are specifying new tag combinations when adding bookmarks to their collections, the most often used tag combinations are too dominant and prevent newly arising tag combinations from being included in the profile.

When comparing these results to those of the Add-A-Tag approach (Figure 5), one can see that the profiles remain dynamic (`dist` stays high) even after prolonged usage. In fact, the degree of change in the user profile in the Add-A-Tag approach starts off higher than in the co-occurrence approach, and remains similar for every time span. This provides evidence that the Add-A-Tag approach meets its goal of adapting the profile to the interests of the user over time.

For a more detailed evaluation, Figure 6 shows a direct comparison of the co-occurrence and the Add-A-Tag method for one user together with the weekly activity of this user expressed as the logarithm of the average number of items added to the bookmark collection (cf. Figure 3). Again, trend lines of type moving average with period 6 are included. The dashed lines show the user's activity.

Figure 6 reveals that both approaches exhibit a change pattern proportional to the user's activity pattern, but Add-A-Tag approach's curve shows a considerably higher amount of change and fits better with the activity pattern. This is particularly true for the results in the time span between week 80 and week 100, where the user's activity level is high and the Add-A-Tag approach reflects the activity pattern, whereas the co-occurrence approach remains quiescent. Inspection of the profiles show that it was putting too much emphasis on the most often used tag combinations and thus failing to adapt to the newly-used ones.

However, one drawback of the Add-A-Tag approach that became evident during the ex-

Figure 6. Direct comparison of co-occurrence and Add-A-Tag approaches for user 5

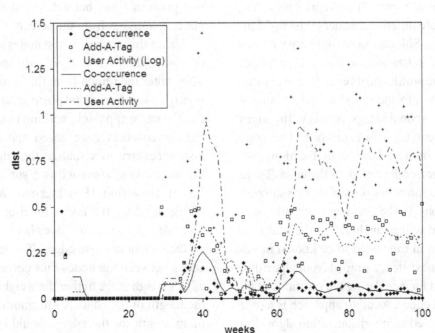

periments is that the value for the evaporation coefficient (parameter ρ) needs to be chosen very carefully. The higher the value for this parameter, the more emphasis is put on those items that were added to the bookmark collection recently. Choosing a value in the range between 0.01 and 0.05 gives reasonable results where the proportion between newly used tag combinations and often-used tag combinations is balanced. Setting the value higher than 0.05 places the emphasis on newly-used tag combinations.

From the results presented so far, it would appear that Add-A-Tag is a plausible method for generating an adaptive user profile. In the next section we show how we can effectively visualize such profiles.

PROFILE VISUALIZATION

Kay (2006) argues that profiles should be *scrutable*, that is, amenable to examination by the user: understandable, controllable and privacy preserving. The first step in making profiles scrutable is to allow the user to visualize them, and to present them in an understandable way.

There is much interest in representing tag clouds in a more intuitive manner (Hassan-Montero & Herrero-Solana, 2006), but here we need a different visualization to show the network structure of the profile and its evolution over time. One approach is to show nodes as dots labeled with their corresponding tags, connected by edges which represent tag co-occurrence. The edge weight can be indicated by length; the higher the weight, the shorter the length of the edge. There are two basic approaches possible for visualizing dynamic graphs. In the first approach, all nodes and edges that will be included in the profile at a certain point in time need to be known in advance. In the next step, a graph layout algorithm can be applied for calculating the positions of all the nodes and edges. Another approach is to use an iteration-based graph visualization algorithm

that incrementally optimizes the layout of the different graph states.

The first approach allows us to choose a good representation for a certain point in time (e.g., the most recent profile). During the animation those nodes that are currently included in the profile are set to visible while all the others are set to invisible. The benefit of this approach is that the nodes do not move, they simply appear or disappear as user activity changes over time. However, the drawback is that while the layout algorithm creates a visually pleasing layout for the complete graph, the layouts of the different graph states shown over time are not optimized and tend to look quite ugly (Michlmayr et al, 2007). Nevertheless, this is an approach worth considering if the dynamic aspects are less important than ensuring that the most up to date profile has an intuitive visualization.

The second approach allows a simpler and more intuitive dynamic visualization, which makes it easier to track the profile evolution over time. In (Michlmayr et al, 2007) this approach is used to show nodes "bubbling up". Tags enter the screen from the bottom and continuously move towards the top. If a tag is included in the user profile at one point of time, but not included in the next state, it vanishes from the screen.

Using this approach, the nodes are shown as dots and labeled with their corresponding tags. They enter the screen from the bottom on a randomly chosen horizontal position, and bubble up. For the naïve approach, nothing more is needed, but for co-occurrence based approaches, it is also necessary to visualize the edges between the nodes. One approach is a spring embedder layout algorithm (Fruchterman & Reingold, 1991), in which the nodes repel or attract each other depending on the edges between them and on the weight of these edges. The lengths of the edges between the nodes thus correspond to the edge's weights; the higher the weight, the shorter the length of the edge. A minimum and a maximum length for the edges should be defined in order to prevent node labels being printed on top of each other, and to avoid nodes being too far away from each other.

The "bubbling up" metaphor and spring embedding work together. If a tag A that newly appears at the bottom of the screen has a connection to a tag B that is already shown on the screen, the spring embedder algorithm will cause tag B to move down on the screen and tag A to move up at the same time. Tag A and tag B will move towards each other until the edge between them has a length according to its weight.

A screen shot of Michlmayr's visualization tool is shown in Figure 7. The screen is divided into a main part and a control panel at the bottom of the screen. The control panel contains radio buttons which allow the user to select one of the profile creation methods and a button to start or pause the

visualization. After starting a visualization, the user profile is presented as an animation over time. The bottom panel shows a date and the main part of the screen shows the state of the user profile at this date. A button allows the user to pause and resume the animation. The tool was implemented as a Java applet, and the graph visualization is based on the JUNG framework[5]

The vertical positions of the profile's components divide themselves into active and not active as well as into long-term, mid-term, and short-term interests of a user. The subgraphs at the centre of the screen, for example research and travel in Figure 7, are those that change over time, because as new nodes connect to the sub graph, this older tags are pulled down again. They refer to long- and midterm interests of a user that are currently active. By contrast, those subgraphs

Figure 7. Visualization of a user profile. The user (name obscured here) can select a profile creation method using one of the radio buttons (here labeled Method A/B/C). The animation can be started or paused using the large button at the bottom right.

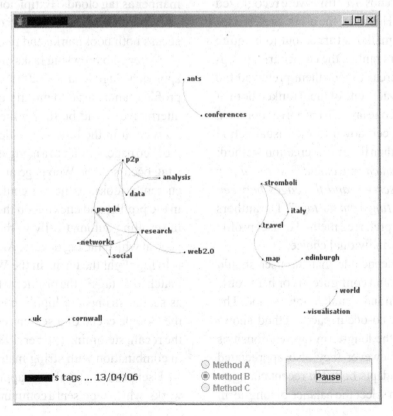

that do not change but are still included in the profile move to the top of the screen, such as ants-conferences, refer to long-term interests of a user that are currently not active. The third category comprises tags that move in from the bottom and vanish shortly after, such as uk-cornwall, which refer to the short-term interests of a user.

In (Michlmayr et al, 2007) a small user study was conducted in order to get feedback about user's acceptance of profile creation and visualization methods. Six users were provided with the visualization tool just described, and verbally interviewed using a questionnaire. The names of the three profile creation methods were not mentioned in order not to influence the results of the user study. In general, the system provoked a positive response similar to the one described by (Golder & Huberman, 2006) in their study of visualizing users' email archives. A subsequent comment we have received about this tool (*pers. comm.*) is that *"It's like looking at your mind"*. Both being able to view the relationships between the tags and the trends over time were recognized and appreciated. However, the users' preferences for the different methods turned out to be quite diverse. Two users ranked the co-occurrence approach first, whereas two of them preferred the Add-A-Tag approach, one of them ranked both of them equally, and one favored the naive approach. This may have been down to the visualization algorithm rather than the profile creation method: *"there was too much movement and too many changes on the screen, and the edges between them were detracting from the tags"*. The authors conclude that the preferred method of user profile creation is a very individual choice.

Therefore we conclude that the user should be able to choose and configure his or her profile creation algorithm and visualization method. The popularity of the co-occurrence method shows that users value the long-term tag relationships in their profile; however they also appreciated that Add-A-Tag adapts better to recent changes. Allowing users to select the balance of long-term

and short-term interests would provide control without over-burdening the user.

APPLICATION OF USER PROFILES

In the previous section we have described methods for building and visualizing a rich and dynamic user profile. To what use can we put it?

If the person knows what he or she is looking for, e.g., when performing a targeted search, knowing the user's additional interests outside the immediate search context could be used to predict the user's intention for ambiguous queries. Certainly this mode of personalized search seems to be of increasing importance to the major vendors, like Google[6]. Knowing the user's interests becomes more important if the person does not know what he or she is looking for, e.g., when browsing the Web for no specific purpose. Perhaps the most obvious approach is to use the profile for accessing web resources in the same manner as tag clouds. Extipicious[7] is a prototype interface that uses a delicious.com tag cloud to access both bookmarks and photographs.

Other web browsing tasks are enabled by this approach. Sugiyama et al (2004) describe how user profiles can be used to modify query results. An alternative would be to use the profile directly, showing it in the browser's sidebar or as part of the Web page: similar to a navigation menu. When a tag occurs in the Web page at which the user is currently looking, the tag could be highlighted in the profile, and clicking on the tag could result in scrolling automatically to the position on the page at which the tag occurs. Another possibility is to highlight the terms in the Web page that are matched by tags in the profile, in the same manner as search strings are highlighted when viewing the Google cache of a search result. To improve the recall, stemming (Porter, 1980) could be used in combination with string matching.

User profiles can also be applied to social networks, which represent a community of people and their connections. Using such networks to find an expert, or a colleague, or a community of interest, is a well known problem (Adamic & Adar 2005, Leskovec et al. 2007). User profiles allow such searches to be personalized and hence provide context dependent help, even when the searcher is not part of the network themselves.

In this section we will choose one example to study in more depth: the use of such profiles for personalized access to enterprise information systems. We use the HP Technical Reports[8] as an example for such a data source (Michlmayr & Cayzer, 2007). The social network me@hp (described earlier) is also integrated with the system and made searchable via the user profile.

This example simplifies matters because users are typically not interested in their dynamic, historic profile for information access: rather they need the most up to date 'snapshot'. Indeed, visualizing the relationships between the tags and the time-based aspects at the same time might be counterproductive, cognitively overloading users. So here we focus on visualizing the relationships between the tags in the profile at a fixed point in time.

Enterprise data sources are often annotated with metadata, such as title, author(s), date of publication, number of pages, abstract, and keywords. So the user profile can be matched, not only to the content of the data source, but also to its metadata. Technical or structural metadata, such as number of pages, resolution of a photograph, or date of publication, are generally not helpful for matching, but can be exploited for additional navigational options in the interface. Descriptive metadata on the other hand, including keywords, tags, subject indicators and geographical information, can be profitably used to match content against a user profile. Full text or abbreviated (e.g. title, abstract) content can also be used, although such approaches tend to carry computational expense (Byde et al, 2007).

In our example the user profile tags are simply compared to technical report keywords. Since tags are most commonly in lower-case letters, whereas keywords are usually in capitalized letters, the matching was performed in a case-insensitive way. Simple stemming (Porter, 1980) was also used. In general, this resulted in a partial overlap between the user's profile and the technical report content. Coverage can be extended considerably by using related keywords and authors as explained below.

The user interface layout is shown and annotated in Figure 8. The top left shows a representation of the profile. The user can select a tag from the profile to show only those resources in the main screen on the right that match with the selected tag. However, the data source will also contain content for which no corresponding tags are included in the profile. Such content would be therefore inaccessible using only the profile for navigation. This could be avoided by offering additional navigation options to the user, such as a simple query interface. Alternatively, providing additional context enables better coverage of the data source. Figure 8 illustrates that using 2 navigation panels. The first shows a list of related keywords, each of which co-occurs with the selected keyword. Co-occurrence in this case means that the keywords in question are both attached to a single technical report. These related keywords are likely to cover between them many technical reports, including those which do not have any keyword matching a user's tags. The second navigation panel is similar, but this time shows all authors that have used the selected keyword to mark up one or more of their technical reports. Again, the union of all technical reports authored by one of these people is likely to include those that would not be covered by the profile alone.

The user profile can also be used to link enterprise information systems together; to integrate data relevant to a particular user from a number of sources. Figure 8 shows a [community] section in which the 'self-tagging' system me@hp.com (described earlier) is used to recommend people, not necessarily technical report authors, who have

Figure 8. Interface layout. The top left shows the profile. The main screen (right) shows the resources that match with the tag from the profile selected by the user. The bottom left allows the user to navigate via related authors and keywords, and shows a community of interest related to the current search (section not populated for reasons of privacy)

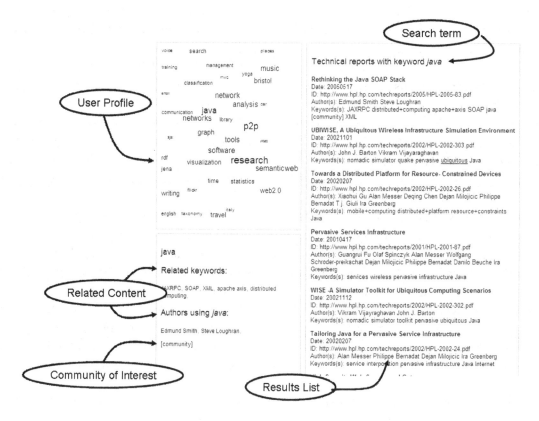

'self tagged' with the selected term. This provides a collaborative aspect to the search; linking the user to a context sensitive community of interest. Since me@hp.com is an internal system, this section has been left unpopulated in the screenshots for reasons of privacy.

The question of profile representation can be addressed from two viewpoints. One of them is the *profile-centric viewpoint* which focuses on visualizing the structure of the profile. For visualizing the relationships between the tags in the profile, a spring embedder layout algorithm is used to position related tags next to each other. The font size of each tag reflects the relative importance, i.e. number of uses of that tag, just as in a tag cloud. As explained above, the dynamic

aspects are not exploited in this interface. In fact, after some initial user feedback, the co-occurrence links have also been removed as they lead to some confusion.

It is also necessary to take a *data-centric viewpoint* by adapting the profile to the data that is available. The profile may contain tags for which there is no corresponding content, and such tags should be removed from the profile. For the remaining tags, an optional possibility would be to print the number of resources that exist next to the tag name, as in faceted browsing. The problem with this option is that combining font sizes (for relative importance of tags) and numbers (for number of resources) can be misleading to users.

It should be clear that Figure 8 does not present the last word in profile visualization. There are many open issues and areas of research including: alternatives to graph based visualization (e.g., hierarchies); representation of dynamic aspects; scrutability and control; adaptation to content. These themes will be discussed in the next section.

Figure 9 shows an 'storyboard' illustrating how a user might navigate through the system. This user is interested in techniques for enterprise information management. Firstly, they click on the tag 'graph' from their user profile because graph based user profiles is their current research interest. A list of relevant technical reports is displayed, and one of the keywords (not contained in the user's profile) is 'browser'. Clicking on this yields a second set of technical reports. The researcher knows Dick Cowan, so browses to see what else this author has published. Finding a technical report on agent technology, our user clicks on the link to get access to this research. This illustrative story shows how the system integrates personal and collaborative aspects in order to provide a richer and more context sensitive search experience.

FUTURE TRENDS

As collaborative knowledge management systems grow, we expect that personalized access will become increasingly important. Users need to be able to view a large and complex information space in a way that makes sense to them. We have outlined such an approach here. However it is likely that improvements will be needed in profile representation, editing and in interface design. We have already talked about gathering user profile information from a range of systems, such as email, browsing, file activity, newsgroups and so on. There is clearly a research challenge in merging the information from these different sources. The data needed to populate the profile will need to be gathered implicitly, as a side effect of work the user is already doing. However it is essential that the user has some ownership of the profile, and is able to inspect, change, correct and tweak the profile to better match his or her needs (Ahn et al, 2007): the twin requirements of scrutability and privacy must be met.

We also foresee improvements in profile interface design. Graph based profiles are not always intuitive, and users may need an alternative. A hierarchy, for example, would have advantages of simplicity and familiarity. Multiple inheritance issues, such as a tag having two parents, do not preclude such a representation; as such a tag would simply appear at two places in the hierarchy. We tested this possibility using an approach loosely similar to the one of Heymann and Garcia-Molina (2006), who used centrality measures to derive a taxonomy from tagging data based on the entirety of a collaborative tagging system's data. Two steps were executed for every subgraph. First, the node with the highest betweenness centrality was determined as the root node of the tree. Second, Prim's algorithm (Prim, 1957) was used for computing the maximum spanning tree based on the weights. However, this approach is not well suited for profile representation of the type we are interested in. One problem is that the resulting tree can be quite unbalanced, which gives an unsatisfying browsing experience. In addition, nodes that frequently co-occur often belong conceptually together and should exist at the same hierarchy level. For one user the tags "semantic" and "web" were used to represent a composite tag 'semantic web'. The spanning tree approach forces these tags to exist at different levels which was confusing for this user.

But the spectrum of layout algorithms is far from exhausted; given the utility of such profiles to the user it seems this would be a promising direction for future work. The current trend is tag based clustering. Chapter *"Analyzing Communal Tag Relationships for Enhanced Navigation and User Modeling"* examines this topic in more detail.

Figure 9. Storyboard showing browsing behaviour of a user who first selects a term from her profile (1), then browses by related keyword (2) and author (3) and finally selects a technical report to examine in more detail (4)

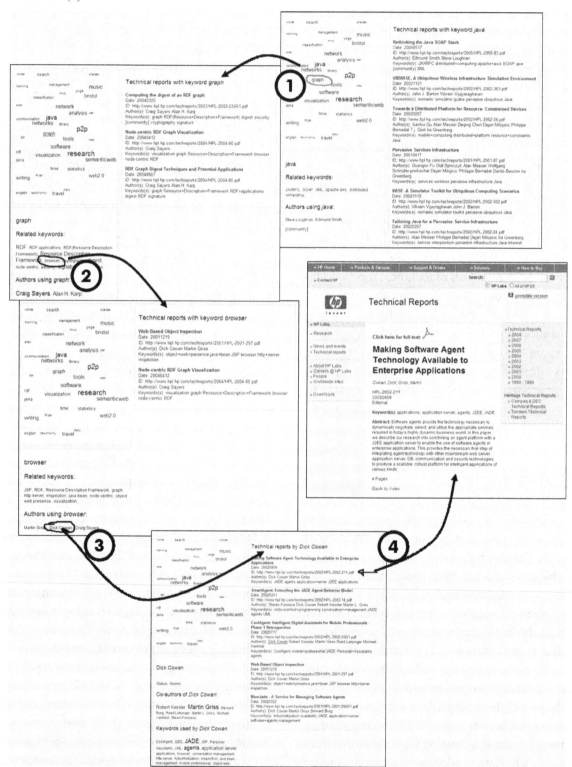

We also draw the reader's attention to the work of Begelman et al (2006), and to the more recent promising approach of Kim & Chan (2008), who split a co-occurrence graph into clusters, and arrange the clusters hierarchically.

The matching of profiles to information sources has to date been achieved using simple mechanisms, such as string matching in combination with stemming and case conversion. This could be enhanced by backing the comparison algorithm with a thesaurus such as WordNet, which would link tags with synonym keywords. Tools like ZigTag[9] and EntityDescriber[10] are providing facilities to link tags with such structured knowledge bases. Another possibility would be to use a data-centric approach, such as clustering, to find implicit relationships between tags or technical report keywords. Although we have already shown clusters of user interest in generated profiles, such clusters are subjective. It would be possible to apply any formal clustering algorithm that can be applied to weighted graphs (Brandes et al, 2003; Begelman et al, 2006). Again, this mechanism would allow a tag to be matched to a larger number of possible keywords.

The time varying nature of a profile is also important. Evaporation, as described here, provides a simple and effective way of applying such changes. Alternative approaches can be found in the literature, for example imposing a maximum/minimum weight (Stützle & Hoos, 2000). In any case, the user needs to be kept informed, and we have shown in this chapter how one can visualize these profile changes over time. Incorporating these changes into an effective interface over knowledge sources remains a research challenge.

Finally, there needs to be a balance between personal, idiosyncratic profiles and those representing shared topics in a community of interest. Too far to one extreme, and we lose the possibility of collaboration: too far to the other, and we have removed the advantages of personalization.

CONCLUSION

In this chapter we have described techniques for building a profile from a user's browsing behaviour. It does not seem adequate to take account of tag frequency alone as co-occurrence information is needed to make the profiles make sense to the user. User profiles demonstrably adapt over time and it is possible to derive appropriate metrics to measure this change. Mechanisms like evaporation can be used to deal with transient and changing interests. Visualization of the generated profiles is not straightforward but seems genuinely useful.

Profiles can also be used to access other information sources in a way that makes sense to the user. We have shown an example where tag profile information guides access to both documents (HP Labs technical reports) and communities (me@hp.com). However the principles are much more generic and can be applied to collaborative knowledge management systems in general. Much work remains to be done – in profile gathering, data integration, visualization, privacy control and interface design.

ACKNOWLEDGMENT

We would like to thank Mark Butler and Edwin Simpson for discussion and feedback on this chapter.

REFERENCES

Abdi, H. (2007). Kendall rank correlation. In N. Salkind (Ed.), *Encyclopedia of Measurement and Statistics* (pp 508-510). Thousand Oaks, CA: Sage.

Adamic, L., & Adar, E. (2005). How to Search a Social Network. *Social Networks, 27*(3), 187-203.

Ahn J., Brusilovsky, P., Grady, J., He, D., & Syn, S. Y. (2007). Open User Profiles for Adaptive News Systems: Help or Harm? In *Proceedings of the 16th International World Wide Web Conference (WWW2007)*, Banff, Alberta, Canada, May 2007.

Begelman, G., Keller, P. & Smadja, F. (2006). Automated Tag Clustering: Improving Search and Exploration in the Tag Space. *World Wide Web Conference 2006*, Edinburgh, UK. Retrieved 23 February 2008, from http://www.pui.ch/phred/automated_tag_clustering/

Brandes, U., Gaertler, M., & Wagner, D. (2003). *Experiments on graph clustering algorithms. Lecture Notes in Computer Science*, Di Battista and U. Zwick (Eds.) 2832, 568-579. Retrieved 23 February 2008, from http://citeseer.ist.psu.edu/brandes03experiments.html

Buckley, F., & Harary, F. (1990) *Distance in graphs*. Reading, MA: Addison-Wesley.

Byde, A., Wan, H., & Cayzer, S. (2007). Personalized Tag Recommendations via Social Network and Content-based Similarity Metrics. *In Proceedings of the International Conference on Weblogs and Social Media (ICWSM'07)*. Boulder, Colorado.

Chen, H., & Lynch, K. J. (1992). Automatic Construction of Networks of Concepts Characterizing Document Databases. *IEEE Transactions on Systems, Man and Cybernetics, 22*(5):885-902.

Dorigo, M., & Caro, G. D. (1999). The Ant Colony Optimization Meta-Heuristic. New Ideas in Optimization, (pp 11-32), McGraw-Hill.

Gauch, S., Speretta, M., Chandamouli, A., & Micarelli, A. (2007). User Profiles for Personalized Information Access. In Brusilovsky, P., Kobsa, A., and Nejdl, W. (Eds.), *The Adaptive Web*, (pp. 54-89), Springer LCNS 4321.

Goecks, J. and Shavlik, J. (2000). Learning users' interests by unobtrusively observing their normal behavior. In *Proceedings of the 5th international Conference on Intelligent User interfaces* (New Orleans, Louisiana, United States, January 09 - 12, 2000). IUI '00. ACM, New York, NY, 129-132.

Godoy, D., & Amandi, A. (2005). User Profiling for Web Page Filtering. *IEEE Internet Computing* 9 (4) 56-64.

Golder, S., & Huberman, B. A. (2006). Usage patterns of Collaborative Tagging Systems, *Journal of Information Science, 32*(2), 198-208. Retrieved 25 January 2007, from http://www.hpl.hp.com/research/idl/papers/tags/tags.pdf

Hassan-Montero, Y. & Herrero-Solana, V. (2006). Improving Tag-Clouds as Visual Information Retrieval Interfaces. International Conference on Multidisciplinary Information Sciences and Technologies, Merida, Spain. Retrieved 15 February 2008, from http://www.nosolousabilidad.com/hassan/improving_tagclouds.pdf

Karat, C. M., Brodie, C., Karat, J., Vergo, J., & Alpert, S. R. (2003). Personalizing the user experience on ibm.com. *IBM Systems Journal, 42*(4).

Kay, J. (2006). *Scrutable Adaptation: Because We Can and Must*. AH 2006: 11-19.

Kim, H., & Chan, P. K. (2008). Learning implicit user interest hierarchy for context in personalization. *Applied Intelligence, 28*, 2(Apr. 2008), 153-166.

Leskovec, J., Krause, A., Guestrin, C., Faloutsos, C., VanBriesen, J., & Glance, N. (2007). Cost-effective Outbreak Detection in Networks. In: *Proceedings of the 13th ACM SIGKDD International Conference on Knowledge Discovery and Data Mining*, (pp. 420-429), San Jose, California, USA.

Michlmayr, E., & Cayzer, S. (2007). Learning User Profiles from Tagging Data and Leveraging them for Personal(ized) Information Access. In: *Proceedings of the Workshop on Tagging and Metadata for Social Information Organization,*

16th International World Wide Web Conference (WWW2007), Banff, Alberta, Canada.

Michlmayr, E., Cayzer, S., & Shabajee, P. (2007). *Adaptive User Profiles for Enterprise Information Access*, HP Labs Technical Report HPL-2007-7. Retrieved 24 January 2008, from http://www.hpl. hp.com/techreports/2007/HPL-2007-72.pdf

Middleton, S. E., De Roure, D. C., & Shadbolt, N. R. (2001). Capturing knowledge of user preferences: ontologies in recommender systems. In *Proceedings of the 1st international Conference on Knowledge Capture* (Victoria, British Columbia, Canada, October 22 - 23, 2001). K-CAP '01. ACM, New York, NY, 100-107. DOI= http://doi. acm.org/10.1145/500737.500755

Mika, P. (2005). Ontologies are us: A unified model of social networks and semantics. Y. Gil, E. Motta, R. V. Benjamins & M. Musen (Eds.), *Proceedings of the Fourth International Semantic Web Conference*, Heidelberg, Germany: Springer. Retrieved 25 January 2008, from http://www. cs.vu.nl/~pmika/research/papers/ISWC-folksonomy.pdf

Nanas, N., Uren, V., & de Roeck, A. (2004). Exploiting Term Dependencies for Multi-Topic Information Filtering with a Single User Profile. *Lecture Notes in Computer Science, 3025*: 400-409

Pazzani, M., & Billsus, D. (1997). Learning and Revising User Profiles: The identification of interesting web sites, Machine Learning, *27*, 313-331.

Porter, M. F. (1980). An algorithm for suffix stripping, *Program*, *14*(3) pp 130–137.

Prim, R. C. (1957). Shortest connection networks and some generalizations. *Bell System Technical Journal, 36.*

Stützle, T., & Hoos, H. (2000) MAX-MIN Ant System. Journal of Future Generation Computer Systems, *16*, 889 – 914.

Sugiyama, K., Hatano, K., and Yoshikawa, M. (2004). Adaptive web search based on user profile constructed without any effort from users. In *Proceedings of the 13th International Conference on World Wide Web* (New York, NY, USA, May 17 - 20, 2004). WWW '04. ACM, New York, NY, 675-684.

Wasserman, S., & Faust, K. (1994). *Social Network Analysis.* Cambridge, UK: Cambridge University Press.

Xu, Z., Mao, F. J., & Su, D. (2006). Towards the Semantic Web: Collaboration Tag Suggestions. *In Proceedings of the Collaborative Web Tagging Workshop, World Wide Web Conference (WWW 2006).*

ENDNOTES

[1] http://office.microsoft.com/en-us/sharepointserver/

[2] RSS stands for 'really simple syndication' (RSS2.0: http://cyber.law.harvard. edu/rss/rss.html) or 'RDF site summary' (RSS1.0: http://web.resource.org/rss/1.0/). It is a machine readable syndication format for websites, blogs, newsfeeds and so on. Atom (http://tools.ietf.org/html/rfc4287) is a similar but newer standard.

[3] http://www.techcrunch.com/2006/09/25/delicious-reports-1-million-users-post-yahoo-growth-tops-all-of-digg/

[4] http://www.techcrunch.com/2007/09/06/exclusive-screen-shots-and-feature-overview-of-delicious-20-preview/

[5] http://jung.sourceforge.net

[6] http://www.google.com/preferences

[7] http://kevan.org/extispicious.cgi

[8] http://www.hpl.hp.com/techreports

[9] http://www.zigtag.com/

[10] http://www.entitydescriber.org/

Chapter V
Modeling Users for Adaptive Information Retrieval by Capturing User Intent

Eugene Santos, Jr.
Dartmouth College, USA

Hien Nguyen
University of Wisconsin - Whitewater, USA

ABSTRACT

In this chapter, we study and present our results on the problem of employing a cognitive user model for Information Retrieval (IR) in which a user's intent is captured and used for improving his/her effectiveness in an information seeking task. The user intent is captured by analyzing the commonality of the retrieved relevant documents. The effectiveness of our user model is evaluated with regards to retrieval performance using an evaluation methodology which allows us to compare with the existing approaches from the information retrieval community while assessing the new features offered by our user model. We compare our approach with the Ide dec-hi approach using term frequency inverted document frequency weighting which is considered to be the best traditional approach to relevance feedback. We use CRANFIELD, CACM and MEDLINE collections which are very popular collections from the information retrieval community to evaluate relevance feedback techniques. The results show that our approach performs better in the initial runs and works competitively with Ide dec-hi in the feedback runs. Additionally, we evaluate the effects of our user modeling approach with human analysts. The results show that our approach retrieves more relevant documents to a specific analyst compared to keyword-based information retrieval application called Verity Query Language.

INTRODUCTION

We studied the problem of employing a user model for Information Retrieval (IR) in which knowledge about a user is captured and used for improving a user's performance. A user model addresses the "one size fits all" problem of the traditional IR system (Brusilovsky & Tasso, 2004). It takes into consideration a user's knowledge, preferences, interests, and goals of using an IR system to deliver corresponding documents that are relevant to an individual and to present different parts of the same documents to a user according to his/her preferred ways of perceiving information. Modeling a user in an information seeking task also addresses the gap between what a user thinks as relevant versus what an IR system assumes that any user would think as relevant (Saracevic et al., 1997). The main purpose of user modeling for IR is to determine what the user intends to do within a system's environment for the purpose of assisting the user to work more effectively and efficiently (Brown, 1998). The common approach for an IR application that employs a user model usually consists of two main steps: (i) to construct a static, or a dynamic user profile; and (ii) to adapt the target IR application to the user's profile. An example of a static user profile is his/her demographic data such as gender, age, profession, and zip code. An example of a dynamic user profile is his domain knowledge, goals, and preferences. The first step is referred to as elicitation and the second step is referred to as adaptation. Elicitation of user models is a knowledge acquisition process. It is well-known in the artificial intelligence (AI) community that knowledge acquisition is the bottleneck of intelligent system design (Murray, 1997). Determining when and how to elicit the user's knowledge is a domain and application-dependent decision. Adaptation involves how to retrieve documents that are relevant to the user's profile and how to present these relevant documents according to the user's preferred ways of perceiving information.

User modeling techniques have been used to improve a user's performance in information seeking since the late 80s (examples of some early works are (Allen, 1990; Brajnik et al., 1987; Saracevic et al., 1997)). Modeling a user for information seeking poses many challenges to both the information retrieval and the user modeling communities. We have identified five main challenges as follows:

(i)   the partial-observability of a user's knowledge (e.g. as identified in (Wilson, 1981)). A user's information needs is a subjective experience that only exists in a user's mind and therefore, it is not directly accessible to outsiders (Case, 2002; Wilson, 1981).

(ii)   the uncertainty when modeling a user (e.g. as identified in (Greenberg & Witten, 1985; Chin, 1989)). Even within a very small domain, the number of possible actions that a user can perform may increase exponentially over time. To make matters worse, modeling every possible action in the user's world unfortunately does not lead to the most accurate model (DeWitt, 1995).

(iii)   the vagueness of an individual's information needs (e.g. as identified in (Case, 2002; Wilson, 1981;)). These challenges are caused by a user's inexperience in problem solving, a user's unfamiliarity with the search subjects, or a user's lack of required computer skills. If a user does not know exactly what he/she is looking for, he/she often constructs queries with terms that are either too broad or too specific and are not closely related to what he/she actually needs.

(iv)   the dynamics of a user's knowledge which changes over time as a result of new information (e.g. as identified in (Belkin, 1993; Ingwersen, 1992)). The traditional IR framework assumes that a user's information needs are static. This means that the content of retrieved documents did not have any effect on a user. However, studies have shown that a user's knowledge is updated over time by interacting with information (Ingwersen, 1992; Campbell, 1999).

(v) the absence of a standard, unified evaluation framework on the effectiveness of such a model (e.g. as identified in (Weibelzahl, 2003)). After all, the goal of a user model is to make an IR system better serve a user. Unfortunately, empirical evaluation is often overlooked even within the user modeling (UM) community (Chin, 2001). There are two main schools of thought regarding the evaluation of effectiveness of a user model from the UM and IR communities. The techniques from the UM community focus more on the issues of assessing an individual user's performance (Chin, 2003) whereas the techniques from the IR community focus more on the issues of assessing an IR system's performance. In the IR community, standard metrics such as precision and recall (Salton & McGill, 1983) and benchmark data collections are used to evaluate how many documents assessed as relevant by a group of experts have been retrieved. In the last few years, the evaluation methods in the IR community have shifted towards more concerns for the end users, for example, the interactive track at TREC conference (Craswell et al., 2003; Wilkinson & Wu, 2004), but this is still in its infancy with limited attention and participation from the IR community. The reasons for this situation are that the evaluations involving real users are expensive, time-consuming, and contain a lot of measurement noise. The key to solving this problem is to develop testbeds, metrics and procedures that take into account a user's experience in a search as well as an IR system's performance.

Unfortunately, traditional IR does not offer a way to overcome these challenges because its framework supports very little users' involvement (Saracevic, 1996).

In Collaborative IR (Karamuftuoglu, 1998) and Social IR (Goh & Foo, 2007), modeling a user is a very critical issue. In order to do a good job in CIR and SIR, we need to understand a user's behaviors in an information seeking task. In other words, we need to capture an individual's experience, knowledge, interests, and cognitive styles and use this information to assist the user in stand-alone and collaborative retrieval tasks. The research on using user models for information retrieval will help answer some of the most important research questions for CIR and SIR: how to capture a user's behaviors in an information seeking task and how to improve a user's performance and satisfaction using the captured information.

The current approaches to building user models for information retrieval are classified into three main groups (Saracevic et al., 1997): system-centered, human-centered, and connections (which we will refer in this chapter as hybrid approaches). The methods belonging to the system-centered group focus on using IR techniques such as relevance feedback and query expansion to create a user model. The methods belonging to the human-centered group focus on using human computer interaction (HCI) approaches to create a user model. The methods belonging to the hybrid group combine IR, HCI or Artificial Intelligence (AI) techniques to construct a user model. As Saracevic and his colleagues (1997) have succinctly pointed out, there is very little crossover between IR and AI communities with regards to building user models for IR. This is quite unfortunate because many techniques and evaluation methods are often reinvented by both sides. The main objective of our approach is to take advantage of well-established evaluation frameworks in IR, and use the strength of knowledge representation techniques in AI to build and evaluate a user model for improving retrieval performance.

In this chapter, we present our effort in improving a user's effectiveness in an IR application by building a user model to capture user intent dynamically. We assess its effectiveness with an evaluation methodology which allows us to compare with the existing approaches from the IR community as well as validates its effectiveness with human subjects. This chapter brings together some of our past results and user modeling experiments providing a unified formal framework and evaluations with synthesized data sets and human testing (Santos et al., 2003a; Santos et al., 2003b; Nguyen et al., 2004a; Nguyen et al., 2004b; Nguyen, 2005). Uncertainty is one of the key challenges in modeling a user for IR, as mentioned earlier. While there are some other approaches to modeling uncertainty such as Dempster-Shafer theory (Shafer, 1976), we selected Bayesian networks (Pearl, 1988) since it provides a mathematically sound model of uncertainty and we have expertise in efficiently building and reasoning over them (Santos et al., 2003c; Santos & Dinh, 2008). The novelty of our approach lies with the fine-grained representation of a user model, the ability to learn user knowledge incrementally and dynamically, and the evaluation framework to assess the effectiveness of a user model.

The goal of our user model is to capture a user's information seeking intent. We observe that a document's content reflects its authors' intent (termed as author intent) because the authors want to convey certain messages through their writings. The intent of a user engaged in an information seeking task is reflected in his/her information needs. When a user indicates which documents are relevant to his/her needs, the user intent and the author intent are probably overlapped. Therefore, capturing a user's intent by analyzing the contents of retrieved relevant documents is an intuitive task to do. Moreover, a user's intent is characterized by the goals that the user is trying to achieve, the methods used to achieve them, and the reasons why a user wants to accomplish a certain goal. Therefore, we partition a user's intent into three formative components: interests, preferences, and context which captures what goals a user

focuses on, how a user is going to achieve them, and why a user wants to achieve these goals. We refer to our user model as the *IPC* user model. While previous efforts at building a user model for information retrieval and filtering have either focused exclusively on learning any one of these aspects alone (e.g., Balabanovic & Shoham, 1997; Billsus & Pazzani, 2000; Horvitz et al., 1998; Hwang, 1999; Maes, 1994), or combining dynamic interests and/or local context with static ontology (e.g., Hernandez et al., 2007; Liu & Chu, 2007; Mylonas et al., 2008), we focus on generating an individual's context dynamically from the concepts relevant to his/her information seeking tasks. We construct our user model over time and incrementally from retrieved relevant documents as indicated by the users in an interactive IR framework. Our user model also focuses on interactions among a user's interests, preferences and context in a dynamic fashion. In particular, our emphasis is on deriving and learning the context for each user which is essentially the relations between concepts in a domain dynamically. The difference of our approach versus the existing work in this direction is that we provide a learning capability for the system to discover new knowledge based on analyzing the documents relevant to the user and their context, i.e., why a user is focusing on the given information by exploring the structure of information instead of frequency.

In our evaluation framework, we assess the effectiveness of our user model with regards to the target application in terms of its influence on retrieval performance as well as its effects on helping humans to retrieve more documents that are relevant to an individual's needs (Santos et al., 1999; Santos et al., 2003a; Santos et al., 2003b; Nguyen et al., 2004a; Nguyen et al., 2004b; Nguyen, 2005). We discuss the results of our evaluation on the effectiveness of our user model with regards to retrieval performance using the CRANFIELD, CACM, and MEDLINE collections (Salton & Buckley, 1990). We compare against the best traditional approach to relevance feedback

– the Ide dec-hi approach using term frequency inverted document frequency (TFIDF) weighting (Salton & Buckley, 1990). Even though the Ide dec-hi approach is old, it is still very competitive, especially in evaluations with small data sets such as CRANFIELD, CACM and MEDLINE, as shown in more recent studies (Drucker et al., 2002; Lóper-Pujalte et al., 2003). The difference between our user modeling approach and the Ide dec-hi approach is that our model is long-lived and changes overtime while the user model created by using the Ide dec-hi is short-lived and only affects the current query. Therefore, we simulate the traditional procedure as laid out in (Salton & Buckley, 1990) by starting with an empty user model. We also create a new procedure in which we assess new features offered by our user model such as the use of prior knowledge and the use of information learned from one query to the same query and related queries. We show that our approach performs better than TFIDF in the initial run; works competitively with Ide dec-hi in the feedback run; and, improves retrieval performance when knowledge about users and search domains have been learned over time. In addition to the evaluation with synthesized data, we conduct an evaluation with human analysts. Our evaluation with three intelligence analysts was conducted at the National Institute of Standard Technology (NIST). The results show that our approach retrieves more relevant documents that are unique for each user.

This chapter is organized as follows: We begin by reviewing important related work in IR and UM communities with regards to capturing user intent, using relevance feedback and Bayesian networks to improve retrieval performance. Next, our approach will be presented, followed by a description of the evaluation procedures with synthesized data and the analysis of the results. Then, a description of the evaluation with intelligent analysts will be reported. Finally, we present our conclusions and future work.

RELATED WORK

Our approach builds a user model by capturing user intent for improving the user's effectiveness in an IR application. Our technique makes use of relevance feedback and Bayesian networks for building our user model dynamically and uses information about a user's interests, context and preferences to modify a user's query proactively. In this section, we first review some work on capturing user intent from the IR community and then present some related research on relevance feedback, Bayesian networks and context for IR.

According to the Webster dictionary (online version available at http://www.merriam-webster.com/, based on *Merriam-Webster's Collegiate® Dictionary, Eleventh Edition)*, intent is defined as "a usually clearly formulated or planned intention". We define intent as composed of the user's desired end-states (goals), the reason for pursuing such end-states, methods to achieve these goals, and the levels of commitment behind them. An important aspect behind intent is to capture as much as possible of the user's knowledge, experience, and individual cognitive style to improve a user's effectiveness in an information seeking task. In the IR community, researchers have recently focused on identifying the goals of a user's search to retrieve more relevant information to the tasks that the user is doing (Broder, 2002; Baeza-Yates et al., 2006; Jansen et al., 2007; Lee et al., 2005; Rose & Levinson, 2004). However, two questions need to be addressed in order to capture a user's intent:

(i)   Does a user have predictable goals in information seeking and which factors can affect the user's goals?

(ii) How can we identify a user's goals automatically?

In (Rose & Levinson, 2004), data collected from a user study has been analyzed and the goals of a user's queries are classified into two categories: navigational and informational. Navigational queries refer to the ones issued by a user who knows exactly which web pages he/she is going to visit. Informational queries refer to the ones issued by a user who does not have any specific web pages in mind and use IR applications for learning or exploring a specific topic. One more category added by Broder (2002) and later explored by Jansen et al. (2007) is transactional, which refers to "the intent to perform some web-mediated activity" (Broder, 2002). Another similar classification scheme is introduced in (Baeza-Yates et al., 2006), which include informational, not informational, and ambiguous. These categories can be determined manually (for example in (Broder, 2002; Jansen et al., 2007)) and automatically (for example, in (Lee et al., 2005), goals are determined using frequency information from click and anchor link distributions). Yahoo used to maintain a research site (http://mindset.research.yahoo.com) that allowed users to sort the retrieved web sites into commercial and non-commercial based on whether a user is shopping or seeking information. In our approach, we infer a user's intent automatically and dynamically using information from a user's queries and documents that they have indicated as relevant. Even though the query is important, it may not be enough to represent a user's information needs because of various reasons, including vagueness due to the user's inexperience and partial-observability due to the user's inability to map his/her information needs into words. Therefore, we believe that additional information such as document contents may shed some light on the actual intention of a user.

Relevance feedback is an effective method for iteratively improving a user's query by learning from the relevant and non-relevant documents of a search (Spink & Losee, 1996). Relevance feedback and query expansion techniques have been used widely in the IR community since the early 60s (Frake & Baeza-Yates, 1992). Several comprehensive reviews of research in relevance feedback and query expansion are (Borlund, 2003; Efthimis, 1996; Ruthven & Lalmas, 2003; Spink & Losee, 1996). Not only did the IR community focus on the development of different techniques for improving retrieval performance using relevance feedback and query expansion, IR researchers also focused on the evaluation of the effectiveness of these two approaches early on. In particular, Salton and Buckley (1990) have laid out an evaluation framework to assess and compare any technique using relevance feedback and query expansion. Twelve different relevance feedback techniques including Ide dec-hi, Ide regular (Ide, 1971), and Rochio (1971) have been evaluated for vector space and probabilistic models using 6 collections: CACM, CISI, CRANFIELD, INSPEC, MEDLINE and NPL. Two important issues raised by this evaluation are the use of a residual collection and the computation of average precision at three specific recall points of 0.25, 0.5, and 0.75 (or as it is called, three point fixed recall). A residual collection is created by removing all documents previously seen by a user regardless of whether they are relevant or not from the original collection. Evaluation is done using the reduced collection only. The main idea for using the residual collection is to assure that we assess a technique based on new information retrieved (Salton & Buckley, 1990). The average precision at particular fixed recall points offers an opportunity for easy comparison among different techniques. The best technique found in this evaluation over all tested collections is Ide dec-hi in which the terms from all relevant documents and the first non-relevant document are added to the original query. Ide dec-hi is still very competitive in some newer studies, as pointed out in (Drucker et al., 2002; López-Pujalte et al., 2003). Relevance feedback or query expansion techniques represent a user's information needs explicitly by words or terms that the user is looking for or has found in relevant or non-relevant documents. This type of model captures only the user's immediate interests for a specific query. This model is only good for the current query and is completely reset as the user changes from one query to the next. The content of the model is not reused if a similar query is issued. In summary, there is no history of user search behaviors except the relevance feedback for the current query.

In our approach, we made use of Bayesian networks to build our user model. Bayesian networks also have been applied to IR for improving ranking (deCristo et al., 2003) and improving relevance feedback and query expansion (Decampos et al., 1998; Haines & Croft, 1993). The techniques proposed in (deCristo et al., 2003; Haines & Croft, 1993) take advantage of the expressiveness of Bayesian networks to represent the relationships among queries, documents, and keywords while the approach in (Decampos et al., 1998) uses the inference power of Bayesian networks with relevance feedback set as evidence. In our approach, we focus on exploring the structure of information based on syntactic analyses of sentences and noun phrases instead of frequency as have been done in other Bayesian networks approaches above. We also use Bayesian networks to reason about a user's preferences in choosing a class of tools to modify a query.

The techniques for using feedback from users as inputs for machine learning mechanisms to build user models are widely used in information filtering and text recommendation systems. Please see Zukerman & Albrecht (01) for a comprehensive survey on statistical approaches. Some techniques have successfully captured a user's interests in information seeking such as (Balabanovic, 1998; Billsus & Pazzani, 2000). The work of Adaptive News Filtering (Billsus & Pazzani, 2000) is a typical example of how to use machine learning techniques to build user models while the work by Balabanovic (1998) on a text recommender system is a typical example of using decision theoretic principles to represent preference rankings over a set of documents. Each of the two UM approaches above is evaluated using their own collections

and evaluation procedures. Therefore, it is very difficult to compare them against different techniques. Other studies from the UM community (Bueno & David, 2001; Magnini & Strapparave, 2001) also use their own users, collections and procedures.

Even though context in information retrieval is considered a very important research topic in the IR community (e.g., early work from Saracevic (1996) and Dervin (1997)), until recently, IR researchers have emphasized more on capturing contextual information for improving retrieval effectiveness (e.g., special issues on context for information retrieval edited by Cool and Spink (2002); another special issue edited by Crestani & Ruthven (2007); or, paper by Mylonas and colleagues (2008)). The studies presented in the special issue on context for information retrieval edited by Cool and Spink (2002) shed some light on how to capture a user's context at different levels (e.g., environment, information seeking, interaction, and query levels). The studies in the special issue edited by Crestani and Ruthven (2007) are directly related to our work in this chapter. In particular, in the approach proposed by Campbell et al. (2007), a naive Bayesian classifier is created and used to find relationships between documents. One problem with this approach is that it requires many instances of training data for the classifier to start working. Another direction to explore contextual information is to use a domain ontology to support text retrieval (Hernandez et al., 2007; Liu & Chu, 2007). Our approach is different from these two approaches in that we construct individual contextual information dynamically instead of using static domain ontology. Another work that is very closely related to our approach is Mylonas et al. (2008). In this work, domain ontology is combined with individual context information extracted from annotations, and queries are used to provide context information for IR. In our work, we currently extract individual context information from analyzing the whole content. However, our approach does work with annotations or snippets as well.

In summary, our approach is different from other approaches reviewed in this section in two aspects. First, we define and capture the user's intention in an information seeking task dynamically by exploring the structural information from retrieved relevant documents. Second, we focus on assessing whether our technique retrieves more relevant documents for an individual user as well as comparing our results with the existing techniques from the IR community.

IPC USER MODEL

The main goal of our user model is to accurately capture and represent a user's intent in order for the main IR application to be able to assist the user in getting more relevant documents for the tasks at hand (Santos et al., 2001). We partition a user's intent in information seeking into three formative components. The first, Interests, captures the focus and direction of the individual's attention. The second, Preferences, describes the actions and activities that can be used to carry out the goals that currently hold the individual's attention, with a focus on how the individual tends to carry them out. The third, Context, provides insight into the user's knowledge and deeper motivations behind the goals upon which the individual is focused and illuminates connections between goals. In other words, Interests component captures what a user is doing, Preferences component captures how the user might do it, and Context component infers why the user is doing it. Within the context of an IR application, our user model uses the information captured on what a user is currently interested in, how a query needs to be constructed, and why the user dwells on a search topic in order to modify a user's queries pro-actively and autonomously, and send the modified queries to the search engine to retrieve documents for the user.

In our user model, we capture the context, interest, and preference aspects of a user's intent with a context network, an interest set, and a prefer-

ence network, correspondingly. Before describing the details of the IPC model and how queries are modified on behalf of the user, we first introduce the document and query representation called document graph and query graph. Each document is represented as a document graph (DG). A *DG* is a directed acyclic graph (DAG) in which each node represents a concept (called concept node) or a relation among the concepts (called relation node). Concept nodes are noun phrases such as *"surface heat transfer"* or *"transfer rate distribution"*. Relation nodes are either nodes labeled *"isa"* or *"related to"*. A relation node of a DG should have concept nodes as its parent and its child. The algorithm for extracting concepts and relations between these concepts from a text file is included in Appendix. A query graph (QG) is similar to the document graph but it is generated from a user's query. DG and QG will be used in our description of the algorithms for constructing our user model.

Interest Set

The Interest set determines what is currently relevant to a user. Each element in the interest set consists of an interest concept and interest level. Interest concepts refer to the concepts the user is currently focusing on, and interest levels are real numbers from 0 to 1 representing how much emphasis the user has on a particular concept. The concept with an interest level of 1 is a concept of maximum interest while one with an interest level of 0 is of minimum interest to the user. An interest set is created and updated based on the intersection of retrieved relevant documents. Since a user's interests change overtime, we incorporate a fading function to make the irrelevant interests fade away.

The concepts in an interest set are determined from the set of documents that the user has indicated as relevant. Denote each interest concept as a and its associated interest level as $L(a)$. We compute $L(a)$ after every query by:

$$L(a) = 0.5 * (L(a) + \frac{p}{q})$$

where p is the number of retrieved relevant documents containing a and q is the number of retrieved documents containing a. If $L(a)$ falls below a user-defined threshold value, the corresponding interest concept a is removed from the interest set. After we find the set of DGs in the intersection of retrieved relevant documents, as described in the next section, each concept in this set will be added to the current interest set with the interest level being computed as the ratio of frequency of a specific concept over the total frequency of all concepts in the intersection.

Context Network

The Context network captures a user's knowledge of concepts and the relations among concepts in a specific domain. Figure 1 shows a portion of the context network of a user model from one of the experiments conducted in this chapter. The representation of a context network is similar with that of a document graph. It is basically a directed acyclic graph (DAG) that contains two kinds of nodes: concept nodes and relation nodes. We use DAG to represent a context network because of its expressiveness in representing the relations among concepts in a specific domain visually. Each node is associated with a weight,

value and bias. The weight of a node represents its importance assigned initially by the system. The concept nodes and "*isa*" relation nodes have initial weights equal to 1 while the "*related to*" relation nodes have initial weight equals to 0.8. We choose these values to emphasize that with "*isa*" relation, one node can transfer all of its energy to the other node while with "*related to*" relation, only a part of its energy can be transferred to another node. The value of a node represents its importance to a user and is any real number from 0 to 1. The bias of a node represents whether this node is actually in the user's interests or not. Each node's weight, value and bias will be used by a spreading activation propagation algorithm to reason about concepts of a user's interests used in determining the modified query graph. The main idea is that a node that is located far from an evidently been interested concept will be of less interest to the user.

The spreading activation propagation algorithm consists of the followings:

- The inputs to this spreading activation algorithm are the current interest set, current query graph and current context network of our user model. The output of this algorithm is a new interest set.
- We set the bias equal to 1 for every concept found both in the current context network and in the current query graph. We set the

Figure 1. An example of a context network

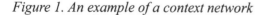
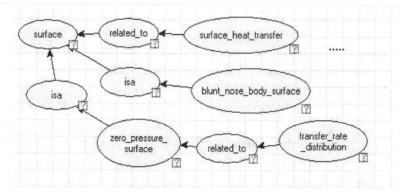

bias equal to the interest level for every interest concept found both in the current context network and in the current interest set.

- We sort all the nodes based on its depth in the context network. Denote a node as *a*, its depth as *d(a)*.

  $d(a) = 0$ if the node has no parents

  $d(a) = \max(d(p(a))) + 1$ with $p(a)$ is a parent of *a*.

- For each node *a* in the existing context network

  If this node doesn't have any parents:

  $sum = 0$

  $$value = \frac{(sum + bias)}{2} \quad \text{if } bias > sum$$

  value =0 Otherwise

  If this node has one parent node:

  $sum = value(p(a)) * weight(p(a))$

  $$value = \frac{(sum + bias)}{2} \quad \text{if } bias > sum$$

  value = sum Otherwise

  If this node has multiple parent nodes:

  $$sum = \frac{1}{1 + e^{\frac{\sum value(p_i(a))*weight(p_i(a))}{n}}}$$

in which $p_i(a)$ is a parent of a node *a*, *n* is the total number of all parent nodes. We chose this function to ensure that the value of each node is converged to 1 as the values and weights of its parents are increasing.

$$value = \frac{(sum + bias)}{2} \quad \text{if } bias > sum$$

value = sum Otherwise

- Sort all concept nodes by their values and pick the nodes whose values are greater than a user-defined threshold to form a new interest list.

We treat nodes with one parent and multiple parents differently in this algorithm to stress the important influences a child node received from the only parent versus received from many different parents.

In the example shown in Figure 2, a user's query is about "*transfer rate distribution*". The node corresponding to the query term found in the existing context network has initial weight and bias being 1 (shown as a shaded node in Figure 2). We assume further that the existing interest list contains two concepts: "*surface*" with interest level being 0.6 and "*surface heat transfer*" with interest level being 0.7. We apply this algorithm and recompute the values for the concepts nodes

Figure 2. Example illustrates spreading activation algorithm on a context network

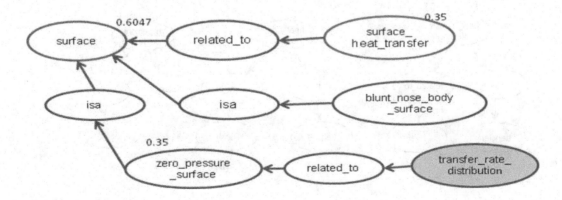

in this context network. The value of the node *"surface"* is slightly increased from 0.6 to 0.6047 while the node *"surface heat transfer"* is sharply decreased from 0.7 to 0.35. The node *"surface heat transfer"* is located farther from the concept in the query node compared to the node *"surface"*. If the threshold for values of interest list is set as 0.4 for example, then the new interest list will consist of only two nodes: *"transfer rate distribution"* and *"surface"*.

We construct a context network dynamically by finding the intersection of all document graphs representing retrieved relevant documents. The algorithm for finding intersections of retrieved relevant document graphs consists of the following:

Denote the set of retrieved relevant documents as $D=\{D_1, D_2, ..D_m\}$. Denote intersection set as J which is initially empty.

For each document D_i belongs to D do
 For each node c in D_i do sum=0
if this node is a concept node then
 For j from 0 to m
     if (i does not equal to j) and (Dj contains concept node c)
     then sum++
if (sum $\geq$ user-defined-threshold)
     then Add concept node c to J

For each document D_i belongs to D do
For each node r in D_i do
    sum =0
    if this node is a relation node and (its parent and its child are in J)
    then sum++
    if sum > 0 then add this fragment r's parent - r -r's child to J

The common set of sub-graphs of the two documents described in Figure 3 is shown in Figure 4. The set of common sub-graphs is used to update our context network. We will check if a sub-graph is not currently in the context network, and add it accordingly. We will also ensure that the update will not result in a loop in the existing context network. If it does, we skip this addition. We avoid loops in our context network to make sure that our context network is a directed acyclic graph. A new link between two existing concepts in a context network will also be created if two concepts are indirectly linked in the set of common sub-graphs and the frequency of these links exceeds a certain user-defined threshold.

Preference Network

The Preference network represents how a user wants to form the query. We use Bayesian networks to represent a preference network because

Figure 3. A portion of document graphs for two documents

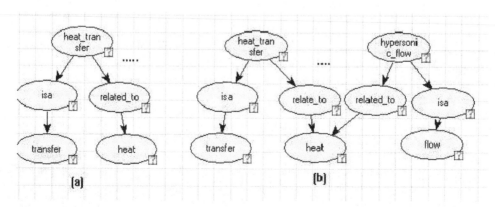

Figure 4. A portion of common set of sub-graphs of two documents in Figure 3

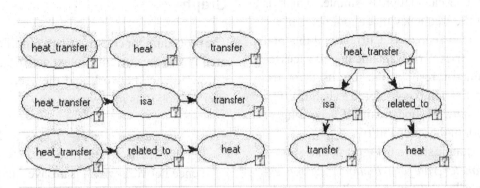

of its expressiveness and power for modeling uncertainty. A user's preference is reflected by how a user prefers to use a class of tools. A tool is defined as an operator to perform specific actions to transform the information that the user needs based on his preferences. There are three kinds of nodes in a preference network. The first type is a precondition node (*Pc*) which represents the requirements of a tool. A user's query and the concepts contained in the current interest relevancy set are examples of pre-condition nodes. The second type is a goal node (*G*) which represents a tool. An example of a tool is a filter that searches for documents that narrows down the search topics semantically. Another example of a tool is an expander that searches for documents that broaden up the search topics semantically. The third type of node is an action node (A) which is associated with each goal node. For each pre-condition node representing a user's current interest, its prior probability will be set as the interest level of the corresponding interest concept. The conditional probability table of each goal node is similar to the truth table for logical AND. In the current model, each goal node is associated with only one action node. The conditional probability of the action node will be set to 1 if the corresponding tool is chosen and to 0, otherwise.

A preference network is built when a user issues a new query and is updated when a user gives relevance feedback after each query. Every query is considered a pre-condition node in a preference network. If this query or some parts of it have been encountered before, the existing pre-condition nodes representing previously asked queries in the preference network that match the current query will be set as evidence. Each interest concept from the current interest set is added to the preference network as a pre-condition node and set as evidence. If the user's query is totally new and the preference network is empty, the tool being used by the user is set to the default value (a filter) and a goal node representing the filter tool is added to the preference network. Otherwise, it is set to the tool being represented by the goal node with highest marginal probability. Each action node represents a way to construct a modified query based on the current tool, interests and user query.

In our user model, the preference network adapts based on the observation of interactions between a user and our system. The idea is based on Brown's work on interface agents (Brown et al., 1998). In our current version, there are two different tools, filter and expander. Therefore, two new preference networks are created, one of them contains an additional new tool labeled as filter, and another contains a new tool labeled as expander. We will then calculate the probability that a new network will improve the user's effectiveness for both of the two new preference networks. The calculation is simple, which is to find out the frequency that a tool helps in the previous retrieval process. Currently, if the total number of retrieved relevant documents excesses a user-defined threshold, the tool used for the query modification is considered as helpful. The preference network updates itself according to the one with higher probability.

In the example shown in Figure 5, those nodes labeled "*transfer_rate_distribution*", "*zero_pressure_surface*", and "*heat_transfer*" are pre-condition nodes created from a user's current interest list while the nodes "*query_01*" and "*query_02*" nodes are pre-condition nodes created to represent a user's queries. The nodes "*filter_01*" and "*expander_01*" are two goal nodes and "*proactive_query_01*" and "proactive_query_02" are action nodes. After we set as evidences three nodes labeled "*transfer_rate_distribution*", "*query_01*", and "*zero_pressure_surface*" (shown as shaded nodes in the Figure 5), we can perform belief updating on this preference network. The node "*filter_01*" has value 1 for state "true" and 0 for false while node "expander" has value 0.42 for state "true" and 0.58 for state "false", and therefore, we will use the filter to modify the original query.

Construction of Modified Query Graph

The procedure for constructing a modified query graph from the current context network, interest set, preference network and the user's original query graph is as follows:

- Given a user model $M=\{I, P, C\}$ and a query graph q. I is an interest set. P is a preference network which is a Bayesian network to reason about the tool used for modifying a query. C is a context network which is a directed acyclic graph containing concepts and relation nodes.
- Use spreading activation algorithm to reason about the new set of interest I'.
- Set as evidence all concepts of the interest set I' found in the preference network P.
- Find a pre-condition node a representing a query in the preference network P which has associated QG that completely or partially matches against the given query graph q. If such a node a is found, set it as an evidence.
- Perform belief updating on the preference network P. Choose top n goal nodes from preference network with highest marginal probability values. Call this set of goals as suggested goal nodes.

Figure 5. An example of a preference network

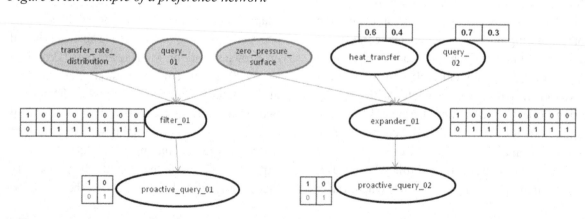

- For every goal node in the set of suggested goal nodes, do

If the query has been asked before and the user has used this goal, replace the original query subgraph with the graph associated with the action node of this goal.

If the query has not been asked before and the goal node represents a filter: For every concept node q_i in the user's query graph q, we search for its corresponding node cq_i in the context network C. For every concept i in I', we search for its corresponding node ci_i in the context network such that ci_i is an ancestor of cq_i. If such ci_i and cq_i are found, we add the paths from context network between these two nodes to the modified query graph.

If the query has not been asked before and the goal node represents an expander: For every concept node q_i in the user's query graph q, we search for its corresponding node cq_i in the context network C. For every concept i in I', we search for its corresponding node ci_i in the context network such that ci_i is a progeny of cq_i. If such ci_i and cq_i are found, we add the paths from context network between these two nodes to the modified query graph.

Figure 6 shows an example of an original query graph. In this example, we assume that the query has not been asked and currently the goal node fired in the preference network representing a filter. Furthermore, the concept "*transfer_rate_distribution*" is currently in the interest list. The current context network contains the following relations:

transfer_rate_distribution → related to → transfer
transfer_rate_distribution → related to → zero_pressure_surface → related to → surface

In the modified query graph in Figure 7, the concept nodes representing "*transfer rate distribution*", and "*zero pressure surface*", and their relations with the concepts "*transfer*" and "*surface*" are newly added. The relation "transfer_rate_distribution → related to → transfer" is added first because the node "*transfer_rate_distribution*" is found both in the interest list and context network and is an ancestor of the node "*transfer*" in the query graph. Similarly, the relation "*transfer_rate_distribution → related to → zero_pressure_surface → related to → surface*" is added.

Figure 6. A user's original query graph

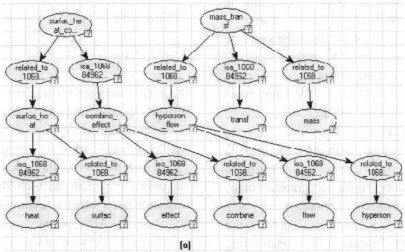

Figure 7. A modified query graph

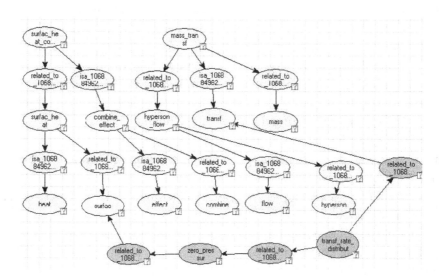

Integrating IPC into Information Retrieval Application

In our approach, we generate a document graph for each document automatically in an offline process. In this process, we use LinkParser Program (Sleator & Temperley, 1993) to parse each sentence in a document and extract noun phrases, prepositional phrases from a parsed tree to construct a document graph using three heuristics listed in Appendix. Even though LinkParser package comes with the capability with a full parser, we mainly use it for recognizing the noun phrases and prepositional phrases. The running time for LinkParser is $O(l^3)$ for each sentence in which l is the number of words in the sentence to be parsed. The complexity of the process of creating relations from the phrases extracted from the Link Parser is $O(l \log l)$. We generate a query graph for each query in the same way as we generate a document graph. Therefore, we always maintain the consistency between a query graph and a document graph. While we are trying to maximize the quality of document graphs as much as possible, the consistency between query graph and document graph is very important to ensure good retrieval performance. For constructing

Bayesian networks, we use Smile package from the Decision Systems Laboratory, University of Pittsburgh, to implement our preference network (Druzdzel, 1999).

The architecture of our IR application includes five modules as shown in Figure 8. The user model module takes as input a query graph and generates as output a modified query graph for the search module. The search module matches the modified query graph against each document graph representing a record in the database of documents, chooses those records that have the number of matches greater than a user-defined threshold, and displays the output to the user. A match between a QG q and a DG d_i is defined as:

$$sim(q, d_i) = \frac{c}{2 * C} + \frac{r}{2 * R}$$

in which c and r are the number of concepts and relation nodes of the query graph found in the document graph while C and R are the total numbers of concept and relation nodes of the query graph. Note that two relation nodes are matched if and only if its parents and its child are matched. In this similarity, we treat relation nodes and concept nodes equally. After the search module returns the search results, the feedback module allows a user

Figure 8. Overall architecture of IR application using our user model

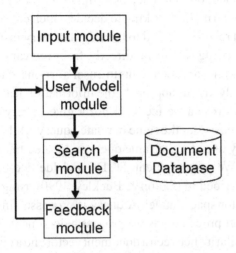

to indicate whether the search result is relevant or not. The document graphs of relevant documents will be used to update the three component of the user model as describe earlier.

In our approach, we use some thresholds such as for filtering out concepts in the short-term interest lists and thresholds for finding common sub-graphs. These thresholds are determined based on empirical tests with the above collections.

Analysis of User Model Complexity

We now focus on the running time cost of our approach.

Construction/Update: Denote n as the size of a document graph with the largest number of nodes of all the retrieved relevant documents. Denote m as the number of retrieved relevant documents. The complexity of the construction of an interest set is $O(n+nm)$. The complexity of the spreading activation propagation algorithm to construct an adaptive interest set is $O(|C|^3)$ where $|C|$ is the size of the context network C. In our implementation, we have used a hash table to index the nodes in a document graph. The running time complexity of finding a set of common

subgraphs in the intersections of m document graphs is $O(m^2 n+mn)$.

The complexity of construction our preference network is $O((|I|+ |q|^2)|P|)$ where q is the given query graph.

Inference: The complexity of inference on C is $O(|C|)$. The complexity of inference on P is polynomial because we are using an inference algorithm for poly-trees (Pearl, 1988).

EMPIRICAL EVALUATION WITH SYNTHESIZED DATA SET

The main goals of this empirical evaluation are to assess the effectiveness and competitiveness of our user model with regards to retrieval of relevant documents. We view the effectiveness of a user model as its ability to produce a desired effect when integrated with an IR application. Specifically, the desired effect in our case is to improve the number of retrieved relevant documents early in the process of searching for information. We aim at a unified set of empirical evaluations which offers an opportunity to compare our user modeling approach with existing approaches using relevance feedback from the IR community. We begin with a description of our testbed, present the technique we are comparing against, describe the experimental procedure, and finally present our results and discussion.

Testbed

Our evaluation uses the CRANFIELD (Cleverdon, 1967), MEDLINE and CACM collections (Salton and & Buckley, 1990). CRANFIELD contains 1398 papers on aerodynamics and 225 queries with relevancy assessment. A relevant document with regards to a specific query is rated on a numerical scale from 1 to 4. 1 represents the most valuable reference and 4 represents the least valuable reference while -1 represents a document that is irrelevant. CACM contains 3204 documents and

64 queries in computer science and engineering (CSE) domain while MEDLINE contains 1033 documents and 30 queries in the medicine domain. Our main reason for choosing these collections is that they have been used for evaluating the effectiveness of techniques that use relevance feedback and query expansion (Lóper-Pujalte et al., 2003; Salton & Buckley, 1990). Additionally, the sizes of these collections seem to be appropriate for a user modeling application to start with.

For CRANFIELD, we choose this set of 43 queries with the property that at least 6 relevant documents are not in the top 15. For MEDLINE and CACM, we use the whole query set.

In our experiment, we use both original and residual collections. Original is referred to the document set obtained when the same query is run again without removing the relevant document retrieved when this query is issued for the first time. Residual collection is created by removing all documents from top 15 in the initial run regardless to whether or not they are relevant or not from the original collection.

TFIDF and Ide dec-hi Approach

We compare the effectiveness of our user model approach against Ide dec-hi with term weighting using TFIDF (Salton & Buckley, 1990). There are several reasons for this. First of all, TFIDF and Ide dec-hi techniques are very well-documented (Frake & Baeza-Yates, 1992; Lóper-Pujalte et al., 2003; Salton & Buckley, 1990), and thus make it easier and more reliable for re-implementation. Secondly, the Ide dec-hi approach was considered to be the best traditional approach in the IR community and is still competitive with other recent approaches (Drucker et al., 2002; Lóper-Pujalte et al., 2003; Salton & Buckley, 1990). It offers an opportunity to see where we stand with other approaches as well because others also report their results comparing against Ide dec-hi.

To briefly summarize, the differences between our approach and Ide dec-hi using TFIDF are three-fold. First, we capture the structure of information instead of frequency of individual terms. Second, our approach determines a user's intent in information seeking to decide which concepts and relations to add to the original query instead of adding the terms directly from relevant and non-relevant documents to a user's original query. Lastly, in our approach, the information learned from relevance feedback for a given query can be reused for the same or related query while it is only used for the same query in Ide dec-hi.

We re-implement TFIDF and Ide dec-hi as described in (Salton & Buckley, 1990) using the vector space model. A query is processed in the exact procedure as we process a document. The similarity between a document vector and a query vector is defined as the cosine between them as shown in (Frake & Baeza-Yates, 1992, chapter 14, page 366).

The main idea of Ide dec-hi is to merge the relevant document vectors into the original query vector. This technique automatically reweighs the original weight for each term in the query vector by adding its corresponding weights from relevant documents directly and subtracting its corresponding weight from the first non-relevant document. For the terms which are not from the original query vector but appear in the relevant documents, they are added automatically to the original query vector with their associated weights. For the terms which are not from the original query vector but appear both in the relevant document and non-relevant documents, their weight would be the difference between the total weights of all relevant documents and the weight in the first non-relevant document. For the terms which are not from the original query vector but appear only in non-relevant documents, they are not added to the original queries vector with negative weights (Frake & Baeza-Yates, 1992). The formula for Ide dec-hi is:

$$Q_{new} = Q_{old} + \sum_i D_i - D_j$$

in which Q_{new} and Q_{old} represent the weighting vector for the modified query and the original query, respectively. D_i represents the weighting vector for any relevant document and D_j represents the weighting vector for the first non-relevant document. Denote n as the size of the biggest vector representing a relevant document. Denote m as the number of relevant documents. The running time for Ide dec-hi approach is $O(m*n)$.

Traditional Procedure Applied to Ide dec-hi/TFIDF and User Modeling

We simulate the procedure laid out by Salton and Buckley (1990). For the Ide dec-hi/TFIDF, each query in the testbed is converted to a query vector. The query vector is compared against each document vector in the collection. For our approach, we construct a QG for each query in the testbed. After we issue each query, the relevant documents found in the first 15 returned documents are used to modify the original query. For the Ide dec-hi/TFIDF, the weight of each term in the original query is modified from its weights in relevant documents and the first non-relevant document. The terms with the highest weights from relevant documents are also added to the original query. For our approach, we start with an empty user model and add the concept and relation nodes to the original QG based on the procedure described in next section. We then run each system again with the modified query. We refer to the first run as *initial run* and the second run as *feedback run*. After the feedback run, we reset the user model to empty. For each query, we compute average precision at three point fixed recall (0.25, 0.5, and 0.75).

New Procedure for User Modeling Approach

The new procedure is similar to the traditional procedure described earlier except that we start with an empty user model in one experiment and

with a *seed* user model in some experiments. The seed user model is the model that is created after we run the system through the set of queries once. For each query, we still use the same set of documents. The new procedure assesses the effects of prior knowledge and the combination of prior knowledge with knowledge learned from a query or a group of queries. We would like to separate what we term "short-term" and "long-term" effects. Short-term effects are the effects obtained by using the user model to modify the same query immediately after a user is giving feedback. Long-term effects are the effects obtained by using user model to modify any queries regardless of whether feedback has been given or not. Our goals for this new procedure are to evaluate:

- How does the long-term effect of our user model affect the retrieval performance?
- How do the combination of short-term and the use of prior knowledge affect the retrieval performance?
- How do the combination of short-term, long-term and the use of prior knowledge affect the retrieval performance?

These requirements lead to our decision to perform 4 experiments:

- **Experiment 1:** We start with an empty user model. We update the initial user model based on relevance feedback and we do not reset our user model unlike the traditional procedure above. The user model obtained at the end of this experiment is used as the seed user model for the next 3 experiments.
- **Experiment 2:** We start with the seed user model. For each query, we do not update our user model and don't run the feedback run. This experiment assesses how the prior knowledge helped improve retrieval performance.
- **Experiment 3:** We start with the seed user model and run our system following

the traditional procedure described above. However, after each query, we reset our user model to the seed user model. This experiment assesses the effects of the combination of prior knowledge and knowledge learned from a given query on retrieval performance.

- **Experiment 4:** We start with the seed user model. For each query, we update our user model based on relevance feedback and we do not reset our user model. This experiment assesses the effects of combination of prior knowledge, and knowledge learned immediately from each query and knowledge learned from previous queries on retrieval performance.

The modified query graph from all experiments will be matched against every document graph in the database. We compute the similarity based on the formula previously described. We return every document which has a similarity greater than zero.

For all experiments in the traditional and new procedure, except experiment 2, we compute average precision at three point fixed recall (0.25, 0.5, and 0.75) for both initial run and feedback run using original collection and residual collection. For Experiments 2 in the new procedure, we compute the average precision at three point fixed recall for only the initial run.

Figure 9. Average precision at three point fixed recall for traditional procedure

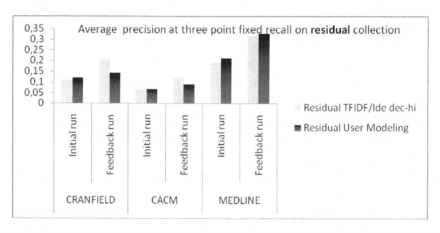

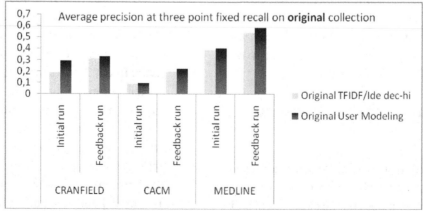

Results

The result of the traditional evaluation of Ide dec-hi using TFIDF and our user modeling approach is shown in Figure 9. For CRANFIELD collection, the precision of the initial run and feedback run using residual collection are close to the numbers reported by (Lóper-Pujalte et al., 2003) and (Salton & Buckley, 1990). Those in previous publications for CACM and MEDLINE achieved a slightly better results compared to ours because (i) we used the entire set of queries, while others, for example (Lóper-Pujalte et al., 2003), used a subset of queries; and (ii) we treat the terms from title, author, and content equally. Figure 9 shows that we achieved competitive performance in both runs for residual and original collections for MEDLINE collection. For CRANFIELD and CACM collections, the Ide dec-hi approach obtained higher precision in the feedback run with

residual collection. However, we still obtained competitive results for both two collections in the feedback run with original collection. The reason is further investigated and presented in more details in the discussion section.

The results of our new procedure evaluation are reported in Figure 10.

Results of Experiment 1: The first experiment also shows that the user model did improve the retrieval performance in the feedback run compared to the initial run for all three collections.

Results of Experiment 2: The precision of this experiment is higher than the experiment in the traditional procedure for CRANFIELD and MEDLINE collections. That said, the seed user model is doing its job by changing the user's queries and improves the retrieval performance in the initial run.

Figure 10. Average precision at three point fixed recall for new procedure

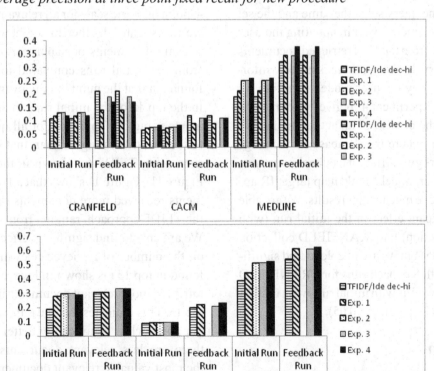

Results of Experiment 3: The precision of this experiment, as shown in Figure 10, indicates that there is a relatively good improvement of the feedback run compared to the initial run on residual collection for CRANFIELD and MEDLINE. This experiment shows that the more knowledge a user model has about a user and search domain, the better it helps improve retrieval performance.

Results of Experiment 4: For CRANFIELD collection, the precision of the feedback run using residual collection is slightly less than the precision of Experiment 3, but is better than the precision of traditional procedure and Experiment 1. For both CACM and MEDLINE, we can see that among the four experiments, Experiment 4 performs competitively compared to Ide dec-hi in the feedback run while it offers the advantages of having higher precision in the initial run compared to TFIDF. The reason for this is that within the design of this experiment, we use the same seed user model in Experiments 2 and 3, the database is the same, the query set is the same and the set of relevant documents used in updating the user model is taken from top 15 of retrieved documents for every query. Probably, there is no new information learned by the user model, therefore we can't expect Experiment 4 to give better results. However, in the context of an actual interactive IR framework where the database may change overtime, users give different feedback over time; as such our user model should help target IR application achieve much better results. We are able to find significant effect in the initial run (with original collection) for CRANFIELD collection (p-value < 0.05) but we are unable to find significant effect with feedback runs for CRANFIELD collection, as well as with initial runs with CACM and MEDLINE (p-value > 0.05).

Discussion

Our goals initially set for these experiments have been met.

- Effectiveness of the user model in terms of improving the retrieval performance: Experiments 1, 3, and 4 show that by using our user model, the precision of the feedback run is always higher using residual and original collections compared to the initial run.
- Competitiveness of the improvement obtained by using our user model compared with the improvement obtained by using TFIDF and Ide dec-hi approach: Among two procedures and 5 experiments in total, we can see that for CRANFIELD Experiment 3 of new procedure performed competitively well compared to Ide dec-hi while it offers the advantages of having higher precision in the initial run compared to TFIDF. For both CACM and MEDLINE, the Experiment 4 of new procedure performs competitively with Ide dec-hi in the feedback run.

Moreover, as the CRANFIELD collection has classified the relevancy of a document on a 4-point numeric scale for all relevant documents, we investigated further to see how many good relevant documents our approach has retrieved from the initial runs compared to TFIDF. We found out that the number of relevant documents in the top 15 of the initial runs in all six experiments using our approach for all queries in the testbed is always higher than that of the initial runs using TFIDF (as shown in the last row of Figure 11). Figure 11 shows that all of our experiments retrieved more documents ranked 1 than the TFIDF approach, ranging from 46% to 69%. We are able to find significant effect using t-test on the number of retrieved relevant documents found in top 15 (as shown in Figure 11). We also retrieved more relevant documents in all ranks in top 15. This indicates that the retrieval quality of our approach is significantly better. As a result, there are less relevant documents, especially, the most valuable relevant documents, left to be retrieved in the feedback run. This is the main reason why the improvement of precision in the feedback run on the residual collection for our approach is less than that achieved by Ide dec-hi approach.

Regarding the evaluation methodology, the traditional procedure offers us a chance to compare with the TFIDF and Ide dec-hi approaches using their evaluation procedures on the same collections. For any user modeling approach, the ultimate goal is to test the approach with a group of end users. This test however, often times is considered as expensive and contains many variables to control. Our evaluation methodology helps us to prepare better for the test with end users because the testbed contains knowledge spreading over several domains and the tested queries are as complicated as the ones asked by any end user. The evaluation procedure fortunately is lightweight and they can be easily used to evaluate adaptive systems before hiring the real subjects. This maintains objectivity and serves as a baseline comparison for future extensions.

There are four main conclusions that we have after conducting our experiments:

- Our approach of capturing user intent in information seeking and using the information captured to modify user queries does produce better performance in the initial runs compared to TFIDF. The quality of retrieval in our initial run is significantly better than TFIDF for CRANFIELD collection.

- Our user model is trying to combine and balance between the long term and short-term interests of a user in information seeking. The model is long-lived, therefore, even its long-term effects can help modify queries and improve retrieval performance in a search session.

- We show how we can compare the user modeling approaches using procedures, collections and metrics of the IR community while still being able to assess special features of the models such as the use of prior knowledge, knowledge learned from one query or from a group of queries.

EVALUATION WITH HUMAN ANALYSTS

After our evaluation with synthesized data sets, we had an opportunity to conduct an evaluation with three human analysts (Santos et al., 2005). The evaluation took place at a laboratory at the National Institute of Standards and Technology (NIST) in May, 2004. This system was compared with commercial off-the-shelf keyword based application called Verity Query Language (VQL). We used a data collection from the Center for Nonproliferation Studies (CNS, Sept. 2003 distribution. http://cns.miis.edu/). The UM system package, which includes the pre-processed CNS

Figure 11. Retrieved relevant documents in top 15 for CRANFIELD and t-test results

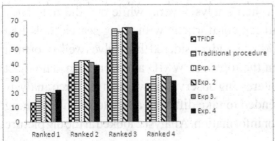

Degree of freedom	Experiment	t, p-value
3	Traditional vs. TFIDF/Ide dec-hi	t=3.77 p-value=0.033
3	Exp. 1 vs. TFIDF/Ide dec-hi	t= 5.13 p-value=0.014
3	Exp. 2 vs. TFIDF/Ide dec-hi	t=3.86 p-value=0.031
3	Exp. 3 vs. TFIDF/Ide dec-hi	t=3.73 p-value=0.034
3	Exp. 4 vs. TFIDF/Ide dec-hi	t=3.22 p-value=0.048

database with 4000 documents on weapons of mass destruction (WMD) domain, was delivered to and installed at the NIST laboratory. Three evaluators, who were naval reservists assigned to NIST with intelligence analysis background participated in the experiments. During the evaluation, the UM system and the VQL system were run side by side. The same queries were input into both systems and the retrieved documents were compared. For the VQL system, analysts needed to note on paper which documents were relevant to their interests for each query; for the UM system, in addition to recording the relevancy, they were asked to mark check boxes beside the documents if they were relevant ones. There was a short tutorial session to show the analysts how to work with the UM system, such as indicating the relevancy. The VQL system has a graphic user interface (GUI) similar to Google, thus, it is straightforward to use.

Procedure

The experimental session lasted about 4 hours. Each participant was asked to perform a search on Qumar research and development of biological weapons. Note that the country name has been replaced. Because of the time constraint, the participants were asked to check the first 10 returned documents for relevancy only, and the task was limited with just 10 fixed queries. We scripted 10 queries to avoid adding more variables into our experiments such as errors in natural language processing. The queries were extracted from the log of query sequences of working analysts and re-arranged from a database that collected other intelligence analysts IR activities at NIST laboratory.

The UM system started with an empty user model, which means that the user model initially knew nothing about the analyst, and had to start learning about the user from the very beginning. The procedure went as follows:

- **Step 1:** Each of the analysts was asked to fill out an entry questionnaire about their background and experience with searching programs; and, respond to an exit questionnaire about their experience on working with the UM system.
- **Step 2:** Start with the first query in the query list, each analyst starts both systems with the same query.
- **Step 3:** After the system with the user model approach returns a set of documents, each analyst is asked to look at the first 10 returned documents and indicate which one is relevant to the current query. Each analyst only sees the same set of retrieved documents for the first query but after that depending on which retrieved documents are marked as relevant, each analyst's model will be built and used to proactively modify subsequent queries. Therefore, the set of retrieved documents after the first query may be different for these three analysts.
- **Step 4:** After deciding relevant documents, each analyst clicks on "Put Feedback" option.
- **Step 5:** Start a new query for both systems.
- **Step 6:** After finishing all queries, each analyst is asked to fill out the exit questionnaire about the workload spent.

Results and Analysis

The experience in intelligence analysis for the three participants ranged from five months to seven years. Two of them use computers as a tool in their analysis work, while one did not. They all felt comfortable with using search tools like Google, and considered themselves well-informed on the topics of WMD and terrorism. The most interesting observation was that the three analysts tended to take different approaches in searching for information. Analyst 2 looked at the big picture first; while Analyst 3 likes to start with the details. Analyst 1 practice a mixed approach that depend on his knowledge of the topic. If much was already known, then he would try to create an outline of the useful information; otherwise, he would look for some details first. After 4 hours, two analysts finished the 10 queries that we provided, and Analyst 3 finished 9 queries. All of them managed to identify more relevant documents when working with the UM system than they did with the VQL system. The precisions were 0.257 and 0.312 for the VQL system and the UM system, respectively. Since a document could be returned and identified multiple times as relevant for different queries, we also counted the numbers of unique (or distinct) documents that have been returned by the system and found as relevant by each participant. The data showed that when they were using the UM system, each of them was presented with more unique documents, and selected more unique documents as relevant as shown in Table 1. The total number of unique relevant documents for all 10 queries returned by the UM system is 39, while the number is 27 by the VQL system, a 44% increase. The number of documents selected as relevant by more than 2 analysts are 15 in the UM system and 19 in the VQL system, respectively. Notice that the number of documents marked as relevant by just one analyst is 24 when using the UM system, while this number is only 12 for the VQL system. This suggests that more information that is specifically relevant to each analyst's individual interests had been retrieved by the UM system. By using the UM system, the analysts displayed their differences in identifying the docu-

ments that were relevant to their individualized interests and searching styles. By the end of the experiment, the analysts were asked to fill out the exit questionnaire. When asked about the system performance and their satisfaction, they scored the UM system as above medium (3.7/5.0) (as shown in Table 2). Notice that they felt the UM system was somewhat demanding, especially in mental effort and the temporal effort. Since relevancy assessment is a mentally demanding process by itself, and the analysts were required to finish the experiment in about 4 hours, which included 10 queries (i.e., more than 100 documents to review, of which some of them may be quite long), and working with 2 different systems at the same time, we think this is a result of the workload the analysts had in the experiments. As the data shows, the UM system presented more unique documents to the analysts, and helped analysts retrieve more relevant documents. In particular, it helped them retrieve more information that is relevant to their individual interests, which suggests that the user model was tracking the user's personalized interests.

CONCLUSION AND FUTURE WORK

In this chapter, we have described the development and the evaluation of a user model to capture a user's intent in information seeking for improving retrieval performance. The difference between ours and the existing relevance feedback approaches in the IR community is that we capture the structure of information while existing

Table 1. Unique relevant documents retrieved by two systems

	VQL	UM
Total unique relevant documents	27	39
Document marked as relevant by all 3	3	8
Documents marked as relevant by more than 2 analysts	19	15
Document marked as relevant by only one analyst	12	24

Table 2. Average score for user satisfaction of the User Modeling approach

Questions	Score
How confident were you of your ability to use the system to accomplish the assigned task? (1-5, 1: less confident, 5 more confident)	3.0
Given that you were performing this task outside of your standard work environment, without many of your standard resources, were you comfortable with the process of preparing your report? (1-5, 1: less comfortable, 5: more comfortable)	3.7
Given that you were performing this task outside of your standard work environment, with access to a restricted set of documents, were you satisfied with the quality of the report/answers that you were able to find for this scenario? (1-5, 1: not satisfied, 5: satisfied)	2.7
How satisfied are you with the overall results for this task using system with user model? (1-7. 1: most satisfied, 7: least satisfied)	4.3
How confidence are you with the results that they cover all possible aspects of the task? (1-7. 1: most confident, 7: least confident)	4.7
The regarding this task, do you think that user modeling approach helped you to retrieve critical document earlier in the process than the VQL? (1-7. 1: strongly agree, 7: strongly disagree)	3.7
Ranking of mental demand. (1-7, 1: little, 7: high)	5.3
Ranking of physical demand. (1-7, 1: little, 7: high)	2.0
Ranking of temporal demand. (1-7, 1: little, 7: high)	5.0
Ranking of performance demand. (1-7, 1: little, 7: high)	4.7
Ranking of frustration. (1-7: 1: little, 7: high)	5.3
Ranking of effort. (1-7. 1: little, 7: high)	6.0

approaches in IR focuses on frequency of individual terms. Also, we use the information about a user's intent to guide the process of modifying the user's queries instead of merging individual terms directly from relevant and non-relevant documents into the user's original queries. Our user model is long-lived. This means that feedback information can be used for a specific query or any other queries on the same or related topics. We have shown that our approach offers better performance in the initial runs and competitive performance in the feedback runs. The results from our research show that a user model can be a very effective tool for improving retrieval performance in an IR interactive framework.

Our evaluation with three intelligence analysts partially answered the question on impacts of user modeling on an IR system by measuring the number of relevant documents presented to the analysts. This user modeling approach also tracks the individual differences among analysts and presents uniquely relevant documents to each analyst. By combining these results, we can assess if the user modeling is actually follows the user's individual interests, and ultimately improve the user's performance in an IR system.

There are issues that we wish to address from this research. First, our user model currently can only modify a user's query. We are looking at a methodology to allow the user model to modify other parameters and attributes of the target IR system in a decision theoretic framework. For example, the similarity measure or threshold can be adaptively changed based on a user's searching behaviors. We have pushed our effort further to develop a hybrid user model as an extension of the IPC model (Nguyen et al., 2006). Secondly, the process of constructing a model for a user is done automatically by the system using inputs from a user's query and reference feedback. Relevance feedback is a lightweight way to get a user's inputs and build a model. However, in the long run, a user may become frustrated because he/she did not know how the feedback is used. This is also pointed out in our experiment with human analysts. We plan to employ an explanation mechanism which uses context network, interest and preference network to provide natural language description of why a query is modified in a certain way. We also allow users to manually re-start the model when a new topic is issued and the model has not changed fast enough and allow users to manually edit context network at any time.

Next, our user modeling approach works best if a user has demonstrated his/her searching styles. So, we will consider re-ordering the queries to affect different search styles (e.g users explore a topic, its subtopics, and then change to a new topic). It will help to closely relate the experiment to real life situations while maintaining its objectivity. Fourth, we would like to explore some other semantic relationships such as "links to", "associated with", and "caused by" by using discourse analyses, heuristics such as (Greffenstette & Hearst, 1992). More specifically, we investigate the possibility to reason about these relationships given a sequence of actions, snippet and annotation associated with each action. Fifth, we would like to push our effort further in evaluation the effectiveness of our approach. We plan to extend our empirical evaluation on data from recent TREC conferences. The scalability issue should be taken into consideration while we are working with large scale testbeds. We would like to explore the possibilities of working with abstracts of large documents instead of considering entire documents and the use of the parallel computing to accelerating the process. Additionally, we want to strength our evaluation results on internal accuracy of our user model (Nguyen & Santos, 2007a) as well as the use of

prior knowledge in our user modeling approach (Nguyen & Santos, 2007b). Finally, we are mapping our current approach to modeling context into Bayesian knowledge-bases (Santos & Santos, 1998; Santos & Dinh, 2008) to better utilize probabilistic semantics for uncertainty like its use in our preference network.

ACKNOWLEDGMENT

This work has been supported in part by grants from the Advanced Research Development Activity, the Intelligence Advanced Research Projects Activity, the Air Force Office of Scientific Research, and the Air Force Research Laboratory. Special thanks to the anonymous reviewers whose comments helped to greatly improve this chapter.

REFERENCES

Allen, R. (1990). User Models: theory, method and practice. *International Journal of Man-Machine studies, 32*, 511–543.

Baeza-Yates, R., Calderón-Benavides, L., & Gonzalez-Caro, C. (2006). The Intention Behind Web Queries. In *Proceedings of String Processing and Information Retrieval 2006* (pp 98-109). Glasgow, Scotland.

Balabanovic, M., & Shoham, Y. (1997). Content-based collaborative recommendation. *Communications of the ACM, 40(3)*, 66–72.

Balabanovic, M. (1998). Exploring versus Exploiting when Learning User Models for Text Recommendation. *Journal of User Modeling and User-Adapted Interaction, 8(1)*, 71–102.

Belkin, N. J. (1993). Interaction with text: Information retrieval as information seeking behavior. *Information Retrieval, 10*, 55–66.

Billsus, D., & Pazzani P. M. (2000). User modeling for adaptive news access. *Journal of User Modeling and User-Adapted Interaction, 10*, 147–180.

Borlund, P. (2003). The Concept of Relevance in Information Retrieval. *Journal of the American Society for Information Science and Technology, 54*, 913–925.

Brajnik, G., Guida, G., & Tasso, C. (1987). User modeling in intelligent information retrieval. *Information Processing and Management, 23(4)*, 305–320.

Broder, A. (2002). A taxonomy of Web Search. In *SIGIR Forum, 36(2)*.

Brown, S. M. (1998). *Decision Theoretic Approach for Interface Agent Development.* Ph.D dissertation. Air Force Institute of Technology.

Brown, S. M., Santos, E. Jr., Banks, S. B., & Oxley, M. (1998). Using explicit requirements and metrics for interface agent user model construction. In *Proceedings of the Second International Conference on Autonomous Agents* (pp. 1–7).

Brusilovsky, P., & Tasso, C. (2004). Preface to Special Issue on User Modeling for Web Information Retrieval. *User Modeling and User-Adapted Interaction, 14(2-3)*, 147-157.

Bueno, D., & David, A. A. (2001). METIORE: A personalized information retrieval system. In Bauer, M., Vassileva, J. and Gmytrasiewicz, P. (Eds.). *User Modeling: Proceedings of the Eight International Conference, UM 2001,* (pp. 168–177).

Campbell, D. R., Culley, S. J., Mcmahon, C. A., & Sellini F. (2007). An approach for the capture of context-dependent document relationships extracted from Bayesian analysis of users' interactions with information. *Information Retrieval, 10*(2), (Apr. 2007), 115-141.

Campbell, I. (1999). Interactive Evaluation of the Ostensive Model, using a new Test-Collection of Images with Multiple Relevance Assessments. *Information Retrieval, 2(1),* 89-114.

Case, D. (2002). *Looking for Information: A Survey of Research on Information Seeking, Needs, and Behavior.* Academic Press

Chin, D. (1989). KNOME: Modeling What the User knows in UC. In A. Kobsa and W. Wahlster (Ed.), *User models in dialog systems,* (pp. 74—107). Springer Verlag, Berlin.

Chin, D. (2001). Empirical Evaluation of User Models and User-Adapted Systems. *User Modeling and User-Adapted Interaction, 11(1-2),* 181-194.

Chin, D. (2003). Evaluating the Effectiveness of User Models by Experiments. *Tutorial presented at the Ninth International Conference on User Modeling (UM 2003).* Johnstown, PA

Cleverdon, C. (1967). The Cranfield test of index language devices. In *Reprinted in Reading in Information Retrieval Eds.* 1998. (pp. 47–59).

Cool, C., & Spink, A. (2002). Issues of context in information retrieval (IR): an introduction to the special issue. *Information Processing Management 38(5)* (Sep. 2002), 605-611.

Craswell, N., Hawking D., Upstill, T., McLean, A., Wilkinson, R., & Wu, M. (2003). TREC 12 Web and Interactive Tracks at CSIRO. *NIST Special Publication 500-255. The Twelfth Text Retrieval Conference,* (pp 193-203).

Crestani, F., & Ruthven, I. (2007). Introduction to special issue on contextual information retrieval systems. *Information Retrieval, 10 (2) (Apr. 2007),* 111–113.

Decampos, L., Fernandez-Luna, J., & Huete, J. (1998). Query expansion in information retrieval systems using a Bayesian network-based thesaurus. In *Proceedings of the Fourteenth Annual Conference on Uncertainty in Artificial Intelligence (UAI-98),* (pp. 53–60). Sanfrancisco, CA.

deCristo, M. A. P., Calado, P. P., da Silveria, M. L., Silva, I., Munzt, R., & Ribeiro-Neto, B. (2003). Bayesian belief networks for IR. *International Journal of Approximate Reasoning, 34*, 163–179.

Dervin, B. (1997). Given a context by any other name: methodological tools for taming the unruly beast. In P.Vakkari, R.Savolainen, & B.Dervin (Eds.), *Information seeking in context: Proceedings of an international conference on research in information needs, seeking and use in different contexts,* (pp.13–38). London: Taylor Graham.

DeWitt, R. (1995). Vagueness, Semantics, and the Language of Thought. *Psyche, 1.* Available at http://psyche.cs.monash.edu.au/index.html.

Drucker, H., Shahrary, B., & Gibbon, C. (2002). Support vector machines: relevance feedback and information retrieval. *Information Processing and Management, 38(3),* 305–323.

Druzdzel, J. M. (1999). SMILE: Structural Modeling, Inference, and Learning Engine and GeNIe: A development environment for graphical decision-theoretic models (Intelligent Systems Demonstration). In *Proceedings of the Sixteenth National Conference on Artificial Intelligence (AAAI-99),* (pp. 902-903), AAAI Press/The MIT Press, Menlo Park, CA.

Efthimis, E. N. (1996). Query Expansion. In Williams, M. (Ed.). *Annual Review of Information Science and Technology, 31,* 121–187.

Frake, W. B., & Baeza-Yates, R. (1992). *Information Retrieval: Data Structures and Algorithms.* Prentice Hall PTR, Upper Saddle River, NJ 07458.

Goh, D., & Foo, S. (2007). *Social Information Retrieval Systems: Emerging Technologies and Applications for Searching the Web Effectively.* Premier Reference Source.

Greenberg, S., & Witten, I. (1985). Adaptive personalized interfaces - A question of viability.

Behaviour and Information Technology, 4(1), 31-45

Greffenstette, G., & Hearst, M. A. (1992). A method for refining automatically-discovered lexical relations: Combining weak techniques for stronger results. In *Proceedings of the Workshop on Statistically-Based Natural Language Programming Techniques,* AAAI Press, Menlo Park, CA.

Haines, D., & Croft, W. B. (1993). Relevance feedback and inference networks. In *Proceedings of the Sixteenth Annual International ACM SIGIR Conference on Research and Development in Information Retrieval, Pittsburgh, PA.* (pp. 2–11).

Hernandez, N., Mothe, J., Chrisment, C., & Egret, D. (2007). Modeling context through domain ontologies. *Information Retrieval, 10* (2) (Apr. 2007), 143-172.

Horvitz, E., Breeze, J., Heckerman, D., Hovel, D., & Rommelse, K. (1998). The Lumiere project: Bayesian user modeling for inferring goals and needs of software users. In: *Proceedings of the Fourteenth Annual Conference on Uncertainty in Artificial Intelligence,* (pp. 256–265).

Hwang, C. H. (1999). Incompletely and imprecisely speaking: Using dynamic ontologies for representing and retrieving information. *Knowledge Representation Meets Databases,* 14-20

Ide, E. (1971). New experiment in relevance feedback. In: *The Smart system-experiments in automatic documents processing,* (pp. 337–354).

Ingwersen, P. (1992). *Information Retrieval Interaction.* London, Taylor Graham.

Jansen B., Booth D., & Spink A. (2007). Determining the User Intent of Web Search Engine Queries. In *Proceedings of the International World Wide Web Conference,* (pp 1149-1150). Alberta, Canada.

Karamuftuoglu, M. (1998). Collaborative information retrieval: toward a social informatics view of IR interaction. *Journal of the American Society for Information Science, 49(12)*, 1070 -1080.

Lee U., Liu Z., & Cho J. (2005). Automatic identification of user goals in web search. In *Proceedings of the International World Wide Web Conference 2005*, (pp. 391–400), Chiba, Japan.

Liu, Z., & Chu, W. W. (2007). Knowledge-based query expansion to support scenario-specific retrieval of medical free text. *Information Retrieval, 10(2) (Apr. 2007)*, 173 – 202.

Lóper-Pujalte, C., Guerrero-Bote, V., & Moya-Anegon, F. D. (2003). Genetic algorithms in relevance feedback: a second test and new contributions. *Information Processing and Management, 39(5)*, 669–697.

Maes, P. (1994). Agents that reduce work and information overload. *Communications of the ACM, 37(7)*, 31–40.

Magnini, B., & Strapparava, C. (2001). Improving user modeling with content-based techniques. In: *Bauer, M., Vassileva, J., and Gmytrasiewicz, P. (Eds). User Modeling: Proceedings of the Eighth International Conference, UM 2001.* (pp. 74–83).

Murray, T. (1997). Expanding the knowledge acquisition bottleneck for intelligent tutoring systems. *International Journal of Artificial Intelligence in Education, 8*, 222-232.

Mylonas, Ph. Vallet, D., Castells, P., Fernandez, M., & Avrithis, Y. (2008). Personalized information retrieval based on context and ontological knowledge. *Knowledge Engineering Review, 23*(1), 73-100. Cambridge University Press

Nguyen, H. (2005). *Capturing User Intent for Information Retrieval*. Ph.D dissertation. University of Connecticut.

Nguyen, H., & Santos, E., Jr. (2007a). An Evaluation of the Accuracy of Capturing User Intent for Information Retrieval. In *Proceedings of the 2007 International Conference on Artificial Intelligence* (pp. 341-350). Las Vegas, NV.

Nguyen, H., & Santos, E., Jr. (2007b). Effects of prior knowledge on the effectiveness of a hybrid user model for information retrieval. In *Proceedings of the Homeland Security and Homeland Defense VI conference, 6538*. Orlando, FL. March 2007.

Nguyen, H., Santos, E. Jr., Zhao, Q., & Lee, C. (2004a). Evaluation of Effects on Retrieval Performance for an Adaptive User Model. In *Adaptive Hypermedia 2004: Workshop Proceedings -Part I*, (pp. 193–202), Eindhoven, the Netherlands

Nguyen, H., Santos, E., Jr., Schuet, A., & Smith, N. (2006). Hybrid User Model for Information Retrieval. In *Technical Report of Modeling Others from Observations workshop at AAAI-2006 conference.*

Nguyen, H., Santos, E.J., Zhao, Q. & Wang, H. (2004b). Capturing User Intent for Information Retrieval. In: *Proceedings of the Human Factors and Ergonomics society 48th annual meeting.* (pp. 371–375), New Orleans, LA.

Pearl, J. (1988). *Probabilistic Reasoning in Intelligent Systems: Networks of Plausible Inference.* Morgan Kaufmann, San Mateo, CA.

Rochio, J. J. (1971). Relevance feedback in information retrieval. *The Smart retrieval system- experiments in automatic document processing,* (pp. 313–323).

Rose, D., & Levinson D. (2004). Understanding User Goals in Web search. In *Proceedings of the International World Wide Web Conference 2004,* (pp 13–19), New York, USA.

Ruthven, I., & M. Lalmas. (2003). A survey on the use of relevance feedback for information access systems. *Knowledge Engineering Review, 18(2)*, 95 – 145.

Salton, G. & Buckley, C. (1990). Improving Retrieval Performance by Relevance Feedback. *Journal of the American Society for Information Science, 41(4)*, 288–297.

Salton, G., & McGill, M. (1983). *Introduction to Modern Information Retrieval*. McGraw-Hill Book Company.

Santos, E. Jr, Nguyen, H., Zhao, Q. & Pukinskis, E. (2003b). Empirical Evaluation of Adaptive User Modeling in a Medical Information Retrieval Application. In: *Proceedings of the ninth User Modeling Conference UM 2003*, (pp. 292–296). Johnstown. Pennsylvania.

Santos, E. Jr, Nguyen, H., Zhao, Q., & Wang, H. (2003a). User Modelling for Intent Prediction in Information Analysis. In: *Proceedings of the 47th Annual Meeting for the Human Factors and Ergonomincs Society (HFES-03)*, (pp. 1034–1038).

Santos, E. Jr., & Dinh, H. T. (2008). Automatic Knowledge Validation for Bayesian Knowledge Bases. *Data and Knowledge Engineering, 64*, 218-241.

Santos, E. Jr., Brown, S. M., Lejter, M., Ngai, G., Bank, S., & Stytz, M. R. (1999). Dynamic User Model Construction with BayesianNetworks for Intelligent Information Queries. In: *Proceedings of the 12th International FLAIRS Conference*. pp. 3–7. Orlando. FL.

Santos, E. Jr., Nguyen, H., & Brown, M. S. (2001). Kavanah: An active user interface Information Retrieval Application. In: *Proceedings of 2ⁿᵈ Asia-Pacific Conference on Intelligent Agent Technology*, (pp. 412–423).

Santos, E. Jr., Santos, E. S., & Shimony, S., E. (2003c). Implicitly Preserving Semantics During Incremental Knowledge Base Acquisition Under Uncertainty. *International Journal of Approximate Reasoning 33(1)*, 71-94.

Santos, E. Jr., Zhao, Q., Nguyen, H., & Wang, H. (2005). Impacts of User Modeling on Personalization of Information Retrieval: An evaluation with human intelligence analysts. In Weibelzahl, S., Paramythis, A., & Masthoff, J. (Eds.). Proceedings of the Fourth Workshop on the Evaluation of Adaptive Systems, held in conjunction with the 10th International Conference on User Modeling (UM'05), (pp 19-26).

Saracevic, T. (1996). Relevance reconsidered. In: Ingwersen, P & Pors, P.O. (Eds.), *Proceedings of the Second International Conference on Conceptions of Library and Information Science: Integration in Perspective. Copenhagen: The Royal School of Librarianship*, (pp. 201–218).

Saracevic, T., Spink A., & Wu, M. (1997). Users and Intermediaries in Information Retrieval: What Are They Talking About? In *Proceedings of the 6ᵗʰ International Conference in User Modeling UM 97*, (pp. 43–54).

Shafer, G. (1976). *A Mathematical Theory of Evidence*, Princeton University Press.

Sleator, D. D., & Temperley, D. (1993). Parsing English with a link grammar. In: *Proceedings of the Third International Workshop on Parsing Technologies*, (pp. 277–292).

Spink, A., & Losee, R. M. (1996). Feedback in information retrieval. In Williams, M., (Ed.), *Annual Review of Information Science and Technology, 31*, 33–78.

Weibelzahl, S. (2003). *Evaluation of Adaptive Systems*. Ph.D Dissertation. University of Trier, Germany.

Wilkinson, R. & Wu, M. (2004). Evaluation Experiments and Experience from Perspective of Interactive Information Retrieval. In *Adaptive Hypermedia 2004 - Workshop Proceedings -Part I. Eindhoven,* (pp 221-230), Eindhoven, the Netherlands.

Wilson, T. D. (1981). On user studies and information needs. *Journal of Documentation, 37(1),* 3–15.

Zukerman I., & Albrecht, D. (2001). Predictive statistical models for user modling. In A. Kobsa (Ed.), *User Modeling and User-Adapted Interaction Journal, 11*(1-2), 5-18. Kluwer Academic Publishers.

APPENDIX

The flowchart of the algorithm for extracting a document graph from a natural language text file is shown in Figure 12.

1. Note that in this flowchart, we used Link Parser (Sleator & Temperley, 1993) as a tool to parse a natural language sentence.
2. The relations are extracted based on three heuristic rules which are *noun phrase heuristic, noun phrase-preposition phrase heuristic* and *sentence heuristic*. Noun phrase heuristic captures taxonomy relations within a noun phrase. For example: for the noun phrase of *"experimental investigation"*, we have extracted the relation: *experimental investigation – isa – investigation*.
    Noun phrase-preposition phrase heuristic attaches prepositional phrases to adjacent noun phrases. For example: *"boundary layer transition at supersonic speeds"*. We have extracted the relation: *boundary layer transition -related to -supersonic speeds*.
    Sentence heuristic relates two noun phrases associated with a verb in a sentence. For example: *"the discussion here is restricted to two-dimensional incompressible steady flow"*. We have extracted the relation: *discussion - related to - two dimensional incompressible steady flow*.
3. We use "related to" to represent relations in a conjunctive noun phrase. For example: with the phrase *"heat transfer and zero pressure transfer"*, we extracted the relation *"heat transfer - related to - zero pressure transfer"*. We do not have any special rules for pronouns currently.

Figure 12. Flowchart of the algorithm to extracting document graph

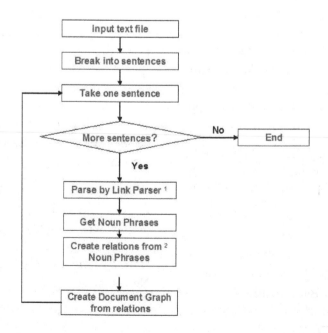

Chapter VI
Ontology–Based User Competencies Modeling for E–Learning Recommender Systems

Mihaela Brut
Alexandru Ioan Cuza University of Iasi, Romania

Florence Sedes
Institut de Recherche en Informatique de Toulouse, France

Corinne Zayani
Institut de Recherche en Informatique de Toulouse, France

ABSTRACT

Inside the e-learning platforms, it is important to manage the user competencies profile and to recommend to each user the most suitable documents and persons, according to his or her acquired knowledge, to their long-term interests, but also according to his very current goals. The authors of this chapter explore a Semantic Web-based modeling approach for the document annotations and user competencies profile development, based on the same domain ontology set. The ontologies constitute the binder between the materials and users. For the user profile development and for the personalized recommendations facilities, the authors' solution propose a hybrid recommender approach: first the user navigation inside the ontology is monitored (instead of user navigation inside the e-learning platform) and the next concept of interest is recommended through a collaborative filtering method; then a content-based recommendation of documents is provided to the user, according the selected concept and his competencies profile. In both phases, a variant of the nearest neighbor algorithm is applied.

INTRODUCTION

An E-learning platform is a real source of knowledge due to the available materials, but also to its users competencies. The demands for personalization are very important in this context. There are two main application types which provide personalization: *Hypermedia Adaptive Systems* and *Recommender Systems*. Each of them make use or develop personalization techniques which are specific to the World Wide Web space, but also there is a beginning in adopting the semantic Web specific techniques.

The Adaptive Systems and Recommender Systems are focused in exploring a certain hypermedia structure in order to help user finding the best way for their interests, while the Recommender Systems are focused on a network of Web resources, bind by existing or virtual relations, aiming to provide users with individual views on Web data (Baldoni et al., 2005). For acquiring this, *Web Mining* techniques are applied, both over the Web usage and Web content.

In this paper we explore the user modeling and user model development for recommender systems by using Web semantic techniques, especially the ontology-related ones. Our purpose is to develop a competence-oriented user model which to accompany the corresponding person in various on-line communities, with a focus on e-learning systems. We will consider the case in which the competencies are expressed through ontological constructs. On the strength of this model the recommendations will be made. A further service-oriented solution could enable the migration of the recommender module from a system to another.

Unlike the e-commerce or on-line news sites, where the content-based recommendations explore especially the user navigational activity, an e-learning platform could exploit its specific supplementary information available about users, namely the users knowledge and their long-term interests, beside their current goals illustrated by the navigational activity. We structured this information into a three-layered user competence profile, which constitutes a complex framework for providing recommendations to the user, especially when the profile as well as the documents annotations have an ontology-based model.

The particularity of our approach consists in considering the user conceptual navigation into ontology instead of the site navigation for providing him with recommendations. For monitoring the conceptual navigation and selecting the next focused concept into the ontology, a collaborative filtering approach is used, based on the nearest neighbors algorithm. In order to effectively recommend documents corresponding to the selected concept, a content-based recommendation is accomplished, considering the user competencies profile, and also applying a nearest neighbor algorithm. The advantage of our ontology-oriented approach consists in the possibility of migrating the user profile from a system to another, and also in the platform-independent character of the recommendation system itself.

Our paper explores various existing approaches for ontology-based document and user models, presenting the proposed models based on the e-learning specific standards. Then, the existing ontology-based recommendation techniques are presented, followed by our hybrid recommendation approach which combines a collaborative filtering technique and a content-based method. The conclusions are then exposed together with further work directions.

USING DOMAIN ONTOLOGIES FOR USER MODELING AND CONTENT ANNOTATION

The Current Modeling Approaches

The idea of managing competencies through one or more ontologies was explored by multiple ontology-driven applications.

The CommOn framework facilitates the development of Competency-Based Web Services dedicated to Human Resource Management (Trichet & Leclere, 2003), where self-defined competence schemes are used, organized as ontology. Within the same framework, the project COMONCV faciltates the use of the above mentioned rich network of competencies for CV development and search.

(Draganidis et al., 2006) describe a prototype ontology based system for competencies management, intended to be integrated with e-learning and other human resource functions. (Noda, 2006) proposes an ontology for evaluating skill-based human performance. (Schmidt & Kunzmann, 2006) develop an ontology destined for Human Resource Development reasons inside a corporation, which include a part for competence management. But the competencies themselves are not necessary expressed through ontological concepts.

(Dorn & Pichlmair, 2007) present an information system for storing, evaluating and reasoning about competencies of students at universities, based on a fine-grained representation of skills and a competence ontology. Also in the area of education, (Dolog & Schäfer, 2005) present the conceptualization and implementation of a framework which provides a common base for exchanging learner profiles between several sources. The exchange representation of learner profiles is based on standards, and includes a competency management.

(Tsiriga & Virvou, 2003) present ICALL - a student modeling module inside Web-PVT platform aiming to provide individualized tutoring to each student in learning English. The developed student models are both long term and short term. The short term student model is responsible for diagnosing possible errors accomplished by students while they solve exercises. In developing the long term student model, the stereotype and the overlay technique is used. A bidirectional interaction of two sub-components could be noticed: the set of stereotypes that the student belongs to and the individual student model that is inferred based on direct observations of the student's behavior. The domain model is represented in the Web-PVT as a conceptual network that depicts the interrelations between the several grammatical concepts. Three kinds of link between nodes are used: part-of, is-a, and prerequisite. The domain concepts are associated with hypertext pages of the platform.

As could be observed, many of these approaches consider the ontology-based annotation of the documents, but the explicitly usage of exactly the same set of ontologies as external model for both developing an user competencies model and for documents indexing is still incipient, although has many advantages: it is reliable for the case of dynamic changing the documents or users space by adding, modifying or removing items (Brusilovsky & Henze, 2007).

The Proposed Ontology-Based User Competencies Model

A user modeling approach aims to create and maintain an up-to-date user model, in order to provide each user with the most suitable information (Brusilovsky & Millán, 2007). User models consider five most popular and useful features for user as an individual: the user's knowledge, interests, goals, background, and individual traits.

The overlay model, which represents an individual user's knowledge as a subset of the domain model, is the most popular model not only for user knowledge, but also for user interests and goals (Brusilovsky & Millán, 2007). We adopt the overlay model in our user competencies focused profile, considering a domain ontology as domain model, as (Dolog et al., 2004) or (Kay & Lum, 2004) do.

In our approach, the user model regards the first three features: into a system which aims the user competencies management and development, the *user knowledge* could be identified with the actual, acquired, *competencies* (e.g. through previous acquired certificates), the *user interests* – as the desired, foresighted, competencies (e.g., which will be acquired through actual courses), and the *user goals* – constituted by the particular interests encountered into the current moment and expressed through concepts illustrated by the accessed documents, which we are denoting by *fingerprints*. Thus, in our ontology-based user modeling approach, the user profile is split into three layers:

1. *Competencies* – ontology concepts selected according the his acquired certificates and qualifications. For the automatically construction of this layer, a rule-based approach (Henze et al., 2004) is applied. For example, a certain certificate should have assigned some competencies (ontology concepts). In function of the score associated with the certificate, the user gains those knowledge at a certain level (beginner, intermediate, advanced). In ExpertizeNet system (Song et al., 2005) some relational and evolutionary graph models are used in order to automatically detect the user knowledge from his published papers.

2. *Interests* – the concept in which the user is interested for a long period. In order to develop this profile layer, a rule-based approach is also adopted: if a user is enrolled to a certain training session, or is working to a certain project, the topics (ontology concepts) assigned to these are included automatically in his long term interests profile. In the CourseAgent system (Farzan & Brusilovsky, 2005), a taxonomy of career job profiles is used to model the user interests in order to recommend him relevant courses.

3. *Fingerprints* – ontology concepts in which the user is interested at the current moment, while accomplishes a specific task (e.g., accesses some interest documents). By

developing the fingerprints profile, we will illustrate how could be traced the conceptual navigation through ontology instead of the site navigation.

For expressing these three layers, we depart from one of two main user profile models standardized and imposed in the e-learning domain: IMS Learner Information Specification and IEEE PAPI – Public And Private Information. We choose PAPI for our user profile model, because we intend to use IEEE LOM standard for structuring the educational content.

The PAPI model structure includes 6 categories (Collett et al., 2001) – all optional: Personal, Learner Relations, Preferences, Portfolio, Learner Performance, Security Information. The *personal* category contains information about names, contacts and addresses of a user. *Relations* category serves as a category for specifying relationships between users (e.g. classmate, teacherIs, teacherOf, instructorIs, instructorOf, belongsTo, belongsWith). *Preference* indicates the types of devices and objects, which the user is able to recognize. The *Learner Performance* category is for storing information about measured performance of a user through learning material (i.e. what does a user know). It is in charge with competence management, including support for tracking the competencies level and validity. *Portfolio* is for accessing previous experience of a user. *Security* aims to provide slots for credentials and access rights. Each category can be extended. Of course, we will focus on the *Learner Performance* category in order to define the three-layered user competencies profile.

In order to enable the unique reference to a certain competence, a special IEEE specification for competencies was recently developed: Data Model for Reusable Competency Definitions (RCD) (Ostyn & Lewis, 2007), which provides support for specifying that the referred competence belongs to a certain ontology:

```
reusable _ competency _ definition :
record ( identifier : long _ identi-
fier _ type,
         title : bag of langstring _
type(1000),
         description : bag of lang-
string _ type(4000))
```

The *long_identifier_type* enables the reference to a specific concept belonging to a specific ontology: the catalog element is a namespace-scheme, and the entry element is a namespace-specific string.

```
type long _ identifier _ type =
record ( catalog: characterstring(iso-
10646),
       entry: characterstring(iso-
10646) );
```

So, in our approach, the competencies are uniquely referred by using the RCD format within the PAPI Learner Performance category. The identifier of a Reusable Competence Definition is particularized by a specific concept from the domain-specific ontology. This approach is conformant with the framework of integrating RCD with competence data established by (Ostyn & Lewis, 2007) and illustrated in the Figure 1: the PAPI Learner Performance category to express a competence *evidence* (such an exam, certificate etc.), and also its temporal validity; the domain ontology provides the competence or documents

Figure 1. RCD integration with competency data

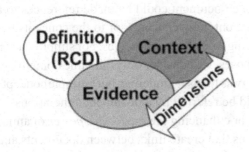

context inside a specific domain; and the RCD standard provides unique references to competency *definition*.

Below is an extras of such user competence model:

```
<papi:recording _ date _ time>20080507
</papi:recording _ date _ time>
<papi:granularity>course</papi:granu-
larity>
<papi:performance _ metric>
       A B C D F</papi:performance _
metric>
<papi:peformance _ value>A</papi:pe-
formance _ value>
<certificate _ list>
<certificate>
   <certification _ source>
   X  University</certification _
source>
   <certification _ parameter _ list>
     <rcd:rdceo>
       <rcd:identifier> ACM-I.2.6.5 </
rcd:identifier>
       <rcd:title>"Knowledge Aquisi-
tion"</rcd:title>
     </rcd:rdceo>
   </certification _ parameter _ list>
          ...
</certificate>
</certificate _ list>
```

When a student *X* starts working with an e-learning platform, the system could acquire knowledge about her/his proficiency level of the domain by developing his competence profile based on his current certificates *Ce* and associated scores. Ideally, the certificates should express the acquired competencies through the current domain ontology concepts *Co*. If some certificates refer to new ontologies, a mapping between these and the platform competencies ontology could be accomplished:

```
certificate(Ce, Co), hasAcquired(X,
Ce) →
hasCompetence(X,Co)
```

For expressing and developing the user interests level, we make use of stereotypes.

A *stereotype user modeling* approach (Rich, 1978) classifies users into *stereotypes*: users belonging to a certain class are assumed to have the same characteristics. According to (Kay, 2000) a stereotype consists of:

1. A set of *trigger conditions*, which are boolean expressions that activate a stereotype,
2. a set of *retraction conditions* that are responsible for deactivating an active stereotype, and
3. a set of *stereotype inferences* that serve as default assumptions once a user is assigned to a stereotype category.

In our user modeling approach, the user interests level could be considered as a combination of stereotypes: the set of ontology concepts corresponding to each course in which the student is currently enrolled could be considered as a stereotype since it defines a set of interests common to all students enrolled in the course. The competencies level is more diverse since the acquired certificates could be issued by various academic institutions. However, during the university years, many long-term interests become competencies when students successfully finish their current courses. Thus, a student X enrolment into a course C constitutes a trigger condition for assigning to him the course concepts Co as long-term interests (so assigning him into the course stereotype). A course graduation accomplished by a student through an exam E, with a mark M, is a retraction condition for eliminating the course concepts from his interest profile (deactivating his course stereotype), but also for transferring the concepts into his competence profile, according the obtained scores.

```
certificate(Ce), concept(Co),
hasCompetences(Ce,Co), learner(X),
obtainedCertificate(X, Ce) →
```

```
hasCompetences(X,Co)
course(C,Co), hasEnrolled(X,C) →
hasInterest(X,Co)
course(C,Co), hasGraduated(X,C) →
deleteInterest(X,Co)
course(C,Co), exam(E,C), obtainedMark
(X,E,M) →
  {if (M<5) hasCompetence(X,Co,0)
else {hasGraduated(X,C)
  if (M<7) hasCompetence(X,Co,1)
      else if (M<9)
hasCompetence(X,Co,2)
      else hasCompetence (X,Co,3)}}
}
```

The Document Model and its IR-Based Construction

Alongside with the standards for user profile modeling, some other standards were developed in the e-learning field addressing the educational materials organization and management. In order to facilitate the Semantic Web technologies integration, inside these standards, various support to make reference to ontologies was provided. For example, inside the IEEE/LOM (Learning Object Metadata) standard - considered as the most enabling for semantic extensions (Al-Khalifa & Hugh, 2006) -, the *Classification* category enables to specify that the Learning Object (LO) belongs to a certain classification system, including domain ontology. It is possible to specify the information for identifying the ontology and the particular concept which want to refer.

Using such a document structuring standardized approach, a certain document could be related to a single concept (single-concept indexing) or to many concepts (multi-concepts indexing). Also, from a document could be made references to a single ontology concepts, or to the concepts belonging to multiple ontologies. For simplification purposes, we consider only the same domain ontology as for user modeling, but multiple concepts could be referred by a document annotations.

For enhancing the *expressive power* of annotations that create links between documents and ontology concepts, some techniques of associating *roles* and/or *weights* with these relations were conceived. The roles are important for distinguish the various kind of connections between concepts and documents. The most common role is *prerequisite*, which indicates that a certain document is a prerequisite for understanding the corresponding concept (Brusilovsky et al., 1998). In (Brusilovsky & Cooper, 2002), 30 roles are defined and used in order to identify the context within which a certain concept appears. In the KBS-HyperBook system, the documents could be marked as "problem statement", "example", "theory" for a certain concept (Henze & Nejdl, 2001).

The e-learning standards provide support for specifying the relations a new material possesses with the existing ones, when the new material is added to the platform. Usually, the Dublin Core/LOM relations set between LOs is used, as the IEEE/LOM *Relation* category adopts: The semantics of these relations is refined or modified in (Engelhardt et al., 2006), and also some new relations are introduced for the purpose of relating various LOs in a more semantic manner: isNarrowerThan / isBroaderThan, isAlternativeTo, Illustrates / isIllustratedBy, isLessSpecificThan / isMoreSpecificThan. As a remark, instead of using these relations between different LOs, they could be used for relating the concepts of an ontology which models the domain knowledge. Indirectly, the relations between concepts illustrate the relations between the corresponding annotated LOs.

In order to differentiate the importance of a concept-based LO annotation, as well as of the user competence level, we propose two new attributes which could be integrated in the Classification IEEE/LOM category:

- *relationType*: to express the relevance degree of the referred concept for the current LO, through 3 possible values, expressing this relevance into a decreasing order:

- *isOnTopic* – for a LO which is especially destined to a certain topic;
- *usesTheConcept* – expressing the ordinary concepts encountered into LO;
- *makesReferenceTo* – for designating the other concepts from ontology encountered inside LO as hyperlinks or explicit references.
- *userType*: expressing the type of the user to which the LO is destined - beginner, intermediate, advanced.

We can consider that the user level for which is destined a document (beginner, intermediate, advanced) is established – during the above described editing phase - by the document author (or by the person which include the document in the educational repository), and is propagated to all the concepts to which the document is related.

Let us consider the general case in which a LO available into PDF or HTML format, in which the titles and hyperlinks could be automatically located. We expose below a solution for automatically generating the ontology-based LO annotations inside the *Classification* category, by adapting some existing Web information retrieval techniques.

The *relationType* attribute could be related to the place inside the LO where the ontology concept reference is encountered. For this purpose, the document is distributed in 3 classes:

1. the document *title and subtitles* will be considered for the *isOnTopic* relation;
2. the *hyperlinks and the bibliographical references* will be processed for the generation of the *makesReferenceTo* relation;
3. the *document body* (the rest of the document) will be processed in order to obtain *usesTheConcept* relation.

The existing Web information retrieval (Web-IR) techniques consider a larger number of classes, corresponding to 12 categories (Lin et al., 2002) or 6 categories (Cutler et al., 1997) of HTML tags. We selected only these 3 classes which are relevant for our considered relations.

Each of the three document classes are separately processed in order to be mapped to the set of concepts provided by the current ontology. The existing approaches consider the *Latent Semantic Indexing techniques* (Dumais, 1993), which represent a document through concepts rather than through index terms, as in term-based classical information retrieval. First there is built the matrix of terms frequency, and then is obtained the matrix of concepts frequency, by applying *the Singular Value Decomposition* technique (Micarelli et al., 2007).

An alternative solution for locating the concepts inside a document and computing their frequency consists in building the *concept semantic cluster* using the *Wordnet* relations, and then in computing each cluster frequency using information retrieval techniques (Baziz et al., 2005). Thus, for each of the above mentioned 3 document classes, the corresponding set of concepts is obtained, together with their occurrence number.

- The corresponding relations *isOnTopic* and *makesReferenceTo* are generated based on the first two categories, storing also the occurrences number.
- The concepts belonging to the document body are used for generating the third category - *usesTheConcept*.

For example, the following metadata associated with a certain educational document express that the current document is destined to the *intermediate* users in the field on *Knowledge acquisition*, being a material exactly *on this topic*. The topic is identified as a concept inside the ACM classification system:

```
<Classification>
    <Purpose> competency </Purpose>
    <TaxonPath relationType="isOnTopic"
occurrences="3"
```

```
userType="intermediate">
        <Source> ("en", "ACM") </
Source>
    <Taxon> <id>I.2.6.5</id>
        <entry> ("en","Knowledge
Aquisition") </entry>
    </Taxon>
  </TaxonPath>
</Classification>
```

In the following section we will illustrate how the ontology-based user and document models could be exploit in order to provide users with personalized recommendations.

ONTOLOGY-BASED RECOMMENDER SYSTEMS APPROACHES

The Semantic Web Enhancement

The traditional recommendation techniques could be classified according the information analyzed and processed in: content-based, collaborative, demographic, utility-based, and knowledge-based recommendations (Burke, 2007).

- *Content-based recommendation*: Exploits information derived from document contents, correlating it with the user profile information, in order to recommend the most suitable documents. We will apply the content-based filtering for documents selection according to an interest concept, the documents annotations and user profile.
- *Collaborative recommendations* (social information filtering): Documents/items are recommended to a user according to the "ratings of the similar users", where the similarity is measured on the basis of the user profile values. The main problem in this case is the so-called "cold start" issue: a critical mass of users is required before the system can make recommendations; a

new added document/item has no ratings initially, so how could be considered for recommendations? Also, for a new user, the system has initially little or no information. We will apply the collaborative filtering for predicting and recommending to the user the next focused concept inside the ontology, according to the activity performed by the other users belonging to the same stereotype. The cold start issue is solved by assigning a certain weight to the current stereotypes' concepts inside the ontology, according to their superposition and enchainment.

- *Demographic recommendations:* The "ratings of the similar users" are considered also in this case, where the similarity is computed upon the demographic data
- *Utility-based recommendations*: The users preferences are coded by a utility function, which is applied to all the documents/items in order to select among them for recommendations.
- *Knowledge-based recommendations*: There is used an auxiliary body of knowledge that describes how items can meet various needs, and an inference process is applied in order to match the description of the user's needs and to select the most useful items.

The main limitation of these techniques is caused by their requirement for a critical mass of data before the adopted machine learning algorithms produce results of sufficient quality. A technique for obtaining a better performance adopted by researchers is to combine recommendation techniques in order to build hybrid recommender systems.

Seven main types hybrid recommender systems are obtained by combining the above mentioned recommendation techniques: weighted, switching, mixed, feature combination, feature augmentation, cascade, meta-level (Burke, 2007). Among these, the meta-level hybrid type provide the framework for our solution, as will be described in the section "A Hybrid Solution for Personalized Recommendations". A meta-level hybrid uses a user model learned by one recommender as input for another, completely replacing its original knowledge source. An example is provided by the (Pazzani, 1999): the restaurant recommender build the models of users' preferences through a content-based approach by using the naive Bayes technique. The developed models are then used in a collaborative approach which identify the user clusters. We will develop the user fingerprints model through a collaborative filtering technique, and will use this model into a content-based recommendation approach in order to recommend him the relevant documents.

A significant enhancement of the recommender systems is brought by the Semantic Web techniques, as they provide the Web resources (users and documents) with a level of comprehensibility for computer applications, by associating them a machine-processable semantics. Ontology-based annotations are a major example of such semantics. Thus, the use of a wide variety of reasoning techniques is made possible, which could be applied for enhancing the personalization quality.

(Baldoni et al., 2005) underline that all of this reasoning techniques go one step beyond the ontology layer because, in fact, pure ontological annotation and ontological reasoning techniques (though necessary) are not sufficient to produce, in an automatic way, the desired personalization.

Inside e-learning systems, the ontology-based semantic annotations of the learning objects could facilitate the localization of certain relations between these, based on the ontological relations. In order to recommend certain learning objects to a specified user, a representation of the user's goals (interests) and competencies is necessary (as our modeling approach provides), and a supplementary reasoning process which to correlate these with the knowledge about the learning objects provided by the semantic annotations. For a such process, the goal-directed reasoning techniques seem particularly suitable (Baldoni et al., 2005).

The collaborative part of our hybrid recommender adopts a goal-directed reasoning technique by considering the stereotypes provided by the user interest profile in order to predict the next concept of interest for the user.

Various systems integrated an ontological layer in user profiling in order to enhance the personalized functionalities. The *CourseAgent* system (Dolog et al., 2004) uses a taxonomy of career job profiles to model the user interests in order to recommend him relevant courses. *Onto-Seek* system (Guarino et al., 1999) enable users to formulate queries by navigating the ontology in order to improve the content-based search.

Foxtrot recommender system uses a machine learning technique for classifying the research papers according a paper topic ontology, and the user interest profile is developed in term of ontology concepts according to browsed and visited papers, as well as to his feed-back. Collaborative filtering is used to find sets of interesting papers. Then the content-based user profile is used to select the papers of most interest (Middleton et al., 2004). Our approach is similar with Foxtrot's as functionalities, but avoids the explicit user feedback and considers two supplementary layers in user profile.

Using Ontologies for Web Personalization

Using the domain ontologies for enhancing characterization of user segments and objects could enable a system to recommend different types of complex objects (Dai & Mobasher, 2003). Ontology-based annotated documents are such complex objects, since their characteristics are structured concept sets.

The most general method for developing the user profile in order to provide him with suitable recommendations (or, morel general, with personalization) is by analyzing the user's navigational activity. Usage-based Web personalization systems involve three main phases:

data preparation and transformation, pattern discovery, and recommendation. The last one is the only real-time component, while the other two phases are performed offline. Integrating domain ontology into these phases involves (Dai & Mobasher, 2003):

- *Data preparation*: The site Web pages should be analyzed together with domain information in order to generate the site ontology; in our use case, the documents to be recommended are previously annotated based on established domain ontology.
- *Pattern discovery*: The already performed user choices are analyzed from the ontology perspective in order to establish semantic usage patterns; in our system case, the common interests of users are provided also in advance, through the stereotypes composing the long term interest user profiles. So the first two phases are assured in our system by the document and user models development preliminary steps.
- *Recommendation* matches the semantic representation of the user's active session (called current user profile) against the discovered domain-level aggregate profiles. In our system, the current user profile compose the fingerprints level of his profile. The mentioned matching process involves in fact the adoption of a consecrated recommendation techniques (Mobasher, 2007) or a hybrid one.

Instead of tracing the user's site navigation, some approaches were recently developed for modeling users' navigation behavior at "higher" abstraction levels. In the adaptive *InterBook* system, the concept-based navigation was introduced [8]: each concept used to index documents constitutes also a navigation hub - providing links to all content pages indexed with this concept; also, from each page, all its related concepts are accessible.

In (Farzan & Brusilovsky, 2005), Web documents are first clustered based on users' navigational data, and then user behavior models are built at this document cluster level.

(Jin et al., 2005) adopts the proposed task-oriented user modeling approach. The relations between the common navigational "tasks" and Web pages or users are characterized through the Probability Latent Semantic Analysis (PLSA) model. The user model development is accomplished through an algorithm based on Bayesian updating, and the Web recommendation technique is based on a maximum entropy model.

In our approach, the domain ontology used for modeling documents annotations and user knowledge and interests provides the abstraction level for user conceptual navigation modeling. This modeling is performed through a nearest neighbor technique for predicting the next focused ontology concept by the user in order to provide him with personalized recommendations.

A Hybrid Solution for Personalized Recommendations

Exploring the presented document annotation and user profile models, our hybrid recommendation solution combine two techniques in different phases:

- First a collaborative filtering approach implemented through the Nearest Neighbors Algorithm is accomplished, monitoring the user's ontology conceptual navigation, in order to predict the next concept(s) of interest (which are integrated into the user fingerprints profile).
- Then, a content-based recommendation technique selects the most content relevant documents for the user according to his competence profile and to the selected concept.

When user selects a certain document, its corresponding main concept is detected, in order to reiterate the first collaborative phase. More precisely, at a certain moment, our system will display to the user:

- the chronological list of the already reached concepts in the current session;
- the currently chosen concept, c_0, accompanied by a list of recommended documents;
- the recommended concepts for being further accessed, displayed in the predicted importance order;
- a link to "Other" concept list, for the case user is not satisfied by the recommended concepts.

Collaborative Filtering for Recommending the Next Focused Ontology Concepts

The collaborative filtering (CF) algorithms could be classified as (Schafer et al., 2007):

1. *Non-probabilistic algorithms* - are widely used by practitioners. The main such algorithms are:
    - The nearest neighbor algorithms (kNN) – constitute the most well-known CF algorithms, differentiated in two main classes: user-based nearest neighbor and item-based nearest neighbor.
    - Algorithms that transform or cluster the ratings space to reduce the ratings space dimensionality;
    - Graph-based algorithms (Aggarwal et al., 1999)
    - Neural networks (Billsus & Pazzani, 1998)
    - Rule-mining algorithms (Heckerman et al, 2001).
2. *Probabilistic algorithms* - based on an underlying probabilistic model: they represent

probability distributions when computing predicted ratings or ranked recommendation lists. The most popular collaborative filtering probabilistic algorithms adopt Bayesian-network models that derive probabilistic dependencies among users or items. Probabilistic models have been gaining favor particularly in the machine learning community.

We adopted the user-based nearest neighbor algorithm based on ratings from similar users, adapted for our particular situation: when a user reach a certain concept, the candidates for recommending the next focused concepts are selected according the ontology structure (among the concept's parent and children). Their relevance for recommendation is established according to the ratings of user's neighbors.

Generally, user-based algorithms generate a prediction for an item i destined to a user u by analyzing ratings for i from users in u's neighborhood. If we denote by:

- r_{ni} – the neighbor n's rating for item i
- $userSim(u,n)$ – the measure of the similarity between the user u and one of his neighbors n

then, the prediction for item i to be of interest for user u could be computed as:

$$pred(u,i) = \frac{\sum_{n \subset neighbors(u)} userSim(u,n) \cdot r_{ni}}{\sum_{n \subset neighbors(u)} userSim(u,n)}$$

(1)

For computing the similarities between two users $userSim(u,n)$, a current approach is to use the *Pearson correlation*, as in the *GroupLens* system for Usenet newsgroups (Resnick et al., 1994), or in the *Foxtrot* system (Middleton et al., 2004). The Pearson correlation coefficient is calculated by comparing ratings for all items rated by both the target user and the neighbor (e.g. *corated* items). If we denote by $CR_{u,n}$ the set of corated items

between the users u and n, and by $\bar{r}_u$ the average rating of the user u, the similarity between the users u and n could be expressed through:

$$userSim(u,n) =$$

$$\frac{\sum_{i \subset CR_{u,n}} (r_{ui} - \bar{r}_u)(r_{ni} - \bar{r}_n)}{\sqrt{\sum_{i \subset CR_{u,n}} (r_{ui} - \bar{r}_u)^2} \sqrt{\sum_{i \subset CR_{u,n}} (r_{ni} - \bar{r}_n)^2}}$$

(2)

In our approach, we are storing the user navigation activity through ontology as his fingerprints profile, and we are using the user-based nearest neighbor algorithm for predicting his next focused concept. We provide below a detailed description.

The ontology itself is basically stored in OWL (Web Ontology Language) format:

```
<owl:Class rdf:ID="Knowledge _ acqui-
sition">
    <rdfs:subClassOf>
        <owl:Class rdf:about="#I.2.6 _
Learning"/>
    </rdfs:subClassOf>
    <rdfs:label xml:lang="en">
    Knowledge  acquisition</rdfs:la-
bel>
    </owl:Class>
```

For the easy development of user profile, the ontology is processed and converted into two paired vectors:

- *concept* – the vector containing the IDs of all concepts: concept[i] = the ID of the concept i extracted from the OWL ontology format, i = 1,n.
- *parent* – the vector of parent concept indexes: parent[i] = the index in the concept vector for the parent of the concept[i], i = 1,n. As possible values, parent[i] ∈ {0, n-1}.

An advantage for this representation is reflected by the ontology development: when a new concept is added (as leave) in the ontology, its corresponding information is added also in the end of the two vectors, the previous values are not affected.

The user interests profile consist into a set of stereotypes. Let us consider the system defines a total set of *s* stereotypes. Their representation consists into a *nxs* matrix of 0 and 1 values: $S[i,j]$ = 1 if the *concept[i]* belongs to the stereotype *j*, and 0 otherwise. The addition of a new stereotype into the system involves simply a new row in the matrix S.

Let us denote by *m* the total number of the users. Their profiles are represented as 3 matrix, corresponding to the three profile layers:

- UC_{nxm}, where $UC[i,k]$ = the competence of the user k concerning the concept[i], $UC[i,k]$ $\in$ {0, 1, 2, 3} (meaning no competence, beginner, intermediate, advanced);
- UI_{nxm}, where $UI[i,k]$ = the interest of user k concerning the concept[i]. $UI[i,k]$ $\in$ {0, 1, 2, ...}, depending the number of stereotypes composing the user k's interest profile and including the concept[i]. The matrix *UI* is obtained by multiplying the matrix *S x US*, where US_{sxm} is the matrix identifying each user's stereotypes: $US[j,k]$ = 1 if the stereotype j belongs to the interest profile of the user k, and 0 otherwise.
- UF_{nxm}, where $UF[i,k]$ = the fingerprints of user k concerning the concept[i], expressing the current interest for a certain topic similarly to the manner adopted by Foxtrot system (but avoiding the user explicit feedback): $UF[i,k]$ = 1 if the user browsed a document on the concept[i] topic, $UF[i,k]$ = 2 if the user followed a recommendation on this topic. In addition, $UF[i,k]$ = -2 if the user choose the "Other..." link from the recommendation list. These values are added to the previous *UF[i,k]* value, and are

propagated with a 50% de-valorization to the concept[i] topic's super-classes: interest value for super-class per instance= 50% of sub-class. Thus, a user fingerprints profile express his current rating for each ontology concept, providing the r_{ui} vector in the equation (2).

The initialization of a user fingerprints profile is accomplished by normalizing his interest profile

$$UF[i,k] = \frac{UI[i,k]}{\sum_{i=1,n} UI[i,k]}.$$

Thus, the cold start issue is addressed: from the very beginning, all users gain a fingerprint profile. Pedagogically, this approach is justified by the necessity of recommending to users – at least for the first sessions – the items corresponding to their official interest profile (shared with the similar users). When many users become actives, their fingerprints profile become more customized, contributing to the recommendations for the current user.

For testing purposes, we considered a fragment of the ACM topic ontology depicted in the Figure 2 below. Let's suppose a certain course on *Hypermedia Systems* has associated the set of bolded concepts on the ACM tree, and another course on *Multimedia Systems* has associated the italic concepts inside the ACM tree. The concepts which appear bold as well as italic belong to both courses. For a student enrolled in both courses, the initialization of the fingerprints profile part corresponding to H.5.1-H.5.5 concepts involves the assignment of a double value to concepts belonging to both courses in comparison to those belonging to a single course; such, the value distribution is 0.16, 0.33, 0.00, 0.33, 0.16.

We developed a training set of fingerprint profiles values considering different user categories (beginner, intermediate, advanced), in different phases of course attendance. The last information was exploited for establishing the current focused concept. Such, the training set used by the nearest neighbor classifier has a similar structure as the fingerprint profile itself:

```
(<userID>,  (<conceptFingerprints>)*,
<focusedConcept>).
```

Based on the training set, given a certain user fingerprint profile, the classification of the *focusedConcept* is accomplished: the probabilities the *focusedConcept* to belongs to each concept class are provided.

If we denote by k_0 the current user, and concept[i_0] his current focused concept, the following steps are performed for the Nearest Neighbor-based implementation of the next focused concept recommender module:

- The users with common interests are first selected according to the stereotypes to which they belong – the matrix *US* is used;
- This users set is further filtered according to their stored *focusedConcept*: only the concepts related (via ontology relations) with the current focused concept by the current user are selected;
- The similarity between user k_0 and each of its neighbors k_1 is computed according to the equation derived from, considering the common concepts encountered in their fingerprints profile $CF(k_0, k_1)$ (2):

$$userSim(k_0,k_1)=\frac{\sum_{i\subset CF_{k_0,k_1}}(UF[i,k_0]-\overrightarrow{UF[k_0]})(UF[i,k_1]-\overrightarrow{UF[k_1]})}{\sqrt{\sum_{i\subset CF_{k_0,k_1}}(UF[i,k_0]-\overrightarrow{UF[k_0]})^2}\sqrt{\sum_{i\subset CF_{k_0,k_1}}(UF[i,k_1]-\overrightarrow{UF[k_1]})^2}} \quad (3)$$

where

$$UF[k_0]=\frac{\sum_{i\subset CR_{k_0,k_1}}UF[i,k_0]}{\sum_{i\subset CR_{k_0,k_1}}1}$$

(the normalized value of user k_0 fingerprints concerning the common interest concepts with user k_1).

Figure 2. A fragment of the ACM topic hierarchy, where the concepts belonging to two courses are emphasizes

- H. Information Systems
  - H.1 MODELS AND PRINCIPLES
    - H.1.1 Systems and Information Theory
    - H.1.2 User/Machine Systems
  - H.2 DATABASE MANAGEMENT
    - H.2.1 Logical Design
    - H.2.2 Physical Design
    - H.2.3 Languages
    - H.2.4 Systems
    - H.2.5 Heterogeneous Databases
    - H.2.6 Database Machines
    - H.2.7 *Database Administration*
    - H.2.8 *Database Applications*
  - H.3 ***INFORMATION STORAGE AND RETRIEVAL***
    - H.3.1 *Content Analysis and Indexing*
    - H.3.2 **Information Storage**
    - H.3.3 ***Information Search and Retrieval***
    - H.3.4 *Systems and Software*
    - H.3.5 **Online Information Services**
    - H.3.6 Library Automation
    - H.3.7 **Digital Libraries**
  - H.4 INFORMATION SYSTEMS APPLICATIONS
    - H.4.1 Office Automation
    - H.4.2 *Types of Systems*
    - H.4.3 Communications Applications
  - H.5 ***INFORMATION INTERFACES AND PRESENTATION (e.g., HCI)***
    - H.5.1 *Multimedia Information Systems*
    - H.5.2 ***User Interfaces***
    - H.5.3 Group and Organization Interfaces
    - H.5.4 ***Hypertext/Hypermedia***
    - H.5.5 *Sound and Music Computing*

- The first k neighbors (according the computed similarity with user k_0) are selected;
- The classification of k_0 is performed according the classes of its neighbors (in terms of *focusedConcept*). The classification is provided as a vector of probabilities that estimates the *focusedConcept* to be each of the ontology concepts. The biggest probability provide the most likely estimation of the *focusedConcept*. This concept is then transmitted to the second recommender (see further) in order to establish the concrete documents to be recommended. According to the user selection, the correction of the *focusedConcept* is accomplished and the current user fingerprints profile is transferred to the training data set.

The Weka machine-learning library (Witten & Frank, 2000) was used for testing the kNN algorithm: IBk classifier was adopted, boosted by the AdaBoostM1, as the Foxtrot recommender system adopted (Middleton et al., 2004). We will compare our approach to Foxtrot in the end of the next section.

The space dimension of our solution is relatively big because of using matrix and vectors with sparse values. However, the time complexity is polynomial: all operations are performed by a single vector covering. If we reduce the space dimension by using data structures with variable dimension for storing the references to certain elements, the time complexity increases. E.g., if the user fingerprints profile stores only the current reached concepts (through their index into the *concept* vector, a supplementary record is necessary for counting and normalizing the visits and after each new visit a check is necessary for verifying the current concept was or not previously visited. The matrix and vectors solution has the main advantage of facilitating the direct access to the elements.

Content-Based Recommendation of Documents

This recommender is activated when the user selects a concept among those recommended in the previous phase. We remind that the user could select the "Other..." link if he is not satisfied by the concept recommendation, and the recommendation will be continued with the children and parents of the existing concepts.

The content-based recommender receives as input a concept c_0 and provide the user k_0 with a list of documents indexed with c_0 and with as many as possible concepts from his competencies profile (the most personal profile level for a certain user).

For a uniform representation, the documents' annotations are processed such as the *Documents'* collection is represented as a matrix D_{pxn} where p is the total number of documents, n is the total number of concepts, and D[j,i] = the weight of concept[i] inside the annotations of document j, $D[j,i] \in \{1, 0.66, 0.33, 0\}$, corresponding to the annotation based on the isOnTopic, usesTheConcept, makesReferenceTo relations respectivelly (the 0 value means "no relation").

The candidate documents for recommendation are selected by analyzing the column i_0 in the matrix D, corresponding to c_0 (concept[i_0] = c_0). The selected documents are sorted according the value of D[j, i_0].

Due to the similar representation of documents and user competencies (vectors with the n dimension, where n = the total number of ontology concepts), the competencies profile could be considered as the etalon "document" for which the nearest neighbors should be computed. Thus, the candidate documents will be considered for computing the nearest neighbors for the competencies profile. The similarity between a document and the user competence profile could be expressed as:

$$userDocSim(k_0, D_j) =$$

$$\frac{\sum_{i \subset CC_{k_0,D_j}} (UC[i,k_0] - \vec{UC[k_0]})(D[j,i] - \vec{D[j]})}{\sqrt{\sum_{i \subset CC_{k_0,D_j}} (UC[i,k_0] - \vec{UC[k_0]})^2} \sqrt{\sum_{i \subset CC_{k_0,D_j}} (D[j,i] - \vec{D[j]})^2}}$$

where $CC(k_0, D_j)$ is the common concept set of user k_0 competencies profile and the annotations of the document j, $\vec{UC}[k_0]$ is the normalized value (the average) of the $UC[i, k_0]$ considered values, as well as the $\vec{D}[j]$ is the normalized value of the $D[j, i]$ considered values.

After the neighbor documents are selected and their similarity degree with the competence profile is computed, the final sorted document list is established also according to the prediction computed with a formula similar to (1):

$$pred(k_0, D_k) =$$

$$\frac{\sum_{j \subset docNeighbors(k_0)} userDocSim(k_0, D_j) \cdot D[k,j]}{\sum_{j \subset docNeighbors(k_0)} userDocSim(k_0, D_j)}$$

The first 10 documents are recommended to the user. If the user selects a certain document, it is marked in order to be no more recommended. In the same time, the main concept of the selected document (annotated with *isOnTopic* relation) is transmitted to the collaborative filtering recommender, in order to update the user fingerprint profile.

Comparison to Foxtrot

As we mentioned earlier, *Foxtrot* (Middleton et al., 2004) is the most closed system to our approach because it also adopts an ontology-based user profiling and a hybrid recommendation technique, combining a collaborative and a content-based approach. We discuss bellow some advantages of our approach due to the adopted user and document models.

In Foxtrot, a document is assigned to a single ontology concept, and the user profile is developed by the concepts corresponding to the browsed documents. An interest value is assigned to each ontology concept. Our approach adopts a multi-concept document indexing (with a single concept as dominant, established by *isOnTopic* relation). The user profile fingerprints layer includes concepts corresponding to the browsed documents, but two supplementary user profile layers contribute to the recommendation refinement: user interests layer is used to initialize the user fingerprints profile, and also to select the users belonging to the same stereotypes for the collaborative filtering recommender; user competencies profile is used to select the most relevant documents for the user.

Foxtrot first generates the term-vectors for each paper, and then uses the kNN algorithm (IBk classifier, boosted by AdaBoostM1) in order to classify the papers according the ontology concepts. A manually-developed training set of classified papers is used. In our approach, the kNN algorithm is applied first for establishing the user next focused concept, and the training set starts with records created on the interest profile basis and exploiting some generic users characteristics.

In *Foxtrot*, user interest profiles are computed daily by correlating previously browsed research papers with their classifications, and the recommendations are provided once for each day of the system usage. We tried to find a solution to provide real-time recommendations, as user performs his very current tasks.

CONCLUSION AND PERSPECTIVES

In this article, we presented a modeling approach for the content annotations and user competencies profile within e-learning platforms, based on the same domain ontology. The ontology constitutes the binder between the materials and users. We exploited the specificity of e-learning platforms of detaining information about users' competencies and long-term interests in order to develop a three layers user profile.

The paper also provides a solution for applying the current personalized recommendation techniques in the case of using domain ontologies for developing both the user and document model. The procedure differences are discussed, as well as the semantic enhancement brought by the ontology usage. Our hybrid recommendation solution combines a collaborative and a content-based approach:

- By using a collaborative filtering approach, the user's ontology conceptual navigation is monitored in order to predict the next concept(s) of interest.
- Then, a content-based recommendation technique selects the most content relevant documents for the user according to the selected concept and user's competence profile.

The main advantage of our approach consists in its independence by the navigational structure of a particular site. Moreover, the conceptual navigation supports the user in receiving recommendations according to his current main interests. Our approach avoids the difficulty of the cold start problem (encountered currently in the collaborative filtering recommendations methods), as well as the monitoring of the user navigational activity (considered especially by the content-based recommender systems).

Moreover, if a such user model could be transferred from a system to another, together with the descriptive ontology – for example, through certain Web services – the recommendation approach could be also imported. We intend to extend our prototype in order to provide such support, and also to consider the multimedia documents for recommendations.

The exposed recommendation hybrid approach is in fact independent by the e-learning field: we exposed the pre-processing phase of user and documents models which transforms them into matrix of numeric values. Only the concept references are considered in this pre-process activity, not also the e-learning specific elements. Thus, the recommendation technique remains applicable to each model which could be similarly pre-processed. We will consider in the future a generic ontology-based user and document model suitable for our hybrid recommendation approach.

REFERENCES

Aggarwal, C. C., Wolf, J., Wu, K. L., & Yu, P. S. (1999). Horting Hatches an Egg: A New Graph-Theoretic Approach to Collaborative Filtering. *Proceedings of the Fifth ACM SIGKDD International Conference on Knowledge discovery and data mining.* San Diego, California. ACM Press p. 201-212.

Al-Khalifa, H.S., & Hugh, D. (2006). The Evolution of Metadata from Standards to Semantics in E-Learning Applications. *Proceedings of Hypertext'06*, ACM Press.

Baldoni, M., Baroglio, C., Henze, N. (2005). Personalization for the Semantic Web. In Eisinger, N. Maluszynski, J. (Eds.), *REWERSE 2005, LNCS 3564*, pp. 173–212, Springer-Verlag, 2005.

Baziz, M., Boughanem, M., & Traboulsi, S. (2005). A concept-based approach for indexing documents in IR. *Actes du XXIII-eme Congres INFORSID*, Grenoble.

Billsus, D., & Pazzani, M. J. (1998). Learning Collaborative Information Filters. *Proceedings of the Fifteenth National Conference on Artificial Intelligence (AAAI-98)*. Menlo Park, CA. Morgan Kaufmann Publishers Inc. p 46-94

Brusilovsky, P., & Cooper, D. W. (2002). Domain, Task, and User Models for an Adaptive Hypermedia Performance Support System. In Gil, Y., Leake, D.B. (eds.) *Proc. of 2002 International*

Conference on Intelligent User Interfaces (pp. 23-30). ACM Press

Brusilovsky, P., Eklund, J., & Schwarz, E. (1998). Web-based education for all: A tool for developing adaptive courseware. In Ashman, H., Thistewaite, P. (Eds.) *Proc. of Seventh International World Wide Web Conference, 30*(pp. 291-300).. Elsevier Science B. V.

Brusilovsky, P., & Henze, N. (2007). Open corpus adaptive educational hypermedia. In Brusilovsky, P., Kobsa, A., Neidl, W. (Eds.): *The Adaptive Web, LNCS 4321*, Springer.

Brusilovsky, P., & Millán, E. (2007). User Models for Adaptive Hypermedia and Adaptive Educational Systems, in P. Brusilovsky, A. Kobsa, W. Nejdl (Eds.): *The Adaptive Web, LNCS 4321*, Springer

Burke, R. (2007). Hybrid Web Recommender Systems. In P. Brusilovsky, A. Kobsa, W. Nejdl (Eds.): *The Adaptive Web, LNCS 4321* (pp. 377 – 408), Springer

Collett, M., Linton. F., Goodman, B., & Farance, F. (2001). IEEE P1484.2.25 - Draft Standard for Learning Technology. Public and Private Information (PAPI) for Learners (PAPI Learner) — Learner Performance Information, IEEE Computer Society Press, Piscataway, NJ, USA

Cutler, M., Shih, Y., & Meng, W. (1997). Using the structure of HTML documents to improve retrieval. In *USENIX Symposium on Internet Technologies and Systems* (pp. 241–252)

Dai, H., & Mobasher, B. (2003). A Road Map to More Effective Web Personalization: Integrating Domain Ontologies with Web Usage Mining. *Proceedings of Int. Conference on Internet Computing – IC03*

Dolog, P., Henze, N., Nejdl, W., & Sintek, M. (2004). Personalization in distributed e-learning environments. In *Proc. of The Thirteenth Inter-*

national World Wide Web Conference, WWW 2004 (pp. 161-169). ACM Press

Dolog, P., & Schäfer, M. (2005). Learner Modeling on the Semantic Web. *In Proc. of PerSWeb'05, Workshop on Personalization on the Semantic Web, User Modeling Conference*, 2005

Dorn, J., & Pichlmair, M. (2007). A Competence Management System for Universities, *Proceeding of the European Conference on Artificial Intelligence*, St. Gallen

Draganidis, F., Chamopoulou, P., & Mentzas, G. (2006). An Ontology Based Tool for Competency Management and Learning Path. *6th International Conference on Knowledge Management (I-KNOW 06), Special track on Integrating Working and Learning*, Graz, Austria.

Dumais, S. T. (1993). Latent semantic indexing (LSI) and TREC-2. In *Text REtrieval Conference (TREC) TREC-2 Proceedings* 105–116 NIST Special Publication 500-215.

Engelhardt, M., Hildebrand, A., Lange, D., & Schmidt, T. C. (2006). Reasoning about eLearning Multimedia Objects. *Procedings of SWAMM 06*, Springer

Farzan, R., & Brusilovsky, P. (2005). Social Navigation Support through Annotation-Based Group Modeling, *Proceedings of the 10th Conference on User Modeling*, LNCS 3538, Springer.

Guarino, N., Masolo, C., & Vetere, G. (1999). OntoSeek: Content-based access to the Web. *IEEE Inteligent Systems, 14*, 3

Heckerman, D., Chickering, D.M., Meek, C., Rounthwaite, R., & Kadie, C. (2001). Dependency Networks for Inference, Collaborative Filtering, and Data Visualization. *Journal of Machine Learning Research*, (pp. 49-75).

Henze, N., Dolog, P., & Nejdl, W. (2004) Reasoning and Ontologies for Personalized E-Learning in the Semantic Web. *Educational Technology & Society, 7*(4), 82-97

Henze, N., & Nejdl, W. (2001). Adaptation in open corpus hypermedia. *International Journal of Artificial Intelligence in Education 12*(4), 325-350.

Jin , X., Zhou, Y., & Mobasher, B. (2005). Task-Oriented Web User Modeling for Recommendation, In *Proceedings of the 10th International Conference on User Modeling (UM'05),* Edinburgh, Scotland, LNAI 3538, pp.109-118, Springer

Kay, J. (2000). Stereotypes, Student Models and Scrutability. In Gauthier, G., Frasson, C. and VanLehn, K. (eds.), *Lecture Notes in Computer Science 1839* (pp. 19-30), Springer

Kay, J., & Lum, A. (2004) Ontologies for Scrutable Learner Modeling in Adaptive E-Learning. In Aroyo, L., Tasso, C. (Eds.) *Proc. of Workshop on Application of Semantic Web Technologies for Adaptive Educational Hypermedia.* Technische University Eindhoven

Lin, W., Alvarez, S. A., & Ruiz, C. (2002). Efficient adaptive-support association rule mining for recommender systems. *Data Mining and Knowledge Discovery,* 6(2002) 83–105.

Micarelli, A., Sciarrone, F., & Marinilli, M. (2007). Web document modeling. In Brusilovsky, P., Kobsa, A., Nejdl, W. (Eds.), *The Adaptive Web: Methods and Strategies of Web Personalization.* LNCS 4321. Springer

Middleton, S. E., Shadbolt, N. R., De Roure, D. C. (2004). Ontological User profiling in Recommender Systems, *ACM Transactions on Information Systems, 22*(1), 54-88.

Mobasher, B. (2007).Data Mining for Web Personalization. In Brusilovsky, P., Kobsa, A., Nejdl, W. (Eds.), *The Adaptive Web: Methods and Strategies of Web Personalization.* LNCS. Springer

Noda, K. (2006). Towards a Representational Model of Evaluation Ontology, *Proceedings of International Symposium on Large Scale Knowledge Resources: LKR2006,* 159-160.

Ostyn, C., & Lewis, S. (Eds.) (2007). IEEE 1484.20.1 - Draft Standard for Learning Technology. Data Model for Reusable Competency Definitions, IEEE Computer Society Press, Piscataway, NJ, USA

Pazzani, M. J. (1999). A Framework for Collaborative, Content-Based and Demographic Filtering. *AI Review, 13*(5/6), 393-408.

Resnick, P., Iacovou, N., Suchak, M., Bergstrom, P., & Riedl, J. (1994). Grouplens: An Open Architecture for Collaborative Filtering Of Netnews. In *Proceedings of the 1994 ACM conference on Computer supported cooperative work.* Chapel Hill, North Carolina. ACM Press (p. 175-186).

Rich, E. (1978). User modeling via stereotypes. *Cognitive Science, 3,* 329–354.

Schafer, B., Frankowski, D., Herlocker, J., & Sen, S. (2007). Collaborative Filtering Recommender Systems. In: Brusilovsky, P., Kobsa, A., Nejdl, W. (Eds*.), The Adaptive Web: Methods and Strategies of Web Personalization.* LNCS 4321. Springer

Schmidt, A., & Kunzmann, C. (2006). Towards a Human Resource Development Ontology for Combining Competence Management and Technology-Enhanced Workplace Learning, In *Proceedings of OntoContent 2006 ,* LNCS, Springer

Song, X., Tseng, L., Lin, C-Y., & Sun, M-T. (2005). ExpertiseNet: Relational and Evolutionary Expert Modeling, *LNCS 3538,* Springer

Trichet, F., & Leclere, M. (2003). A Framework for building competency-based systems. In N. Zhong et al. (Eds.): *ISMIS 2003,* LNAI 2871, 633–639, Springer.

Tsiriga, V., & Virvou, M. (2003) Modelling the student to individualise tutoring in a web-based ICALL, *International Journal of Continuing Engineering Education and Life Long Learning,* Vol 13; Part 3/4, pp. 350-365, Switzerland, ISSN 1560-4624

Witten, I. H., & Frank, E. (2000). Weka. Machine Learning Algorithms in Java. In *Data Mining: Practical Machine Learning. Tools and Techniques with Java Implementations*, Morgan Kaufmann Publishers

Section III
Improved User Modeling:
Application of CSIRA

Chapter VII
Combining Relevance Information in a Synchronous Collaborative Information Retrieval Environment

Colum Foley
Dublin City University, Ireland

Alan F. Smeaton
Dublin City University, Ireland

Gareth J. F. Jones
Dublin City University, Ireland

ABSTRACT

*Traditionally information retrieval (IR) research has focussed on a single user interaction modality, where a user searches to satisfy an information need. Recent advances in both Web technologies, such as the sociable Web of Web 2.0, and computer hardware, such as tabletop interface devices, have enabled multiple users to collaborate on many computer-related tasks. Due to these advances there is an increasing need to support two or more users searching together at the same time, in order to satisfy a shared information need, which we refer to as **Synchronous Collaborative Information Retrieval**. **Synchronous Collaborative Information Retrieval** (SCIR) represents a significant paradigmatic shift from traditional IR systems. In order to support an effective SCIR search, new techniques are required to coordinate users' activities. In this chapter we explore the effectiveness of a sharing of knowledge policy on a collaborating group. **Sharing of knowledge** refers to the process of passing relevance information across users, if one user finds items of relevance to the search task then the group should benefit in the form of improved ranked lists returned to each searcher. In order to evaluate the proposed techniques the* *authors simulate two users searching together through an incremental feedback system. The simulation assumes that users decide on an initial query with which to begin the collaborative search and proceed through the search by providing relevance judgments to the system and receiving a new ranked list. In order to populate these simulations we extract data from the interaction logs of various experimental IR systems from previous Text REtrieval Conference (TREC) workshops.*

INTRODUCTION

The phrase *"Collaborative Information Retrieval"* has been used in the past to refer to many different technologies which support collaboration in the information retrieval (IR) process. Much of the early work in collaborative information retrieval has been concerned with asynchronous, remote collaboration via the reuse of previous search results and processes in collaborative filtering systems, collaborative re-ranking, and collaborative footprinting systems. Asynchronous collaborative information retrieval supports a passive, implicit form of collaboration where the focus is to improve the search process for *an individual*.

Synchronous collaborative information retrieval (SCIR) is an emerging form of collaborative IR in which *a group* of two or more users are explicitly collaborating in a synchronised manner in order to satisfy a shared information need. The motivation behind these systems is related to both the ever-growing corpus of human knowledge on the web, the improvement of social awareness on the internet today, and the development of novel computer interface devices. SCIR systems represent a significant paradigmatic shift in focus and motivation compared with traditional IR systems and asynchronous collaborative IR systems. The development of new IR techniques is needed to exploit this. In order for collaborative IR to be effective there needs to be both an appropriate *division of labour*, and an effective *sharing of knowledge* across collaborating searchers (Zeballos, 1998; Foley et al., 2006). **Division of labour** enables each collaborating group member to ex-

plore a subset of a document collection in order to reduce the redundancy associated with multiple people viewing the same documents. **Sharing of knowledge** enables collaborating users to benefit from the knowledge of their collaborators. Early SCIR systems provided various awareness cues such as chat windows, shared whiteboards and shared bookmarks. By providing these cues, these systems enabled the collaborating searchers to coordinate their activities in order to achieve a division of labour and sharing of knowledge. However, coordinating activities amongst users can be troublesome, requiring too much cognitive load (Adcock et al., 2007).

Recently we have seen systems to support a more system-mediated division of labour by dividing the results of a search query amongst searchers (Morris and Horvitz, 2007), or defining searcher roles (Adcock et al., 2007). However, there has been no work to date which addresses the system-mediated sharing of knowledge across collaborating searchers. In this chapter we introduce our techniques to allow for effective system-mediated sharing of knowledge. We evaluate how a sharing of knowledge policy affects the performance of a group of users searching together collaboratively. But first, in the next section, we provide a comprehensive account of work to date in synchronous collaborative information retrieval.

SYNCHRONOUS COLLABORATIVE INFORMATION RETRIEVAL

Information retrieval (IR), as defined by Baeza-Yates and Ribeiro-Neto (1999), is concerned with the representation, storage, organisation of and access to information items. The purpose of an IR system is to satisfy an information need.

Synchronous collaborative information retrieval (SCIR) systems are concerned with the realtime, explicit, collaboration which occurs when multiple users search together to satisfy a shared information need; these systems represent a significant paradigmatic shift in IR systems from an individual focus to a group focus. As such these systems represent a more explicit, active form of collaboration, where users are aware that they are collaborating with others towards a common, and usually explicitly stated, goal. This collaboration can take place either remotely, or, in a co-located setting. These systems have gained in popularity and now with the ever-growing popularity of the social web (or *Web 2.0*), support for explicit, synchronous collaborative information retrieval is becoming more important than ever.

The benefit of allowing multiple users to search together in order to satisfy a shared information need is that it can allow for a *division of labour* and a *sharing of knowledge* across a collaborating group. **Division of labour** means that each member of a collaborating group can explore a subset of information thereby reducing the redundancy associated with two or more people viewing the same documents, and improving the efficiency of a search. Some methods proposed here include increasing the awareness amongst users of each collaborative searcher's progress (Diamadis and Polyzos, 2004; Smeaton et al., 2006) or system-mediated splitting of a task (Foley et al., 2006; Adcock et al., 2007). The ability to effectively share information is the foundation of any group activity (Yao et al., 1999). **Sharing of knowledge** across group members involved in a collaborative search can occur by providing awareness of other searchers' progress through the search, and this can be achieved by enabling direct chat facilities (Gianoutsos and Grundy, 1996; Gross, 1999; Krishnappa, 2005) or group blackboards (Gianoutsos and Grundy, 1996; Cabri

et al., 1999) so that brainstorming activities can be facilitated.

The first examples of SCIR tools were built using a distributed architecture where software enabled communication across groups of remote users. Recently the development of new computing devices has facilitated the development of co-located SCIR tools. We will now outline research to date in each of these areas.

Synchronous Remote Collaborative Information Retrieval

SCIR systems have been developed to enable remote users to search and browse the web together. These systems often require users to log-in to a particular service or may require the use of particular applications in order to facilitate collaboration.

GroupWeb (Greenberg and Roseman, 1996) represents an early collaborative browsing environment and was built upon the GroupKit groupware toolkit (Roseman and Greenberg, 1996). In GroupWeb, several users could log onto a collaborative browsing session and the web browser was used as a group "presentation tool". A master browser (or "presenter") selected a page and this page was displayed to each group member using a form of "What You See Is What I See" (WYSIWIS). The system also supported synchronous scrolling and independent scrolling on a web page and supported the use of telepointers (showing others' mouse pointers on the page) in order to allow users to focus the attention of the group and to enact gestures. GroupWeb provided an annotation window where groups could attach shared annotations to pages when viewing and these annotations could be viewed by all group members. In GroupWeb, group members were tightly coupled. Enabling each user to see the same documents increases awareness amongst group members but can be an inefficient technique for exploring the vastness of the web.

The W4 browser (Gianoutsos and Grundy, 1996) extended the GroupWeb system to allow users to browse the web independently whilst synchronising their work. In W4, a user could view all pages viewed by other users, they could chat with each other, share bookmarks (i.e. documents deemed relevant), and see a shared WYSIWIS white-board to brainstorm. Users could also embed chat sessions, links and annotations directly into a web-page. A similar approach was employed by Cabri et al. (1999), which used a proxy server to record documents viewed by others. These documents were then displayed to each user in a separate browser window. The system also made others aware of these viewed documents by editing the HTML mark-up in pages viewed by each collaborating searcher (links to pages already viewed by other users in a session were indicated using different colours).

The above systems all required users to explicitly log onto a service to support collaborative searching. Systems have been developed in order to make users who are browsing the web aware of others who may be *nearby* in order to facilitate a more spontaneous collaboration. Donath and Robertson (1994) developed a tool which enabled people to see others currently viewing the same web page as themselves. The system also allowed them to interact with these people and coordinate their activities in order to travel around the web as a group. Sidler et al. (1997) extended this approach in order to allow users to identify other searchers within their *neighbourhood* to enable spontaneous collaboration.

SearchTogether (Morris and Horvitz, 2007) was a prototype system which incorporated many synchronous and asynchronous tools to enable a small group of remote users to work together to satisfy a shared information need. SearchTogether was built to support *awareness* of others, *division of labour*, and *persistence* of the search process. Awareness of others was achieved by representing each group member with a screen name and photo. Whenever a team member performed a new search

the query terms were displayed in a list underneath their photo. By clicking on a search query a user could see the results returned for this query, and this reduced the duplication of effort across users. When visiting a page, users could also see which other users had visited that page previously. Users could also provide ratings for pages using a thumbs-up or thumbs down metaphor. Support for division of labour was achieved through an embedded text chat facility, a recommendation mechanism, and a split search and multi-search facility. Using split search a user could divide the results of their search with a collaborating searcher and, using multi-search, a search query could be submitted to different search engines, each associated with different users.

The Adaptive Web Search (AWS) system proposed by Dalal (2007) represented a combination of personalised, social and collaborative search. The system was a type of meta-search system in which users' could search using multiple search engines and maintain a preference vector for a particular engine based on their long and short term search contexts, user goals and geographic location. Users could perform social searching by having their preference vector influenced by others depending on a level of trust.

A commercial application of synchronous collaborative IR is available in the popular Windows Live Messenger, an instant messaging service. During a chat session, users can search together by having the results from a search displayed to each user (Windows Live Messenger, 2007). Netscape Conferencer (Netscape Conferencer, 2001) allows multiple users to browse the web together using WYSIWIS, where one user controls the navigation and chat facilities and whiteboards are implemented to facilitate communication.

Synchronous Co-Located Collaborative Information Retrieval

Recent advances in ubiquitous computing devices such as mobile phones and PDAs have allowed researchers to begin exploring techniques for spontaneous collaborative search.

Maekawa et al. (2006) developed a system for collaborative web browsing on mobile phones and PDAs. In this system a web page was divided into several components and these components were distributed across the devices of collaborating users. WebSplitter (Han et al., 2000) was a similar system for providing partial views to web pages across a number of users and potentially across a number of devices available to a user (e.g. laptop, PDA).

Advances in single display groupware (SDG) technology (Stewart et al., 1999), have enabled the development of collaborative search systems for the co-located environment. The advantages of such systems are that they improve the awareness of collaborating searchers by bringing them together in a face-to-face environment. Increased awareness can enable both a more effective division of labour and a greater sharing of knowledge.

Let's Browse (Lieberman et al., 1999) was a co-located web browsing agent which enabled multiple users standing in front of a screen (projected display onto a wall) to browse the web together based on their user profiles. A user profile in the system consisted of a set of weighted keywords of their interests and was built automatically by extracting keywords from both the user's homepage and those pages around it. Users wore electronic badges so that they could be identified as they approach the screen. A collaborating group of users using Let's Browse were shown a set of recommended links to follow from the current page, ordered by their similarity to the aggregated users' profiles.

The tangible interface system developed by Blackwell et al. (2004), allowed a group of users to perform "Query-By-Argument" whereby a series of physical tokens with RFID transmitters could be arranged on a table to develop a team's query.

The TeamSearch system developed by Morris et al. (2006) enabled a group of users collaborating around an electronic tabletop to sift through a stack of pictures using collaborative Boolean query formulation. The system enabled users to locate relevant pictures from a stack by placing query tokens on special widgets which corresponded to predefined metadata categories for the images.

Físchlár-DiamondTouch (shown in Figure 1) was a multi-user video search application devel-

Figure 1. Físchlár-DiamondTouch

oped by the authors and others at the Centre for Digital Video Processing at Dublin City University (Smeaton et al., 2006). Físchlár-DiamondTouch was developed on an interactive table known as DiamondTouch (Dietz and Leigh, 2001) and used the groupware toolkit DiamondSpin (Shen et al., 2004) from Mitsubishi Electric Research Labs (MERL). The system allowed two users to collaborate in a face-to-face manner in order to interact with a state-of-the-art video retrieval application, Físchlár (Smeaton et al., 2001). Users could enter a free text query using an on-screen keyboard. This query was then issued to the search engine and a list of the 20 top ranked keyframes (an image from a video chosen as a representative of a particular video shot) were displayed upon the screen (the most relevant in the middle and decreasing in relevance as the images spiralled out). Keyframes were rotated to the nearest user in order to provide for an implicit division of labour. Two versions of Físchlár-DiamondTouch were evaluated in TRECVid 2005 (Foley et al., 2005), one which provided for increased awareness amongst users and one which was designed for improved group efficiency. This represented the first time any group had performed collaborative search in any TREC or TRECVid workshop.

In an effort to improve collaborative search effectiveness through "algorithmically-mediated collaboration", the "Cerchiamo" system was developed by the FXPAL TRECVid team (Adcock et al., 2007). Cerchiamo was designed to support two users working together to find relevant shots of videos. Two users worked under predefined roles of "prospector" and "miner". The role of the prospector was to locate avenues for further exploration, while the role of the miner was to explore these avenues. The system used information from users' interactions to determine the next shots to display on-screen and provide a list of suggested query terms.

In this section we have described work to date in synchronous collaborative information retrieval (SCIR). Early SCIR systems focussed on providing tools to increase awareness across collaborating users. Research has suggested that the performance of a group searching in a SCIR system can be improved by allowing for a division of labour and sharing of knowledge. In early SCIR systems, the onus for coordinating the group's activities was placed on the users. Work has been done into allowing for a system-mediated division of labour, but no work, as yet, has attempted to implement a system-mediated sharing of knowledge in order to improve the quality of ranked lists returned to users searching together in an adhoc search task.

SHARING OF KNOWLEDGE IN SYNCHRONOUS COLLABORATIVE INFORMATION RETRIEVAL

Suppose two users are searching together to satisfy a shared information need using a state-of-the-art SCIR system as described in the previous section. When two or more users come together in an SCIR environment, there are several ways in which to initiate the collaborative search. For example, users may each decide to formulate their own search query, or users may decide on a shared, group query. Having generated an initial ranked list for an SCIR search, either as a result of a shared query or a separate query for each collaborator, these results can be divided across users using a simple *round-robin* strategy. Where, for a collaborative search involving two users with a shared initial query, user 1 would receive the first document in the ranked list, user 2 would receive the second ranked document, user 1 the third, and so on until all results are distributed across the users. This is the approach proposed by Morris and Horvitz (2007). As users examine documents and find those relevant to the search, they may save them to a "bookmarked" area. What these users are doing is providing *explicit relevance judgments* to the search engine. In traditional, single-user IR, these relevance judgments are often used in a process known as *relevance feedback* to improve the quality of a user's query by reformulating it based on this relevance information. Over a number of relevance feedback iterations, an IR system can build a short term profile of the user's information need. At present, SCIR systems do not use this new relevance information directly in the search process to re-formulate a user's query, instead it is used simply as a bookmark and therefore we believe that this information is wasted. No attempt is made to utilise this relevance information during the course of an SCIR search to improve the performance of a collaborating group of users. As a consequence, the collaborating group does not see the benefit of this relevance information in their ranked lists.

Relevance feedback is an IR technique which has been proven to improve the performance of the IR process through incorporating extra relevance information provided by users (in the form of documents identified as relevant by a user) into an automatic query reformulation process. The basic operation of relevance feedback consists of two steps: (1.) query expansion – whereby significant terms from documents judged relevant are identified and appended to the user's original query, and (2.) relevance weighting – which biases weights of each query term based on this relevance information.

If we provided a relevance feedback mechanism in an SCIR system, then when a member of an SCIR group initiates a relevance feedback operation, if their search partner has provided relevance judgments to the system, we could incorporate both users' relevance judgments into the feedback process. This could enable better quality results to be returned to the user. Furthermore such a sharing of knowledge policy could allow users to benefit from the relevance of a document without having to view the contents of the document. It is not clear, however, how multi-user relevance information should be handled in a relevance feedback process.

Collaborative Relevance Feedback

One of the simplest ways to incorporate multi-user relevance information into a feedback process is to assume that one user has provided all the relevance judgments made by all users and then initiate a standard, single-user, relevance feedback process over these documents. There may, however, be occasions where it is desirable to allow for a user-biased combination of multi-user relevance information. Therefore, we will outline how the RF process can be extended to allow for a weighted combination of multi-user relevance information in a *collaborative relevance feedback process*. Combination of evidence is an established research problem in IR (Croft, 2002), in our work we are interested in investigating the combination of multi-user relevance information within the relevance feedback process. In our work we use the probabilistic model for retrieval which is both theoretically motivated, and proven to be successful in controlled TREC experiments first shown in (Robertson et al., 1992). In the probabilistic retrieval model the relevance feedback processes of *Query Expansion* and *Term Reweighting* are treated separately (Robertson, 1990). Figure 2 presents a conceptual overview of the collaborative relevance feedback process for two users are searching together. When the relevance feedback process is initiated, user 1 has provided 3 relevance judgments and user 2 has provided 4. As we can see, we have a choice as to what stage in the relevance feedback process we can combine this information.

In particular we have identified three stages in the process at which we can combine relevance information.

Combining Inputs to the Relevance Feedback Process (A)

The relevance feedback process uses all available relevance information for a term in order to assign it a score for both query expansion and

Figure 2. Combining relevance information, the 3 choices

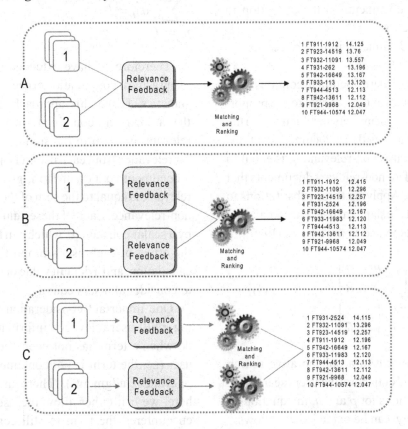

term reweighting. If we have relevance information from multiple co-searchers, combining this information before performing relevance feedback should result in an improved combined measure of relevance for these terms. This is the rationale behind this novel method for combining relevance information, which we refer to as ***partial-user weighting***, as the evidence for relevance or non-relevance of a term is composed of the combined partial evidence from multiple users.

We will now outline the derivation for the partial-user relevance weight and partial-user offer weight. From Robertson and Spärck Jones (1976), we can see that the probability of relevance of a term is defined as:

$$w(i) = \log \frac{p(1-q)}{q(1-p)} \qquad (1)$$

where

p = probability that a document contains term i given that it is relevant

q = probability that a document contains term i given that it is non-relevant

The appropriate substitutions for p and q are the proportions:

$$p = \frac{r_i}{R} \qquad (2)$$

$$q = \frac{n_i - r_i}{N - R} \qquad (3)$$

where

r_i = Number of relevant documents in which term i occurs

R = Number of identified relevant documents
n_i = Number of documents in the collection in which term i occurs
N = Number of documents in the collection

The probability that a document contains term i given that it is relevant, p, is equal to the proportion of all relevant documents in which the term i occurs. The probability that a document contains term i given that it is non-relevant, q, is equal to the proportion of all non-relevant documents that contain the term. Applying these substitutions to equation 1 we get the standard relevance weighting formula (Robertson and Spärck Jones (1976)):

$$rw(i) = log \frac{\left(\frac{r_i}{R}\right)\left(1 - \frac{n_i - r_i}{N - R}\right)}{\left(\frac{n_i - r_i}{N - R}\right)\left(1 - \frac{r_i}{R}\right)} \quad (4)$$

If we assume that in a collaborative search session we have U collaborating users searching. Then the proportions for p and q, in equations 2 and 3 respectively, can be extended as follows:

$$p = \sum_{u=0}^{U-1} \alpha_u \frac{r_{ui}}{R_u} \quad (5)$$

$$q = \sum_{u=0}^{U-1} \alpha_u \frac{n_i - r_{ui}}{N - R_u} \quad (6)$$

where

n_i, N are as before
r_{ui} = Number of relevant documents identified by user u in which term i occurs
R_u = Number of relevant documents identified by user u
α_u = Determines the impact of user u's proportions on the final term weight, and

$$\sum_{u=0}^{U-1} \alpha_u = 1$$

Therefore we have extended the proportions using a linear combination of each user's relevance statistics. Using this approach, the probability that a document contains term i, given that it is relevant, is equal to the sum of the proportions for relevance from each user. The probability that a document contains term i, given that it is not relevant, is equal to the sum of the proportions of non-relevance. Each of these values is multiplied by a scalar constant α, which can be used to vary the effect of each user's proportion in the final calculation, and a default value of $\frac{1}{U}$ can be used to consider all users equally.

One important consideration when combining multi-user relevance information is what to do when a term has not been encountered by a user (i.e. the term is not contained in the user's relevance judgments). There are two choices here, we can either allow the user that has not encountered the term to still contribute to the shared weight, or we can choose to assign a weight to a term based solely on the relevance and non-relevance proportions of users that have actually encountered the term.

If we wish to incorporate a user's proportions for a term regardless of whether the term appears in any of the user's relevance judgments, then the term will receive a relevance proportion, p, of 0 ($\frac{0}{R}$) and a non relevance proportion, q, of $\frac{n}{N - R}$, from a user who has not encountered the term (as $r_i = 0$ for that user).

If we do not wish to incorporate a user's proportion for a term, in the case that they have not encountered the term, then the shared relevance and non-relevance proportions of p and q in equation 5 and equation 6 respectively will only be composed of the proportions from users who have encountered the term.

Applying the extended proportions of p and q, in equations 5 and 6 respectively, to the probability of relevance from equation 1, results in our *partial-user relevance weight* (*purw*):

$$purw(i) = log \frac{\left(\sum_{u=0}^{U-1} \alpha_u \frac{r_{ui}}{R_u}\right)\left(1 - \sum_{u=0}^{U-1} \alpha_u \frac{n_i - r_{ui}}{N - R_u}\right)}{\left(\sum_{u=0}^{U-1} \alpha_u \frac{n_i - r_{ui}}{N - R_u}\right)\left(1 - \sum_{u=0}^{U-1} \alpha_u \frac{r_{ui}}{R_u}\right)} \qquad (7)$$

For practical implementation of the standard relevance weighting formula (equation 4), and to limit the errors associated with zeros such as dividing by zero, a simple extension is commonly used that adds a constant to the values in the proportions. Applying the proportions suggested in Robertson and Spärck Jones (1976), known as the Jeffrey prior, to equation 7, results in:

$$purw(i) = log \frac{\left(\sum_{u=0}^{U-1} \alpha_u \frac{r_{ui} + 0.5}{R_u + 1}\right)\left(1 - \sum_{u=0}^{U-1} \alpha_u \frac{n_i - r_{ui} + 0.5}{N - R_u + 1}\right)}{\left(\sum_{u=0}^{U-1} \alpha_u \frac{n_i - r_{ui} + 0.5}{N - R_u + 1}\right)\left(1 - \sum_{u=0}^{U-1} \alpha_u \frac{r_{ui} + 0.5}{R_u + 1}\right)} \qquad (8)$$

So far we have shown how the partial-user method can be applied to the standard relevance weighting formula which is used for reweighting terms in the relevance feedback process. Now we will consider applying the scheme to the offer weighting formula (Robertson (1990)), which is used to rank terms for query expansion:

$$ow_i = r_i \times rw_i \qquad (9)$$

Using a linear combination approach the r_i value in equation 9, can be extended to include a weighted combination of each collaborating user's r_i value, to produce a *partial-user offer weight* (*puow*):

$$puow(i) = \left(\sum_{u=0}^{U-1} \alpha_u r_{ui} \times purw(i)\right) \qquad (10)$$

where

α_u = Determines the impact of each user's r_i value on the final weight, and

$$\sum_{u=0}^{U-1} \alpha_u = 1$$

Combining Outputs of the Relevance Feedback Process (B)

This method of combination operates at a higher level of granularity than the previous method by treating the relevance process as a black box. In this method, for each user, relevance weighting and offer weighting are calculated separately using only a searcher's own relevance statistics (i.e. terms from documents identified as relevant by the user and their distribution in these relevant documents). The outputs from these processes (i.e. the scores) are combined to produce a combined weight. Combination is therefore performed at a later stage in the relevance feedback process than the method proposed in the previous section.

For relevance weighting, we calculate the combined relevance weight (*crw*) using a linear combination of relevance weight scores from all users:

$$crw(i) = \sum_{u=0}^{U-1} \alpha_u \times rw_{ui} \qquad (11)$$

For offer weighting we can follow the same approach, by calculating the offer weight separately for each user and then combining afterwards to produce a combined offer weight (*cow*):

$$cow(i) = \sum_{u=0}^{U-1} \alpha_u \times ow_{ui} \qquad (12)$$

where

α_u = determines the impact of each user's contribution on the final score, and

$$\sum_{u=0}^{U-1} \alpha_u = 1$$

As with the partial-user method, we can either include or leave-out a user's contribution to either the combined relevance weight or combined offer weight if they have not encountered the term in their own set of relevance judgments. Once again the α variable can be used to control the impact of each user's evidence on the combination and a default value can be set to $\frac{1}{U}$ for all users to give all users the same weighting.

Combining Outputs of the Ranking Process (C)

This stage of combination operates at a higher level of granularity than either of the previous methods, as here we treat the entire search engine as a black box and combination is performed at the ranked list or document level.

Combining the outputs from multiple ranking algorithms has become a standard method for improving the performance of IR systems' ranking (Croft, 2002).

In order to produce a combined ranked list, a reformulated query is generated for each collaborating user, based on their own relevance information, and these relevance feedback queries are then submitted to the search engine in order to produce separate ranked lists, one for each user. These ranked lists are then combined in order to produce a combined ranked list. Combination at the document level can be achieved, as before, by performing a linear combination of the document scores produced by the search engine, to arrive at a combined document score (*cds*):

$$cds(d,q) = \sum_{u=0}^{U-1} \alpha_u \times s_{ud} \qquad (13)$$

where

s_{ud} = the relevance score for document d in relation to user u's query
α_u = determines the impact of each user's contribution on the final document score, and

$$\sum_{u=0}^{U-1} \alpha_u = 1$$

In this section we have outlined how a system-mediated sharing of knowledge can be achieved in an SCIR search, by incorporating each group member's relevance judgments into a collaborative relevance feedback process. We have proposed three methods by which the standard relevance feedback formula can be extended into a collaborative relevance feedback process. Evaluating these techniques will allow us to establish how a sharing of knowledge policy, via collaborative relevance feedback, impacts on the performance of a collaborating group. In the next section we will outline how we plan to evaluate these techniques.

Experimental Setup

In this chapter, we are evaluating many different approaches to combining relevance information. It would have been infeasible to evaluate each of these approaches thoroughly using real user experiments. Instead, by using *simulations* we can evaluate our proposed approaches effectively while ensuring that our evaluations are realistic.

Requirements Analysis

Previous IR experiments that have used user simulations have focussed on a single user's interactions with an IR system. Here we are attempting to simulate a synchronous collaborative IR environment, a dynamic, collaborative simulation. We are conscious that the simulation should be realistic of future systems in any device or interface which could support SCIR search, i.e. desktop search, tabletop search, PDA or Apple iPhone search, etc.

Our **SCIR simulations** will simulate a search involving *two* collaborating users. Recent studies of the collaborative nature of a search task have shown how the majority of synchronous collaborative search sessions involve a collaborating group of size two (Morris and Horvitz, 2007), and therefore we believe that this group size is the most appropriate to model, though the techniques proposed could scale to larger groups.

One of the important considerations for any SCIR system is how to begin a collaborative search. For the experiments reported here the search assumes that one initial query has been formulated. In a real system, this query could be formulated by one user or by both users collaboratively. By only requiring one query from the set of users, we can limit the interactions needed by users with the search system. Although querying may be easy using the standard keyboard and mouse combination, interactions with phones or other handheld devices can be difficult.

In these experiments we are interested in evaluating how a system-mediated sharing of knowledge policy can operate alongside an explicit division of labour policy. Therefore, the simulated SCIR system will implement a system-mediated division of labour where the results returned to a searcher at any point in the search are automatically filtered in order to remove:

1. Documents seen by their search partner.
2. Documents assumed seen by their search partner. These are documents that are in their search partner's current ranked list.

In our simulations, users do not manually reformulate their queries during the search, instead, in order to receive new ranked lists during the search, users use a simple relevance feedback mechanism. In any SCIR search, users may provide multiple relevance assessments over the course of the search session, and therefore we have a choice as to when to initiate a relevance feedback operation. For example, we could choose to perform feedback after a user provides a relevance judgment, or after the user has provided a certain number of relevance judgments. For the purposes of the experiments reported in this chapter, our SCIR simulations operate by initiating a relevance feedback operation for a user each time they provide a relevance judgment, thereby returning a new ranked list of documents to the user. This approach is known as *Incremental Relevance Feedback*, a method first proposed by Aalbersberg (1992). Using the Incremental RF approach, a user is provided with a new ranked list of documents after each relevance judgment, rather than accumulating a series of relevance judgments together and issuing them in batch to the RF process. This can enable users to benefit immediately from their relevance judgments. Furthermore, studies have shown that applying feedback after only one or two relevant documents have been identified can substantially improve performance over an initial query (Spärck Jones, 1997).

Another choice for any SCIR system, related to feedback granularity, is whether to present a user with a new ranked list only when they perform feedback themselves or when they *or their search partner* provides feedback. Presenting users with a new ranked list when their search partner performs relevance feedback may allow users to benefit more quickly from their partner's relevance judgments. However deployment of such an intensive SCIR system would require designers to develop novel interface techniques to allow for the seamless updating of a user's ranked list. Furthermore, users searching in such an intensive system may suffer from *cognitive overload* by being presented with new ranked lists, seemingly, at random. In this chapter we will evaluate the effects of both of these interaction environments on an SCIR search.

Figure 3, presents a conceptual overview of the SCIR system we will simulate in our evaluations.

Referring to Figure 3, the data required to populate our SCIR simulations is:

- An initial query (Q) – as outlined above, the simulated SCIR session begins with an initial query entered by the set of two users.

- Series of relevance judgments (RJ) – these are explicit indications of relevance made by a user on a particular document.

- Timing information – this represents the time, in seconds, relative to the start of the search session at which relevance judgments were made. This timing information is used to order relevance judgments in an SCIR simulation and allows us to model SCIR sessions in which collaborating searchers are providing relevance information at distinct times and at different rates in the process.

Methodology

In order to populate these simulations we have mined data from previous TREC interactive search experiments. The **Text REtrieval Conference** (TREC) is an annual workshop established in 1992 under the auspices of the National Institute for Standards and Technology (NIST) in an attempt to promote research into IR. For each TREC, a set of tasks or *tracks* are devised, each evaluating different aspects of the retrieval process. The purpose of the **TREC** (Text REtrieval Conference) interactive task is for a searcher to locate documents of relevance to a stated information need (a search "topic") using a search engine and to save them. For the interactive track at TREC 6 – TREC 8 (1997-1999), each participating group that submitted results for evaluation was required to also include *rich format data* with their submission. This data consisted of transcripts of a searcher's significant events during a search, such as their initial query, the documents saved (i.e. relevance judgments), and their timing information. For our simulations we extracted data from several groups' submissions to TREC 6 – TREC 8. Unfortunately, it was not possible to extract data for our simulations from all participating groups' submissions to these

Figure 3. A simulated SCIR session

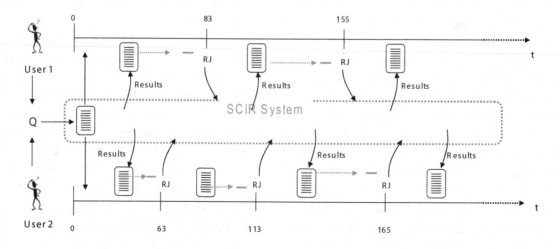

TRECs. This was due to a variety of reasons but typically some groups had either failed to submit rich format data or the data they submitted was not complete as it lacked some of the data needed to build our simulations. In our simulations we used this extracted data to simulate two users, who originally searched the topic separately as part of their group's submission, searching together with an SCIR system.

Figure 4 shows a conceptual overview of a simulated SCIR session involving two users whose rich format data was extracted from TREC data, searching on a TREC topic entitled "Hubble Telescope Achievements". From Figure 4, we can see that the search begins with the group query "positive achievements hubble telescope data", which is the concatenation of both users' original queries. By the time user 1 provides their first relevance judgment on document *FT921-7107*, user 2 has already provided a relevance judgment, on document *FT944-128*. By the time user 2 makes their second relevance judgment on document *FT924-286*, user 1 has made their first relevance judgment on *FT921-7107*.

By extracting rich format data associated with different users' interactions on a search topic, we can acquire multiple heterogeneous simulations, where the data populating our simulations is from

real users searching to satisfy the same information need on a standardised corpus. There were a total of 20 search topics used in these TREC workshops, with varying degrees of difficulty and therefore our simulations were evaluated across these 20 topics.

Relevance Judgments

The **SCIR simulations** proposed thus far are based on taking *static* rich format data, which records a user's previous interactions with a particular search engine, and imposing our SCIR simulated environment on this data. By imposing our own simulated environment on this rich format data, we cannot assume that users would have saved the same documents as that they did during their original search, as recorded in the rich format data. Before we can proceed with our simulations we need to replace these static relevance judgments with relevance judgments based on the ranked lists that simulated users are presented with. Although in any simulation we can never predict, with absolute certainty, the actions of a user, in the simulations used in our experiments it is important that the relevance judgments are a reasonable approximation of real user behaviour. Our solution is to simulate the user providing a

Figure 4. Conceptual overview of two searchers searching together

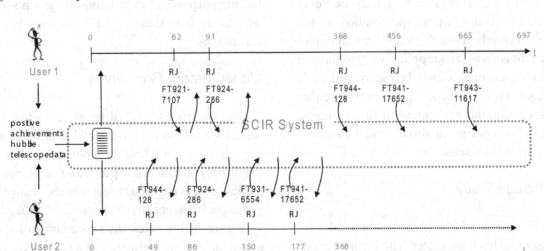

relevance judgment on the first relevant document, i.e. highest ranked, on their current ranked list, where the relevance of the documents is judged according to the TREC relevance assessments for the topic ("qrels").

Although we can never be fully certain that a user will always save the *first* relevant document that they encounter on a ranked list (i.e. rather than the second or third), recent studies have shown that users tend to examine search results from top to bottom, "deciding to click each result before moving to the next" (Craswell et al., 2008). Therefore we believe that this approximation of a real user's action is reasonable.

Before finalising our simulations, we also need to enforce an upper limit on the number of documents a user will examine in order to locate a document on which to provide a relevance judgment. For example, it would be unreasonable to assume that a user would look down as far as rank *900* in the ranked list in order to find a relevant document. Instead, we limit the number of documents that a simulated user will examine to the top 30 documents in their ranked list. Although in a real world system, users may be willing to examine more or less documents according to the device they are using for searching, we feel that 30 is a reasonable figure to assume users will examine in any SCIR search.

After performing relevance feedback, the relevance judgments made by a user are never returned to them again for the duration of that search. As our baseline SCIR system will implement a division of labour policy, we also remove these *seen* documents from their search partner's subsequent list. Furthermore, as we assume that users will examine a maximum of 30 documents, our baseline system will also remove these documents from their search partner's ranked list.

Evaluation Metric

At each stage in an SCIR session, each collaborating user will have associated with them a ranked list of documents. This list could have been returned to the user either as a result of the initial query or after performing relevance feedback. In traditional, single-user IR the accuracy of each individual searcher's ranked lists can be evaluated using standard IR measurements such as average precision (AP), a measure which favours systems that rank relevant documents higher in a returned ranked list of documents. In our work we are concerned with the performance of a *group* of users, and therefore we need to be able to assign a score to the collaborating group at any particular point in the search process. What we need is a measure which captures the quality and diversity across collaborating users' ranked lists. Our solution is to calculate the *total number of unique relevant documents across user's ranked lists* at a certain cut-off and use this figure as our **group score**. In our simulations as we assume that users will examine the top 30 documents in the ranked list, our measure of quality is taken at a cut-off of 30 documents from each users list (i.e. a total of 60 documents). This performance measure will enable us to capture both the quality and diversity across collaborating users' ranked lists and in particular the parts of the list that they will examine.

As described earlier, in our simulations, before returning a new list to a searcher, all relevance judgments made by the searcher are removed. For the purposes of calculating the group score we also include these saved documents in the calculation.

Measurement Granularity

In our simulations of SCIR search, a user is presented with a new ranked list of documents each time they make a relevance judgment. Taking a measurement of the group performance after each of these events allows us to capture the change in group performance over the course of a search.

Figure 5 illustrates the procedure followed to calculate the performance of a group over the duration of an SCIR simulation involving two collaborating users. The SCIR simulation begins with a shared query, at this point we measure the total number of relevant documents in the top 60 positions of this list (top 30 for each user). As this figure represents the initial group score before any relevance feedback is provided to the system, it is plotted at position 0 on the x-axis of the graph at the bottom of Figure 5. The first relevance feedback iteration is initiated after user 2 provides a relevance judgment after 63 seconds. At this point, user 2's current list is updated as a result of a feedback iteration, however user 1 is still viewing the results of the initial query. We calculate

the group score at this point by counting the total number of unique relevant documents across these two ranked lists (labelled "GS") including the one relevance judgment made. As this is the first relevance feedback iteration in the SCIR session, the AP for this merged list is plotted at position 1 on the graph. The measurement proceeds in this manner, by calculating the number of unique relevant documents across each user's current ranked list after each relevance judgment, these figures are plotted after each relevance feedback iteration in order to show the group's performance over the course of the entire search.

Figure 5. Measurement granularity used in experiments

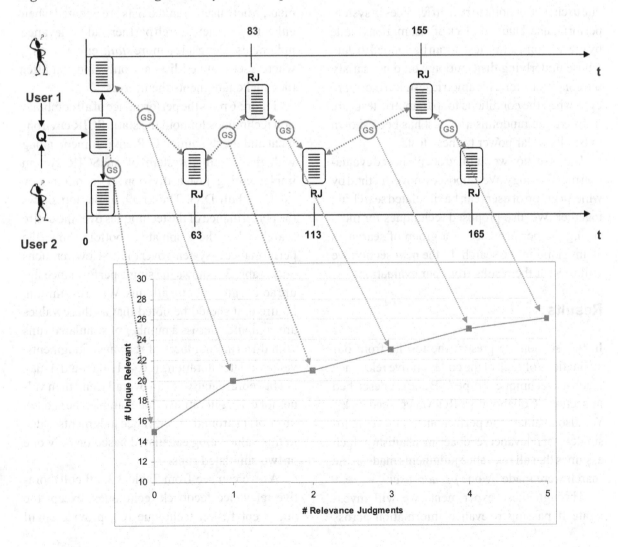

From this graph, we can also generate a single performance figure for the entire search, by averaging the group score after the initial query and each subsequent feedback iteration.

Significance Testing

We will use this single performance figure in order to test for significance in our results. In this chapter we use randomisation testing (Kempthorne and Doerfler, 1969), a non-parametric significance test, to test for statistical significance and use a significance threshold of $p < 0.05$. All results with p values less than this threshold are considered as *significant*. These tests will allow us to understand whether observed differences in performance are due to chance or point to real differences in system performance. Due to the lack of assumptions made by the randomisation test, it can be applied to data whose underlying distribution would not satisfy the conditions for a parametric test. Furthermore even when the conditions for parametric tests are justified, the randomisation test has been shown to be of similar power to these tests.

In this section we outlined our proposed evaluation methodology. We proposed a novel method by which a group of users can be simulated searching together. We also proposed techniques for measuring the performance of a group of searchers at any point in the search. In the next section we will present the results from our evaluation.

Results

In this section we present the results from our evaluations of each of the collaborative relevance feedback techniques (Type A, B and C), described in section "Collaborative Relevance Feedback". We also evaluate the performance of a standard single-user relevance feedback mechanism, which assumes that all relevance judgments made in the search were made by one *pseudo-user*.

Through these experiments we will investigate if passing relevance information across searchers in the feedback process can improve an SCIR search over a baseline SCIR system that implements just a division of labour policy. For both the partial-user (A) and combined weighting technique (B), we will run two variations of the technique, one which allows a user who has not encountered a term in their relevance judgments to contribute to its relevance and offer weight (*Contr*), and another which only considers the weighting for a term from the user that has encountered (*No Contr*).

As outlined in the previous section, an important consideration for any SCIR system is when to provide users with the relevance information from their search partner. In these experiments, we evaluated both a *dynamic* intensive environment, where users' ranked lists are updated when either they or their search partner make relevance judgments, alongside a more *static* environment, where users ranked lists are only updated after they make judgments themselves.

Figure 6 plots the performance of all combination techniques for both the static SCIR environment and the dynamic SCIR environment, along with the baseline system of an SCIR system implementing just a division of labour policy (SCIR + Full Div). The graph at the top shows the performance of the techniques over the entire search, while the graph at the bottom shows the performance of systems over the first few iterations only. Table 3.3 shows the single performance figure across all topics for all runs. When examining Figure 6, it should be noted that as these values are computed across a number of simulated runs with differing numbers of relevance judgments, values at later iterations (i.e. > 11 on x-axis) may not be representative of an overall trend than values for earlier iterations. For example, the sudden drop-off at around 35 relevance judgments is due to this value being calculated based on only one or two simulated runs.

As we can see from Table 3.3, all collaborative relevance feedback techniques, except the document fusion technique (C), provide small improvements in performance over the SCIR + Full Div system. With the best performing system, the dynamic partial user (A) no contr technique, providing a 1.5% improvement. Running significance testing over the single performance figures, however, reveals no significant difference between any SCIR system implementing a collaborative relevance feedback process for either feedback environment (i.e. static or dynamic), and the SCIR system with no combination of relevance information (SCIR + Full Div). When we relax the significance threshold, we find in the static environment, that the combined weighting (contr) (B) method and the pseudo user method outperform the SCIR + Full Div system at significance values of $p = 0.165$ and $p = 0.186$ respectively. While in the dynamic environment, the partial user (no contr) (A) and combined weighting (B) technique outperform the SCIR + Full Div system at significance values of $p = 0.186$, and $p = 0.169$ respectively.

Comparing the performance across collaborative RF techniques from Figure 6 and Table 3.3, it does appear that the document fusion technique for both the static and dynamic environments does not perform as well as the term-based techniques. Significance tests reveal that the dynamic collaborative RF techniques of pseudo user, partial-user (A), and combined weighting (B) all significantly outperform the dynamic document fusion technique (C). However, no difference could be found at the significance threshold between any static term-based technique and the static document fusion technique. When we relax our significance threshold to a threshold of $p < 0.1$, we do find that the techniques of pseudo user, partial-user, and combined weighting perform better than the static document fusion technique. Although not strictly significant according to our threshold, these p values, suggest that the results are unlikely due to chance.

Comparing the overall performance of the contribution versus no contribution techniques for both partial-user (A) and combined weighting (B), we find no significant difference.

Examining the bottom graph in Figure 6, we can see that the combination of relevance information techniques do provide a more substantive increase in performance over the SCIR system with just a division of labour for the first few iterations. Our significance tests confirm that for iterations 2 - 5 all collaborative RF techniques, for both static and dynamic environments, significantly outperform the SCIR system with full division. With the best performing system, the dynamic combined weighting no contr technique (B) providing a 4.8% improvement over the SCIR + Full Div system for these iterations.

Next we compare the performance of static versus dynamic feedback environments. From Figure 6 and Table 3.3, it appears that the SCIR systems operating in a dynamic feedback environment provide a modest increase in performance over their static counterparts. Our significance tests reveal that only the partial-user technique (A) shows any significant difference between the running of the technique in static versus dynamic mode and no significant improvement could be found between any dynamic collaborative relevance feedback technique and the static combined weighting technique.

Discussion

We explored the effects of a collaborative relevance feedback technique operating alongside an explicit division of labour policy in a synchronous collaborative information retrieval system. We hypothesised that by incorporating each user's relevance information into a collaborative relevance feedback mechanism, the ranked lists returned to the searchers could be improved.

Firstly, comparing the performance of the collaborative relevance feedback techniques, we found that the term-based techniques of pseudo-user, partial user and combined weighting all outperform the document fusion technique. However no significant difference could be found at a significance threshold of $p < 0.05$. When we

Figure 6. Comparison of collaborative relevance feedback techniques and baseline division of labour system across all topics

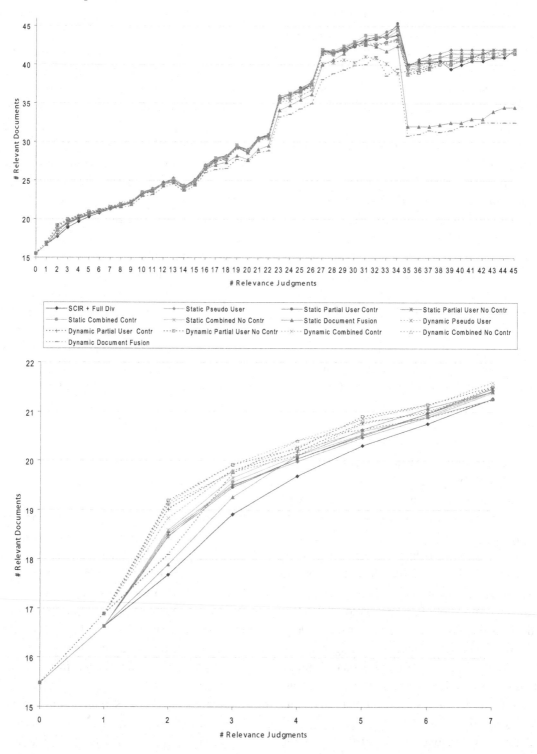

Table 3.3. Single performance figure comparison of collaborative relevance feedback techniques and baseline division of labour system across all topics

Topic #	SCIR + Full Div	Static Pseudo User	Static Partial User Contr	Static Partial User No Contr	Static Combined Contr	Static Combined No Contr	Static Document Fusion	Dynamic Pseudo User	Dynamic Partial User Contr	Dynamic Partial User No Contr	Dynamic Combined Contr	Dynamic Combined No Contr	Dynamic Document Fusion
303	6.00	6.00	6.00	6.00	6.00	6.00	6.00	6.00	6.00	6.00	6.00	6.00	6.00
307	35.75	35.92	36.32	36.32	36.17	36.46	35.37	35.90	36.42	36.67	36.55	36.41	35.88
322	2.99	2.90	2.90	2.90	2.90	2.90	2.99	2.97	2.97	2.99	2.98	3.01	3.07
326	35.43	34.64	34.70	34.74	34.63	34.60	35.27	35.20	35.16	35.26	35.09	35.34	35.59
339	5.93	5.94	5.94	5.94	5.94	5.95	5.94	5.93	5.93	5.93	5.94	5.94	5.93
347	25.69	26.29	26.04	26.02	26.11	25.99	26.00	26.01	26.10	26.10	26.05	25.89	26.26
352	31.88	34.51	34.83	34.89	34.40	34.62	33.90	36.64	36.39	36.89	36.18	36.72	34.91
353	30.82	31.03	30.66	30.68	30.80	31.27	30.91	31.71	31.40	31.63	31.52	32.01	30.87
357	28.69	24.84	24.74	24.80	25.20	24.65	25.73	24.26	24.18	24.22	25.14	24.28	24.83
362	2.96	2.96	2.96	2.96	2.96	2.96	2.96	2.96	2.96	2.96	2.96	2.96	2.96
365	10.97	10.97	10.97	10.97	10.97	10.97	10.97	10.97	10.97	10.97	10.97	10.97	10.97
366	17.98	17.54	17.91	17.96	17.97	18.03	17.12	17.17	17.47	17.48	17.38	17.56	16.05
387	8.99	9.15	9.13	9.15	9.13	9.16	9.03	9.15	9.15	9.13	9.11	9.08	9.03
392	31.10	32.18	32.19	32.26	32.00	32.07	31.70	31.85	32.44	32.38	32.38	32.44	31.64
408	15.67	15.37	15.53	15.02	15.52	14.75	15.47	15.01	15.25	14.68	15.24	14.47	15.24
414	9.63	9.67	9.56	9.61	9.59	9.59	9.54	9.42	9.36	9.34	9.23	9.22	9.40
428	25.80	26.26	26.22	26.39	26.43	26.71	25.49	26.17	25.67	26.01	25.86	26.17	25.00
431	29.77	29.93	29.51	29.47	29.90	29.90	26.78	29.17	29.18	29.45	29.03	29.21	24.90
438	31.87	32.35	32.25	32.23	32.21	32.20	32.38	32.73	32.68	32.77	32.85	33.07	32.84
446	29.79	30.95	30.56	30.61	30.47	30.58	30.72	31.35	30.90	31.19	30.85	31.10	30.45
Overall	20.79	20.97	20.95	20.95	20.97	20.97	20.71	21.03	21.03	21.10	21.07	21.09	20.59

relax the threshold we do find that all term-based techniques outperform the document fusion technique. These results suggest that for both the dynamic and static environments a term-based technique can outperform the document based fusion technique.

Over the entire search, no significant differences could be found across term-based techniques. In particular the collaborative techniques of partial user and combined weighting perform similarly to the standard single user (pseudo-user) method.

Our results show small improvements can be made over some techniques by implementing an intensive, dynamic environment. However due to the slenderness of these differences and the fact that not all static techniques can be significantly improved upon, it may not be worthwhile implementing such a policy due to the discussed difficulties that such an environment presents for both the system designer and the user.

Our results show that over the entire search, the collaborative relevance feedback techniques

do provide modest increases in performance over the SCIR system with just a division of labour. Although at the significance threshold of $p < 0.05$ no significance can be found, improvements could be found at lower significance thresholds. However when we examine the performance of the group over the first few iterations of feedback, we do find that all the collaborative relevance feedback techniques in both the static and dynamic environments significantly improve the performance over the SCIR + Full Div system. This result is interesting, and suggests that although users may benefit from gaining relevance judgments from their search partner early in the search, that after a number of iterations this benefit is reduced.

We believe that the collaborative relevance feedback process of aggregating relevance information is causing users' ranked lists to become too similar. Although, by implementing the division of labour policy we are ensuring unique documents across the top 30 ranked positions for both users, we feel that the aggregation may be causing a loss of uniqueness across users' lists. In order to

Figure 7. Comparisons of the total amount of unique documents across users' ranked lists for SCIR system with collaborative RF and without, across all topics

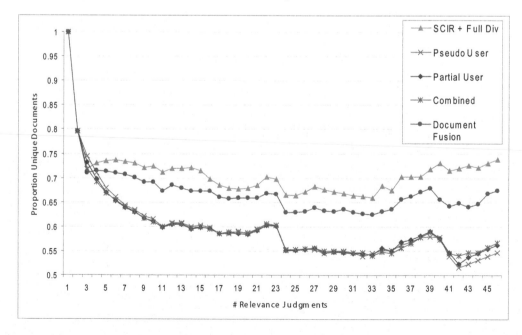

investigate this hypothesis, in Figure 7 we plot the proportion of unique documents across the top 1000 documents of each user's ranked lists for the SCIR system with full division only and all static collaborative relevance feedback techniques.

As we can see, there is a clear difference in the total number of unique relevant documents across users between the collaborative relevance feedback systems and the SCIR + Full Div system. This difference is significant for all techniques and across all topics. This result confirms our hypothesis, that the collaborative relevance feedback process is causing users' ranked lists to become too similar. This finding is intuitive- one of the great advantages of having multiple users tackle a search task is that the task can be divided. By ensuring a complete division of labour, in the SCIR + Full Division system, we are allowing users to make unique relevance judgments, however by implementing a collaborative relevance feedback process in such an environment, where the relevance feedback process for a user uses the relevance information of their search partner, we are causing users to loose this uniqueness. Interestingly however, the gap is less substantial between the SCIR system with full division and the SCIR system implementing document fusion. The fact that the document fusion technique provides substantially more unique documents than all the term-based techniques suggests that the term-based techniques are causing the selection of similar terms for expansion between users. The document fusion technique, allowing for a later stage of combination does not suffer from this problem, however as our results in this section have shown this does not lead to this technique outperforming the others in terms of discovering relevant unique documents. This does not, of course, mean that the introduction of unique documents degrades performance, but that the collaborative relevance feedback mechanism needs to strive to allow for the introduction of more unique relevant documents.

FUTURE TRENDS

Our results have shown that the proposed, term-based, collaborative relevance feedback techniques perform similarly to the standard single-user relevance feedback formula. This result is not surprising as all techniques are attempting to aggregate each user's relevance information. The advantages of the collaborative techniques over the standard single user technique are that they can allow for a user-biased combination (by changing the α value associated with each user), but in these experiments this α has set to 0.5 to consider all users equally. In a real-world system, an SCIR system could exploit this α value in order to allow users to bias the relevance feedback process in favour of their own relevance judgments or in favour of their search partner. Alternatively an SCIR system could use this α value to enable an SCIR system to bias the collaborative relevance feedback process in favour of expert searchers through an *authority weighting* mechanism.

Our results have shown how a collaborative relevance feedback mechanism causes a loss of uniqueness across collaborating users' ranked lists. An alternative way of using multiple users' relevance judgments in an SCIR search is to implement a *Complementary Relevance Feedback* technique. Whereas the collaborative relevance feedback techniques discussed in this chapter attempt to make user's queries more similar, a complementary technique would make them more distinct.

CONCLUSION

Synchronous collaborative information retrieval refers to an explicit and active form of collaboration whereby users are collaborating in realtime to satisfy a shared information need. The benefits that such a system can provide over users searching independently are that it can enable both a *division of labour* and a *sharing of knowledge* across collaborating searchers. Although there has been some work to date into system-mediated division of labour, there has been no work which has investigated how a system-mediated sharing of knowledge can be realised in an adhoc search which can be either remote or co-located, despite the fact that SCIR systems in the literature have allowed users to make explicit relevance judgments in the form of bookmarks.

In this chapter, we have outlined how to make use of these bookmarks in order to benefit the group. We have proposed several techniques by which the standard relevance feedback formula can be extended to allow for relevance information from multiple users to be combined in the process. We have also outlined a novel evaluation methodology by which a group of users, who had previously searched for a search topic independently as part of a TREC interactive track submission, were simulated searching together.

Our results have shown that over an entire SCIR search, the passing of relevance information between users in an SCIR search does not improve the performance of the group. However, over the first few iterations of feedback only, the combination of relevance information does provide a significant improvement. This is an interesting result and encourages us and others to pursue further work in this area.

REFERENCES

Aalbersberg, I. J. (1992). Incremental relevance feedback. In *SIGIR '92: Proceedings of the 15th annual international ACM SIGIR conference on Research and Development in information retrieval*, pages 11–22, Copenhagen, Denmark. ACM Press.

Adcock, J., Pickens, J., Cooper, M., Anthony, L., Chen, F., & Qvarfordt, P. (2007). FXPAL Interactive Search Experiments for TRECVID 2007. In *TRECVid2007 - Text REtrieval Conference TRECVID Workshop*, Gaithersburg, MD, USA.

Baeza-Yates, R., & Ribeiro-Neto, B. (1999). *Modern Information Retrieval*. Addison Wesley.

Blackwell, A. F., Stringer, M., Toye, E. F., & Rode, J. A. (2004). Tangible interface for collaborative information retrieval. In *CHI '04: extended abstracts on Human factors in computing systems*, pages 1473–1476, Vienna, Austria. ACM Press.

Cabri, G., Leonardi, L., & Zambonelli, F. (1999). Supporting Cooperative WWW Browsing: A Proxy-based Approach. In *7th Euromicro Workshop on Parallel and Distributed Processing*, pages 138–145, University of Maderia, Funchal, Portugal. IEEE Press.

Craswell, N., Zoeter, O., Taylor, M., & Ramsey, B. (2008). An experimental comparison of click position-bias models. In *Proceedings of WSDM*, pages 87 – 94, Palo Alto, CA, ACM Press.

Croft, W. B. (2002). *Advances in Information Retrieval*, volume 7 of *The Information Retrieval Series*, chapter Combining Approaches to Information Retrieval, pages 1–36. Springer, Netherlands.

Dalal, M. (2007). Personalized social & real-time collaborative search. In *WWW '07: Proceedings of the 16th international conference on World Wide Web*, pages 1285–1286, Banff, Alberta, Canada. ACM Press.

Diamadis, E. T., & Polyzos, G. C. (2004). Efficient cooperative searching on the web: system design and evaluation. *Int. J. Hum.-Comput. Stud.*, *61*(5), 699–724.

Dietz, P., & Leigh, D. (2001). DiamondTouch: A multi-user touch technology. In *UIST '01: Proceedings of the 14th annual ACM symposium on User interface software and technology*, pages 219–226, Orlando, Florida, USA. ACM Press.

Donath, J. S., & Robertson, N. (1994). The Sociable Web. In *Proceedings of the Second International WWW Conference*, Chicago, IL, USA.

Foley, C., Gurrin, C., Jones, G., Lee, H., Mc Givney, S., O'Connor, N., Sav, S., Smeaton, A. F., & Wilkins., P. (2005). TRECVid 2005 Experiments at Dublin City University. In *TRECVid 2005 - Text REtrieval Conference TRECVID Workshop*, Gaithersburg, MD. National Institute of Standards and Technology, MD USA.

Foley, C., Smeaton, A. F., & Lee., H. (2006). Synchronous collaborative information retrieval with relevance feedback. In *CollaborateCom 2006 - 2nd International Conference on Collaborative Computing: Networking, Applications and Worksharing, pages 1-4.*, Adelaide, Australia, IEEE Computer Society.

Gianoutsos, S., & Grundy, J. (1996). Collaborative work with the World Wide Web: adding CSCW support to a Web browser. In *Procedingss of Oz-CSCW'96, DSTC Technical Workshop Series, University of Queensland*, pages 14-21 University of Queensland, Brisbane, Australia.

Greenberg, S., & Roseman, M. (1996). GroupWeb: A WWW browser as real time groupware. In *CHI '96: Conference companion on Human factors in computing systems*, pages 271–272, Vancouver, British Columbia, Canada. ACM Press.

Gross, T. (1999). Supporting awareness and cooperation in digital information environments. In *Basic Research Symposium at the Conference on Human Factors in Computing Systems - CHI'99*, Pittsburgh, Pennsylvania, USA. ACM Press.

Han, R., Perret, V., & Naghshineh, M. (2000). WebSplitter: a unified XML framework for multi-device collaborative Web browsing. In *CSCW '00: Proceedings of the 2000 ACM conference on Computer supported cooperative work*, pages 221–230, Philadelphia, Pennsylvania, USA. ACM Press.

Kempthorne, O., & Doerfler, T. E. (1969). The behavior of some significance tests under experimental randomization. *Biometrika*, 56(2):231-248.

Krishnappa, R. (2005). Multi-user search engine (MUSE): Supporting collaborative information seeking and retrieval. Master's thesis, University of Missouri-Rolla, University of Missouri-Rolla, Rolla, USA.

Lieberman, H., Van Dyke, N. W., & Vivacqua, A. S. (1999). Let's browse: a collaborative web browsing agent. In *IUI '99: Proceedings of the 4th international conference on Intelligent user interfaces*, pages 65–68, Los Angeles, California, USA. ACM Press.

Maekawa, T., Hara, T., & Nishio, S. (2006). A collaborative web browsing system for multiple mobile users. In *PERCOM '06: Proceedings of the Fourth Annual IEEE International Conference on Pervasive Computing and Communications (PERCOM'06)*, pages 22–35, Washington, DC, USA. IEEE Computer Society.

Morris, M. R., & Horvitz, E. (2007). SearchTogether: An interface for collaborative web search. In *UIST '07: Proceedings of the 20th annual ACM symposium on User interface software and technology*, pages 3–12, Newport, Rhode Island, USA. ACM Press.

Morris, M. R., Paepcke, A., & Winograd, T. (2006). TeamSearch: Comparing Techniques for Co-Present Collaborative Search of Digital Media. In *TABLETOP '06: Proceedings of the First IEEE International Workshop on Horizontal Interactive Human-Computer Systems*, pages 97–104, Washington, DC, USA. IEEE Computer Society.

Netscape Conferencer (2001). http://www.aibn.com/help/Software/Netscape/communicator/conference/.

Robertson, S. E. (1990). On term selection for query expansion. *Journal of Documentation*, 46(4):359–364.

Robertson, S. E., & Spärck Jones, K. (1976). Relevance weighting of search terms. *Journal of the American Society for Information Science*, 27(3), 129–146.

Robertson, S. E., Walker, S., Hancock-Beaulieu, M., Gull, A., & Lau, M. (1992). Okapi at TREC. In Harman, D., editor, *Proceedings of the First Text REtrieval Conference (TREC)*, pages 21–30, Gaithersburg, MD. NIST, USA.

Roseman, M., & Greenberg, S. (1996). Building real-time groupware with GroupKit, a groupware toolkit. *ACM Trans. Comput.-Hum. Interact.*, 3(1), 66–106.

Shen, C., Vernier, F. D., Forlines, C., & Ringel, M. (2004). DiamondSpin: An extensible toolkit for around-the-table interaction. In *CHI '04: Proceedings of the SIGCHI conference on Human factors in computing systems*, pages 167–174, Vienna, Austria. ACM Press.

Sidler, G., Scott, A., & Wolf, H. (1997). Collaborative Browsing in the World Wide Web. In *Proceedings of the 8th Joint European Networking Conference*, Edinburgh, Scotland. Springer.

Smeaton, A. F., Lee, H., Foley, C., & Mc Givney., S. (2006). Collaborative Video Searching on a Tabletop. *Multimedia Systems Journal*, 12(4):375–391.

Smeaton, A. F., Murphy, N., O'Connor, N., Marlow, S., Lee, H., Donald, K. M., Browne, P., & Ye., J. (2001). The Físchlár Digital Video System: A Digital Library of Broadcast TV Programmes. In *JCDL 2001 - ACM+IEEE Joint Conference on Digital Libraries*, pages 312–313, Roanoke, VA, USA.

Spärck Jones, K. (1997). Search term relevance weighting given little relevance information. *Readings in information retrieval* pages 329–338, Morgan Kaufmann Publishers Inc.

Stewart, J., Bederson, B. B., & Druin, A. (1999). Single display groupware: a model for co-present collaboration. In *CHI '99: Proceedings of the SIGCHI conference on Human factors in computing systems*, pages 286–293, Pittsburgh, Pennsylvania, USA. ACM Press.

Windows Live Messenger (2007). http://get.live.com/messenger/overview.

Yao, K.-T., Neches, R., Ko, I.-Y., Eleish, R., & Abhinkar, S. (1999). Synchronous and Asynchronous Collaborative Information Space Analysis Tools. In *ICPP '99: Proceedings of the 1999 International Workshops on Parallel Processing*, page 74, Washington, DC, USA. IEEE Computer Society.

Zeballos, G. S. (1998). Tools for Efficient Collaborative Web Browsing. In *Proceedings of CSCW '98 workshop on Collaborative and co-operative information seeking in digital information environment*.

Chapter VIII
DemonD:
A Social Search Engine Built Upon the Actor-Network Theory

Charles Delalonde
EDF R&D, France

Eddie Soulier
Université de Technologie de Troyes, France

ABSTRACT

This research leverages information retrieval activity in order to build a network of organizational expertise in a distributed R&D laboratory. The authors describe traditional knowledge management practices and review post-cognitivists theories in order to define social creation in collaborative information retrieval activity. The Actor-Network theory accurately describes association processes and includes both human and non-human entities. This chapter compares this theory with the emergence of Social Search services online and Experts' Retrieval Systems. The chapter authors suggest afterward, a social search engine named DemonD that identifies documents but more specifically users relevant to a query. DemonD relies on transparent profile construction based upon user activity, community participation, and shared documents. Individuals are invited to participate in a dedicated newsgroup and the information exchanged is capitalized. The evaluation of our service both ergonomic and through a simulation provides encouraging data.

INTRODUCTION AND CONTEXT DESCRIPTION

During the early years of the Personal Computer research, two rather distinctive philosophical approaches competed. Artificial Intelligence believers wished to replace humans by machine whereas Human Intelligence Augmentation project, led by Douglas Engelbart, envisioned computers as a technology to augment human mind and eventually network each other's (Markoff, 2005).

This debate is still vibrant in the Information Retrieval community where the algorithmic approach is recently challenged by human approaches leveraging individual's social capital to identify pertinent knowledge sources. Our work contributes to this "Social Search movement", in a corporate environment, and identifies the challenges of a Research and Development laboratory, of 80 persons, in a French telecommunication company. The laboratory observed is distributed, in France, among three cities: Grenoble, Sophia Antipolis and Caen. Its mission is to plan, conceive and support the production of original telecommunication services for businesses. This process involves each distributed team of the laboratory. Ideas are suggested utilizing an email discussion list. Then, marketing teams identify a potential market. Business development teams confirm the financial opportunities of such project. When validated by the steering committee, the service is prototyped and developed. A partner company usually accepts to experiment the service. Business units of the telecommunication company might then decide to market this innovation. In such context, cooperation is a necessity. Teams must be well coordinated to remain creative in order to shorten the time to market of the services. Information Retrieval being a critical task for laboratory members, the company previously attempted two strategies in order to create and share organizational information in a distributed context.

First, they produced an exhaustive knowledge database, trying to externalize and share explicit knowledge. Intranet's folders were also utilized to share content among coworkers. Yet, interviewed employees revealed that the knowledge database was usually obsolete and shared folders not accessible (privileges needed to be granted on each folder) and content was not properly indexed.

Second, the organization, conscious about the shortcomings of a systemic approach of knowledge management, deployed communities of practice (Wenger, 1998). The 'not-so-informal' communi-

ties shared a virtual collaborative workplace and face to face member's meetings were scheduled monthly. Yet, this second strategy also turned out to be unsatisfactory. Employees were reluctant to ask/share information with individuals they had never met.

Unlike content, which is perishable and quickly becomes obsolete, experts' informal networks are rather permanent in R&D context. We assert that the real value of information systems is connecting people to people and encouraging them to share their expertise rather than collecting and storing de-contextualized information. (Hertzum & Pejtersen, 2000) already evidenced that individual looking for information usually explore and contact personal communications prior to using documents or knowledge bases. Following this strategy and in order to identify pertinent individuals, we need to evaluate their relevance on a specific subject along with social indicators. Thus, we leverage transparent user's profile modeling techniques to match a knowledge demand with one or many knowledge offers (Delalonde & Soulier, 2007). Relying on Bruno Latour and Michel Callon Actor Network Theory (named ANT throughout this article) our objective is then to validate a hybrid information retrieval model. This model helps specifying DemonD (Demand&responD) a search engine dedicated to collaborative information retrieval and favoring the emergence of a lightly structured information network.

The remainder of this paper is structured as follows. In section "Actor network theory in information retrieval activity" we present Actor Network Theory and its application in Information Retrieval. In section "Related works on social search" we review related work on Social Search. Section "DemonD a social search engine" describes DemonD's specifications. Section "Evaluation" is shared between a simulation of DemonD and its ergonomic evaluation. Section "Conclusion and future works" finally concludes our work with a discussion of future directions for research in this area.

ACTOR NETWORK THEORY IN INFORMATION RETRIEVAL ACTIVITY

As mentioned in the introduction of the article, we believe that information retrieval and acquisition is necessarily a social process, creating ties between individuals and expanding their social capital (Huysman & Wulf, 2003). This section aims to define our vision of "social", constructed through a review of post-cognitivists theory including the activity, the situated cognition, the distributed cognition and eventually the Actor Network theories.

Activity Theory

The Activity Theory (Vygotsky, 1978) is helpful for examining the social dimension of Information Retrieval. (Leontiev, 1979) proved user's actions only make sense in a social context of a shared work activity distinguishing between *activities*, which satisfy a need, and the *actions* that constitute the activities. Engeström's recent contributions to the Activity theory expanded Vygotsky's mediating triangle with a social component (Engeström, 1987) providing the activity theoretical community with a powerful tool for social systems analysis. Yet, the social dimension of activity, in this theory shall be better specified and not "taken for granted" as pre-existing groups (such as family, colleagues). We retain however the importance of artifacts to mediate user's thoughts.

Situated Action Theory

The situated action theory is another helpful framework to analyze information retrieval as a social process. Situated action theory was formulated in contradiction to artificial intelligence formalism. Indeed, Lucie Suchman's research demonstrated the inefficiency of action plans and suggested that activity was constantly constructed and reconstructed from dynamic interactions with the material and social worlds "situated" (Suchman, 1987). Yet, the situated action theory refuses to generalize its observations. Furthermore, the "social", in this theory, is restricted to local interactions. Distributed cognition is then appeared as a coherent theory to apprehend social information retrieval in organizations depicted in the introduction.

Distributed Cognition Theory

Relying on ethnographical methods, Edwin Hutchins analyzed sophisticated activities such as flying airplanes or sailing (Hutchins, 1995) (Hutchins, 1991). His research identified an exhaustive cognitive system formed by human and the artifacts they utilized to achieve their activity. As (Wood, 1993) indicated, "cognition is never simply 'amplified' or 'externalized', but rather cognition is 'mediated' through the external artifacts and collaborators such that the new cognitive system which is formed has a radically different character, structure and functionality than the cognition of the unsupported individual". This theory illustrates efficiently the distribution between human and non-human in the analysis of a cognitive system yet, the social dimension of the system being observed, lacks specification.

Situated Cognition Theory

Diffusion and acquisition of knowledge, in a distributed group, shall also be observed with Albert Stutz theory of social knowledge (Schütz, 1946). The author regards the knowledge as socially derived and transmitted to the individual by relations of all kinds. He describes three forms of knowledge. The store of experiences is a form of knowledge strictly individual that includes recipe and routines practical or theoretical. Second, the socially transmitted knowledge created when interacting with other agents. Third, the approved knowledge validated by members considered as cognitive authorities of a group. We are particularly interested in the second form of knowledge, since, this distribution of knowledge justifies cooperation between individuals and is built through a relation that coordinates a demand and an offer of information. When this relation is extended to multiple individuals, cooperation occurs and a community is created. Numerous researches have been conducted to utilize information technologies to support cooperation among agents distributed in the organization or geographically in virtual teams. Computer Supported Cooperative Work and Groupware developments results from this evolution.

We investigated existing typologies of communities offering a new paradigm for social information retrieval activity. The theory of socially shared cognition recognizes the importance of a network or a community in the study of human cognition (Resnick *et al.*, 1991).

Cognition as a social and cultural phenomenon requires, in a computer mediated environment, artifacts able to transmit individuals awareness and create a context for the completion of collaborative activities (Erickson & Kellogg, 2000). R&D teams which we observed share knowledge and cooperate with information technology (cf. introduction). In the related literature we found three forms of communities, observed in the organizations, and supporting the transmission of knowledge like: community of interest, epistemic or of practice. When considering the activity of information retrieval as a social practice, we are interested in a network, slightly structured, whose principal objective is the transmission of knowledge.

In communities of interest (Bergé & Périn, 2002), members share information on a specific subject whereas epistemic communities (Conein, 2003) are conducting a cognitive activity relying on globally distributed individuals. Communities of practice (Lave, 1988) (Lave & Wenger, 1991) (Soulier, 2004), initiated by employees willing to improve their professional practice, do not

describe either the networks of information we observed in R&D teams. As a consequence, we suggest a new form of information network, relying on information retrieval activity as a social process in order to build an organizational network of expertise (Twidale & Nichols, 1998).

Actor Network Theory

ANT constitutes a distinctive approach to represent a society of heterogeneous entities both humans and non-humans. Bruno Latour suggests a dynamic vision of social ties constructed when entities interacts with each other (Latour, 2006). The result of this movement leaves footprints named a "social reassembled".

Other post-cognitivists theories (activity theory, situated cognition, distributed cognition, situated action) previously investigated to describe Social Information Retrieval activity usually envisioned the social aspect prior to the activity. ANT appeared as the only theory crystallizing social components to achieve an activity. This theory does not assume existing social ties between entities (humans and non-humans) but constantly create them during each query. Furthermore, ANT's non-distinctive inclusion of both human and non-human entities seemed to be the most suitable to describe a hybrid information retrieval system relying on assembled heterogeneous resources.

ANT's author utilize a specific vocabulary including the terms "entities", "intermediaries", "mediators" and "associations" that we will describe below.

In the information retrieval activity, entities might be: a query, personal or shared documents, discussions taking place on a dedicated environment, articles extracted from a knowledge base, votes, tags, colleague's profiles... Each query catalyzes a network containing at least one entity. Entities are related between one another. The relationship between each related items is described in Figure 1. The various arrows between entities

Table 1. Post-cognitivists theories to define "social" activities

	What is the "social" made of ?
Activity Theory	Takes the social for granted.
Situated Action Theory	The social is restricted to local interactions.
Distributed Cognition Theory	The social is only a consequence of a distribution / repartition between elements of a system.
Situated Cognition Theory	The social results from a dialectic between micro and macro structures.
Actor Network Theory	Does not pre-assume existing social ties between entities (humans and non-humans) but observes their creation through various associations.

describe some type of association. For instance, tags might be set on documents, profiles, articles or discussions. Votes evaluate the quality of comments or articles.

Intermediaries are in charge of conveying information without any kind of modification.

Mediators modify the information they are conveying. In fact, mediators are in charge of translating information to facilitate its propagation in a distributed system. The association of heterogeneous entities relies on such mediators.

Associations represent different stages of a network of intertwined entities. Three types of associations are relevant for the information retrieval activity we will describe: social vacuity, hybrid community and society.

The first association is a social vacuity and describes a state where entities are not linked between one another (Soulier *et al.*, 2007). The hybrid community designates a dynamic stage where entities are incessantly associating. The association eventually stabilized and give birth to a society (Whitehead, 1929/1995).

Information retrieval creates social capital in distributed teams. ANT appeared as a pertinent theoretical framework to represent such social search practices. We will now review specific implementation of this theory in Social Search services online and in organizations.

RELATED WORKS ON SOCIAL SEARCH

Considering the activity of information retrieval as a social practice, we are interested in a network, slightly structured, whose principal objective is the transmission of knowledge.

A non exhaustive definition of social search services could be: *a type of search engine that determines the relevance of search results by considering users' interactions or contributions.* Within the huge amount of available information

Figure 1. Relationships between various entities

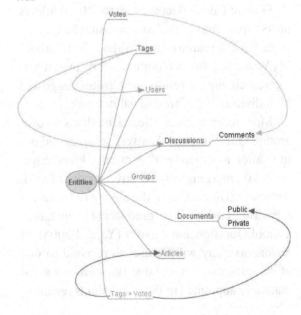

and sources and due to frequent search engines manipulations, Social Search is recently garnering a lot of attention on the Web 2.0. In order to increase the ranking of their websites in Google search engine, unscrupulous webmasters utilize fake blogs to promote goods and services. As a matter of fact, a page will be ranked higher if the sites linking to that page use consistent anchor text.

Two significant social search services are emerging including navigating on previously recommended web sites and addressing a question to pertinent individuals. After reviewing recent social search initiatives online, we will identify Expert Retrieval Systems ERS in the corporate environment (Referral Web, Agilience and Answer Garden 2).

Social Search Initiatives Online

Social Search takes many forms online. Among them, navigating on content previously approved or recommended by other has been implemented in the Web Of People. This service has been developed by (Plu *et al.*, 2003) and helps individuals sharing relevant information with their peers. The system eventually propagates the pertinent resources to a network of individuals.

Google Co-op (Google Co-op, 2006) allows users to personalize the list of websites being suggested by the search engine. Yahoo! 360 (Yahoo! My Web 2.0, 2006) acts quite similarly by restricting search engine results to websites suggested by individual's declared social network.

More recently, Social Search methods revolve around Questions and Answers services and put in relation a demand and an offer of knowledge. Web 2.0 emerging collaborative services (wiki, weblogs) give each user the ability to be an information consumer or producer. For instance, Yahoo! Question and Answer (Yahoo! 2005) let anyone ask any willing user to respond to one of his question. Yet, the questions are not automatically appointed to the respondents resulting

in many unanswered questions. Yedda (Yedda, 2007) adopts another strategy leveraging light profiling techniques and to forward unanswered questions to pertinent profiles. Profile creation is unfortunately quite poor and relies only on declared keywords.

Expert Retrieval Systems

Information technologies also contribute to sharing and constructing knowledge in distributed organizations thru specific systems named: Expert Retrieval Systems (ERS). Multiple ERS have been deployed but usually failed for not taking in consideration the importance of informal social networks in the construction of knowledge or not allowing final users to manage their profiles.

Referral Web (Kauntz *et al.*, 1996) is an ERS created in AT&T labs. User's profile is constructed based on keywords extracted from web pages or shared documents where individual's name appears. Social network is also drawn based on co-occurring names on published research or public documents. Individual utilizing Referral Web selects the reach of his request and the number of hopes between him and knowledge offer.

Agilience (Agilience, 2006), another ERS, relies on sent email messages to create user's profile. During initiation phase, emails are analyzed and significant words extracted and compared to an existing taxonomy. User is able to manage his profile by adding or deleting keywords. To retrieve pertinent individuals, users send an email with a description of his request. The content of the message is analyzed by Agilience that returns back a list of documents, a list of individuals and a list of individuals able to forward the request to other potential respondents. Requests and responses are leveraged to accurately define user's profile. Agilience conceptualize knowledge construction or sharing as a dialogue between a demand and an offer. In reality, knowledge usually emerges from collaboration between multiple individuals. The creation of a dedicated collaborative workspace could definitely enhance this solution.

Answer Garden 2 (Ackerman & McDonald, 1996) follows the realization of an earlier version and relies on a multi agent system to select a recipient for a request. AG2 replicates progressively user's request based on recipient's proximity, privileging first near-by contacts. Recipients are invited to cooperate on specific discussions groups with instant messaging and emails functionalities. This powerful ERS presents a major constraint for end-users: individuals do not control the reach of their request. In fact, AG2 retransmits the request without prior approval.

In conclusion, the description of three ERS (Agilience, Referral Web and AG2) presents three challenges that need to be addressed. First of all, user's profile modeling must be extracted from heterogeneous sources (documents, user's activity, social networks…) (challenge 1). Second, a knowledge exchange should take place in a collaborative environment, with multiple participants (challenge 2). Finally, user must be able to manage the reach of his request and ensure privacy, especially in R&D teams depicted in the introduction (challenge 3). Furthermore, social search initiatives online or thru ERS usually rely on preexisting social networks of individuals. Our approach is rather different, following Actor-Network theory, a query catalyze a network of entities, human or non-human. Online social search services and Expert Retrieval Systems that we reviewed are summarized in Table 2.

DEMOND A SOCIAL SEARCH ENGINE

In opposition to the solitary information retrieval activity, we model information retrieval as a social process of association able to structure an organizational network of expertise. The information seeking process is not restricted to content retrieval / distribution but initiate a negotiation between a demand and one or many offers. The negotiation is followed by the capitalization of exchanged information and the social structure

utilized. The recurrence of the exchanges of information supports the constitution of mutual aid (caring) network and eventually the emergence of a knowledge community. ANT's specific vocabulary includes "entities", "intermediaries", "mediators" and "associations".

In the information retrieval activity, entities might be: a query, personal or shared documents, discussions taking place on a dedicated environment, articles extracted from a knowledge base, votes, tags, colleague's profiles… Each query catalyzes a network containing at least one entity. Entities are related between one another.

As mentioned previously, intermediaries are in charge of conveying information without any kind of modification. The information retrieval engine, we conceived, contains three intermediaries including a database, a collaborative environment and a knowledge base. Intermediaries are indeed indispensable in the association process.

The information retrieval engine, described in the following section, contains three mediators: the Profiler, the ContactRank and the Coop. Profiler creates, for each individual, a transparent profile based on tags declared, shared documents, and groups created. ContactRank sorts each knowledge offer (including human or non human entities) based on their proficiency on a specific subject and their propensity to respond. Coop creates a dedicated collaborative workplace and invites pertinent individuals to contribute.

DemonD is available in the corporate information systems (intranet). It is comprised of four main stages including initialization and information retrieval - diffusion - negotiation and capitalization that we will describe successively. A workflow of information retrieval activity in DemonD is available in Figure 2.

Initialization and Information Retrieval

The user's profile is modeled with the "Profiler" algorithm and consists of a list of weighted keywords also named tags. Distinct profiling

Table 2. Social search services

Type of service	Name	Description	
Browsing On Trusted Websites	SoMeOne	SoMeOne arranges user's documents in shared folders along with discussion groups and suggests contacts based on a specific query.	Online
	Google Co-op	Google Co-op is a customized search engine allowing user to query pre-defined websites.	
	My Web 2.0 Yahoo!	My Web 2.0 from Yahoo! is also a customized search engine querying websites previously approved by members of a defined community.	
Questions And Answers	Yahoo! Answers	A knowledge-sharing community where anyone can ask and answer questions on any topic.	
	Yedda	A knowledge-sharing community where questions asked by users are transmitted to pertinent respondents based on basic profiling techniques.	
	Google Answers	A social search service for users to get help from other with expertise in a specific domain. Users post a question and specify the price they are willing to pay for an answer.	
	LinkedIn	A business social network service giving each member methods to question his network.	
Expert Retrieval Systems	Responsive	Instant messaging service in charge of broadcasting a query to user's existing contact-list.	In Organizations
	Agilience	Service relying on email logs to create user's profile. Agilience eventually suggests documents or pertinent individuals able to respond to any question.	
	Referral Web	Referral Web creates user's profile based on keywords extracted from web pages or shared documents where individual's name appears.	
	Answer Garden 2	AG2 creates users profile and replicates progressively user's request based on recipient's proximity. Recipients are invited to cooperate on specific discussions groups.	

techniques are utilized to provide web personalization (Brusilovsky & Kobsa, 2007) but in order to overcome the first challenge presented in 3.2, user's profile is modeled from multiple sources and updated when individual utilizes DemonD. It is important to underline that modeled profile are not utilized to personalize search engine results based on user's characteristics since profiling is leveraged to match a query with pertinent knowledge offers.

In DemonD, corporate information system directly provisions socio demographic data including (name, address, email, phone, occupation...). Individual also declares a list of competency through keywords complementing his profile (cf. Figure 6).

To enrich his profile, individual shares a set of documents (curriculum vitae, publications, patents) with the rest of the community. Recurrent keywords are extracted from these documents and enhance user's profile.

User also creates workgroups known as a list of contacts. DemonD utilized the group creation activity to extract recurrent keywords from group member's profiles. Such keywords are also utilized to complement user's profile.

Individuals are able to add or delete tags (keywords) on any resources on DemonD (his/others profile, his/others documents, and discussions) (cf. Figure 7). Various tags utilized by the individual are added to his profile.

Figure 2. Workflow DemonD

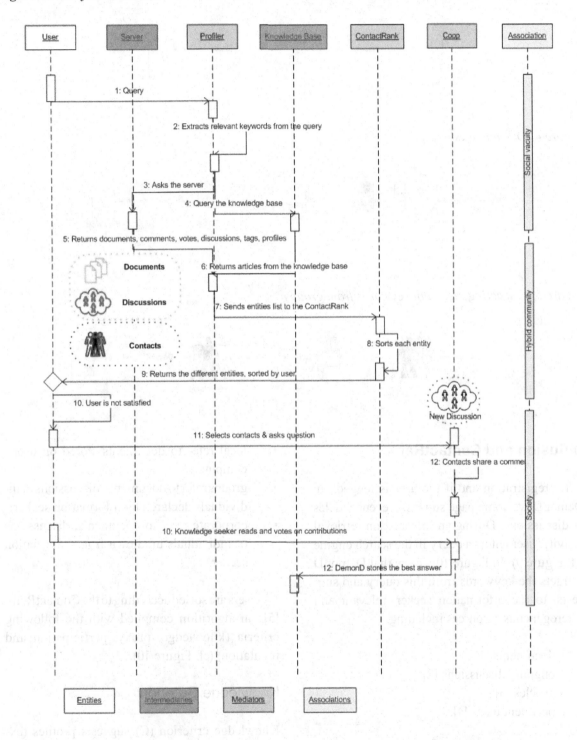

Figure 3. User's registration

Figure 4. Documents sharing

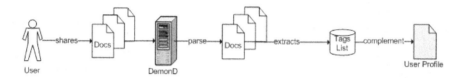

Figure 5. Extracting recurrent keywords from groups

Diffusion and ContactRank

After registration and if the user is logged on, DemonD welcome page suggests recent articles or discussions. During an information retrieval activity, user enters a query in the search engine (cf. Figure 9). In Figure 10 we see that DemonD extracts the keywords from this query and suggests, to the information seeker, relevant and heterogeneous resources including:

- documents [1];
- ongoing discussions [2];
- articles [3];
- pertinent users [4].

The results are sorted according to their provenance:

- local refer to documents stored on user's computer;
- groups refer to documents, discussions or individuals declared by information seeker;
- corporate refer to documents, discussions or individuals unknown from information seeker.

Users are sorted according to the ContactRank [5], an algorithm compiled with the following criteria (knowledge, proxy, participation and reputation) (cf. Figure 10).

Knowledge Criterion

Knowledge criterion (C) suggests profiles (extracted from Profiler cf. 4.1) containing tags directly embedded in seeker's query. After being calculated, this criterion is utilized as a coefficient

Figure 6. User's registration

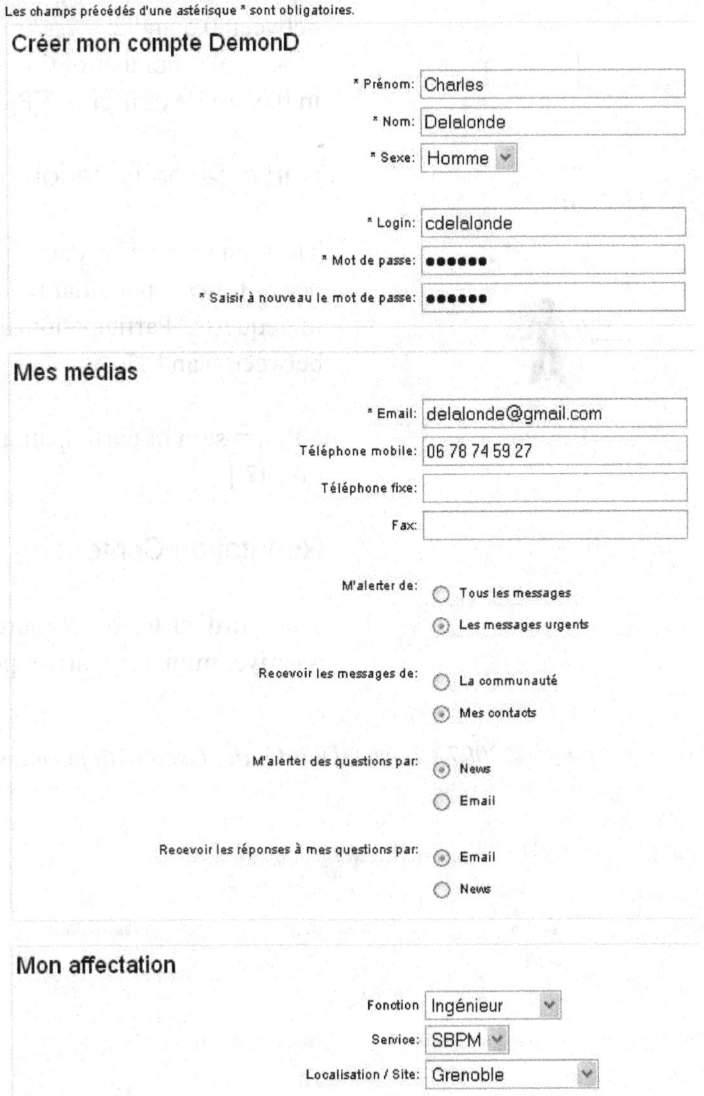

Les champs précédés d'une astérisque * sont obligatoires.

Créer mon compte DemonD

* Prénom: Charles
* Nom: Delalonde
* Sexe: Homme

* Login: cdelalonde
* Mot de passe: ●●●●●
* Saisir à nouveau le mot de passe: ●●●●●

Mes médias

* Email: delalonde@gmail.com
Téléphone mobile: 06 78 74 59 27
Téléphone fixe:
Fax:

M'alerter de:
○ Tous les messages
◉ Les messages urgents

Recevoir les messages de:
○ La communauté
◉ Mes contacts

M'alerter des questions par:
◉ News
○ Email

Recevoir les réponses à mes questions par:
◉ Email
○ News

Mon affectation

Fonction: Ingénieur
Service: SBPM
Localisation / Site: Grenoble

Figure 7. User's tags declared

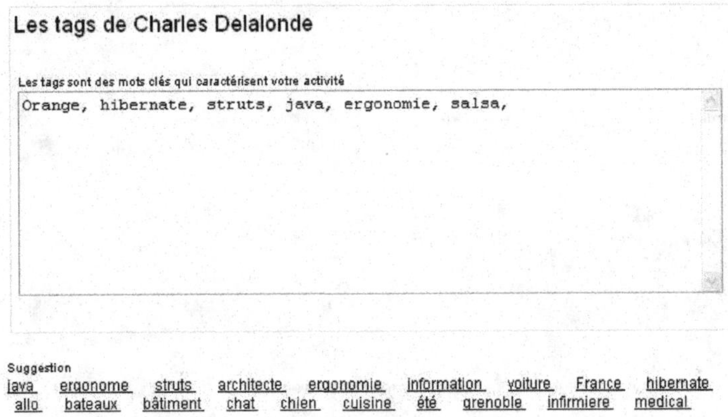

Les tags de Charles Delalonde

Les tags sont des mots clés qui caractérisent votre activité

Orange, hibernate, struts, java, ergonomie, salsa,

Suggestion
java ergonome struts architecte ergonomie information voiture France hibernate
allo bateaux bâtiment chat chien cuisine été grenoble infirmiere medical

Figure 8. Tagging activity

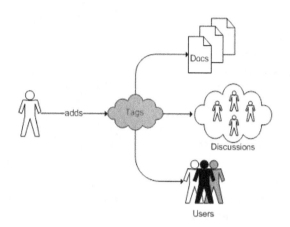

of the overall sum of proxy, participation and reputation criterion. This coefficient is comprised between 0,5 and 2:

C(t)[o] = number of times that tag (t) is found in the profile of user o; ∑P[o] e [0.5 ; 2].

Participation Criterion

The second criterion Participation (P) is the number of times a potential recipient has responded to requests. Participation is a sum comprised between 0 and 17:

∑P[o] = sum of participations of user o; ∑P[o] e [0 ; 17].

Reputation Ccriterion

The third criterion Reputation (R) compiles positive minus negative potential recipients'

Figure 9. DemonD's welcome page (©2007 Charles Delalonde. Used with permission)

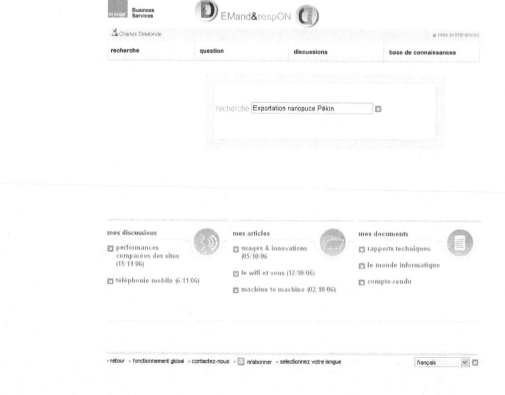

participations. Reputation is comprised between 0 and 17:

$$\sum R[o] = \text{sum of reputation of user o}; \sum R[o] \in [0;17].$$

Proxy Criterion

The fourth criterion Proxy (Pr) is the number of contacts of a potential recipient unknown from the information seeker. This criterion is also comprised between 0 and 17:

$$\sum Pr[o] = \text{sum of contacts from user o's unknown from an information seeker and}$$

$$\sum Pr[o] \in [0;17].$$

Overall ContactRank

The ContactRank algorithm is in charge of sorting potential recipients of a request according to four criteria including: knowledge, participation, reputation and proxy. For a recipient "o" following a query on tag "t" ContactRank is:

$$C(t)[o](\sum P[o] + \sum R[o] + \sum Re[o]); \text{ et } C(t)[o] \in [0;102].$$

If documents or existing discussions does not match seeker's query, he chooses to send a request. In order to follow the second challenge (cf. 3.2), knowledge seekers manage the reach of their requests by selecting one or many recipients.

Negotiation and Capitalization

The recipients selected are invited to provide a collaborative answer on a dedicated workspace (cf. Figure 11). Such workflow follows the third challenge of ERS (cf. 3.3).

When an individual initiates a request the "Coop" algorithm automatically creates a dedicated workspace. Coop also invites previously selected recipients to provide a collaborative answer. Validation takes place with peer reviewing and grading other member's participations.

During the capitalization phase, the best answer validated by the community is inserted in the organizational knowledge base. Information network constructed previously is also available on DemonD.

Figure 10. Potential Recipients sorted with ContactRank (©2007 Charles Delalonde. Used with permission)

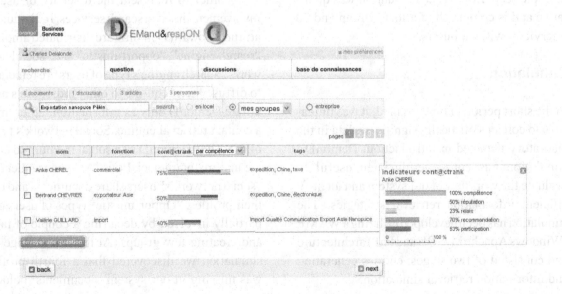

Figure 11. Dedicated collaborative workspace. (©2007 Charles Delalonde. Used with permission)

EVALUATION

To evaluate our Social Search engine we collected quantitative and qualitative data. First evaluation was a simulation of DemonD allowing us to test multiple scenario. Second evaluation was qualitative and is comprised of a focus group and 50 interviews with end-users.

Simulation

In the short period of time granted, it was unfeasible to collect statistically significant data in the laboratory depicted in introduction. DemonD's simulation has consequently been useful to evaluate the workflow of our system and identify efficient information retrieval strategies. The simulation has been developed utilizing a WAMP (Windows Apache MySQL and PhP) architecture and consisted of two stages: entities generation and information retrieval simulation.

Entities Generation

Before running multiple search cycles, we generated 100 users, theirs documents, their groups and built their profiles as presented in Figure 12.

In order to represent the diversity of user's involvement in social search services, Individuals' attitudes toward DemonD are distributed among: "search engine", "opportunistic" and "social network". Search engine's type of users are reluctant to diffuse their requests to other individuals and utilize DemonD only as information rather than a contact retrieval engine. Social network's type of users use DemonD as a social medium to create and maintain social ties. As a consequence, "social network's" users share documents and tag their profiles. "Opportunistic" types of users get partially involved by declaring a couple of tags and creating few groups. At the initial stage of simulation we discovered that a fourth profile was missing in our system: documents' holder.

Figure 12. Data generation

Générateur

Profil	Nombre	Tags-Déclarés	Documents partagés	Groupes	ProbaP*	ProbaR**
Lurker	1	0	0	0	0	0
Opportuniste	5	5	0	0	15	30
Communautaire	5	5	8	0	30	50
Documentaire	0	0	5	0	0	0

* ProbaP : Probabilité pour l'utilisateur de poser une question
** ProbaR : Probabilité pour l'utilisateur de répondre à une question

Probabilité de répondre correctement	Minimum 0	Maximum 30
Probabilité de ne pas répondre correctement	Minimum 0	Maximum 30

Générer ces données

Indeed, the system could not function without the 200 documents initially shared by this last profile whom represents organizations' knowledge bases (okb). Two likelihoods are also added to each profile including the odds that this individual initiates a query at any given time (likelihood 1); the odds that this individual responds to any demand from another (likelihood 2). Each profile and information associated is described in Table 3.

Search Cycles

After generating the users and their documents, we ran multiple search cycles.

For each query, users might be:

- satisfied by documents ongoing, discussions / articles recommended by DemonD;
- satisfied by the responses brought by other individuals;
- not satisfied at all.

Four situations lead to an evolution of users' profiles (Likelihood 1 and 2 cf. Table 3) including:

- probability to ask a new question if a user is satisfied with previous responses received;

- probability to respond to a question if a user is satisfied with previous responses received.

During 50 cycles, 100 fictitious users queried DemonD resulting in 2133 queries and an overall satisfaction greater than 70%. 621 users were satisfied by documents / discussions and 877 were satisfied by responses given by other individuals. In addition, users (regardless of their profiles) trust DemonD's ability to retrieve the right information since 45% of the "search engine" profiles and 70% of the "social network" profiles queried the system. Furthermore profiles tend to become altruistic. Search engine's profile had an initial probability to respond to other's request of 10%. At the end of the 50 cycles their probability to respond is above 48%. The activity model of DemonD appeared coherent and able to retrieve information through pre-existing shared entities (documents, articles) or social ties.

Yet, such encouraging data hide the fact that 82% of the responses were given by users with "social network's" profile. A thorough analysis of user's selected profile indicates a malfunction in the ContactRank. Indeed, the ContactRank algorithm (cf. 4.2) selects, for each query, 10 potential respondents based on a set of criteria that auto-aliment each other. An effective meth-

Table 3. Data generated (Search Engine, Opportunistic, Social Network)

Profiles	SE	O	SN	OKB
Number of this profile	50	25	25	1
Number of declared-tags	5	10	15	0
Shared documents Number of tags per doc.	0 0	2 10 tags	5 25 tags	200 5
Groups created Number of tags per group	0 0	2 10 tags	5 20 tags	0 0
Likelihood 1	30	40	50	0
Likelihood 2	10	20	50	0

ods to correct this sorting algorithm have been deployed and limit the size of certain criterion. As a reminder, ContactRank is for a user "o" and a tag "t":

$$C(t)[o](\sum P[o] + \sum R[o] + \sum Re[o]), \text{ where:}$$

- $C(t)[o]$ = number of times a tag (t) exists in a profile o;
- $\sum P[o]$ = number of times a user o has responded to user's questions;
- $\sum R[o]$ = difference between negative and positive evaluations from user o;
- $\sum Re[o]$ = number of unknown contacts between o and other potential knowledge giver.

ContactRank is frequently maximized with the criteria $\sum P[o]$ et $\sum R[o]$ auto alimenting each other. Indeed, if reputation and participation are high, knowledge giver (o) has a greater ContactRank. As a consequence he gets selected more often, participate more often increasing naturally the criterion $\sum P[o]$ and $\sum R[o]$. To avoid this situation, we maximized the size of the following : $\sum P[o]$, $\sum R[o]$, $\sum Re[o]$.

Focus Group and 50 Interviews

In order to confirm potential usages of DemonD qualitative data were also needed. An ergonomic study, with 50 respondents and potential end-users followed by a focus group, simulated a geographically distributed company willing to export "nanotechnologies" in China.

As mentioned earlier, existing ERS we evaluated usually face three challenges (cf. 3.2) that we attempted to address. DemonD's workflow appeared coherent to most surveyed users whom reacted very positively to DemonD's approach of collaborative information retrieval.

Yet, two challenges need to be taken in consideration. First, the collaborative tagging approach, critical in DemonD (users tags their/other's documents, their/other's profiles...), must be assisted. As Richard (one of the respondents) indicated:

"Tagging is costly to the User, you should consider automatic tagging functionalities. Metadata on documents should be extracted automatically" Richard B.

In fact, tagging might create inaccuracy (noise) if it does not rely on a semi-structured ontology. Furthermore, tagging is time consuming and not yet included in worker's practice. To respond to this first challenge, we are contemplating the possibility to suggest tags based on user's context following Nicolas Pissard's algorithm (Pissard, 2007).

Knowledge capitalization is also a challenge that need to be addressed. Wiki's technology are progressively entering organizations (certainly due to wikipedia's success) and constitutes a strategy to structure user generated content produced in DemonD. SweetWiki a semantic wiki is a technology that could replace DemonD unstructured knowledge base (Buffa *et al.*, 2007).

In addition, our sharing assumption embedded in DemonD must be leveraged by proper incentives. Users usually rely on their personal network of information. Sharing knowledge with unknown co-workers must be secured (in terms of intellectual property) and encouraged. To respond to this second challenge, we included a "confidential" functionality to restrain and control information diffusion. We also gave "proactive users" a specific status on DemonD.

CONCLUSION AND FUTURE WORKS

In conclusion, Social Search certainly constitutes a promising alternative to traditional information retrieval methods. Our model, relying on Actor-Network Theory, has revealed very encouraging data both quantitative and qualitative however certain flaws identified during evaluation needs to be corrected.

The Actor Network Theory utilized to specify our system might also be slightly criticized for two reasons.

First, treating humans and non-humans in an equivalent manner might also be criticized (Bloor, 1999). For instance, in social search activities, tags given by a user to define his profile and tags inherited automatically from the documents he is sharing must be treated differently. We suggest to include coefficients on tags based on their provenance when Profiler creates user's profile. Furthermore, as (Mutch, 2002) indicated in (Pentland & Feldman, In Press), ANT has been criticized as being "flat". Associations are observed at a given time but fail to encompass the history or context of the network. When social information retrieval takes place in organizations

like the one described in introduction we must take into account the context.

A new version of DemonD is currently in progress and will be deployed in the laboratory depicted in the introduction. Quantitative data will then be collected based on user's improved effectiveness when utilizing the system. A beta version will also be experimented and the telecommunication company, funding this research, protected DemonD's algorithms thru a French then a European patent (Delalonde *et al.*, 2006) and plans to commercialize the system.

REFERENCES

Ackerman, M., & McDonald, D. (1996). *Answer garden 2: Merging organizational memory with collaborative help.* Paper presented at the Proceedings of the 1996 ACM conference on Computer supported cooperative work, Boston, Mass.

Agilience. (2006). Expertise location and management. Retrieved January 3rd 2007, from http://www.agilience.com/

Bergé, J.-M., & Périn, P. (2002). Contexte et enjeux des communautés d'intérêt. *Mémento technique du conseil scientifique de France Télécom, 18.*

Bloor, D. (1999). Anti-latour. Studies in history and philosophy of science, *30*(1), 81-112.

Brusilovsky, P., & Kobsa, A. (2007). *The adaptive web.* Springer.

Buffa, M., Ereteo, G., & Gandon, F. (2007, 2 au 6 Juillet). *Wiki et web sémantique.* Paper presented at the 18e Journées Francophones d'Ingénierie des Connaissances, Grenoble.

Conein, B. (2003). Communautés épistémiques et réseaux cognitifs: Coopération et cognition distribuée. *Revue d'Economie Politique* (Numéro spécial).

Delalonde, C., Chevrier, B., Soulier, E., & Potiron, J. (2006). Procédé et système de communication pour fournir au moins une réponse à une requête d'un utilisateur. France.

Delalonde, C., & Soulier, E. (2007, From 25 to 29 Juin). *Demond: Leveraging social participation for collaborative information retrieval.* Paper presented at the 1st Workshop on Adaptation and Personalisation in Social Systems: Groups, Teams, Communities. 11th International conference on User Modelling, Corfu, Greece.

Engeström, Y. (1987). *Learning by expanding.* Helsinki: Orienta-Konsultit Oy.

Erickson, T., & Kellogg, W. (2000). Social translucence: An approach to designing systems that support social processes. *ACM Transactions on Computer-Human Interaction, 7*(1), 59-83.

Google Co-op. (2006). Google co-op. Retrieved Septembre 15th 2006, from http://www.google.com/coop/

Hertzum, M., & Pejtersen, A. M. (2000). The information-seeking practices of engineers: Searching for documents as well as for people. *Information Processing and Management, 36*(5), 761-778.

Hutchins, E. (1991). *How a cockpit remembers its speed.* San Diego.

Hutchins, E. (1995). *Cognitition in the wild.* Cambridge MA: The MIT Press.

Huysman, M., & Wulf, V. (2003). *Social capital and information technology.* Cambridge MA.

Kauntz, H., Selman, B., & Shah, M. (1996). Referral web: Combining social networks and collaborative filtering. *Communications of the ACM, 40*(3), 63-65.

Latour, B. (2006). Changer de société - refaire de la sociologie. Paris: Armillaire.

Lave, J. (1988). Cognition in practice: Mind, mathematics and culture in everyday life. Cambridge: Cambridge University Press.

Lave, J., & Wenger, E. (1991). *Situated learning: Legitimate peripheral participation.* Cambridge: Cambridge University Press.

Leontiev, A. (1979). The problem of activity in psychology. In J. V. Wertsch (Ed.), *The concept of activity in soviet psychology* (pp. 135-143). Armonk: Sharpe.

Markoff, J. (2005). What the dormouse said: How the 60s counterculture shaped the personal computer: Viking Adult.

Mutch, A. (2002). Actors and networks or agents and structures: Towards a realist view of informations systems. *Organization, 9*(3), 477-496.

Pentland, B. T., & Feldman, M. S. (In Press). Narrative networks: Patterns of technology and organization. *Organization Science - Special issue on Information Technology and Organizational Form.*

Pissard, N. (2007). Etude des interactions sociales médiatées: Méthodologies, algorithmes, services. Paris Dauphine, Paris.

Plu, M., Bellec, P., Agosto, L., & Van De Velde, W. (2003). *The web of people: A dual view on the world wide web.* Paper presented at the Twelfth International World Wide Web Conference, Budapest.

Resnick, L. B., Levine, J. M., & Teasley, S. D. (1991). *Perspectives on socially shared cognition.* Washington DC: American Psychological Association (APA).

Schütz, A. (1946). The well-informed citizen. An essay on the social distribution of knowledge. *Social Research, 13*(4), 463-478.

Soulier, E. (2004). Les communautés de pratique au cœur de l'organisation réelle des entreprises. *Systèmes d'Information et Management (SIM), 9*(1).

Soulier, E., Delalonde, C., & Petit, O. (2007, Du 28 au 31 août). *Subjectivation et singularisation dans la perspective de l'apprentissage situé et de l'acteur-réseau.* Paper presented at the Congrès international AREF 2007 (Actualité de la Recherche en Education et en Formation), Strasbourg.

Suchman, L. A. (1987). Plans and situated actions - the problem of human-machine communication. Cambridge: Cambridge University Press.

Twidale, M. B., & Nichols, D. M. (1998). Designing interfaces to support collaboration in information retrieval. *Interacting with Computers. The Interdisciplinary Journal of Human-Computer Interaction, 10*(2), 177-193.

Vygotsky, L. S. (1978). *Mind in society.* Cambridge MA: Harvard University Press.

Wenger, E. (1998). Communities of practice. Learning, meaning, and identity. Cambridge: University Press.

Whitehead, A. N. (1929/1995). *Procès et réalité. Essai de cosmologie.* Paris: Editions Gallimard.

Wood, C. C. (1993). *A cognitive dimensional analysis of idea sketches.* University of Sussex, Falmer, Brighton.

Yahoo! (2005). Yahoo! Questions/réponses. Retrieved July 5th 2006, from http://fr.answers.yahoo.com/

Yahoo! My Web 2.0. (2006). My web 2.0. Retrieved March 12th 2006, from http://myweb2.search.yahoo.com/

Yedda. (2007). *Yedda.* Retrieved February 9th 2007, from http://www.yedda.com/

Chapter IX
COBRAS:
Cooperative CBR Bibliographic Recommender System

Hager Karoui
Université Paris XIII, France

ABSTRACT

In this chapter, the authors propose a case-based reasoning recommender system called COBRAS: a Peer-to-Peer (P2P) bibliographical reference recommender system. COBRAS's task is to find relevant documents and interesting people related to the interests and preferences of a single person belonging to a like-minded group in an implicit and an intelligent way. Each user manages their own bibliographical database in isolation from others. Target users use a common vocabulary for document indexing but may interpret the indexing vocabulary differently from others. Software agents are used to ensure indirect cooperation between users. A P2P architecture is used to allow users to control their data sharing scheme with others and to ensure their autonomy and privacy. The system associates a software assistant agent with each user. Agents are attributed three main skills: a) detecting the associated user's hot topics, b) selecting a subset of peer agents that are likely to provide relevant recommendations, and c) recommending both documents and other agents in response to a recommendation request sent by a peer agent. The last two skills are handled by implementing two inter-related data-driven case-based reasoning systems. The basic idea underlying the document recommendation process is to map hot topics sent by an agent to local topics. Documents indexed by mapped topics are then recommended to the requesting agent. This agent will provide later, a relevance feedback computed after the user evaluation of the received recommendations. Provided feedbacks are used to learn to associate a community of peer agents to each local hot topic. An experimental study involving one hundred software agents using real bibliographical data is described. The Obtained results demonstrate the validity of the proposed approach.

INTRODUCTION

Recommender systems (Resnick & Varian, 1997) aim at learning users' preferences over time in order to automatically suggest products that fit the learned user model. For example, recommender systems are used in e-commerce web sites to help customers in selecting products more suitable to their needs. Various techniques are used in order to compute recommendations such as:

- *Collaborative filtering*: is the most popular recommendation technique that aggregates data about customer's preferences (products' ratings) to recommend new products. A popular example is Amazon.com (Linden et al., 2003) wich recommends items to customers. Another example is MovieLens (Miller et al., 2003) which recommends movies.
- *Content-based filtering* exploits the preferences of a specific customer to build new recommendations to the customer. Content-based filtering approaches recommend items for the user based on the description of previously evaluated items. User profiles are created using features extracted from these items and each user is assumed to operate independently. NewsDude (Billsus & Pazzani, 1999) recommends news stories that follow up on stories the user read previously. It observes what online news stories the user has read and not read and learns to present the user with articles he/she may be interested to read. Letizia (Lieberman, 1995) wich recommends Web pages during browsing based on user profile.
- *Hybrid filtering* exploits features of content-based and collaborative filtering. For example, Fab (Balabanovic, 1997) for document recommendation where user profiles based on content analysis are maintained and closely compared to determine users with similar preferences for collaborative recommendation. COSYDOR (Jéribi et al.,

2001) is a system for user's assistance by helping the users to reformulate their queries based on the experience reuse and on the user's profiles. WebWatcher (Armstrong et al., 1995) presents an agent recommending appropriate hyperlink given the current Web page viewed by the user.

In collaborative filtering the recommendation depends on customers information, and a large number of previous user/system interactions are required to build reliable recommendations. In content-based systems only the data of the current user are exploited in building a recommendation. It requires a description of user interests that is either matched in the items catalog or provided as input for the learned user model to output a recommendation. Both approaches, if not trained with lot of examples (product ratings or pattern of user preferences), deliver poor recommendations. This limitation mostly motivated a third approach, knowledge-based, that tries to better use preexisting knowledge specific of the application domain (e.g. travels vs. computers) to build a more accurate model requiring less training instances (Lorenzi & Ricci, 2003). The knowledge-based approach is considered complementary to the other approaches (Burke, 2000). In this approach, knowledge about customers and the application domain are used to reason about what products fit the customers preferences. The most important advantage is that this approach does not depend (exclusively) on customers rates, hence avoiding the mentioned difficulty in bootstrapping the system. Case-Based Reasoning (CBR) is one of the most successful machine learning methodologies that exploits knowledge-rich representation of the application domain (Vatson, 1997; Aha, 1998), It is a cyclic and integrated problem solving process that supports learning from experience (Aamodt & Plaza, 1994) and is based on human reasoning. In this chapter, we propose a general CBR approach for object recommendation such as document, musique, image, etc.. In the treated example, the system recommends documents or more precisely bibliographical references. For the different types of recommendation, the vocabulary and the similarity functions will differ but the principle is the same. We situate in a contexte of user's assistance based on offering cooperation tool. This cooperation will be direct via groupware tools or is indirect via assistant agents. We belong to this indirect cooperation to offer implicit recommendation to users and to avoid them making extra effort needed for experience sharing. According to Montaner classification (Montaner, 2003), Cobras is a document recommender where the user model is presented by her/his topics of interest and their interpretation by some keywords and also by the collaborator's list. The system starts with an empty profil and uses implicit feedback by monitoring the user's actions (because we think that users are not willing to give explicit relevance feedback) based on the user behavior in front of the proposed recommendations (e.g. adding some proposed references, navigating on the reference list, ...). The profil adaptation is done by adding new information extracted from the user relevance feedback.

A number of systems have been proposed in the scientific literature to cope with the problem of document sharing and recommendation within a group of like-minded people. A common point of these systems is the use of some kind of hierarchy to model user's interest topics. According to the sharing policy of such a topic hierarchy, we can classify existing systems in one of the following classes:

1. Systems where all users share the same topic hierarchy with the same interpretation of each topic. These systems have often a centralised architecture (Glance et al., 1998). A document repository is shared by all users where they can add documents to sub-directories. In some systems a user can associate a relevance note to each added document. In such systems, the problem is

to compute how relevant would be a document d for a user u knowing the relevance of d to others.

2. Systems where each user manages her/his own topic's hierarchy. This is frequently the case in collaborative bookmarking systems were each user manages her/his own bookmark collection. The main issue here is to compute a mapping between each couple of users bookmark directories (Kanawati & Malek, 2007).

3. Systems where users share a the same hierarchy of topics but each has her/his own interpretation of topics. This is commonly the case in research teams where a common hierarchy of topics is defined but each user is free to associate a reference to a topic that is different from the one selected by other users.

Cobras falls in the third class where we assume that users speak a common language. The general architecture is illustrated on Figure 1. Each user maintains its personal bibliographic database. The goal of Cobras is to allow sharing these personal bibliographic knowledge in an implicit and and intelligent way. It is implicit because users are not asked to provide any extra effort for helping in the sharing process.

It is intelligent, since a user will be recommended with data that are relevant to her/his current interests when needed. The system associates a software personal agent with each user. The role of a personal agent is to observe user's interactions with her/his own bibliographic database in order to detect the user's hot topics and the user's own interpretation of the shared topic hierarchy.

Each agent cooperates with peer agents in order to find bibliographic data that are relevant to the associated user's hot topics. Two skills are necessary for an agent to achieve this task:

1. *Learning to ask*: the goal is to select a subset of the available peer agents that are likely

Figure 1. COBRAS's architecture

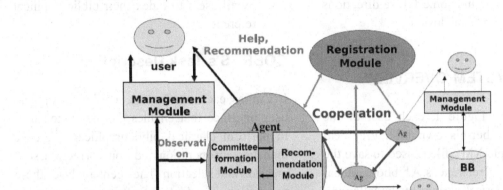

to provide the most relevant documents to a given hot topic.

2. ***Learning to recommend***: the goal is to find local documents that best match the received recommendation request.

In Cobras, we experiment an approach that enables each agent to achieve both learning tasks by exploring interaction data among agents. Each agent uses two inter-related case-based reasoners; one for implementing each learning task. CBR is a problem solving methodology (Aamodt & Plaza, 1994). A new problem is solved by finding a similar previous case, and reusing it in the new problem situation. It is a paradigm for learning and reasoning through experience. An important feature is that CBR is an approach to incremental and sustained learning since a new experience is retained each time a problem has been solved, making it immediately available for future problems.

A CBR cycle contains mainly four phases:

1. In the **retrieve phase**, the system searches for similar topics of interest and their

interpretation in the case base in order to find out where to search on the local agent bibliographical base for relevant documents associated to the found topics. Similarity measures are based on topic and keyword similarities.

2. In the **reuse phase**, the set of topics and keywords are used to find relevant documents on the bibliographical base.

3. In the **revision phase**, the relevance feedback of the user is used in order to retain the new case.

4. In the **retain phase,** the new case will be added to the case base if it is judged to be interesting for the learning.

The reminder of the chapter is organised as follows. Next we explain the system functioning in an informal way. Section "Recommendation computation" details the proposed approach for reference recommendation computation. The computation of the query community is described in section "Community computation". Experimental results are presented and discussed in section "System Evaluation". Related work are summarized in section "Related Work", and finally a conclusion and some future directions are given in section "Conclusion".

COBRAS: SYSTEM OVERVIEW

As illustrated on Figure 1, each user of the system manages her/his own bibliographical database. A simple XML file is used to save the user bibliographical references. A bibliographical reference element r is described by the following informations:

- *Bibliographical data* (denoted r.data): these are classical bibliographical data such as the type of the reference (Article, proceedings, report, etc.), the list of authors, the title, the date. The classical bibtex format is used to model this part of data.

- *Reference description* (denoted r.desc): this is a user-defined list of keywords describing the reference content. If no keywords are given by the user, the field will contain the list of nominal groups extracted from the reference title. A more elaborated method will be used for document description such as a vector of weighted terms VSM (Salton, 1971), TF-IDF (Salton and McGill, 1983).

- *Topics* (denoted r.topics): this is a list of topics that are relevant to the reference. These topics are selected by the user out from a system-provided topic hierarchy shared by all users. Each reference should be indexed by at least one topic. Obviously, different users may assign different topics to the same reference. For example one may index all CBR-related papers to the same topic, let's say CBR, while another user may index the same papers differently: some related to memory organization in CBR systems and others for CBR case maintenance. A third may index the same references as all related to lazy learning. In the current implemented

prototype, The ACM[1] topic hierarchy is used by all users to index their bibliographical references.

COBRAS's Task Description

In Cobras, each assistant agent offers a graphical user interface that enables the associated user to perform classical bibliographical reference management operations: edition, correction, suppression and selection. The agent analyses these user actions in order to infer the user's current hot topics. The more the user manipulates references indexed by a topic T the more this topic is hot. Topics importance decreases with time enabling to detect only current interests of the user. Details about the applied algorithm for detecting the user's hot topics are given in section "Hot topic detection". For each detected hot topic the agent computes a keyword vector representing the user interpretation of this topic. This vector is computed by aggregating keyword lists of references assigned directly or indirectly to that topic. A reference is indirectly related to a topic T if it is related to a topic T' more specific than T. Details are given in (Karoui et al., 2004).

Community computation. Once a hot topic T is detected by an agent, the agent computes a community of peer agents to which a recommendation request will be sent. Informally, a community is composed of agents that have provided relevant recommendations to similar queries in the past and from agents that are recommended by relevant agents. A Case-based reasoner is used in order to explore the history of the agent interaction with peer agents in order to compute the most relevant agents for a given query. If no relevant community is found, which is typically the case for a new detected hot topic, the agent will select a random set of available peer agents. This set will form the starting set of forming a more relevant query-community based on provided recommendations and on user evaluation of these recommendations. The process of community computation is detailed in section "Community computation".

Recommendation computation. When an agent receives a recommendation request from a peer agent; it searches for local references that match the received request. Recall, that a recommendation request contains a topic label T (selected from the shared topic hierarchy) and a list of keywords giving the sender agent interpretation of the topic label T. Matching is a two-step process:

1. First, the agent will match the received topic T (with its interpretation) with local topics that have contributed in the past in providing relevant recommendations for past received requests that are similar to the current one (the search occurs on the local case base).

2. Next, documents assigned locally to these computed topics will be recommended back to the sender agent (the search occurs on the bibliographical base).

The sender agent will merge all recommendations provided by different contacted peer agents and will provide a list of top ranked documents to the user. Some recommended documents will be approved by the user, others may not. Based on the implicit user evaluation of the provided recommendations, the user's agent sends back to each contacted peer agent an evaluation of recommendations provided by that agent. This information is used to assess the local topic's relevance for the initial recommendation request. A second case-based reasoner is used for reference recommendation computation. This is detailed in the next section.

Hot Topic Detection

As stated before all users share the same topic hierarchy that has a tree structure. All topics are not equally interesting for each user. In addition for each user the set of interesting topics changes over time. It is crucial for any recommender system to provide recommendations in the area that interests the most the user. Recommendation providing should not be intrusive. In addition, if users are really interested in the recommendation area they will be more willing to evaluate provided advices. In order to compute a user's hot topics list we apply a simple algorithm that measures the "temperature" of each topic. Topics that have a temperature above a given threshold σ will be labelled as hot topics. Initially, all topics have a zero temperature. Each action executed by the user involving a topic T will increase the temperature of that topic by a specified amount. Typical actions that modify a topic's temperature are: adding, editing or searching for a reference related to the topic. Different actions add different values to the current topic temperature. A cooling function is also applied in order to decrease the temperature of topics no more used by the user. Now because the topic hierarchy can be used differently by different users, we need to determine the most specific topics (e.g. most deep topics) on which the user's activity is centered on. To do so, a temperature propagation function is applied. Starting from the leaves of the the topic tree, each topic propagates its current temperature to the parent topic. Topics with temperature above a system threshold r will cease to propagate their temperature and will be added to the list of hot topics. The most n hot topics that has been added to the hot topics lists after visiting the tree in a bottom-up way will be returned. The heuristic is to return the most specific topics which concentrate a given level of the user's focus.

RECOMMENDATION COMPUTATION

Principle

This section explains the recommendation computation process applied by an agent when receiving a recommendation request, called also a query, from a peer agent.

Figure 2. Recommendation computation module

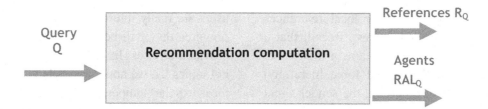

A query Q is given by the triple Q =< A_u, T, I^u_T > where:

- A_u is the sender agent identifier.
- T is a topic label selected by Au as a hot interest topic of user u.
- I^u_T is the interpretation of the topic T by the user u. Actually, this is a set of keywords extracted from keyword lists associated to references assigned directly or indirectly by user u to the topic T (Karoui et al., 2006b).

An agent answers a recommendation request by sending back two ranked lists:

- R_Q is a list of recommended bibliographical references that match, from the agent point of view the received query,
- RAL_Q is a list of recommended peer agents that are relevant, from the local agent point of view, to the received query. Each recommended agent is associated with a trust degree that express the relevance of its recommended references to the topic T.

Three types of agents can be recommended: agents that are known to the local one to have relevant documents, agents that are known to the local one to don't have relevant documents and those that have sent in the past queries similar to Q:

1. ***Interesting agents*** (IA): agents that have relevant documents and then judged to be interesting by the local agent according the interest topic.
2. ***Not interesting agents*** (NIA): agents judged to be not interesting according to the interest topic from the local agent point of view.
3. ***Similar agents*** (SA): in terms of interest topics. They are agents who asked similar request but not yet evaluated by the local agent.

$$RAL_Q \leftarrow (\{SA\} \cup \{IA\} \cup \{NIA\}).$$

Recommended references are evaluated by the user u. Agent Au sends back to the recommender agent an overall evaluation of the recommended references. The evaluation is expressed by the local precision of recommended references (see equation 9). The local precision is given by the ratio of the number of recommended references that are accepted by the user u over the size of the set of recommended references provided by the recommender agent.

A data-driven case-based reasoner is used for computing references that are relevant to the received query (Malek & Kanawati, 2004). Unlike classical CBR systems, the memory of a data-driven CBR reasoner is composed of two main repositories: a case-base and a raw data base. To solve a new problem pb, the reasoner acts first as an ordinary CBR reasoner: it searches for past solved cases that are similar to pb. It proposes a solution sol(pb) to the current problem by reusing solutions of found similar cases.

sol(pb) can be revised by the user or by another software module and the reasoner may add the couple < pb, sol(pb) > to the case base if this new case can improve the system capacity for solving new problems. If for some reasons, no relevant solution can be proposed following the classical CBR cycle, a data-driven CBR reasoner elaborates new potential source cases by exploring available raw data. Potential cases that contribute to solve the problem pb will be added to the case base. This reasoning strategy allows to continuously revise and maintain the case base in order to fit the profile of new problems submitted to the system (Malek & Kanawati, 2004).

Similarity Measures

In this section, we define the different similarity functions used in the recommendation computation process (mainly in the retrieval and reuse phases).

Keywords Similarity: noted simKeywords(A,B), computes the similarity of two keyword lists A and B. It is a simple function measuring the number of common words between two lists. This similarity is used to compare lists that have comparable cardinalities. This is the case of two interpretations of two topics.

$$sim_{Keywords}(A,B) = \frac{|A \cap B|}{|A \cup B|} \quad (1)$$

Topic Similarity: noted simTopics(T1, T2), computes the similarity of two topics selected in the common topic's hierarchy. Figure 3 illustrates the general architecture of a topic's hierarchy. Nodes (i.e. topic's labels) can be related by two types of arcs (i.e. relations):

1. *Specialization relation is* an is-a relation (represented on the figure by continuous lines) which structures the set of topics in a tree.
2. *RelatedTo relation* (represented on the figure in a dashed lines) that expresses some semantic relationship between linked topics.

The similarity between two topics is defined as the inverse of the distance that separates these topics following both arcs types. Two distance functions are hence defined, one for each type of arcs:

- A first distance (d_s) is defined using the Specialization arcs as:

$$d_s(T_1, T_2) = \frac{path(T_1, msca(T_1, T_2)) + path(T_2, msca(T_1, T_2))}{path(T_1, root) + path(T_2, root)}$$

Where:

- path(x, y) returns the number of is-a arcs that separate x from y,
- msca(x, y) returns the most specific common ancestor of both nodes,
- root is the root node of the hierarchy.

This function expresses the idea that two nodes separated by the same number of arcs as another couple of nodes are closer if they are deeper in the hierarchy (Jaczynski & Trousse, 1999).

- A second distance (d_r) is defined using the RelatedTo arcs as follows:

$$d_r(T_1, T_2) = min_{(T_i \in V(T_1), T_j \in V(T_2), T_i \rightarrow T_j)} \frac{path(T_i, T_1) + path(T_j, T_2)}{2 \times p}$$

Where:

- V(T) is the set of nodes in the neighbourhood of T following the *is-a* relation. The neighbourhood is the set of successors and ancestors of a node including the node itself.
- p is the depth of the topics hierarchy (p > 0) and x → y express the fact that nodes x and y are linked by a *RelatedTo* arc.

Notice that if T1 → T2 then we have d_r(T1, T2) = 0. The similarity value according to *RelatedTo* relation is maximal if the two topics are directly linked (we have an arc connecting both topics) and decreases in proportion as the two topics are indirectly linked. Two topics are indirectly linked

Figure 3. The two types of relations in the topic hierarchy

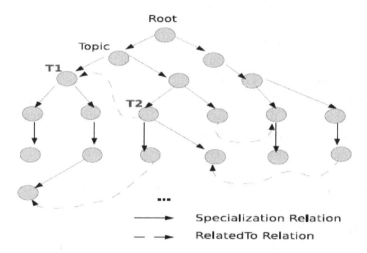

if one of the descendants or ascendants of the first topic is linked with one of the descendants or ascendants of the second topic.

The similarity of two topics is then defined by:

$$sim_{Topics}(T_1, T_2) = \alpha(1 - d_s(T_1, T_2)) + (1 - \alpha)(1 - d_r(T_1, T_2))$$

Where α in [0, 1] is a weighting parameter. Two topics are said similar if $sim_{Topics}(T1, T2) > \sigma_t$ where σ_t is a system parameter.

Reference Relevance

We define the relevance of a reference r to a query Q as a weighted aggregation of two basic similarities by:

$$(2)$$

$$relevance(r, Q) =$$

$$Max_{T_i \in r.topics}(\beta sim_{Topics}(T_i, Q.T)) + (1 - \beta)\frac{|r.desc \cap Q.I_T^u|}{|r.desc|}$$

Where β in [0, 1] is a weighting parameter. A reference r is said to be relevant to a query Q if relevance(r,Q) > σ_r where σ_r is a given specified threshold.

Notice that we use Max simTopics because a reference will have several topics and for keyword

similarity, we divide by the description reference size because the two sets don't have comparable cardinalities ($|r.desc| \ll |Q.I_t^u|$).

Case Structure

In our application, the raw data set is the local bibliographical reference database. Remember that each reference should be assigned, at least, one topic selected from the shared topic's hierarchy. A source case, in the case base has the following structure < pb, sol(pb) > where:

- **The problem part** involves a current topic of interest. It is given by pb = (A_u, T, I_T^u) where:
  - Au is the identity of the initiator agent,
  - T is a topic label,
  - I_T^u is an interpretation of this topic provided by a user u.
- **The solution part** presents the mapping of the topic label and its interpretation to local topics. It is given by: sol(pb) = (TL_s, KL_s, E, t) where:
  - TL_s is a set of topics that index references relevant to the query given in the problem part,

- KL$_s$ is a keyword list that represents the set of documents that have been recommended in response to the query cited in the problem part and that have been approved by the user,
- E is the evaluation of the recommended references provided by the user u,
- t is the date of the case elaboration.

Notice that a case solution gives a set of topics to search rather than enumerating documents (i.e. references) to recommend. This allows the system to recommend new documents that have been added to the local reference database after the case edition. More precisely a source case expresses a kind of mapping between the topic T expressed by user u and topics TLs managed by the local user.

Recommendation Computation

As stated before an answer to a query Q is composed of two lists: R$_Q$ a list of recommended references and RAL$_Q$ a list of recommended agents. Next we explain how both lists R$_Q$ and RAL$_Q$ are computed.

Computing R$_Q$

In order to compute the list of references to recommend in answer to Q, the recommender agent will search for cases in the local case base that are similar to Q. Similarity between a request Q $= <A_u, T, I^u_T>$ and a source case sc $= <$pb $= (A_{u'},$ T', $I^u_{T'}$), sol(pb) $>$ is evaluated using a weighted aggregation of basic similarity functions defined over the set of topics and lists of keywords (see section "Similarity measures"). Depending on the output of the source case research phase, we distinguish between two possible situations: a) no similar cases are found and b) some similar cases are retrieved. Next we explain the applied process in both situations.

Computing RAL$_Q$

In addition to the list R$_Q$, each agent Au maintains for each local hot topic T , a square evaluation matrix E$_u$(T) where an entry e$^u_{ij}$(T) represents the relevance of agent A$_i$ as evaluated by agent A$_j$ concerning the topic T as currently known to agent A$_u$.

$$E^u(T) = \begin{pmatrix} e_{11} & e_{12} & \cdots & e_{1i} & \cdots & e_{1n} \\ e_{21} & e_{22} & \cdots & e_{2i} & \cdots & e_{2n} \\ \vdots & \vdots & \vdots & \vdots & \vdots & \vdots \\ e_{i1} & e_{i2} & \cdots & e_{ii} & \cdots & e_{in} \\ \vdots & \vdots & \vdots & \vdots & \vdots & \vdots \\ e_{n1} & e_{n2} & \cdots & e_{ni} & \cdots & e_{nn} \end{pmatrix}_T$$

(3)

Evaluation values are taken from the set: $\{-1\}$ U $\{0\}$ U $]0, 1]$ where:

1. e$^u_{ij}$(T) $= -1$ if agent A$_u$ is aware that agent A$_j$ judges agent A$_i$ as irrelevant to the topic T . An agent A$_i$ is irrelevant to a topic T if the precision of recommendations provided by A$_i$ is null (which means that agent A$_i$ did not recommend relevant references concerning the topic T).
2. e$^u_{ij}$(T) $= 0$ if A$_u$ has no information about the relevance of A$_i$ as computed by A$_j$ concerning the topic T .
3. $0 < $ e$^u_{ij}$(T) $=< 1$ if agent A$_u$ is aware that agent A$_j$ judges agent A$_i$ as relevant to the topic T. e$^u_{ij}$(T) value is the reference precision of recommendations provided by A$_i$ to A$_j$ concerning the topic T .

The list of agents to recommend in relation to a query Q is given by the union of agents that have submitted queries similar to Q, all agents A$_j$ for which e$^r_{jr}$(T') $> \sigma_e$ such as Sim(T, T') $> \sigma_t$ and agents for which e$^r_{jr}$(T) $= -1$ in order to penalize them concerning to topic T . This is to say that an agent recommends peer agents that have submitted similar queries, those who have provided good results for local recommendation requests relative to similar topics and also irrelevant agents in order to avoid contacting them for this topic.

1. Raw data exploration

If no similar cases are found, which is typically the case when the query's topic is new, the recommender agent will try to answer Q by exploring the local references database. The shared topic's hierarchy is explored in order to find references that match the query. Starting from the node that has the label Q.T, a depth-first searching strategy is applied in order to find k references that are relevant to Q where k is a system parameter. If no more nodes can be visited the agent will explore the tree starting from the parent of Q.T. The rationale here is to give priority for references assigned to the same topic as the query, then for those assigned to more specific topics and at last for those assigned to more general topics. The tree exploration ends if k relevant references are found or if the similarity between the query topic and the currently visited topic is under a given threshold σ_e.

The list R_Q (i.e. recommended references) is then composed of the list of retrieved references ranked by their relevance to the query Q. Formally we have:

$$R_Q = \{(r_1, \text{relevance}(r_1,Q)), (r_2, \text{relevance}(r_2,Q)), \ldots, (r_l, \text{relevance}(r_l,Q))\}$$ where l<= k and v i, j: i < j, relevance(r_i,Q) => relevance(r_j,Q).

The recommender agent answers Q by sending back to the asking agent both lists R_Q and RAL_Q and edits a new potential case *pc* where the problem part is given by the couple $<Q.A_u, Q.T, Q.I_u^T>$.

The solution part is given by:

- TLs = U{ri.topics}, ri in R_Q. This is the set of topics assigned to retrieved documents.
- KLs = U{inter{r_i.desc}(T_i)}, r_i. in R_Q, T_i in TL_s. This is a keyword list describing the retrieved documents.

Agent A_u sends back to the recommender agent an overall evaluation of the recommended references (i.e. R_Q list). The evaluation is expressed by the local precision of recommended references. The local precision is given by the ratio of the number of recommended references that are accepted by the user u over the size of the set of recommended references provided by the recommender agent. If the evaluation is not null then the recommender agent will add the potential case to the case base after adding the received evaluation E and the date t of the case elaboration to the solution part (see section "Case structure").

2. CBR cycle

When the recommender agent finds similar cases (i.e. search phase) in its reference case base, then it goes to the reuse phase. Having all similar source cases, the agent builds the solution of the target problem. The solution of the reuse phase is a set of signs indicating where to search in the bibliographical base. Sign set includes topics and keywords lists used to search for references in the bibliographical database. Note that if the base content changes (ex. the user adds some new references), the system will retrieve them if they are indexed by the found signs. The solution of the target problem is composed by a topic and keyword lists of the different selected source cases SC_Q. The recommender agent answers by the list R_Q which will be formed of the list of documents indexed by the set of topics returned by all retrieved source cases SC_Q that match the query Q. The list R_Q is given by: $R_Q = \{(r_i, \text{relevance}(r_i,Q))\}$ with r_i.topics in sc.TL_s and sc in SC_Q.

Besides of this signs, the system returns a list of recommended agents (named RAL_Q). Each agent belonging to this list, is assigned a score (as defined in section "Recommendation computation") which presents its assessment by the recommender agent for the query's topic.

COMMUNITY COMPUTATION

This section explains the community computation process applied by an agent when detecting a hot topic of its user. For each detected user's hot topic, the agent tries to compute a relevant agent community. In order to find those communities, the agent exploits its historical interactions and its experiences of collaboration in order to learn to form relevant community per interesting topic.

Once the community is computed, the query is sent then to the agents composing the returned community. The contacted community is evaluated by the user u depending on their contributions (reference recommendations) according to the request and then its agent A_u updates the community case base.

The community evaluation is expressed by the local agent precision of recommended references. The local precision is given by the ratio of the number of interesting agents that proposed references that are accepted by the user u over the size of the community (number of all contacted agents) by the asking agent A_u.

Another data-driven case-based reasoner is used for computing agents that will be relevant to the interest topic (Karoui et al., 2006a). To solve a new problem pb, the reasoner acts first as an ordinary CBR reasoner: it searches for past solved cases that are similar to pb. If no relevant solution can be proposed following the classical CBR cycle, a data-driven CBR reasoner elaborates new potential source cases by exploring available agents.

Case Structure

A case presents an agent's collaboration experience according to a topic of interest and has the following structure: Case = ((T), (C, E, t)) where:

- **The problem part**: pb=(T) is a detected hot topic,
- **The solution part**: sol(pb) = (C,E, t) where:
  - C is the community composed by interesting agents according to the topic T ,
  - E is the evaluation of the community,
  - t is the date of the case elaboration.

Evaluation function In order to evaluate agent relevance, each agent applies the following agent evaluation function:

$$Eval_u(A_i, T) = \sum_{\{T, sim_{Topics}(T',T) > \delta\}} sim_{Topics}(T',T) \times \sum_{j=1}^{n} e_{j,u} \times e_{i,j}$$

(4)

This function expressess the idea that the evaluation of an agent A_i by the agent Au according to a topic T depends on the evaluation of the other agents (A_j) for the agent A_i weighted by the evaluation of the local agent A_u for the recommender agents (A_j). This reasoning exploits other peer's experiences and past collaboration with others relating to some topics. Each agent will learn from its own experience and also from other's experiences.

Community Computing

The community search is based on the topic similarity (defined in equation 2) which compares the target topic with the one of the case in the agent's case base. If this similarity value is above a given threshold σ_t, then the case will be recalled and we go to the next step. If the search phase does not lead to source cases, the system will contact a number of available agents randomly selected and a set of agents that had been recommended according to the theme T by consulting its evaluation matrix. The next phase aims at building the solution to the target problem from the set of source cases found in the previous phase.

The steps are:

- Determining the evaluation matrix to be considered: matrix corresponding to the matching found topics: {E^u(T')} such as simTopics(T', T) > x, x is a system threshold.
- Determining the candidate agents CAg for whom the system computes their relevance values. Indeed, instead of considering all columns of the related matrix (and thus all agents), we consider only the columns corresponding to the found community agents. The agents of a matrix that will have their relevance computed are agents who have been recommended by the community agents. The same treatment will be carried out on each matrix corresponding to a topic belonging to the found topics TL.
- Calculating the total relevance for all found agents: $Eval_u(A_i, T)$ where A_i in CAg.
- Selecting a subset of the found candidate agents. The selection can be done depending on the number of required agents, and depending on their evaluation value by choosing the n best for example.

The recommendation request is broadcast to all peer agents composing the computed community. The community is then evaluated by the asking agent according to its user's behavior with respect to the recommended references. If the user is interested on a set of recommended references (e.g. the user adds some references to its local base), then their associated cases and agents will be well evaluated.

Computing Retained Community

The retained community is built as follows:

- The first step is to group all agents having their local precision value strictly positive (i.e. agents proposing at least a good reference).
- Then the agents are classified according to their precision value.
- Finally, the retained community will be composed by the n best ordered agents.

The idea is to retain only those interesting agents, which are evaluated in comparison with others. Once a community is formed, a new corresponding case (T , C, E, t) will be developed such as:

- T : the topic of the sent query,
- C: community of the retained agents,
- E: the community evaluation (precision). The community precision is the average of its agents precision (see equation 9 of section "System evaluation").
- t: the date of the case elaboration. The date will be useful mainly for the maintenance phase but we did not interested at this time.

The update of an agent i relevance in the evaluation matrix of the initiator agent j, corresponding to a given topic T is as follows: if the agent is already evaluated then its evaluation value is updated such:

$$e_{ij}^{t+1}(T) = (e_{ij}^t(T) + New(e_{ij}(T)))/2,$$

Else its evaluation value takes the new one:

$$e_{ij}^{t+1}(T) = New(e_{ij}(T)) \qquad (5)$$

If the research phase has not resulted in any source cases, the new elaborated potential source case will be added to the base case of the agent if the evaluation is satisfactory (E). If the research phase has resulted in source cases, and whether the case is well assessed by the agent, then, if a case already exists for the same topic, then it will be updated by replacing the values of E and t with the new ones. Otherwise, the case will be added to the case base.

SYSTEM EVALUATION

In order to validate the proposed approaches, we have made a simulation study involving 100 Jade[2] agents. Each agent maintains its own bibliographic database that corresponds to a whole conference inproceedings (e.g. AI05 for Artificial Intelligence proceedings of 2005, MI98 for Machine Learning conference of 1998) extracted from the open source DBLP[3] database. The ACM hierarchy is used as a shared topic hierarchy. Each document in the used DBLP has been attributed, using an heuristic automatic classification scheme, one or several topics from the ACM hierarchy and keywords extracted from the document title to simplify the experimentation.

In our simulation, we assume that all agents have the same initial state: empty case bases and no knowledge about others. Each agent has a hot topic presenting the topic with the maximum number of attached references and consequently the submitted query is related to that hot topic. An interesting agent is agent who recommend at least one good reference and we suppose that a good reference is a reference having a similarity above a given threshold to the request. Most of the used parameters are resulting from previous experiments.

The request of each agent will be sent several times, the system will use its two CBR components to handle that request. We measure each time the values of recall and precision of the system

(defined hereafter) and we evaluate the system, based on these criteria. We compute for each agent the list of all interesting agents and the list of all relevant references by sending the request to all agents in the system, necessary to compute the system recall and precision. Then we compute at each request launching, the values of the selected criteria, for each agent, then those for the system. The system performances have been evaluated using the recall and the precision measures for both modules: community computation and reference recommendation:

1. ***Community computation***: the recall of the system, respectively the precision, is the average of the local recalls (Agent Recall$_i$), respectively the local precisions (Agent Precisioni) of each agent, defined respectively in equations 6 and 7. The local recall of an agent i is the rate of interesting contacted agents from all interesting agents. The local precision of an agent is the rate of interesting contacted agents from all contacted agents by the agent i for a given query.

$$Agent\_Recall_i = \frac{|(Interesting\_contacted\_agents)_i|}{|All\_interesting\_Agents|}$$

$$Agent\_Precision_i = \frac{|(Interesting\_contacted\_Agents)_i|}{|(All\_contacted\_Agents)_i|}$$

(6,7)

2. ***Reference recommendation***: the recall of the system, respectively the precision, is the average of the local recalls (Reference Recalli), respectively the local precisions (Reference Precisioni) of each agent, defined respectively in equations 8 and 9. The local reference recall of an agent i is the rate of good recommended references from all good references existing in the system by all the agents. The local reference precision of an agent is the rate of good recommended references from all recommended references by the agent i for a given query.

$$Reference\_Recall_i = \frac{|(Good\_recommended\_references)_i|}{|Good\_references|}$$

$$Reference\_Precision_i = \frac{|(Good\_recommended\_references)_i|}{|(All\_recommended\_references)_i|}$$

$$(8,9)$$

Figure 4 shows the recall and the precision variation according to the number of CBR cycles for the reference recommendation module. We notice that the precision of the reference recommendation is very important (average > 0.75) which means that the system recommends relevant references according to a given request. The reference recall is satisfactory (average > 0.25) which means that the system retrieves a part of the relevant references. The system learns progressively to find more relevant references according to a given topic of interest.

Figure 5 shows the recall and the precision variation according to the number of CBR cycles for the community computation module. We notice that the precision of the agent is very important (precision > 0.9 from the 3rd cycle) while the recall is satisfactory (nearly 0.4). The system learns progressively to form relevant community according to a given topic of interest.

The system has an important precision for selecting interesting agent and recommending relevant references while its recall is satisfactory. Notice that the experience is made without any preliminary learning phase, with empty case bases and close environment wich explains the stagnation of the results. Our first goal is to validate our approaches. A next more elaborate experience will be made in large scale environement in order to evaluate and to compare the system performances (recall, precision, exchanged messages numbers per request, community size) with other similar systems.

RELATED WORK

One interesting work directly related to our system is the Bibster system (Broekstra et al., 2004). The main goal of Bibster is to allow a group of people to search for bibliographical references in each other personal database. A peer-to-peer architecture is used. However, only exact searching is supported. Peer selection is based on the expertise notion (Haase et al., 2004). The expertise is a set of topics selected by the

Figure 4. Recall and precision variation for reference recommendation

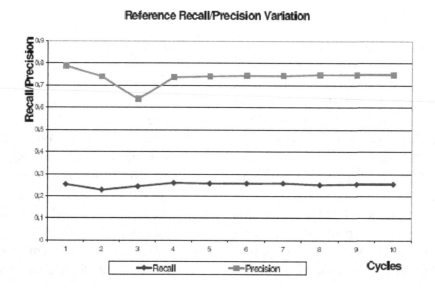

Figure 5. Recall and precision variation for community computation

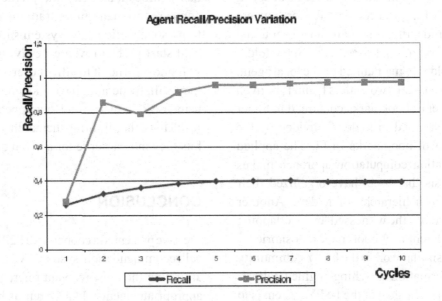

user herself/himself from a shared hierarchy of topics. All peers share a common ontology for publishing semantic descriptions of their expertise. When a peer receives a request, it decides to forward the query to peers whose expertise is similar to the subject of the query. Peers decide autonomously to whom advertisements should be sent and which advertisements to accept. This decision is based on the semantic similarity between expertise descriptions. This strategy gives good results compared with broadcasting the query to all or to a random set of peers but does not exploit past experience to learn and improve the formed semantic topology. The system also uses an important exchanged message number. Our system represents, in a way, an extension of Bibster where similarity-based searching is used. In addition the search is made by software agents instead of being initiated by the users themselves and the number of exchanged messages is linear to the community size,

Collaborative P2P bookmarking systems address a similar problem (Kanawati & Malek, 2000). However in the peer-to-peer collaborative bookmarking system (Kanawati & Malek, 2001), we lack a unified hierarchy of topics making the matching evaluation harder to compute. CoWING is a multi-agent collaborative bookmark management system. The CoWING system allows users to share their bookmarks, in a personalized way without asking users to do extra task except for defining other access control on their repositories. Each user is assisted by a personal agent, the CoWING agent that uses a hybrid neural/CBR classifier that learns the users' strategy in classifying bookmarks. A WING agent observes the user's behaviour when managing her/his own bookmark collection. It learns how the user classifies her/his bookmarks. The learned classification strategy is used to construct associations between bookmark folders belonging to other users. The system is composed of a central CoWING agent and a WING agent per registred user. The CoWING agent acts as WING agent registry. It provides WINGS with each other addresses. The bookmark recommendation computation is performed as follows. Each WING agent maintains localy two data structures: an agenda and a folder correlation matrix FCM. The agenda is a dictionary structure where keys represent identifiers of peer WING agents to contact and values are next contact dates. The FCM is a mXn matrix where m is the number of folders in the local repository and the number of peer agents known to the local agent. An entry FCM[i, j] is a couple $< f^l_k, cor_{ij} >$ where f^l_k is a folder identifier maintained by user u_i and cor_{ij} is the correlation degree between the folder f^l_k and the folder f^l_k maintained by the local agent. Correlation between two folders f_1 and f_2 is given by the number of bookmarks contained in folder f_2 that are classified in folder f_1 divided by the total number of bookmarks in f2. The applied recommendation computation approach makes the hypothesis that users have organized their bookmarks in a hierarchy of folders. Another related problem is the witnessed low overlapping between different user bookmark repositories.

Another similar work is the I-SPY community oriented information searching engine (Balfe & Smyth, 2004). The goal of the I-SPY system is to allow a group of like-minded people to share their search results in an implicit way. The system uses a case-based reasoning technique and is built in a centralised way where a hit matrix H_{ij} records for each submitted query the documents selected by the user. An element hij gives the number of times that a document d_j was selected by users from the response list of a query q_i. When a new query is submitted, results that have been selected by other users in response to similar past queries are provided by the system. In our system, the set of topics can be viewed as a set of pre-specified queries. The overlap between the users'queries is more likely to happen than in the case of open vocabulary queries. The system uses a collaborative search for two reasons: first, to attract communities of users with similar information needs and second, by monotoring user selections for a query it is possible to build a model of query-page relevance based on the probability that a given page pi will be selected by a user when returned as a result for query q_i. The system has the ability to personalize search results for the needs of a community is possible without the need to store individualised search histories; no individual user profiles are stored

and no user identification is necessary. This has significant security and privacy advantages compared to many more traditional approaches to personalization. The system suffers from the cold-start problem where newly indexed pages will find it difficult to attract user attention since they will, by default, have a low relevancy score using I-SPY's metric and thus appear far down in result lists, thus limiting their ability to attract the hits they may deserve for a given query.

CONCLUSION

We have presented a cooperative P2P bibliographical recommendation system COBRAS. It aims at finding the most relevant references from the appropriate agents. The system is based on two CBR components collaborating each other in order to compute relevant recommendations. The first CBR reasoner aims at finding an appropriate community to ask for a given recommendation request. The second CBR reasoner aims at finding the most relevant references from the previous computed community. Experimental results show the validity of the proposed approaches and that the use of a cooperative CBR approach for community and reference recommendation promise good recommender system performances. The proposed approach doesn't deal with the vocabulary problem (synonyms, metaphors, ...) (Furnas et al., 1987). A large application and a real user test are required to compare the results with used and existing approaches.

FUTURE TRENDS

Several trends of this work can be handled to improve the proposed system such as:

* more specific similarity measures proposal in order to take into account the similarity of references in relation to the request and

also the diversity of the proposed recommendations (references diversity between them).

- large-scale experiment to analyze the system performances and to compare it with other systems.

REFERENCES

Aamodt, A., & Plaza, E. (1994). Case-based reasoning: Foundational issues, methodological variations, and system approaches. *AI Communications IOS Press*, 7(1), 39–59.

Aha, D. W. (1998). The omnipresence of case-based reasoning in science and application. *Knowledge-Based Systems*, 11(5-6), 261–273.

Armstrong, R., Freitag, D., Joachims T., & Mitchell T. (1995). WebWatcher: A Learning Apprentice for the World Wide Web. *In AAAI Spring Symposium on Information Gathering*, pages 6-12.

Balabanovic, M., & Shoham, Y. (1997). Combining Content-Based and Collaborative recommendation. *In the communications of the ACM*.

Balfe E., & Smyth, B. (2004). Case-based collaborative web search. In *the* 7th *European Conference on Advances in Case-based Reasoning (ECCBR'04)*, volume 3155 of *LNCS*, pages 489–503, Madrid, Spain, Springer.

Billsus, D., & Pazzani, M. (1999). A hybrid user model for news story classi¢cation. I*n User Modeling (Proceedings of the Seventh International Conference)*. Banff, Canada, pp. 99-108.

Broekstra, J., Ehrig, M., Haase, P., Harmelen, F., Menken, M., Mika, P., Schnizler, B., & Siebes, R. (2004). Bibster- a semantics-based bibliographic peer-to-peer system. In *Proceedings of SemPGRID'04,* 2ⁿᵈ *Workshop on Semantics in Peer-to-Peer and Grid Computing*, pages 3–22, New York, USA.

Burke, R. (2000). Knowledge-based Recommender Systems. In J. E. Daily, A. Kent, and H. Lancour, editors, *Encyclopedia of Library and Information Science, 69*. Marcel Dekker.

Furnas, G. W., Landauer, T. K., Gomez, L. M., & Dumais, S. T. (1987). The vocabulary problem in human-system communication. *Communications of the ACM, 30*(11), 964-971.

Glance, N., Arregui, D., & Dardenne, M. (1998). Knowledge pump: Supporting the flow and use of knowledge. In U. Borghoff and R. Pareschi, editors, *Information technology for knowledge management*, pages 35–51. Springer.

Haase, P., Siebes, R., & Harmelen, F. (2004). Peer selection in peer-to-peer networks with semantic topologies. In *International Conference on Semantics of a Networked World: Semantics for Grid Databases*, Paris.

Jaczynski, M., & Trousse, B. (1999). Broadway: A case-based system for cooperative information browsing on the world-wide-web. In Julian A. Padget, editor, *Collaboration between Human and Artificial Societies, 1624* of *LNCS*, pages 264–283. Springer.

Jéribi, L., Rumpler, B., & Pinon, J.M. (2001). Système d'aide à la recherche et à l'interrogation de bases documentaires, basé sur la réutilisation d'expériences. *In Congrès Informatique des Organisations et Systèmes d'Information et de Décision (INFORSID'2001)*, pages 443–463, Martigny, Suisse.

Kanawati, R., & Malek, M. (2000). Informing the design of shared bookmark systems. In *the proceedings of RIAO'2000: Content-based Multimedia Information Access*, pages 170–180, Collège de France, Paris, France.

Kanawati, R., & Malek, M. (2001). Cowing: A collaborative bookmark management system. In *the International workshop on Cooperative Information Agents (CIA'01), 2182* of *LNAI*, pages 34–39.

Kanawati, R., & Malek, M. (2007). Computing Social Networks for Information Sharing: A Case-based Approach. In Schuler Douglas, editor, *Second international conference on Online Communities and Social Computing*, *4564* of *LNCS*, pages 86–95, Beijing, China, Springer.

Karoui, H., Kanawati, R., & Petrucci, L. (2004). An intelligent peer-to-peer multi-agent system for collaborative management of bibliographic databases. In *Proceedings of the 9th UK Workshop on Case-Based Reasoning*, pages 43–50, Queens' College, Cambridge, UK.

Karoui, H., Kanawati, R., & Petrucci, L. (2006). COBRAS: Cooperative CBR system for bibliographical reference recommendation. In Thomas Roth-Berghofer, Mehmet H.Göker, and H. Altay Güvenir, editors, *the 8th European Conference on Case-Based Reasonning (ECCBR'06)*, volume 4106 of *LNCS*, pages 76–90, Ölüdeniz/Fethiye, Turkey, Springer.

Karoui, H., Kanawati, R., & Petrucci, L. (2006). An intelligent peer-to-peer multi-agent system for collaborative management of bibliographic databases. In *SGAI's expert update magazine*, volume 8, pages 22–31. Springer.

Lieberman, H. (1995). Letizia: An Agent That Assists Web Browsing. In *Proceedings of the 1995 International Joint Conference on Artificial Intelligent*, Montreal, Canada.

Linden, G., Smith, B., & York, J. (2003). Amazon.com recommendations: items-to-item collaborative filtering. *Internet Computing, IEEE, 7*(1), 76-80.

Lorenzi, F., & Ricci, F. (2003). Case-Based Recommender Systems: A Unifying View. *ITWP*, page 89-113, Acapulco, Mexico, Springer, Lecture Notes in Computer Science, 3169.

Malek, M., & Kanawati, R. (2004). A data driven CBR approach: A contineous maintenance strategy. *In the International Conference on Advances in Intelligent Systems: Theory and Applications*, pages 281–290, Luxemburg.

Miller, B., Albert, I., Lam, S., Konstan, J., & Riedl, J. (2003). Movielens unplugged: Experiences with an occasionally connected recommender system. *In Proceedings of ACM 2003 International Conference on Intelligent User Interfaces (IUI'03)*. ACM Press.

Montaner, M. (2003). Collaborative Recommender Agents Based on Case-Based Reasoning and Trust. *PHD Thesis*, Universitat de Girona.

Resnick, P., & Varian, H.R. (1997). Recommender systems. *Communications of the ACM, 40*(3), 56–58.

Salton, G. (1971). *The SMART Retrieval System-Experiments in Automatic document Processing*. Prentice-Hall, Inc., Upper Saddle River, NJ, USA.

Salton, G. (1989). *Automatic Text Processing : The Transformation, Analysis, and Retrieval of Information by Computer*. Addison-Wesley.

Watson, I. (1997). *Applying Case-Based Reasoning: Techniques for Enterprise Systems*. Morgan Kaufmann.

ENDNOTES

[1] ACM: Association for Computing Machinery, http://www.acm.org/
[2] JADE: Java Agent DEvelopment Framework
[3] DBLP: Digital Bibliography and Library Project, http://dblp.uni-trier.de/

Chapter X
Music Recommendation by Modeling User's Preferred Perspectives of Content, Singer/Genre and Popularity

Zehra Cataltepe
Istanbul Technical University, Turkey

Berna Altinel
Istanbul Technical University, Turkey

ABSTRACT

As the amount, availability, and use of online music increase, music recommendation becomes an important field of research. Collaborative, content-based and case-based recommendation systems and their hybrids have been used for music recommendation. There are already a number of online music recommendation systems. Although specific user information, such as, demographic data, education, and origin have been shown to affect music preferences, they are usually not collected by the online music recommendation systems, because users would not like to disclose their personal data. Therefore, user models mostly contain information about which music pieces a user liked and which ones s/he did not and when.

INTRODUCTION

The authors of this chapter introduce two music recommendation algorithms that take into account music content, singer/genre and popularity information. In the entropy-based recommendation algorithm, they decide on the relevant set of content features (perspective) according to which the songs selected by the user can be clustered as compactly as possible. As a compactness measure, they use entropy of the distribution of songs a user listened to in the clustering. The entropy-based recommendation approach enables both a dynamic user model and ability to consider a different subset of features appropriate for the specific user.

In order to improve the performance of this system further, the authors introduce the content, singer/genre and popularity learning algorithm. In this algorithm, they first evaluate the extent to which content, singer/genre or popularity components could produce successful recommendations on the past songs listened to by the user. The number of songs in the final recommendation list contributed according to each component is chosen according to the recommendation success of each component.

Experiments are performed on user session data from a mobile operator. There are 2000 to 500 sessions and of length 5 to 15 songs. Experiments indicate that the entropy-based recommendation algorithm performs better than simple content-based recommendation. Content, singer/genre and popularity learning algorithm is the best algorithm investigated. Both algorithms perform better as the session length increases.

BACKGROUND

Widespread use of mp3 players and cell-phones and availability of music on these devices according to user demands, increased the need for more accurate Music Information Retrieval (MIR) Systems. Music recommendation is one of the subtasks of MIR Systems and it involves finding music that suits a personal taste (Typke et al., 2005). The content search in MIR systems could also be used to identify the music played, for example query-by-humming (Ghias et al., 1995), to identify suspicious sounds recorded by surveillance equipment, to make content-based video retrieval more accurate by means of incorporating music content, to help theaters and film makers find appropriate sound effects (Typke et al. 2005), to produce audio notification to individuals or groups (Jung & Heckmann, 2006).

Music recommendation tasks could be in the form of recommending a single album/song (Logan 2004) or a series of them as in playlist generation (Aucouturier & Pachet, 2002; Alghoniemy & Tewfik, 2000). In addition to containing interesting songs for the user or the user group, a playlist have to obey certain conditions, such as containing all different songs, having a certain duration, having continuity and progression from one song to the next (Aucouturier & Pachet, 2002). Therefore, playlist generation is a harder task than single music item recommendation.

The songs to recommend could contain the audio or MIDI content, as well as, genre, artist, lyrics and other information. The audience of a music recommendation system could be a single person or a group of people (Baccigalupo & Plaza, 2007; McCarthy et al., 2006). The audience or the songs could be dynamic or mostly static. Depending on these task and user requirements, different algorithms have to be employed for music recommendation. Yahoo Launch!, Last. FM, Pandora (music genome project), CDNow, Audioscrobbler, iRate, MusicStrands, inDiscover (Celma et al., 2005) are some of the music recommendation projects.

In this chapter, we first review collaborative, content-based and case-based recommendation systems and their hybrids for music recommendation. We also discuss the user models that have been considered for music recommendation. We then introduce two music recommendation algorithms. In our algorithms, we find the perspective of music such as different subsets of audio features, singer/genre or popularity, which affect the song choice of users most. Then we recommend songs to users based on the perspective selected for that specific user.

The rest of the chapter is organized as follows: Section "Literature review" includes literature review on collaborative, content-based, case-based recommendation systems, hybrid music recommendation systems and user models for music recommendation. In Section "Motivation", we go through the motivation for our entropy-based and learning recommendation approaches. Section "Structure" contains the data set we used, the evaluation criteria to compare recommendation algorithms, details on content, popularity and singer/genre information we use for recommendation, our entropy and learning based recommendation algorithms and experimental results and discussions. Section "Conclusions and future work" concludes the chapter.

LITERATURE REVIEW

According to Burke (2002), a recommendation system has three components: the background data, user input data and a recommendation algorithm to combine the background and input data to come up with a recommendation. Based on these three components, Burke (2002) comes up with five different types of recommendation systems: collaborative, content-based, demographic, utility based and knowledge based. Among these, collaborative, content-based and case-based recommendation systems are the most used ones.

In this section, we first give an overview of collaborative, content-based and case-based recommendation systems. Then we give examples of hybrid recommendation systems, mostly music recommendation systems, which combine two or more recommendation schemes. We also discuss user models in music recommendation systems.

Collaborative, Content-Based and Case-Based Recommendation

Collaborative recommendation systems take as input the users' ratings and generate recommendations based on items selected by users who previously selected similar items. This recommendation scheme does not use the content of

the background data and hence has the advantage of being applicable for various data types from movies, to books to food. When there are a lot of users, it takes a lot of time to compute the similarity between them. Item-based collaborative filtering algorithm analyzed in (Sarwar et al. 2001) overcomes this problem by finding items that are similar to the items that the user liked previously. They show that item-based collaborative filtering performs better than user-based collaborative filtering. Ringo (Shardanand & Maes, 1995) is one of the well-known collaborative music recommendation systems. Based on the ratings given for various artists by the user, Ringo finds other users who have similar taste and recommends groups or music pieces liked by those similar users. GroupLens is another collaborative recommendation system which was used for filtering of usenet news articles (Resnick et al., 1994).

Collaborative recommendation systems use a user-item matrix, which contains the ratings given by each user to different items. Users who have similar ratings (similar rows of this matrix) are put into the same user group. Pure collaborative recommendation systems suffer from the cold start (or latency) problem, which means a new item which has not been rated by any user will not be recommended to anybody, until some users rate them. Another problem is if a user is unusual, then there will not be users similar enough to him and he will not be able to get reliable recommendations.

Content-based recommendation systems, use similarities of extracted features of items, in order to come up with recommendations. These systems assume that users tend to like to items similar to the ones they liked in the past and compute similarity according to some features based on the content of items. NewsDude of Billsus & Pazzani (1999) is one of the earlier examples of content-based recommendation systems. The main disadvantages of content-based recommendation systems are the difficulty of expressing content similarities, the time it takes to compute content similarities when there are many of them and finally the diversity problem, the fact that the user may not ever be recommended items which are not like the items he has seen in the past but may have actually liked.

There are also *case-based* recommendation systems. A case-based reasoning system stores solutions to old problems. When a new problem arrives, it fetches a problem which is likely to have a similar solution. Based on the user response, i.e. whether the solution is what the user required or not, the system learns the new case also. In case-based recommendation systems, user answers some questions on what s/he likes and s/he is asked some other questions and based on those answers the best item to recommend is found. Wasabi Personal Shopper (Burke, 1999) is one of the early case-based recommendation systems, where users are recommended wines based on answers they give to questions related to quality, price and other properties of wines. Burke (2000) also mentions Entrée and Recommend.com for restaurant and movie recommendation respectively. All of these recommendation systems are based on the FindMe knowledge-based recommender systems where users are asked questions and they can "tweak" the solution they receive according to the answers they provide. Burke (2000) identifies certain aspects of similarity that are important for the recommendation task at hand, for example, cuisine, price and location for a restaurant. Then he produces retrieval strategies which order the similarity metrics according to their importance, for example: first price, second cuisine, and then location. It is mentioned in (Burke, 2000) that collaborative and case-based recommendation could be combined in order to come up with a better recommendation scheme. Another case-based recommendation system is introduced in (Göker & Thompson, 2000). In this system, user models are used for case-based recommendations. The user models are used not only to increase accuracy, but also to enable the user to reach to information s/he seeks, with as small number of questions as possible.

Hybrid Music Recommendation Systems

There have been a lot of work on *hybrid* recommendation systems, where collaborative, content-based or case-based recommendation schemes are used together for a better recommendation scheme which does not have the weaknesses of the original ones (Burke, 2002). A hybrid recommender can be built out of existing ones using a number of different methods. A weighted sum that comes from the votes or scores from the existing algorithms can be used to produce recommendations. The system could switch between base recommenders depending on the amount of data available. An example of a switching system is in (Pazzani, 1999), where they decide on which recommender to use based on each recommender's success on the user's past items. Their approach is similar to our work here based on the incorporation of past session history to decide on the recommender. Instead of deciding on a single recommender, recommendations from several different recommenders could also be presented to the user at the same time (Smyth & Cotter, 2000). Using collaborative information as another type of feature in addition to the content feature and then performing content-based recommendation is another option (Basu et. al., 1998). Cascading, feature augmentation and meta-level combination of recommenders are the other types of hybrid recommendation techniques mentioned in (Burke, 2002).

Among the hybrid recommender systems, (Popescul et al., 2001) built a hybrid method of content-based and collaborative filtering approaches and extended Hofmann & Puzicha's (1994) aspect model to incorporate three-way co-occurrence data among users, items, and item content. They showed that secondary content information can often be used to overcome sparsity. Experiments on data from the ResearchIndex library of Computer Science publications showed that appropriate mixture models incorporating secondary data produce significantly better quality recommenders than k-nearest neighbor (k-NN). Probabilistic models were also used for recommendation. (Smyth & Cotter, 2000) used content-based and collaborative recommendation techniques to come up with a list of programs a person may want to watch on TV. They found out that collaborative approach always resulted in better recommendations than the content-based approach for this problem. Two different types of information: domain and program preferences are kept in the user profile for collaborative recommendation. (Jin et al., 2005) used both content and user rating information to produce probability of recommendation for each web page.

Yoshii et al. (2006) introduced a new hybrid music recommendation system incorporating both content-based and collaborative filtering approaches by means of a Bayesian Network. In this method, the distribution of mel-frequency cepstral coefficients (MFCCs) was modeled as music content. Representations of user preferences differs between collaborative and content-based methods. The former represents a preference of user as a vector that contains rating scores of all pieces. The latter represents the preference as a set of feature vectors of favorite pieces. In order to build a hybrid recommender system, they used a Bayesian network called a three-way aspect model proposed by Popescul et al. (2001). Their test results showed that their method outperforms the two conventional methods in terms of recommendation accuracy and artist variety and can reasonably recommend pieces even if they have no ratings.

Chedrawy & Abidi (2006) introduce PRE-CiSE, a collaborative case-based recommendation system and use it for music playlist recommendation. First an item based collaborative filtering (Linden, 2003 ; Sarwar et al., 2001) is performed, instead of a single value for item-item similarity, a vector of similarities is used. Each component of this vector represents the similarity of items from a perspective, for example lyrics, tune, band

etc. The user chooses the relevant perspectives himself. The context similarity of two items is then computed by taking a weighted and normalized sum of perspective similarities. According to this context similarity, for each item rated by the user the closest items are found and a recommendation list is produced based on those closest items. Although (Chedrawy & Abidi, 2006) report that using more (3 instead of 1) perspectives result in better recommendation performance, we believe that if more and more dimensions are added, they could be useless or even harmful because they introduce noise into the context similarity values. In the second stage of the recommendation process, they use case-based reasoning mediation of past cases. They select cases which are most similar to the current user and based on their appropriateness degree with the user, produce recommendations. A weighted sum of the past similar cases are stored into the case database to represent the current user. According to F1 measure, (Chedrawy & Abidi, 2006) show that they get significantly better results with the addition of the case-based reasoning stage.

Li et al. (2004, 2005 and 2007) showed that using content in addition to user ratings help with collaborative recommendation's three basic problems related to lack of enough data: user bias, non-association, and cold start problems in capturing accurate similarities among items. They performed their experiments on music and video data sets. They use ring tones for cell phones users as their recommendation items. Li et al. used ratings by users and item attributes together and produced item clusters. They first clustered items together according to their features. Assuming that the ratings of a user in an item community are distributed according to a Gaussian distribution, they produce pseudo-ratings for items that are not yet rated by a user. Both real and pseudo ratings are used to create item groups. An item which has not yet been rated by a user is rated assuming a Gaussian parametric model for ratings for each user. This produces a solution to the cold start problem. In their work, Li et al., also used the audio features produced by Marsyas (Tzanetakis & Cook, 2002) and experimented with combinations of different features. In our system, we are able to use the Marsyas feature group which best groups the music taste of a user. Another similarity between our and Li et al.'s work is the cell-phone user data. They work on ring-tones, whereas we work on the songs downloaded by users so that people who call them can listen to instead of the ring-back tone.

Chen & Chen (2005) used both content and user ratings for MIDI music data and achieved better recommendation when using them both. Wang et al. (2006) perform experiments on collaborative filtering both in text and music recommendation areas.

User Models in Music Recommendation Systems

User models contain information about a user. By means of the user model, collaborative recommenders or their hybrids are able to find similar users. In a very simplistic sense, once similar users are found, recommendations can be made based on the items they chose and the items the user chose to in the past.

The user information could be gathered explicitly (for example a survey to get sex, age, education, origin etc., see, for example, (Kuo et al., 2005)) or implicitly, through observation of the user's behavior in the system and then use of machine learning or knowledge-based techniques. Explicit information indirectly and implicit information can be directly used by a recommendation system. The user model can be useful to increase accuracy of recommendation (Sarwar et al., 2001) as well as making the recommendation process shorter (Goker & Thomson, 2000).

The user's preferences change over time, therefore the user model needs to be dynamic. In their work, Billsus and Pazzani (1999) use two user models, a short term and a long term model,

which are modeled using a k-Nearest Neighbor and Naïve Bayes classifiers respectively. In (Rolland 2001) a user model which changes over time as user's preferences change is suggested. Rolland uses alignment similarity between notes in MIDI files of songs to determine their similarity. (Kumar et al., 2001) used probabilistic user models in their analysis. In this model users select items from different clusterings with some probability and they select each clustering also with some other probability. The probabilistic framework allows analysis of recommendation algorithms in terms of their behavior for different conditions. The work of (Lekakos & Giaglis, 2007) includes lifestyle segmentation of a user for digital interactive television advertisements. Lifestyle includes external (culture, demographics, social status, etc.) and internal factors (perception, motives, personality, etc.). They start with a recommendation algorithm based on the lifestyle of the user and then enrich the algorithm to become a better performing hybrid. They consider both segment level and user-level personalization of recommendations and suggest different levels of personalization based on the amount of data available for the user.

There have been some work to come up with a common language (see UMIRL (User Modeling for Information Retrieval Language) (Chai & Vercoe, 2000), USERML (User model Markup Language) (Heckmann & Kruger, 2003)), in which different systems may describe the user in this standard format to make the user model sharable and reusable.

According to (Chai & Vercoe, 2000), user models are necessary in music recommendation systems due to a number of reasons. User models are needed to specify some perceptual features, for example, to get a happy music, since it depends on all of them, we may need a tuple: <music, user, context, feature, value> to describe it, because a music piece could sound happy to a user based on where s/he listens to it. Demographic and personality factors (such as age, origin, occupation, socio-economic background, personality factors, gender, musical education) have been shown to affect music preference (Uitdenbogerd & van Schyndel, 2002; Yapriady & Uitdenbogerd, 2005), therefore, whenever they are available, they should be included in the user model.

There are a number of internet radio stations which use music recommendation to come up with good songs for users. Among those, Last. FM [www.last.fm] (Aucouturier & Pachet, 2002) creates a user profile based on immediate user feedback and uses collaborative filtering for users. On Pandora Music [www.pandora.com], users provide their approval or disapproval on the individual song choices which later is taken into account. Slacker [www.slacker.com] also operates very similarly. Due to the fact that most people would be unwilling to share their personal information, these radio stations do not ask users about their education, origin, age, sex, etc.

MOTIVATION

We aim to use different sources of information, for example audio content, genre/similarity and popularity, in order to come up with better user models and hence better recommendations, for each user individually. Users tend to make choices based on different aspects of music. For example, while someone may like songs based on whether they contain a fast beat, someone else may like them due to their slow beat. In such a case, using only the beat information about a song, we can tell whether these two users would like a song or not. First of all, for all possible feature groups (beat, mfcc etc.), we produce clusterings of all available songs. For each user we choose the feature set that can be used to cluster the songs the user has listened to as compact as possible. If songs are distributed all over the clusters, then it means that the particular feature set is not suitable for that user. Otherwise, the similarity measure could be used to recommend new songs to the user. As a measure of compactness, we use an entropy

(Cover, 2006) criterion. When we recommend a certain number of songs, to a user at a certain time, we recommend a certain percentage of songs based on the content of the songs the user has listened to so far and the remaining songs based on the popularity information about songs (Cataltepe, 2007a).

Different feature groups we consider correspond to perspectives of (Chedrawy & Abidi, 2006) which had to be explicitly selected by the user. Finding out the appropriate feature group in this way also automatically allows for dynamic user modeling as in (Rolland, 2001). We should also note that, traditionally recommendation systems build clusters of songs or users in order to make faster recommendations. However, the clustering we do here has the sole purpose of determining the right feature set for the user.

Combinations of different audio content features have been previously used for music recommendation. Li et al. (2004) combined different audio features based on the proximity of songs and found out that their combination may result in better recommendation performance. Our approach differs from them in that we use all combinations of subsets of audio features in different number of dimensions. We also incorporate song selections by other users in the system. Li et al. (2004) performed their experiments on a different real-world music corpus, which has 240 pieces of music and 433 users with 1,150 ratings. Our music corpus has 730 audio files and more than 1,350,000 users. Vignoli & Pauws (2005) also combined different audio features. We differ from them in calculation of timbre, genre and mood. They used all features whereas we used different subsets of features. Performance of different subsets of audio features have been examined in (Logan, 2004). Logan found out that for the song set recommendation problem, using MFCC features with k-means clustering, minimum distance is a better measure than median or average. For MIDI songs, features extracted from MIDI features could be used, for example (Chen & Chen,

2005). The framework we use in this chapter can be used for MIDI or audio features.

Entropy has been used within the collaborative filtering framework. Pavlov & Pennock (2002) developed a maximum entropy approach for generating recommendations. In order to minimize the case that the recommendations will cross cluster boundaries and then recommending only within cluster, they addressed sparsity and dimensionality reduction by first clustering items based on user access patterns. They performed experiments on data from ResearchIndex and they showed that their maximum entropy formulation outperforms several competing algorithms in offline tests simulating the recommendation of documents to ResearchIndex users.

Every user may also choose songs based on popularity or singer/genre of the songs, and again the importance they give to these properties may also be different for each user. We introduce a framework that lets us estimate the weight of content, popularity and singer/genre for each user based on his/her listening history and make recommendations based on those weights.

STRUCTURE

Data Set

User session data is the most important component of a recommendation system. Although there have been recent attempts to produce publicly accessible audio databases (McKay et al., 2006), we are not aware of a music recommendation database that contains considerable amount of users, sessions and songs.

In the system we consider, cell-phone users pay for and download songs that will stay active in their accounts for upto six months. When someone calls them, instead of the regular ring-back tone, the caller hears one of the songs downloaded by the user. The ring-tone melody of the mobile phones

have been colored and the phone melodies have become a huge market. Subscribers have paid and are still paying for their customized, popular ring tones. There are many operators sharing revenues with the ring tone content providers. Now the market that is created by the ring tones may be expanded to the ring back tones. Traditionally, subscribers listen to the infrastructure based tones before connecting to the other party. The traditional tones are played at the call states of alerting, busy, not reachable, and no answer. In the system from which our data set comes, customers change the traditional ring back tones with the melodies they select. Although the choice of songs downloaded may be affected by the identity of people who call the user, the user is the person who picks the songs not the calling party. On the other hand, the song preferences of a user may also change in time. Since the songs downloaded in the previous part of a session are used for the same purpose as the songs downloaded at the later parts, in other words, the characteristics of the recommendation task does not change, we believe that this is a legitimate music recommendation task. We should also note the fact that the songs downloaded are not gifts for other people.

We are provided with the identity of the songs and the times they are selected for each user. There were sessions containing different number of songs, however, we concentrated only on sessions of length 5, 10 and 15 songs. There were a total of 11398, 1215 and 518 user sessions of length 5, 10 and 15. Due to time limitations, in our experiments, we used 2000, 1000 and 500 of these sessions respectively. There were a total of 730 songs, whose audio features we obtained as described below.

In our recommendation system, no feedback about the recommendation is given to the users and we can not evaluate the live system performance. We evaluate the system performance based on how well we can predict what user selects at a particular point in time.

Evaluation of Recommendation Algorithms

Many metrics have been proposed to evaluate recommendation algorithms. (Herlocker et al., 2004) provides a detailed review of evaluation metrics and their suitability for different tasks, number of items and users in the recommendation system and the kind of input available from the user. In terms of the tasks, the task we consider in this chapter is the task of "Find Good Items". Although, a live evaluation would be a lot more reliable, it was not possible to perform it for the recommendation system proposed, hence the evaluation results are based on user requests that already happened. However, we make sure that the evaluation results are for test items only, we separate the last item in a session for a user and evaluate the performance of the system for that item. Since we have timestamps for each item request, we make sure that we only use information available at the time of recommendation.

In order to evaluate our recommendations, we can not use metrics that rely on multi-valued ratings, since they are not available. In our system, what we really have are, what (Herlocker et al., 2004) calls "unary" ratings, since we only have a record of items user selected, an item which has not been selected in the past is not necessarily disliked by the user. The metrics we could have used are precision, recall, F1 metric, ROC (Receiver Operating Characteristic) curve and AUC (Area Under ROC Curve or Swet's A Measure). Precision is the number of selected and relevant items divided by the number of selected items. Recall is the probability that a relevant item is selected and it is computed by dividing the number of relevant and selected items to the number of relevant items. As the number of recommended items increases, recall increases and precision decreases. F1 measure attempts to combine both metrics into one. While F1 measure combines precision and recall for a single recommendation list length, ROC curve provides a curve of precision and recall values for all possible recommendation list lengths. The AUC is the area under an ROC curve and it makes comparison of algorithms' performance easier. If a recommender is able to find the items at the beginning of the recommendation list, it would have higher values of precision at the beginning of the ROC curve and hence a higher AUC value.

In our study, we use percentage of times the correct song was in the list of recommendations returned as an evaluation measure. The same metric has been used in (Logan, 2004) for a number of different recommendation list lengths. We use a recommendation list of length 20 for all algorithms. As the recommendation list gets bigger this evaluation measure would increase. (Logan, 2004) also used a more relaxed metric where she assumed that a recommendation was correct if the composer name was correct. Error rate (which is one minus percentage of times correct) has been used in, for example, Jester joke recommendation system (Goldberg et al., 2001). Yoshii (2006) also used accuracy to evaluate their recommendation system.

Content Information

For each song in our data set, we have the audio files, from which we extract the audio features described below. Singer and genre of each song is also known. Based on the songs listened within a certain number of days, we also obtain a popularity measure for each song.

Audio Features

Several features including low-level parameters such as zero-crossing rate, signal bandwidth, spectral centroid, root mean square level, band energy ratio, delta spectrum, psychoacoustic features, MFCC and auditory filter bank temporal envelopes have been employed for audio classification (Uitdenbogerd & van Schyndel, 2002). In our experiments, we obtained the following content-based audio features using Tzanetakis's Marsyas software [opihi.cs.uvic.ca/marsyas] with default parameter settings (Tzanetakis & Cook, 2002).

Timbral Features (MFCC and STFT)

Timbral features are generally used for music-speech discrimination and speech recognition. They differentiate mixture of sounds with the same or similar rhythmic content. In order to extract the timbral features, audio signal is divided into small intervals that can be accepted as stationaryl. The following timbral features are calculated for these small intervals: spectral centroid, spectral rolloff, spectral flux, time domain zero crossing, low energy, mel-frequency cepstral coefficients (MFCC).

Means and variances of the spectral centroid, spectral rolloff, spectral flux, zero crossing (8 features) and low energy (1 feature) results in the 9 dimensional feature vector and it is represented in experimental results using the STFT label. Means and variances of the first five MFCC coefficients yield a 10 dimensional feature vector, which is labeled as MFCC in the experiments.

Rhythmic Content Features (BEAT)

Rhythmic content features characterize the movement of music signals over time and contain such information as the regularity of the rhythm, the beat, the tempo, and the time signature (Tzanetakis & Cook, 2002; Li & Tzanetakis, 2003). The rhythm structure is detected based on the most pronounced periodicities of the signal. Rhythmic content features are calculated by beat histogram calculation and yield a 6 dimensional feature vector which is represented using BEAT label.

Pitch Content Features (MPITCH)

The melody and harmony information about the music signal is obtained by pitch detection techniques. Although musical genres may not be characterized fully by their pitch content, there are certain patterns that could lead to useful feature vectors (Tzanetakis & Cook, 2002). Pitch content features are calculated by pitch histogram calculation and yield a 5 dimensional feature vector which is labeled as MPITCH in the experimental results.

The following is a list of audio features we use and their length:

- BEAT (6 features)
- STFT (9 features)
- MFCC (10 features)
- MPITCH (5 features)
- ALL (all 30 features above)

Using CLUTO (Karypis, 2002) software and graph clustering option, we obtain 8 different clusterings of all the 730 songs in our database.

We use the Euclidean distance between song features as the distance between songs. If $\underline{x}$ and $\underline{y}$ are audio feature vectors of dimension d for two songs x and y, the distance between x and y is:

$$d_{audio}(x, y) = \left\| \underline{x} - \underline{y} \right\| = \sqrt{\frac{1}{d} \sum_{i=1}^{d} (x(i) - y(i))^2}$$

(1)

We also considered the cosine similarity between song features, however did not observe a significant performance difference. We obtained 8 clusterings using the following (*audio*) feature combinations: MFCC, MPITCH, STFT, BEAT, MFCC+MPITCH, STFT+BEAT, MPITCH+BEAT and ALL. We considered all 15 possible feature set combinations, but discarded combinations for which the clustering algorithm can not perform well (i.e. very non-homogenous clusters, many songs outside clusters, etc.).

Singer/Genre Information

Singer/genre distance value is calculated according to the 4 level hierarchy presented to the cellphone users: Turkish/Foreign song, genre, singer and song (Figure 1). Because users are presented the song information in this way, what they select is affected by it. Using singer/genre distance, we wanted to take the effect of this presentation into account. If two songs share the same singer (lowest category) then their singer/genre distance is 0, if they do not share the same highest category, their singer/genre distance is 1. We denote the singer/genre distance between two songs x and y as $d_{\sin ger}(x,y)$.

Popularity Information

For any day of recommendation, we group songs into popular and non-popular. We compute the popularity ratio as the number of times a song is listened within the last t days divided by the number of times all songs are listened within the last t days. We compute the mean popularity ratio for all songs and group songs whose popularity ratio are below the average as unpopular and the rest as popular. (Ahn, 2006) is another study that uses popularity for recommendation.

We use the popularity matrix in order to compute the popularity values (Table 1). The popularity matrix contains the count of the times a specific song is requested by a user and the count of how many songs were requested among all 730 songs. In order to compute the popularity ratio of a song on a specific day, we take the ratio of these two counts (Table 2).

Recommendation Algorithms

In this section, we first introduce the notation that will be used for our recommendation algorithms. Then we give the two recommendation algorithms: entropy-based and content, singer/genre, popularity learning based recommendation.

Figure 1. Some of the singer/genre categories

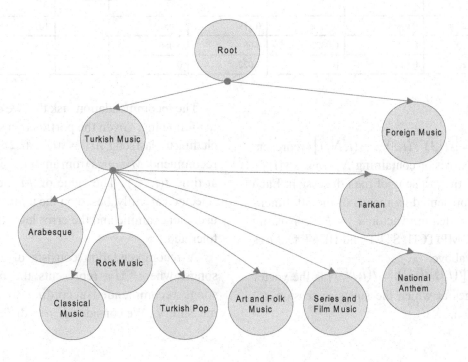

Table 1. A sample table showing the number of times each song is listened on a day (Popularity Matrix)

Day	Bryam Adams-I need Somebody	50 Cent-Just A Little Bit	Jennifer Lopez-Play	Paris Avenue-I Want You	...	All Songs Listened
01.01.2006	3	0	2	1	...	34
02.01.2006	5	1	4	2	...	78
03.01.2006	6	2	12	5	...	101
04.01.2006	11	4	10	7	...	124
05.01.2006	25	0	1	0	...	45
...	...	...	...	...	...	...

Table 2. A sample table showing the popularity values computed Table 1

Day	Bryam Adams-I need Somebody	50 Cent-Just A Little Bit	Jennifer Lopez-Play	Paris Avenue-I Want You	...	All Files Listened
01.01.2006	0.088	0	0.058	0.029	...	34
02.01.2006	0.064	0.013	0.051	0.015	...	78
03.01.2006	0.059	0.02	0.119	0.05	...	101
04.01.2006	0.089	0.032	0.08	0.056	...	124
05.01.2006	0.556	0	0.022	0	...	45

Notation

Let $s(i) = [s(i,1)\ s(i,2),...,s(i,N_i)]$ represent the i'th user session containing N_i songs. $s(i,j)$ represents the j'th song of the i'th session. Each song is represented by means of the 30 dimensional audio feature vector, $x_{i,j} \in R^{30}$ consisting of MFCC, MPITCH, STFT and BEAT features described above.

$t(i) = [t(i,1)\ t(i,2),...,t(i,N_i)]$ is the vector of the times at which the songs in session *s(i)* were chosen.

The recommendation task that we consider is the following: Given the portion of a session excluding the last song, $s(i)^- = s(i,1), s(i,2),...,s(i,N_{i-1})$ recommend M songs from among the 730 songs at time $t(i,N_i)$. The value of M needs to be selected carefully, based on the number of items user can examine and the error level that can be tolerated.

A recommendation consists of $M = \sum_{k=1}^{K} M_k$ songs, where M_k represents the number of songs recommended according to similarity measure k. We consider $K = 8$ different types of information. $k = 1...8$ correspond to the 8 different subsets of audio features MFCC, MPITCH, STFT, BEAT, MFCC+MPITCH, STFT+BEAT, MPITCH+BEAT and ALL.

We describe the recommendation algorithms used in this study below. The experimental results for each algorithm are given in the Experimental Results section.

Entropy-Based Recommendation

When we need to recommend M songs using $s(i)^- = s(i,1) \; s(i,2),...,s(i,N_{i-1})$ at time $t(i,N_i)$, for each clustering $k = 1...8$, we compute the number of songs to recommend from this clustering as follows. For the clustering c, we first find the cluster to which each song belongs. Let:

$$p_c = n_c \; / \; (N_i - 1) \qquad (2)$$

be the ratio songs in session $s(i)^-$ which fall into a cluster c. In equation (2), n_c is the number of

songs in $s(i)^-$ assigned to the cluster c, where $c \leq C = 20$ and C is the number of clusters. The (Shannon) entropy (Cover, 2006) value for this clustering is computed as:

$$H_k = -\sum_{c=1}^{C} p_c \log p_c \qquad (3)$$

The number M_k of songs to recommend from clustering k, should decrease as the value of H_k increases. Because a high value of entropy means songs in the session $s(i)^-$ are distributed all over the clustering k.

In this study, we use a *discrete scheme* to compute M_k. The clustering whose entropy is minimum is selected as the clustering to which the user belongs, because it is the clustering that can group the songs user has listened to in the best possible way. All M songs are recommended from that clustering. Figure 2 shows an example depiction of the entropy-based recommendation.

When popularity P, where $0 \leq P \leq 1$, is also included in recommendation, first $P*M$ most

Figure 2. A depiction of the entropy-based recommendation. Different perspectives/feature groups of songs are shown with small rectangles. User1's songs can be grouped as having common black second property, User2's songs have their first property gray. The second property can be used to select songs for the first user and the first property can be used to select songs for the second user. Hence song4 can be recommended to User1 and song5 can be recommended to User2.

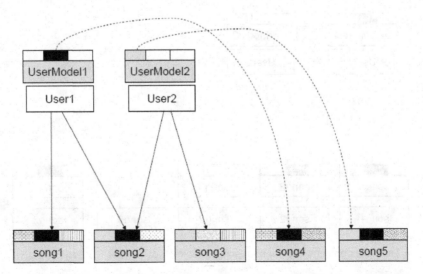

popular songs at the time of recommendation are recommended. The remaining *(1-P)*M* are selected according to the entropy-based scheme above.

Content, Popularity and Singer/Genre Learning Based Recommendation

Entropy-based recommendation recommends a certain percentage *P* popular songs for all users in the system. However, just like favoring different sets of audio features, users could show different preferences for songs based on their popularity or singer/genre. In content, popularity and singer/genre learning based recommendation, in addition to user's preferred set of song features based on entropy, we also learn his/her degree of preference for songs based on their popularity and singer/genre. This way, instead of system wide values for *P*, we can have a different *P* value per user based on the user's history of songs. We can also incorporate the singer/genre preferences for the specific user.

In this method we consider all three components (content similarity, singer/genre similarity and the popularity) and learn the percentage values for each component. We do the learning as follows: For each $s(i, j) \in s_i^-$, $j < N_i$, we try to find *s(i,j)* based on all remaining $N_i - 2$ songs in the session. We use content, singer/genre and popularity components all by themselves for finding song *s(i,j)* when they give *M* recommendations. We choose the number of songs to recommend from each of the content, singer/genre and popularity components proportional to their number of successes in recommending item *s(i,j)*.

As seen in Figure 3, each user could be given recommendations from a different recommender based on the success of content, singer/genre (not shown) or popularity recommenders on the past user session data.

Experimental Results

In Table 3, we give the results of simple recommendation, based on a single set of song features

Figure 3. A depiction of the popularity, singer/genre learning based algorithm. The songs requested by User1 are always the most popular songs therefore the recommendation for that user is song5, which is the most popular song when recommendation is requested. On the other hand, songs listened by user 2 are not always the most popular, therefore, user model 2, not the popular songs, is used to get the recommendation for user 2.

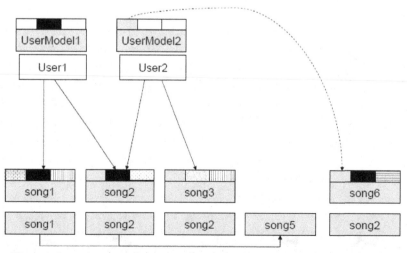

The most popular song when a song is requested

for all users and entropy-based recommendation, which uses the minimum entropy set of features for each specific user.

Results are shown for varying ratio P of recommendations from the popular songs. The number of sessions considered are 2000, 1000 and 500 for sessions of length 5, 10 and 15 respectively. A recommendation is considered successful if the N_i'th song is among the recommended songs. M=20 songs are recommended in all cases, therefore if songs to be placed on the recommendation list were selected randomly without replacement from among the 730 songs, the probability of success would be 20/730=2.74%.

Percentage of songs recommended from among the popular songs at the time of recommendation are shown on the second column. As more popular songs are considered for recommendation, success increases. The remaining songs are recommended using entropy-based method. Column 3 in the table shows the recommendation success when the entropy of clusterings of songs in user history are used to select the best clustering for the user among 8 different clusterings. Columns 4, 5 and 6 shows the recommendation success when only

a static set of features and hence clustering (ALL, MPITCH+MFCC, BEAT+STFT) are used. The entropy-based recommendation results in 10 to 62 percent better recommendation success. With increasing the session length the entropy-based method becomes even more successfull, because feature set and hence the clustering valued by the user in selecting a song can be predicted more reliably. When content-based recommendation is done based on only a static set of features, using ALL features results in better recommendation success than using any subset of features.

Table 4 compares all the algorithms considered in this study. As seen in the table, content, singer/genre and popularity learning performs best and entropy-based recommendation method follows. Both methods perform better than content-based recommendation based on all the available song features.

As the session length increases, there is more information available about user's preferences. While simple recommendation has not benefited much from this information, both entropy-based and content, singer/genre and popularity learning based recommendation algorithms were able to

Table 3. Recommendation success when 8 clusterings and entropy measure vs. a static single clustering is used

Session Length	P = %Popular Recommend	%RecomSuccess Entropy-based	%RecomSuccess All Features	%RecomSuccess MFCC+MPTCH	%RecomSuccess STFT+BEAT
5	20	**21**	19	11	11
5	40	**30**	22	16	13
5	60	**40**	28	14	17
5	80	**44**	33	22	19
10	20	**22**	18	13	13
10	40	**32**	25	16	18
10	60	**41**	27	13	13
10	80	**46**	29	20	17
15	20	**22**	17	8	11
15	40	**33**	21	16	13
15	60	**44**	27	15	15
15	80	**50**	32	17	17

Table 4. Comparison of Recommendation Accuracies of Simple (Using ALL features), Entropy-based, Popularity and Singer/Genre Learning and User Group Learning Algorithms

Session Length	%RecomSuccess Simple Recommendation Using ALL features (P=80%)	%RecomSuccess Entropy-based Recommendation (P=80%)	%RecomSuccess Content, Popularity, Singer/Genre Learning
5	33	44	**70**
10	29	46	**71**
15	32	50	**73**

get better. When session length is very small, the entropy values computed become less reliable. It could be a good idea to incorporate the session length into the content, singer/genre and popularity learning algorithm.

CONCLUSION AND FUTURE WORK

In this chapter, we introduced a number of new ideas for music recommendation based on different types of available information. First of all, we introduced a framework that lets us use different subsets (portions) of audio features for each user so that we can do recommendation to a user, based on the most relevant subsets of features for that user. We used the entropy measure to decide on which subset of features to use for a particular user. We then introduced a recommendation algorithm where content, popularity and singer/genre preference for each user are computed and the best performing recommender is selected for that user.

Analyzing the performance of these recommendation systems on a running system and using them not only for music recommendation, but also for web page recommendation are among the future work that we consider.

ACKNOWLEDGMENT

We thank Argela for providing the user session data, G. Tzanetakis for Marsyas software, G. Karypis for Cluto software. We thank Prof. Sule Gunduz-Oguducu of Istanbul Technical University for useful discussions and proofreading. Author Cataltepe would like to thank Dr. Tanju Cataltepe for his continuous support and also proofreading this work. Authors also appreciate anonymous referees' comments which greatly helped improve the quality of this work.

REFERENCES

Ahn, H. J. (2006). Utilizing Popularity Characteristics for Product Recommendation. *International Journal of Electronic Commerce, 11*(2), 59–80.

Alghoniemy, M., & Tewfik, A.H. (2000). User-defined Music Sequence Retrieval. *Proceedings of the eighth ACM international conference on Multimedia.* (pp. 356 – 358).

Aucouturier, J. J., & Pachet, F. (2002). Scaling up Music Playlist Generation. *Proc IEEE Intl Conf on Multimedia Expo.*

Baccigalupo, C., & Plaza, E. (2007). A Case-Based Song Scheduler for Group Customised Radio. *ICCBR* 2007, LNAI 4626, pp. 433–448.

Billsus, D., & Pazzani, M. J. (1999) A Hybrid User Model for News Story Classification. *Proc. the Seventh International Conference on User modeling,* Banff, Canada, 99 - 108.

Billsus, D., & Pazzani, M. (2000). User Modeling for Adaptive News Access. *User-Modeling and User-Adapted Interaction, 10*(2-3), 147-180.

Burke, R. (1999). The Wasabi Personal Shopper: A Case-Based Recommender System. *Proceedings of the 11th Conference on Innovative Applications of Articifial Intelligence.* American Association for Artificial Intelligence. (pp. 844-949)..

Burke, R. (2000). A Case-Based Approach to Collaborative Filtering. *Advances in Case-Based Reasoning,* pp. 370–379, *5th European Workshop EWCBR 2000.* Springer-Verlag, New York.

Burke, R. (2002). Hybrid Recommender Systems: Survey and Experiments. *User Modeling and User-Adapted Interaction,* 12: 331-370.

Cataltepe, Z., & Altinel, B. (2007a). Hybrid Music Recommendation Based on Different Dimensions of Audio Content and Entropy Measure. *Proc. of Eusipco 2007 Conference,* Poznan, Poland, September 2007.

Cataltepe, Z., & Altinel, B. (2007b). Hybrid Music Recommendation Based on Adaptive Feature and User Grouping. *Proc. of ISCIS 2007 Conference,* Ankara, Turkey, October 2007.

Celma, O., Ramirez, M., & Herrera, P. (2005). Foafing the Music: A Music Recommendation System Based on RSS Feeds and User Preferences. *Proc. of the International Conference on Music Information Retrieval (ISMIR) 2005.*

Chai, W., & Vercoe, B. (2000). Using User Models in Music Information Retrieval Systems. *Proc. of the International Conference on Music Information Retrieval (ISMIR) 2000.*

Chedrawy, Z., & Abidi, S. S. R. (2006). An Adaptive Personalized Recommendation Strategy Featuring Context Sensitive Content Adaptation,

Adaptive Hypermedia and Adaptive Web-Based Systems. *LNCS* Volume 4018/2006, 61-70.

Chen, H. C., & Chen, A. L. P. (2005). A music recommendation system based on music and user grouping. *Journal of Intelligent Information Systems, 24*(2-3), 113-132.

Cohen, W., & Fan, W. (2000). Web-collaborative filtering: Recommending music by crawling the Web. *Computer Networks, 33*(1–6), 685–698.

Cover, T. M., & Thomas, J. A. (2006). *Elements of Information Theory.* Wiley.

Ghias, A., Logan, J., Chamberlin, D., & Smith, B. C. (1995). Query by humming - musical information retrieval in an audio database. *Proceedings ACM Multimedia.*

Goker, M. H., & Thompson, C. A. (2000) Personalized Conversational Case-Based Recommendation. *Advances in Case-Based Reasoning,* LNCS 1898/2000, 29-82.

Heckmann, D., & Kruger, A. (2003) A user modeling markup language (UserML) for ubiquitous computing. *Lecture Notes in Artificial Intelligence, 2702*(2003) 393–397.

Herlocker, J. L., Konstan, J. A., Terveen, L. G., & Riedl, J. T. (2004) Evaluating Collaborative Filtering Recommender Systems. *ACM Transactions on Information Systems, 22*(1), January 2004, 5–53.

Hoashi, K., Matsumoto, K., & Inoue, N. (2003). Personalization of user profiles for content-based music retrieval based on relevance feedback. *ACM Multimedia,* 110–119.

Hofmann, T., & Puzicha, J. (1999). Latent Class Models for Collaborative Filtering. *Proceedings of IJCAI'99.*

Jin, X., Zhou, Y., & Mobasher, B. (2005). A Maximum Entropy Web Recommendation System: Combining Collaborative and Content Features. *KDD'05,* August 21–24, 2005, Chicago, Illinois, USA.

Jung, R., & Heckmann, D. (2006). Ambient Audio Notification with Personalized Music. *UM ECAI'06.*

Karypis, G. (2002). *Cluto A Clustering Toolkit Manual.* University of Minnesota, Department of Computer Science Technical Report.

Kumar, R., Raghavan, P., Rajagopalan, S., & Tomkins, A. (2001) Recommendation Systems: A Probabilistic Analysis. *Journal of Computer and System Sciences, 63,* 42-61.

Kuo, F. F., Chiang, M. F., Shan, M. K., & Lee, S. Y. (2005). Emotion-based Music Recommendation by Association Discovery from Film Music. *Proc. 13th annual ACM international conference on Multimedia,* Hilton, Singapore, 507 - 510.

Lekakos, G., & Giaglis, G.M. (2007) A Hybrid Approach for Improving Predictive Accuracy of Collaborative Filtering Algorithms. *User Model User-Adap Inter., 17,* 5–40.

Li, T., & Tzanetakis, G. (2003). Factors in automatic musical genre classification of audio signals. *Proc. IEEE Workshop on Applications of Signal Processing to Audio and Acoustics (WASPAA).*

Li, Q., Kim, B. M., Guan, D. H., & Oh, D. W. (2004). A Music Recommender Based on Audio Features. *SIGIR'04,* July 25-29, 2004, Sheffield, South Yorkshire, UK.

Li, Q., Myaeng, S. H., Guan, D. H., & Kim, B.M. (2005). A Probabilistic Model for Music Recommendation Considering Audio Features. *Information Retrieval Technology.* Lecture Notes in Computer Science, *3689,* 72-83.

Li, Q., Myaeng, S. H., & Kim, B. M. (2007). A probabilistic music recommender considering user opinions and audio features. *Information Processing and Management, 43,* 473–487.

Lia, Y., Lu, L., & Xuefeng, L. (2005). A hybrid collaborative filtering method for multiple-interests and multiple-content recommendation in E-Commerce. *Expert Systems with Applications, 28,* 67–77.

Linden, G., Smith, B., & York, J. (2003). Amazon.com recommendations: Item-to-item collaborative filtering. *IEEE Internet Computing, 4*(1).

Logan, B. (2004). Music recommendation from song sets. *Proc. of the International Conference on Music Information Retrieval (ISMIR) 2004.*

McCarthy, K., Salao, M., Coyle, L., McGinty, L., Smyth, B., & Nixon, P. (2006) Group Recommender Systems: A Critiquing Based Approach. *IUI'06,* January 29–February 1, 2006, Sydney, Australia.

McKay, C., McEnnis, D., & Fujinaga, I. (2006). A Large Publicly Accessible Prototype Audio Database for Music Research. *Proc. of the International Conference on Music Information Retrieval (ISMIR) 2006.*

Pavlov, D. Y., & Pennock, D. M. (2002). A Maximum Entropy Approach To Collaborative Filtering in Dynamic, Sparse, High-Dimensional Domains. *Neural Information Processing Systems (NIPS) 2002.*

Pavlov, D. Y., Manavoglu, E., Giles, C. L., & Pennock, D. M. (2004). Collaborative Filtering with Maximum Entropy. *IEEE Intelligent Systems, 19*(6), 40- 47.

Pazzani, M. J. (1999). A Framework for Collaborative, Content-Based and Demographic Filtering. *Artificial Intelligence Review, 13*(5/6), 393-408.

Popescul, A., Ungar, L. H., Pennock, D. M., & Lawrence, S. (2001). Probabilistic Models for Unified Collaborative and Content-Based Recommendation in Sparse-Data Environments. *Proc. of the Seventeenth Conference on Uncertainty in Artificial Intelligence (UAI-2001).*

Resnick, P., Iacovou, N., Suchak, M., Bergstrom, P., & Riedl, J. (1994). GroupLens: An Open Architecture for Collaborative Filtering of Netnews.

Proceedings of the Conference on Computer Supported Cooperative Work, Chapel Hill, NC, 175-186.

Rolland, P. Y. (2001). Adaptive User Modeling in a Content-Based Music Retrieval System. *Proc. of the International Conference on Music Information Retrieval (ISMIR) 2001.*

Sarwar, B., Karypis, G., Konstan, J., & Riedl, J. (2001). Item-Based Collaborative Filtering Recommendation Algorithms WWW10, May 15, 2001, Hong Kong.

Shardanand, U., & Maes, P. (1995). Social information filtering: Algorithms for automating. Word of Mouth. *ACM CHI'95 Conference on Human Factors in Computing Systems*, 210–217.

Smyth, B., & Cotter, P. (2000). A Personalized Television Listings Service. *Communications of the ACM, 43*(8).

Smyth, B., & Cotter, P. (2000). A personalised TV listings service for the digital TV age. *Knowledge-Based Systems, 13*, 53-59.

Typke, R., Wiering, F., & Veltkamp, R. C. (2005). A Survey of Music Information Retrieval Systems. *Proc. of the International Conference on Music Information Retrieval (ISMIR) 2005.*

Tzanetakis, G., & Cook, P. (2002). Musical genre classification of audio signals. *IEEE Transactions on Speech and Audio Processing, 10*(5), 293–302.

Uitdenbogerd, A., & van Schyndel, R. (2002). A review of factors affecting music recommender success. *Proc. of the International Conference on Music Information Retrieval (ISMIR).*

Vignoli, F., & Pauws, S. (2005). A Music Retrieval System Based on User-Driven Similarity and Its Evaluation. *Proc. of the International Conference on Music Information Retrieval (ISMIR).*

Wang, J., de Vries, A. P., & Reinders, M. J.T. (2006). A User-Item Relevance Model for Log-Based Collaborative Filtering. *ECIR 2006*, LNCS 3936, pp. 37–48.

Yapriady, B., & Uitdenbogerd, A.L. (2005). Combining Demographic Data with Collaborative Filtering for Automatic Music Recommendation. *Knowledge-Based Intelligent Information and Engineering Systems, LNCS* Volume 3684/2005.

Yoshii, K., Goto, M., Komatani, K., Ogata, T., & Okuno, H.G. (2006). Hybrid Collaborative and Content-based Music Recommendation Using Probabilistic Model with Latent User Preferences. *Proc. of the International Conference on Music Information Retrieval (ISMIR).*

Chapter XI
Web Content Recommendation Methods Based on Reinforcement Learning

Nima Taghipour
Amirkabir University of Technology, Iran

Ahmad Kardan
Amirkabir University of Technology, Iran

ABSTRACT

Information overload is no longer news; the explosive growth of the Internet has made this issue increasingly serious for Web users. Recommender systems aim at directing users through this information space, toward the resources that best meet their needs and interests. In this chapter the authors introduce their novel machine learning perspective toward the Web recommendation problem, based on reinforcement learning. Our recommendation method makes use of the Web usage and content data to learn a predictive model of users' behavior on the Web and exploits the learned model to make Web page recommendations. Unlike other recommender systems, this system does not use the static patterns discovered from Web usage data, instead it learns to make recommendations as the actions it performs in each situation. In the proposed method the authors combined the conceptual and usage information in order to gain a more general model of user behavior and improve the quality of web recommendations. A hybrid Web recommendation method is proposed by making use of the conceptual relationships among Web resources to derive a novel model of the problem, enriched with semantic knowledge about the usage behavior. The method is evaluated under different settings and it is shown how this method can improve the overall quality of recommendations.

INTRODUCTION

The amount of information available on-line is increasing rapidly with the explosive growth of the World Wide Web and the advent of e-Commerce. Although this surely provides users with more options, at the same time makes it more difficult to find the "relevant" or "interesting" information from this great pool of information. This problem is commonly known as *information overload*: The state of having too much information to make a decision or remain informed about a topic. To address the problems caused by information overload, recommender systems have been introduced (Resnick & Varian, 1997). These systems can be defined as the personalized information technologies used to predict a user evaluation of a particular item (Deshpande & Karypis, 2004) or more generally as systems that guide users toward interesting or useful objects in a large space of possible options (Burke, 2002).

Recommender systems have been used in various applications ranging from predicting the products a customer is likely to buy (Shany *et al.*, 2005), movies, music or news that might interest the user (Konstan *et al.,* 1998; Zhang & Seo, 2001) and web pages that the user is likely to seek (Cooley *et al.*, 1999; Fu *et al.*, 2000; Joachims *et al.*, 1997; Mobasher *et al.*, 2000a), which is also the focus of this chapter. Web page recommendation is considered a user modeling or web personalization task (Eirinaki *et al.*, 2004). One research area that has recently contributed greatly to this problem is web mining. Most of the systems developed in this field are based on web usage mining which is the process of applying data mining techniques to the discovery of usage patterns form web data (Srivastava *et al.*, 2000). These systems are mainly concerned with analyzing web usage logs, discovering patterns from this data and making recommendations based on the extracted knowledge (Fu *et al.*, 2000; Mobasher *et al.*, 2000a; Shahabi *et al.*, 1997; Zhang & Seo, 2001). One important characteristic of these systems is that unlike traditional recommender systems, which mainly base their decisions on user ratings on different items or other explicit feedbacks provided by the user (Deshpande & Karypis, 2004; Herlocker *et al.*, 2000), these techniques discover user preferences from their implicit feedbacks, e.g. the web pages they have visited. More recently, systems that take advantage of domain knowledge, e.g. a combination of content, usage and even structure information of the web, have been introduced and shown superior results in the web page recommendation problem (Li & Zaiane, 2004; Mobasher *et al.*, 2000b; Nakagawa & Mobasher, 2003).

In this chapter we will introduce a different machine learning perspective toward the web recommendation problem, which we believe is suitable to the nature of the problem and has some intrinsic advantages over previous methods. Our recommendation method falls in the category of methods that aim at supporting user's short-term information needs on a single website by recommending web pages to the user based on their navigation, such as previous works presented in (Mobasher *et al.*, 2000a,b; Li & Zaiane, 2004; Nakagawa & Mobasher, 2003). The proposed recommendation method makes use of the web usage and content data to learn a predictive model of users' behavior on the web and exploits the learned model to make web page recommendations to the users (Taghipour *et al.*, 2007; Taghipour & Kardan, 2007; Taghipour & Kardan, 2008). We model the recommendation process as a Reinforcement Learning (RL) problem (Sutton & Barto, 1998) or more specifically a Q-Learning problem. For this purpose we have devised state and action definitions and rewarding policies, considering common concepts and techniques used in the web mining domain. Then we train the system using web usage logs available as the training set, by adapting a variation of Q-learning algorithm. Our recommendation method differs from the previous methods in which the purpose was to find explicit and static patterns or rules, e.g. association rules or clusters of similar sessions, from the data. Here the system learns to make recommendations, i.e. predictions of interesting web pages, as the actions to perform in each situation (state). The choice of reinforcement learning was due to several reasons: It provides a framework appropriate to the nature of web page recommendation problem, mainly due to the concept of delayed reward or temporal difference in RL. Also, due to the characteristics of this type of learning and the fact that we are not making decisions explicitly from the static patterns discovered from the data, it provides us with a system which can potentially be constantly in the learning process and hence does not need periodic updates and can adapt itself to changes in website structure and content and more importantly to the new trends in user behavior.

We begin by introducing our method for web recommendations from web usage data (Taghipour *et al.*, 2007), i.e. usage logs available at web servers. Although the mentioned technique has shown promising results in comparison to common techniques like collaborative filtering and association rules, an analysis of the system's performance, shows how this method still suffers from the problems commonly faced by other usage-based techniques, such as the inability to generalize the learnt usage-based model which might results various problems such as the low coverage of recommendations or the "new item" problem commonly faced in collaborative filtering recommendations (Burke, 2002). To address these problems and to enhance our solution furthermore, we make use of the conceptual relationships among web pages and derive a novel model of the problem, enriched with semantic knowledge about the usage behavior (Taghipour & Kardan, 2008). We use existing methods to derive a conceptual structure of the website (Godoy & Amandi, 2005). Then we come up with new definitions for our states, actions and rewarding functions which capture the semantic implications of users' browsing behavior. Our new hybrid, i.e. usage- and content-based, model for the web page

recommendation problem shows the flexibility of the reinforcement learning framework for the recommendation problem and how it can be extended to incorporate other sources of information. We evaluate our method under different settings and show how this method can improve the overall quality of web recommendations.

BACKGROUND

Web Recommender Systems

Recommender systems have been developed using various approaches and can be categorized in various ways (Burke, 2002). From an architectural point of view, recommendation generation approaches fall into two main categories: memory-based and model-based (Breese *et al.*, 1998). Memory based approaches memorize all the previous historical data, e.g. ratings, and make use of this data in the recommendation generation phase. Therefore, these techniques are more prone to scalability issues. Model-based approaches, on the other hand, use the available data to learn a model for recommendation. In these systems the computationally expensive learning phase is performed offline and hence they generally tend to scale better than memory based systems. It should be noted that as more data becomes available, memory based systems generally adapt better to changes in user interests. While in model based techniques, models must either be incremental or be rebuilt periodically to reflect the new trends.

From an algorithmic point of view recommender systems can be categorized into four general categories (Burke, 2002): knowledge-based systems, content-filtering systems, collaborative filtering systems and hybrid systems. Knowledge-based recommender systems make use of explicit domain knowledge about the items (such as their position in a concept hierarchy of the domain the items belong to) or the users (such as their demographic characteristics) to generate recommendations (Burke, 2000). Most of these recommenders employ some kind of knowledge-based decision rules for recommendation. This type of recommendation is heavily dependant on knowledge engineering by system designers to construct a rule base in accordance to the specific characteristics of the domain. While the user profiles are generally obtained through explicit interactions with users, there have also been some attempts at exploiting machine learning techniques for automatically deriving decision rules that can be used for personalization, e.g. (Pazzani, 1999).

In Content-based filtering systems, the user profile represents a content model of items in which that user has previously shown interest (Pazzani & Bilsus, 2007).These systems are rooted in information retrieval and information filtering research. The content model for an item is represented by a set of features or attributes characterizing that item. The recommendation generation is usually comprised of comparing extracted features from new items with content model in the user profile and recommending items that have adequate similarity to the user profile.

Collaborative techniques (Resnick & Varian, 1997; Herlocker *et al.*, 2000) are the most successful and the most widely used techniques in recommender systems, e.g. (Deshpande & Karypis, 2004; Konstan *et al.,* 1998; Wasfi, 1999). In the simplest from, in this class of systems, users are requested to rate the items they know and then the target user will be recommended the items that people with similar tastes had liked in the past. Recently, Web mining and especially web usage mining techniques have been used widely in web recommender systems (Cooley *et al.*, 1999; Fu *et al.*, 2000; Mobasher *et al.*, 2000a; Mobasher *et al.*, 2000b). Common approach in these systems is to extract navigational patterns from usage data by data mining techniques such as association rules and clustering, and making recommendations based on the extracted patterns. These approaches differ fundamentally from our method in which no static pattern is extracted from data.

More recently, systems that take advantage of a combination of content, usage and even structural information of the websites have been introduced and shown superior results in the web page recommendation problem (Li & Zaiane, 2004; Mobasher *et al.,* 2000b; Nakagawa & Mobasher, 2003). In (Nakagawa & Mobasher, 2003) the degree of connectivity based on the link structure of the website is used to choose from different usage based recommendation techniques, showing that sequential and non-sequential techniques could each achieve better results in web pages with different degrees of connectivity. A new method for generating navigation models is presented in (Li & Zaiane, 2004) which exploits the usage, content and structure data of the website. This method introduces the concept of user's *missions* to represent users' concurrent information needs. These missions are identified by finding content-coherent pages that the user has visited. Website structure is also used both for enhancing the content-based mission identification and also for ranking the pages in recommendation lists. In another approach (Eirinaki *et al.*, 2004, 2003) the content of web pages is used to augment usage profiles with semantics, using a domain-ontology and then performing data mining on the augmented profiles. Most recently, concept hierarchies were incorporated in a novel recommendation method based on web usage mining and optimal sequence alignment to find similarities between user sessions in (Bose *et al.*, 2007).

Markov Decision Process and Reinforcement Learning

Reinforcement learning (Sutton & Barto, 1998) is primarily known in machine learning research as a framework in which agents learn to choose the optimal action in each situation or state they are in. The agent is supposed to be in a specific state s, in each step it performs some action and transits to another state. After each transition the agent receives a reward. The goal of the agent is to learn which actions to perform in each state to receive the greatest accumulative reward, in its path to the goal states. The set of actions chosen in each state is called the agent's policy. One variation of this method is Q-Learning in which the agent does not compute explicit values for each state and instead computes a value function $Q(s,a)$ which indicates value of performing action a in state s (Sutton & Barto, 1998; Mitchell, 1997). Formally the value of $Q(s,a)$ is the discounted sum of future rewards that will be obtained by doing action a in s and subsequently choosing optimal actions. In order to solve the problem with Q-Learning we need to make appropriate definitions for our states and actions, consider a reward function suiting the problem and devise a procedure to train the system using web logs available to us.

The learning process of the agent can be formalized as a Markov Decision Process (MDP). The MDP model of the Problem includes:

1. **Set of states S**, which represents the different 'situations' that the agent can observe. Basically, a state s *in* S must define what is important for the agent to know in order to take a good action. For a given situation, the complete set of states is called the *state space*.

2. **Set of possible actions A,** that the agent can perform in a given state s ($s \in S$) and that will produce a transition into a next state s' $\in S$. As we mentioned, the selection of the particular action depends on the *policy* of the agent. We formally define the policy as a function that indicates for each state s, the action $a \in A$ taken by the agent in that state. In general, it is assumed that the environment, with which the agent interacts, is non-deterministic, i.e., after executing an action, the agent can transit into many alternative states.

3. **Reward function *rew(s,a)*** which assigns a scalar value, also known as the *immediate reward*, to the performance of each action

$a \in A$ taken in state $s \in S$. For instance, if the agent takes an action that is satisfactory for the user, then the agent should be rewarded with a positive immediate reward. On the other hand, if the action is unsatisfactory, the agent should be punished through a negative reward. However, the agent cannot know the reward function exactly, because the reward is assigned to it through the environment. This function can play a very important role in an MDP problem.

4. **Transition function $T(s, a, s')$** which gives the probability of making a transition from state s to state s' when the agent performs the action a. This function completely describes the non-deterministic nature of the agent's environment. Explicit use of this function can be absent in some versions of Q-Learning.

Reinforcement Learning in Recommender Systems

Reinforcement Learning (RL) has been previously used for recommendations in several applications. Web Watcher (Joachims *et al.,* 1997), exploits Q-Learning to guide users to their desired pages. Pages correspond to states and hyperlinks to actions, rewards are computed based on the similarity of the page content and user profile keywords. There are fundamental differences between Web Watcher and our approach, two of the most significant are: (a) our approach requires no explicit user interest profile in any form, and (b) unlike our method, Web Watcher makes no use of previous usage based data. In most other systems, reinforcement learning is used to reflect user feedback and update current state of recommendations. A general framework is presented in (Golovin and Rahm, 2004), which consists of a database of recommendations generated by various models and a learning module that updates the weight of each recommendation by user feedback. In (Srivihok & Sukonmanee, 2005) a travel recommendation agent is introduced which considers various attributes for trips and customers, computes each trip's value with a linear function and updates function coefficients after receiving each user feedback. RL is used for information filtering in (Zhang & Seo, 2001) which maintains a profile for each user containing keywords of interests and updates each word's weight according to the implicit and explicit feedbacks received from the user. In (Shany *et al.*, 2005) the recommendation problem is modeled as an MDP. The system's states correspond to user's previous purchases, rewards are based on the profit achieved by selling the items and the recommendations are made using the theory of MDP and their novel state-transition function. In a more recent work (Mahmood & Ricci, 2007) RL is used in the context of a conversational travel recommender system in order to learn optimal interaction strategies. They model the problem with a finite state-space based on variables like the interaction stage, user action and the result size of a query. The set of actions represent what the system chooses to perform in each state e.g. executing a query, suggesting modification. Finally RL is used to learn an optimal strategy, based on a user behavior model. To the best of our knowledge our method differs from previous work, as none of them used reinforcement learning to train a system in making web site recommendations merely from web usage data.

REINFORCEMENT LEARNING FOR USAGE-BASED WEB PAGE RECOMMENDATION

The specific problem which our system is supposed to solve, can be summarized as follows: the system has, as input data, the log file of users' past visits to the website, these log files are assumed to be in any standard log format, containing records each with a user ID, the sequence of pages the user visited during a session and typically the time of each page request. A user session is defined as a sequence of temporally compact accesses by a user. Since web servers do not typically log usernames, sessions are considered as accesses from the same IP address such that they satisfy some constraints, e.g. the duration of time elapsed between any two consecutive accesses in the session is within a pre-specified threshold (Cooley et al., 1999).

A user enters our website and begins requesting web pages, like a typical browser mostly by following the hyperlinks on web pages. Considering the pages this user has requested so far, the system has to predict in what other pages the user is probably interested and recommend them to her. Table 1 illustrates a sample scenario. Predictions are considered successful if the user chooses to visit those pages in the remaining of that session, e.g. page *c* recommended in the first step in Table 1. Obviously the goal of the system would be to make the most successful recommendations.

Modeling Recommendations as a Q-Learning Problem

Using the Analogy of a Game

In order to better represent our approach toward the problem we try to use the notion of a game. In a typical scenario a web user visits pages sequentially from a web site, let's say the sequence a user *u* requested is composed of pages *a, b, c* and *d*. Each page the user requests can be considered a step or move in our game. After each step the user takes, it will be the system's turn to make a move. The system's purpose is to predict user's next move(s) with the knowledge of his previous moves. Whenever the user makes a move (requests a page), if the system has previously predicted the move, it will receive positive points and otherwise it will receive none or negative points. For example predicting a visit of page *d* after viewing pages *a* and *b* by the user in the above example yields in positive points for the system. The ultimate goal

Table 1. A sample user session and system recommendations

Visited Page	a	b	c	d	e	f
Navigation Trail	a	ab	abc	abcd	abcde	abcdef
System Prediction	c	d	e	s	f	h

of the system would be to gather as much points as possible during a game or actually during a user visit from the web site.

Some important issues can be inferred from this simple analogy: first of all, we can see the problem certainly has a stochastic nature and like most games, the next state cannot be computed deterministically from our current state and the action the system performs due to the fact that the user can choose from a great number of moves. This must be considered in our learning algorithm and our update rules for Q values; the second issue is what the system actions should be, as they are what we ultimately expect the system to perform. Actions will be prediction or recommendation of web pages by the system in each state. Regarding the information each state must contain, by considering our definition of actions, we can deduct that each state should at least show the history of pages visited by the user so far. This way we'll have the least information needed to make the recommendations. This analogy also determines the basics of rewarding function. In its simplest form it shall consider that an action should be rewarded positively if it recommends a page that will be visited in one of the consequent states, not necessarily the immediate next state. Of course, this would be an over simplification and in practice the reward would depend on various factors described in the coming sections. One last issue which is worth noting about the analogy is that this game cannot be categorized as a typical 2-player game in which opponents try to defeat each other, as in this game clearly the user has no intention to mislead the system and prevent the system from gathering points. It might be more

suitable to consider the problem as a competition for different recommender systems to gather more points, than a 2-player game. Because of this intrinsic difference, we cannot use self-play, a typical technique used in training RL systems (Sutton & Barto, 1998) to train our system and we need the actual web usage data for training.

Modeling States and Actions

Considering the above observations we begin the definitions. We tend to keep our states as simple as possible, at least in order to keep their number manageable. Regarding the states, we can see keeping only the user trail can be insufficient. With that definition it won't be possible to reflect the effect of an action a performed in state s_i, in any consequent state s_{i+n} where $n>1$. This means the system would only learn actions that predict the immediate next page which is not the purpose of our system. Another issue we should take into account is the number of possible states: if we allow the states to contain any given sequence of page visits clearly we'll be potentially faced by an infinite number of states. What we chose to do was to limit the page visit sequences to a constant number. For this purpose we adopted the notion of N-Grams which is commonly applied in similar personalization systems based on web usage mining (Mobasher *et al.,* 2000a; Mobasher *et al.,* 2000b). In this model we put a sliding window of size w on user's page visits, resulting in states containing only the last w pages requested by the user. The assumption behind this model is that knowing only the last w page visits of the user, gives us enough information to predict his future page requests. The same problem rises when considering the recommended pages' sequence in the states, for which we take the same approach of considering w' last recommendations.

Regarding the actions, we chose simplicity. Each action is a single page recommendation in each state. Considering multiple page recommendations might have shown us the effect of the combination of recommended pages on the user, in the expense of making our state space and rewarding policy much more complicated.

Thus, we consider each state s at time t consisting of two sequences V, R indicating the sequence of visited and previously recommended pages respectively:

$$V_S = <v_{t-w+1}, v_{t-w+2}, ..., v_t> \qquad (1)$$

$$R_S = <r_{t-w'+1}, r_{t-w'+2}, ..., r_t>$$

Where v_{t-w+i} indicates the ith visited page in the state and r_{t-w+i} indicates the ith recommended page in the state s. The corresponding states and actions of the user session of Table 1 are presented in Figure 1, where straight arrows represent the actions performed in each state and the dashed arrows represent the reward received for performing each action.

Choosing a Reward Function

The basis of reinforcement learning lies in the rewards the agent receives, and how it updates state and action values. As with most stochastic environments, we should reward the actions performed in each state with respect to the consequent

state resulted both from the agent's action and other factor's in the environment on which we might not have control. These consequent states are sometimes called the after-states (Sutton & Barto, 1998). Here this factor is the page the user actually chooses to visit. We certainly do not have a predetermined function $rew(s,a)$ or even a state transition function $\delta(s, a)$ which gives us the next state according to current state s and performed action a.

It can be inferred that the rewards are dependent on the after state and more specifically on the intersection of previously recommended pages in each state and current page sequence of the state. Reward for each action would be a function of $V_{s'}$ and $R_{s'}$ where s' is our next state. One tricky issue worth considering is that though tempting, we should not base on rewards on $|V_s' \cap R_{s'}|$ since it will cause extra credit for a single correct move. Considering the above example a recommendation of page b in the first state shall be rewarded only in the transition to the second state where user goes to page b, while it will also be present in our recommendation list in the third state. To avoid this, we simply consider only the occurrence of the last visited page in state s', in the recommended pages list to reward the action performed in the previous sate s. To complete our rewarding procedure we take into account common metrics used in web page recommender systems. One issue is considering when the page was predicted by the system and when the user actually visited the page. According to the goal of the system this might influence our rewarding. If we consider shortening user navigation as a sign of successful guidance of user to his

Figure 1. States and actions in the recommendation problem

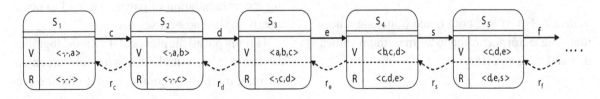

required information, as is the most common case in recommender systems (Li & Zaiane, 2004; Mobasher *et al.*, 2000a) we should consider a greater reward for pages predicted sooner in the user's navigation path and vice versa. Another factor commonly considered in theses systems (Mobasher *et al.*, 2000a; Liu *et al.*, 2004; Fu *et al.*, 2000) is the time the user spends on a page, assuming the more time the user spends on a page the more interested he probably has been in that page. Taking this into account we should reward a successful page recommendation in accordance with the time the user spends on the page. The rewarding can be summarized as follows:

Algorithm 1. Usage Based Reward Function

1: **Assume** $\delta(s, a) = s'$

2: $K_{s'} = V_{s',w} \cap R_{s'} = v_{t+1} \cap R_{s'}$
3: **If** $K_{s'} \neq \emptyset$
4:   **For each** *page k* in $K_{s'}$
5:     $rew(s,a) \mathrel{+}= UBR(Dist(R_{s'}, k), Time(v_{t+1}))$
6:   **End For**
7: **End If**

In line 1, $\delta(s,a) = s'$ shows that the transition of the system to the next state *s'* after performing *a* in state *s*. $K_{s'}$ represents the set of correct recommendations in each step and *rew(s,a)* is the reward of performing action *a* in state *s*. $Dist(R_{s'}, k)$ is the distance of page *k* from the end of the recommended pages list in state *s'* and $Time(v_{t+1})$ indicates the time user has spent on the last page of the state. Here, *UBR* is the Usage-Based Reward function, combining these values to calculate the reward function *rew(s,a)*. We chose a simple linear combination of these values as Equation (2):

$$UBR(Dist, Time) = \alpha \times Dist + \beta \times Time \qquad (2)$$

Where $\alpha + \beta = 1$ and both α and β include a normalizing factor according to the maximum values dist and time can take.

The last modification we experimented was changing our reward function. We noticed as we put a sliding window on our sequence of previously recommended pages, practically we had limited the effect of each action to *w'* next states as can be seen in Figure 2. As can be seen in the example presented in this figure, a correct recommendation of page *f* in state s_i will not be rewarded in state s_{i+3} when using a window of size 2 on the *R* sequence (*w'=2*). After training the system using this definition, the system was mostly successful in recommending pages visited around *w'* steps ahead. Although this might be quite acceptable while choosing an appropriate value for *w'*, it tends to limit system's prediction ability as large numbers of *w'* make our state space enormous. To overcome this problem, we devised a rather simple modification in our reward function: what we needed was to reward recommendation of a page if it is likely to be visited an unknown number of states ahead. Fortunately our definition of states and actions gives us just the information we need and this information is stored in *Q* values of each state. The basic idea is that when an action/recommendation is appropriate in state s_i, indicating the recommended page is likely to occur in the following states, it should also be considered appropriate in state s_{i-1} and the actions in that state that frequently lead to s_i. Following this recursive procedure we can propagate the value of performing a specific action beyond the limits imposed by *w'*. This change is easily reflected in our learning system by considering value of $Q(s',a)$ in computation of *rew(s,a)* with a coefficient like γ. It should be taken into account that the effect of this modification in our reward function must certainly be limited as in its most extreme case where we only take this next *Q* value into account we're practically encouraging recommendation of pages that tend to occur mostly in the end of user sessions.

Having put all the pieces of the model together, we can get an initial idea why reinforcement learning might be a good candidate for the rec-

Figure 2. An example of limited action effectiveness due to the size of the recommendation window

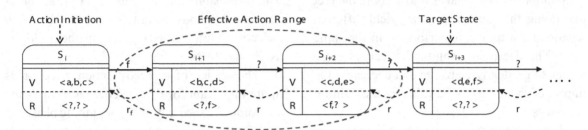

ommendation problem: it does not rely on any previous assumptions regarding the probability distribution of visiting a page after having visited a sequence of pages, which makes it general enough for diverse usage patterns as this distribution can take different shapes for different sequences. The nature of this problem matches perfectly with the notion of delayed reward or what is commonly known as temporal difference: the value of performing an action/recommendation might not be revealed to us in the immediate next state and sequence of actions might have led to a successful recommendation for which we must credit rewards. What the system learns is directly what it should perform, though it is possible to extract rules from the learned policy model, its decisions are not based on explicitly extracted rules or patterns from the data. One issue commonly faced in systems based on patterns extracted from training data is the need to periodically update these patterns in order to make sure they still reflect the trends residing in user behavior or the changes of the site structure or content. With reinforcement learning the system is intrinsically learning even when performing in real world, as the recommendations are the actions the system performs, and it is commonplace for the learning procedure to take place during the interaction of system with its environment.

Training the System

We chose Q-Learning as our learning algorithm. This method is primarily concerned with estimat-

ing an evaluation of performing specific actions in each state, known as Q-values. Each $Q(s,a)$ indicates an estimate of the accumulative reward achievable, by performing action a in state s and performing the action a' with highest $Q(s',a')$ in each future state s'. In this setting we are not concerned with evaluating each state in the sense of the accumulative rewards reachable from this state, which with respect to our system's goal can be useful only if we can estimate the probability of visiting the following states by performing each action. On the other hand Q-Learning provides us with a structure that can be used directly in the recommendation problem, as recommendations in fact are the actions and the value of each recommendation/action shows an estimation of how successful that prediction can be. Another decision is the update rule for Q values.

Because of the non-deterministic nature of this problem we use the following update rule (Sutton & Barto, 1998):

$$Q_n(s,a) = (1-\alpha_n)Q_{n-1}(s,a) + \alpha_n[r(s,a) + \gamma \max_{a'} Q_{n-1}(\delta(s,a),a')]$$

$$(3)$$

With

$$\alpha_n = \frac{1}{1+visits_n(s,a)} \qquad (4)$$

Where $Q_n(s,a)$ is the Q-Value of performing a in state s after n iterations, and $visits_n(s,a)$ indicates the total number of times this state-action pair, i.e. *(s,a)*, has been visited up to and including the nth iteration. This rule takes into account the fact that doing the same action can yield different rewards each time it is performed in the same state. The decreasing value of a_n causes these values to gradually converge and decreases the impact of changing reward values as the training continues.

What remains about the training phase is how we actually train the system using web usage logs available. As mentioned before these logs consist of previous user sessions in the web site. Considering the analogy of the game they can be considered as a set of opponent's previous games and the moves he tends to make. We are actually provided with a set of actual episodes occurred in the environment, of course with the difference that no recommendations were actually made during these episodes. The training process can be summarized as Algorithm 2

One important issue in the training procedure is the method used for action selection. One obvious strategy would be for the agent in each state *s* to select the action *a* that maximizes *Q(s,a)* hereby exploiting its current approximation. However, with this greedy strategy there's the risk of over-committing to actions that are found during early training to have high Q values, while failing to explore other actions that might have even higher values (Mitchell, 1997). For this reason, it is common in Q learning to use a probabilistic approach to selecting actions. A simple alternative

is to behave greedily most of the time, but with small probability ε, instead select an action at random. Methods using this near-greedy action selection rule are called ε-greedy methods (Sutton & Barto, 1998).

The choice of ε-greedy action selection is quite important for this specific problem as the exploration especially in the beginning phases of training, is vital. The Q values will converge if each episode, or more precisely each state-action pair is visited infinitely. In our implementation of the problem convergence was reached after a few thousand (between 3000 and 5000) visits of each episode. This definition of the learning algorithm completely follows a *TD(0)* off-policy learning procedure (Sutton & Barto, 1998), as we take an estimation of future reward accessible from each state after performing each action by considering the maximum *Q* value in the next state.

EXPERIMENTAL EVALUATION OF THE USAGE BASED APPROACH

We evaluated system performance in the different settings described above. We used simulated log files generated by a web traffic simulator to tune our rewarding functions. The log files were simulated for a website containing 700 web pages. We pruned user sessions with a length smaller than 5 and were provided with 16000 user sessions with average length of eight. As our evaluation

Algorithm 2. Training procedure

- Initial values of *Q(s,a)* for each pair *s,a* are set to zero
- Repeat until convergence
  - A random episode is chosen from the set of training episodes.
  - *s* is set to the first step/state of the episode.
  - For each step of the episode do
    - Choose an action *a* of this state using the ε-greedy policy.
    - Perform action a observe the next state and compute *rew(s,a)* as described before.
    - Update value of *Q(s,a)* with the above equation.
    - $s \leftarrow s'$.

---

data set we used the web logs of the Depaul University website, one of the few publicly available and widely used datasets, made available by the author of (Mobasher *et al.*, 2000a). This dataset is pre-processed and contains 13745 user sessions in their visits on 687 pages. These sessions have an average length around 6. The website structure is categorized as a dense one with high connectivity between web pages according to (Nakagawa & Mobasher, 2003). 70% of the data set was used as the training set and the remaining was used to test the system. For our evaluation we presented each user session to the system, and recorded the recommendations it made after seeing each page the user had visited. The system was allowed to make r recommendations in each step with $r<10$ and $r < \sqrt{O_v}$ where O_v is the number of outgoing links of the last page v visited by the user. This limitation on number of recommendations is adopted from (Li & Zaiane, 2004). The recommendation set in each state is composed by selecting the *top-r* actions of the sates with the highest Q-values, again by a variation of the ε-greedy action selection method.

Evaluation Metrics

To evaluate the recommendations we use the metrics presented in (Li & Zaiane, 2004) because of the similarity of the settings in both systems and the fact that we believe these co-dependent metrics can reveal the true performance of the system more clearly than simpler metrics. Recommendation Accuracy and Coverage are two metrics quite similar to the precision and recall metrics commonly used in information retrieval literature.

Recommendation accuracy measures the ratio of correct recommendations among all recommendations, where correct recommendations are the ones that appear in the remaining of the user session. If we have M sessions in our test log, for each visit session m after considering each page p, the system generates a set of recommenda-

tions $Rec(p)$. To compute the accuracy, $Rec(p)$ is compared with the rest of the session $Tail(p)$ as Equation (5). This way any correct recommendation is evaluated exactly once.

$$Accuracy = \frac{\sum_m \frac{\left|\cup_p(Tail(p) \cap Rec(p))\right|}{\left|\cup_p Rec(p)\right|}}{M} \quad (5)$$

Recommendation coverage on the other hand shows the ratio of the pages in the user session that the system is able to predict before the user visits them:

$$Coverage = \frac{\sum_m \frac{\left|\cup_p(Tail(p) \cap Rec(p))\right|}{\left|\cup_p Tail(p)\right|}}{M} \quad (6)$$

As is the case with precision and recall, these metrics can be useful indicators of the system performance only when used in accordance to each other and lose their credibility when used individually. As an example, consider a system that recommends all the pages in each step, this system will gain 100% coverage, of course in the price of very low accuracy.

Another metric used for evaluation is called the shortcut gain which measures how many page-visits users can save if they follow the recommendations. The shortened session is derived by eliminating the intermediate pages in the session that the user could escape visiting, by following the recommendations. A visit time threshold is used on the page visits to decide which pages are auxiliary pages as proposed by Li and Zaiane (2004). If we call the shortened session m', the shortcut gain for each session is measured as follows:

$$ShortcutGain = \frac{\frac{|m|-|m'|}{|m|}}{M} \quad (7)$$

Evaluation Results

In the first set of experiments we tested the effect of different decisions regarding state definition, rewarding function, and the learning algorithm on the system behavior. Afterwards we compared the system performance to the other common techniques used in recommendation systems.

Sensitivity to Active Window Size on User Navigation Trail

In our state definition, we used the notion of N-Grams by putting a sliding window on user navigation paths. The implication of using a sliding window of size w is that we base the prediction of user future visits on his w past visits. The choice of this sliding window size can affect the system in several ways. A large sliding window seems to provide the system a longer memory while on the other hand causing a larger state space with sequences that occur less frequently in the usage logs. We trained our system with different window sizes on user trail and evaluated its performance as seen in Figure 3. In these experiments we used a fixed window size of 3 on recommendation history.

As our experiments show the best results are achieved when using a window of size 3. It can

be inferred form this diagram that a window of size 1 which considers only the user's last page visit does not hold enough information in memory to make the recommendation, the accuracy of recommendations improve with increasing the window size and the best results are achieved with a window size of 3. Using a window size larger than 3 results in weaker performance (only shown up to *w=4* in Figure 3 for the sake of readability), it seems to be due to the fact that, as mentioned above, in these models, states contain sequences of page visits that occur less frequently in web usage logs, causing the system to make decisions based on weaker evidence. In our evaluation of the short cut gain there was a slight difference when using different window sizes.

Sensitivity to Active Window Size on Recommendations

In the next step we performed similar experiments, this time using a constant sliding window of size 3 on user trail and changing size of active window on recommendations history. As this window size was increased, rather interesting results was achieved as shown in Figure 4.

In evaluating system accuracy, we observed improvement up to a window of size 3, after that increasing the window size caused no improve-

Figure 3. System performance with various user visit windows sizes (w)

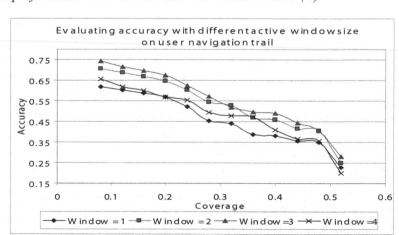

ment while resulting in larger number of states. This increase in the number of states is more intense than when the window size on user trail was increased. This is manly due to the fact that the system is exploring and makes any combination of recommendations to learn the good ones. The model consisting of this great number of states is in no way efficient, as in our experiments on the test data only 25% of these states were actually visited. In the sense of shortcut gain the system achieved, it was observed that shortcut gain increased almost constantly with increase in window size, which seems a natural consequence as described in section "Reinforcement learning for usage-based web page recommendation".

Evaluating Different Reward Functions

Next we changed the effect of parameters constituting our reward function. First we began by not considering the *Dist* parameter, described in section "Reinforcement learning for usage-based web page recommendation", in our rewards. We gradually increased it's coefficient in steps of 5% and recorded the results as shown in Table 2. These results show that increasing the impact of this parameter in our rewards up to 15% of total reward can result both in higher accuracy and higher shortcut gain. Using values greater than 15% has a slight negative effect on accuracy with a slight positive effect on shortcut gain and keeping it almost constant. This seems a natural

Figure 4. System performance with different active recommendation windows (w')

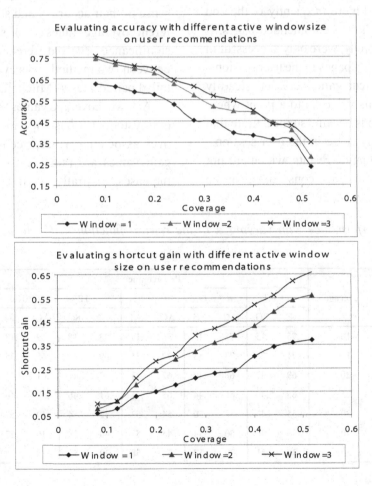

235

consequence since although we're paying more attention to pages that tend to appear later in the user sessions, the system's vision into the future is bounded by the size of window on recommendations. This limited vision also explains why our accuracy is not decreasing as expected.

The next set of experiments tested system performance with the reward function that considers *next state Q-value* of each action in rewarding the action performed in the previous state, as described in section "Reinforcement learning for usage-based web page recommendation". We began by increasing the coefficient of this factor (γ) in the reward function the same way we did for the *Dist* parameter. In the beginning increasing this value, lead to higher accuracy and shortcut gains. After reaching an upper bound, the accuracy began to drop. In these settings, recommendations with higher values were those targeted toward the pages that occurred more frequently in the end of user sessions. These recommended pages, if recommended correctly, were only successful in predicting the last few pages in the user sessions. As expected, shortcut gain increased steadily with increase in this value up to a point where the recommendations became so inaccurate that rarely happened anywhere in the user sessions. More detailed evaluation results, which are not presented here due to space constraints, can be found in (Taghpour *et al.*, 2007).

A Comparison with Other Methods

Finally we observed our system performance in comparison with two other methods: (a) association rules, as one approach based on of the usage-pattern and one of the most common approaches in web mining based recommender systems (Mobasher *et al.*, 2000a,b); and collaborative filtering which is commonly known as one of the most successful approaches for recommendations. We chose item-based collaborative filtering with probabilistic similarity measure (Deshpande & Karypis, 2004), as a baseline for comparison because of the promising results it had shown. It should be noted that these techniques have already shown significantly superior results compared to common sense methods such as recommending most popular items (pages) of a collection. In Figure 5 the performance of these systems in the sense of their accuracy and shortcut gain in different coverage values can be seen. The statistical significance of any differences in performance between two methods was evaluated using two-tailed paired t-tests (Mitchell, 1997).

At lower coverage values we can see although our system still has superior results especially over association rules, accuracy and shortcut gain values are rather close. As the coverage increases, naturally accuracy decreases in all

Table 2. System performance with varying α in the reward function. (AC=Accuracy, SG=Shortcut Gain)

Coverage	Performance									
	α = 0.1		α = 0.15		α = 0.20		α = 0.25		α = 0.30	
	AC	SG	AC	SG	AC	SG	AC	SG	AC	SG
10	.75	.15	.78	.17	.76	.17	.73	.18	.69	.18
15	.71	.28	.73	.33	.72	.35	.69	.34	.65	.35
20	.69	.37	.68	.40	.67	.41	.67	.41	.61	.41
25	.65	.40	.66	.44	.65	.44	.61	.46	.58	.46
30	.55	.43	.57	.50	.54	.53	.52	.54	.49	.57
40	.48	.48	.50	.54	.45	.57	.40	.58	.36	.57
50	.36	.51	.39	.57	.33	.58	.29	.58	.27	.59

systems, but our system gains much better results than the other two systems. It can be seen the rate in which accuracy decreases in our system is lower than other two systems; at lower coverage values where the systems made their most promising recommendations (those with higher values), pages recommended were mostly the next immediate page and as can be seen had an acceptable accuracy. At lower coverage rates, where recommendations with lower values had to be made our system began recommending pages occurring in the session some steps ahead, while the other approaches also achieved greater short-cut gains, as the results show their lower valued recommendations were not as accurate and their performance declined more intensely. Regardless

of the size of the difference at different coverage values, all the differences in Accuracy and Short-cut Gain between our proposed method and the baseline approaches are statistically significant ($p<0.001$ on the *t*-test).

INCORPORATING CONTENT FOR HYBRID WEB RECOMMENDATIONS

In this section we exploit the idea of combining content and usage information to enhance the reinforcement learning solution, we had devised for web page recommendations based on web usage data. Although the mentioned technique showed promising results in comparison to common tech-

Figure 5. Comparing our system's performance with two other common methods

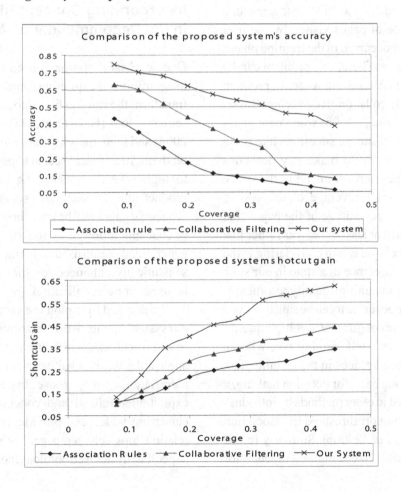

niques like collaborative filtering and association rules, an analysis of the system's performance, reveals that this method still suffers from the problems commonly faced by other usage-based techniques. To address these problems, we made use of the conceptual relationships among web pages and derived a new model of the problem, enriched with semantic knowledge about the usage behavior. We used existing methods to derive a conceptual structure of the website. Then we came up with new definitions for our states, actions and rewarding functions which capture the semantic implications of users browsing behavior.

Observations on Performance of the Usage-Based Approach

In our evaluation of the system, we noticed that although we were faced with a rather large number of states, there were cases where the state resulted from the sequence of pages visited by the user had actually never occurred in the training phase. Although not the case here, this problem can be also due to the infamous "new item" problem commonly faced in collaborative filtering (Burke, 2002; Mobasher *et al.,* 2000b) when new pages are added to the website. In situations like these the system was unable to make any decisions regarding the pages to recommend to the users. Moreover, the overall coverage of the system on the website, i.e. percentage of the pages that were recommended at least once, was rather low (55.06%). Another issue worth considering is the fact that the mere presence of a state in our state space cannot guarantee a high quality recommendation, to be more accurate it can be said that even a high Q-value cannot guarantee a high quality recommendation by itself. Simply put, when a pattern has few occurrences in the training data it cannot be a strong basis for decision making, a problem addressed in other methods by introducing metrics like support threshold in association rules (Mobasher *et al.,* 2000b). Similarly in our case a high Q-value, like a high confidence for

an association rule, cannot be trusted unless it has strong supporting evidence in the data. In summary, there are cases when historical usage data provides no evidence or evidence that's not strong enough to make a rational decision about user's need or behavior.

This is a problem common in recommender systems that have usage data as their only source of information. Note that in the described setting, pages stored in the V sequence of each state S are treated as items for which the only information available is their id. The system relies solely on usage data and thus is unable to make any generalization. One common solution to this problem is to incorporate some semantic knowledge about the items being recommended, into the system. In the next section we describe our approach for adopting this idea.

Incorporating Concept Hierarchies in the Recommendation Model

One successful approach used to enhance web usage mining, is exploiting content information to transform the raw log files into more meaningful semantic logs (Bose *et al.,* 2006; Eirinaki *et al.,* 2004) and then applying data mining techniques on them. In a typical scenario pages are mapped to higher level concepts e.g. catalogue page, product page, etc and a user session consisting of sequential pages will be transformed to a sequence of concepts followed by the user. Consequently, generalized patterns are extracted from these semantically enhanced log files which can then be used for personalization.

We decided to exploit the same techniques in our system to improve our state and action model. In order to make our solution both general and applicable, we avoided using an ad-hoc concept hierarchy for this purpose. Instead we chose to exploit hierarchical and conceptual document clustering which can provide us with semantic relationships between pages without the need of a specifically devised ontology, concept hierarchy or manual assignment of concepts to pages. An important factor in our selection was the ability of the method to perform incremental document clustering, since we prefer to come up with a solution that is able to cope with the changes in the web site content and structure. In order to map pages to higher level concepts, we applied the DCC clustering algorithm (Godoy & Amandi, 2005) on the web pages. It is an incremental hierarchical clustering algorithm which is originally devised to infer user needs and falls in the category of conceptual clustering algorithms as it assigns labels to each cluster of documents. In this method each document would be assigned to a single class in the hierarchy. This method has shown promising results in the domain of user profiling based on the web pages visited by the user from web corpuses. We use this method to organize our documents similar to the manner in which they're assigned to nodes of a concept hierarchy. It should be noted that the output of other more sophisticated approaches like the one proposed in (Eirinaki *et al.*, 2004) for generating C-Logs could also be used for this purpose without affecting our general RL model.

Conceptual States and Actions

After clustering the web pages in the hierarchy, our state and action definition change as follows. Instead of keeping a sequence V of individual page visits by the user, each state would consist of a sequence of concepts visited by the user. Considering a mapping like $C : P \rightarrow H$ which transforms each page p in the set of pages P to the corresponding concept c in the concept hierarchy H, the states s in each time step t would now be defined as:

$$V_s = <C(v_{t-w+1}), C(v_{t-w+2}),...,C(v_t)>$$
$$R_s = <C(r_{t-w'+1}), C(r_{t-w'+2}),...,C(r_t)>$$

$$(8)$$

Also, the actions are now recommendation of pages that belong to a specific concept. In order to do so we need a module to find the node each page belongs to in the concept hierarchy and transform each usage log to a sequence of concepts in the training phase. The other aspects of the system like the reward function and the learning process would remain the same, e.g. an action a recommending a concept c is rewarded if the user visits a page belonging to concept c later in his browsing session.

This definition results in a much smaller state-action space as now the state space size is dependant on the number of distinct page clusters instead of the number of distinct web pages in the website. Consequently, the learning process will become more efficient and the system will have a more general model of users' browsing behavior on the site. With this generalized definition, the chance of confronting an unseen state will be much less and actually minimized as our evaluation results show. We'll no longer make decisions based on weak usage patterns as now the states represent a generalized view of many single visit sequences, and the average number of times a state is visited in user sessions is now 10.2 times the average visit of states in the usage-based setting. A general view of the system is depicted in Figure 6.

In the test phase, the user's raw session will be converted to a semantic session, the corresponding state will be found and the page cluster with the highest value is identified. When a concept is chosen as the action, the next step would be to recommend pages from the chosen cluster(s). Initially we chose to recommend the pages with a probability corresponding to their similarity to the cluster mean vector. This new definition of actions enables the system to cover a wider range of pages to be recommended as our evaluations show, and also the potential ability of avoiding the "new item" problem as any new page will be categorized in the appropriate cluster and have a fair chance of being recommended.

Figure 6. Architecture of the Hybrid Recommender System

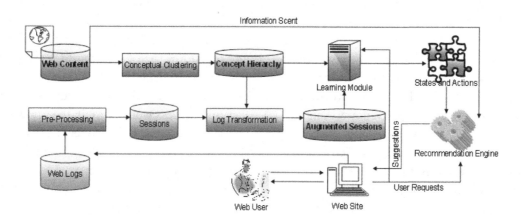

A Content-Based Reward Function

We can also make use of the content information of web pages and their relative positioning in the concept hierarchy in our reward function. The new rewarding function takes the content similarity of the recommended and visited pages into account. The basic idea behind this method is to reward recommendation of a concept c in s_i which might not be visited in s_{i+1} but is semantically similar to the visited page v, or more precisely, to the concept that v belongs to. The new reward function would be basically same as the one presented in Algorithm 1, the only difference is that instead of using $rew(s,a)$ in step 5, now the reward would be computed by the new function $HybridRew(s,a)$ shown in Equation 9.

$$HybridRew(s,a)= \quad\quad\quad\quad (9)$$
$$UBR(Dist(R_s,a),Time(v_{t+1}))\times CBR(a, v_{t+1})$$

Here CBR represents the content-based reward of an action and UBR is the usage based reward which is our previous reward function used in step 5 of Algorithm 1.

In order to compute the content based reward we use the method for computing similarity of nodes in a concept hierarchy proposed in (Bose et al., 2006). In this method, first a probability $p(c)$ is assigned to each concept node c which is proportional to the frequency of pages belonging to this node and its descendants in user sessions. The information content of each node is then defined as:

$$I(c) = - \log p(c) \quad\quad\quad\quad (10)$$

Then a set LCA is found which contain the Least Common Ancestors, those occurring at the deepest level, of the pair of concept nodes. And the similarity score between those are computed as:

$$Sim(c_1,c_2) = \max_{a\in LCA} \{I(a)\} \quad\quad (11)$$

The CBR for each recommended page a will be equal to the similarity score:

$$CBR(a, v_{t+1})=Sim(C(a),C(v_{t+1})) \quad (12)$$

This method seems specifically appropriate for the off-line training phase where recommendations are evaluated using the web usage logs. In this phase actions are predictions of the user's next visit and web pages are not recommended to the user in the on-line browsing sessions. As a result actual user reactions towards pages cannot be assessed and the assumption is made that users interest toward a recommendation can be estimated as function of conceptual similarity between the recommended and visited pages.

The situation is a bit different when the system provides on-line recommendations to the user. Here the usage-based reward is given more weight than the reward based on content similarity. This is based on the idea that the overall judgment of users can be trusted more than the content similarity of pages, since satisfying user information need is the ultimate goal of personalization.

Selection of Pages in a Concept

Based on the actions, we can decide which concept the user is interested in. In order to make recommendations, we should select a page belonging to that concept, which is not a trivial task especially when we're faced with large clusters of pages. Our initial solution was to rank pages with respect to their distance from cluster center. Our experiments show that this method does not yield in accurate recommendations. In order to enhance our method we exploited the content information of web pages and the hyperlinks that the users have followed in each state. The text around the chosen hyperlinks in each page has been used as an indicator of user information need in user modeling, based on the information scent model (Chi *et al.*, 2001). We also employ the information scent to compute a vector representing user information need in each state. The method we used is basically similar to (Chi *et al.*, 2001), using the text around the hyperlink, the title of the out going page etc., with the exception that we assign more weight to the hyperlinks followed later in each state. After computing this vector we use the cosine based similarity to find the most relevant pages in each selected page cluster for recommendation.

Overall, we experimented with three different methods for ranking pages for selection from a given concept c' (pages with lower ranks have higher probability of being selected):

1. Ranking based on the distance of a page from Cluster Mean (*HCM*): The basic idea here is that pages which are closer to the cluster mean vector are more relevant to the given concept and hence might be more relevant to a user interested in that concept. Considering $W_{c'}$ as the mean content vector of concept c', and the vector W_i, representing each web page p_i ($p_i \in P$ and $C(p_i) = c'$), the selection rank of each p_i, shown by $SelRank_{CM}(p_i)$, would be computed according to (14). This rank is in reverse relation with the distance of W_i from $W_{c'}$. In these experiments we computed the distance using the cosine of these two vectors.

$$SelRank_{CM}(p_i) \leq SelRank_{CM}(p_j) \Leftrightarrow$$
$$Dist(W_{C'}, W_i) \leq Dist(W_{C'}, W_j)$$

$$(13)$$

2. Ranking based on the occurrence frequency of a page (*HFreq*): this method is primarily based on historical usage data. The rationale is that pages which are more frequently visited by users might more popular in the collection of pages related to a concepts and therefore more probable to be sought by the target user. Considering $Frq(p_i)$ as the occurrence frequency of each p_i ($p_i \in P$ and $C(p_i) = c'$), the selection rank of each p_i, shown by $SelRank_{Freq}(p_i)$, would be in reverse relation with the distance this frequency.

$$SelRank_{Freq}(p_i) \leq SelRank_{Freq}(p_j) \Leftrightarrow$$
$$Frq(p_i) \geq Frq(p_j)$$

$$(14)$$

3. Ranking based on the Information Scent model (*HIS*): in this approach, based on the information foraging theory, it is assumed that the information need of the user van be estimated by the proximal cues that the user follows in his navigation on the web. Here, pages are ranked in accordance to their similarity to the vector derived by the information scent model from the sequence

of pages visited in each state. Considering W_{IS} as the information scent vector, and the vector W_i, representing each web page p_i ($p_i \in P$ and $C(p_i) = c'$), the selection rank of each p_i, shown by $SelRank_{IS}(p_i)$, would be computed according to (15). This rank is in accordance with the similarity of W_i to W_{IS}. In our experiments, the similarity of two vectors was computed using the cosine-based similarity function commonly used in information retrieval.

$$SelRank_{IS}(p_i) \le SelRank_{IS}(p_j) \Leftrightarrow$$

$$Sim(W_{IS}, W_i) \ge Sim(W_{IS}, W_j) \qquad (15)$$

EXPERIMENTAL EVALUATION OF THE HYBRID RECOMMENDATION METHOD

Evaluation Metrics

We pointed out the main weaknesses of the usage-based method in the previous section and proposed the hybrid approach as a solution to overcome these shortcomings. In order to assess the success of the proposed method in this regards, we need metrics that directly address these characteristics of the system. Thus, metrics beyond the ones used in evaluation of the usage-based method in the previous section should be used. We used the following metrics for this purpose, many of which were used by Bose *et al.* (2007). We also used some modifications of these metrics as needed. The metrics used are:

- **Recommendation Accuracy** *(RA)*: Percentage of correct recommendations between all the recommendations made by the system. A correct recommendation is, as before, a specific recommended web page that the user chooses to visit. These recommendations are generated in the hybrid approach by applying one of the page selection methods.

- **Predictive Ability** *(PA)*: Percentage of pages recommended at least once. Bose *et al.* (2007) mention this metric as one that measures how useful the recommendation algorithm is.

- **Prediction Strength** *(PS)*: Measures the average number of recommendation the system makes in each state (for each sequence of page visits). This metric aims at evaluating the ability of the recommender in generating recommendations for various scenarios of user behavior. It can specially reflect the performance of the system in the presence of the "new state" problem.

- **Shortcut Gain** *(SG)*: average percentage of pages skipped because of recommendations. This is the same metric we used to evaluate the usage-based approach.

- **Recommendation Quality** *(RQ):* average rank of a correct recommendation in the recommendation lists. This metric emphasizes the importance of ranking pages for recommendations (somehow similar to the manner in which ranking is valued in the results returned by a search engine).

Sensitivity to Visited Sequence Window Size

The first experiments were performed to evaluate system sensitivity to the size of visited concept sequence V in our states. To evaluate the choice of different window sizes, regardless of other parameters e.g. the page selection method, we used a new metric called *Concept recommendation Accuracy (CRA)* and *Concept Predictive Ability (CPA)* which are based on recommendation and visit of concepts instead of pages. For example, a recommendation of concept c_l is considered successful if the user later visits any page p belonging to c_l, i.e. $C(p) = c_l$. Our evaluations indicate the best performances are achieved when using window sizes of 3 and 4 (Table 3). This is due to the fact that smaller values of w keep insufficient infor-

Table 3. Comparison of different window sizes in the hybrid approach

Window Size	Metric		
	CRA	CPA	RQ
1	42	76	1.88
2	63	81	3.21
3	79.50	96	2.80
4	81.30	98	2.11
5	66.66	95	3.78

mation about navigation history and larger values of w result in states that are numerous and less frequently visited, as the average session length in our data is 8.6. We choose $w=3$ in the rest of the experiments as it results in smaller number of states with a negligible decrease in accuracy.

Comparison with Other Methods

We compared the proposed method with the previous usage-based approach *(UB-RL)* and a content-based approach that uses the info scent model to recommend pages from the whole website *(CIS)*. The latter method was used because of the promising results achieved in the system while using the page selection method based on information scent. Note that *UB-RL* has shown superior results than common usage-based methods, and is considered as the baseline usage-based method we aim to improve. We used three different methods for page selection in our hybrid approach: based on the distance from cluster mean *(HCM)*, using the frequency of occurrence in user sessions *(HFreq)* and the one based on Information Scent *(HIS)*. We also compared our method to a state of the art recommendation method proposed by Bose *et al.* (2007). This method makes use of concept hierarchies and sequence alignment methods in order to cluster user sessions and making recommendations based on the resulted clusters. It is abbreviated by *HSA* in the results. The results presented here are based different experiments of having 3, 5 and 10 as the maximum number

of recommendations in each stage (length of the recommendation list).

An issue worth considering is that based on the experiments performed in the previous section (sensitivity to the *V* sequence), we have an upper bound estimation of the performance of our hybrid recommendation methods. For example, the *CRA* achieved by the system is the maximum *RA* the hybrid methods can achieve. Since now the methods have to select a specific page from a concept and we know the ability of the system in predicting the correct concept is limited by *CRA*. In fact, these results can be used to compare the performance of various page selection methods in the hybrid approaches.

As our evaluation shows (Table 4), *HIS* out performs the rest of the methods except with respect to *RA*, compared to *UB*-RL. Note that the *UB-RL* method shows a much lower *PA*, as it's a purely usage-based approach. An initial glance on the results can show the success of our hybrid methods in overcoming the shortcomings of the usage-based approach, especially in the sense of *PA* and *PS* metrics (both significant at $p<0.001$ on the *t*-test). Our hybrid approaches, especially *HIS* and *HFreq*, can also outperform the state of the art *HSA* recommendation method in almost every situation, although the better performance is marginal and less significant in *PS* measure, it is more significant on *PA* ($p<0.01$) and more emphasized and also statistically significant on RA, SG and RQ (all with $p<0.001$ on the *t*-test). The results achieved when using different

Table 4. Comparison of different recommendation methods

Method	Metric				
	RA	PA	PS	SG	RQ
Max. Number of Recommendation in Each Step=3					
UB-RL	**53.76**	51.06	2.73	10.26	**1.96**
CIS	35.09	67.12	2.99	7.01	2.54
HSA	45.11	93.60	2.97	21.07	2.26
HCM	38.09	91.01	**2.97**	11.33	2.39
HFreq	46.34	93.40	**2.97**	**24.11**	2.19
HIS	**51.66**	**94.10**	2.97	22.31	**2.15**
Max. Number of Recommendation in Each Step=5					
UB-RL	**49.81**	55.06	3.64	13.17	**2.21**
CIS	32.11	69.29	4.98	7.21	3.90
HSA	40.01	96.91	4.95	24.21	3.58
HCM	33.09	91.67	**4.96**	12.56	3.76
HFreq	42.12	95.91	**4.96**	**26.80**	3.11
HIS	**46.28**	**97.20**	4.96	25.76	**2.89**
Max. Number of Recommendation in Each Step=10					
UB-RL	**44.91**	58.15	5.69	14.17	**2.79**
CIS	29.82	73.12	9.96	8.14	8.11
HSA	34.31	96.91	9.79	25.18	6.27
HCM	30.09	92.23	9.82	14.62	6.97
HFreq	39.36	96.31	9.82	27.77	5.94
HIS	**42.17**	**97.20**	9.84	27.95	5.33

lengths for recommendation lists almost show the same relative performance from different recommendation methods, while some features of the methods are more emphasized in higher or lower number of recommendations which we'll point out in the rest of this section. One important issue in analyzing the evaluation results is considering the logical dependencies that exist between various evaluation metrics, e.g. between *PS* and *RQ*. Considering dependencies, naturally there's not a single recommendation method that outperforms the rest with respect to *all* evaluation metrics. What should be noted is the importance of

evaluating recommendation methods based their overall performance in all the evaluation metrics and also considering their relative performance in dependent evaluation metrics. As we will investigate further in the following subsections, we conclude from these results that our two hybrid approaches *HIS* and *HFreq* show an overall superior performance compared to the other methods and could be considered our suggestions for further development and implementation in real world applications, especially the *HIS* method which is the superior method in the majority of the metrics and the usually the second best in the rest. We will discuss the performance of various recommendation methods with respect to each metric in the following sub sections.

Predictive Ability

It can also be seen that all the hybrid approaches can achieve better predictive ability than the content based recommendation method *CIS* (significant at $p<0.001$ on the t-test). This issue is more emphasized when using shorter recommendation lists. This shows that semantic grouping of the web pages and then recommending a page from the *correct* can actually increase the chance of each page to be recommended appropriately. While, the *CIS* method which considers the whole set of pages as the search space is less successful in covering the web site.

Predictive Strength

Regarding the prediction strength metric, the *UB-RL* method is the weakest recommendation method, as expected. Various reasons for this phenomena such as the "new state" problem were mentioned in the previous section. On the other hand, the purely content-based *CIS* approach can achieve the perfect *PS* performance as there have always been some pages with some minimum similarity with the resulted content model. This can be an intrinsic characteristic of each content-based method, when not considering a lower bound on similarity. It should be noted that beside the number of recommendations shown by the *PS* value, the quality of the recommendation list is also of uttermost importance. In this regard, our hybrid approaches are able to achieve better results in almost every evaluation metric, while also achieving a *PS* very close to the optimal *CIS* approach. For example the *HIS* method achieves a 36% increase in compared to the baseline *UB-RL* method which is also statistically significant ($p<<0.001$). These results illustrate the strength of the generalized models of user behavior, em-

ployed in the hybrid approaches, in capturing user behavior patterns and avoiding unseen navigation scenarios at a higher level of abstraction resulted from the generalized state and action model.

Recommendation Accuracy

While the *UB-RL* method receives the highest accuracy as expected, our proposed hybrid approaches *HIS* and *HFreq* are the second bests in almost every case with a rather small difference. This performance is especially important due to the fact that the hybrid approaches have lost the information at the detail level of page visits because of their generalized view of user behavior. Like any generalization this information loss is supposed to come inevitably with some loss in model accuracy. These results show the success of the page selection methods employed in *HFreq* and *HIS* and the importance of this selection. The rather low *RA* value achieved by *HCM* indicates the importance of page selection method in the process. It is also an indicator of the existing trade-off between generalized and detailed knowledge. As we can see this approach has a high *CRA* value (Table 3), but because of the information loss occurred at a higher level of abstraction and lack of an appropriate page selection method (at lower level of abstraction), it performs even worse than *CFreq* which is based on a rather simple metric, i.e. popularity of a page. The weaker performance of *CIS* (statistically significant at $p<0.001$) might be considered as further evidence in support of the importance of usage patterns in accurate inference of user information needs.

Shortcut Gain

Regarding the shortcut gain metric, the content-based *CIS* approach which makes no use of usage information receives the weakest results. The usage-based UB-RL method is able to achieve better shortcut gain in recommendations and *HIS* and *HFreq* hybrid recommendation methods achieve the best results in this regard (significant at $p<0.001$). The weaker performance of *HCM* in comparison to *UB-RL* is again due to the inappropriate page selection method in *HCM*, although it still manages to beat *CIS*, because of having a usage-based component. An interesting point is the ability of HIS and HFreq to achieve an increase of almost 100% in comparison to the usage-based approach. Of course, it should be mentioned that beside the higher accuracy and diversity of recommendations generated by these methods, the greater number of recommendation (*PS*) is also an effective factor in this regard.

Recommendation Quality

This metric shows the rank of correct recommendations in the recommendation lists. It can be seen that the *UB-RL* receives the best results in this regard, while our hybrid approaches are second bests and the content based approach is the weakest. The difference between the usage-based and the hybrid approaches is marginal in almost every case. One important issue is the logical dependency between the *RQ* and the *PS* metrics. Naturally, a recommender that makes fewer recommendations is more likely to achieve lower *RQ* values, e.g. a recommender that does not make more than 2 recommendations will definitely have $RQ \leq 2$. In fact, it is more appropriate to consider *RQ* in respect to the *PS* metric, e.g. the ratio *RQ/PS*. Considering this, we can see that the *HIS* method has better performance between all recommendation methods used in the experiments (significant at p<0.001 compared to all the baseline methods).

CONCLUSION AND FUTURE WORKS

In this chapter we presented novel web page recommendation methods based on reinforcement learning. First a usage-based method for web recommendation was proposed, which was based the reinforcement learning paradigm. This system learns to make recommendations from web usage data as the actions it performs in each situation rather than discovering explicit patterns from the data. We modeled web page recommendation as a Q-Learning problem and trained the system with common web usage logs. System performance was evaluated under different settings and in comparison with other methods. Our experiments showed promising results achieved by exploiting reinforcement learning in web recommendation based on web usage logs.

Afterwards we described a method to enhance our solution based on reinforcement learning, devised for web recommendations from web usage data. We showed the restrictions that a usage-based system inherently suffers from (e.g. low coverage on items, inability to generalize, etc.) and demonstrated how combining conceptual information regarding the web pages can improve the system. Our evaluation results show the flexibility of the proposed RL paradigm to incorporate different sources of information and to improve overall the quality of recommendations.

There are other alternatives that can potentially improve the system and constitute our future work. In the case of the reward function used, various implicit feedbacks from the user rather than just the fact that the user had visited the page can be used, such as those proposed in (Zhang & Seo, 2001). Another option is using a more complicated reward function rather than the linear combination of factors; a learning structure such as neural networks is an alternative. The hybrid method can also be extended in various ways. One is to find more sophisticated methods for organizing a website into a concept hierarchy. More accurate methods of assessing implicit feed-back can also be used to derive a more precise reward function. Integration of other sources of domain knowledge e.g. website topology or a domain-ontology into the model can also be another future work for this research. Finally, devising a model to infer higher level goals of user browsing, similar to the work done in categorizing search activities can be another future direction.

REFERENCES

Bose, A., Beemanapalli, K., Srivastava, J., & Sahar, S. (2006). Incorporating concept hierarchies into usage mining based recommendations. In O. Nasraoui, M. Spiliopoulou, J. Srivastava, B. Mobasher, B. M. Masand (Eds.), *Advances in Web Mining and Web Usage Analysis, 8th International Workshop on Knowledge Discovery on the Web, Lecture Notes in Computer Science 4811* (pp. 110-126). Berlin, Heidelberg, Germany: Springer.

Breese, J., Heckerman, S., & Kadie, C. (1998, July). Empirical analysis of predictive algorithms for collaborative filtering. In G. F. Cooper, S. Moral (Eds.), *UAI '98: Proceedings of the Fourteenth Conference on Uncertainty in Artificial Intelligence* (pp. 43-52). University of Wisconsin Business School, Madison, Wisconsin, USA: Morgan Kaufmann.

Burke, R. (2000). Knowledge-based recommender systems. In A. Kent (Ed.), *Encyclopedia of Library and Information Systems, 69*. New York: Marcel Dekker.

Burke, R. (2002). Hybrid recommender systems: survey and experiments. *User Modeling and User-Adapted Interaction, 12(4)*, 331-370.

Chi, E. H., Pirolli, P., & Pitkow, J. (2001).Using information scent to model user information needs and actions on the web. *Proceedings of the ACM SIG-CHI on Human Factors in Computing Systems* (pp.490-497). Seattle, WA, USA: ACM Press.

Cooley, R., Mobasher, B., Srivastava, J. (1999). Data preparation for mining World Wide Web browsing patterns. *Knowledge and Information Systems, 1*(1), 5-32.

Deshpande, M., & Karypis, G. (2004). Item-based top-N recommendation algorithms. *ACM Transactions on Information Systems, 22*(1), 143-177.

Eirinaki, M., Vazirgiannis, M., & Varlamis, I. (2003). SEWeP: using site semantics and a taxonomy to enhance the web personalization process. In L. Getoor, T. E. Senator, P. Domingos, C. Faloutsos (Eds.), *Proceedings of the Ninth ACM SIGKDD International Conference on Knowledge Discovery and Data Mining* (pp. 99-108), Washington, DC, USA: ACM Press.

Eirinaki, M., Lampos, C., Paulakis, S., & Vazirgiannis, M. (2004). Web personalization integrating content semantics and navigational patterns. In A. H. Laender, D. Lee, M. Ronthaler (Eds.), *Proceeding of the Sixth ACM CIKM International Workshop on Web Information and Data Management* (pp.72-79), Washington, DC, USA: ACM Press.

Fu, X., Budzik, J., & Hammond, K. J. (2000). Mining navigation history for recommendation. In *IUI 2000: Proceedings of the 5ᵗʰ International Conference on Intelligent User Interface* (pp. 106-112). New Orleans, LA, USA: ACM Press.

Godoy, D., & Amandi, A. (2005). Modeling user interests by conceptual clustering. *Information Systems, 31*(4-5), 245-267.

Golovin, N., & Rahm, E. (2004). Reinforcement learning architecture for web recommendations. In *Proceeding of the International Conference on Information Technology: Coding and Computing, 1*, 398-403. Las Vegas, Nevada, USA: IEEE Computer Society.

Herlocker, J., Konstan, J., Brochers, A., & Riedel, J. (2000). An Algorithmic Framework for Performing Collaborative Filtering. In *SIGIR '99: Proceedings of the 22nd Annual International ACM SIGIR Conference on Research and Development in Information Retrieval* (pp. 230-237). Berkeley, CA, USA: ACM Press.

Joachims, T., Freitag, D., & Mitchell, T. M. (1997). Web Watcher: A tour guide for the World Wide Web. In *Proceedings of the Fifteenth International Joint Conference on Artificial Intelligence* (pp. 770-777). Nagoya, Japan: Morgan Kaufmann.

Konstan, J., Miller, B., Maltz, D., Herlocker, J., Gordon, L. R., & Riedl. J. (1997). GroupLens: applying collaborative filtering to Usenet news. *Communications of the ACM, 40*(3), 77-87.

Li, J., & Zaiane, O. R. (2004). Combining usage, content and structure data to improve web site recommendation. In K. Bauknecht, M. Bichler, B. Pröll (Eds.), *Proceeding of 5th International Conference E-Commerce and Web Technologies, Lecture Notes in Computer Science 3182* (pp. 305-315). Berlin, Heidelberg, Germany: Springer.

Mahmood, T, & Ricci F. (2007, August). Learning and adaptivity in interactive recommender systems. In M. L. Gini, R. J. Kauffman, D. Sarppo, C. Dellarocas, & F. Dignum (Eds.), *Proceedings of the 9th International Conference on Electronic Commerce: The Wireless World of Electronic Commerce* (pp. 75-84). University of Minnesota, Minneapolis, MN, USA: ACM Press.

Mitchell, T. (1997). *Machine Learning.* New York, NY: McGraw-Hill.

Mobasher, B., Cooley, R., & Srivastava, J. (2000). Automatic personalization based on Web usage mining. *Communications of the ACM, 43*(8), 142-151.

Mobasher, B., Dai, H., Luo, T., Sun, Y., & Zhu, J. (2000). Integrating web usage and content mining for more effective personalization. In K. Bauknecht, S. K. Madria, G. Pernul (Eds.), *Proceeding of First International Conference E-Commerce and Web Technologies, Lecture Notes in Computer Science 1875* (pp. 165–176). Munich, Germany: Springer.

Nakagawa M., & Mobasher, B. (2003). A hybrid web personalization model based on site con-

nectivity. In R. Kohavi, B. Liu, B. Masnad, J. Srivastava, O. R. Zaiane (Eds.), *Web Mining as a Premise to Effective and Intelligent Web Applications, Proceedings of the Fifth International Workshop on Knowledge Discovery on the Web* (pp. 59-70). Washington DC, WA, USA: Quality Color Press.

Pazzani, M. (1999). A framework for collaborative, content-based and demographic filtering. *Artificial Intelligence Review, 13*(5-6), 393–408.

Pazzani, M., & Billsus, D. Content-based recommendation systems. In P. Brusilovsky, A. Kobsa, and W. Nejdl (Eds.), *The Adaptive Web: Methods and Strategies of Web Personalization, Lecture Notes in Computer Science 4321* (pp. 325-341). Berlin, Heidelberg, Germany: Springer-Verlag.

Resnick, P., & Varian, H. R. (1997). Recommender systems. *Communications of the ACM, 40*(3), 56-58.

Shany, G., Heckerman, D., & Barfman, R. (2005). An MDP-based recommender system. *Journal of Machine Learning Research 6*(9), 1265-1295.

Srivastava, J., Cooley, R., Deshpande, M., & Tan, P.N. (2000). Web usage mining: discovery and applications of usage patterns from web data. *SIGKDD Explorations, 1*(2), 12–23.

Srivihok, A., & Sukonmanee, V. (2005). E-commerce intelligent agent: personalization travel support agent using Q-Learning. In Q. Li, & T. P. Liang (Eds.): *Proceedings of the 7th International Conference on Electronic Commerce* (pp. 287-292). Xi'an, China: ACM Press.

Sutton, R. S., & Barto, A. G. (1998) *Reinforcement Learning: An Introduction,* Cambridge, MA, USA: MIT Press.

Taghipour, N., & Kardan, A. (2008, March). A hybrid web recommender system based on Q-Learning. In R. L. Wainwright, & H. Haddad (Eds.), *Proceedings of the 2008 ACM Symposium on Applied Computing* (pp. 1164-1168). Fortaleza, Brazil: ACM Press.

Taghipour, N., & Kardan, A. (2007, September). Enhancing a recommender system based on Q-Learning. In A. Hinneburg (Ed.), *LWA 2007: Lernen - Wissen - Adaption, Workshop Proceedings, Knowledge Discovery, Data Mining and Machine Learning Tack,* (pp. 21-28). Halle, Germany: Martin-Luther-University Publications.

Taghipour, N., Kardan, A., & Shiry Ghidary, S. (2007, October). Usage-based web recommendations: a reinforcement learning approach. In J. A. Konstan, J. Riedl, & B. Smyth (Eds.), *Proceedings of the First ACM Conference on Recommender Systems* (pp. 113-120). Minneapolis, MN, USA: ACM Press.

Wasfi, A. M. (1999). Collecting User Access Patterns for Building User Profiles and Collaborative Filtering. In: *IUI '99: Proceedings of the 4ʰ International Conference on Intelligent User Interfaces* (pp. 57-64).

Zhang, B., & Seo, Y. (2001). Personalized web-document filtering using reinforcement learning. *Applied Artificial Intelligence, 15*(7), 665-685. Los Angels, CA, USA: ACM Press.

Chapter XII
Collaborating Agents for Adaptation to Mobile Users

Angela Carrillo-Ramos
Pontificia Universidad Javeriana, Colombia

Manuele Kirsch Pinheiro
Université Paris 1 Panthéon-Sorbonne, France

Marlène Villanova-Oliver
Grenoble Computer Science Laboratory, France

Jérôme Gensel
Grenoble Computer Science Laboratory, France

Yolande Berbers
Katholieke Universiteit Leuven, Belgium

ABSTRACT

The authors of this chapter present a two-fold approach for adapting content information delivered to a group of mobile users. This approach is based on a filtering process which considers both the user's current context and her/his preferences for this context. The authors propose an object-based context representation, which takes into account the user's physical and collaborative contexts, including elements related to collaboration tasks and group work in which the user is involved. They define the notion of preference for an individual or a group of people that develops a collaborative task and give a typology of preferences before proposing a formalism to represent them. This representation is exploited by a context matching algorithm in order to select only user preferences which can be applied according to the context of use. This chapter also presents the framework PUMAS which adopts a Multi-Agent System approach to support our propositions.

INTRODUCTION

Nowadays, through the Web or wireless networks, *Mobile Devices* (*MD*), such as cellular phones, *PDA*, *etc.*, can be used, to access distant *Information Systems* (*IS*), which allows mobile users to share and to collaborate with communities of users anytime, anywhere. This freedom of keeping connected and keeping the contact with the colleagues in any situations represents an opportunity for collaborating groups. Users are not anymore constrained to work isolated at their offices; they can work and interact with other users at different places and in unpredictable situations. For instance, a user can keep collaborating and use a wiki system to write a document with her/his colleagues even when she/he (or her/his colleagues) is traveling, may prepare a meeting with these colleagues being kilometers far away from the meeting place, share her/his impressions about a photo with her/his friends, *etc.* All these opportunities to collaborate are rendered possible through new mobile technologies.

However, mobile technologies present several physical and technical constraints, such as a limited battery lifetime and display size, for common used *MD*, and intermittent and poor quality connections, for wireless networks. In addition to these constraints, *mobile users* are often confronted to environmental constraints, like noisy and uncomfortable environments. Moreover, *mobile users* typically use these *MD* in brief time intervals, in order to perform activities and to consult small, but relevant, amount of information. All these constraints significantly affect *mobile user*'s expectations regarding the content supplied by *IS*. This content should, for instance, match the capacities of the client device and the quality of the network connection used by the user. If this content corresponds to a video, it should use a format that is accepted by the client device and a quality acceptable for a network transmission. And even if these conditions are satisfied, the video should match the environmental conditions (*e.g.*, no sound if the user is in a noisy environment) and social aspects of the current situation, having, for example, a duration that matches the user's current activity. Indeed, mobile user's interests and needs change according to the user's activities. The supplied content should match these interests in order to satisfy the users and help them in their own activities and when they are working (collaborating) with other users.

Through the example presented above, one can note that *mobile users* have multiple needs regarding content adaptation. More than traditional users, *mobiles users* need an informational content that suits her/his current *context of use*, which provides in particular a description of the (changing) conditions (temporal, spatial, hardware, physical and environmental) under which a user accesses one or several *IS*. In the remainder of this chapter we use "*context*" and "*user's context*" like synonyms of "*context of use*".

In this chapter, we propose to study how a *collaborative and social technology* such as *Multi-Agent System* (*MAS*) can be used for adapting services and information supplied to *mobile users* belonging to a social community of people. Adaptation is performed according to the user's profile (essentially here her/his preferences in terms of activity, content, and presentation) and according to the contexts (environmental but also collaborative) in which she/he uses the system.

We aim at providing *mobile users* who access an *IS* through a *MD* with the most relevant information according to the characteristics of the *context of use*. In a previous work (Carrillo-Ramos *et al.*, 2006), we have defined *PUMAS* (acronym of *Peer Ubiquitous Multi-Agent System*), a framework for retrieving information distributed among several *IS* and/or accessed through different types of *MD*. The architecture of *PUMAS* relies on four *MAS* (a *Connection MAS*, a *Communication MAS*, an *Information MAS* and an *Adaptation MAS*), each one encompassing several ubiquitous software agents which collaborate in order to achieve the different tasks handled by *PUMAS* (*e.g.*, *MD* connection/disconnection, information storage and retrieval, content and presentation adaptation, *etc.*). Beyond the management of accesses to *IS* through *MD*, *PUMAS* is also in charge of performing an adaptation process over information.

We present a new version of *PUMAS* which takes into consideration the notion of community of users (equipped with *MD*) and especially supports the work of a group by describing a collaborative context exploited for adaptation purpose. This notion of collaborative context refers to elements that describe and characterize the work performed by a group of users, such as the activities they are performing together or the objects they are sharing. In order to represent the (personal or collaborative) context of a group of people who communicate and work together in ubiquitous environments, we use the context model we have proposed in Kirsch-Pinheiro *et al.* (2004). This model represents both user's physical context and collaborative context. It takes into consideration the context of a *mobile user*, who is involved, as member of one or more groups, in one or more collaborative processes. The goals of the group as whole, the activities performed by its members as well as the role of these members are also considered by the model. We are especially interested in groups of people who communicate (between them) and access *IS* using *MD*, and whose objective is to perform collaborating activities. In order to represent the user and the group profiles (composed of preferences related to activities, to the expected results and the way they are displayed on *MD*), we use the model proposed by Carrillo-Ramos *et al.* (2007).

This chapter is organized as follows: Section *"Background"* describes how the emergence of ubiquitous computing influences the user's adaptation needs, the opportunities and the constraints the *MD* offers for collaborating mobile users.

Section *"Adaptation to collaborating mobile users with PUMAS"* presents the new *PUMAS* framework. We present the context model and the user preferences model we propose in this framework, as well as its architecture. In Section *"Example"*, we present an example which illustrates our proposal. Finally, we conclude and present future works.

BACKGROUND

Mobile Users and Collaboration

Mobile technologies make it now possible for users to access distant *Information Systems* (*IS*), from various kinds of device, *anytime* and *anywhere*. This is the underlying idea of the *Ubiquitous Computing* defined by the *W3C* (*World Wide Web Consortium*) (Heflin, 2004) as the paradigm of *"Personal Computing"* which is characterized by the use of small wireless devices. *Ubiquitous Computing* has given birth to a new type of users, called *mobile users*, who connect to the *IS* from different locations (*e.g.* from home, from the airport, from the office) or using different devices (*e.g.*, a laptop, a *Personal Digital Assistant—PDA—*, a cellular phone), sometimes without interrupting their login sessions. In parallel, the recent development of Web 2.0 technologies makes it simpler for users to share information and to collaborate with each other. The underlying notions of *social networks* and *communities* are a main concern for Web 2.0 (Ankolekar *et al.*, 2007). Then, not surprisingly, combining mobile technologies together with some of the principles of the Web 2.0 has given rise to a new generation of *IS* which allows *mobile users* to share data and contextualized information (*i.e.*, location-aware annotations or photos exchanged by Flyckr users, *http://flickr.com/*) and to collaborate with other users (through groupware systems, wikis or blogs, for example). However, this new mode of accessing and sharing information is only at its beginning and, still, many problems have to be overcome.

First of all, *mobile users* have to cope with the intrinsic limitations of *MD* (such as battery lifetime, screen size, intermittent network connections, *etc.*) and with the characteristics of their nomadic situation (noisy or uncomfortable environment). All these aspects and their implications (*i.e.* the quantity of information to be delivered, its type, *etc.*) have to be considered when searching for and displaying information (Krüger *et al.*, 2007).

Second, what is expected through collaboration is gains in terms of productivity (in the case of workers, for instance) but also in terms of facility and efficiency in retrieving and accessing some information that match the needs of each member of a collaborative group. Such gains depend on the capability of exploiting the social dimension of large communities of users but also of smaller groups (for instance in some collaborative work). *Folksonomies* (*http://www.vanderwal. net/folksonomy.html*) built in social bookmarking approaches or the *FOAF* initiative (Brickley & Miller, 2007) are examples of this recent trend. An idea, more and more widely accepted, is that by taking into account the characteristics of the group a user is a member of (*i.e.*, considering the group's common goal to be reached, the things that other members like/dislike, what they have bought, *etc.*) helps in better selecting information she/he needs.

In order to provide any member of a community with some appropriate and relevant information when she/he uses a *MD,* some adaptation mechanisms are required. Adaptation, as a general issue, has to be tackled from different perspectives: What has to be adapted (*i.e.* data, service, *etc.*)? To whom / to what is adaptation required? What are the guidelines or strategies for the adaptation? How adaptation can be performed? What are the subjacent technologies?

The Adaptation Issue

In this chapter, we do not intend to address every aspect of adaptation. Rather, we limit our study of adaptation to the case of an *IS* accessed through a *MD*, with some collaborative and social considerations. More particularly, we consider users involved in some collaborative process, such as participating in a given community of users or using a wiki system. We consider the user as a member of a social network, member of a group. When a user is member of a community, a user may share, with their colleagues, activities, goals, interests, *etc.* These common aspects influence the adaptation process, together with other target features. These target features include the user's personal characteristics, preferences, background, culture, history in the system, current location, *etc.*, and/or the characteristics of the access device, of the network, *etc.* These characteristics or criteria are generally (and sometimes in different ways) assembled together to build so-called users' profiles and/or models of context (Conlan *et al.*, 2006; Harvey *et al.*, 2005; Preuveneers *et al.*, 2006). According to Dey (2001), the "*Context is any information that can be used to characterize the situation of an entity. An entity is a person, place, or object that is considered relevant to the interaction between a user and an application, including the user and applications themselves*" (p. 6). Some propositions of model of context, such as Daoud *et al.* (2007) and Preuveneers *et al.* (2001), include the user's personal characteristics and preferences which generally constitute the main components of the *user's profile.* This notion of user profile can also be composed of the user interests, history in the system or information needs in order to adapt information to users.

As a matter of fact, a user's profile or/and a model of context are the foundations of any adaptation process. *Context-aware computing* (Chaari *et al.*, 2007; Dey, 2001; Moran & Dourish, 2001) is a field of research which studies how the user's current context can be exploited for adaptation purpose. Context-awareness is defined as the capacity of the system to perceive and analyze the user's situation and to adapt itself (*i.e.,* its behavior, services, interface, *etc.*) accordingly.

Often, the user's interests and preferences differ according to the context: while some information may be valuable when she/he works at her/his office, it may well be completely useless when she/he travels even for professional reasons. According to Greenberg (2001), the actions and expectations of the user directly depend on the context in which she/he interacts with the *IS*. Thus, in order to improve the adaptation process, we consider both the user's current context (extended by some information related to her/his activities and to the collaboration processes in which she/he is involved) and her/his preferences (in terms services, data, presentation, *etc.*) for this context.

The majority of context models cover concepts related to the user's location and to the characteristics of the *MD* (Bardram *et al.* 2005; Indulska *et al.*, 2003; Preuveneers *et al.*, 2006). However, most of the context models proposed in the literature consider user as an isolated individual and do not consider the activities performed by the user. Other works only use context models for adapting the system components and services, and do not cover the content delivered by the system to mobile users, ignoring often the user's preferences (Geihs *et al.*, 2006; Rouvoy *et al.*, 2006).

Some authors (Brusilovsky, 2000; Kurumatani, 2003; Murray *et al.*, 2000; Yudelson *et al.*, 2005) propose to observe different aspects (such as user's needs, goals, tasks, knowledge or preferences) when designing and modeling Adaptive Hypermedia systems and applications. However, these works do not specify precisely how to adapt information to the characteristics of mobile environments, such as location (which can modify the information needs of users), and *MD* features (which constrain the information display on the access devices of users). Moreover, some works such as Daoud *et al.* (2007) define the *user*

profile in a multidimensional way. These authors expose a two dimensions profile, represented by the *history of the information requests* and the *recurrent information needs* of the user (based on the *user interests*). The work in Birukov *et al.* (2005) proposes a generic model of profiles composed of six dimensions: *i) personal data; ii) user interests; iii)* the *expected quality; iv)* the *delivery preferences; v) security; vi)* the *history* of user interactions. It is important to note that none of these works associate the user's preferences with the context of use. Consequently, user's preferences remain unchanged even when the context of use evolves.

It is important to note that the user is not an isolated individual. She/he interacts with other users through the collaboration processes she/he is involved in. This interaction must be taken into account when considering some contextual information (Grudin, 2001) and integrated in decisions made during the adaptation process. Indeed, the goals and activities of a group usually highly influence the actions of an individual when considered as a member of a group of users involved in a collaborative process. Consequently, information related to this process, such as the concepts of *group, role* and *collaborative activity* must be considered as part of each user's context. We call this set of information the *user's collaborative context.* This notion of the user's collaborative context is based on the concept of *group awareness. Awareness* (Dourish & Bellotti, 1992; Schmidt, 2002) refers to the knowledge a user has about her/his colleagues and their actions inside the group's work. We claim that this knowledge is part of the user's context since it forms the common knowledge on which the users' actions inside the group are based. Taking into consideration this knowledge in the adaptation process allows new *IS* to supply users in a community with a content more adapted to their activities inside this community.

Finally, the collaborative and social dimensions of the group can be exploited by offering users the opportunity to share their profiles and preferences so that they benefit from the experiences of each other.

The Multi-Agent Systems: A 'Social and Collaborative' Technology for Adaptation

The *Multi-Agent System* (*MAS*) approach is defined by El Fallah-Seghrouchni *et al.* (2004) as a credible paradigm to design distributed and collaborative systems based on the agent technology. Ramparany *et al.* (2003) underline the interest of *MAS*, when a *mobile user* accesses and exchanges information through *MD* (also called "*smart devices*"). In this case, agents are useful because they can be used to represent the user's characteristics inside the system, they can help users in achieving their individual or collective activities and they can collaborate in the information exchange and communication between people performing collaborative tasks using *MD* (by collaborative tasks we mean tasks performed conjointly by several collaborating users). In this way, agents make *MD* work like "*collaborative devices*".

A *MAS* is a set of agents which collaborate in order to achieve their activities. The *W3C* Heflin (2004) defines an agent as "*a concrete piece of software or hardware that sends and receives messages*". These messages can be used (by agents which represent and help users to perform their assigned activities) to access an *IS* and to exchange and adapt information by means of applications executing on *MD*.

Rahwan *et al.* (2003) recommend the use of agent technology in *MD* applications because agents that execute on the user's *MD* can inform the system accessed by the user about her/his contextual information. However, in the case of a *mobile user*, the agent must take into account that the ever changing location could make the activity and the information needs of the user evolve. Then, the agent must be proactive, and

needs to reason about the user's goals and the way they can be reached. At the same time, an agent is a social entity because it communicates with other agents in order to achieve its assigned tasks (which can be individual or collective tasks). In a collaborative task, direct communications between agents allow them to accomplish their assigned tasks without lost of autonomy. In conclusion, *MAS* are social systems by essence. In these systems, agents can be organized in communities, having their own goals and rules. Through *MAS*, it is also possible to describe the user's activities and their interactions with other users (and other user's activities). These agents can be trained to analyze or capture the user preferences and collaborate with other agents in order to provide user information according to her/his context and her/his characteristics and preferences.

Some agent-based works such as Albayrak *et al.* (2005), Gandon & Sadeh (2004), Kurumatani (2003) and Sashima *et al.* (2004) take into consideration the notion of *context of use* in order to adapt information for nomadic users. However, these proposals only consider some characteristics of the context of use, ignoring others characteristics. For instance, Kurumatani (2003) does not consider the user location or the characteristics of the *MD*. The *PIA* system (Albayrak *et al.*, 2005) limits the information handling to text format and does not consider user location. Works such as Albayrak *et al.* (2005) and Sashima *et al.* (2004) do not consider the adaptation of the information to the *MD*.

Some works offer explicit mechanisms to personalize the information for the user considering *user preferences,* in the case of *MADSUM* (acronym of *MultiAgent Decision Support via User Modeling*) (Harvey *et al.*, 2005), and their context, in the case of *AmbieAgents* (Lech *et al.*, 2005). However, these proposals do not consider together the *context of use* and the *user preferences* in order to adapt information.

ADAPTATION TO COLLABORATING MOBILE USERS WITH PUMAS

In this section, we present the models, algorithms and architecture of the *PUMAS* framework (acronym of *Peer Ubiquitous Multi-Agent System*) we propose for an adaptation of both the content and the way it is displayed to collaborating mobile users. This framework adopts the *MAS* approach and provides a mobile user with information adapted according to her/his characteristics, preferences and contextual features (*e.g.*, location, *MD* constraints, *etc.* but also aspects of the collaborative context). In this chapter, we focus on: *i)* the context modeling which on the one hand addresses the representation of both the collaborative and the *mobility* aspects of users' contexts, and on the other hand, is used to select the users' preferences which can be applied for a session; *ii)* the user preferences model we have proposed in *PUMAS* and the *contextual matching algorithm* allowing the dynamic construction of context-aware profiles for the users; and *iii)* the *PUMAS* architecture. The next sections present each one of these topics.

Context Modeling for Collaborating Mobile Users

This section presents how the *PUMAS* framework models the mobile user's context and how collaborative aspects are taken into consideration.

The objective of our work is to provide *mobile users* with information which corresponds as much as possible to the current *context of use* (*i.e.*, the context of use corresponding to the current session). When considering mobile users accessing an *IS* through a *MD*, one of the challenges an adaptation process has to cope with is the fact that the notion of context of use refers to a large concept made of aggregated values which are in constant evolution. On the one hand, the *context of use* is a set of both *i)* elements describing the situation in terms of spatio-temporal features,

software and materials (such as location, connection time, current application, characteristics of a device, *etc.*) and, *ii)* goals and intentions of the user during a session of information searching (Schmidt, 2002). On the other hand, context refers to a set of data which allows the characterization of the interaction between the user and the *IS* (Dey, 2001). The *context of use* is composed of several different elements such as the activities achieved by the user, the characteristics of the used access device and the location and/or moment of connection. These elements and their dynamic character should be represented in a model in order to be considered for adaptation purposes. The work we have developed in Kirsch-Pinheiro *et al.* (2004) constitutes a proposal in this direction.

We have proposed in Kirsch-Pinheiro *et al.* (2004) an object-oriented *context* model, based mainly on a set of *UML* diagrams. This model represents both the user's physical *context* (including the concepts of location, device and application) and the user's collaborative context (which includes the concepts of group, role, member, calendar, activity, shared object and process). We claim that collaborative context should be taken into account since users belonging to communities are considered. In this case, information related to the group, such as its goals, its composition, its activities, *etc.*, becomes relevant for the users, and consequently should be included into the user's context. Figure 1 shows all the concepts that constitute this model.

In this model (see Figure 1), the concept of *context* is represented by a class `Context Description` which is a composition of both physical (`Location`, `Device` and `Session`) and collaborative elements (`Group`, `Role`, `Activity`, `Shared Object`, etc.). These elements are represented by classes that are specializations of a common super class, called `Context Element`. Furthermore, these context elements are related to each other, defining associations between the corresponding concepts. Each element of context is not isolated information

Figure 1. A context description is seen as a composition of context elements

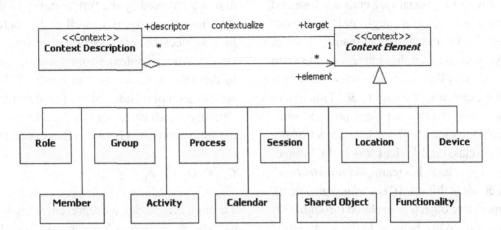

but does belong to a more complex representation of the user's situation. For instance, we consider that a user is the member of a group through the roles she/he plays in this group, and that a user executes an activity, which is composed by a set of system functionalities, and so on. Figure 2 illustrates these associations and a complete description of these associations is given in Kirsch-Pinheiro *et al.* (2004). We would underline here the `Activity` and `Functionality` concepts). From the point of view of the system, an *activity* is a set of functionalities (*i.e.*, the invocation of a service, the execution of an application) which must be executed in order to achieve this activ-

ity. These concepts are not only used to represent current user's actions and intentions, but they also participate to the user's profile definition, allowing the association of user's preferences to particular actions.

The context of a user (member of a group/community) is then represented in this model by an instance of the class `Context Description` which is linked by a composition relation to instances of the class `Context Element` and its subclasses (see Figure 1). Figure 3a illustrates an example of this context model. In this figure, we consider a user ("*Alice*"), who is coordinating ("*coordinator*" role) a team ("*administration*"

Figure 2. Associations forming the context model

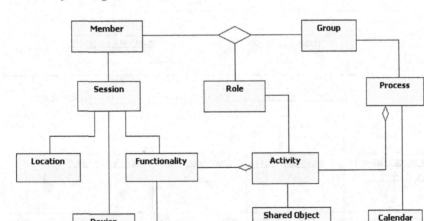

group) which is editing a document (activity) through a wiki functionality. Let us suppose that Alice is accessing the *IS* through her *PDA* in order to consult the document that her team is writing. When Alice requests it, her current context can be represented by the `context description` object represented in the Figure 3b. This object is composed by the context elements representing Alice's location ("*officeD322*" object of the `Location` class) and device ("*PocketPC*" object of the `Device` class), her team ("*administration*" object), her role in this team ("*coordinator*" object), and so on. These objects are related through a set of associations: Alice belongs to the administration group through the role coordinator; this role allows Alice to perform the 'report edition' activ-

ity, which handles the shared object 'report2007' and is composed by the functionality 'wiki', *etc.* All these associations, as well as the context elements objects they connect together, compose the current Alice's context. In other words, according to this model, the context of a user (C_u) can be seen as a set of related objects (O_u) describing the situation in which a user interacts with a *IS*, and the association (A_u) between these objects:

$$C_u = O_u \cup A_u$$

Through this model, we represent not only active users' current context, but also the descriptions of potential contexts set up for the different users. For the active user's current context, instances of

Figure 3. Example of a context description for a given user (Alice)

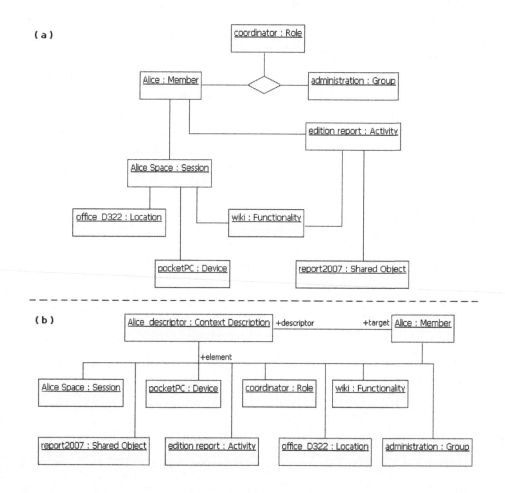

this model are created and dynamically updated by the *IS* during each user's session, according to her/his behavior. Concerning the potential contexts, their instances represent a knowledge that is permanently stored and that represents situations in which the user can potentially find herself/himself during her/his interaction with the system.

The model presented above has been previously used (Kirsch-Pinheiro *et al.*, 2004) in order to describe potential *contexts of use* in which the system knows how to react, *i.e.*, knows how to adapt. The work presented here goes further, by adopting a different approach. Instead of using preliminary definition of potential context, such as in Kirsch-Pinheiro *et al.* (2004), we replace this definition by a description of a set of *user preferences*. These preferences render the wishes of the user according to activities that she/he must or wants to achieve, the contents that the system delivers and the way information has to be displayed. Their level of satisfaction is evaluated according to the current *context of use*: all preferences can, indeed, be unsatisfied if certain conditions are not guaranteed. This is, for example, the case when a user expresses that she/he prefers to get video data although the access device does not support this type of data. The next section introduces the *user preferences* model we propose.

In order to illustrate how the notion of *activity* can be exploited in the user preferences, let us consider a user who wants to organise her/his week-end. In our example, the user may specify in her/his preferences the moment when the user wants the *activity* "*Organise week-end*" to be performed (for instance, every Friday at 6pm to plan her/his week-end occupations). This activity is composed by two functionalities, "*Consult the weather prediction*" and "*Set agenda*". For the first functionality, the user preferences specify that she/he is only interested by a *content* composed of the predictions concerning the city where the user is, for the next two days, and with the temperature data given in Fahrenheit degrees.

The user preferences also indicate that the user prefers images to be displayed rather than as text. According to the results returned by the first *functionality*, it is possible to define that the second *functionality* must be committed or selecting another functionality to be performed. For example, if the weather predictions announce rain (*content* analysis), then these preferences state to execute automatically the *functionality* "*Consult the cinema schedule*".

User Preferences Model for Mobile Users

This section proposes a model for representing user's preferences, taking into account the user's activities and the *context of use* (considering also the collaborative dimension of the context). From an instance of this model, a *contextual matching algorithm* generates a contextual profile applying for the current context of a *mobile user*. This algorithm is presented in a later section.

In addition to the notion of *context of use*, an adaptation process can exploit *user preferences*. We advocate that *IS* designers should provide users with tools that empower them to express their preferences, that is: *i)* to choose and classify information that they want to obtain from the *IS*; *ii)* to specify what they want to achieve using the *IS* (*i.e.*, activities of a user or a group such as consultation, insertion, deletion or modification of data); *iii)* to define the way they want information to be displayed on their *MD*. Through these tools, mobile users could provide the system with some knowledge about their *own preferences* in order to adapt information. Kassab & Lamirel (2006) explain how information about user preferences can be acquired : *i)* provided by the user by means of interfaces dedicated; *ii)* defined like general user profiles; *iii)* deduced from the history of the user, *i.e.*, from her/his previous sessions.

We define a "*user preference*" as a set of descriptions including:

- the activities (including collaborative activities) that a user plans to achieve in the system (*e.g.*, consultation and data management) and the way in which this is achieved (*e.g.*, sequential, concurrent, conditional);
- the type and order of results of these activities (that we call "*content*");
- the way the user wants information to be displayed on her/his *MD* (specification of the expected format – image, video, text – with its characteristics).

It is worth noting that we are particularly interested in tools and mechanisms representing these preferences only. Other elements that may compose a user profile, such as a user expertise level or socio-cultural characteristics (*e.g.*, gender, age, cultural background, *etc.*) are not studied here nor exploited in our approach.

In our approach, the notion of *user preferences* refers to three types of *preferences* (see Figure 4): *activity preferences, result preferences,* and *display preferences*. *Activity preferences* concern the activities that a user wants and can perform in the system in order to achieve an individual or group task. We focus here on *data consultation activities* which are composed of functionalities built upon selection queries and return the queries results to the user. *Result preferences* concern the *content* returned when executing the queries of consultation functionalities: a user can choose which results to be delivered are relevant (among those obtained after the execution of the queries) and determine their order of presentation. *Display preferences* concern the way the user wants the information to be displayed on his *MD*. This includes on the one hand appearance, style of characters, *etc.*, and, on the other hand, the characteristics of the display formats (*i.e.*, characteristics of the video, images, or sound).

For each type of *user preference*, we distinguish between *general preferences* (which are applied for all the sessions; this is the default value) and *specific preferences* (which apply only to the current session). A *session* starts when a user connects to the system and starts executing an activity. We describe below more precisely the three types of *user preference* (*activity, result* and *display*) and the way they are interconnected.

The ***Activity preferences*** define how a user aims at achieving her/his activities in the system:

$$(i)$$

```
Activity_Preference (type, criteria,
characteristics, A)
```

where **type** takes as values "*general*" or "*specific*", and **criteria** is a set of adaptation criteria (*e.g.*, the location and the type of *MD*) considered for the execution of activities in a session. These criteria, expressed accordingly to the terms of the context model, are used to check the compatibility of activities with the current context in order to decide whether they have to be proposed to the user or not. **Characteristics** represent the characteristics of the activity such as events for launching it (*e.g.*, time, location, another user's activity, *etc.*). **A** is the *activity* that the user wants to execute in the system. This *activity* is expressed using a *chain of functionalities* executed in a sequential, concurrent or conditional way. This string is expressed using a grammar defined in *BNF* ("*Backus Naur Form*") notation as follows:

Activity:= functionality [op functionality] |conditional | loop | nil ;
functionality::=fname"(<" input[, input]">,<" output[, output]">")";
fname::=String;
input::=String;
output::=String;
op::= sequence|concurrent ;
sequence ::= «;»;
concurrent ::= «|» ;
conditional ::= "if" <condition> "then" Activity ["else" Activity] "end if" ;

loop ::= "while" <condition> "do" Activity "end while" ;

We designate as F a *functionality* whose name is *fname* and which is defined as a tuple constituted by a list of input parameters ($<i_1, i_2 \ldots i_n>$) and a list of output parameters ($<o_1, o_2 \ldots o_k>$).

Thus, an *activity preference* for F_i, "*general*" and with no adaptation criterion is defined by:

```
Activity_Preference (General, (), (),
F_i)
```

(ii)

Every functionality F_i can be associated with a *result preference* as follows:

```
Activity _ Preference (General, (),(), (F_i,
ResPrefF_i))
```

(iii)

where `ResPrefF_i` is a ***Result preference*** which allows a user to choose and order the pieces of content returned after the execution of a functionality (*i.e.* the results or "*ouput parameters*" above).

We define a ***Result Preference*** as follows:

```
ResPrefF_i= Result_Preference (type,
<(o_1, DisplayP_1),
(o_2, DisplayP_2)...(o_k, DisplayP_k)>)
```

(iv)

where **type** takes as values "*general*" or "*specific*", and the last term is an ordered list of pairs (o_i, `DisplayP_i`) where o_i represents a result of F_i. The order of the list expresses the presentation order of the results. Finally, `DisplayP_i` is the *display preference* applied to this result. A user can choose, among the results delivered by the functionality, those she/he wants to get (*e.g.* only o_3, o_5, o_8). In this case, the *result preference* is defined as follows:

Result_Preference (type,$<(o_3, DisplayP_1),(o_5,nil),$
$(o_8, DisplayP_3)>)$

where *nil* means that the user did not define preferences for displaying this result. Let us consider the example of the activity "*Organise week-end*" we have previously given. This activity is composed by the functionality "*Consulting weather predictions*", for which the user can set the following result preference:

```
Result _ Preference(General,<(city _
map,DisplayP _ image_1),(Temp,DisplayP _
text_1),(Rain?,DisplayP _ text_2)>)
```

This preference represents that the user only wants to obtain the results concerning her/his city presented using a map (*i.e.*, an image having an associated *display preference* `DisplayP _ image_1`), the *temperature in Fahrenheit degrees* and the rain possibility (defined by text *Temp, Rain?*, respectively associated with the *display preferences* `DisplayP _ text_1` and `DisplayP _ text_2`).

The ***Display preferences*** describe the way the user wishes information to be displayed on her/his *MD* (*e.g.*, image format). These *user preferences* are defined as follows:

```
DisplayP_k= Display _ Preference (format,
{characteristics}, substitution)
```

(v)

In these tuples, the ***format*** can take as values: "*video*", "*text*", "*image*" or "*audio*" and ***characteristics*** specify the values taken by the attributes which characterize the format. The term *substitution* corresponds to another *display preference* that the system will try to use instead of that defined if it cannot be satisfied (*substitution* can take as value *nil*). The *display preference* P_1 given below corresponds to a preference for the display of a video, giving its dimensions and the file type (*e.g.*, width, height, type):

```
P_1 = Display _ Preference (video, {200,300,
AVI}, P_2)
```

where P_2 is the *substitution preference* of P_1 and contains the characteristics for the text (*e.g.*, police, size, color, file type):

```
P₂ = Display _ Preference (text, {Arial,
10, bleu, .doc}, nil)
```

It is worth noting that the display preferences can be referenced by the result preferences (see equation (iv)). In this case, they constitute preferences that will be applied to a format independently of a particular content (*e.g.,* in order to privilege text format for a session).

The *UML* Class Diagram in Figure 4 represents the relations between the three types of *user preferences* explained above:

The Adaptation Process

The notion of user's preferences we proposed previously is naturally related to several concepts from the context model. This can be observed through the different associations in Figure 4. These associations express the fact that preferences are related to the characteristics of the context of use of the user's session. In other words, only the preferences which can be applied according to the current *context of use* are selected for composing the user's profile. This selection process is achieved by the *Contextual Matching Algorithm* that we propose and which uses the *user preferences* and the model of *context of use* presented in order to define a *contextual profile* for a given user, during a given session. The *Contextual Matching Algorithm* analyzes each user preference to evaluate if this preference can be satisfied according to the *context of use*. This context allows the system to select only the *preferences* which are compatible with the user's current activities. For example, the contextual profile generated by the algorithm can be composed of display preferences which can be taken into consideration in function of characteristics of the access device or of activity and result preferences which are not in contradiction with user access rights. The preferences retained are components of the contextual user profile. It is important to note that the *contextual user profile* only covers here user preferences.

Figure 4. UML Class Diagram of user preferences and their relations

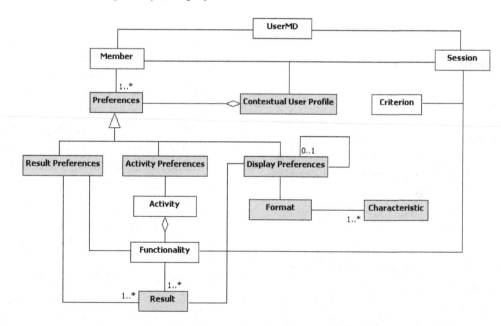

Figure 5. Adaptation process

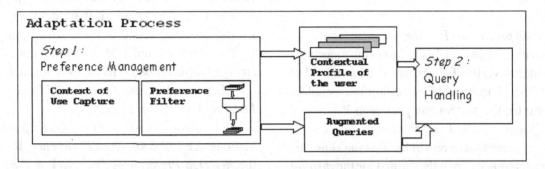

We show how the *Contextual User Profile* (*CUP*) is generated with help of the *Contextual Matching Algorithm*, using a user profile and the current context of use. In order to adapt information to user characteristics and to those of her/his *MD*, we adopt a process in two steps (see Figure 5):

The *Preference Management* step (*step 1*) is achieved by the *Contextual Profile Management System* (*CPMS*). This step consists, on the one hand, in capturing the *context of use* of the session and, on the other hand, in selecting the *user preferences* which can be applied considering the current session (see Figure 5, *Preference Filter*). For example, for the location capture, it is possible to use a *GPS* device or methods such as the *SNMP* ("*Simple Network Management Protocol*") proposed in Nieto-Carvajal *et al.* (2004). The result of *step 1* is a *CUP* (composed of the selected *user preferences*) and one or several *queries* which are "*augmented*". An augmented query corresponds to the initial *query* associated with a consultation functionality involved in the achievement of an *activity*, to which the *CPMS* adds information about the *result* and *display* preferences. The *CUP* and the augmented queries are input parameters for the *Query Handling* step (namely step 2, out of scope of this chapter, but detailed in Carrillo-Ramos *et al.* (2006). The following section details the *Preference Management* step, achieved by the *CPMS*.

Definition of the Contextual User Profile (CUP)

The *CUP* (*u, s, MD*) = {P_1, P_2, P_3...P_k} of a user "*u*", who is connected through a device "*MD*" during a session "*s*" is the set of the *k* preferences which are retained considering the context of use. We can note that the *CUP* is built by means of the analysis of the set P_u = {P_1, P_2,...,P_i, ..., P_n} constituted of *all* preferences defined by the user *u*, which include preferences defined independently of the context of use ("*general*" preferences) and those defined for this particular session ("*specific*" preferences). The analysis of the set P_u by the algorithm described in the following section relies on a preliminary phase which aims at organizing the user preferences. We do not detail here the priority system established for the organization of the preferences, we only present its main principles: *i) activity preferences* are analyzed, then *result preferences* and finally *display preferences*. *ii)* In each type of *user preferences* (*activity, result, display*), *specific preferences* have the higher priority. *iii)* If no *user preference* is defined, the system considers the *history of the user* in the *IS* and, in as last resort, the inherent constraints of the user's *MD* (in this case, the system builds itself the *preferences*).

The Contextual Matching Algorithm (CMA)

For each *preference P_i* of the complete set of *user preferences P*, we apply the following algorithm in order to verify if P_i can be added to the *CUP* (see lines 2 to 4 of the algorithm presented in Figure 6): the system analyzes each P_i (for i ∈ [1, n]) and the set of *substitution preferences* of P_i. It is important to remember that the *substitution preferences* are only defined for the *display preferences*. The analysis of P_i ends if: P_i can be satisfied (see line 5) or, if a *substitution preference* of P_i can be satisfied (see lines 15 to 35) or finally if the *substitution preference* is *nil*. The analysis of the *substitution preference* of P_i starts

if P_i cannot be satisfied (see line 13). When the preference P_i (respectively, the *substitution preference* of P_i) can be satisfied, P_i (respectively, the *substitution preference* of P_i) is added into the *CUP* (see lines 7 and 15). The remainder of the *string of substitution preferences* is not analyzed (*i.e.*, they are added into the *Rejected Preference List*, see lines 11, 14, 24, 32).

In the algorithm, we use the following abbreviations: **AP** is the *Analyzed Preference*, **RPL** is the *Rejected Preferences List*, **NAP** is the *New Analyzed Preference,* and **CUP** is the *Contextual User Profile.*

We use a *RPL* to maintain *user preferences* which are not retained in the *CUP*, for two reasons. First, some of these rejected preferences can still

Figure 6. Contextual Matching Algorithm described in pseudo-code

```
(1) i=1
(2) While (i <= n) do // For each Pi where i ∈ [1,n] :
(3)     AP = Pi     //Preference which is analyzed in this iteration
(4)     if (Pi∉CUP AND Pi∉RPL) then
(5)         if (Pi can be satisfied) then
(6)             Add Pi into CUP
(7)             AP = Substitution preference of Pi
(8)             While (AP <> nil) do
(9)                 NAP = AP;
(10)                AP = Substitution preference of NAP
(11)                Add NAP into the RPL if and only if NAP∉CUP AND NAP∉RPL
(12)             end While
(13)         else
(14)             Add Pi into the RPL if and only if Pi∉CUP AND Pi∉RPL
(15)             AP = Substitution preference of Pi
(16)             While (AP <> nil) do
(17)                 if (AP can be satisfied AND AP∉CUP AND AP∉RPL) then
(18)                     NAP = AP;
(19)                     AP = Substitution preference of NAP
(20)                     Add NAP in CUP if and only if NAP∉CUP AND NAP∉RPL
(21)                     While (AP <> nil) then
(22)                         NAP = AP;
(23)                         AP = Substitution preference of NAP
(24)                         Add NAP in RPL if and only if NAP∉CUP AND NAP∉RPL
(25)                     end While
(26)                 else
(27)                     if (AP∈CUP OR AP∈RPL) then
(28)                         AP = Substitution preference of AP
(29)                     else
(30)                         NAP = AP;
(31)                         AP = Substitution preference of NAP
(32)                         Add NAP in RPL if and only if NAP∉CUP AND NAP∉RPL
(33)                     end if
(34)                 end if
(35)             end While
(36)         end if
(37)     end if
(38)     Increment i. // i = i + 1
(39) End While
```

be useful. For example, let us suppose that a *user preference "a"* is the *substitution preference* of the preferences *"b"* and *"c"*. If *"b"* is satisfied, *"a"* will be added to the *RPL*. In the case where *"c"* cannot be satisfied, *"a"* should be analyzed again in order to determine if it can be satisfied. Secondly, certain *user preferences* of the *RPL* can describe the characteristics of a format of media which must be displayed. For example, let us suppose that *"a"* is the *substitution preference* of *"b"*. *"a"* specifies the characteristics associated with the text and *"b"* specifies the characteristics associated with the video. If the video is supported by the *MD*, the system adds *"a"* (the characteristics of text) to the *RPL* privileging in this way the *user preference* concerning the video. Whenever some information cannot be displayed as a video, the system is able to find again in the *RPL* characteristics preferred by the user for text (*"a"*) and can therefore be applied.

In order to illustrate the *CMA*, we suppose that the set P_u of preferences of a user is the one presented in Figure 7. If P_1 is satisfied, P_5, P_2 and P_4 are added into the *RPL*. Different *CUP* generated by the algorithm are presented in Table 1.

Each *CUP* corresponds to a given session and is generated in function of the *context of use* of the session. For example, let us suppose that one of the *MD* of the user only supports text. In this case, all *user preferences* associated to the display of images will not be satisfied for the sessions during which the user is connected through this *MD*. These preferences will not appear in the *CUP* generated for these sessions; they belong to the *RPL*. Table 1 presents for instance that the profile CUP_1 is composed of the *user preferences* P_1, P_3 and P_6 (P_2, P_4 and P_5 are in the *RPL*) and that the CUP_{19} is *"empty"* (*i.e.*, it does not contain any *user preference*).

If there are no *strings of substitution preferences* (no *user preference* has *substitution prefer-*

Figure 7. User preferences and their substitution preferences

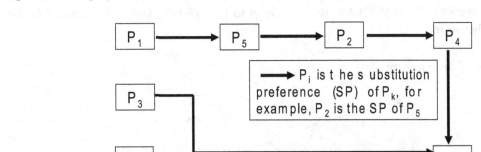

Table 1. Profiles generated by the CMA

	CUP1	CUP2	CUP3	CUP4	CUP5	CUP6	CUP7	CUP8	CUP9	CUP10	CUP11	CUP12	CUP13	CUP14	CUP15	CUP16	CUP17	CUP18	CUP19	CUP20
P 1	X	X	X	X																
P 2								X	X	X	X									
P 3	X		X		X	X			X	X			X	X			X	X		
P 4													X		X	X				
P 5						X	X													
P 6	X	X			X		X		X		X		X		X		X			X

ences) in a set of "*p*" *user preferences*, then the number of profiles (*P*) will be calculated in the following way:

$$P = f(p) = \sum_{i=1}^{p} C_p^i = \sum_{i=1}^{p} \binom{p}{i} = \sum_{i=1}^{p} \frac{p!}{(p-i)!i!}$$

(vi)

In order to calculate the number of *CUP* that the *CMA* generates considering the set of *user preferences* which contains the strings of *substitution preferences*, we calculate *P* using the equation (vi). The number of *CUP* is obtained by subtracting from *P* the number of combinations which contain a *user preference* with one or several of its *substitution preferences*. For the example shown in Figure 7, the *CMA* generates 20 different *CUP* (a *CUP* by session considering the contextual characteristics of this session). For a set of 6 preferences without strings of *substitution preferences*, we have 63 different *CUP* (6 combinations of 1 preference, 15 of 2, 20 of 3, 15 of 4, 6 of 5 and 1 of 6), but 43 of these combinations contain a preference with one or several of its *substitution preferences*. So, only 20 *CUP* are generated by the algorithm.

The Framework PUMAS

This section introduces briefly a framework called *PUMAS* which, additionally to the management of accesses to *IS* performed through *MD*, is also in charge of performing an adaptation of information according to both user profiles (which refers to their needs, preferences, histories in the system, current location, *etc.*) and the technical capabilities of her/his *MD*. A detailed description of *PUMAS* can be found in Carrillo-Ramos *et al.* (2006).

The architecture of *PUMAS* is composed of four *MAS* (see in Figure 8 the logical architecture). Each *MAS* encompasses several *ubiquitous software agents* which collaborate to achieve different tasks handled by *PUMAS* (*e.g.*, *MD* connection/disconnection, communications between agents, information exchange, storage and retrieval, etc.). *i*) The *Connection MAS* provides mechanisms for facilitating the connection to the system from different types of *MD*. *ii*) The *Communication MAS* ensures a transparent communication between *MD* and the system. *iii*) The *Information MAS* receives users' queries, redirects them to the "*right*" *IS* (*e.g.*, the nearest *IS*, the

Figure 8. The PUMAS Architecture

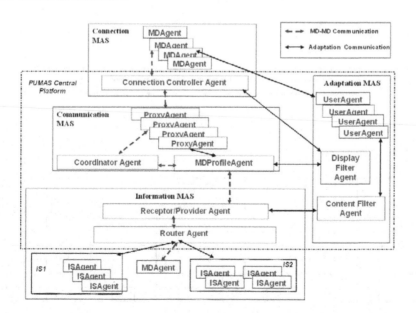

more consulted one) and returns results to the *Communication MAS. iv)* The *Adaptation MAS* communicates with agents of the three other *MAS* in order to transfer to them information adapted according to user, connection and communication features, *MD* characteristics, *etc.* This information is adapted executing a two filters process: a *Content Filter* to adapt information according to user profile in the system (*e.g.,* last connections, queries, preferences) and a *Display Filter* to adapt and display information according to the technical constraints of the user's *MD.* The services and tasks of its agents essentially consist in managing specific *XML* files which contain information for performing these filters.

Using User Preferences and Context of Use Notions in PUMAS

We present how we make *PUMAS* evolve to exploit the models and algorithm we have previously presented. Our objective is to offer a new version of the framework able to support efficiently the work of a group, and of each member of this group, by describing a collaborative context exploited for adaptation purpose.

Since a user can access one or several *IS* using her/his *MD* and can achieve different activities at the time of her/his connections to the *IS,* the *Contextual Profile Management System* (*CPMS*) uses a set of five *XML* files, stored in the *MD,* in order to keep contextual information (represented in the context model), define the *CUP* and adapt the information. First, the **context.XML** file contains contextual elements related to the user's collaborative context, mainly the *activities* (and their associated functionalities) of a session. In this file, each *functionality* is represented by means of a list of tuples (*functionality, parameters, results, status*). The *status* of a *functionality* can take as values "*started*", "*finished*", "*suspended*", *etc.* Second, the **session.XML** file stores information about the characteristics of the session: who is the connected user, when has begun the session

and of which type is the connected *MD.* Third, the **location.XML** file manages the physical and logical location of the user: city, country, street, IP address, orientation, speed. Fourth, the **profile.XML** file contains *user preferences.* Finally, the **device.XML** file holds the characteristics of the *MD* (such as the screen size, the memory or battery capacity) used in order to connect to the system. These five files describe the corresponding concepts of the context model (session, location device…) using extensions of the *CC/PP* model proposed by Indulska *et al.* (2003).

The adaptation capabilities rely on a two step filter process. First, the *Content Filter* allows the selection of relevant information according to the *CUP* defined in the system. Second, the *Display Filter* applies to the results of the first filter and considers the characteristics and technical constraints of the user's *MD.* These filters are applied by the agents of *PUMAS* as explained below (see Figure 9).

The *MDAgent* sends the *profile.XML,* the *context.XML* and the *session.XML* files to the *UserAgent* (*UA*). (**2**) If a *session.XML* file does not already exist, the *UA* asks for this information from the *Connection Controller Agent* (which controls all the *MD* connections). (**3**) The *UA* and the *Content Filter Agent* (*CFA*) check if conflicts between the *activity* and *results preferences* are present. The *CFA* checks each *activity* and *result preferences* against the user access rights in the system. (**4**) The *UA* and the *Display Filter Agent* (*DFA*) check if there are conflicts between the *display preferences.* The *DFA* checks each *display preference* against both the characteristics of the *MD* (defined in the *device.XML* file) and its knowledge about previous problems presented whenever this kind of *MD* has been connected to the system. (**5**) The *UA,* the *CFA* and the *DFA* check if conflicts exist between each *activity* (respectively each *result preference*) and each *display preferences.* If problems related to the format supported by the *MD* are identified, the *UA* and the *DFA* change the *result preferences* (the field related to the preferred *format*). The information about the supported formats is extracted from the *device.XML* file and the *knowledge base* of the *DFA*. When the field "*format*" of the *result preference* is changed from one supported by the *MD*, the *DFA* searches whether there is any *user preference* related to the new format. If one exists at least, the *DFA* verifies if this (or these) preference(s) can be applied according to the current context (information represented in the *context.XML* file). (**6**) The *UA* selects the *activity* and *results preferences* and sends them to the *CFA*. Then, the *UA* selects the *display preferences* and sends them to the *DFA*. Finally, the *UA* generates the *CUP* (executing the *CMA*) with the *user preferences* which do not generate conflicts and sends this profile to the *CFA*. The latter stores a registry of the *CUP* in the system. (**7**) When the *Receptor/Provider Agent* (*R/PA*) receives a user request, it asks from the *CFA* for the *CUP* and adds this information into the request. The *R/PA* adds to the query information about the *user preferences* and sends this *augmented query* (i.e. "*original query*" + "*context of use* + *user preferences*") to the *Router Agent* which is in charge of analyzing the query and

redirecting it to the information sources able of answering it. In conclusion, the functionalities of the *Contextual Profile Management System* are performed in *PUMAS* by the agents of the *Adaptation MAS*.

EXAMPLE

The Scenario

In this section we present an example which illustrates our proposal. Let us consider the following scenario: a group of doctors located in different places organizes a meeting in order to study the case of a patient. They want to get the results of the medical tests of this patient, especially the ultrasound scans in order to decide if a surgery is required. This meeting starts at 2:00 p.m., using chat. We consider here the activity "*Attending a medical meeting*" which is composed of the following functionalities:

- Connecting to the meeting
- Verifying the presence of every summoned participant

Figure 9. Information filtering process by means of the user preferences analysis

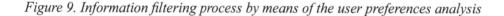

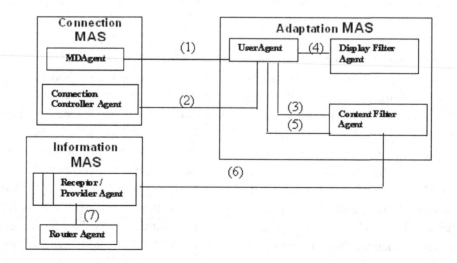

- Checking the medical tests
- Giving an opinion
- Making a decision
- Disconnecting from the meeting

This activity can be represented in the following way:

$PActC_1$= Activity_Preference(General, (), ("2:00 p.m", "by chat"), $F_1;F_2;F_3;F_4;F_5;F_6$)

Where:

F_1= *Connecting_to_the_meeting(<login,password>, <session>)*
F_2= *Verifying_summoned_participant(<list of participants, date, hour>, <list of absent participant>)*
F_3= *Checking_medical_test(<patient_name, medical_test_type, date>, <medical_tests>)*
F_4= *Giving_an_opinion(<login, password, opinion, arguments>, <doctor_opinion>)*
F_5= *Making_a_decision(<doctor_opinions>, <decisions>)*
F_6= *Disconnecting_from_the_meeting (<>, <>)*

Preferences Related to the Non Collaborative Dimension of the Context and their Processing

Each doctor in the group can express (and share with the other doctors in the group) her/his preferences concerning, for instance, the way she/he wants to get the medical tests of the patient. For example, the *activity* and *result preferences* of a doctor named "Smith" are defined as follows:

$PResI_1$= Doctor Smith wants to obtain the images and the video of the ultrasound scan.

```
PResI₁= Result _ Preference (Specific, <(re-
sult _ us, DisplayP _ image), (result _ us,
DisplayP _ video)>)
```

$PActI_2$ = Doctor Smith wants to obtain the text of the analysis prepared by the radiologist who did this ultrasound scan.

```
F₁₁= Consult _ analysis _ ultrasound _
scan(<patient _ name>, <ultrasound _ scan,
date>, <analysis _ radiologist>)
PActI₂= Activity _ Preference (Specific,
(), (), F₁₁)
```

$PResI_3$ = Doctor Smith wants to obtain the analysis of the previous ultrasound scans in a graphical format (images or video).

```
PResI₃= Result _ Preference (Specific, <(re-
sult _ us, DisplayP _ image), (result _ us,
DisplayP _ video)>)
```

$PActI_4$ = Each time that Doctor Smith asks for the results of a ultrasound scan, he also wants to consult the last registry (in the clinical history of the patient) of the doctor who prescribed this ultrasound scan.

```
F₁₂= Consult _ ultrasound _ scan (<patient _
name, date>, <result _ us>)
F₁₃= Consult _ last _ registry (<patient _
name, doctor, ultrasound _ scan>, <last _
registry>)
PActI₄= Activity _ Preference (General,
(), (), F₁₂;F₁₃)
```

$PActI_5$ = Each time that Doctor Smith asks for the results of an ultrasound scan, he also wants to consult the previous ultrasound scans of the same type (*e.g.*, if the ultrasound scan is a kidney one, the results of the previous kidney ultrasound scans must be presented).

```
F₁₄= Consult _ previous _ us (<patient _
name, type>, <result _ us>)
PActI₄= Activity _ Preference (General,
(), (), F₁₁;F₁₄)
```

We suppose that the display preferences of Doctor Smith are: {DisplayP_image, DisplayP_text1, DisplayP_text2, DisplayP_text3} where:

- *DisplayP_image* expresses the characteristics of the images that Doctor Smith wants to get for the current session.
- *DisplayP_text1* expresses that, if for the current session his *MD* does not support images, then information have to be displayed as text (*DisplayP_text1* is a substitution preference of *DisplayP_image* and shows the characteristics of the text to be displayed).
- *DisplayP_text2* expresses the preferences of Doctor Smith for the display of the text, for the current session. Finally,
- *DisplayP_text3* expresses his preferences for the display of the text, for all his sessions.

The system analyzes each preference from *DisplayP_image* to *DisplayP_text3*. *DisplayP_image*, *DisplayP_text1* and *DisplayP_text2* have an upper priority than *DisplayP_text3* because the formers are specific preferences and the latter is a general preference. If the images specified in *DisplayP_image* are supported by the *MD*, this preference is added to the contextual profile and *DisplayP_text1* is added to the *Rejected Preferences List*. If they are not, *DisplayP_image* is added to the *Rejected Preferences List* and *DisplayP_text1* is included in the contextual profile. Moreover for the current session, the text will be displayed according to the characteristics defined in *DisplayP_text2*.

Since the *activity* and the *result preferences* of the user are also constraints by the user access rights, the system must verify if the user can access the information or not. These access rights define if the *activity* and *results preferences* can be applied in a specific session. They notably express : *i)* the fact that a user can or cannot access the required information; for example, only the enterprise manager can consult the salaries of all the employees, while an employee can only consult her/his salary; *ii)* some constraints on the display format of information; for example, a specialist doctor can obtain ultrasound scan in video but a physician can only obtain the text of the analysis

done by the radiologist; *iii)* some constraints on the content; for instance, a physician can only obtain some excerpts of the clinical history of a patient while a specialist doctor can get the whole set of information. In order to define these access rights, we have defined some rules which impose some restrictions for different types of users with regard to the content and format of the required information. It is important to note that the fulfillment of these rules can change the content and display of the results obtained from the *IS* queried by users. In this example, let us suppose that the hospital has established certain rules concerning the consultation of the medical tests for the different types of doctors. A medical test is defined by means of a tuple *Medical_Test* (type, prescribed_by) where type can take as values "ultrasound scan", "blood test", and prescribed_by is the doctor who has prescribed it. A doctor is represented by the tuple *Doctor* (name, type) where name corresponds to the doctor and the type takes as value "physician" or "specialist". The rules for the doctors who access to the *IS* are expressed in the following way:

If (Medical_Test.prescribed_by.name == Doctor. name) OR (Doctor.type == "specialist") OR (Medical_Test.prescribed_by.type == Doctor. type) then access_granted

If (Medical_Test.prescribed_by.type == "specialist" AND Doctor.type == "physician") then access_denied

The way the rules and the facts are expressed here relies on the definitions given in Carrillo-Ramos *et al.* (2006).

Concerning the doctor Smith's *MD*, we suppose two facts: first, his *PDA* (*MD₁*) supports video and images, but can not display them at the same time. Second, his cellular phone (*MD₂*) only supports text. These constraints are defined as a *CC/PP* (*Composite Capabilities/Preference Profiles*) profile. This profile is stored in the user's *MD*.

In order to define the doctor Smith's contextual profile, the system must analyze his preferences and, notably, compare them with the formats supported by his *MD*. For a session "s_1", the contextual profile CP_1 ("*doctor Smith*", s_1, MD_1) is composed of {$PResI_1$, $PActI_2$, $PResI_3$, $PActI_4$ and $PActI_5$} after the analysis done by the system. First, $PResI_1$ and $PActI_2$ are satisfied because MD_1 supports the video, the text and the images. Second, $PResI_3$ can also be satisfied when we suppose, for example, that the previous ultrasound scans have been prescribed by doctor Smith or by other physicians (following the hospital rules). In a similar way, $PActI_4$ can be also satisfied considering that the doctor who has prescribed this ultrasound scan and who has done the last registry is a physician. Finally, $PActI_5$ is also satisfied if the previous ultrasound scans of the same type have been prescribed by him or by other physicians. Moreover, if the previous ultrasound scans have been prescribed by specialist doctors, then $PResI_3$ is not included into the contextual user profile due to the rules established in the hospital. The same consideration is taken into account for $PActI_4$ and $PAct_5$.

Actually, we suppose that the result preferences, $PResI_6$ and $PResI_7$ are respectively associated with F_{13} in $PActI_4$ and F_{14} in $PActI_5$. We define:

```
PResI₆= Result _ Preference (Specific, < (
last _ registry, nil ) >)
```

```
PResI₇= Result _ Preference (Specific, <
(result _ us, nil ) >)
```

PResI$_6$ and *PResI$_7$* are not associated with *display preferences* (the user did not precise display preferences in *PResI$_6$* and *PResI$_7$*). The system changes the value of "< (result_us, nil)>)" by "<(result_us, DisplayP_image),(result_us, DisplayP_video)>)" in *PResI$_7$*:

```
PResI₇=Result _ Preference (Specific, <(re-
sult _ us,  DisplayP _ image),(result _ us,
DisplayP _ video)>)
```

because doctor Smith expresses in $PResI_1$ that all information associated with an ultrasound scan have to be displayed as images or video. Then, the system changes the value of "nil" in $PResI_6$ by DisplayP_text2 because the last registry of the clinical history of the patient retrieved is in text format:

```
PResI₆=Result _ Preference (Specific, <(re-
sult _ us, DisplayP _ text2)>)
```

DisplayP_text2 is used because *DisplayP_text2* expresses the preferences of doctor Smith for the display of the text, for the current session. Please note that *DisplayP_text1*, substitution preference of *DisplayP_image*, is not taken into account since doctor's *MD* supports images.

Preferences Related to the Collaborative Dimension of the Context and their Processing

The preferences presented in the section above have been defined for an individual user (Doctor Smith) which is free to propose for sharing these preferences with his colleagues. In this case, his colleagues import these preferences, creating new individual preferences based on these original ones and that can be modified by their new owners. This import acts as an important knowledge sharing mechanism in a team, in which good preferences, approved by a team member, can be imported by other team members. Moreover, these preferences, even if they are individual, have been defined considering the collaborative process in which the activity "*Attending a medical meeting*" takes place. By personalizing the results of the functionalities related to this activity, the *PUMAS* framework proposes to improve individual user actions into a collaborative context, which directly contributes with the group as a whole.

In addition to the individual preferences, the models proposed by *PUMAS* framework allow also the definition of collaborative preferences, which are defined for the group, influencing the collaborative process itself. In this medical meeting example, since the list of absent participants in F_2 can be not empty, it is necessary to define an alternative *activity preference*: "*Summoning other participants*", composed by the following functionalities:

F_7= *Verifying_type_of_absents (<list_of_absent_participants>, <type_of_absent>)*
F_8= *Generating_list_of_participants_by_type (<type>, <list_of_participants>*
F_9= *Selecting_participants_by_type(<type, (conditions)>, < list_of_participants>)*
F_{10}= *Calling_new_participants(<list_of_participants>, <>)*

This activity is expressed in the following way:

```
PActC₂= Activity _ Preference (General,
(), ("2:30 p.m"), "by chat"), F₇; i=0;while
(i<size (list _ of _ type) do {F₈;F₉})
```

We can observe here some conditions for selecting the participants of a certain type (see the parameter "conditions" in $\mathbf{F_9}$). For example, the organizer of the meeting can establish some conditions which take into account the context of use in order to select other participant of the same type of that absent of the meeting: participant located in the same city, participant with an access device supporting the exchanged information, *etc*. This kind of condition is used in this example to assure the presence of different specialist necessary for obtaining a large view of the patience situation. By doing this, this activity and the corresponding preferences influence the collaborative process as a whole according to the current context.

CONCLUSION AND FUTURE WORK

In this chapter, we have presented how the emergence of ubiquitous computing offers opportunities for collaborating mobile users and influences their adaptation needs. In order to take into account these needs, we have presented *PUMAS*, an agent-based framework which provides mobile users with information adapted according to their profile (composed of user's preferences) and the characteristics of the context of use. We present the context model and the user preferences model proposed in this framework, as well as its architecture. The context model we propose here integrates not only the concepts of user's location and *MD*, but also the notion of collaborative context, which includes the concepts of activity and functionality used by the user preferences model. The formalism of user preferences allows representing in the system the activities the user wants to execute, the order and the specific results expected from these activities and the way in which these results must be displayed on the user's access device. We have presented an example which illustrates how our proposal can apply. In this example, we have defined personal and group preferences in order to perform a group activity.

The context and user preference models, as well as the *PUMAS* architecture have been implemented using Java technology. On the one hand, the context model has been represented using the object-based knowledge representation system AROM (Page *et al.*, 2001), which supplies a Java API allowing the manipulation of the model and its instances kept in memory in a specific knowledge base. On the other hand, the user preferences are modeled using ontologies expressed in OWL (Ontology Web Language). We have translated the concepts of each ontology in facts described in *JESS* (*http://herzberg.ca.sandia.gov/*) in order to exploit its inference engine and the coupling facilities with *JADE* (Java Agent DEvelopment Framework, *http://jade.tilab.com/*) it offers. The different *MAS* have been implemented in *JADE* and tested by means of a chat application. In order to integrate and manipulate OWL ontologies in JADE, we have used AgentOWL (*http://agentowl. sourceforge.net/*). These ontologies represent the agents' knowledge in *PUMAS*. The adaptation *MAS* of *PUMAS* is responsible of managing the different models in order to adapt information. The mobile device characteristics are represented as a *CC/PP* (*Composite Capability/Preference Profiles, http://www.w3.org/TR/2007/WD-CCPP-struct-vocab2-20070430/*) profile. We look further for testing these implementations with real mobile users for a usability tests in real world situations.

The *PUMAS* architecture and the associated models represent an alternative allowing user modeling considering physical and collaborative context, in which users activities are directly related to collaborative and social activities. By allowing such modeling, the *PUMAS* architecture allows users to represent their preferences considering the collaborative environment in which they interact with other users, and supplies an adaptation process aware of these preferences.

REFERENCES

Albayrak, S., Wollny, S., Varone, N., Lommatzsch, A., & Milosevic D. (2005). Agent Technology for Personalized Information Filtering: the PIA-System. In L.M. Liebrock (Ed.), *20th Annual ACM Symposium on Applied Computing*: *Vol. 1. Agents, interactions, mobility, and systems* (pp. 54-59). ACM Press.

Ankolekar, A., Krötzsch, M., Tran, T., & Vrandecic, D. (2007). The two cultures: Mashing up Web 2.0 and the Semantic Web. In C. Williamson & M.E. Zurko (GC), *International World Wide Web Conference* (*WWW 2007*): *Vol. 1. Semantic web and web 2.0* (pp. 825-834). ACM Press.

Bardram, J. E. (2005). The Java Context Awareness Framework (JCAF) – a service infrastructure and programming framework for context-aware applications. In H.W. Gellersen, R. Want & A. Schmidt (Ed.), *Third International Conference in Pervasive Computing* (*Pervasive'2005*): *Vol.*

3468. Lecture Notes in Computer Science (pp. 98-115). Springer-Verlag.

Birukov, A., Blanzieri E., & Giorgini, P. (2005). Implicit: An Agent-Based Recommendation System for Web Search. In M. Pechoucek, D. Steiner & S. Thompson (PC), *4th International Conference on Autonomous Agent and MAS* (*AAMAS 2005*): *Vol. 1. Information agents, brokering and matchmaking* (pp. 618-624). ACM Press.

Brickley, D., & Miller, L. (2007). FOAF Vocabulary Specification 0.91, 2007. Retrieved January 2008, from http://xmlns.com/foaf/spec/

Brusilovsky, P. (2000). Adaptive Hypermedia: From Intelligent Tutoring Systems to Web Based Education. In G. Gauthier, C. Frasson, K. VanLehn (Ed.), *5th International Conference on Intelligent Tutoring Systems* (*ITS 2000*): *Vol. 1839. Lecture Notes in Computer Science* (pp. 1-7). Springer-Verlag.

Carrillo-Ramos, A., Villanova-Oliver, M., Gensel, J., & Martin, H. (2006). Knowledge Management for Adapted Information Retrieval in Ubiquitous Environments. In J. Filipe, J. Cordeiro, V. Pedrosa (Ed.), *2nd International Conference on Web Information Systems and Technologies* (*WebIST 2006*): *Vol. 1. Lecture Notes in Business Information Processing* (pp. 84-96). Springer-Verlag.

Carrillo-Ramos, A., Villanova-Oliver, M., Gensel, J., & Martin, H. (2007). Contextual User Profile for Adapting Information in Nomadic Environments. In M. Weske, M.-S. Hacid, C. Godart (Ed.), *Personalized Access to Web Information* (*PAWI 2007*), *Workshop of the 8th International Web Information Systems Engineering* (*WISE 2007*): *Vol. 4832. Lecture Notes In Computer Science* (pp. 337-349). Springer-Verlag.

Chaari, T., Dejene, E., Laforest, F., & Scuturici, V.-M. (2007). A comprehensive approach to model and use context for adapting applications in pervasive environments. *Journal of Systems and Software, 80*(12), 1973-1992.

Conlan, O., O'Keeffe, I., & Tallon, S. (2006). Combining adaptive hypermedia techniques and ontology reasoning to produce dynamic personalized news services. In V. P. Wade, H. Ashman & B. Smyth (Ed.), *4th International Conference on Adaptive Hypermedia and Adaptive Web-Based Systems (AH'2006): Vol. 4018. Lecture Notes In Computer Science* (pp. 81-90). Springer-Verlag.

Daoud, M., Tamine, L., Boughanem, M., & Chabaro, B. (2007). Learning Implicit User Interests Using Ontology and Search History for Personalization. In M. Weske, M.-S. Hacid & C. Godart (Ed.), *Personalized Access to Web Information (PAWI 2007), Workshop of the 8th International Web Information Systems Engineering (WISE 2007): Vol. 4832. Lecture Notes In Computer Science* (pp. 325-336). Springer-Verlag

Dey, A. (2001). Understanding and using context. *International ACM Journal of Personal and Ubiquitous Computing, 5(1)*, 4-7.

Dourish, P., & Bellotti, V. (1992). Awareness and Coordination in Shared Workspaces. In M. Mantel & R. Baecker (GC), *ACM Conference on Computer-Supported Cooperative Work (CSCW 92), 1,* 107-114. ACM Press.

El Fallah-Seghrouchni, A., Suna, A. (2004). CLAIM: A Computational Language for Autonomous, Intelligent and Mobile Agent. In M. Dastani, J. Dix, A. El Fallah-Seghrouchni (Ed.), *PROMAS 2003: Vol. 3067. Lecture Notes In Artificial Intelligence* (pp. 90–110). Springer-Verlag.

Gandon, F., & Sadeh, N. (2004). Semantic Web Technologies to Reconcile Privacy and Contexte Awareness. *Journal of Web Semantics, 1(3)*, 241-260

Geihs, K., Khan, M., Reichle, R., Solberg, A., & Hallsteinsen, S. (2006). Modeling of component-based self-adapting context-aware applications for mobile devices. In S. Boston (Ed.), *Software Engineering Techniques: Design for Quality: Vol.*

227. *IFIP International Federation for Information Processing* (pp. 85-96). Springer.

Grudin, J. (2001). Desituating action: digital representation of context. *Journal of Human-Computing Interaction, 16(2/4)*, 269-286.

Greenberg, S. (2001). Context as a dynamic construct. *Journal of Human Computer Interaction, 16(2/4)*, 257-268.

Harvey, T., Decker K., Carberry, S. (2005). Multi-Agent Decision Support Via User Modeling. In M. Pechoucek, D. Steiner & S. Thompson (PC), *4th International Conference on Autonomous Agent and MAS (AAMAS 2005): Vol. 1. Cooperation I* (pp. 222-229). ACM Press.

Heflin, J. (2004). OWL Web Ontology Language Use Cases and Requirements. W3C Recommendations. Retrieved January 2008, from http://www.w3.org/TR/webont-req/

Indulska, J., Robinson, R., Rakotonirainy, A., & Henricksen, K. (2003). Experiences in Using CC/PP in Context-Aware Systems. In M.-S. Chen, P.K. Chrysance, M. Sloman & A. Zaslavsky (Ed.), *4th International Conference on Mobile Data Management (MDM 2003): Vol. 2574. Lecture Notes in Computer Science* (pp. 247-261). Springer-Verlag.

Kassab, R. & Lamirel, J.C. (2006). An innovative approach to intelligent information filtering. In H. Haddad (Ed.), *ACM Symposium on Applied Computing 2006 (SAC 2006): Vol. 1. Information access and retrieval* (pp. 1089-1093). ACM Press.

Kirsch-Pinheiro, M., Gensel, J., & Martin, H. (2004). Representing Context for an Adaptive Awareness Mechanism. In G.-J. de Vreede, L. A. Guerrero & G. Marín Raventós (Ed.), *10th International Workshop on Groupware (CRIWG 2004): Vol. 3198. Lecture Notes In Computer Science* (pp. 339-348). Springer-Verlag.

Krüger, A., Baus, J., Heckmann, D., Kruppa, M., & Wasinger, R. (2007). Adaptive mobile guides. In P. Brusilovsky, A. Kobsa & W. Nejdl (Ed.), *The Adaptive Web: Vol. 4321. Lecture Notes in Computer Science* (pp. 521-549). Springer-Verlag.

Kurumatani, K. (2003). Mass User Support by Social Coordination among Citizen in a Real Environment. In K. Kurumatani, S. Chen & A. Ohuchi (Ed.), *International Workshop on Multi-Agent for Mass User Support (MAMUS 2003): Vol. 3012. Lecture Notes In Artificial Intelligence* (pp. 1–16). Springer-Verlag.

Lech, T., & Wienhofen, L. (2005). AmbieAgents: A Scalable Infrastructure for Mobile and Context-Aware Information Services. In M. Pechoucek, D. Steiner & S. Thompson (PC), *4th International Conference on Autonomous Agent and MAS (AAMAS 2005): Vol. 1. Information agents, brokering and matchmaking* (pp. 625-631). ACM Press.

Moran, T., & Dourish, P. (2001). Introduction to this special issue on context-aware computing. *Journal of Human-Computer Interaction, 16 (2/4)*, 87-95.

Murray, T., Piemonte, J., Khan, S., Shen, T., & Condit, C. (2000). Evaluating the Need for Intelligence in an Adaptive Hypermedia System. In G. Gauthier, C. Frasson & K. VanLehn (Ed.), *5th International Conference on Intelligent Tutoring Systems (ITS 2000): Vol. 1839. Lecture Notes In Computer Science* (pp. 373-382). Springer-Verlag.

Nieto-Carvajal, I., Botia, J.A., Ruiz, P.M., & Gomez-Skarmeta, A.F. (2004). Implementation and Evaluation of a Location-Aware Wireless Multi-Agent System. In L. Yang, M. Guo, G.R. Gao & N.K. Jha (Ed.), *Embedded and Ubiquitous Computing (EUC 2004): Vol. 3207. Lecture Notes in Computer Science* (pp. 528-537). Springer-Verlag.

Page, M., Gensel, J., Capponi, C., Bruley, C., Genoud, P., Ziébelin, D., Bardou, D. & Dupierris, V. (2001) A New Approach in Object-Based Knowledge Representation: the AROM System. In L. Monostori, J. Váncza & M. Ali (Ed.), *14th International Conference on Industrial & Engineering Applications of Artificial Intelligence & Expert Systems, (IEA/AIE2001): Vol. 2070. Lecture Notes in Artificial Intelligence* (pp. 113-118). Springer-Verlag.

Preuveneers, D.; Vandewoude, Y.; Rigole, P.; Ayed, D., & Berbers, Y. (2006). Context-aware adaptation for component-based pervasive computing systems, In T. Pfeifer, A. Schmidt, W. Woo, G. Doherty, F. Vernier, K. Delaney, B. Yerazunis, M. Chalmers & J. Kiniry (Ed.), *Advances in Pervasive Computing 2006. Adjunct Proceedings of the 4th International Conference on Pervasive Computing: Vol. 207.* (pp. 125-128). Austrian Computer Society (OCG), Vienna.

Rahwan, T., Rahwan, T., Rahwan, I., & Ashri, R. (2003). Agent-Based Support for Mobile Users Using AgentSpeak(L). In P. Giorgini, B. Henderson-Sellers & M. Winikoff (Ed.), *5th International Bi-Conference Workshop on Agent-Oriented Information Systems (AOIS2003): Vol. 3030. Lecture Notes In Artificial Intelligence* (pp. 45-60). Springer-Verlag.

Ramparany, F., Boissier, O., & Brouchoud, H. (2003, May). *Cooperating Autonomous Smart Devices.* Paper presented at the Smart Objects Conference (sOc'2003), Grenoble, France.

Sashima, A., Izumi, N., & Kurumatani, K. (2004). Bridging Coordination Gaps between Devices, Services, and Humans in Ubiquitous computing. *Workshop on Agents for Ubiquitous Computing (UbiAgents04)*. Retrieved January 2008, from http://www.ift.ulaval.ca/~mellouli/ubiagents04/

Rouvoy, R. & Merle, P. (2006, July). Leverage Component-Oriented Programming with Attribute-Oriented Programming. Paper presented at the *11th International ECOOP Workshop on Component-Oriented Programming* (*WCOP'06*), Nantes, France. Retrieved January 2008, from http://research.microsoft.com/~cszypers/events/WCOP2006/rouvoy-wcop-06.pdf

Schmidt, K. (2002). The problem with 'awareness': introductory remarks on 'Awareness in CSCW'. *Computer Supported Cooperative Work*, *11(3-4)*, 285-298.

Yudelson, M., Gavrilova, T., & Brusilovsky, P. (2005). Towards User Modeling Meta-ontology. In L. Ardissono, P. Brna & A. Mitrovic (Ed.), *10th International Conference on User Modeling* (*UM 2005*): *Vol. 3538. Lecture Notes In Computer Science* (pp. 448-452). Springer-Verlag.

Section IV
Selected Readings

Chapter XIII
A User–Centered Approach to the Retrieval of Information in an Adaptive Web Site

Cristina Gena
Università di Torino, Italy

Liliana Ardissono
Università di Torino, Italy

ABSTRACT

This chapter describes the user-centered design approach we adopted in the development and evaluation of an adaptive Web site. The development of usable Web sites, offering easy and efficient services to heterogeneous users, is a hot topic and a challenging issue for adaptive hypermedia and human-computer interaction. User-centered design promises to facilitate this task by guiding system designers in making decisions, which take the user's needs in serious account. Within a recent project funded by the Italian Public Administration, we developed a prototype information system supporting the online search of data about water resources. As the system was targeted to different types of users, including generic citizens and specialized technicians, we adopted a user-centered approach to identify their information needs and interaction requirements. Moreover, we applied query analysis techniques to identify further information needs and speed up the data retrieval activity. In this chapter, we describe the requirements analysis, the system design, and its evaluation.

INTRODUCTION

The development of a *Web-based information system* targeted to different types of users challenges the Web designer because heterogeneous requirements, information needs, and operation modes have to be considered. As pointed out by Nielsen (1999) and Norman and Draper (1986), the user's mental model and expectations have to be seriously taken into account to prevent her/him from being frustrated and rejecting the services offered by a Web site. Indeed, this issue is particularly relevant to Web sites offering task-oriented services, because most target users utilize them out of their leisure time, if not at work. Being under pressure, these users demand ease of use as well as efficient support to the execution of activities.

The positive aspect of a technical Web site is, however, the fact that the users can be precisely identified and modeled; moreover, their information needs, representing strong requirements, can be elicited by means of a suitable domain analysis. Therefore, utilities, such as data search and retrieval, can be developed to comply with different goals and backgrounds. Of course, users' involvement and testing have to be carried out also in this case because they support the development of effective and usable services (see Dumas & Redish, 1999; Keppel, 1991).

In our recent work, we faced these issues in the development of ACQUA, a prototype Web-based information system for the Italian Public Administration presenting information about water resources (a demo is available at http://acqua.di.unito.it). During the system design phase, we put in practice traditional *usability* principles and *adaptive hypermedia* best practices and we derived general guidelines for the development of *usable Web-based systems* for technical users (see Brusilovsky, 1996, 2001; Fink, Kobsa, & Nill, 1999; Maybury & Brusilovsky, 2002). The system described in the rest of this chapter is targeted to two main classes of users:

- Generic users, such as the citizen, who want to be informed about the general health state of rivers, lakes, and underground waters.
- Technical users, such as the public administration employees, who retrieve specific pieces of information for analysis purposes.

In this chapter we describe the requirements analysis, the design, and the evaluation of ACQUA, focusing on the *user-centered approach* adopted in the prototype design and development phases. We involved domain experts and end users since the beginning of our work in order to assess the usefulness and suitability of the functionality offered by the system, as well as of its user interface. For further information about the system, see Gena and Ardissono (2004).

The rest of this chapter is organized as follows: Section "Background" provides an overview of the relevant user-centered design research. Section "The ACQUA Project" presents our work. Specifically, Section "Application Requirements" describes the interaction and user interface requirements that emerged during the design phase; Section "Adaptive Features" presents the adaptive features we developed for our system; Section "Association Rules" describes the techniques supporting the personalized information search; Section "Evaluation of ACQUA" presents the results of an evaluation we carried out to test the system functionality with real users; and Section "Comparison with Other Solutions" compares our proposal with some related work. Finally, section "Future Trends" discusses some open technical issues and suggests how to address them, and Section "Conclusion" concludes the chapter.

BACKGROUND

Several researchers suggested to address usability issues by developing *adaptive systems*. For instance, Benyon (1993) proposed adaptivity as a solution, because a single interface cannot be designed to meet the usability requirements of all the groups of users of a system. However, it is possible to prove that adaptivity enhances the usability of a system only if it can be shown that, without the adaptive capability, the system performs less effectively. Benyon identifies five interdependent activities to be considered when designing an adaptive system:

1. *Functional analysis*, aimed at defining the main functions of the system.
2. *Data analysis*, concerned with understanding and representing the meaning and structure of data in the application domain.
3. *Task knowledge analysis*, focused on the cognitive characteristics required by the system users, such as the user's mental model, cognitive load, and the required search strategy.
4. *User analysis*, aimed at determining the scope of the user population to which the system is targeted. This analysis concerns the identification of the user attributes that are relevant for the application, such as required intellectual capability, cognitive processing ability, and similar. The target population is analyzed and classified according to the aspects of the application derived from the above-mentioned points.
5. *Environment analysis* is aimed at identifying the characteristics of the environment in which the system is going to operate.

Notice that these phases are similar to the steps followed during the requirements analysis phase of a generic software system (Preece, Rogers, Sharp, & Benyon, 1994). Benyon underlined the fact that adaptive systems should benefit more than other systems from a requirements analysis before starting any kind of evaluation, because the development of these systems has to take a high number of features into account. The recognition that an adaptive capability may be desirable leads to an improved system analysis and design. As a demonstration, he reported an example of an adaptive system development, wherein he prototyped and evaluated the system with a number of users. Several user characteristics were examined to determine their effects on the interaction. Then,

further task knowledge and functional analysis were carried out.

Also Oppermann (1994) proposed a user-centered perspective and suggested a *design-evaluation-redesign* approach. He noticed that the adaptive features can be considered as the main part of a system and thus have to be evaluated during every development phase. The problem is circular:

- A problem solvable by means of the adaptivity has to be identified.
- The user characteristics related to the problem have to be selected.
- Ways of inferring user characteristics from interaction behavior have to be found.
- Adaptation techniques offering the right adaptive behavior have to be designed.

This process requires a bootstrapping method: first some initial adaptive behavior is implemented, then tested with users, revised, and tested again. The reason is that it is hard to decide which particular adaptations should be associated to specific user actions. Furthermore, the adaptations must be potentially useful to the user. The necessity of an iterative process is due to the fact that the real behavior of users in a given situation is hard to foresee; therefore, some evidence can be shown only by monitoring the users' activity. From the iterative evaluation point of view, the design phases and their evaluation have to be repeated until good results are reached.

Oppermann's iterative process is very similar to the *user-centered system design* approach originally phrased by Gould and Lewis (1983) and extended by Norman and Draper (1986).

Dix, Finlay, Abowd, and Beale (1998) pointed out that the iterative design is also a way to overcome the inherent problems of incomplete requirements specification, as only a subset of the requirements for an interactive system can be determined from the start of the project. The iterative evaluation process requires empirical knowledge about the users' behavior from the first development phases. In the case of an adaptive system, prior knowledge about the real users, the context of use, and domain experts facilitates the selection of the relevant data for the user model, such as personal features, goals, plans, domain knowledge, and context. Deep knowledge about users also offers a broad view of the application goals and prevents the system designer from serious mistakes, especially when dealing with innovative applications.

Petrelli, De Angeli, and Convertino (1999) proposed the user-centered approach to user modeling as a way to move from designer questions to guidelines by making the best use of empirical data; they advocated incremental system design as a way to satisfy large sets of users. They reported that at the early stage of development of a mobile device presenting contextual information to museum visitors, they decided to revise some of their initial assumptions about the user model. Indeed, they made this decision after having analyzed the results of a questionnaire distributed to 250 visitors. For instance, they discarded the former user modeling techniques based on stereotypes (because the sociodemographic and personal data taken in consideration did not characterize the users' behavior in a satisfactory way) in favor of a socially oriented and context-aware perspective. For instance, they noticed that people do not like to visit museums on their own and prefer looking at paintings to interacting with a device.

As discussed by Höök (2000), intelligent user interfaces may violate many usability principles developed for direct manipulation systems. The main problem is that these systems may violate many good principles, such as enabling the user to control the system, making the system predictable (given a certain input, the system always generates the same response), and making the system transparent so that the user understands at least partially how it works. In addition, most adaptive interface developers are more concerned

with defining inference strategies than with interface design. For Höök, intelligent user interfaces sometimes require a new way of addressing usability, different from the principles outlined for direct-manipulation systems. Instead of measuring factors such as task completion time, number of errors, or number of revisited nodes, other aspects have to be considered. For instance, "if the system should do information filtering, then we must check whether subjects find the most relevant information with the adaptive system and not necessarily whether they find it fast. This is not to say that the traditional measurements are always wrong—this of course depends upon the task that user and (adaptive) system should solve together" (Höök, 2002, p. 12).

Finally, Palmquist and Kim (2000) investigated the effects of (field independent and field dependent) *cognitive style* and online database search experience on WWW search performance. They concluded that cognitive style significantly influences the performance of novice searchers. In contrast, experienced searchers display a common behavior: they usually do not get lost in Web pages including many links, but they are able to choose useful navigation strategies. Therefore, Palmquist and Kim suggested that novice users should benefit from Web pages that have a simple design and few links providing information necessary to perform analytic search.

THE ACQUA PROJECT

Application Requirements

In 2003, the Water Resources Division (*Direzione Risorse Idriche*) of the Piedmont Region and the University of Torino started a project for the development of ACQUA, a Web-based information system presenting data about water resources derived from the monitoring activities on the territory. The goal was to make information available on a Web site that describes the

Division and supports a search for data in real time, in order to limit the distribution of information on a one-to-one basis via e-mail messages and paper publications. The technicians of the Division guided us in the system development by specifying application requirements and by sharing with us a repository of e-mail messages they exchanged with users asking for information throughout the years. The repository provided us with evidence about the users' interested in water resources data, the inspected information, and the regularities in the search for data. Most questions were posed by the following:

- Employees of other Public Administrations, such as technicians and researchers, who are often interested in environmental impact studies, construction feasibility studies, and historical data.
- Technicians, such as companies working at the construction of bridges and houses.
- Attorneys, who are typically interested in the examination of data concerning specific regions, for example, as a consequence of an environmental disaster.
- Farmers, who wish to monitor the biochemical state of their fields.
- Students attending secondary school, university, and also doctoral programs. These users collect information for the preparation of reports concerning, for example, historical changes in biological and chemical composition of waters, or the evolution of the capacity and hydrometric levels of rivers, and similar.

Following a user-centered approach, we developed the system by involving domain experts and end users since the first design phases. After a requirements analysis phase, we developed a number of mock-ups, which we discussed and redesigned after several focus group sessions with the experts and the users involved in the project. We decided to adopt a cooperative design approach

(Greenbaum & Kyng, 1991) in order to utilize the experience of domain experts and technicians in the design of an effective user interface. We based the development of our first prototype on the collected feedback. As the ACQUA system is devoted to the Public Administration, we had to satisfy usability and predictability requirements that imposed the design of a simple user interface. Specifically, our interlocutors suggested the following:

- The interface should be usable and intuitive in order to satisfy user needs and expectations. This first requirement should be followed in every interface design project; however, Public Administrations have the mandatory goal of satisfying all the citizens, thus usability is also intended as a service for the collectivity.
- The system behavior should be highly predictable (Dix et al., 1998) to support first-time visitors in their search task, but also to avoid frustrating professional users who would regularly use it at work. Notice that the predictability requirement has some subtle aspects: for instance, not only the user should foresee what is going to happen next, but also what should *not* be expected from the service. This is very important to prevent the user from starting the exploration of paths that will not provide her/him with the information, or the functionality (s)he is looking for.
- The system should provide the user with data that can be analyzed without preprocessing. Therefore, search results should be presented in machine-processable formats, in addition to the pictorial ones suitable for a general-purpose presentation in Web pages.
- For the sake of accessibility, the pages of the user interface should be optimized for standard browsers, without the need of special equipments or software environments.

In order to maximize the usefulness of the information that can be retrieved from the Web site, we decided to make the system generate the search results in formats, such as MS Excel® tables and textual (TXT) files, directly supporting the data analysis and interpretation at the user side. We also tried to address efficiency in the retrieval of information by reconsidering the design of the general Web site to be presented. We wanted to offer the right information the user is looking for; thus, we decided to show the main search functions in the home page of the Web site, and to move textual information, such as the pages describing the Public Administration divisions, in secondary pages, which can be reached by following hypertextual links.

Moreover, having analyzed the data about the users interested in water resources, we identified two main targets to which the system should adapt. For shortness, we denote these categories as novices and experts.

- *Novice users*, such as students and generic citizens, visit the Web site on an occasional basis and are not familiar with the content presented by the information system.

- *Expert users*, such as technicians, farmers, and the personnel of other Public Administrations, frequently visit the site and are familiar with the domain-specific information provided by the system.

In order to take the interaction requirements of these users into account, we defined two search functions:

(i) The *simple search* is a geographical search modality and guides the user step by step in the retrieval of information;

(ii) The *advanced search* offers forms where the expert user may compose the queries in single step. Figure 1 shows the user interface of the ACQUA prototype supporting the advanced search; the menus enable the user to specify the river ("Scegli il corso d'acqua"), observation point ("Scegli il punto di monitoraggio"), start date ("Data Inizio"), and end date ("Data Fine"). Moreover, the

Figure 1. Searching quantitative data (continuous hydrometric and chemical-physical parameters) about Po River in the Torino-Murazzi observation point

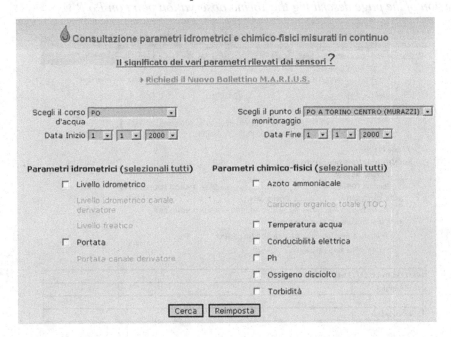

user interface enables the user to select the hydrometric and chemical-physical parameters to be inspected.

Thus, novice users may search for information in a friendly modality and the eligible choices are restricted and presented along the path, while expert users benefit from a faster search function.

As a matter of fact, the information about water resources exploited by the system is unavoidably incomplete. For instance, some data are collected by automatic stations, which have been set up at different times over the years and sometimes are out of order. Moreover, unfortunately, data collected in manual observation points have been stored in unstructured formats and the historical series has been reconstructed only for the very recent past.

For the sake of predictability, the simple and advanced search functions prevent the user from composing any queries that are incorrect, or are aimed at searching for unavailable data. The idea is that, in both cases, the system should only present the choices leading to available results.

For instance, as shown in Figure 1, the labels of the parameters, which are not available for the Po River, are shaded and cannot be selected by the user to define a query.

Adaptive Features

The information about water resources concerns rivers, lakes, and underground waters and includes the following:

- Descriptive data about resources and observation points: for example, maps of the points, charts representing environmental changes, pictures, documents, publications, and descriptions of the monitoring stations. For instance, Figure 2 ("Caratteristiche della stazione di monitoraggio TORINO" ["Features of the Torino monitoring station"]) shows the coordinates and other information about the observation point on Po River located in Torino, Parco Michelotti.

- Measurement parameters concerning physical dimensions and other features, which

Figure 2. Portion of the page describing the Torino observation point on Po River

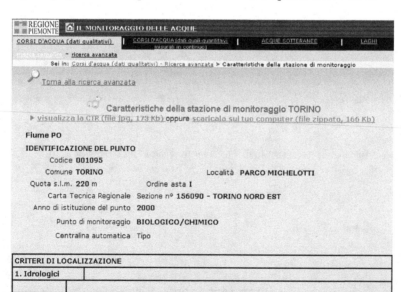

characterize the environmental state of the resources. These parameters are grouped in two main classes:

- *Qualitative parameters*, which are periodically measured: technicians visit the observation points, collect data, and take samples for laboratory tests.
- *Quantitative parameters*, which are monitored by automatic stations.

These stations carry out the measurements on a daily basis.

The ACQUA Web site is organized in four main sections, respectively devoted to the presentation of qualitative and quantitative information about rivers, information about lakes, and information about underground waters. The system enables the user to retrieve data about water resources by performing a simple or advanced search in all the sections of the site. Therefore, a large amount of heterogeneous data is accessible, ranging from biological and chemical data to capacity measurement and hydrometric levels (for details, see Gena & Ardissono, 2004).

We noticed that, by performing queries aimed at selecting a large number of data items, belonging to different categories, the results returned by the system were complex and hard to present in an intuitive results table. However, as shown by the repository of user requests we analyzed, users often need to combine heterogeneous data to accomplish their goals. For example, in construction feasibility studies, users are interested in qualitative and quantitative parameters of rivers and underground waters, considering the historical series. In order to keep the user interface simple and to guarantee that the presented results are not confusing, we decided to limit the user's freedom in composing the queries: to retrieve very heterogeneous types of information, the user must define more than one search query. For example, as shown in Figure 1, the ACQUA query interface enables the user to choose from different rivers,

observation points, years, and data types. Other categories, such as qualitative and quantitative data about rivers, lakes, and underground waters are treated as separate sections of the Web site and have their own query functions.

Unfortunately, although this approach enforces the clarity of the results, it makes the search for multiple types of information a lengthy task. Therefore, a compromise between clarity and efficiency must be found. In order to address this issue, we extended the system with an *intelligent search component*, which complements the user's explicit queries with *follow-up queries* (Moore & Mittal, 1996) frequently occurring together in navigation paths. When possible, the system anticipates the user's queries and makes the extended search results available as personalized suggestions that can be downloaded on demand. If the user is interested in the recommended information, (s)he can retrieve it by clicking on the adaptive suggestion links, without performing any further queries. At the same time, the system retrieves the extended results only after the user clicks on a suggestion link in order to avoid precaching possibly useless data.

For instance, Figure 3 shows the recommendations generated by the system in the lower portion of the page ("Ti consigliamo anche i valori dei parametri chimici e microbiologici" ["We also suggest results about chemical and microbiological parameters"]).

During different interaction sections, the same user may be interested in rather different types of information; therefore, we decided to base the system's recommendations on the analysis of her/his navigation behavior, leaving the management of a long-term user model apart. One immediate advantage is the fact that the user can interact with the system in an anonymous way, without signing up for the service. The follow-up queries are generated as follows: the search queries performed by the user while (s)he browses the Web site are monitored and association rules which suggest other, strictly related queries are applied.

Figure 3. Annotated link for the suggested information and descriptions of the monitoring stations

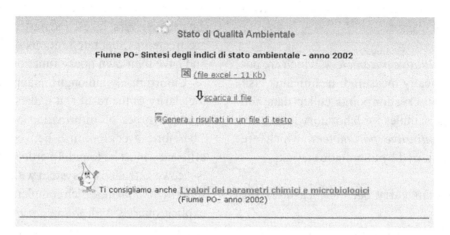

Each association rule has a condition part specifying constraints on the previous navigation behavior, and an action part defining a relevant follow-up query to be performed in order to retrieve complementary information. The rules we defined in our current prototype are mutually exclusive and they are selected and fired by applying a very tiny and efficient inference engine. This engine would not be suitable to manage a large set of conflicting rules: a general-purpose rule-based engine should be employed to that purpose. However, we prefer to maintain a simple set of adaptation rules, and to avoid embedding complex rule-based engines in order to keep the adaptive features as lightweight as possible. In fact, the management of the interaction is subject to a relevant overload due to the generation of results in multiple formats, which is a main requirement for the information system. In this situation, minimalist but efficient adaptation to the user is strongly preferred to flexible but complex one.

Association Rules

In order to define the *association rules* to be applied for anticipating the user's information needs, we analyzed a repository of requests, which real users posed to the Water Resources Division over the years; the requests consisted of e-mail messages and fax documents. As we noticed that different kinds of information frequently occurred together in these requests, we decided to analyze the frequency of co-occurrence in order to identify the regularities. Specifically, we analyzed 97 requests and we selected a set of features describing the requests in a systematic way. These features concerned rather different aspects of the requests; thus, for clarity purposes, we grouped them in subcategories. In the following, we report the subcategories we defined and for each one we list some sample features:

- *Kind of request:* for example, environmental impact study, construction feasibility studies, and lawyers' studies.
- *Request features:* for example, information about one or more rivers, about lakes or underground waters, about one or more observation points on a river or lake.
- *Kind of data:* for example, qualitative or quantitative parameters, biological and chemical data, hydrometric level, average daily capacity.
- *Data features:* for example, raw data, or elaborated data such as medium, maximum, and minimum values during a time interval.

- *User features:* for example, research center, Public Administration, technicians, farmers, and attorneys.

We computed the frequency with which the features co-occurred in the requests: if the frequency exceeded a given threshold, the set of involved features became a possible candidate for an association rule. Then we compared the extracted associations with their original requests in order to validate our findings with factual knowledge, and finally we asked the technicians of the Water Resources Division if our conclusions were correct. After this last check, we selected the correct associations and we encoded the rules in the system.

For instance, a rule suggests to retrieve qualitative parameters about a water resource if the user has asked for quantitative historical data for more than one observation point on that resource, supposing that (s)he is looking for information for a construction feasibility study. Another rule suggests retrieving the environmental state indexes of a resource if the user has requested biological and chemical data, under the hypothesis that (s)he is involved in an environmental impact study.

Evaluation of ACQUA

We first evaluated the ACQUA prototype in a usability test by involving external users who were not cooperating at the project (see Dumas & Redish, 1999, for methodological details). The evaluation highlighted some usability problems concerning the presentation of basic information, such as the choice between simple and advanced search and the background color of the menus. After having solved those problems, we tested the final prototype with real end users representative of the users the Web site is devoted to. In particular, we involved technicians working at the Water Resources Division in different fields (rivers, lakes, underground rivers, etc.) and not collaborating to the design of the project. We

carried out both an experimental evaluation and a qualitative session to assess the suitability of the adaptive features offered the system.

Subjects. We evaluated 10 potential users of the ACQUA system, four females and six males, aged 30–50. All the users worked in the water resource area and none of them was involved in the project.

Procedure. The subjects were split up in two groups (five subjects each) and randomly assigned to one of the two groups. The experimental group had to solve some tasks using the adaptive Web site, which applies the association rules described in Section "Adaptive Features" to compute the results of follow-up queries related to the users' explicit queries. Instead, the control group had to solve the tasks without adaptation.

Experimental tasks. Every subject had to solve seven tasks, each one representing a real task the user can perform in the Web site. As suggested by our correlation study, the tasks were strictly correlated and could be grouped in three search activities the user often performs together. The first activity conveyed the whole information useful to an environmental impact study. The second one supported construction feasibility studies. The third activity supported lawyers' studies and activities.

- In the control group, the users had to submit a new query for every task, in order to obtain the requested results. The new queries were submitted by filling in the query specification forms (see, e.g., Figure 1).
- In the experimental group, the users could obtain the extra information related to the next task to be performed by clicking on an adaptive suggestion link that supports the immediate retrieval of the suggested information (see, e.g., Figure 3).

Experimental design. Single-factor (the adaptivity) between-subjects design.

Measures. The subjects' navigation behavior was recorded by using Camtasia Studio®. We measured the task completion time and then the subjects' satisfaction, by means of a post-task walk-through.

Hypothesis. We hypothesized that the users working in the experimental group could obtain better performance results than those of the control group.

Results. The ANOVA (analysis of variance) showed that the subjects of the experimental group achieved the best performance results. In addition, we calculated the effect size (treatment magnitude) and the power (sensitivity) as suggested in Chin (2001). The effect size (ω^2) measures the strength, or the magnitude, of the treatment effects in an experiment. In behavioral sciences, small, medium, and large effects of ω^2 are 0.01, 0.06, and >0.15, respectively. The power of an experiment (n') is the ability to recognize treatment effects and the power can be used for estimating the sample size. In social science, the accepted value of the power is equal to 0.80, which means that the 80% of repeated experiments will give the same results. In the following, we show a summary of the results:

Task 2.
ANOVA: $F(1.8) = 12.45$ $p < 0.01$; $\omega^2 = 0.53$; $n' = 3.49$

Task 3.
ANOVA: $F(1.8) = 12.12$ $p < 0.01$; $\omega^2 = 0.53$; $n' = 3.60$

Task 5.
ANOVA: $F(1.8) = 14.16$ $p < 0.01$; $\omega^2 = 0.57$; $n' = 3.04$

Task 7.
ANOVA: $F(1.8) = 9.23$ $p < 0.05$; $\omega^2 = 0.45$; $n' = 4.86$

It should be noticed that all the results are significant and have a large estimate of the magnitude of the treatment effect. In addition, by exploiting a power of 0.80 and the corresponding ω^2 for each task we could determine the requested sampled size, which fits our sample size ($n=5$) (for details about statistics, see Keppel, 1991).

Post-task walk-through. During any *post-task walk-through*, test subjects are asked to think about the event and comment on their actions. Thus, after each test we talked to the subjects to collect their impression and to discuss their performance and the problems encountered during the test. In this session, we also aimed at retrieving useful feedback for a qualitative evaluation of the site. In fact, although our experimental evaluation reported significant results supporting our hypothesis, the actual user behavior could be different. As recently pointed out by Nielsen (2004), statistical analyses are often false, misleading, and narrow; in contrast, insights and qualitative studies are not affected by these problems because they strictly rely to the users' observed behavior and reactions.

In most cases, the interviewed users were satisfied with the site. Most of them encountered some problems in the execution of the starting query of task 2, thus we modified the interface form.

- All the users of the experimental group followed the adaptive suggestion link provided by the system but they did not realize that it represented a personalization feature. When we explained the adaptations, they noticed the particularity of the suggestion ("We also recommend you ..."). Anyway, they were attracted from the suggestions and they appreciated the possibility of skipping the execution of a new query. The adaptive suggestions were considered visible and not intrusive.
- The users of the control group reported similar considerations when we described the adaptive features offered by the Web site.

Even if they did not receive any suggestions during the execution of tasks, they explored the result pages in order to find a shortcut to proceed in the task execution. After having followed some links, they went back to the previous query page or to the home page by clicking on the "Back" button of the browser.

Both groups displayed a common behavior pattern: the users explored a results page before starting a new search. Nevertheless, their behavior could be influenced by the test condition, because tested users tend to pay a lot of attention to their own actions and to the page design.

We conclude by admitting that although the test subjects were satisfied with the adaptation features, only the real system usage can demonstrate our hypothesis. However, both quantitative and qualitative test results are encouraging and we think that the adaptations are correctly placed. After this test, we presented the adaptive version of the Web site to the technicians of the Water Resources Division collaborating on the project. They confirmed the correctness of association rules we defined and they decided to replace the non-adaptive version of the prototype system with the adaptive one.

Comparison with Other Solutions

The ACQUA system has a plain user interface, designed to meet simplicity, usability, and predictability requirements, but it offers advanced interactive features enabling the user to create a personal view of the information space. Two search features, targeted to novice and expert users, are available, and the search results are presented in both pictorial and machine-readable formats in order to support direct data manipulation at the user side. Moreover, the system analyzes the user's queries to identify her/his information needs, and it employs association rules to propose follow-up queries complementing the search results with

strictly related information. The follow-up queries are applied on demand; thus, the user can ignore them if (s)he is not interested in the additional data, and the system does not need to retrieve any uninteresting information.

The advanced search features we presented differ from the related work in various aspects. On the one hand, the inferences performed by our system are simpler than the probabilistic ones applied in other automated assistants, such as Lumière (Horvitz, Breese, Heckerman, Hovel, & Rommelse, 1998) and ACE (Bunt & Conati, 2003), which exploit Bayesian networks to capture the dependencies among the user actions. The point is that the user interacting with the ACQUA system does not carry out a complex task requiring a problem-solving activity. Therefore, lightweight rules associating contextually related search queries are sufficient to predict the implicit information needs and to complement the search for information accordingly. Our approach also differs from the follow-up question answering techniques proposed by Moore and Mittal (1996): in order to efficiently manage the query selection process, our follow-up queries are precompiled in a set of association rules, instead of being generated by a planner.

On the other hand, we apply query analysis techniques to identify regularities in search patterns. This differs from the typical inferences carried out in recommender systems, which reason about the features of the selected items to identify the user's priorities (see, e.g., Billsus & Pazzani, 1999), or about the regularities in the selection of individual items (see, e.g., the work by Cotter & Smyth, 2000; GroupLens, 2002).

Liu, Yu, and Meng (2002) propose other query analysis strategies for personalized Web search. However, instead of personalizing the proposed results, their system supplies a small set of categories as a context for each query. The system combines the user's search history with a general user profile automatically extracted from a category hierarchy to offer a personalized context for disambiguating the proposed query results. In ACQUA, we do not manage long-term user preferences because we noticed that, in different interaction sections, the same users are interested in rather different types of information. We thus decided to base the recommendations only on the analysis of the user's search behavior.

FUTURE TRENDS

It is worth mentioning that the manual definition of the first set of association rules supporting the user's search task was a lengthy work and might not be easily replicated to revise the rules along time. However, if the Water Resources Division employs the ACQUA system as its official Web site, the log files generated by the system will provide structured evidence about user behavior (in addition to e-mails and faxes). Thus, data-mining techniques could be exploited to automatically recognize usage patterns and revise the association rules accordingly.

Indeed, we believe that these techniques can support the analysis of user behavior in an effective way, but they still have to be coupled with human analysis, in order to validate and interpret results: in several cases, these techniques have generated some very interesting results, but also other irrelevant or hardly understandable findings, which have been discarded.

At any rate, Web usage mining techniques, derived from machine learning methods such as knowledge discovery in data (KDD or data mining) can contribute to automate the adaptation of Web-based systems to the users. According to the scheme proposed by Pierrakos, Paliouras, Papatheodorou, and Spyropoulos (2003), ACQUA can be classified as a Web personalization system offering *task performance support*: this functionality involves the execution of a particular action on behalf of the user. In our case, the system generates queries and makes the results available as links to some files storing them. This

functionality is considered as the most advanced personalization function and it is seldom offered by Web-based personalized services.

The most suitable data-mining technique, given the adaptive goals of the ACQUA system, is the *sequential pattern discovery*, which is aimed at identifying navigational patterns (event sequences) in the analyzed data (in our case, Web usage data). This methodology supports the discovery of event sequences that can be summarized as follows: "If event A, B, and C occur in that order, then events D, E, and F always follow." Two types of methods are generally applied to discover sequential patterns: *deterministic techniques*, which record the navigational behavior of the users and extract knowledge from the analyzed data, and *stochastic methods*, which use the sequence of already-visited Web pages to predict the behavior occurring in the next visits. Once sequential patterns have been discovered, the extracted knowledge can be automatically integrated in the personalization process, and the system behavior adapted accordingly.

CONCLUSION

We presented our experience in the design and development of ACQUA, an interactive prototype Web site for the Public Administration. The system presents information about water resources and supports the user in the search for generic information, as well as technical information about the rivers, lakes, and underground waters.

The usability and functional requirements that emerged during the design of the ACQUA system were very interesting and challenging, as they imposed the development of functions supporting the efficient retrieval of data by means of a simple user interface. We found out that the introduction of basic adaptivity features, aimed at understanding the user's information needs in detail, was very helpful to meet these requirements.

We were asked to develop a system having a simple user interface, designed to meet usability and predictability requirements. This fact limited our freedom to add advanced interaction features, desirable in a Web site visited by heterogeneous users; however, it challenged us to find a compromise between functionality and simplicity. In order to address this issue, we developed two interactive features enabling the user to create a personal view on the information space:

- The system offers a simple and an advanced search functions targeted to novice and expert users, respectively.
- Moreover, the system carries out a query analysis aimed at identifying the user's information needs, and applies association rules to extend the user's queries and complete the search results with data that is usually retrieved together by end users.

Qualitative and quantitative evaluation results showed that the adaptive user interface was more successful than the nonadaptive one. The reason was probably the concrete help offered by the adaptive suggestions, which speed up the execution of time-consuming search tasks. Moreover, the adaptive features were not perceived as intrusive and the user was allowed to skip useless suggestions. Furthermore, the system did not impose a previous annoying and discouraging registration phase.

As discussed in Section "Future trends," the adaptive features offered by the ACQUA system could be improved by the integration of Web-usage mining techniques aimed at discovering real usage patterns. In that way, the association rules employed to identify the user's implicit information needs could be automatically updated along time. However, we believe that the rules we manually defined provide a knowledge base that cannot be replaced with automatically extracted rules. In principle, both kinds of rules could be integrated in order to enhance the effectiveness of the system adaptations.

ACKNOWLEDGMENTS

This work was funded by Regione Piemonte, Direzione Risorse Idriche. We thank Giovanni Negro, Giuseppe Amadore, Silvia Grisello, Alessia Giannetta, Maria Governa, Ezio Quinto, Matteo Demeo, and Vincenzo Pellegrino, who assisted us during the system development and provided the domain-specific knowledge.

REFERENCES

Benyon, D. (1993). Adaptive systems: A solution to usability problems. *International Journal of User Modeling and User-Adapted Interaction, 3*, 65–87.

Billsus, D., & Pazzani, M. (1999). A personal news agent that talks, learns and explains. *In Proceedings of 3rd International Conference on Autonomous Agents* (pp. 268–275).

Brusilovsky, P. (1996). Methods and techniques of adaptive hypermedia. *International Journal of User Modeling and User-Adapted Interaction, 6*(2–3), 87–129.

Brusilovsky, P. (2001). Adaptive hypermedia. *International Journal of User Modeling and User-Adapted Interaction, 11*(1–2), 87–110.

Bunt, A., & Conati, C. (2003). Probabilistic student modelling to improve exploratory behaviour. *International Journal of User Modeling and User-Adapted Interaction, 13*(3), 269–309.

Chin, D. N., (2001). Empirical evaluation of user models and user-adapted systems. *International Journal of User Modeling and User-Adapted Interaction, 11*(1–2), 181–194.

Cotter, P., & Smyth, B. (2000). WAPing the Web: Content personalization for WAP-enabled devices. *Proceedings of International Conference on Adaptive Hypermedia and Adaptive Web-Based Systems* (pp. 98–108).

Dix, A., Finlay, J., Abowd, G., & Beale, R. (1998). *Human computer interaction* (2nd ed.). Prentice Hall.

Dumas, J. S., & Redish, J. C. (1999). *A practical guide to usability testing.* Norwood, NJ: Ablex.

Fink, J., Kobsa, A., & Nill, A. (1999). Adaptable and adaptive information for all users, including disabled and elderly people. *New Review of Hypermedia and Multimedia, 4,* 163–188.

Gena, C., & Ardissono, L. (2004). Intelligent support to the retrieval of information about hydric resources. *Proceedings of 3rd International Conference on Adaptive Hypermedia and Adaptive Web-Based Systems* (pp. 126–135).

Gould, J. D., & Lewis, C. (1983). Designing for usability: Key principles and what designers think. *Proceedings of CHI '83* (pp. 50–53).

Greenbaum, J., & Kyng, M. (1991). *Design at work: Cooperative design of computer systems.* Hillsdale, NJ: Lawrence Erlbaum.

GroupLens. (2005). GroupLens Research. Retrieved November 2, 2005, from www.GroupLens.org

Höök, K. (2000). Steps to take before IUIs become real. *Journal of Interacting With Computers, 12*(4), 409–426.

Horvitz, E., Breese J., Heckerman D., Hovel D., & Rommelse, K. (1998). *The* Lumière project: Bayesian user modeling for inferring the goals and needs of software users. *Proceedings of 14th Conference on Uncertainty in Artificial Intelligence,* San Francisco.

Keppel, G. (1991). *Design and analysis: A researcher's handbook.* Englewood Cliffs, NJ: Prentice-Hall.

Liu, F., Yu, C., & Meng, W. (2002). Personalized Web search by mapping user query to categories. *Proceedings of the 2002 ACM Conference on Information and Knowledge Management,* McLean, VA.

Maybury, M., & Brusilovsky, P. (Eds.). (2002). The adaptive Web. *Communications of the ACM, 45.*

Moore, J. D., & Mittal, V. O. (1996). Dynamically generated follow-up questions. *IEEE Computer, 29*(7), 75–86.

Nielsen, J. (1999). *Web usability.* Indianapolis, IN: New Riders Publishing.

Nielsen, J. (2004). *Risks of quantitative studies.* Retrieved March 9, 2004, from www.useit.com/alertbox/20040301.html

Norman, D. A., & Draper, S. W. (1986). *User centered system design: New perspective on HCI.* Hillsdale, NJ: Lawrence Erlbaum.

Oppermann, R. (1994). Adaptively supported adaptivity. *International Journal of Human-Computer Studies, 40,* 455–472.

Palmquist, R. A., & Kim, K. S. (2000). Cognitive style and on-line database search experience as predictors of Web search performance. *Journal of the American Society for Information Science, 51*(6), 558–566.

Petrelli, D., De Angeli, A., & Convertino, G. (1999). A user centered approach to user modeling. *Proceedings of the 7th International Conference on User Modeling* (pp. 255–264).

Pierrakos, D., Paliouras, G., Papatheodorou, C., & Spyropoulos, C. D. (2003). Web usage mining as a tool for personalization: A survey. *International Journal of User Modeling and User-Adapted Interaction, 13*(4), 311–372.

Preece, J., Rogers, Y., Sharp, H., & Benyon, D. (1994). *Human-computer interaction*. Addison Wesley.

Chapter XIV
Personalized Information Retrieval in a Semantic–Based Learning Environment

Antonella Carbonaro
University of Bologna, Italy

Rodolfo Ferrini
University of Bologna, Italy

ABSTRACT

Active learning is the ability of learners to carry out learning activities in such a way that they will be able to effectively and efficiently construct knowledge from information sources. Personalized and customizable access on digital materials collected from the Web according to one's own personal requirements and interests is an example of active learning. Moreover, it is also necessary to provide techniques to locate suitable materials. In this chapter, we introduce a personalized learning environment providing intelligent support to achieve the expectations of active learning. The system exploits collaborative and semantic approaches to extract concepts from documents, and maintaining user and resources profiles based on domain ontologies. In such a way, the retrieval phase takes advantage of the common knowledge base used to extract useful knowledge and produces personalized views of the learning system.

INTRODUCTION

Most of the modern applications of computing technology and information systems are concerned with information-rich environments, the modern, open, large-scale environments with autonomous heterogeneous information resources (Huhns & Singh, 1998; Cooley, Mobasher, & Srivastava, 1997). The effective and efficient management of the large amounts and varieties of information they include is the key to the above applications.

The Web inherits most of the typical characteristic of an information-rich environment: information resources can be added or removed in a loosely structured manner, and it lacks global control of the content accuracy of those resources. Furthermore, it includes heterogeneous components with mutual complex interdependencies; it includes not just text and relational data, but varieties of multimedia, forms, and executable code. As a result, old methods for manipulating information sources are no longer efficient or even appropriate. Mechanisms are needed in order to allow efficient querying and retrieving on a great variety of information sources which support structured as well as unstructured information.

In order to foster the development of Web-based information access and management, it is relevant to be able to obtain a user-based view of available information. The exponential increase of the size and the formats of remotely accessible data allows us to find suitable solutions to the problem. Often, information access tools are not able to provide the right answers for a user query, but rather, they provide large supersets thereof (e.g., in Web search engines). The search for documents uses queries containing words or describing concepts that are desired in the returned documents. Most content retrieval methodologies use some type of similarity score to match a query describing the content, and then they present the user with a ranked list of suggestions (Belkin & Croft, 1992). Designing applications for supporting the user in accessing and retrieving Web information sources is one of the current challenges for the artificial intelligence community.

In a distributed learning environment, there is likely to be large number of educational resources (Web pages, lectures, journal papers, learning objects, etc.) stored in many distributed and differing repositories on the Internet. Without any guidance, students will probably have great difficulty finding the reading material that is relevant for a particular learning task. The metadata descriptions concerning a learning object (LO) representation provide information about properties of the learning objects. However, the sole metadata does not provide qualitative information about different objects nor provide information for customized views. This problem is becoming particularly important in Web-based education where the variety of learners taking the same course is much greater. In contrast, the courses produced using adaptive hypermedia or intelligent tutoring system technologies are able to dynamically select the most relevant learning material from their knowledge bases for each individual student. Nevertheless, generally these systems cannot directly benefit from existing repositories of learning material (Brusilovsky & Nijhavan, 2002).

In educational settings learning objects can be of different kinds, from being files having static content (like HTML, PDF, or PowerPoint presentation format) or in sophisticated interactive format (like HTML pages loaded with JavaScript or Java applet, etc.). Audio files, video clips, or Flash animations could also constitute learning objects. An LO comprises a chunk of content material, which can be re-used or shared in different learning situations. Such a re-use of content from one system to another makes LO standardized so that it can be adopted across different computer platforms and learning systems. The IEEE Standard for Learning Object Metadata (LOM)[1] is the first accredited standard for learning object technology.[2]

Presently there are countless LOs available for commercial and academic use. Because of time and capability constraints, however, it is almost impossible both for a learner and a teacher to go through all available LOs to find the most suitable one. In particular, learning object metadata tags may facilitate rapid updating, searching, and management of content by filtering and selecting only the relevant content for a given purpose (Carbonaro, 2004). Searchers can use a standard set of retrieval techniques to maximize their chances of finding the resources via a search engine (Recker,

Walker, & Lawless, 2003). Nevertheless, the value searching and browsing results depend on the information and organizational structure of the repository. Moreover, searching for LOs within heterogeneous repositories may become a more complicated problem. What we are arguing in this chapter is that one can alleviate such difficulties by using suitable representations of both available information sources and a user's interests in order to match as appropriately as possible user information needs, as expressed in his or her query and in any available information. The representation we propose is based on ontologies representing the learning domain by means of its concepts, the possible relations between them and other properties, the conditions, or regulations of the domain. In the digital library community, a flat list of attribute/value pairs is often assumed to be available. In the Semantic Web community, annotations are often assumed to be an instance of an ontology. Through the ontologies the system will express hierarchical links among entities and will guarantee interoperability of educational resources. Recent researches on ontologies have shown the important role they can play in the e-learning domain (Dzbor, Motta, & Stutt, 2005).

In this context, standard keyword search is of very limited effectiveness. For example, it does not allow users and the system to search, handle, or read concepts of interest, and it does not consider synonymy and hyponymy that could reveal hidden similarities potentially leading to better retrieval. The advantages of a concept-based document and user representations can be summarized as follows: (i) ambiguous terms inside a resource are disambiguated, allowing their correct interpretation and, consequently, a better precision in the user model construction (e.g., if a user is interested in computer science resources, a document containing the word 'bank' as it is meant in the financial context could not be relevant); (ii) synonymous words belonging to the same meaning can contribute to the resource model definition (for example, both 'mouse' and

'display' bring evidence for computer science documents, improving the coverage of the document retrieval); (iii) synonymous words belonging to the same meaning can contribute to the user model matching, which is required in recommendation process (for example, if two users have the same interests, but these are expressed using different terms, they will considered overlapping); and (iv) classification, recommendation, and sharing phases take advantage of the word senses in order to classify, retrieve, and suggest documents with high semantic relevance with respect to the user and resource models.

For example, the system could support computer science last-year students during their activities in courseware like bio computing, internet programming, or machine learning. In fact, for these kinds of courses, it is necessary to have the active involvement of the student in the acquisition of the didactical material that should integrate the lecture notes specified and released by the teacher. Basically, the level of integration depends both on the student's prior knowledge in that particular subject and on the comprehension level he wants to acquire. Furthermore, for the mentioned courses, it is necessary to continuously update the acquired knowledge by integrating recent information available from any remote digital library.

The rest of the chapter is organized as follows. The next section describes background and literature review proposing significant examples of semantic-based e-learning systems. We then illustrate our personalized learning retrieval framework detailing proposed system requirements and architecture. We propose a concept-based semantic approach to model resource and user profiles providing word sense disambiguation process and resource representation, and provide some notes about test implementation and experimental sessions. Some final considerations and comments about future developments conclude the chapter.

BACKGROUND AND LITERATURE REVIEW

The research on e-learning and Web-based educational systems traditionally combines research interests and efforts from various fields, in order to tailor the growing amount of information to the needs, goals, and tasks of the specific individual users. Semantic Web technologies may achieve improved adaptation and flexibility for users, and new methods and types of courseware which will be compliant with the semantic Web vision. In the following sections we will describe some examples of existing projects thanks to which we will be able to outline what the current research on these fields offers. They are based on ontologies and standards that have an important role in the representation of LOs. Heflin (2004) defined an ontology as a structure in which defined terms are used to describe and represent an area of knowledge. Moreover, ontologies include computer-usable definitions of basic concepts in the domain and the relationships among them. Ontologies could be used to share domain information in order to make that knowledge reusable. The W3C standard language for ontology creation is OWL. More detailed review on ontology-based applications in education can be found in Kanellopoulos, Kotsiantis, and Pintelas (2006).

Edutella

Edutella (*http://edutella.jxta.org/*) is defined as a multi-staged effort to scope, specify, architect, and implement an RDF-based[3] metadata infrastructure for P2P-networks for exchanging information about learning objects. Edutella P2P architecture is essentially based on JXTA and RDF. JXTA (*http://www.jxta.org/*) is an open source technology that provides a set of XML-based protocols supporting different kinds of P2P applications.

According to Mendes and Sacks (2004), three types of services that a peer can offer are defined in an Edutella network:

- **Edutella query service:** This is the basic service in the framework. It presents a common, RDF-based query interface (the Query Exchange Language–RDF-QEL) for metadata providing and consuming through the Edutella network.
- **Edutella replication:** This provides replication of data within additional peers to ensure data persistence
- **Edutella mapping, mediation, clustering:** This kind of service manages metadata allowing semantic functionality of the global infrastructure.

An important point to underline is that Edutella does not share resource content but only metadata.

Smart Space for Learning

Smart Space for Learning is the result of the Elena project work (*http://www.elena-project. org*). According to Stojanovic, Stojanovic, and Volz (2002), a Smart Space for Learning can be defined as a set of service mediators which support the personalized consumption of heterogeneous educational services provided by different management systems. Learning services are entities designed to satisfy a specific purpose (e.g., the delivery of a course). They may use resources as learning objects (e.g., exercises and exams) and Web services to interface the formers with learners. WSDL and WSDL-S are languages to syntactically and semantically describe a Web service.

The system architecture of a Smart Space for Learning is essentially composed of two building blocks: an Edutella network and a set of ontologies. In a Smart Space for Learning, providers of learning services are connected to a learning management system that is based on Edutella. Ontology has to describe the learning domains using concepts and relations that may be referred to in the annotations of the learning services.

HyCo

HyCo (García, Berlanga, Moreno, García, & Carabias, 2004) stands for Hypermedia Composer; it is a multiplatform tool that supports the creation of learning materials. HyCo is the result of the development of an authoring tool created in order to define ALDs.

According to Berlanga and García (2005), ALDs are learning units that contain personalized behavior in order to provide each student with a learning flow which is to be adequate to his or her characteristics. ALDs are semantically structured in order to allow reusability.

The last version of HyCo also manages a kind of resource named SLO. An SLO is a learning object compliant with IMS metadata (*http://www. imsglobal.org/metadata/index.cfm*). Every resource created with HyCo is turned into an SLO. Whenever the conversion process is finished, an XML file is generated for the new SLO and stored in a repository.

Magpie

Magpie (*http://kmi.open.ac.uk/projects/magpie/*) provides automatic access to complementary Web sources of knowledge by associating a semantic layer to a Web page. This layer depends on one of a number of ontologies, which the user can select. When an ontology is selected, the user can also decide which classes are to be highlighted on the Web page. Clicking on an instance of a class from the selected ontology gives access to a number of semantic services. Magpie is proposed in a learning context to help students of a course in climate science understand the subject. The provided semantic services are integrated into the browsing navigation both in active and passive

user involvement.

Ontology Mapping

The *ontology space* holds all the ontologies used by the system. The distributed nature of ontology development has led to a large number of different ontologies covering the same or overlapping domains. In this scenario it is possible that a particular sub-domain can be modeled by using different ontologies and, in general, if the ontology space contains n elements, the same sub-domain can be modeled n times, one for each ontology maintained by the system. This could be very useful in ontology mapping. *Ontology mapping* is the process whereby two ontologies are semantically related at the conceptual level, and the source ontology instances are transformed into the target ontology entities according to those semantic relations. Ontology mapping though is not an easy task; it has been widely treated in literature, and some crucial problems are listed below:

1. **The lack of a universally recognized standard for ontology:** On the Web a number of ontologies are available, but they are developed using different languages.
2. **The difficulty of commonly modeling the knowledge domain:** Different developers could have different visions of the domain, and they could give most weight to some aspect rather than other one.
3. **The granularity of the domain to be represented may be different in different communities:** Different communities may have overlapping sub-domains, but concepts and relations could have been developed with a different granularity.

While the first point represents a technical problem, the last two are related to the physical ontology design and development. In particular, the second case represents a fixed domain in which different developers produce different ontologies, while the third case refers to different communities having the same domain but with a different perspective of the involved semantics.

In the literature, one can distinguish three different approaches for ontology mapping. For each of them we propose an example application:

Automatic Mapping

- **MAFRA** (Maedche, Motik, Silva, & Volz, 2002) aims to automatically detect similarities between entities belonging to source and target ontologies. The overall process is composed of five steps. First, data are normalized; second, similarity between entities are calculated according to a previously proposed algorithm, then the mapping is obtained through the semantic bridging phase, and finally transformation of instances and checking of the achieved results are executed.
- **IF-Map** (Kalfoglou, 2003) is a semi-automatic method for ontology mapping. The authors make the assumption that if two communities want to share their knowledge, they must refer their local ontologies to a reference ontology. The overall process is obtained by composing the following four major steps: ontology harvesting, in which ontologies are acquired; translation, as the IF-Map method is specified in Horn logic, the data are translated in prolog clauses; IF-Map, the main mapping mechanism; and, finally, the display result step.

Manual Mapping

- **SKOS** (SKOS Core Vocabulary specification, *http://www.w3.org/TR/swbp-skos-core-spec/ 2005*; SKOS Mapping Vocabulary specification, *http://www.w3.org/2004/02/skos/ mapping/spec/ 2005*) is a group of RDF-based vocabularies developed to support the interoperability between

different types of knowledge organization systems. In particular, SKOS consists of three RDF vocabularies:

- ○ *SKOS Core:* Provides a model for expressing contents and structures of different kind of concept schemas.
- ○ *SKOS Mapping:* Provides vocabularies for describing mappings between concept schemas.
- ○ *SKOS Extension:* Contains extensions to the SKOS Core useful for specialized applications.

For example one could use SKOS Core to translate knowledge structures like taxonomies or thesauri into a common format, and subsequently he can create a mapping between them by using SKOS Mapping.

Semi-Automatic Mapping

As an example of semi-automatic tool for ontology mapping, we would like to illustrate the one proposed in Ehrig and Sure (2004). The implemented approach is based on manually encoded mapping rules. The rules are then combined to achieve better mapping results compared to one obtained using only one at a time. In order to learn how to combine the methods, both manual and automatic approaches are introduced.

PERSONALIZED LEARNING RETRIEVAL FRAMEWORK

System Requirements

Traditional approaches to personalization include both content-based and user-based techniques (Dai & Mobasher, 2004). If, on one hand, a content-based approach allows the definition and maintenance of an accurate user profile (for example, the user may provide the system with a list of keywords reflecting his or her initial interests, and the profiles could be stored in form of weighted keyword vectors and updated on the basis of explicit relevance feedback), which is particularly valuable whenever a user encounters new content, on the other hand it has the limitation of concerning only the significant features describing the content of an item. Differently, in a user-based approach, resources are processed according to the rating of other users of the system with similar interests. Since there is no analysis of the item content, these information management techniques can deal with any kind of item, being not just limited to textual content. In such a way, users can receive items with content that are different from those received in the past. On the other hand, since a user-based technique works well if several users evaluate each item, new items cannot be handled until some users have taken the time to evaluate them, and new users cannot receive references until the system has acquired some information about the new user in order to make personalized predictions. These limitations are often referred to as sparsity and start-up problems (Melville et al., 2002). By adopting a hybrid approach, a personalization system is able to effectively filter relevant resources from a wide heterogeneous environment like the Web, taking advantage of common interests of the users and also maintaining the benefits provided by content analysis.

A hybrid approach maintains another drawback: the difficulty of capturing semantic knowledge of the application domain—that is, concepts, relationships among different concepts, inherent properties associated with the concepts, axioms or other rules, and so forth.

A semantic-based approach to retrieving relevant LOs can be useful to address issues like trying to determine the type or the quality of the information suggested from a personalized learning environment. In this context, standard keyword search has a very limited effectiveness. For example, it cannot filter for the type of information (tutorial, applet or demo, review questions, etc.),

the level of information (aimed to secondary school students, graduate students, etc.), the prerequisites for understanding information, or the quality of information. Some examples of semantic-based e-learning systems can be found in Mendes and Sacks (2004), in Lytras and Naeve (2005), and in the last paragraph of this chapter.

The aim of this chapter is to present our personalized learning retrieval framework based on both collaborative and semantic approaches. The collaborative approach is exploited both in retrieving tasks (to cover recommendation and resource sharing tasks) and in semantic coverage of the involved domain. The semantic approach is exploited introducing an ontology space covering domain knowledge and resource models based on word sense representation. The ontologies are updated as time goes on to reflect changes in the research domain and user interests. Also the ontology level exploits system collaborative aspect.

In Carbonaro (2005), we introduced the InLinx (Intelligent Links) system, a Web application that provides an online bookmarking service. InLinx is the result of three filtering components integration, corresponding to the following functionalities:

1. **Bookmark Classification (content-based filtering):** The system suggests the more suitable category that the user can save the bookmark in, based on the document content; the user can accept the suggestion or change the classification by selecting another category he considers the best for such a given item.

2. **Bookmark Sharing (collaborative filtering):** The system checks for newly classified bookmarks and recommends them to other users with similar interests. Recipient users can either accept or reject the recommendation once they receive the notification.

3. **Paper Recommendation (content-based recommendation):** The system periodically checks if a new issue of some online journal

has been released; then, it recommends the plausible appealing documents, according to the user profiles.

Over the years we have designed and implemented several extensions of the original architecture such as personalized category organization and mobile services (Andronico, Carbonaro, Colazzo, & Molinari, 2004). Most recently, we have introduced concepts for classification, recommendation, and document sharing in order to provide a better personalized semantic-based resource management. Generally, recommender systems use keywords to represent both the users and the resources. Another way to handle such data is by using hierarchical concept categories. This issue will enable users and the system to search, handle, or read only concepts of interest in a more general manner, providing a semantic possibility. For example, synonymy and hyponymy can reveal hidden similarities, potentially leading to better classification and recommendation. We called the extended architecture EasyInfo.

In this chapter we present the introduction of an ontology layer in our e-learning domain to describe the content and the relations between the various resources. It will formulate an exhaustive representation of the domain by specifying all of its concepts and the existing relations. Through the ontologies the system will express hierarchical links between entities and will guarantee interoperability of educational resources. We decide to maintain the several existing ontologies that each user knows. This approach allows us to easily compare the knowledge of a user with his or her personal ontologies without having a single consensual ontology that will accommodate all his or her needs. In this section we describe our approach to support personalization retrieval of relevant learning resources in a given Web-based learning system. This framework distinguishes between the generic user and the system administrator points of view.

Marco: A User Seeking Resources

Web technologies will continue to mature, and learning through the World Wide Web will become increasingly popular, particularly in distance education systems. Teachers can distribute lecture notes and other required materials via the Web, so Marco gets the opportunity to freely and autonomously use learning materials by collecting other related materials on the Web as well.

Active learning is the ability of learners to carry out learning activities in such a way that they will be able to effectively and efficiently construct knowledge from information sources. That is, Marco should be able to acquire, apply, and create knowledge and skills in the context of personal requirements and interests (Lee, 1999). Marco expects more than being able to filter, retrieve, and refer to learning materials. He prefers to have personalized access to library materials that he can customize according to his personal requirements and interests.

Therefore, new tools should allow the learners to integrate their selections from digital information sources and create their own reference sources. Moreover, in order to give intelligent support to achieve the expectations of active learning, it is also necessary to provide techniques to locate suitable materials. These mechanisms should extend beyond the traditional facilities of browsing and searching, by supporting active learning and by integrating the user's personal library and remote digital libraries. The user will be able to carry out learning activities when browsing both the personal and the remote digital libraries, therefore he can build personalized views on those materials while turning them into an accessible reference collection.

Because of the complexity of the system as well as the heterogeneity and amount of data, the use of semantics is crucial in this setting. For example, semantic description of resources and student profiles can be used to cluster students or resources with similar content or interests.

From a functional point of view, Marco needs a procedure to submit new material integrating the existing personal and remote libraries which consist of the following two phases:

1. An interface to submit new resources to the system, and
2. An interface to propose the mapping between the submitted resource and the ontology concepts.

Francesco: Learning System Administrator

Francesco wants to offer a personalized e-learning system that is able to respond to the effective user needs and modifiable user behavior and interests. The keyword profiling approach suffers because of a polysemy problem (the presence of multiple meanings for one term) and a synonymy problem (the presence of multiple words having the same meaning). If user and resource profiles do not share the same exact keywords, relevant information can be missed or wrong documents could be considered as relevant. Francesco wants an alternative method that is able to learn semantic profiles capturing key concepts, and which represents user and resource contents. The concepts should be defined in some ontologies. Moreover, Francesco wants to offer a procedure to map resources with respect to an ontology by creating an open and flexible ontology space describing the learning domain, in order to avoid specialized retrieving.

From a functional point of view, Francesco needs a procedure to organize the ontology space consisting of the following three phases:

1. An interface to add, remove, and modify ontologies belonging to the ontology space;
2. An interface to execute ontology mapping; and
3. An interface to propose the mapping between resources submitted by users and the ontology concepts.

System Architecture

As shown in Figure 1, the proposed architecture is divided into five different layers:

- **Search layer:** In this layer the user can specify his or her query and subscribe new resources to the system.
- **Ontology space layer:** In this the layer the system logically maintains the system ontologies.
- **Mapping layer:** This layer organizes the structure in which the mapping between resources and ontology concepts.
- **DB layer:** In this layer are stored all the meta-information about the resources, that is, information like title, author, physical location, and so on.
- **Resource layer:** This layer stores the different learning resources.

The following sections describe in more detail each layer.

Search Layer

This is the layer where the user can query the system for resources and propose new ones. Through the GUI the user composes his or her query by using the *Query Composition* module (see Figure 2). A simple query specifying only keyword is not enough for a semantic search. The query composer interacts with the ontology management middleware in order to navigate the ontology and allows the user to choose not only the concept, but also a property associated with it.

Once the query has been composed, the Query Composition module passes the query to the Resource Search Engine. This module interacts with the ontology space and queries the mapping layer retrieving a list, eventually empty, of resources to be proposed to the user.

Figure 1. System architecture

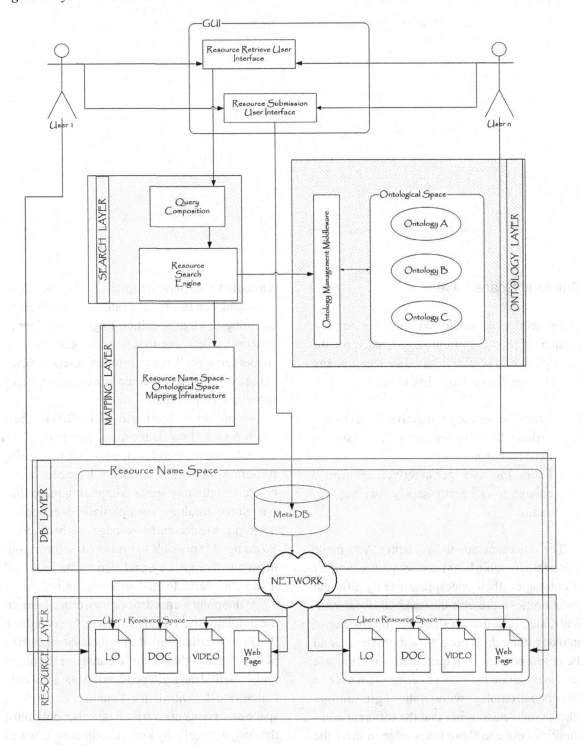

Figure 2. Query composition GUI

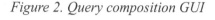

Ontology Space Layer

In this section we would like to center our discussion on the kind of ontology needed for the description of a semantic-based system domain. In particular, the ontology has to be:

- **From the system perspective:** large enough to describe all the resources that the system must manage; and
- **From the user perspective:** descriptive enough to efficiently satisfy user requirements.

The emergence of the semantic Web made it possible to publish and access a large number of ontologies; their widespread use by different communities represents the backbone for semantically rich information sharing. The sharing of ontology, though, is not a solved problem. With the proposed domain requirements in mind, we need to maintain the view of each system user on the personal ontology without altering its original schema, while assuming that the different communities desire to share knowledge to infer the relationships among their concepts and to amplify the effectiveness of the system response. For example, let us consider an example taken from

Kalfoglou and Schorlemmer (2003) that shows the issues one has to take into account when attempting to align specified English and French concepts. We argue that promoting services to support group collaboration among users involved in the learning process could be a useful approach to solve such problems.

According to Stutt and Motta(2004), there are a lot of 'knowledge neighborhoods' built around some topic by handling different learning resources, ontologies, and users. It is necessary to create an ontology space comprising more than one global ontology, even partially overlapping, belonging to different knowledge neighborhoods. So doing, it is possible to propose to a huge user-maintained repository, and also create links and automatic search to another community.

At this point we need to outline a crucial aspect: the ontology space analysis phase. We can think that Francesco has built the perfect system, but the performance—that is, the accuracy in the query reply—will strongly depend on the ontology used to describe the knowledge domain. The ontology space analysis is not a trivial task; not only must the designer perfectly know the domain he wants to describe, but he must also have an excellent knowledge both of the living ontologies in the various communities and the kind of users that the system must serve. For example, if the target of Francesco's system is an user with an in-depth knowledge about a particular domain, the ontology space must be as detailed as possible. On the contrary, if the expected user is at a more scholastic level, the domain will be more general and with less detailed information. These choices are related to the design phase of the system, but they cannot be a binding obstacle for future improvements. Communities and their domains evolve in time, and as a consequence, the representation of the overall system domain must evolve.

Ontology mapping is not a trivial task. If, at first glance, the biggest problem seems to be related to highly time-consuming aspects of the subsequent process, it is easy to verify that matching of concepts belonging to different ontologies can be considered the hardest part of the work. Initially, the purpose of manually mapping different ontologies can seem a titanic effort, so the first idea is the development of an automatic tool able to solve the task. Unfortunately, this approach has problems with accuracy of matching. An automatic tool such as MAFRA could solve the mapping process in little time and certainly the results are not prone to classical human errors. But other errors may occur and we think that they can be even more dangerous. An automatic tool, for example, will find it difficult to detect semantic differences between concepts belonging to different and complex ontologies. Moreover, the accuracy of algorithms and rules used for automatic semantic relationship deduction between different schemas could not be satisfactory.

In particular, a human error could be related to the absent-mindedness of the mapper and can be categorized as syntactical mistakes. These kinds of errors, or a big percentage of them, can be detected through the help of a parser. On the contrary, an accuracy problem is a semantical error and is much more difficult to identify. This kind of error could reduce the expected performance improvement deriving from ontology use.

A manual process is necessary because the semantic relationships that can occur between ontologies are too complex to be directly learned by machines. For this reason, in order to avoid semantic errors, one can adopt a manual mapping approach; however, it could be unacceptably expensive.

At the time of writing, the mapping process is an open problem in our architecture. For our test cases we used a manual mapping, but a semi-automatic ontology mapping tool is in development.

Mapping Layer

Another crucial aspect of the proposed system is the resource mapping phase. The resource representation may be accomplished using two different strategies:

1. **By using a list containing ontology concepts**: this solution represents a good resource representation and it is easily practicable;

2. **By using a subgraph of the ontology space**: this solution could represent in more detail the learning resources, but it is more difficult to implement.

The main difference between the two mentioned strategies is related to concept properties. Without the properties the subgraph can be conformed to the concept list; nevertheless, the properties allow differentiation between similar resources.

Generally, the choice depends on the domain one has to manage. If the resource space is composed of resources made up of generic domain topics, then the first solution may be the best one. On the contrary, if the resources are extremely detailed, the graph model may be the best choice. We have chosen the first proposed model; our choice is limited by the interaction with the resource representation produced by the disambiguation module of EasyInfo, which is similar to a concept list expressed in an XML-based language. In future works we intend to go through this limitation also supporting the graph model.

In the last part of this section, we describe the resource ontology mapping task. As shown in Figure 1, all the information about resources are maintained within the DB; through the DB layer it provides a Resource Name Space to other system modules. More precisely, the Resource Name Space is the set of logical names of the resources managed by the system. For this reason, the list of ontology concepts is mapped with a record of the database.

Most of the efforts in the field of mapping between ontologies and databases have been spent in the directions of heterogeneous database integration. The purpose of such an approach is to map a database record to a list of ontology concepts in order to give a semantical representation of the data they represent.

In our architecture the database maintains all the meta information about the learning resources such as title, author, physical location, and so on. Through the DB, the system provides a Resource Name Space in which each element represents a single resource. Both system and users can refer to resources by using their logical name and all the other information handled within the Database Layer. In order to give an ontological–logical–resource representation, we have to create an ontological–physical–database mapping. In the rest of this section, we refer to some existing techniques of mapping between databases and ontologies.

- *Kaon reverse* (Stojanovic et al., 2002) is a KAON plug-in for semi-automatically mapping relational database to ontologies. In the first step of this approach, the relational database model is transformed into an ontology structure expressed in F-Logic (Kifer, 1995). In the second step, the database content is migrated into the created ontology. If needed, the F-Logic structure can be translated in RDF.

- *D2R* (Bizer, 2003) is defined as a declarative XML-based language used to describe mappings between relational database schemas and OWL[4] ontologies without changing the database schema. The D2R mapping process comprises the following steps:
  - selection of a record set from the database,
  - grouping of the record set by the d2r: group By attribute,
  - creation of class instances, and
  - mapping of the grouped record set data to instance properties.
- *Deep annotation* (Handschuh, Staab, & Volz, 2003) is defined as a manual annotation process that uses information properties, information structures, and information context in order to derive mapping between database schema and ontologies. This approach proposes the annotation of Web pages maintaining DB content by using information about the database schema. In this way, a client can map the public mark up of the Web page to its own ontology.

Our first approach was inspired by the ones proposed in Kaon Reverse. We studied a two-step process for the semi-automatic mapping between database schemas and ontologies. We had taken into consideration the approach proposed in D2R, and we have developed an XML-based language to express the resulting mapping (see Figure 3). In order to improve the accuracy of the mapping process, we have adopted the idea of manual mapping proposed in Deep Annotation. Although the resource manual mapping can be considered time consuming, we have preferred the accuracy of the resource representation rather than the quickness of the overall process.

DB Layer

In the DB layer we maintain all the meta-information about the resources, information like title, author, physical location, and so on. As previously

Figure 3. XML-based language to express the resource mapping process

```
<?xml version="1.0" encoding="UTF-8" ?>
<!DOCTYPE Map (View Source for full doctype...)>
- <Map>
  - <DBConnection>
    <NameDB>testDB</NameDB>
    <Login>root</Login>
    <Password />
  </DBConnection>
  - <Ontologies>
    + <Ontology>
    + <Ontology>
    + <Ontology>
    + <Ontology>
  </Ontologies>
  - <ClassesMap>
    + <ClassMap type="Inferred">
    + <ClassMap type="Asserted">
    - <ClassMap type="Inferred">
      <TableName>animali</TableName>
    + <IDRow>
      <PrefixOntology>pean</PrefixOntology>
      <IDObject>animal</IDObject>
    </ClassMap>
    - <ClassMap type="Asserted">
      <TableName>animali</TableName>
      - <IDRow>
        <KeyValue>2</KeyValue>
      </IDRow>
      <PrefixOntology>pean</PrefixOntology>
      <IDObject>duck</IDObject>
    </ClassMap>
  </ClassesMap>
</Map>
```

Figure 4. A screenshot of the GUI for the mapping phase

described, this layer provides the Resource Name Space, which is the set of resource logical names managed by the system.

Resource Layer

This is the layer of resources. A resource can be maintained both on the same machine in which

the system is running and in a remote accessible machine. All the information about resources are stored in the DB layer.

CONCEPT-BASED SEMANTIC APPROACH TO MODEL RESOURCE AND USER PROFILES

Word Sense Disambiguation Process

In order to substitute keywords with univocal concepts into user and resource profiles, we must build a process called Word Sense Disambiguation (WSD). Given a sentence, a WSD process identifies the syntactical categories of words and interacts with an ontology both to retrieve the exact concept definition and to adopt some techniques for semantic similarity evaluation among words. We use GATE (Cunningham, Maynard, Bontcheva, & Tablan, 2002) to identify the syntactic class of the words and WordNet (Fellbaum, 1998), which is one of the most used reference lexicons in the Word Sense Disambiguation task.

The use of the described Word Sense Disambiguation step reduces classification errors due to ambiguous words, thus allowing better precision in the succeeding recommendation and sharing phases. For example, if the terms "procedure," "subprogram," and "routine" appear in the same resource, we consider three occurrences of the same sysnset "{06494814}: routine, subroutine, subprogram, procedure, function (a set sequence of steps, part of larger computer program)" and not one occurrence for each word.

Moreover, the implemented WSD procedure allows more accurate document representation. For example, let us process two sentences containing the "mouse" polysemous word. The disambiguation process applied to the first sentence "The white cat is hunting the mouse" produces the following WordNet definition:

{2244530}: mouse (any of numerous small rodents typically resembling diminutive rats having pointed snouts and small ears on elongated bodies with slender usually hairless tails), while the same process applied to the second sentence "The mouse is near the pc" produces the following result:

{3651364}: mouse, computer mouse (a hand-operated electronic device that controls the coordinates of a cursor on your computer screen as you move it around on a pad; on the bottom of the mouse is a ball that rolls on the surface of the pad; "a mouse takes much more room than a trackball").

To the best of our knowledge, no systems use a concept-based semantic approach to model resource and user profiles in a learning environment.

Resource Representation

Many systems build document and user representations by taking into account some word properties in the document, such as their frequency and their co-occurrence. Nevertheless, we described how a purely word-based model is often not adequate when the interest is strictly related to the resource semantic content. We now describe how the novice user and resource semantic profiles differ from the old ones in taking into account word senses representing user and resource contents.

In the early version of our system, we adopted a representation based on the Vector Space Model (VSM), the most frequently used model in information retrieval (IR) and text learning. Since the resources of the system are Web pages, it was necessary to apply a sequence of contextual processing to the source code of the pages in order to obtain a vector representation. To filter information resources according to user interests, we must have a common representation both for the users and the resources. This knowledge representation model must be expressive enough to synthetically and significantly describe the information content. The use of the VSM allows updates of the user profile in accordance with consulted information resources (Salton, 1989).

To guarantee a customizable architecture, the system needs to construct and maintain user profiles. For a particular user, it is reasonable to think that processing a set of correctly classified relevant and inappropriate documents from a certain domain of interest may lead to identifying the set of relevant keywords for such a domain at a certain time. Thus, the user domain-specific sets of relevant features, called prototypes, may be used to learn how to classify documents. In particular, in order to consider the peculiarity of positive and negative examples, we define positive prototype for a class c_j, a user u_i at time t, as a finite set of unique indexing terms, chosen to be relevant for c_j, up to time t. Then we define a negative prototype as a subset of the corresponding positive one, whereas each element can be found at least once in the set of documents classified as negative examples for class c_j. Positive examples for a specific user u_i and for a class c_j are represented by the explicitly registered documents or accepted by u_i in c_j, while negative examples are either deleted bookmarks, misclassified bookmarks, or rejected bookmarks that happen to be classified into c_j.

After the WSD, our resources are represented by using a list of WordNet concepts obtained by the described architecture from the words in the documents and their related occurrence. Our hypothesis is that concept-based document and user representations produce retrieved documents with high semantic relevance with respect to the user and resource models.

EXPERIMENTAL DOMAIN

The following paragraphs describe how we consider the resource content to propose a fitted technique in a personalized information retrieval framework. The automatic retrieval of relevant learning objects is obtained by considering students and learning material profiles, and by adopting filtering criteria based on the value of selected metadata fields. Our experiments are based on SCORM[5]-compliant LOs. For example, we use the student's knowledge of domain concept to avoid recommendation of highly technical papers to a beginner student or popular magazine articles to a senior graduate student. For each student, the system evaluates and updates his or her skill and technical expertise levels.

We use artificial learners to get a flavor of how the system works. We created SCORM-compliant learning material using the abstract of several papers in .html version from scientific journals published on the Web. We linked an imsmanifest SCORM file to each paper. Then, we simulated 10 users with different initial profiles (based on the field of interest and on the skill level) and saved, in four turns, 10 learning resources for each user, obtaining 400 LOs. The main advantage of the described approach is the semantic accuracy growth. To give a quantitative estimation of the improvement induced by a concept-based approach, we are executing a comparative experiment between word-based user and resource models on one side and concept-based user and resource models on the other one. In particular, in order to evaluate the collaborative approach, we have considered different initial student profiles. The several components influencing the choice of recommendation receivers are:

- **User interest in the category of recommended resource:** The system maintains a user vs. category matrix that, for a specific user, stores the number of times he or she shows interest for a certain class, saving a bookmark in that class.
- **Confidence level between users:** We use a matrix maintaining the user's confidence factor, ranging from 0.1 to 1, to represent how many documents recommended by a specific user are accepted or rejected by another one. The confidence factor is not bi-directional.
- **Relation between the class prototype of recommended resource and the class prototype of other categories:** To obtain a fitting recommendation, we apply the Pearson-r correlation measure to a weighted user-category matrix in which classes related to the class of the recommended bookmark are enhanced.

To verify the effectiveness of the EasyInfo module on the recommendation process, we considered a certain snapshot of the user/category matrix and of the confidence factor matrix. Then, we observed the behavior of the system while performing the same recommendation task both using and without using the EasyInfo extension.

For simplicity, we have considered three users, user1, user2 and user3, and three resources, r1, r2, and r3. In the first case, whenever user1 saves (or accepts) r1, the system will recommend it to user2 who has a high interest in that topic (independent of similarity among user profiles). The same resource will not be recommended to user3 because the system is not able to discover similarity between two students by simply using word-based user and resource models. In the second case, the same resource could also be recommended to user3 who is conceptually similar to user1, even if the similarity is not evident in a simple word matching system. Moreover, the system is able to discover word sense similarities between r1 and r3 and to propose r3 both to user2 and user3, thus allowing better personalization.

CONSIDERATIONS

This chapter addresses key limitations with existing courseware on the Internet. Humans want immediate access to relevant and accurate information. There has been some progress in combining learning with information retrieval, however, these advances are rarely implemented in e-learning courseware. With this objective in mind, we described how to propose a personalized information retrieval framework, considering student and learning material profiles, adopting filtering criteria based on the value of selected metadata fields, and capturing not only structural but also semantics information. We showed how the semantic technologies can enhance the traditional keyword approach by adding semantic information in the resource and user profiles.

Summarizing, the key elements of the described system could be highlighted as follows. The system provides immediate portability and visibility from different user locations, enabling access to a personal bookmark repository just by using a Web browser. The system assists students in finding relevant reading material providing personalized learning object recommendations. The system directly benefits from existing repositories of learning material by providing access to large amounts of digital information. The system reflects continuous ongoing changes of the practices of its members, as required by a cooperative framework. The system proposes resource and student models based on word senses rather than simply on words exploiting a word sense-based document representation.

REFERENCES

Andronico, A., Carbonaro, A., Colazzo, L., & Molinari, A. (2004). Personalisation services for learning management systems in mobile settings. *International Journal of Continuing Engineering Education and Lifelong Learning.*

Belkin, N.J., & Croft, W.B. (1992). Information filtering and information retrieval: Two sides of the same coin. *Communications of the ACM, 35*(12), 29-38.

Berlanga, A.J., & García, F.J. (2005). IMS LD reusable elements for adaptive learning designs. *Journal of Interactive Media in Education,* 11(Special Issue).

Bizer, C. (2003). D2R MAP—a database to RDF mapping language. *Proceedings of the 12th International World Wide Web Conference.*

Brusilovsky, P., & Nijhavan, H. (2002). A framework for adaptive e-learning based on distributed re-usable learning activities. *Proceedings of the World Conference on E-Learning* (E-Learn 2002), Montreal, Canada.

Budanitsky, A., & Hirst, G. (2001). Semantic distance in WordNet: An experimental, application-oriented evaluation of five measures. *Proceedings of Workshop on WordNet and Other Lexical Resources of the 2nd Meeting of the North American Chapter of the Association for Computational Linguistics,* Pittsburgh, PA.

Carbonaro A. (2004). Learning objects recommendation in a collaborative information management system. *IEEE Learning Technology Newsletter, 6*(4).

Carbonaro, A. (2005). Defining personalized learning views of relevant learning objects in a collaborative bookmark management system. In *Web-based intelligent e-learning systems: Technologies and applications.* Hershey, PA: Idea Group.

Cooley R., Mobasher, B., & Srivastava, J. (1997). Web mining: Information and pattern discovery on the World Wide Web. Proceedings of the 9th International Conference on Tools with Artificial Intelligence (ICTAI '97).

Cunningham, H., Maynard, D., Bontcheva, K., & Tablan, V. (2002). GATE: A framework and graphical development environment for robust NLP tools and applications. *Proceedings of the 40th Anniversary Meeting of the Association for Computational Linguistics,* Budapest.

Dai, H., & Mobasher, B. (2004). Integrating semantic knowledge with Web usage mining for personalization. In A. Scime (Ed.), *Web mining: Applications and techniques* (pp. 276-306). Hershey, PA: Idea Group.

Dzbor, M., Motta, E., & Stutt, A. (2005). Achieving higher-level learning through adaptable semantic Web applications. *International Journal of Knowledge and Learning, 1*(1/2).

Ehrig, M., & Sure, Y. (2004, May). Ontology mapping—an integrated approach. In C. Bussler, J. Davis, D. Fensel, & R. Studer (Eds.), *Proceedings of the 1st European Semantic Web Symposium* (pp. 76-91), Heraklion, Greece. Berlin: Springer-Verlag (LNCS 3053).

Fellbaum, C. (Ed.). (1998). *WordNet: An electronic lexical database*. Cambridge, MA: MIT Press.

García, F.J., Berlanga, A.J., Moreno, M.N., García, J., & Carabias, J. (2004). *HyCo—an authoring tool to create semantic learning objects for Web-based e-learning systems* (pp. 344-348). Berlin: Springer-Verlag (LNCS 3140).

Handschuh, S., Staab, S., & Volz, R. (2003). On deep annotation. *Proceedings of the 12th International World Wide Web Conference.*

Heflin, J. (2004, February). OWL Web Ontology Language use cases and requirements. Retrieved from http://www.w3.org/TR/Webont-req/

Huhns, M.N., & Singh, M.P. (1998). *Multiagent systems in information-rich environments. Cooperative information agents II* (pp. 79-93). (LNAI 1435).

Kalfoglou, Y., & Schorlemmer, M. (2003). IF-Map: An ontology mapping method based on information-flow theory. In S. Spaccapietra et al. (Eds.), *Journal on data semantics.* (LNCS 2800).

Kanellopoulos, D., Kotsiantis, S., & Pintelas, P. (2006, February). Ontology-based learning applications: A development methodology. *Proceedings of the 24th Iasted International Multi-Conference Software Engineering,* Austria.

Kifer, M., Lausen, G., & Wu, J. (1995). Logical foundations of object-oriented and frame-based languages. *Journal of the ACM, 42*(4), 741-843.

Koivunen, M., & Miller, E. (2002). W3C semantic Web activity. In E. Hyvonen (Ed.), *Semantic Web kick-off in Finland* (pp. 27-44). Helsinki: HIIT.

Leacock, C., & Chodorow, M. (1998). Combining local context and WordNet similarity for word sense identification. In C. Fellbaum (Ed.), *WordNet: An electronic lexical database* (pp. 265-283). Cambridge, MA: MIT Press.

Lee, J. (1999). Interactive learning with a Web-based digital library system. *Proceedings of the 9th DELOS Workshop on Digital Libraries for Distance Learning.* Retrieved from *http://courses. cs.vt.edu/~cs3604/DELOS.html*

Lytras, M.D., & Naeve, A. (Eds.). (2005). *Intelligent learning infrastructure for knowledge intensive organizations.* London: Information Science.

Maedche, A., Motik, B., Silva, N., & Volz, R. (2002). MAFRA—a mapping framework for distributed ontologies. *Proceedings of EKAW (Knowledge Engineering and Knowledge Management) 2002.* Berlin: Springer-Verlag (LNCS 2473).

Mendes, M.E.S., & Sacks, L. (2004). Dynamic knowledge representation for e-learning applications. In M. Nikravesh, L.A. Zadeh, B. Azvin, & R. Yager (Eds.), *Enhancing the power of the Internet—studies in fuzziness and soft computing* (vol. 139, pp. 255-278). Berlin/London: Springer-Verlag.

Nagarajan, R. (2002). Content-boosted collaborative filtering for improved recommendations. *Proceedings of the 18th National Conference on Artificial Intelligence,* Canada.

Recker, M., Walker, A., & Lawless, K. (2003). What do you recommend? Implementation and analyses of collaborative filtering of Web resources for education. *Instructional Science, 31,* 229-316.

Resnik, P. (1995). *Disambiguating noun groupings with respect to WordNet senses.* Chelmsford, MA: Sun Microsystems Laboratories.

Salton, G. (1989). *Automatic text processing: The transformation, analysis and retrieval of information by computer.* Reading, MA: Addison-Wesley.

Stojanovic, L., Stojanovic, N., & Volz, R. (2002). Migrating data-intensive Web sites into the semantic Web. *Proceedings of the 17th ACM Symposium on Applied Computing* (pp. 1100-1107).

Stutt, A., & Motta, E. (2004). Semantic learning Webs. *Journal of Interactive Media in Education,* (10).

Tang, T., & McCalla, G. (2005). Smart recommendation for an evolving e-learning system: Architecture and experiment. *International Journal on E-Learning, 4*(1), 105-129.

ENDNOTES

[1] *http://grouper.ieee.org/p1484/wg12/files/LOM_1484_12_1_v1_Final_Draft.pdf*
[2] *http://ltsc.ieee.org*
[3] RDF is the W3C recommendation for the creation of metadata about resources. With RDF, one can make statements about a resource in the form of a subject–predicate–object expression. The described resource is the subject of the statement, the predicate is a specified relation that links the subject, and the object is the value assigned to the subject through the predicate.
[4] OWL is the W3C recommendation for the creation of new ontology optimized for the Web. The Web Ontology Language OWL is a semantic markup language for publishing and sharing ontologies on the World Wide Web. OWL is developed as a vocabulary extension of RDF, and it is derived from the DAML+OIL Web Ontology Language. For these reasons it provides a greater machine interpretability of Web content than the one supported by its predecessors. Essentially, with OWL one can describe a specific domain in terms of class, properties, and individuals. It has three increasingly expressive sublanguages: OWL Lite, OWL DL, and OWL Full.
[5] SCORM (Sharable Courseware Object Reference Model) is a suite of technical standards that enable Web-based learning systems to find, import, share, reuse, and export learning content in a standardized way. It is a specification of the Advanced Distributed Learning Initiative (*http://www.adlnet.org/*).

This work was previously published in Social Information Retrieval Systems: Emerging Technologies and Applications for Searching the Web Effectively, edited by D. Goh and S. Foo, pp. 270-288, copyright 2008 by Information Science Reference (an imprint of IGI Global).

Chapter XV
A Semantic Web Based Approach for Context-Aware User Query Formulation and Information Retrieval

Hanh Huu Hoang
Vienna University of Technology, Austria

Tho Manh Nguyen
Vienna University of Technology, Austria

A Min Tjoa
Vienna University of Technology, Austria

ABSTRACT

Formulating unambiguous queries in the Semantic Web applications is a challenging task for users. This article presents a new approach in guiding users to formulate clear requests based on their common nature of querying for information. The approach known as the front-end approach gives users an overview about the system data through a virtual data component which stores the extracted metadata of the data storage sources in the form of an ontology. This approach reduces the ambiguities in users' requests at a very early stage and allows the query process to effectively perform in fulfilling users' demands in a context-aware manner. Furthermore, the approach provides a powerful query engine, called context-aware querying, that recommends the appropriate query patterns according to the user's querying context.

MOTIVATION

The Semantic Web and ontologies have created a promising background for applying the intelligent techniques in information systems, especially in personal information management (PIM) systems. In PIM systems, effectively retrieving information from a huge amount data of an individual is a challenging issue. The virtual query system (VQS) (Hoang, Andjomshoaa, & Tjoa, 2006) of the SemanticLIFE framework is an approach of using semantic Web techniques with a user-oriented method in order to tackle this challenge.

The SemanticLIFE project (Ahmed, Hoang, Karim, Khusro, Lanzenberger, Latif et al., 2004) is an effort to realize Vanevar Bush's vision of Memex (Bush, 1945) by providing a general semantic PIM system. The SemanticLIFE system integrates a wide variety of data sources and stores them in an ontological repository. In the VQS-enhanced SemanticLIFE, the user is supported in issuing imprecise queries to retrieve the rich semantic information from the user's historical personal data. However, users themselves often do not actually know or remember the specific qualities of what they are looking for, but have some awareness of other things related to the desired items (Quan, Huynh, & Karger, 2003). The VQS supports users in this nature when querying the information from the huge ontological repository effectively not only in the initial phase with offered "virtual information" but during the query process with the "context-based" querying features.

Furthermore, as mentioned above, the user's nature of asking questions is that the user often does not know what the user is looking for; but the user remembers some concepts about related information the user is looking for. This leads us to a way of querying (browsing/navigating) the system by using redefined query templates (patterns) based on the user's querying context.

This would help the user not to be embarrassed in a new phase of query formulation.

The difficulty of query formulation appears not only in the initial phase but it continues in the query process or query refinement. During the query process, the user is asked for new requests using the new knowledge to get the information of interest. In order to ease the user from thinking of new constraints of their queries, we propose a new way based on the users' nature, that is, preferring to customize the query patterns to make new queries. We trace the context of the user's query process and recommend to the user the appropriate query patterns matching up the user's query context.

Our approach originates from the user-side manner in trying to formulate unambiguous requests as early as possible during the querying process. The principle of the approach follows "better known, clearer request" and "customizing than creating." If users are aware of what information they possess, they could ask precise queries against their stored data. This helps the query refinement process of the system by eliminating ambiguities at a very early stage of the query process. These approaches resulted in our query system, the VQS for the SemanticLIFE framework, with a query language called the virtual query language, and with a new way of query formulation entitled *pattern-based* and *context-aware* querying process.

The remainder of this article is organized as follows. The related work to our research is mentioned in Section 2. An overview of the SemanticLIFE project and the VQS is underlined in Section 3. Section 5 describes the details of the "virtual data component." Section 6 presents the VQS's innovative feature for query formulation and information retrieval. Main points of the VQS implementation are pointed out in Section 8. A summarized example is presented in the Section 9. Finally, the article is concluded with a sketch of the intended future work in Section 10.

RELATED WORK

Research activities in ontology-based search/query systems could be classified in to variant categories (Hoang & Tjoa, 2006). In this section we only present two related issues: (a) ontology-enhanced search strategies and (b) query formulation.

Ontology-Enhanced Search Strategies

With the help of ontology technique, OntoLoger (Stojanovic, Gonzalez, & Stojanovic, 2003) builds a query mechanism by recording the user's behaviors in an ontology and recalling it. OntoLoger, similarly to its general version of the Library Agent (Stojanovic, 2003), is a query system based on usage analysis in the ontology-based information portals. Its query mechanism is based on usage-data in form of an ontology, so-called semantic log file. The structure of the ontology reflects the users' needs. By using this, OntoLoger supports the user in fine-tuning of the user's initial query. Moreover, during the refinement process, the system also uses this log ontology for ranking query results and refinements according to the user's needs.

GeoShare (Hübner, Spittel, Visser, & Vögele, 2004) uses ontologies for describing vocabularies and catalogs as well as search mechanisms for keywords to capture more meaning. During the search process, the user narrows a search space's size by selecting specific domain (thematic, spatial, or temporal model). Then the user picks the appropriate concepts from these models and application ontologies, covering all available concepts, to define the concrete query. After that, the user can parameterize the user's query to concertize the retrieval process. In the sequel, the system processes the query and transforms it into the ontology language for the terminological part, where the system looks for equivalent concepts and subconcepts. After processing the query,

the system composes a ranked list of relevant information providers based on the weightings of a specific reasoning process.

Semantic Web data consist of ontological and instance data. The actual data the user is interested in are entities belonging to a class, but the domain knowledge and relationships are described primarily as class relationships in the ontology, and this is exemplified in the SHOE search system (Heflin & Hendler, 2000). In SHOE, the user is first provided a visualization of the ontology, and the user can choose the class of instances the user is looking for. The possible relationships or properties associated with the class are then searched, and the user constrains the instances by applying keyword filters to the various instance properties. A similar approach is also applied in some versions of the SEAL portal (Maedche, Staab, Stojanovic, Studer, & Sure, 2001) and Ontobroker (Decker, Erdmann, Fensel, & Studer, 1998).

However, there are some differences between these systems in their usage ontologies. In SHOE, providers of information can introduce arbitrary extensions to a given ontology. Furthermore, no central provider index is defined. In contrast, Ontobroker relies on the notion of an Ontogroup (Decker et al., 1998) and domain specific ontology defining a group of Web users that agree on an ontology for a given subject.

In a further effort of the above approaches, the authors of Haystack (Huynh, Karger, & Quan, 2002) based their user interface paradigm almost completely on browsing from resource to resource (Quan et al., 2003). This is affirmed by scientific results of a search behavior research (Teevan, Alvarado, Ackerman, & Karger, 2004) that actually most human beings seek information via a process they call "orienteering" rather than carefully formulating a query that precisely defines the desired information target. Users often prefer to start from a familiar location, or a vague search, and "home in" on the desired information through a series of associative steps (Karger, Bakshi, Huynh, Quan, & Vineet, 2005).

Query Formulation

There are two main approaches to reduce the difficulty in formulating queries from user-side. The first trend is going to design a friendly and interactive query interfaces to guide users in generating the queries. The high-rated examples for this trend are geographical RQL (GRQL) (Athanasis, Christophides, & Kotzinos, 2004) and SEWASIE (Catarci, Di Mascio, Franconi, Santucci, & Tessaris, 2003).

GRQL relies on the full power of the RDF/S data model for constructing on the fly queries expressed in RQL (Karvounarakis, Alexaki, Christophides, Plexousakis, & Scholl, 2002). More precisely, a user can first graphically navigate through the individual RDF/S class and property definitions, then transparently generate the required RQL path expressions required to access the resources of interest. These expressions accurately capture the meaning of its navigation steps through the class (or property) subsumption and/or associations. Additionally, users can enrich the generated queries with filtering conditions on the attributes of the currently visited class by specifying the resource's class(es) appearing in the query result.

Another graphical query generation interface is SEWASIE. As a starting point, the user is provided some preprepared domain-specific patterns to choose from as a starting point, which the user can then extend and customize. The refinements to the query can either be additional property constraints to the classes or a replacement of another compatible class in the pattern such as a subclass or superclass. This is performed through a clickable graphic visualization of the neighborhood ontology of the currently selected class.

The second approach of reducing complexity is the effort in creating much lighter query languages than expressive RDF query languages. Following this trend, the approach by Guha and McCool (2003), known as GetData query interface, is a typical example. GetData query interface of TAP[1] expresses the need of a much lighter weight interface for constructing complex queries. The idea of GetData is to design a simple query interface which allows to present network accessible data as directed labeled graph. This approach provides a system which is very easy to build, and supports both type of users, data providers, and data consumers.

THE SEMANTICLIFE DIGITAL MEMORY FRAMEWORK

"SemanticLIFE"

In the physical world, entities are usually interconnected, either by physical or by semantic means; in the latter case, the semantic meaning is added by human interaction (in an abstract sense) with the physical world. Life items in the system proposed can be understood as information entities (in some cases they are representations of such physical entities) stored according to ontologies in a semantic database, which are connected to other information entities according to their semantic meaning. Also ontologies "live" in a way, as they develop and modify permanently during the system- and user-lifetime.

Current (Web) technologies are highly efficient in processing data for human reception; that is, the transformation from data to information, the "generation of meaning" is up to the human. A great deal of effort has already been made, and work is still going on to represent semantics explicitly on the Web. This is required to give computer systems the capability to enhance preprocessing of huge amounts of data for the user. It becomes more important as the "awareness radius" of the contemporary knowledge worker and consumer is continuously increasing. These results from the observation; those users do not limit their information search to specific data repositories, like searching for an address or an event in a calendar. The availability of databases under common or similar interfaces (like Web pages) creates the demand to express more complex queries demanding information aggregated from many different systems using different semantic concepts.

The proposed PIM systems can significantly contribute in overcoming the common inherent human problems such as limited short term memory, memory loss, forgetfulness, high complexity of data, and so forth. Therefore, it is useful for the system to be able to define and capture the user's life-related events and take or trigger appropriate action(s) for it. This process involves the following subprocesses:

1. Capture events and associated information.
2. Process action associated with events (e.g., in the sense of an active database system).
3. Extract metadata from the event, or allow the user to enrich the data manually with semantic meaning.
4. Store the data including semantic context as ontology in an efficient manner.
5. Allow the user to query the data or support the user directly via associated applications and tools with context-sensitive information or action.

Additionally as described by Dolog, Henze, Nejdl, and Sintek (2003), the system is able to adjust to new user features derived from user interactions with the system or from the information being fed. Thus each user may have individual views and navigational possibilities for working with the system. From the technology perspective, new technologies emerge and older ones fade out. If a system has a too tight coupling with some technology, it may become obsolete with the change in technology. A layered approach that provides some extent of separation from the technology is more suitable, making the overall structure still work if there is a change in the technology or even in the case of replacement by the newer ones.

The SemanticLIFE Framework

The SemanticLIFE framework is developed on a highly modular architecture to store, manage, and retrieve the lifetime's information entities of individuals. It enables the acquisition and storage of data while giving annotations to e-mail messages, browsed Web pages, phone calls, images, contacts, life events, and other resources. It also provides intuitive and effective search mechanism based upon the stored semantics, and the semantically enriched user interfaces according to the user's needs. The ultimate goal of the project is to build a PIM system over a human lifetime using ontologies as a basis for the representation of its content.

The whole SemanticLIFE system has been designed as a set of interactive plug-ins that fit into the main application and this guarantees flexibility and extensibility of SemanticLIFE platform. Communication within the system is based on a service-oriented design with the advantage of its loosely coupled characteristics. To compose complex solutions and scenarios from atomic services which are offered by SemanticLIFE plug-ins, the service oriented pipeline architecture (SOPA)[2] has been introduced. SOPA provides a paradigm to describe the system-wide service compositions and also external Web services as pipelines. SOPA provides some mechanisms for orchestration of services and transformation of results.

The SemanticLIFE's system architecture overview is depicted in Figure 1. Data with user annotation is fed into the system using a number of dedicated plug-ins from variety of data sources such as Google Desktop[3] captured data, communication logs, and other applications' metadata. The data objects are transferred to the analysis plug-in via the message handler. The analysis plug-in contains a number of specific plug-ins which provides the semantic mark-up by applying a bunch of feature extraction methods and indexing techniques in a cascaded manner. The semistructured and semantically enriched

Figure 1. The architecture of the SemanticLIFE framework

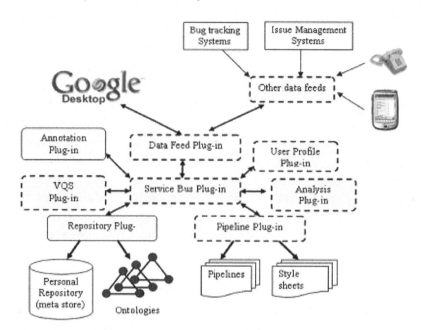

information objects are then ontologically stored via the repository plug-in. In the SemanticLIFE system, data sources are stored in forms of RDF[4] triples with their ontologies and metadata. This repository is called a metastore.

A set of query processing and information visualization tools provides the means for information exploration and report generation. The analysis module and metadata extraction capabilities make associations between the lifetime items/objects and the lifetime events based on user annotation, user profiles, and the system ontologies.

THE VIRTUAL QUERY SYSTEM

An Overview

Formulating nonambiguous queries is always a too demanding task to users as they do not have the awareness of the semantics of the stored information. The goal of the VQS is to overcome this problem by providing an ontology-based virtual information view of the data available in the sys-

tem. If the user can "be aware of" what is inside of the system the use can clearly specify the queries on the "real" data stored in the repository.

The VQS system is primarily based on the reduction of semantic ambiguities of the user query specifications at the very early stage of the retrieving process. The most important point in the VQS approach is that it provides an image of the real system data sources to the user. The user is aware of the data stored in the system when the user generates the queries. As a result, the ambiguities in the user's requests will be much reduced.

As depicted in Figure 2, with the support of a virtual data component containing metadata of real data sources, the user can generate the virtual query against the virtual data. The VQS then analyzes the virtual query based on a common ontology mapped from local ontologies of data sources and user ontology. As the result, subqueries from initial query are generated for the specific underlined data sources. Finally, the results of subqueries are aggregated and represented to the user with regarding the user's profile.

Figure 2. The components and architecture of the virtual query system

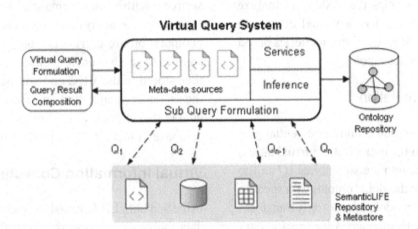

VQS Main Components

The Virtual Data Component

The virtual data component (VDC) contains the metadata of storage sources. This VQS crucial module acts as a virtual information layer to be delivered to the user. It enables the user to be aware of the semantics of the data sources stored and to specify more precise queries.

The VQS collects metadata from data sources in the metadata repository of the SemanticLIFE system. An analysis process is carried out on these metadata sources to get the semantic information. Then the processed information is stored in this module as a *context ontology*. Furthermore, this part is also referred as an image of the system database in further query processing, so-called the *context-aware querying*, which is discussed in detail later on.

The VQS system, with the organization of the "virtual data component" as a context ontology, will guide its users through the system by intelligently recommended query patterns based on the current query context, so-called query space, and that context ontology (the virtual data). In our "front-end" approach, this is the most crucial feature that is different to the current ontology-based query systems (Hoang & Tjoa, 2006a).

The rational behind the idea of this approach is that when users are aware of their data then they could formulate more unambiguous requests. This ultimately leads to the reduction of the query refinement process complexity. Additionally, this VDC plays as a context ontology. This makes the SemanticLIFE system very flexible as the system can adapt to a new scenario by simply changing the context ontology

The VQS Services

- **Ontology Mapping:** This service deals with mapping concepts from the system ontology to the context ontology, including the instances. It can deal with new data sources added with their respective ontologies, so that these ontologies are mapped or integrated to the global ontology. In our approach, we do not reinvest to develop a new ontology mapping framework. Instead, we use the mapping framework (MAFRA) (Maedche, Motik, Silva, & Volz, 2002) for our mapping tasks.
- **Inference:** The ontology-based inference service provides a basis for the deduction process on the relationships (rules) of concepts of the ontologies specified. Inference tasks are performed on the foundation of the

ontologies and the data described by them. This service helps the system to analyze and evaluate the user's virtual queries in the process of generating subqueries based on the inference ontology.

Subquery Formulation

Subqueries formulation is another essential part of the VQS. From the user's initial virtual query, this part parses it into the subqueries (Q_i in the Figure 2) based on the global ontology for specific data sources. This module does not only transform the virtual query to subqueries for specific data sources but additionally perform inference on the user's request in order to create more possible subqueries afterward.

Query Refinement

This is the interactive way (semiautomated) for the VQS dealing with user's ambiguous queries, which is based on incrementally and interactively (step-by-step) tailoring a query to the current information needs of a user (Quan et al., 2003). This VQS service is a semiautomated process, that is, the user is provided with a ranked list of refinements, which leads to a decrease of some of these ambiguities.

THE VIRTUAL DATA COMPONENT

The Goals

From the user perspective, the VDC plays an important role in the process of query generation in the VQS approach. The core of the VDC is the module containing the metadata storage sources (MSS). This module acts as a virtual information layer allowing the user to be aware of the meaning of the stored data sources and the user can then specify more precise queries as the result.

The VDC harvests the metadata of the data sources within the SemanticLIFE metadata repository. An analysis process and a statistical computation are carried out on these metadata sources to get the semantic information which is then stored in the VDC and will be delivered to the user query generation interface. This component is also referred as an "image" of the system database in further query processing.

Virtual Information Collecting

In the SemanticLIFE metastore, there are different data sources' ontologies that exist along with the instances. The SemanticLIFE system manages a huge range of data from common personal information such as contacts, calendar, tasks, notes, documents, files, phone calls, instant messaging logs, and so on, to general data such as maps and weather information (Ahmed et al., 2004).

Figure 3 presents the data feeds covered by the SemanticLIFE framework in the current prototype. The data feeds are about the personal data of an individual's diary. From this ontology and the underlined instances, a VDC service is called to extract the metadata, perform some sta-

Figure 3. A fragment of the SemanticLIFE's datafeeds ontology

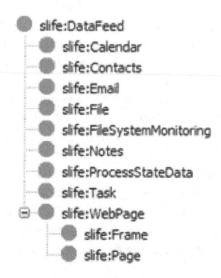

320

tistical computation, and store the information in a new ontology, called the context ontology. This ontology is used in the VDC to provide semantic information on the corresponding data sources to the users.

As mentioned, the core of the VDC is a synthesis ontology which is formed from these variety datafeeds ontologies. This task has been done by using MAFRA ontologies merging framework, with "semantic bridge concept" (Maedche et al., 2002), as the mapping service to merge the ontologies. The process consists of aligning the schemes and merging the instances as well.

Context-Based Support of the VDC

The loosely-coupled organization of the metadata storage sources (an ontology of the "virtual information") reflects the flexibility of the virtual query system as well as the SemanticLIFE system. Based on this ontology, the context-based query templates are also categorized according to the concepts. We can apply the VQS or the SemanticLIFE system in different contexts by simply making changes of this ontology.

The metadata storage sources are constructed as an ontolog,y namely context metadata or context ontology. By doing the taxonomy and reasoning on the concepts and also on the instances, the metadata could be classified into the categories and the data are arranged into the relevant ontology dependent on the context that the SemanticLIFE framework is used for.

Figure 4 shows the ontology constructed by mapping data sources' schemes and the instances. The ontology in the figure is an ontology for a personal diary recording the daily activities of an individual who works in some projects. The extracted metadata will be fetched from system datafeeds ontologies and put into the VDC's context ontology and conformed to its hierarchy. For example, the "Place" class is an abstract concept and formed from classes "Contact," annotations,

Figure 4. An example of the virtual data component ontology

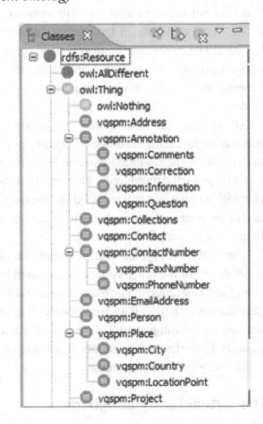

maps, and their instances. This makes the semantic information to become more contextual, and we call this process the concept contextualization.

Definition 1: *A concept contextualization, Con, in VQS is a transformation of concept (class) C of system ontology, O_1, to the context ontology, O_2. The relationships between C and other concepts in O_2 will be reformed.*

Con: $\langle C, O_1 \rangle \mapsto \langle C, O_2 \rangle$

Hence, the context ontology could be redefined based on the concept contextualization as follows:

Definition 2: *The concept ontology, CO, of the VDC is:*
$CO = Con_i$

where, n is the number of concepts.

The metadata in the VDC's context ontology ("context ontology" in short) is still associated to the "real" metadata in the system ontology. The metadata in the new context is used for the VQS's purposed in rendering information for presentation and reasoning during the querying process.

Additionally, the VDC contains the summary information for each data sources over the customized timelines such as total items and the number of items for each data sources. This provides the user with a very good awareness about the user's data in the system. As a result, the user can query the necessary statistic information.

The VDC is the typical feature of our system compared with the other systems mentioned by Hoang and Tjoa (2006a). The basic idea behind it is quite simple: if the user is aware of the user's data, then the user could generate more unambiguous requests. In one hand, this reduces the complexity of the query refinement process.

The Virtual Query Language

The VQL (Hoang & Tjoa, 2006b) is designed for the VQS. The VQL aims to be a lighter weight query language which supports "semantic" queries on the ontological RDF-based storages. VQL is very easy to build and use and to be supported. In context of the VQS, the aims of VQL are as follow:

- VQL helps the clients in making queries without the knowledge of RDF query languages. The user just gives basic parameters of request information in VQL, and would receive the expecting results.
- VQL assists users in navigating the system via semantic links/associations, categorized context queries provided in the powerful query operators based on ontologies.

An example of VQL queries is depicted in Listing 1 in which the VQL query is called "RE-LATED-WITH" query (Hoang & Tjoa, 2006b). This query retrieves the related information from data sources of E-mail and Contact to the e-mail address hta@gmx.at.

The VQL is modeled in extensible markup language (XML)[5] with three supported types: data query type, schema query type, and embedded query types for their own goals. The "data" queries are used to retrieve the data from the SemanticLIFE metastore. The "schema" queries are used to get information from the system's ontologies. The "embedded" queries contain the RDF query statements, which are preprocessed to make the query items unambiguous, transfer them to the execution unit to be executed, and get the results back.

The VQL is designed to help the user easily generate requests according to their nature: *minimum of words, maximum of results*. In order to fulfill this principle, the VQL defines the *virtual query operators* which allow the user to simplify the complex queries:

- *GetInstances* operator is the common form of VQL data queries. The operator retrieves the appropriate information according to the criteria described in the parameters, sources, and constraints of the query.
- *GetInstanceMetadata* operator assists the user in easily retrieving all metadata properties and correspondent result instances. This query operator is very useful when the user does not know exactly what properties of data instances are.
- *GetRelatedData* operator provides the accessible related information to the current found information. In Semantic Web applications, particularly in the SemanticLIFE system, finding relevant or associated information plays an important role.

Listing 1. An example of the VQL GetRelatedData query operator

```
<query type="data">
<params>
  <param name="p1:emailTo" show="0">hta@gmx.at</param>
  <param name="p2:RELATED-WITH" show="1"/>
</params>
<sources>
  <source name="email">Email</source>
  <source name="contact">Contact</source>
</sources>
<relations>
  <relation id="1" param="p1" source="email"/>
</relations>
<resultformat>xml</resultformat>
</query>
```

- *GetLinks* operator operates using the system's ontology and RDF graph pattern traversal to find out the associations/links between the instances and the objects.

For instance, we query for a set of instances of eimails, contacts, and appointments. Normally, we receive these data separately and what we expect here is that the associations between the results are provided additionally. The links are probably properties of e-mail addresses (i.e.,, name of the persons and locations).

- **GetFileContent operator:** The Semanti-cLIFE system covers a large range of data sources, from personal data such as contacts, appointments, and e-mails to files stored in the user's computer, for example, the office documents, PDF files, and media files. Therefore, this operator is about getting the contents of these files for further processing.

CONTEXT-AWARE QUERY FORMULATION IN THE VQS

In the VQS, the user is not only supported in the query formulation by the "virtual" information, but also during the user's querying process by a load of features, which are introduced as follows.

The VQL Query Template

A *VQL query template* (VQL-QT) is an abstract query pattern which is attached with a specific VQL query, containing the concepts and resources for the user querying process.

VQL-QTs are classified on these concepts and resources so that the appropriate template will be recommended to the user based on the user's querying context. VQL-QTs help the user in generating clear requests by only replacing the values into the selected query pattern.

VQL Query Template Syntax

In the VQS, the VQL query templates, so-called VQL query patterns (VQL-QPs), are defined to assist the user in formulating unambiguous queries. The query templates contain the VQL queries with the necessary parameters and the associated data sources. A VQL-QT or VQL-QP mainly consists of:

- A VQL query in form of a *query file name*
- *Parameters* containing the values from the user's input

- *Resources* involved in the querying process

and two optional parts:

- *Description* of the VQL-QT which is used for display to users
- *Query result format* to specify the dedicated format of the results

The structure of a VQL query template is illustrated in Figure 5, in which the components of the VQL query template are shown in a hierarchical tree.

Listing 2 is an example of a VQL query template. That VQL query template is about retrieving the locations of all Web pages found by Google search engine[6] and these Web pages have been browsed by a given person in a period of time. The related sources for the retrieving process are mentioned in the <resources> part. The parameters are put in subparts <param> and these parameters could be changed or added by the user according the information of interest.

Figure 5. The schema of the VQL query template

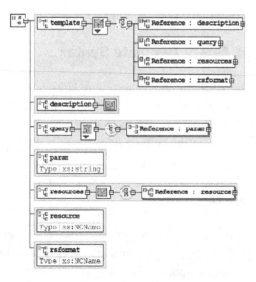

VQL Query Template in Use

The VQL query templates are classified on the concepts of the VDC's context ontology as well as their involved data sources, so-called resources. The concepts of the VDC's context ontology are reflected in parameters of the VQL-QPs. Based on this classification, the VQS will match the VQL-QTs with the user query context and the appropriate VQL-QP will be delivered to the user as a recommendation. When the template is in use, the attached VQL query will be loaded and its variables are then replaced by the template's parameters. The VQL query could be continually edited by the user afterward dependent on the user's interest.

Furthermore, during the VQS user's querying process, a new VQL-QT could be also created. The new VQL-QTs creation can be carried out in two ways: first, it comes from an analysis based on the querying context of the user; second, from the editing of an existing VQL-QT (the user could need to save for later use in the form of another VQL-QT).

VQS User Context

Definition 3: *The VQS user context (VQS-UC) is a set of requested concepts from the context ontology linked to the system ontologies and associated resources, as well as the properties that are in action. Let call U is a VQS-UC, we have:*

Con: $\langle C, R, P \rangle$

where C is the set of the underlying concepts, R is a set of associated resources, and P is a set of queried properties.

In general, in order to formulate a VQS-UC, an analysis process is carried out based on the objects in the querying process. The analysis process counts on the following metadata:

Listing 2. A VQL query template example

```
<template type="vql">
<description>Finding a location of webpage browsed by a person using Googl search engine</de-
scription >
<query name="webpersonse.vql">
 <param>?location</param>
 <param>?tiemStamp</param>
 <param>?person</param >
</query>
<resources>
 <resource>Webpage</resource>
 <resource>Location</resource>
 <resource>Person</resource>
</resources>
<rsformat>xml</rsformat>
</templates>
```

- Querying concepts, their associated resources (based on the system ontologies), and the querying properties.
- The detected semantic links (obtained from VQL's *GetLinks* operator) would help in terms of finding the relationships of the information.
- The query results the last execution of the user's querying process.

A VQS-UC is used to keep the user's querying concepts and querying space, that is, about how the concepts and query results are associated. From that, the new knowledge will be deducted for ideas of further requests.

VQS Query Map

A *VQS query map* (VQS-QM) is a network of VQL query tem-plates, in which the nodes are the VQL query templates and the connections are the related concepts and their properties. $M = \langle T, C, P \rangle$ is a VQS-QM, where T is the set of VQL-QTs, C is the set of concepts of the underlying resources, and P is the set of querying properties.

Generally, with the associated data sources and the VDC's context ontology, the VQL query template creates a *query map* to make the connection network among the templates and underlined resources.

According to the connections between the templates, when a VQL-QT is chosen for making the new queries, the system also recommends the linked VQL-QTs. Besides, when the user selects one or more properties to generate a query, the system could also recommend the relevant templates to the user based on the query map. The connections in the query map are used to determine which templates could be used.

Context-Aware Querying Process

The virtual data component also enhances the query process by a "context-based" querying feature, that is, the query patterns will be proposed by the system according to the context where the user is in. However, a user's query context not only contains all the queried objects and the querying concepts but they are also associated to each other based on the context ontology.

How could the VDC recommend the relevant templates to the user? During context-based information retrieval process, the VDC will do following steps:

1. Keeping track on the concepts queried by the user.
2. From these queried concepts, a context of the user's querying process will be formed. The

context is a graph of queried and querying concepts.

3. When the user asks for a new template from the user's querying context through an interactive interface, then a match of the query map in the virtual data component and the user's querying context will be made.

4. The query patterns/templates will be collected and offered to the user.

For example, the context query being applied is about project management which contains the concepts of project, person, document, publication, partner, time, location, and so on. The user's query context could be a graph of *person, location,* and *Web search for project* as depicted in Figure 6. In this case a query template such as *"finding a person I have contacted in Vienna in a related project found by Google search engine"* will be proposed.

This feature is applied in the VQS's interactive interface, in which the user can right click on the results objects, instance,s or virtual data objects and the system will show dedicated templates based on the user's context.

Context-Aware Query Results Representation

The query results back to the VQS according to the schema the SemanticLIFE metastore. Therefore,

for the user's information consuming, the results is put into the "context" of the query concerning the VDC's ontology before presenting to the user as depicted in Figure 7.

As described in the figure, the results from the SemanticLIFE metastore are based on the system ontologies; therefore, via the VDC, the query results are contextualized with the VDC's context ontology. Moreover, based on the VDC's ontology, the related information associated to the relationships within its hierarchy is also presented as the recommendation to the user.

SEMANTIC NAVIGATION WITH THE VQS

VQS Semantic Traces

The traces are to keep tracing on successful querying sessions. VQS keeps traces in form of query pipelines with annotation and classification, that is, every trace is attached with pipelines, used resources, and annotation of each pipeline.

Definition 4: *A trace is an extended pipeline with the user's annotation and the context applied. Let us call T as a trace and we have:*

$$T = \{P_i, CT_i\}_{i=1-n}$$

Figure 6. An example of context-based querying

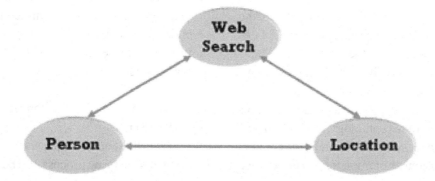

Figure 7. The process of returning query results in the VQS

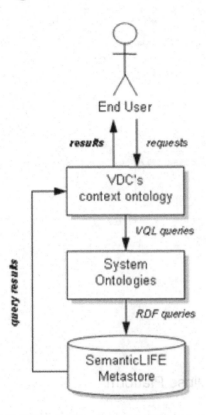

where T is an n-element ordered set with P_i is the ith query pipeline and CT_i is the attached i^{th} context, which is a finite set of m concepts:

$$CT = \{C_k\}_{k=1-m}$$

where C_k is a concept.

Based on these traces, the users could resume and restore last querying sessions. Moreover the traces could be used as the guidelines for the new querying processes as the recommendations.

Context-Aware System Navigation

The VQS is aiming at not only information retrieval aspects, but in inventing a new way of query and processes the query results for the next round. With help of the VQS-UC, VQS-QTs, VQS

semantic traces, the feature of system navigation by semantics (*semantic navigation*) is realized.

Initially, the VQS's user would generate a new query based on the virtual information of the VDC. The user could also select from the commonly used VQL-QTs and customize according the user's interest. After this initial phase, the user enters the process of retrieving information; the system helps the user for the next query formulation. This could be done based on many VQS's features such as the user's querying context, the user's query map, the query patterns in form of the VQL-QTs, as well as the query results, especially the results of the VQL operators which is rich of semantics.

In addition of the semantic traces, the VQS supports the user through the system by navigating source-by-source and concept-by-concept, which would entertain the user by suggestions and offered query patterns associated with the user's querying space (query context and query map).

THE VQS IMPLEMENTATION

VQS Workflow

The detailed workflow of the VQS is described in the UML sequence diagram depicted in Figure 8. Here, at first, is a process of fetching metadata from the SemanticLIFE metastore and organized then into the VDC of the VQS as the context ontology. This process only run once and it would be updated if the ontologies of metastore are changed.

First, as described in the Figure 8 in the phase of query formulation, the user could use the VQL query templates which are predefined query patterns of the VQS. This helps the users in the first steps. The VQL-QTs could be retrieved directly by the user with(out) referring to the selective information of the VDC. Moreover, after the initial phase, the VQL-QTs would be offered automatically based on the user query context.

Figure 8. VQS workflow in its UML sequence diagram

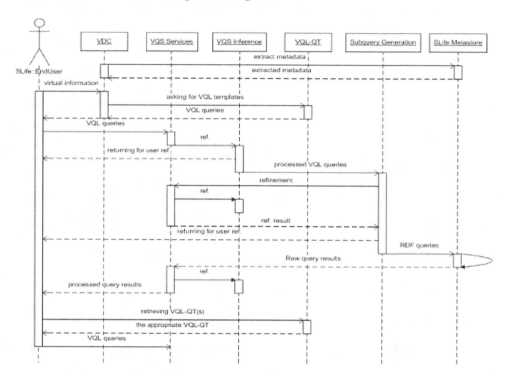

Next, the VQL queries delivered to the subqueries generation phase are semantically clarified based on the system ontologies. The query refinement is performed semiautomatically. Referring to the VQS services to detect the ambiguities during this phase, the generated subqueries are updated by the user if necessary as a feedback to finalize the execution of the RDF queries. Finally, the query results are again "contextualized" by VQS services before representing to the user.

The Used Techniques

In the VQS implementation, we have taken the SemanticLIFE architecture as the baseline and inherited the innovative features of the Eclipse platform. We have used the Java open-source frameworks in form of the Semantic Web applications, the ontology engineering, and the Web services.

The Eclipse Platform

The Eclipse platform gives a technical background not only for developing the basic SemanticLIFE architecture, but also its modules as plug-ins using Eclipse PDE. In the development of the VQS and its components, the help of PDE, RCP, and SWT is very valuable.

The Semantic Web Framework

The Semantic Web framework is mainly used in our development is the Jena Semantic Web Framework[7] of HP Labs. Jena is a leading Java framework in the area of building Semantic Web applications. Jena provides a programmatic environment for RDF, RDFS, OWL, and SPARQL, and includes a rule-based inference engine. Jena is open source and grown out of work with the HP Labs Semantic Web research[8].

With the new releases (since version 2.4), Jena has integrated the Lucene index engine[9] to provide a powerful full-text searching feature for the SPARQL query language. This help to increase the precision in searching documents in the SemanticLIFE framework.

The Ontology Mapping Framework

MAFRA is a conceptual description of the ontology mapping process. Ontology mapping is the process where semantic relations are defined between two ontologies at the conceptual level which in turn are applied at data level transforming source ontology instances into target ontology instances.

The MAFRA toolkit[10] implements a specific architecture for MAFRA. The architecture of the system is based on the notion of service which represents not only the system transformation capabilities, but also the expertise in the manipulation of specific semantic relations.

The Web Services Framework

Finally, for the backbone of the whole system, which connects the services extensions offered and invokes the services or related tasks, the Apache Web Services frameworks[11] have been used in our SemanticLIFE development. The VQS service development inherits from the baseline system for its service extension development.

The XML Parser

A XML parser is an essential part in our approach and development. Our VQL queries, VQL query templates, query pipelines, and traces are coded in XML-format. With the enhanced features, we choose DOM4J[12] as our XML parser in the VQS development.

The VQS Plug-ins

The VQS implementation has been developed with three plug-ins: the core query execution unit, the VQS components, and the VQS query GUI plug-ins.

Query Execution Plug-in

This plug-in is the lowest component in the VQS architecture as it works directly with the back-end database. The query execution unit contains internal service extensions such as the query execution, the query results transformation (e.g., transforming the query results to the specific format such as XML, JSON, RDF graphs, or formatted text), and an aggregated query invocation that consists of the query execution and results transformations. The declaration of this plug-in into the SemanticLIFE master service is shown in the Figure 9.

VQS Components Plug-in

This plug-in is the main implementation of our query system which contains the main features of the VQS. The services are mostly for internal use of the VQS querying process; however, some service extensions are offered to other external uses such as getting the "virtual" information, retrieving the VQS-UC, executing VQL queries, and getting the VQL-QT(s). The declaration of the VQS components plug-in into the SemanticLIFE framework is shown in Figure 10.

VQS User Interface Plug-in

This plug-in is the top layer in the VQS architecture as it works interactively with the SemanticLIFE's users. The query interface plug-in consists of functional windows (views) built on Eclipse RCP ViewParts and SWT widgets. These components are then organized in a separate Eclipse perspec-

Figure 9. The declaration of the query execution plug-in

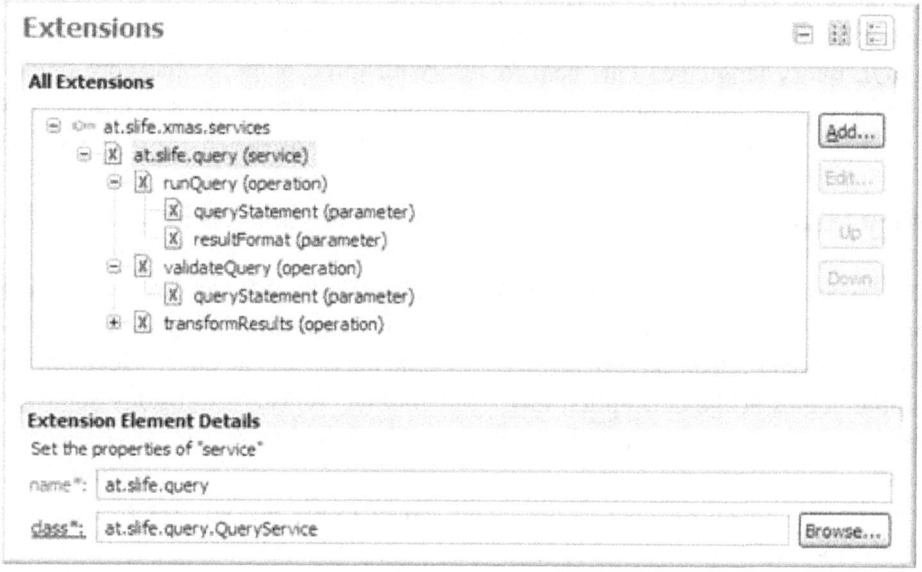

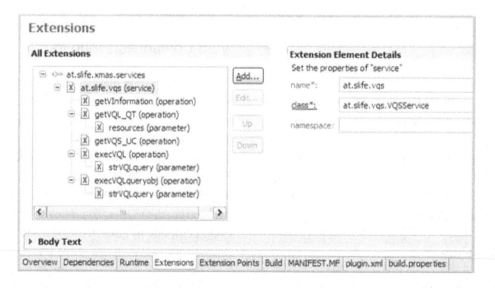

Figure 10. The declaration of the VQS components plug-in

tive associated with the main SemanticLIFE perspective. The declaration of the query interface plug-in into the "backbone" of the SemanticLIFE framework is shown in the Figure 11.

With the above declarations, each plug-in needs an interface to "plug" (register) into the SemanticLIFE plug-in infrastructure so that when the main application runs, all registered plug-ins will automatically be loaded.

The Virtual Data Component

As mentioned in the previous section, the VDC contains the virtual information stored in a context ontology. The context ontology can be customized by the usage of the system and the user. For example, the system could have been used in use case of personal project management system;

Figure 11. The declaration of the query interface plug-in

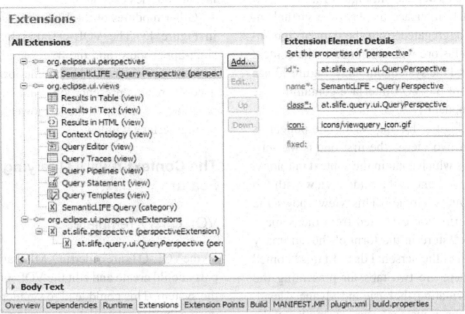

Figure 12. Project management context ontology diagram

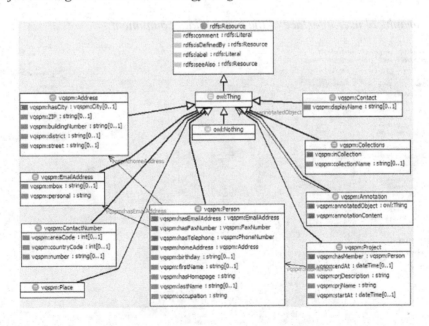

therefore the VDC's context ontology would reflect the scenario as depicted in Figure 12.

The VDC interface displays the virtual information aggregated from the data of SemanticLIFE metastore with reference to the context ontology and the system ontology. Figure 13 is a screenshot of the VQS interface containing the VDC component.

In the Figure 13, the VDC component is reflected in two views: the first one is the left-upper views which contain the context ontology, and the second one is the middle view with tab entitled "Query Home." This view shows the virtual information extracted from the SemanticLIFE metastore in the form of the summary information of the personal data. In this "home" window, there are two tabs for presenting the virtual information: the basic and advanced level. The basic view is just for basic information of the user's personal data and the advanced view presents additional information such as time-based

statistical information, last ten items stored, and last ten queries executed.

Other modules of the VQS are also depicted in Figure 13. The VQL-QT(s) is listed in the right-upper view, and the traces are kept in the right-lower window. The middle-lower part is used for results presentation. Finally, the query pipelines are shown in the left-lower view of the main interface window.

The Context-Aware Querying Feature

VQL Query Templates

As the VQL-QTs are coded in XML that means any party could create and edit the VQL-QTs outside the system. This could lead to syntactical errors during the query template processing. Therefore, we have built a validity checking mechanism for VQL-QTs based on its XSD schema.

Figure 13. The graphical user interface of the virtual data component

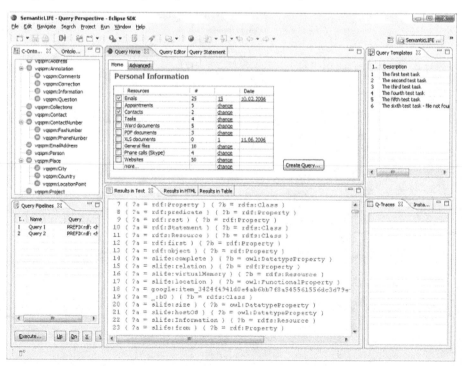

There are two cases of performing this check. First, when the VQS system starts, all VQL-QTs are checked for their validity. Second, this checking procedure will be called upon and a VQL-QT is loaded for using.

The Context-Based Querying

Figure 14 shows the sequence diagram of the VQS context-based querying feature. We make it clear that this feature would be initialized after the first query is successfully executed. First, based on the VQS-UC the necessary resources for the next query are obtained with respect to the context ontology; VQS then retrieves the VQL-QT repository to get the appropriate VQL-QT upon the resources.

The VQL-QT is then returned to the user for editing. Continuously, a procedure of the VQS would consult to the current query map and recommend the relevant VQL-QT(s) to the user.

After execution of the VQL query from the selected VQL-QT, the system will update the VQS-UC for the next round of the querying process. This process will reflect in the change of the VQL-QT view in the VQS GUI main window. The updated VQL-QT view contains only the VQL-QT(s) for the current VQS-UC. Nevertheless, there is an option to see all VQL-QTs at this time.

During the querying process, the user could temporarily save the queries in the form of "traces" shown in the "Traces" window in the main GUI screen. In addition, the user can save the traces into permanent query pipelines for later use because the traces will be removed for the next start of the system. The user could also add, change, or delete the inappropriate VQL-QT(s) to improve the user's query effectiveness.

THE SUMMARIZED EXAMPLE

After having introduced the VQS approach for the ontology-enhanced querying of SemanticLIFE, we want to illustrate in this article by means of an application scenario how our approach could be practically applied and what benefits it offers. This section is a summary of the examples segmented into the previous sections.

Personalized Project Management

A scientist works for several projects at the same time with different roles. Everyday the scientist has a lot of work to do such as reading and sending a lot of e-mails to projects' members, making many phone calls, processing digital documents, browsing the Web sites for tasks, reading the paper/articles, and coding at times. Generally,

Figure 14. UML sequence diagram of the VQS context-based query

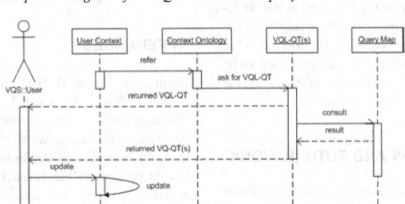

the scientist often makes annotation on what the scientist has done.

The scientist wants the SemanticLIFE system to organize the scientist's large repository in a semantic way in order to retrieve effectively. Searching information in a "mountain" of data of working projects is a challenging task for the scientist. The scientist would like to have the support through the SemanticLIFE's query mechanism, the VQS, to simplify the task of information retrieval.

VQS Contextualization

First, the SemanticLIFE will deal with the issues related to storing data semantically with the user's annotation. A range of covered data could be e-mail messages, contacts (persons), calendar for storing appointments, tasks for keeping projects' tasks and progresses, digital documents, call logs, IM logs, Web browsing sessions, and external publication databases. All these data are kept in the SemanticLIFE metastore with underline ontologies.

Second, the main focus of the example is about the information retrieval in the context of the SemanicLIFE's VQS. This task is divided into two subparts. First, the query formulation should be simple to the user so that the user could have the supportive feeling during the user's information retrieval sessions. The second point is the capabilities of the VQS in returning the aggregated, exact results has the user's interest as well as associated information that may be helpful for the user. It means the VQL-QTs are oriented to the subject of scenario, and the query results must be based on the context ontology for suggesting the information as relevant as possible.

CONCLUSION AND FUTURE WORK

Starting from the idea of users' awareness about their stored data which could help in asking for in-

formation, our front-approach—the virtual query system for the SemanticLIFE framework—offers many features based on the well-organization of the collected metadata from the SemanticLIFE metastore. These metadata are organized as the *virtual information* and stored in an ontology, that is, the *context ontology.*

With VQS, the SemanticLIFE's user is not only supported in the query formulation at the initial phase of querying process, but also in getting help from the VQS during the process. Based on the user context of querying and the VQS's context ontology, the VQS analyzes the user's query space—known as VQS query map—for the new knowledge, and tries to match with the predefined query patterns—known as VQL query templates—and then recommends the most appropriate query patterns to the user. We have considered this feature as an innovative approach to support users in complex query formulation.

As the next steps, we plan to focus on user modeling research for applying them into the VQS's approach to improve the personal aspect of the SemanticLIFE's aims. This would enable the VQS to work towards a more user-oriented future.

ACKNOWLEDGMENT

This work has been generously supported by ASEA-UNINET.

REFERENCES

Ahmed, M., Hoang, H. H., Karim, S., Khusro, S., Lanzenberger, M., Latif, K., et al. (2004). *'SemanticLIFE' - a framework for managing information of a human lifetime.* Paper presented at the 6th International Conference on Information Integration and Web-based Applications and Services. Jarkarta: OCG Books.

Athanasis, N., Christophides, V., & Kotzinos, D. (2004). Generating on the fly queries for the Semantic Web: The ICS-FORTH graphical RQL interface (GRQL). In S. A. McIlraith, D. Plexousakis, & F. van Harmelen (Eds.), *International Semantic Web Conference* (LNCS 3298, pp. 486-501). Springer.

Bush, V. (July 1945). As we may think. *The Atlantic, 176*(1), 101-108.

Catarci, T., Di Mascio, T., Franconi, E., Santucci, G., & Tessaris, S. (2003). An ontology based visual tool for query formulation support. In R. Meersman, & Z. Tari (Eds.), *OTM Workshops* (LNCS 2889, pp. 32-43). Springer.

Decker, S., Erdmann, M., Fensel, D., & Studer, R. (1998). *Ontobroker: Ontology based access to distributed and semi-structured information.* Paper presented at the The IFIP TC2/WG 2.6 Eighth Working Conference on Database Semantics-Semantic Issues in Multimedia Systems (pp. 351-369). Deventer, The Netherlands: Kluwer.

Dolog, P., Henze, N., Nejdl, W., & Sintek, M. (2003). *Towards the adaptive Semantic Web.* Paper presented at the International Workshop on Principles and Practice of Semantic Web Reasoning (LNCS 2901, pp. 51-68). Springer.

Guha, R., & McCool, R. (2003). TAP: A Semantic Web platform. *International Journal on Computer and Telecommunications Networking, 42*(5), 557-577.

Heflin, J., & Hendler, J. (2000). *Searching the Web with SHOE.* Paper presented at the AAAI Workshop (pp. 35-40). AAAI Press.

Hoang, H. H., & Tjoa, A. M. (2006a). *The state of the art of ontology-based query systems: A comparison of current approaches.* Paper presented at the IEEE International Conference on Computing and Informatics.

Hoang, H. H., Andjomshoaa, A., & Tjoa, A. M. (2006). *VQS: An ontology-based query system for the SemanticLIFE digital memory project.* Paper presented at the 2th IFIF WG 2.14 & 4.12 International Workshop on Web Semantics - OTM06 (LNCS 4278, pp. 1796-1805). Montpellier: Springer.

Hoang, H. H., & Tjoa, A. M. (2006b). *The virtual query language for information retrieval in the SemanticLIFE framework.* Paper presented at the International Workshop on Web Information Systems Modeling - CAiSE06 (pp. 1062-1076). Luxembourg.

Hübner, S., Spittel, R., Visser, U., & Vögele, T. J. (2004). Ontology-based search for interactive digital maps. *IEEE Intelligent Systems, 19*(3), 80-86.

Huynh, D., Karger, D., & Quan, D. (2002). *Haystack: A platform for creating, organizing and visualizing information using RDF.* Paper presented at the International Workshop on the Semantic Web.

Hyvönen, E., Saarela, S., & Viljanen, K. (2003). *Ontogator: Combining view- and ontology-based search with Semantic browsing.* Paper presented at the XML Finland Conference: Open Standards, XML and the Public Sector.

Karger, D. R., Bakshi, K., Huynh, D., Quan, D., & Vineet, S. (2005). *Haystack: A general purpose information management tool for end users of semistructured data.* Paper presented at the 2nd Biennial Conference on Innovative Data Systems Research (pp. 13-26).

Karvounarakis, G., Alexaki, S., Christophides, V., Plexousakis, D., & Scholl, M. (2002). *RQL: A declarative query language for RDF.* Paper presented at the Eleventh International World Wide Web Conference (pp. 591-603). ACM Press.

Kerschberg, L., Chowdhury, M., Damiano, A., Jeong, H., Mitchell, S., Si, J., et al. (2004). *Knowledge sifter: Ontology-driven search over heterogeneous databases.* Paper presented at the

16th International Conference on Scientific and Statistical Database Management.

Maedche, A., Motik, B., Silva, N., & Volz, R. (2002). *MAFRA: An ontology mapping framework in the Semantic Web*. Paper presented at the 12th International Workshop on Knowledge Transformation.

Maedche, A., Staab, S., Stojanovic, N., Studer, R., & Sure, Y. (2001). *SEAL: A framework for developing Semantic Web portals*. Paper presented at the 18th British National Conference on Databases (pp. 1-22). London: Springer.

Quan, D., Huynh, D., & Karger, D. R. (2003). *Haystack: A platform for authoring end user Semantic Web applications*. Paper presented at the 12th International World Wide Web Conference (pp. 738-753).

Teevan, J., Alvarado, C., Ackerman, M. S., & Karger, D. R. (2004). *The perfect search engine is not enough: A study of orienteering behavior in directed search*. Paper presented at the SIGCHI Conference on Human Factors in Computing Systems (pp. 415-422). New York: ACM Press.

ENDNOTES

[1] TAP Infrastructure, http://tap.stanford.edu/

[2] JAX Innovation Award 2006 Proposal, http://www.jax-award.com/

[3] Google Desktop, http://desktop.google.com/

[4] Resource Description Framework, http://www.w3.org/RDF/

[5] eXtensible Markup Language, http://www.w3.org/XML/

[6] Google, http://www.google.com/

[7] http://jena.sourceforge.net/

[8] http://www.hpl.hp.com/semweb/

[9] http://lucene.apache.org/

[10] http://mafra-toolkit.sourceforge.net/

[11] http://ws.apache.org/

[12] http://dom4j.org/

This work was previously published in International Journal of Information Technology and Web Engineering, Vol. 3, Issue 1, edited by G. Alkhatib, pp. 1-23, copyright 2008 by IGI Publishing (an imprint of IGI Global).

Compilation of References

Aalbersberg, I. J. (1992). Incremental relevance feedback. In *SIGIR '92: Proceedings of the 15th annual international ACM SIGIR conference on Research and Development in information retrieval*, pages 11–22, Copenhagen, Denmark. ACM Press.

Aamodt, A., & Plaza, E. (1994). Case-based reasoning: Foundational issues, methodological variations, and system approaches. *AI Communications IOS Press*, 7(1), 39–59.

Abdi, H. (2007). Kendall rank correlation. In N. Salkind (Ed.), *Encyclopedia of Measurement and Statistics* (pp 508-510). Thousand Oaks, CA: Sage

Ackerman, M., & McDonald, D. (1996). *Answer garden 2: Merging organizational memory with collaborative help.* Paper presented at the Proceedings of the 1996 ACM conference on Computer supported cooperative work, Boston, Mass.

Adamic, L., & Adar, E. (2005). How to Search a Social Network. *Social Networks, 27*(3), 187-203

Adcock, J., Pickens, J., Cooper, M., Anthony, L., Chen, F., & Qvarfordt, P. (2007). FXPAL Interactive Search Experiments for TRECVID 2007. In *TRECVid2007 - Text REtrieval Conference TRECVID Workshop*, Gaithersburg, MD, USA.

Adomavicius, G., & Tuzhilin, A. (2005). Toward the next generation of recommender systems: A survey of the state-of-the-art and possible extensions. *IEEE Transactions on Knowledge and Data Engineering, 17*(6), 734–749.

Aggarwal, C. C., Wolf, J., Wu, K. L., & Yu, P. S. (1999). Horting Hatches an Egg: A New Graph-Theoretic Approach to Collaborative Filtering. *Proceedings of the Fifth ACM SIGKDD International Conference on Knowledge discovery and data mining.* San Diego, California. ACM Press p. 201-212.

Agilience. (2006). Expertise location and management. Retrieved January 3rd 2007, from http://www.agilience.com/

Agresti, A., & Winner, L. (1997). Evaluating Agreement and Disagreement Among Movie Reviewers. *Chance, 10*, 10-14.

Aha, D. W. (1998). The omnipresence of case-based reasoning in science and application. *Knowledge-Based Systems, 11*(5-6), 261–273.

Ahmed, M., Hoang, H. H., Karim, S., Khusro, S., Lanzenberger, M., Latif, K., et al. (2004). *'SemanticLIFE' - a framework for managing information of a human lifetime.* Paper presented at the 6th International Conference on Information Integration and Web-based Applications and Services. Jarkarta: OCG Books.

Ahn J., Brusilovsky, P., Grady, J., He, D., & Syn, S. Y. (2007). Open User Profiles for Adaptive News Systems: Help or Harm? In *Proceedings of the 16th International World Wide Web Conference (WWW2007)*, Banff, Alberta, Canada, May 2007.

Ahn, H. J. (2006). Utilizing Popularity Characteristics for Product Recommendation. *International Journal of Electronic Commerce, 11*(2), 59–80.

Albayrak, S., Wollny, S., Varone, N., Lommatzsch, A., & Milosevic D. (2005). Agent Technology for Personalized Information Filtering: the PIA-System. In L.M. Liebrock (Ed.), *20th Annual ACM Symposium on Applied Computing: Vol. 1. Agents, interactions, mobility, and systems* (pp. 54-59). ACM Press.

Alghoniemy, M., & Tewfik, A.H. (2000). User-defined Music Sequence Retrieval. *Proceedings of the eighth ACM international conference on Multimedia.* (pp. 356 – 358).

Al-Khalifa, H.S., & Hugh, D. (2006). The Evolution of Metadata from Standards to Semantics in E-Learning Applications. *Proceedings of Hypertext'06*, ACM Press.

Allen, R. (1990). User Models: theory, method and practice. *International Journal of Man-Machine studies, 32*, 511–543.

Alpaydin, E. (2004). *Introduction to Machine Learning. Massachusetts*, USA. MIT Press.

Andronico, A., Carbonaro, A., Colazzo, L., & Molinari, A. (2004). Personalisation services for learning management systems in mobile settings. *International Journal of Continuing Engineering Education and Lifelong Learning.*

Ankolekar, A., Krötzsch, M., Tran, T., & Vrandecic, D. (2007). The two cultures: Mashing up Web 2.0 and the Semantic Web. In C. Williamson & M.E. Zurko (GC), *International World Wide Web Conference* (*WWW 2007*): *Vol. 1. Semantic web and web 2.0* (pp. 825-834). ACM Press.

Armstrong, R., Freitag, D., Joachims T., & Mitchell T. (1995). WebWatcher: A Learning Apprentice for the World Wide Web. *In AAAI Spring Symposium on Information Gathering,* pages 6-12.

Athanasis, N., Christophides, V., & Kotzinos, D. (2004). Generating on the fly queries for the Semantic Web: The ICS-FORTH graphical RQL interface (GRQL). In S. A. McIlraith, D. Plexousakis, & F. van Harmelen (Eds.), *International Semantic Web Conference* (LNCS 3298, pp. 486-501). Springer.

Aucouturier, J. J., & Pachet, F. (2002). Scaling up Music Playlist Generation. *Proc IEEE Intl Conf on Multimedia Expo.*

Baccigalupo, C., & Plaza, E. (2007). A Case-Based Song Scheduler For Group Customized Radio. In *Proceedings of the International Conference on Case Based Reasoning (ICCBR)*. Belfast, Ireland: Springer.

Baccigalupo, C., & Plaza, E. (2007). A Case-Based Song Scheduler for Group Customised Radio. *ICCBR* 2007, LNAI 4626, pp. 433–448.

Baeza-Yates, R., & Ribeiro-Neto, B. (1999). *Modern Information Retrieval*. Addison Wesley.

Baeza-Yates, R., Calderón-Benavides, L., & Gonzalez-Caro, C. (2006). The Intention Behind Web Queries. In *Proceedings of String Processing and Information Retrieval 2006* (pp 98-109). Glasgow, Scotland.

Balabanovic, M. (1998). Exploring versus Exploiting when Learning User Models for Text Recommendation. *Journal of User Modeling and User-Adapted Interaction, 8(1)*, 71–102.

Balabanovic, M., & Shoham, Y. (1997). Content-based collaborative recommendation. *Communications of the ACM, 40(3)*, 66–72.

Baldoni, M., Baroglio, C., Henze, N. (2005). Personalization for the Semantic Web. In Eisinger, N. Maluszynski, J. (Eds.), *REWERSE 2005, LNCS 3564*, pp. 173–212, Springer-Verlag, 2005.

Balfe E., & Smyth, B. (2004). Case-based collaborative web search. In *the 7th European Conference on Advances in Case-based Reasoning (ECCBR'04)*, volume 3155 of *LNCS*, pages 489–503, Madrid, Spain, Springer.

Banerjee, S., & Pedersen, T. (2003). Extended Gloss Overlaps as a Measure of Semantic Relatedness. *Eighteenth International Joint Conference on Artificial Intelligence* (pp 805-810). Retrieved February 15, 2008, from http://citeseer.ist.psu.edu/banerjee03extended.html

Bardram, J. E. (2005). The Java Context Awareness Framework (JCAF) – a service infrastructure and programming framework for context-aware applications. In H.W. Gellersen, R. Want & A. Schmidt (Ed.), *Third International Conference in Pervasive Computing* (*Pervasive'2005*): *Vol. 3468. Lecture Notes in Computer Science* (pp. 98-115). Springer-Verlag.

Basu, C., Hirsh, H., & Cohen, W. (2001). Technical Paper Recommendation: A Study in Combining Multiple Information Sources. *Journal of Artificial Intelligence Research, 14*, 213-252.

Basu, C., Hirsh, H., & Cohen, W. W. (1998). Recommendation as classification: Using social and content-based information in recommendation. In *15th National Conference on Artificial Intelligence* (pp. 714–720).

Baziz, M., Boughanem, M., & Traboulsi, S. (2005). A concept-based approach for indexing documents in IR. *Actes du XXIII-eme Congres INFORSID*, Grenoble.

Begelman, G., Keller, P. & Smadja, F. (2006). Automated Tag Clustering: Improving Search and Exploration in the Tag Space. *World Wide Web Conference 2006*, Edinburgh, UK. Retrieved 23 February 2008, from http://www.pui.ch/phred/automated_tag_clustering/

Begelman, G., Keller, P., & Smadja, F. (2006). Automated Tag Clustering: Improving Search and Exploration in the Tag Space. In *Proceedings of the 15th International Conference on World Wide Web* (pp. 33-42). New York: ACM Press. Retrieved February 15, 2008, from http://www.pui.ch/phred/automated_tag_clustering/

Belkin, N. J. (1993). Interaction with text: Information retrieval as information seeking behavior. *Information Retrieval, 10*, 55–66.

Belkin, N. J., & Croft, B. (1992). Information filtering and information retrieval: Two sides of the same coin? *Communications of the ACM, 34* (12), 29-39. Retrieved January 25, 2008, from http://www.ischool.utexas.edu/~i385d/readings/Belkin_Information_92.pdf

Belkin, N.J., & Croft, W.B. (1992). Information filtering and information retrieval: Two sides of the same coin. *Communications of the ACM, 35*(12), 29-38.

Bell, R., Koren, Y., & Volinsky, C. (2007). Modeling relationships at multiple scales to improve accuracy of large recommender systems. In *13th ACM SIGKDD International Conference on Knowledge Discovery and Data Mining* (pp. 95–104). New York, NY, USA. ACM.

Benyon, D. (1993). Adaptive systems: A solution to usability problems. *International Journal of User Modeling and User-Adapted Interaction, 3,* 65–87.

Bergé, J.-M., & Périn, P. (2002). Contexte et enjeux des communautés d'intérêt. *Mémento technique du conseil scientifique de France Télécom, 18.*

Berlanga, A.J., & García, F.J. (2005). IMS LD reusable elements for adaptive learning designs. *Journal of Interactive Media in Education,* 11(Special Issue).

Bilgic, M. (2004). *Explanation for Recommender Systems: Satisfaction vs. Promotion.* PhD thesis, University of Texas at Austin, Department of Computer Sciences.

Billsus, D., & Pazzani, M. J. (1999) A Hybrid User Model for News Story Classification. *Proc. the Seventh International Conference on User modeling,* Banff, Canada, 99 - 108.

Billsus, D., & Pazzani P. M. (2000). User modeling for adaptive news access. *Journal of User Modeling and User-Adapted Interaction, 10,* 147–180.

Billsus, D., & Pazzani, M J. (1999). A personal news agent that talks, learns and explains. In Etzioni, O., Müller, J.P., & Bradshaw, J.M. (Ed.), *3rd International Conference on Autonomous Agents* (pp. 268-275). ACM Press.

Billsus, D., & Pazzani, M. (1999). A hybrid user model for news story classi¢cation. In *User Modeling (Proceedings of the Seventh International Conference).* Banff, Canada, pp. 99-108.

Billsus, D., & Pazzani, M. (1999). A personal news agent that talks, learns and explains. *In Proceedings of 3rd International Conference on Autonomous Agents* (pp. 268–275).

Billsus, D., & Pazzani, M. (2000). User Modeling for Adaptive News Access. *User-Modeling and User-Adapted Interaction, 10*(2-3), 147-180.

Billsus, D., & Pazzani, M. J. (1998). Learning Collaborative Information Filters. *Proceedings of the Fifteenth National Conference on Artificial Intelligence (AAAI-98).* Menlo Park, CA. Morgan Kaufmann Publishers Inc. p 46-94

Birukov, A., Blanzieri E., & Giorgini, P. (2005). Implicit: An Agent-Based Recommendation System for Web Search. In M. Pechoucek, D. Steiner & S. Thompson (PC), *4th International Conference on Autonomous Agent and MAS (AAMAS 2005): Vol. 1. Information agents, brokering and matchmaking* (pp. 618-624). ACM Press.

Bizer, C. (2003). D2R MAP—a database to RDF mapping language. *Proceedings of the 12th International World Wide Web Conference.*

Blackwell, A. F., Stringer, M., Toye, E. F., & Rode, J. A. (2004). Tangible interface for collaborative information retrieval. In *CHI '04: extended abstracts on Human factors in computing systems,* pages 1473–1476, Vienna, Austria. ACM Press.

Bloor, D. (1999). Anti-latour. Studies in history and philosophy of science, *30*(1), 81-112.

Borchers A., Herlocker J., Konstan J., & Riedl J. (1998). Ganging up on Information Overload. *IEEE Computer, 31,* 106-108.

Borlund, P. (2003). The Concept of Relevance in Information Retrieval. *Journal of the American Society for Information Science and Technology, 54,* 913–925.

Bose, A., Beemanapalli, K., Srivastava, J., & Sahar, S. (2006). Incorporating concept hierarchies into usage mining based recommendations. In O. Nasraoui, M. Spiliopoulou, J. Srivastava, B. Mobasher, B. M. Masand (Eds.), *Advances in Web Mining and Web Usage Analysis, 8th International Workshop on Knowledge Discovery on the Web, Lecture Notes in Computer Science 4811* (pp. 110-126). Berlin, Heidelberg, Germany: Springer.

Brajnik, G., Guida, G., & Tasso, C. (1987). User modeling in intelligent information retrieval. *Information Processing and Management, 23(4),* 305–320.

Brandes, U. (2001). A faster algorithm for betweenness centrality, *Journal of Mathematical Sociology, 25*(2), 163-177. Retrieved February 15, 2008, from http://citeseer.ist.psu.edu/brandes01faster.html

Brandes, U., Gaertler, M., & Wagner, D. (2003). *Experiments on graph clustering algorithms. Lecture Notes in Computer Science,* Di Battista and U. Zwick (Eds.) 2832, 568-579. Retrieved 23 February 2008, from http://citeseer.ist.psu.edu/brandes03experiments.html

Breese, J. S., Heckerman, D., & Kadie, C. (1998). Empirical Analysis of Predictive Algorithms for Collaborative Filtering (Tech Rep. No. MSR-TR-98-12). Redmond, WA: Microsoft Research.

Breese, J., Heckerman, D., & Kadie, C. (1998). Empirical analysis of predictive algorithms for collaborative filtering. In *14th Conference on Uncertainty in Artificial Intelligence* (pp. 43–52). Morgan Kaufman.

Breese, J., Heckerman, S., & Kadie, C. (1998, July). Empirical analysis of predictive algorithms for collaborative filtering. In G. F. Cooper, S. Moral (Eds.), *UAI '98: Proceedings of the Fourteenth Conference on Uncertainty in Artificial Intelligence* (pp. 43-52). University of Wisconsin Business School, Madison, Wisconsin, USA: Morgan Kaufmann.

Brickley, D., & Miller, L. (2007). FOAF Vocabulary Specification 0.91, 2007. Retrieved January 2008, from http://xmlns.com/foaf/spec/

Broder, A. (2002). A taxonomy of Web Search. In *SIGIR Forum, 36(2)*.

Broekstra, J., Ehrig, M., Haase, P., Harmelen, F., Menken, M., Mika, P., Schnizler, B., & Siebes, R. (2004). Bibster-a semantics-based bibliographic peer-to-peer system. In *Proceedings of SemPGRID'04, 2nd Workshop on Semantics in Peer-to-Peer and Grid Computing*, pages 3–22, New York, USA.

Brooks, C. H., & Montanez, N. (2006). Improved annotation of the blogosphere via autotagging and hierarchical clustering. In *Proceedings of the 15th World Wide Web Conference* (pp. 625-632). New York: ACM Press. Retrieved February 17, 2008, from http://www.cs.usfca.edu/~brooks/papers/brooks-montanez-www06.pdf

Brown, S. M. (1998). *Decision Theoretic Approach for Interface Agent Development*. Ph.D dissertation. Air Force Institute of Technology.

Brown, S. M., Santos, E. Jr., Banks, S. B., & Oxley, M. (1998). Using explicit requirements and metrics for interface agent user model construction. In *Proceedings of the Second International Conference on Autonomous Agents* (pp. 1–7).

Brusilovsky, P. (1996). Methods and techniques of adaptive hypermedia. *International Journal of User Modeling and User-Adapted Interaction, 6*(2–3), 87–129.

Brusilovsky, P. (2000). Adaptive Hypermedia: From Intelligent Tutoring Systems to Web Based Education. In G. Gauthier, C. Frasson, K. VanLehn (Ed.), *5th International Conference on Intelligent Tutoring Systems (ITS 2000)*:

Vol. 1839. Lecture Notes in Computer Science (pp. 1-7). Springer-Verlag.

Brusilovsky, P. (2001). Adaptive hypermedia. *International Journal of User Modeling and User-Adapted Interaction, 11*(1–2), 87–110.

Brusilovsky, P., & Cooper, D. W. (2002). Domain, Task, and User Models for an Adaptive Hypermedia Performance Support System. In Gil, Y., Leake, D.B. (eds.) *Proc. of 2002 International Conference on Intelligent User Interfaces* (pp. 23-30). ACM Press

Brusilovsky, P., & Henze, N. (2007). Open corpus adaptive educational hypermedia. In Brusilovsky, P., Kobsa, A., Neidl, W. (Eds.): *The Adaptive Web, LNCS 4321*, Springer.

Brusilovsky, P., & Kobsa, A. (2007). *The adaptive web*. Springer.

Brusilovsky, P., & Millán, E. (2007). User Models for Adaptive Hypermedia and Adaptive Educational Systems, in P. Brusilovsky, A. Kobsa, W. Nejdl (Eds*.): The Adaptive Web, LNCS 4321,* Springer

Brusilovsky, P., & Nijhavan, H. (2002). A framework for adaptive e-learning based on distributed re-usable learning activities. *Proceedings of the World Conference on E-Learning* (E-Learn 2002), Montreal, Canada.

Brusilovsky, P., & Tasso, C. (2004). Preface to Special Issue on User Modeling for Web Information Retrieval. *User Modeling and User-Adapted Interaction, 14(2-3)*, 147-157.

Brusilovsky, P., Eklund, J., & Schwarz, E. (1998). Web-based education for all: A tool for developing adaptive courseware. In Ashman, H., Thistewaite, P. (Eds*.) Proc. of Seventh International World Wide Web Conference, 30*(pp. 291-300).. Elsevier Science B. V.

Buckley, F., & Harary, F. (1990) *Distance in graphs*. Reading, MA: Addison-Wesley.

Budanitsky, A., & Hirst, G. (2001). Semantic distance in WordNet: An experimental, application-oriented evaluation of five measures. *Proceedings of Workshop on WordNet and Other Lexical Resources of the 2nd Meeting of the North American Chapter of the Association for Computational Linguistics,* Pittsburgh, PA.

Budanitsky, A., & Hirst, G. (2001, June). *Semantic Distance in WordNet: An Experimental Application-oriented Evaluation of Five Measures*. Paper presented at Workshop on WordNet and Other Lexical Resources (NAACL), Pittsburgh, PA. Retrieved February 15, 2008, from http://citeseer.ist.psu.edu/budanitsky01semantic.html

Bueno, D., & David, A. A. (2001). METIORE: A personalized information retrieval system. In Bauer, M., Vassileva, J. and Gmytrasiewicz, P. (Eds.). *User Modeling: Proceedings of the Eight International Conference, UM 2001,* (pp. 168–177).

Buffa, M., Ereteo, G., & Gandon, F. (2007, 2 au 6 Juillet). *Wiki et web sémantique.* Paper presented at the 18e Journées Francophones d'Ingénierie des Connaissances, Grenoble.

Bunt, A., & Conati, C. (2003). Probabilistic student modelling to improve exploratory behaviour. *International Journal of User Modeling and User-Adapted Interaction, 13*(3), 269–309.

Burke, R. (1999). The Wasabi Personal Shopper: A Case-Based Recommender System. *Proceedings of the 11th Conference on Innovative Applications of Artificial Intelligence.* American Association for Artificial Intelligence. (pp. 844-949)..

Burke, R. (2000). A Case-Based Approach to Collaborative Filtering. *Advances in Case-Based Reasoning,* pp. 370–379, *5th European Workshop EWCBR 2000.* Springer-Verlag, New York.

Burke, R. (2000). Knowledge-based recommender systems. In A. Kent (Ed.), *Encyclopedia of Library and Information Systems, 69.* New York: Marcel Dekker.

Burke, R. (2002). Hybrid recommender systems: survey and experiments. *User Modeling and User-Adapted Interaction, 12(4),* 331-370.

Burke, R. (2002). Hybrid Recommender Systems: Survey and Experiments. *User Modeling and User-Adapted Interaction,* 12: 331-370.

Burke, R. (2007). Hybrid Web Recommender Systems. In P. Brusilovsky, A. Kobsa, W. Nejdl (Eds.): *The Adaptive Web, LNCS 4321* (pp. 377 – 408), Springer

Bush, V. (July 1945). As we may think. *The Atlantic, 176*(1), 101-108.

Byde, A., Wan, H., & Cayzer, S. (2007). Personalized Tag Recommendations via Social Network and Content-based Similarity Metrics. *In Proceedings of the International Conference on Weblogs and Social Media (ICWSM'07).* Boulder, Colorado.

Cabri, G., Leonardi, L., & Zambonelli, F. (1999). Supporting Cooperative WWW Browsing: A Proxy-based Approach. In *7th Euromicro Workshop on Parallel and Distributed Processing*, pages 138–145, University of Maderia, Funchal, Portugal. IEEE Press.

Campbell, D. R., Culley, S. J., Mcmahon, C. A., & Sellini F. (2007). An approach for the capture of context-dependent document relationships extracted from Bayesian analysis of users' interactions with information. *Information Retrieval, 10*(2), (Apr. 2007), 115-141.

Campbell, I. (1999). Interactive Evaluation of the Ostensive Model, using a new Test-Collection of Images with Multiple Relevance Assessments. *Information Retrieval, 2(1),* 89-114.

Candillier, L., Meyer, F., & Boullé, M. (2007). Comparing state-of-the-art collaborative filtering systems. In Perner, P. (Ed.), *5th International Conference on Machine Learning and Data Mining in Pattern Recognition* (pp. 548–562), Leipzig, Germany. Springer Verlag.

Carbonaro A. (2004). Learning objects recommendation in a collaborative information management system. *IEEE Learning Technology Newsletter, 6*(4).

Carbonaro, A. (2005). Defining personalized learning views of relevant learning objects in a collaborative bookmark management system. In *Web-based intelligent e-learning systems: Technologies and applications.* Hershey, PA: Idea Group.

Carrillo-Ramos, A., Villanova-Oliver, M., Gensel, J., & Martin, H. (2006). Knowledge Management for Adapted Information Retrieval in Ubiquitous Environments. In J. Filipe, J. Cordeiro, V. Pedrosa (Ed.), *2nd International Conference on Web Information Systems and Technologies (WebIST 2006): Vol. 1. Lecture Notes in Business Information Processing* (pp. 84-96). Springer-Verlag.

Carrillo-Ramos, A., Villanova-Oliver, M., Gensel, J., & Martin, H. (2007). Contextual User Profile for Adapting Information in Nomadic Environments. In M. Weske, M.-S. Hacid, C. Godart (Ed.), *Personalized Access to Web Information (PAWI 2007), Workshop of the 8th International Web Information Systems Engineering (WISE 2007): Vol. 4832. Lecture Notes In Computer Science* (pp. 337-349). Springer-Verlag.

Case, D. (2002). *Looking for Information: A Survey of Research on Information Seeking, Needs, and Behavior.* Academic Press

Cataltepe, Z., & Altinel, B. (2007a). Hybrid Music Recommendation Based on Different Dimensions of Audio Content and Entropy Measure. *Proc. of Eusipco 2007 Conference,* Poznan, Poland, September 2007.

Cataltepe, Z., & Altinel, B. (2007b). Hybrid Music Recommendation Based on Adaptive Feature and User Grouping. *Proc. of ISCIS 2007 Conference,* Ankara, Turkey, October 2007.

Catarci, T., Di Mascio, T., Franconi, E., Santucci, G., & Tessaris, S. (2003). An ontology based visual tool for query formulation support. In R. Meersman, & Z. Tari (Eds.), *OTM Workshops* (LNCS 2889, pp. 32-43). Springer.

Cayzer, S., & Aickelin, U. (2002). A Recommender System based on the Immune Network. In *Proceedings of the Fourth Congress on Evolutionary Computation (CEC-2002)*, Honolulu, USA: IEEE.

Celma O., & Lamere, P. (2007, September). Music Recommendation Tutorial. *Presented at the 8th International Conference on Music Information Retrieval*, Vienna, Austria.

Celma, O., Ramirez, M., & Herrera, P. (2005). Foafing the Music: A Music Recommendation System Based on RSS Feeds and User Preferences. *Proc. of the International Conference on Music Information Retrieval (ISMIR) 2005.*

Chaari, T., Dejene, E., Laforest, F., & Scuturici, V.-M. (2007). A comprehensive approach to model and use context for adapting applications in pervasive environments. *Journal of Systems and Software, 80*(12), 1973-1992.

Chai, W., & Vercoe, B. (2000). Using User Models in Music Information Retrieval Systems. *Proc. of the International Conference on Music Information Retrieval (ISMIR) 2000.*

Charikar, M. (2002). Similarity Estimation Techniques From Rounding Algorithms. In *Annual ACM Symposium on Theory of Computing*, Montreal, Canada: ACM Press.

Chedrawy, Z., & Abidi, S. S. R. (2006). An Adaptive Personalized Recommendation Strategy Featuring Context Sensitive Content Adaptation, Adaptive Hypermedia and Adaptive Web-Based Systems. *LNCS* Volume 4018/2006, 61-70.

Chen, H. C., & Chen, A. L. P. (2005). A music recommendation system based on music and user grouping. *Journal of Intelligent Information Systems, 24*(2-3), 113-132.

Chen, H., & Lynch, K. J. (1992). Automatic Construction of Networks of Concepts Characterizing Document Databases. *IEEE Transactions on Systems, Man and Cybernetics,* 22(5):885-902.

Chi, E. H., Pirolli, P., & Pitkow, J. (2001).Using information scent to model user information needs and actions on the web. *Proceedings of the ACM SIG-CHI on Human Factors in Computing Systems* (pp.490-497). Seattle, WA, USA: ACM Press.

Chin, D. (1989). KNOME: Modeling What the User knows in UC. In A. Kobsa and W. Wahlster (Ed.), *User models in dialog systems,* (pp. 74—107). Springer Verlag, Berlin.

Chin, D. (2001). Empirical Evaluation of User Models and User-Adapted Systems. *User Modeling and User-Adapted Interaction, 11(1-2),* 181-194.

Chin, D. (2003). Evaluating the Effectiveness of User Models by Experiments. *Tutorial presented at the Ninth International Conference on User Modeling (UM 2003).* Johnstown, PA

Chin, D. N., (2001). Empirical evaluation of user models and user-adapted systems. *International Journal of User Modeling and User-Adapted Interaction, 11*(1–2), 181–194.

Chirita, P.-A., Nejdl, W., & Zamfir, C. Preventing Shilling Attacks in Online Recommender Systems. In *Proceedings of the 7th Annual ACM International Workshop on Web Information and Data Management.* Bremen, Germany: ACM Press.

Cilibrasi, R., & Vitanyi, P.M.B. (2007). The Google similarity distance. *IEEE Transactions on Knowledge and Data Engineering, 19*(3), 370-383.

Cimiano, P., Hotho, A., & Staab, S. (2004, May). *Clustering Concept Hierarchies from Text by Agglomerative Clustering.* Paper presented at the Fourth International Conference On Language Resources And Evaluation. Lisbon, Portugal. Retrieved February 15, 2008, from http://www.aifb.uni-karlsruhe.de/WBS/pci/lrec04.pdf

Cleverdon, C. (1967). The Cranfield test of index language devices. In *Reprinted in Reading in Information Retrieval Eds.* 1998. (pp. 47–59).

Cohen, W., & Fan, W. (2000). Web-collaborative filtering: Recommending music by crawling the Web. *Computer Networks, 33*(1–6), 685–698.

Cohn, D. A., Ghahramani, Z., & Jordan M. I. (1996). Active Learning with Statistical Models. In *Journal of Artificial Intelligence Research, 4*, 129-145.

Collett, M., Linton. F., Goodman, B., & Farance, F. (2001). IEEE P1484.2.25 - Draft Standard for Learning Technology. Public and Private Information (PAPI) for Learners (PAPI Learner) — Learner Performance Information, IEEE Computer Society Press, Piscataway, NJ, USA

Conein, B. (2003). Communautés épistémiques et réseaux cognitifs: Coopération et cognition distribuée. *Revue d'Economie Politique*(Numéro spécial).

Conference on Cooperative Information Systems. Trento, Italy: Springer.

Conlan, O., O'Keeffe, I., & Tallon, S. (2006). Combining adaptive hypermedia techniques and ontology reasoning to produce dynamic personalized news services. In V. P. Wade, H. Ashman & B. Smyth (Ed.), *4th International Conference on Adaptive Hypermedia and Adaptive Web-Based Systems (AH'2006): Vol. 4018. Lecture Notes In Computer Science* (pp. 81-90). Springer-Verlag.

Cool, C., & Spink, A. (2002). Issues of context in information retrieval (IR): an introduction to the special issue. *Information Processing Management 38(5)* (Sep. 2002), 605-611.

Cooley R., Mobasher, B., & Srivastava, J. (1997). Web mining: Information and pattern discovery on the World Wide Web. Proceedings of the 9th International Conference on Tools with Artificial Intelligence (ICTAI '97).

Cooley, R., Mobasher, B., Srivastava, J. (1999). Data preparation for mining World Wide Web browsing patterns. *Knowledge and Information Systems, 1*(1), 5-32.

Cotter, P., & Smyth, B. (2000). WAPing the Web: Content personalization for WAP-enabled devices. *Proceedings of International Conference on Adaptive Hypermedia and Adaptive Web-Based Systems* (pp. 98–108).

Cover, T. M., & Thomas, J. A. (2006). *Elements of Information Theory.* Wiley.

Craswell, N., Hawking D., Upstill, T., McLean, A., Wilkinson, R., & Wu, M. (2003). TREC 12 Web and Interactive Tracks at CSIRO. *NIST Special Publication 500-255. The Twelfth Text Retrieval Conference,* (pp 193-203).

Craswell, N., Zoeter, O., Taylor, M., & Ramsey, B. (2008). An experimental comparison of click position-bias models. In *Proceedings of WSDM*, pages 87 – 94, Palo Alto, CA, ACM Press.

Crestani, F., & Ruthven, I. (2007). Introduction to special issue on contextual information retrieval systems. *Information Retrieval, 10 (2) (Apr. 2007),* 111–113.

Croft, W. B. (2002). *Advances in Information Retrieval*, volume 7 of *The Information Retrieval Series*, chapter Combining Approaches to Information Retrieval, pages 1–36. Springer, Netherlands.

Cunningham, H., Maynard, D., Bontcheva, K., & Tablan, V. (2002). GATE: A framework and graphical development environment for robust NLP tools and applications. *Proceedings of the 40th Anniversary Meeting of the Association for Computational Linguistics,* Budapest.

Cutler, M., Shih, Y., & Meng, W. (1997). Using the structure of HTML documents to improve retrieval. In *USENIX Symposium on Internet Technologies and Systems* (pp. 241–252)

Dai, H., & Mobasher, B. (2003). A Road Map to More Effective Web Personalization: Integrating Domain Ontologies with Web Usage Mining. *Proceedings of Int. Conference on Internet Computing – IC03*

Dai, H., & Mobasher, B. (2004). Integrating semantic knowledge with Web usage mining for personalization. In A. Scime (Ed.), *Web mining: Applications and techniques* (pp. 276-306). Hershey, PA: Idea Group.

Dalal, M. (2007). Personalized social & real-time collaborative search. In *WWW '07: Proceedings of the 16th international conference on World Wide Web*, pages 1285–1286, Banff, Alberta, Canada. ACM Press.

Daoud, M., Tamine, L., Boughanem, M., & Chabaro, B. (2007). Learning Implicit User Interests Using Ontology and Search History for Personalization. In M. Weske, M.-S. Hacid & C. Godart (Ed.), *Personalized Access to Web Information (PAWI 2007), Workshop of the 8th International Web Information Systems Engineering (WISE 2007): Vol. 4832. Lecture Notes In Computer Science* (pp. 325-336). Springer-Verlag

Decampos, L., Fernandez-Luna, J., & Huete, J. (1998). Query expansion in information retrieval systems using a Bayesian network-based thesaurus. In *Proceedings of the Fourteenth Annual Conference on Uncertainty in Artificial Intelligence (UAI-98)*, (pp. 53–60). Sanfrancisco, CA.

Decker, S., Erdmann, M., Fensel, D., & Studer, R. (1998). *Ontobroker: Ontology based access to distributed and semi-structured information.* Paper presented at the The IFIP TC2/WG 2.6 Eighth Working Conference on Database Semantics-Semantic Issues in Multimedia Systems (pp. 351-369). Deventer, The Netherlands: Kluwer.

deCristo, M. A. P., Calado, P. P., da Silveria, M. L., Silva, I., Munzt, R., & Ribeiro-Neto, B. (2003). Bayesian belief networks for IR. *International Journal of Approximate Reasoning, 34,* 163–179.

Delalonde, C., & Soulier, E. (2007, From 25 to 29 Juin). *Demond: Leveraging social participation for collaborative information retrieval.* Paper presented at the 1st Workshop on Adaptation and Personalisation in Social Systems: Groups, Teams, Communities. 11th International conference on User Modelling, Corfu, Greece.

Delalonde, C., Chevrier, B., Soulier, E., & Potiron, J. (2006). Procédé et système de communication pour fournir au moins une réponse à une requête d'un utilisateur. France.

Dervin, B. (1997). Given a context by any other name: methodological tools for taming the unruly beast. In P.Vakkari, R.Savolainen, & B.Dervin (Eds.), *Information seeking in context: Proceedings of an international conference on research in information needs, seeking and use in different contexts,* (pp.13–38). London: Taylor Graham.

Deshpande, M., & Karypis, G. (2004). Item-based top-N recommendation algorithms. *ACM Transactions on Information Systems, 22*(1), 143-177.

DeWitt, R. (1995). Vagueness, Semantics, and the Language of Thought. *Psyche, 1*. Available at http://psyche.cs.monash.edu.au/index.html.

Dey, A. (2001). Understanding and using context. *International ACM Journal of Personal and Ubiquitous Computing, 5*(*1*), 4-7.

Diamadis, E. T., & Polyzos, G. C. (2004). Efficient cooperative searching on the web: system design and evaluation. *Int. J. Hum.-Comput. Stud., 61*(5), 699–724.

Diederich, J., & Iofciu, T. (2006). Finding Communities of Practice from User Profiles Based on Folksonomies. In E. Tomadaki and P. Scott (Eds.), *EC-TEL 2006 Workshops Proceedings* (pp. 288-297). Aachen, Germany: Redaktion Sun SITE. Retrieved January 25, 2008, from http://www.l3s.de/~diederich/Papers/TBProfile-telcops.pdf

Dietz, P., & Leigh, D. (2001). DiamondTouch: A multi-user touch technology. In *UIST '01: Proceedings of the 14th annual ACM symposium on User interface software and technology*, pages 219–226, Orlando, Florida, USA. ACM Press.

Dix, A., Finlay, J., Abowd, G., & Beale, R. (1998). *Human computer interaction* (2nd ed.). Prentice Hall.

Dolog, P., & Schäfer, M. (2005). Learner Modeling on the Semantic Web. *In Proc. of PerSWeb'05, Workshop on Personalization on the Semantic Web, User Modeling Conference,* 2005

Dolog, P., Henze, N., Nejdl, W., & Sintek, M. (2003). *Towards the adaptive Semantic Web.* Paper presented at the International Workshop on Principles and Practice of Semantic Web Reasoning (LNCS 2901, pp. 51-68). Springer.

Dolog, P., Henze, N., Nejdl, W., & Sintek, M. (2004). Personalization in distributed e-learning environments. In *Proc. of The Thirteenth International World Wide Web Conference, WWW 2004* (pp. 161-169). ACM Press

Donath, J. S., & Robertson, N. (1994). The Sociable Web. In *Proceedings of the Second International WWW Conference*, Chicago, IL, USA.

Dorigo, M., & Caro, G. D. (1999). The Ant Colony Optimization Meta-Heuristic. New Ideas in Optimization, (pp 11-32), McGraw-Hill.

Dorn, J., & Pichlmair, M. (2007). A Competence Management System for Universities, *Proceeding of the European Conference on Artificial Intelligence*, St. Gallen

Dourish, P., & Bellotti, V. (1992). Awareness and Coordination in Shared Workspaces. In M. Mantel & R. Baecker (GC), *ACM Conference on Computer-Supported Cooperative Work* (*CSCW 92*), *1,* 107-114. ACM Press.

Draganidis, F., Chamopoulou, P., & Mentzas, G. (2006). An Ontology Based Tool for Competency Management and Learning Path. *6th International Conference on Knowledge Management (I-KNOW 06), Special track on Integrating Working and Learning*, Graz, Austria.

Drucker, H., Shahrary, B., & Gibbon, C. (2002). Support vector machines: relevance feedback and information retrieval. *Information Processing and Management, 38(3)*, 305–323.

Druzdzel, J. M. (1999). SMILE: Structural Modeling, Inference, and Learning Engine and GeNIe: A development environment for graphical decision-theoretic models (Intelligent Systems Demonstration). In *Proceedings of the Sixteenth National Conference on Artificial Intelligence (AAAI-99),* (pp. 902-903), AAAI Press/The MIT Press, Menlo Park, CA.

Dumais, S. T. (1993). Latent semantic indexing (LSI) and TREC-2. In *Text REtrieval Conference (TREC) TREC-2 Proceedings* 105–116 NIST Special Publication 500-215.

Dumas, J. S., & Redish, J. C. (1999). *A practical guide to usability testing.* Norwood, NJ: Ablex.

Dzbor, M., Motta, E., & Stutt, A. (2005). Achieving higher-level learning through adaptable semantic Web applications. *International Journal of Knowledge and Learning, 1*(1/2).

Eades, P. A. (1984). A Heuristic for Graph Drawing. In Ralph G. (Ed.), *Congressus Numerantium* (pp. 149-160). Winnipeg: Utilitas Mathematica.

Efthimis, E. N. (1996). Query Expansion. In Williams, M. (Ed.). *Annual Review of Information Science and Technology, 31*, 121–187.

Ehrig, M., & Sure, Y. (2004, May). Ontology mapping—an integrated approach. In C. Bussler, J. Davis, D. Fensel, & R. Studer (Eds.), *Proceedings of the 1st European Semantic Web Symposium* (pp. 76-91), Heraklion, Greece. Berlin: Springer-Verlag (LNCS 3053).

Eirinaki, M., Lampos, C., Paulakis, S., & Vazirgiannis, M. (2004). Web personalization integrating content semantics and navigational patterns. In A. H. Laender, D. Lee, M. Ronthaler (Eds.), *Proceeding of the Sixth ACM CIKM International Workshop on Web Information and Data Management* (pp.72-79), Washington, DC, USA: ACM Press.

Eirinaki, M., Vazirgiannis, M., & Varlamis, I. (2003). SEWeP: using site semantics and a taxonomy to enhance the web personalization process. In L. Getoor, T. E. Senator, P. Domingos, C. Faloutsos (Eds.), *Proceedings of the Ninth ACM SIGKDD International Conference on Knowledge Discovery and Data Mining* (pp. 99-108), Washington, DC, USA: ACM Press.

El Fallah-Seghrouchni, A., Suna, A. (2004). CLAIM: A Computational Language for Autonomous, Intelligent and Mobile Agent. In M. Dastani, J. Dix, A. El Fallah-Seghrouchni (Ed.), *PROMAS 2003: Vol. 3067. Lecture Notes In Artificial Intelligence* (pp. 90–110). Springer-Verlag.

Engelhardt, M., Hildebrand, A., Lange, D., & Schmidt, T. C. (2006). Reasoning about eLearning Multimedia Objects. *Procdings of SWAMM 06*, Springer

Engeström, Y. (1987). *Learning by expanding*. Helsinki: Orienta-Konsultit Oy.

Erickson, T., & Kellogg, W. (2000). Social translucence: An approach to designing systems that support social processes. *ACM Transactions on Computer-Human Interaction, 7*(1), 59-83.

Faloutsos, C., & Oard, D. (1995). *A Survey of Information Retrieval and Filtering Methods* (Tech. Rep. No. CS-TR-3514). Maryland, USA: University of Maryland, Department of Computer Science.

Farzan, R., & Brusilovsky, P. (2005). Social Navigation Support through Annotation-Based Group Modeling, *Proceedings of the 10th Conference on User Modeling*, LNCS 3538, Springer.

Fellbaum, C. (Ed.). (1998). *WordNet: An electronic lexical database*. Cambridge, MA: MIT Press.

Fink, J., Kobsa, A., & Nill, A. (1999). Adaptable and adaptive information for all users, including disabled and elderly people. *New Review of Hypermedia and Multimedia, 4*, 163–188.

Foley, C., Gurrin, C., Jones, G., Lee, H., Mc Givney, S., O'Connor, N., Sav, S., Smeaton, A. F., & Wilkins., P. (2005). TRECVid 2005 Experiments at Dublin City University. In *TRECVid 2005 - Text REtrieval Conference TRECVID Workshop*, Gaithersburg, MD. National Institute of Standards and Technology, MD USA.

Foley, C., Smeaton, A. F., & Lee., H. (2006). Synchronous collaborative information retrieval with relevance feedback. In *CollaborateCom 2006 - 2nd International Conference on Collaborative Computing: Networking, Applications and Worksharing, pages 1-4.*, Adelaide, Australia, IEEE Computer Society.

Frake, W. B., & Baeza-Yates, R. (1992). *Information Retrieval: Data Structures and Algorithms*. Prentice Hall PTR, Upper Saddle River, NJ 07458.

Frakes, W., & Baeza-Yates, R. (1992). *Information Retrieval: Data Structures and Algorithms*. Englewood Cliffs, New Jersey: Prentice Hall.

Fu, X., Budzik, J., & Hammond, K. J. (2000). Mining navigation history for recommendation. In *IUI 2000: Proceedings of the 5th International Conference on Intelligent User Interface* (pp. 106-112). New Orleans, LA, USA: ACM Press.

Furnas, G. W., Landauer, T. K., Gomez, L. M., & Dumais, S. T. (1987). The vocabulary problem in human-system communication. *Communications of the ACM, 30*(11), 964-971.

Gandon, F., & Sadeh, N. (2004). Semantic Web Technologies to Reconcile Privacy and Contexte Awareness. *Journal of Web Semantics, 1*(3), 241-260

García, F.J., Berlanga, A.J., Moreno, M.N., García, J., & Carabias, J. (2004). *HyCo—an authoring tool to create semantic learning objects for Web-based e-learning systems* (pp. 344-348). Berlin: Springer-Verlag (LNCS 3140).

Garshol, L. M. (2004). Metadata? Thesauri? Taxonomies? Topic Maps! Making sense of it all. *Journal of Information Science, 30*(4), 378-391. Retrieved February 14, 2008, from http://www.ontopia.net/topicmaps/materials/tm-vs-thesauri.html

Gauch, S., Speretta, M., Chandamouli, A., & Micarelli, A. (2007). User Profiles for Personalized Information Access. In Brusilovsky, P., Kobsa, A., and Nejdl, W. (Eds.), *The Adaptive Web*, (pp. 54-89), Springer LCNS 4321.

Geihs, K., Khan, M., Reichle, R., Solberg, A., & Hallsteinsen, S. (2006). Modeling of component-based self-adapting context-aware applications for mobile devices. In S.

Boston (Ed.), *Software Engineering Techniques: Design for Quality: Vol. 227. IFIP International Federation for Information Processing* (pp. 85-96). Springer.

Gena, C., & Ardissono, L. (2004). Intelligent support to the retrieval of information about hydric resources. *Proceedings of 3rd International Conference on Adaptive Hypermedia and Adaptive Web-Based Systems* (pp. 126–135).

Ghias, A., Logan, J., Chamberlin, D., & Smith, B. C. (1995). Query by humming - musical information retrieval in an audio database. *Proceedings ACM Multimedia.*

Gianoutsos, S., & Grundy, J. (1996). Collaborative work with the World Wide Web: adding CSCW support to a Web browser. In *Procedingss of Oz-CSCW'96, DSTC Technical Workshop Series, University of Queensland*, pages 14-21 University of Queensland, Brisbane, Australia.

Glance, N., Arregui, D., & Dardenne, M. (1998). Knowledge pump: Supporting the flow and use of knowledge. In U. Borghoff and R. Pareschi, editors, *Information technology for knowledge management*, pages 35–51. Springer.

Godoy, D., & Amandi, A. (2005). Modeling user interests by conceptual clustering. *Information Systems, 31*(4-5), 245-267.

Godoy, D., & Amandi, A. (2005). User Profiling for Web Page Filtering. *IEEE Internet Computing* 9 (4) 56-64.

Goecks, J. and Shavlik, J. (2000). Learning users' interests by unobtrusively observing their normal behavior. In *Proceedings of the 5th international Conference on Intelligent User interfaces* (New Orleans, Louisiana, United States, January 09 - 12, 2000). IUI '00. ACM, New York, NY, 129-132.

Goh, D., & Foo, S. (2007). *Social Information Retrieval Systems: Emerging Technologies and Applications for Searching the Web Effectively.* Premier Reference Source.

Goker, M. H., & Thompson, C. A. (2000) Personalized Conversational Case-Based Recommendation. *Advances in Case-Based Reasoning,* LNCS 1898/2000, 29-82.

Goldberg, D., Nichols, D., Oki, B. M., & Terry, D. (1992). Using Collaborative Filtering to Weave an Information Tapestry. *Communications of the ACM, 35*, 61-70. ACM Press.

Goldberg, K., Roeder T., Gupta, D., & Perkins, C. (2000). *Eigentaste: A Constant Time Collaborative Filtering* Algorithm (Tech Rep. No. UCB/ERL M00/41). Berkeley, California: University of California, EECS Department.

Golder, S., & Huberman, B. A. (2006). Usage patterns of Collaborative Tagging Systems. *Journal of Information Science, 32*(2), 198-208. Retrieved January 25, 2007, from http://www.hpl.hp.com/research/idl/papers/tags/tags.pdf

Golder, S., & Huberman, B. A. (2006). Usage patterns of Collaborative Tagging Systems, *Journal of Information Science, 32*(2), 198-208. Retrieved 25 January 2007, from http://www.hpl.hp.com/research/idl/papers/tags/tags.pdf

Golovin, N., & Rahm, E. (2004). Reinforcement learning architecture for web recommendations. In *Proceeding of the International Conference on Information Technology: Coding and Computing, 1*, 398-403. Las Vegas, Nevada, USA: IEEE Computer Society.

Google Co-op. (2006). Google co-op. Retrieved Septembre 15th 2006, from http://www.google.com/coop/

Gould, J. D., & Lewis, C. (1983). Designing for usability: Key principles and what designers think. *Proceedings of CHI '83* (pp. 50–53).

Grcar, M., Fortuna, B., & Mladenic, D. (2005, August). KNN versus SVM in the Collaborative Filtering Framework. In *Workshop on Knowledge Discovery on the Web.*

Greenbaum, J., & Kyng, M. (1991). *Design at work: Cooperative design of computer systems.* Hillsdale, NJ: Lawrence Erlbaum.

Greenberg, S. (2001). Context as a dynamic construct. *Journal of Human Computer Interaction, 16*(2/4), 257-268.

Greenberg, S., & Roseman, M. (1996). GroupWeb: A WWW browser as real time groupware. In *CHI '96: Conference companion on Human factors in computing systems*, pages 271–272, Vancouver, British Columbia, Canada. ACM Press.

Greenberg, S., & Witten, I. (1985). Adaptive personalized interfaces - A question of viability. *Behaviour and Information Technology, 4(1),* 31-45

Greffenstette, G., & Hearst, M. A. (1992). A method for refining automatically-discovered lexical relations: Combining weak techniques for stronger results. In *Proceedings of the Workshop on Statistically-Based Natural Language Programming Techniques,* AAAI Press, Menlo Park, CA.

Gross, T. (1999). Supporting awareness and cooperation in digital information environments. In *Basic Research Symposium at the Conference on Human Factors in*

Computing Systems - CHI'99, Pittsburgh, Pennsylvania, USA. ACM Press.

GroupLens. (2005). GroupLens Research. Retrieved November 2, 2005, from www.GroupLens.org

Grudin, J. (2001). Desituating action: digital representation of context. *Journal of Human-Computing Interaction, 16(2/4)*, 269-286.

Guarino, N., Masolo, C., & Vetere, G. (1999). OntoSeek: Content-based access to the Web. *IEEE Inteligent Systems, 14*, 3

Gudivada, V. N., Raghavan, V. V., Grosky, W. I., & Kasanagottu, R. (1997). Information retrieval on the World Wide Web. *IEEE Internet Computing, 1*(5), 56-68.

Guha, R., & McCool, R. (2003). TAP: A Semantic Web platform. *International Journal on Computer and Telecommunications Networking, 42*(5), 557-577.

Haase, P., Siebes, R., & Harmelen, F. (2004). Peer selection in peer-to-peer networks with semantic topologies. In *International Conference on Semantics of a Networked World: Semantics for Grid Databases*, Paris.

Haines, D., & Croft, W. B. (1993). Relevance feedback and inference networks. In *Proceedings of the Sixteenth Annual International ACM SIGIR Conference on Research and Development in Information Retrieval, Pittsburgh, PA.* (pp. 2–11).

Han, E.-H. S., & Karypis, G. (2005). Feature-based recommendation system. In *14th Conference of Information and Knowledge Management* (pp. 446-452).

Han, R., Perret, V., & Naghshineh, M. (2000). WebSplitter: a unified XML framework for multi-device collaborative Web browsing. In *CSCW '00: Proceedings of the 2000 ACM conference on Computer supported cooperative work*, pages 221–230, Philadelphia, Pennsylvania, USA. ACM Press.

Handschuh, S., Staab, S., & Volz, R. (2003). On deep annotation. *Proceedings of the 12th International World Wide Web Conference.*

Harvey, T., Decker K., Carberry, S. (2005). Multi-Agent Decision Support Via User Modeling. In M. Pechoucek, D. Steiner & S. Thompson (PC), *4th International Conference on Autonomous Agent and MAS (AAMAS 2005): Vol. 1. Cooperation I* (pp. 222-229). ACM Press.

Hassan-Montero, Y., & Herrero-Solana, V. (2006, October). *Improving Tag-Clouds as Visual Information Retrieval Interfaces.* Paper presented at International

Conference on Multidisciplinary Information Sciences and Technologies, Merida, Spain. Retrieved February 15, 2008, from http://www.nosolousabilidad.com/hassan/improving_tagclouds.pdf

Heckerman, D., Chickering, D.M., Meek, C., Rounthwaite, R., & Kadie, C. (2001). Dependency Networks for Inference, Collaborative Filtering, and Data Visualization. *Journal of Machine Learning Research*, (pp. 49-75).

Heckmann, D., & Kruger, A. (2003) A user modeling markup language (UserML) for ubiquitous computing. *Lecture Notes in Artificial Intelligence, 2702*(2003) 393–397.

Heflin, J. (2004). OWL Web Ontology Language Use Cases and Requirements. W3C Recommendations. Retrieved January 2008, from http://www.w3.org/TR/webont-req/

Heflin, J. (2004, February). OWL Web Ontology Language use cases and requirements. Retrieved from http://www.w3.org/TR/Webont-req/

Heflin, J., & Hendler, J. (2000). *Searching the Web with SHOE.* Paper presented at the AAAI Workshop (pp. 35-40). AAAI Press.

Henze, N., & Nejdl, W. (2001). Adaptation in open corpus hypermedia. International Journal of Artificial Intelligence in Education *12*(4), 325-350.

Henze, N., Dolog, P., & Nejdl, W. (2004) Reasoning and Ontologies for Personalized E-Learning in the Semantic Web. *Educational Technology & Society, 7*(4), 82-97

Herlocker J., Konstan J., Terveen, L., & Riedl, J. (2004). Evaluating Collaborative Filtering Recommender Systems. *ACM Transactions on Information Systems, 22*, 5-53.

Herlocker, J. L., Konstan, J. A., Borchers, A., & Riedl, J. (1999). An Algorithmic Framework for Performing Collaborative Filtering. In *Proceedings of the 22nd Annual International ACM SIGIR Conference on Research and Development in Information Retrieval*, Berkley, CA: ACM Press.

Herlocker, J. L., Konstan, J. A., Terveen, L. G., & Riedl, J. T. (2004) Evaluating Collaborative Filtering Recommender Systems. *ACM Transactions on Information Systems, 22*(1), January 2004, 5–53.

Herlocker, J., Konstan, J., & Riedl, J. (2000). Explaining collaborative filtering recommendations. In *ACM Conference on Computer Supported Cooperative Work.*

Herlocker, J., Konstan, J., Brochers, A., & Riedel, J. (2000). An Algorithmic Framework for Performing Collaborative Filtering. In *SIGIR '99: Proceedings of the 22nd Annual International ACM SIGIR Conference on Research and Development in Information Retrieval* (pp. 230-237). Berkeley, CA, USA: ACM Press.

Herlocker, J., Konstan, J., Terveen, L., & Riedl, J. (2004). Evaluating collaborative filtering recommender systems. In *ACM Transactions on Information Systems, 22*(1), 5–53.

Hernandez, N., Mothe, J., Chrisment, C., & Egret, D. (2007). Modeling context through domain ontologies. *Information Retrieval, 10* (2) (Apr. 2007), 143-172.

Hertzum, M., & Pejtersen, A. M. (2000). The information-seeking practices of engineers: Searching for documents as well as for people. *Information Processing and Management, 36*(5), 761-778.

Heymann, P., & Garcia-Molina, H. (2006). Collaborative Creation of Communal Hierarchical Taxonomies in Social Tagging Systems, *Stanford InfoLab Technical Report (2006-10)*. Retrieved February 17, 2008, from http://dbpubs.stanford.edu:8090/pub/2006-10

Hoang, H. H., & Tjoa, A. M. (2006). *The state of the art of ontology-based query systems: A comparison of current approaches.* Paper presented at the IEEE International Conference on Computing and Informatics.

Hoang, H. H., & Tjoa, A. M. (2006). *The virtual query language for information retrieval in the SemanticLIFE framework.* Paper presented at the International Workshop on Web Information Systems Modeling - CAiSE06 (pp. 1062-1076). Luxembourg.

Hoang, H. H., Andjomshoaa, A., & Tjoa, A. M. (2006). *VQS: An ontology-based query system for the SemanticLIFE digital memory project.* Paper presented at the 2th IFIF WG 2.14 & 4.12 International Workshop on Web Semantics - OTM06 (LNCS 4278, pp. 1796-1805). Montpellier: Springer.

Hoashi, K., Matsumoto, K., & Inoue, N. (2003). Personalization of user profiles for content-based music retrieval based on relevance feedback. *ACM Multimedia,* 110–119.

Hofmann, T., & Puzicha, J. (1999). Latent Class Models for Collaborative Filtering. *Proceedings of IJCAI'99.*

Höök, K. (2000). Steps to take before IUIs become real. *Journal of Interacting With Computers, 12*(4), 409–426.

Horvitz, E., Breese J., Heckerman D., Hovel D., & Rommelse, K. (1998). *The* Lumière project: Bayesian user modeling for inferring the goals and needs of software users. *Proceedings of 14th Conference on Uncertainty in Artificial Intelligence,* San Francisco.

Horvitz, E., Breeze, J., Heckerman, D., Hovel, D., & Rommelse, K. (1998). The Lumiere project: Bayesian user modeling for inferring goals and needs of software users. In: *Proceedings of the Fourteenth Annual Conference on Uncertainty in Artificial Intelligence,* (pp. 256–265).

Hotho, A., Jäschke, R., Schmitz, C., & Stumme, G. (2006). Information Retrieval in Folksonomies: Search and Ranking. In Y. Sure & J. Domingue (Eds.), *The Semantic Web: Research and Applications* (pp. 411-426). Heidelberg: Springer. Retrieved January 25, 2008, from http://www.kde.cs.uni-kassel.de/stumme/papers/2006/hotho2006information.pdf

Hübner, S., Spittel, R., Visser, U., & Vögele, T. J. (2004). Ontology-based search for interactive digital maps. *IEEE Intelligent Systems, 19*(3), 80-86.

Huhns, M.N., & Singh, M.P. (1998). *Multiagent systems in information-rich environments. Cooperative information agents II* (pp. 79-93). (LNAI 1435).

Hutchins, E. (1991). *How a cockpit remembers its speed.* San Diego.

Hutchins, E. (1995). *Cognitition in the wild.* Cambridge MA: The MIT Press.

Huynh, D., Karger, D., & Quan, D. (2002). *Haystack: A platform for creating, organizing and visualizing information using RDF.* Paper presented at the International Workshop on the Semantic Web.

Huysman, M., & Wulf, V. (2003). *Social capital and information technology.* Cambridge MA.

Hwang, C. H. (1999). Incompletely and imprecisely speaking: Using dynamic ontologies for representing and retrieving information. *Knowledge Representation Meets Databases,* 14-20

Hyvönen, E., Saarela, S., & Viljanen, K. (2003). *Ontogator: Combining view- and ontology-based search with Semantic browsing.* Paper presented at the XML Finland Conference: Open Standards, XML and the Public Sector.

Ide, E. (1971). New experiment in relevance feedback. In: *The Smart system-experiments in automatic documents processing,* (pp. 337–354).

Indulska, J., Robinson, R., Rakotonirainy, A., & Henricksen, K. (2003). Experiences in Using CC/PP in Context-Aware Systems. In M.-S. Chen, P.K. Chrysance, M. Sloman & A. Zaslavsky (Ed.), *4th International Conference on Mobile Data Management (MDM 2003): Vol. 2574. Lecture Notes in Computer Science* (pp. 247-261). Springer-Verlag.

Ingwersen, P. (1992). *Information Retrieval Interaction.* London, Taylor Graham.

Jack, K., & Duclaye, F. (2007). Etude de la pertinence de critères de recherche en recherche d'informations sur des données structurées. In *PeCUSI, INFORSID* (pp. 285-297). Perros-Guirec, France.

Jack, K., & Duclayee, F. (2008). Improving Explicit Preference Entry by Visualising Data Similarities. In *Intelligent User Interfaces, International Workshop on Recommendation and Collaboration (ReColl).* Spain.

Jaczynski, M., & Trousse, B. (1999). Broadway: A case-based system for cooperative information browsing on the world-wide-web. In Julian A. Padget, editor, *Collaboration between Human and Artificial Societies, 1624* of *LNCS*, pages 264–283. Springer.

Jain, A. K., Murty, M. N., & Flynn, P. J. (1999). Data Clustering: A Review. *ACM Computing Surveys, 31*(3), 264-323. Retrieved May 22, 2008, from http://www.cs.rutgers.edu/~mlittman/courses/lightai03/jain99data.pdf

Jansen B., Booth D., & Spink A. (2007). Determining the User Intent of Web Search Engine Queries. In *Proceedings of the International World Wide Web Conference,* (pp 1149-1150). Alberta, Canada.

Jéribi, L., Rumpler, B., & Pinon, J.M. (2001). Système d'aide à la recherche et à l'interrogation de bases documentaires, basé sur la réutilisation d'expériences. *In Congrès Informatique des Organisations et Systèmes d'Information et de Décision (INFORSID'2001),* pages 443–463, Martigny, Suisse.

Jin, X., Zhou, Y., & Mobasher, B. (2005). Task-Oriented Web User Modeling for Recommendation, In *Proceedings of the 10th International Conference on User Modeling (UM'05),* Edinburgh, Scotland, LNAI 3538, pp.109-118, Springer

Jin, X., Zhou, Y., & Mobasher, B. (2005). A Maximum Entropy Web Recommendation System: Combining Collaborative and Content Features. *KDD'05,* August 21–24, 2005, Chicago, Illinois, USA.

Joachims, T., Freitag, D., & Mitchell, T. M. (1997). Web Watcher: A tour guide for the World Wide Web. In *Pro-ceedings of the Fifteenth International Joint Conference on Artificial Intelligence* (pp. 770-777). Nagoya, Japan: Morgan Kaufmann.

Jung, R., & Heckmann, D. (2006). Ambient Audio Notification with Personalized Music. *UM ECAI'06.*

Kalfoglou, Y., & Schorlemmer, M. (2003). IF-Map: An ontology mapping method based on information-flow theory. In S. Spaccapietra et al. (Eds.), *Journal on data semantics.* (LNCS 2800).

Kanawati, R., & Malek, M. (2000). Informing the design of shared bookmark systems. In *the proceedings of RIAO'2000: Content-based Multimedia Information Access,* pages 170–180, Collège de France, Paris, France.

Kanawati, R., & Malek, M. (2001). Cowing: A collaborative bookmark management system. In *the International workshop on Cooperative Information Agents (CIA'01), 2182* of *LNAI,* pages 34–39.

Kanawati, R., & Malek, M. (2007). Computing Social Networks for Information Sharing: A Case-based Approach. In Schuler Douglas, editor, *Second international conference on Online Communities and Social Computing, 4564* of *LNCS,* pages 86–95, Beijing, China, Springer.

Kanellopoulos, D., Kotsiantis, S., & Pintelas, P. (2006, February). Ontology-based learning applications: A development methodology. *Proceedings of the 24th Iasted International Multi-Conference Software Engineering,* Austria.

Karamuftuoglu, M. (1998). Collaborative information retrieval: toward a social informatics view of IR interaction. *Journal of the American Society for Information Science, 49*(12), 1070 -1080.

Karat, C. M., Brodie, C., Karat, J., Vergo, J., & Alpert, S. R. (2003). Personalizing the user experience on ibm.com. *IBM Systems Journal, 42*(4).

Karger, D. R., Bakshi, K., Huynh, D., Quan, D., & Vineet, S. (2005). *Haystack: A general purpose information management tool for end users of semistructured data.* Paper presented at the 2nd Biennial Conference on Innovative Data Systems Research (pp. 13-26).

Karoui, H., Kanawati, R., & Petrucci, L. (2004). An intelligent peer-to-peer multi-agent system for collaborative management of bibliographic databases. In *Proceedings of the* 9th *UK Workshop on Case-Based Reasoning,* pages 43–50, Queens' College, Cambridge, UK.

Karoui, H., Kanawati, R., & Petrucci, L. (2006). An intelligent peer-to-peer multi-agent system for collaborative management of bibliographic databases. In *SGAI's expert update magazine,* volume 8, pages 22–31. Springer.

Karoui, H., Kanawati, R., & Petrucci, L. (2006). CO-BRAS: Cooperative CBR system for bibliographical reference recommendation. In Thomas Roth-Berghofer, Mehmet H.Göker, and H. Altay Güvenir, editors, *the 8th European Conference on Case-Based Reasonning (ECCBR'06)*, volume 4106 of *LNCS*, pages 76–90, Ölüdeniz/Fethiye, Turkey, Springer.

Karvounarakis, G., Alexaki, S., Christophides, V., Plexousakis, D., & Scholl, M. (2002). *RQL: A declarative query language for RDF.* Paper presented at the Eleventh International World Wide Web Conference (pp. 591-603). ACM Press.

Karypis, G. (2001). Evaluation of item-based top-N recommendation algorithms. In *10th International Conference on Information and Knowledge Management* (pp. 247–254).

Karypis, G. (2002). *Cluto A Clustering Toolkit Manual.* University of Minnesota, Department of Computer Science Technical Report.

Kassab, R. & Lamirel, J.C. (2006). An innovative approach to intelligent information filtering. In H. Haddad (Ed.), *ACM Symposium on Applied Computing 2006 (SAC 2006): Vol. 1. Information access and retrieval* (pp. 1089-1093). ACM Press.

Kauntz, H., Selman, B., & Shah, M. (1996). Referral web: Combining social networks and collaborative filtering. *Communications of the ACM, 40*(3), 63-65.

Kay, J. (2000). Stereotypes, Student Models and Scrutability. In Gauthier, G., Frasson, C. and VanLehn, K. (eds.), *Lecture Notes in Computer Science 1839* (pp. 19-30), Springer

Kay, J. (2006). *Scrutable Adaptation: Because We Can and Must.* AH 2006: 11-19.

Kay, J., & Lum, A. (2004) Ontologies for Scrutable Learner Modeling in Adaptive E-Learning. In Aroyo, L., Tasso, C. (Eds.) *Proc. of Workshop on Application of Semantic Web Technologies for Adaptive Educational Hypermedia.* Technische University Eindhoven

Kelleher, J., & Bridge, D. (2003). Rectree centroid : An accurate, scalable collaborative recommender. In Cunningham, P., Fernando, T., & Vogel, C. (Ed.), *14th Irish Conference on Artificial Intelligence and Cognitive Science* (pp. 89–94).

Kempthorne, O., & Doerfler, T. E. (1969). The behavior of some significance tests under experimental randomization. *Biometrika*, 56(2):231-248.

Keppel, G. (1991). *Design and analysis: A researcher's handbook.* Englewood Cliffs, NJ: Prentice-Hall.

Kerschberg, L., Chowdhury, M., Damiano, A., Jeong, H., Mitchell, S., Si, J., et al. (2004). *Knowledge sifter: Ontology-driven search over heterogeneous databases.* Paper presented at the 16th International Conference on Scientific and Statistical Database Management.

Kifer, M., Lausen, G., & Wu, J. (1995). Logical foundations of object-oriented and frame-based languages. *Journal of the ACM, 42*(4), 741-843.

Kim, H., & Chan, P. (2003). Learning Implicit User Interest Hierarchy for Context in Personalization. In *Proceedings of the 8th International Conference on Intelligent User Interfaces* (pp. 101-108). New York: ACM Press. Retrieved February 15, 2008, from http://cs.fit.edu/~pkc/papers/iui03.pdf

Kim, H., & Chan, P. K. (2008). Learning implicit user interest hierarchy for context in personalization. *Applied Intelligence, 28*, 2(Apr. 2008), 153-166.

Kirsch-Pinheiro, M., Gensel, J., & Martin, H. (2004). Representing Context for an Adaptative Awareness Mechanism. In G.-J. de Vreede, L. A. Guerrero & G. Marín Raventós (Ed.), *10th International Workshop on Groupware (CRIWG 2004): Vol. 3198. Lecture Notes In Computer Science* (pp. 339-348). Springer-Verlag.

Kleinberg, J., & Sandler, M. (2004). Using mixture models for collaborative filtering. In *36th ACM Symposium on Theory of Computing* (pp. 569–578). ACM Press.

Koivunen, M., & Miller, E. (2002). W3C semantic Web activity. In E. Hyvonen (Ed.), *Semantic Web kick-off in Finland* (pp. 27-44). Helsinki: HIIT.

Konstan, J., Miller, B., Maltz, D., Herlocker, J., Gordon, L. R., & Riedl. J. (1997). GroupLens: applying collaborative filtering to Usenet news. *Communications of the ACM, 40*(3), 77-87.

Konstan, J., Miller, B., Maltz, D., Herlocker, J., Gordon, L., & Riedl, J. (1997) GroupLens: Applying Collaborative Filtering to Usenet News. *Communications of the ACM, 40*, 77-87. ACM Press.

Krishnappa, R. (2005). Multi-user search engine (MUSE): Supporting collaborative information seeking and retrieval. Master's thesis, University of Missouri-Rolla, University of Missouri-Rolla, Rolla, USA.

Krüger, A., Baus, J., Heckmann, D., Kruppa, M., & Wasinger, R. (2007). Adaptive mobile guides. In P. Brusilovsky, A. Kobsa & W. Nejdl (Ed.), *The Adaptive*

Web: Vol. 4321. Lecture Notes in Computer Science (pp. 521-549). Springer-Verlag.

Krulwich, B. (1997). LIFESTYLE FINDER: Intelligent User Profiling Using Large-Scale Demographic Data. *AI Magazine* (pp. 37-45).

Kumar, R., Raghavan, P., Rajagopalan, S., & Tomkins, A. (2001) Recommendation Systems: A Probabilistic Analysis. *Journal of Computer and System Sciences, 63*, 42-61.

Kuo, F. F., Chiang, M. F., Shan, M. K., & Lee, S. Y. (2005). Emotion-based Music Recommendation by Association Discovery from Film Music. *Proc. 13th annual ACM international conference on Multimedia,* Hilton, Singapore, 507 - 510.

Kurumatani, K. (2003). Mass User Support by Social Coordination among Citizen in a Real Environment. In K. Kurumatani, S. Chen & A. Ohuchi (Ed.), *International Workshop on Multi-Agent for Mass User Support (MAMUS 2003): Vol. 3012. Lecture Notes In Artificial Intelligence* (pp. 1–16). Springer-Verlag.

Lam, S. K., & Riedl, J. (2004). Shilling recommender systems for fun and profit. In *Proceedings of the 13th international conference on World Wide Web,* New York, NY, USA: ACM Press.

Lam, S. K., Frankowski, D., & Riedl, J. (2006). Do you trust your recommendations? An exploration of security and privacy issues in recommender systems. In *International Conference on Emerging Trends in Information and Communication Security.*

Laniado, D., Eynard, D., & Colombetti, M. (2007, December). *Using WordNet to turn a folksonomy into a hierarchy of concepts.* Paper presented at the Fourth Italian Semantic Web Workshop, Bari, Italy. Retrieved February 14, 2008, from http://ftp.informatik.rwth-aachen.de/Publications/CEUR-WS/Vol-314/51.pdf

Lathia, N., Hailes, S., & Capra, L (2007). Private Distributed Collaborative Filtering Using Estimated Concordance Measures. In *Proceedings of the 2007 ACM Conference on Recommender Systems (RecSys).* Minneapolis, USA: ACM Press.

Lathia, N., Hailes, S., & Capra, L. (2008). The Effect of Correlation Coefficients on Communities of Recommenders. In *23rd Annual ACM Symposium on Applied Computing, Trust, Recommendations, Evidence and other Collaboration Know-how (TRECK) Track.* Fortaleza, Ceara, Brazil: ACM Press.

Latour, B. (2006). Changer de société - refaire de la sociologie. Paris: Armillaire.

Lave, J. (1988). Cognition in practice: Mind, mathematics and culture in everyday life. Cambridge: Cambridge University Press.

Lave, J., & Wenger, E. (1991). *Situated learning: Legitimate peripheral participation.* Cambridge: Cambridge University Press.

Lawrie, D., & Croft, W. B. (2000, April). *Discovering and Comparing Topic Hierarchies.* Paper presented at RIAO 2000, Paris, France. Retrieved February 15, 2008, from http://www.cs.loyola.edu/~lawrie/papers/lawrieRIOA2000.pdf

Leacock, C., & Chodorow, M. (1998). Combining local context and WordNet similarity for word sense identification. In C. Fellbaum (Ed.), *WordNet: An electronic lexical database* (pp. 265-283). Cambridge, MA: MIT Press.

Lech, T., & Wienhofen, L. (2005). AmbieAgents: A Scalable Infrastructure for Mobile and Context-Aware Information Services. In M. Pechoucek, D. Steiner & S. Thompson (PC), *4th International Conference on Autonomous Agent and MAS (AAMAS 2005): Vol. 1. Information agents, brokering and matchmaking* (pp. 625-631). ACM Press.

Lee U., Liu Z., & Cho J. (2005). Automatic identification of user goals in web search. In *Proceedings of the International World Wide Web Conference 2005,* (pp. 391–400), Chiba, Japan.

Lee, J. (1999). Interactive learning with a Web-based digital library system. *Proceedings of the 9th DELOS Workshop on Digital Libraries for Distance Learning.* Retrieved from http:// courses.cs.vt.edu/~cs3604/DELOS.html

Lekakos, G., & Giaglis, G.M. (2007) A Hybrid Approach for Improving Predictive Accuracy of Collaborative Filtering Algorithms. *User Model User-Adap Inter., 17*, 5–40.

Leontiev, A. (1979). The problem of activity in psychology. In J. V. Wertsch (Ed.), *The concept of activity in soviet psychology* (pp. 135-143). Armonk: Sharpe.

Leskovec, J., Krause, A., Guestrin, C., Faloutsos, C., VanBriesen, J., & Glance, N. (2007). Cost-effective Outbreak Detection in Networks. In: *Proceedings of the 13th ACM SIGKDD International Conference on Knowledge Discovery and Data Mining,* (pp. 420-429), San Jose, California, USA.

Li, J., & Zaiane, O. R. (2004). Combining usage, content and structure data to improve web site recommendation. In K. Bauknecht, M. Bichler, B. Pröll (Eds.), *Proceeding* of *5th International Conference E-Commerce and Web Technologies, Lecture Notes in Computer Science 3182* (pp. 305-315). Berlin, Heidelberg, Germany: Springer.

Li, Q., & Kim, B. M. (2003). Clustering Approach for Hybrid Recommender System. In *Proceedings of the 2003 IEEE/WIC International Conference on Web Intelligence*. Beijing, China: IEEE Press.

Li, Q., Kim, B. M., Guan, D. H., & Oh, D. W. (2004). A Music Recommender Based on Audio Features. *SIGIR'04*, July 25-29, 2004, Sheffield, South Yorkshire, UK.

Li, Q., Myaeng, S. H., & Kim, B. M. (2007). A probabilistic music recommender considering user opinions and audio features. *Information Processing and Management, 43*, 473–487.

Li, Q., Myaeng, S. H., Guan, D. H., & Kim, B.M. (2005). A Probabilistic Model for Music Recommendation Considering Audio Features. *Information Retrieval Technology.* Lecture Notes in Computer Science, *3689*, 72-83.

Li, T., & Tzanetakis, G. (2003). Factors in automatic musical genre classification of audio signals. *Proc. IEEE Workshop on Applications of Signal Processing to Audio and Acoustics (WASPAA).*

Lia, Y., Lu, L., & Xuefeng, L. (2005). A hybrid collaborative filtering method for multiple-interests and multiple-content recommendation in E-Commerce. *Expert Systems with Applications, 28*, 67–77.

Lieberman, H. (1995). Letizia: An Agent That Assists Web Browsing. In *Proceedings of the 1995 International Joint Conference on Artificial Intelligent*, Montreal, Canada.

Lieberman, H., Van Dyke, N. W., & Vivacqua, A. S. (1999). Let's browse: a collaborative web browsing agent. In *IUI '99: Proceedings of the 4th international conference on Intelligent user interfaces*, pages 65–68, Los Angeles, California, USA. ACM Press.

Lin, W., Alvarez, S. A., & Ruiz, C. (2002). Efficient adaptive-support association rule mining for recommender systems. *Data Mining and Knowledge Discovery, 6* 83–105.

Linden, G., Smith, B., & York, J. (2003). Amazon.com recommendations: Item-to-item collaborative filtering. In *IEEE Internet Computing, 7*(1), 76–80.

Liu, F., Yu, C., & Meng, W. (2002). Personalized Web search by mapping user query to categories. *Proceedings of the 2002 ACM Conference on Information and Knowledge Management,* McLean, VA.

Liu, Z., & Chu, W. W. (2007). Knowledge-based query expansion to support scenario-specific retrieval of medical free text. *Information Retrieval, 10(2) (Apr. 2007),* 173 – 202.

Logan, B. (2004). Music recommendation from song sets. *Proc. of the International Conference on Music Information Retrieval (ISMIR) 2004.*

Lóper-Pujalte, C., Guerrero-Bote, V., & Moya-Anegon, F. D. (2003). Genetic algorithms in relevance feedback: a second test and new contributions. *Information Processing and Management, 39(5)*, 669–697.

Lorenzi, F., & Ricci, F. (2003). Case-Based Recommender Systems: A Unifying View. *ITWP*, page 89-113, Acapulco, Mexico, Springer, Lecture Notes in Computer Science, 3169.

Lytras, M.D., & Naeve, A. (Eds.). (2005). *Intelligent learning infrastructure for knowledge intensive organizations.* London: Information Science.

Ma, H., King, I., Lyu, M. R. (2007). Effective Missing Data Prediction for Collaborative Filtering. In *Proceedings of the 30th Annual International ACM SIGIR Conference on Research and Development in Information Retrieval.* Amsterdam, Holland: ACM Press.

Maedche, A., Motik, B., Silva, N., & Volz, R. (2002). *MAFRA: An ontology mapping framework in the Semantic Web.* Paper presented at the 12th International Workshop on Knowledge Transformation.

Maedche, A., Motik, B., Silva, N., & Volz, R. (2002). MAFRA—a mapping framework for distributed ontologies. *Proceedings of EKAW (Knowledge Engineering and Knowledge Management) 2002.* Berlin: Springer-Verlag (LNCS 2473).

Maedche, A., Staab, S., Stojanovic, N., Studer, R., & Sure, Y. (2001). *SEAL: A framework for developing Semantic Web portals.* Paper presented at the 18th British National Conference on Databases (pp. 1-22). London: Springer.

Maekawa, T., Hara, T., & Nishio, S. (2006). A collaborative web browsing system for multiple mobile users. In *PERCOM '06: Proceedings of the Fourth Annual IEEE International Conference on Pervasive Computing and Communications (PERCOM'06)*, pages 22–35, Washington, DC, USA. IEEE Computer Society.

Maes, P. (1994). Agents that reduce work and information overload. *Communications of the ACM, 37(7)*, 31–40.

Magnini, B., & Strapparava, C. (2001). Improving user modeling with content-based techniques. In: *Bauer, M.,*

Vassileva, J., and Gmytrasiewicz, P. (Eds). *User Modeling: Proceedings of the Eighth International Conference, UM 2001.* (pp. 74–83).

Mahmood, T, & Ricci F. (2007, August). Learning and adaptivity in interactive recommender systems. In M. L. Gini, R. J. Kauffman, D. Sarppo, C. Dellarocas, & F. Dignum (Eds.), *Proceedings of the 9th International Conference on Electronic Commerce: The Wireless World of Electronic Commerce* (pp. 75-84). University of Minnesota, Minneapolis, MN, USA: ACM Press.

Malek, M., & Kanawati, R. (2004). A data driven CBR approach: A contineous maintenance strategy. *In the International Conference on Advances in Intelligent Systems: Theory and Applications*, pages 281–290, Luxemburg.

Markoff, J. (2005). What the dormouse said: How the 60s counterculture shaped the personal computer: Viking Adult.

Massa, P., & Avesani, P. (2007). Trust-aware Recommender Systems. In *Proceedings of the 2007 ACM Conference on Recommender Systems (RecSys)*. Minneapolis, USA: ACM Press.

Mathes, A. (2004). *Folksonomies: Cooperative Classification and Communication Through Shared Metadata*. Urbana-Champaign, Illinois: Graduate School of Library and Information Science, University of Illinois Urbana-Champaign. Retrieved January 21, 2008, from http://www.adammathes.com/academic/computer-mediated-communication/folksonomies.html

Maybury, M., & Brusilovsky, P. (Eds.). (2002). The adaptive Web. *Communications of the ACM, 45*.

McCarthy, K., Salao, M., Coyle, L., McGinty, L., Smyth, B., & Nixon, P. (2006) Group Recommender Systems: A Critiquing Based Approach. *IUI'06*, January 29–February 1, 2006, Sydney, Australia.

McKay, C., McEnnis, D., & Fujinaga, I. (2006). A Large Publicly Accessible Prototype Audio Database for Music Research. *Proc. of the International Conference on Music Information Retrieval (ISMIR) 2006*.

McLaughlin, M. R., & Herlocker, J. L. (2004). A Collaborative Filtering Algorithm and Evaluation Metric that Accurately Model the User Experience. In *Proceedings of the 27th Annual International ACM SIGIR Conference on Research and Development in Information Retrieval*. Sheffield, United Kingdom: ACM Press.

McNee, S. M., Riedl, J., & Konstan, J. A. (2006, April). Being Accurate is Not Enough: How Accuracy Metrics have hurt Recommender Systems. In *Extended Abstracts of the 2006 ACM Conference on Human Factors in Computing Systems (CHI 2006)*. Montreal, Canada: ACM Press.

Melenhorst, M., & van Setten, M. (2007, September). *Usefulness of Tags in Providing Access to Large Information Systems*. Paper presented at IEEE Professional Communication Society Conference. Retrieved May 13, 2008, from http://www.x-cd.com/ipcc07CD/pdfs/55.pdf

Melville, P., Mooney, R., & Nagarajan, R. (2002). Content-boosted collaborative filtering for improved recommendations. In *18th National Conference on Artificial Intelligence* (pp. 187-192).

Mendes, M.E.S., & Sacks, L. (2004). Dynamic knowledge representation for e-learning applications. In M. Nikravesh, L.A. Zadeh, B. Azvin, & R. Yager (Eds.), *Enhancing the power of the Internet—studies in fuzziness and soft computing* (vol. 139, pp. 255-278). Berlin/London: Springer-Verlag.

Micarelli, A., Sciarrone, F., & Marinilli, M. (2007). Web document modeling. In Brusilovsky, P., Kobsa, A., Nejdl, W. (Eds.), *The Adaptive Web: Methods and Strategies of Web Personalization*. LNCS 4321. Springer

Michlmayr, E., & Cayzer, S. (2007). Learning User Profiles from Tagging Data and Leveraging them for Personal(ized) Information Access. In: *Proceedings of the Workshop on Tagging and Metadata for Social Information Organization, 16th International World Wide Web Conference (WWW2007)*, Banff, Alberta, Canada.

Michlmayr, E., Cayzer, S., & Shabajee, P. (2007). *Adaptive User Profiles for Enterprise Information Access*, HP Labs Technical Report HPL-2007-7. Retrieved 24 January 2008, from http://www.hpl.hp.com/techreports/2007/HPL-2007-72.pdf

Middleton, S. E., De Roure, D. C., & Shadbolt, N. R. (2001). Capturing knowledge of user preferences: ontologies in recommender systems. In *Proceedings of the 1st international Conference on Knowledge Capture* (Victoria, British Columbia, Canada, October 22 - 23, 2001). K-CAP '01. ACM, New York, NY, 100-107. DOI= http://doi.acm.org/10.1145/500737.500755

Middleton, S. E., Shadbolt, N. R., De Roure, D. C. (2004). Ontological User profiling in Recommender Systems, *ACM Transactions on Information Systems, 22*(1), 54-88.

Mika, P. (2005). Ontologies are us: A unified model of social networks and semantics. In Y. Gil, E. Motta, R. V. Benjamins & M. Musen (Eds.), *The Semantic Web – ISWC*

2005 (pp. 522-536). Heidelberg, Germany: Springer. Retrieved January 25, 2008, from http://www.cs.vu.nl/~pmika/research/papers/ISWC-folksonomy.pdf

Miller, B., Albert, I., Lam, S., Konstan, J., & Riedl, J. (2003). Movielens unplugged: Experiences with an occasionally connected recommender system. *In Proceedings of ACM 2003 International Conference on Intelligent User Interfaces (IUI'03).* ACM Press.

Miller, B., Albert, I., Lam, S., Konstan, J., & Riedl, J. (2003). MovieLens unplugged: experiences with an occasionally connected recommender system. In *8th international conference on Intelligent User Interfaces* (pp. 263-266). ACM.

Miller, G. A, Beckwith, R., Fellbaum, C., Gross, D., & Miller, K. J. (1990). Introduction to WordNet: an on-line lexical database. *International Journal of Lexicography, 3*(4), 235-244. Retrieved February 7, 2008, from ftp://ftp.cogsci.princeton.edu/pub/wordnet/5papers.ps

Mitchell, T. (1997). *Machine Learning.* New York, NY: McGraw-Hill.

Mobasher, B. (2007). Data Mining for Web Personalization. In Brusilovsky, P., Kobsa, A., Nejdl, W. (Eds.), *The Adaptive Web: Methods and Strategies of Web Personalization.* LNCS. Springer

Mobasher, B., Burke, R., Bhaumik, R., & Williams, C. (2007). Towards Trustworthy Recommender Systems: An Analysis of Attack Models and Algorithm Robustness. *Transations on Internet Technology (TOIT).* 7, 4.

Mobasher, B., Cooley, R., & Srivastava, J. (2000). Automatic personalization based on Web usage mining. *Communications of the ACM, 43*(8), 142-151.

Mobasher, B., Dai, H., Luo, T., Sun, Y., & Zhu, J. (2000). Integrating web usage and content mining for more effective personalization. In K. Bauknecht, S. K. Madria, G. Pernul (Eds.), *Proceeding of First International Conference E-Commerce and Web Technologies, Lecture Notes in Computer Science 1875* (pp. 165–176). Munich, Germany: Springer.

Montaner, M. (2003). Collaborative Recommender Agents Based on Case-Based Reasoning and Trust. *PHD Thesis*, Universitat de Girona.

Mooney, R., & Roy, L. (1999). Content-based book recommending using learning for text categorization. In *ACM SIGIR'99, Workshop on Recommender Systems: Algorithms and Evaluation.*

Moore, J. D., & Mittal, V. O. (1996). Dynamically generated follow-up questions. *IEEE Computer, 29*(7), 75–86.

Moran, T., & Dourish, P. (2001). Introduction to this special issue on context-aware computing. *Journal of Human-Computer Interaction, 16 (2/4)*, 87-95.

Morris, M. R., & Horvitz, E. (2007). SearchTogether: An interface for collaborative web search. In *UIST '07: Proceedings of the 20th annual ACM symposium on User interface software and technology*, pages 3–12, Newport, Rhode Island, USA. ACM Press.

Morris, M. R., Paepcke, A., & Winograd, T. (2006). TeamSearch: Comparing Techniques for Co-Present Collaborative Search of Digital Media. In *TABLETOP '06: Proceedings of the First IEEE International Workshop on Horizontal Interactive Human-Computer Systems*, pages 97–104, Washington, DC, USA. IEEE Computer Society.

Morville, P., & Rosenfeld, L. (2007). *Information Architecture for the Worldwide Web.* Sebastopol, California: O'Reilly.

Murray, T. (1997). Expanding the knowledge acquisition bottleneck for intelligent tutoring systems. *International Journal of Artificial Intelligence in Education, 8*, 222-232.

Murray, T., Piemonte, J., Khan, S., Shen, T., & Condit, C. (2000). Evaluating the Need for Intelligence in an Adaptive Hypermedia System. In G. Gauthier, C. Frasson & K. VanLehn (Ed.), *5th International Conference on Intelligent Tutoring Systems (ITS 2000): Vol. 1839. Lecture Notes In Computer Science* (pp. 373-382). Springer-Verlag.

Mutch, A. (2002). Actors and networks or agents and structures: Towards a realist view of informations systems. *Organization, 9*(3), 477-496.

Mylonas, Ph. Vallet, D., Castells, P., Fernandez, M., & Avrithis, Y. (2008). Personalized information retrieval based on context and ontological knowledge. *Knowledge Engineering Review, 23*(1), 73-100. Cambridge University Press

Nagarajan, R. (2002). Content-boosted collaborative filtering for improved recommendations. *Proceedings of the 18th National Conference on Artificial Intelligence,* Canada.

Nageswara Rao, K., & Talwar, V.G. (2008). Application domain and functional classification of recommender systems a survey. In *Desidoc journal of library and information technology*, vol 28, n°3, 17-36.

Nakagawa M., & Mobasher, B. (2003). A hybrid web personalization model based on site connectivity. In R. Kohavi, B. Liu, B. Masnad, J. Srivastava, O. R. Zaiane

(Eds.), *Web Mining as a Premise to Effective and Intelligent Web Applications, Proceedings of the Fifth International Workshop on Knowledge Discovery on the Web* (pp. 59-70). Washington DC, WA, USA: Quality Color Press.

Nakamoto, R., Nakajima, S., Miyazaki, J., Uemura, S. (2007, February). Tag-Based Contextual Collaborative Filtering. Paper presented at the 18th IEICE Data Engineering Workshop, Hiroshima, Japan. Retrieved February 15, 2008, from http://www.ieice.org/~de/DEWS/DEWS2007/pdf/m5-6.pdf

Nanas, N., Uren, V., & de Roeck, A. (2004). Exploiting Term Dependencies for Multi-Topic Information Filtering with a Single User Profile. *Lecture Notes in Computer Science, 3025*: 400-409

Netscape Conferencer (2001). http://www.aibn.com/help/Software/Netscape/communicator/conference/.

Newman, M. E. J. (2004). Detecting Community Structure in Networks. *The European Physical Journal B, 38*(2), 321-330. Retrieved May 27, 2008, from http://www-personal.umich.edu/~mejn/papers/epjb.pdf

Newman, M. E. J., & Girvan, M. (2004). Finding and evaluating community structure in networks. *Physical Review E, 69*(2), 6113. Retrieved February 15, 2008, from http://arxiv.org/abs/cond-mat/0308217

Nguyen, A., Denos, N., & Berrut, C. (2007). Improving new user recommendations with rule-based induction on cold user data. In *RecSys2007* (pp. 121-128).

Nguyen, H. (2005). *Capturing User Intent for Information Retrieval*. Ph.D dissertation. University of Connecticut.

Nguyen, H., & Santos, E., Jr. (2007). An Evaluation of the Accuracy of Capturing User Intent for Information Retrieval. In *Proceedings of the 2007 International Conference on Artificial Intelligence* (pp. 341-350). Las Vegas, NV.

Nguyen, H., & Santos, E., Jr. (2007). Effects of prior knowledge on the effectiveness of a hybrid user model for information retrieval. In *Proceedings of the Homeland Security and Homeland Defense VI conference, 6538*. Orlando, FL. March 2007.

Nguyen, H., Santos, E. Jr., Zhao, Q., & Lee, C. (2004). Evaluation of Effects on Retrieval Performance for an Adaptive User Model. In *Adaptive Hypermedia 2004: Workshop Proceedings -Part I*, (pp. 193–202), Eindhoven, the Netherlands

Nguyen, H., Santos, E., Jr., Schuet, A., & Smith, N. (2006). Hybrid User Model for Information Retrieval. In *Technical Report of Modeling Others from Observations workshop at AAAI-2006 conference.*

Nguyen, H., Santos, E.J., Zhao, Q. & Wang, H. (2004). Capturing User Intent for Information Retrieval. In: *Proceedings of the Human Factors and Ergonomics society 48th annual meeting.* (pp. 371–375), New Orleans, LA.

Nielsen, J. (1999). *Web usability*. Indianapolis, IN: New Riders Publishing.

Nielsen, J. (2004). *Risks of quantitative studies*. Retrieved March 9, 2004, from www.useit.com/alertbox/20040301.html

Nieto-Carvajal, I., Botia, J.A., Ruiz, P.M., & Gomez-Skarmeta, A.F. (2004). Implementation and Evaluation of a Location-Aware Wireless Multi-Agent System. In L. Yang, M. Guo, G.R. Gao & N.K. Jha (Ed.), *Embedded and Ubiquitous Computing* (*EUC 2004*): *Vol. 3207. Lecture Notes in Computer Science* (pp. 528-537). Springer-Verlag.

Noda, K. (2006). Towards a Representational Model of Evaluation Ontology, *Proceedings of International Symposium on Large Scale Knowledge Resources: LKR2006*, 159-160.

Norman, D. A., & Draper, S. W. (1986). *User centered system design: New perspective on HCI*. Hillsdale, NJ: Lawrence Erlbaum.

Noruzi, A. (2006). Folksonomies: (Un)Controlled Vocabulary. *Knowledge Organization, 33*(4), 199-203. Retrieved January 25, 2008, from http://eprints.rclis.org/archive/00011286/01/Folksonomy%2C_UnControled_Vocabulary.pdf

O'Conner, M., & Herlocker, J. (1999). Clustering items for collaborative filtering. In *ACM SIGIR Workshop on Recommender Systems.*

Oppermann, R. (1994). Adaptively supported adaptivity. *International Journal of Human-Computer Studies, 40*, 455–472.

Ostyn, C., & Lewis, S. (Eds.) (2007). IEEE 1484.20.1 - Draft Standard for Learning Technology. Data Model for Reusable Competency Definitions, IEEE Computer Society Press, Piscataway, NJ, USA

Page, L., & Brin, S. (1998). The Anatomy of a Large-Scale Hypertextual Web Search Engine. *Computer Networks and ISDN Systems, 30*(1-7), 108-118. Retrieved January 25, 2008, from http://infolab.stanford.edu/~backrub/google.html

Page, M., Gensel, J., Capponi, C., Bruley, C., Genoud, P., Ziébelin, D., Bardou, D. & Dupierris, V. (2001) A New Approach in Object-Based Knowledge Representation: the AROM System. In L. Monostori, J. Váncza & M. Ali (Ed.), *14th International Conference on Industrial & Engineering Applications of Artificial Intelligence & Expert Systems, (IEA/AIE2001): Vol. 2070. Lecture Notes in Artificial Intelligence* (pp. 113-118). Springer-Verlag.

Palmquist, R. A., & Kim, K. S. (2000). Cognitive style and on-line database search experience as predictors of Web search performance. *Journal of the American Society for Information Science, 51*(6), 558–566.

Park, S., Pennock, D., Madani, O., Good, N., & DeCoste, D. (2006). Naïve filterbots for Robust Cold-start Recommendations. In *Proceedings of the ACM Conference on Knowledge Discovery and Data Mining*. Philadelphia, USA: ACM Press.

Paterek A. (2007). Improving regularized singular value decomposition for collaborative filtering. In *KDD cup Workshop at SIGKDD.*

Paterek, A. (2007). Improving Regularized Singular Value Decomposition For Collaborative Filtering. In *Proceedings of the ACM Conference on Knowledge Discovery and Data Mining*. Philadelphia, USA: ACM Press.

Pavlov, D. Y., & Pennock, D. M. (2002). A Maximum Entropy Approach To Collaborative Filtering in Dynamic, Sparse, High-Dimensional Domains. *Neural Information Processing Systems (NIPS) 2002.*

Pavlov, D. Y., Manavoglu, E., Giles, C. L., & Pennock, D. M. (2004). Collaborative Filtering with Maximum Entropy. *IEEE Intelligent Systems, 19*(6), 40- 47.

Pazzani, M. (1999). A framework for collaborative, content-based and demographic filtering. *Artificial Intelligence Review, 13*(5-6), 393–408.

Pazzani, M. J., & Billsus, D. (2007) Content-Based Recommendation Systems. *The Adaptive Web, 4321,* 325-341.

Pazzani, M., & Billsus, D. (1997). Learning and revising user profiles: The identification of interesting web sites. In *Machine Learning, 27,* 313–331.

Pazzani, M., & Billsus, D. (1997). Learning and Revising User Profiles: The identification of interesting web sites, Machine Learning, *27,* 313-331.

Pazzani, M., & Billsus, D. (2007). Content-Based Recommendation Systems. In *The Adaptive Web,* 325-341.

Pazzani, M., & Billsus, D. Content-based recommendation systems. In P. Brusilovsky, A. Kobsa, and W. Nejdl (Eds.), *The Adaptive Web: Methods and Strategies of Web Personalization, Lecture Notes in Computer Science 4321* (pp. 325-341). Berlin, Heidelberg, Germany: Springer-Verlag.

Pearl, J. (1988). *Probabilistic Reasoning in Intelligent Systems: Networks of Plausible Inference.* Morgan Kaufmann, San Mateo, CA.

Pennock, D., Horvitz, E., Lawrence, S., & Giles, C. L. (2000). Collaborative filtering by personality diagnosis: A hybrid memory-and model-based approach. In *16th Conference on Uncertainty in Artificial Intelligence* (pp. 473–480).

Pentland, B. T., & Feldman, M. S. (In Press). Narrative networks: Patterns of technology and organization. *Organization Science - Special issue on Information Technology and Organizational Form.*

Petrelli, D., De Angeli, A., & Convertino, G. (1999). A user centered approach to user modeling. *Proceedings of the 7th International Conference on User Modeling* (pp. 255–264).

Pierrakos, D., Paliouras, G., Papatheodorou, C., & Spyropoulos, C. D. (2003). Web usage mining as a tool for personalization: A survey. *International Journal of User Modeling and User-Adapted Interaction, 13*(4), 311–372.

Pissard, N. (2007). Etude des interactions sociales médiatées: Méthodologies, algorithmes, services. Paris Dauphine, Paris.

Plu, M., Bellec, P., Agosto, L., & Van De Velde, W. (2003). *The web of people: A dual view on the world wide web.* Paper presented at the Twelfth International World Wide Web Conference, Budapest.

Polcicova, G., Slovak, R., & Navrat, P. (2000). Combining content-based and collaborative filtering. In *ADBIS-DASFAA Symposium* (pp. 118-127).

Popescul, A., Ungar, L. H., Pennock, D. M., & Lawrence, S. (2001). Probabilistic Models for Unified Collaborative and Content-Based Recommendation in Sparse-Data Environments. *Proc. of the Seventeenth Conference on Uncertainty in Artificial Intelligence (UAI-2001).*

Porter, M. F. (1980). An algorithm for suffix stripping, *Program, 14*(3) pp 130–137.

Preece, J., Rogers, Y., Sharp, H., & Benyon, D. (1994). *Human-computer interaction.* Addison Wesley.

Preuveneers, D.; Vandewoude, Y.; Rigole, P.; Ayed, D., & Berbers, Y. (2006). Context-aware adaptation for component-based pervasive computing systems, In T. Pfeifer, A. Schmidt, W. Woo, G. Doherty, F. Vernier, K. Delaney, B. Yerazunis, M. Chalmers & J. Kiniry (Ed.), *Advances in Pervasive Computing 2006. Adjunct Proceedings of the 4th International Conference on Pervasive Computing: Vol. 207.* (pp. 125-128). Austrian Computer Society (OCG), Vienna.

Prim, R. C. (1957). Shortest connection networks and some generalizations. *Bell System Technical Journal, 36.*

Quan, D., Huynh, D., & Karger, D. R. (2003). *Haystack: A platform for authoring end user Semantic Web applications.* Paper presented at the 12th International World Wide Web Conference (pp. 738-753).

Rahwan, T., Rahwan, T., Rahwan, I., & Ashri, R. (2003). Agent-Based Support for Mobile Users Using AgentSpeak(L). In P. Giorgini, B. Henderson-Sellers & M. Winikoff (Ed.), *5th International Bi-Conference Workshop on Agent-Oriented Information Systems (AOIS2003): Vol. 3030. Lecture Notes In Artificial Intelligence* (pp. 45-60). Springer-Verlag.

Ramparany, F., Boissier, O., & Brouchoud, H. (2003, May). *Cooperating Autonomous Smart Devices.* Paper presented at the Smart Objects Conference (sOc'2003), Grenoble, France.

Rashid, A. M., Albert, I., Cosley, D., Lam, S. K., McNee, S. M., Konstan, J. A., & Riedl, J. (2002). Getting to Know You: Learning New User Preferences in Recommender Systems. In *International Conference on Intelligent User Interfaces (IUI 2002).* Miami, Florida: ACM Press.

Rashid, A. M., Lam, S. K., Karypis G., & Riedl, J. (2006, August). ClustKNN: A Highly Scalable Hybrid Model- & Memory-Based CF Algorithm. In *The 12th ACM Conference on Knowledge Discovery and Data Mining* Philadelphia, Pennsylvania, USA: ACM Press.

Recker, M., Walker, A., & Lawless, K. (2003). What do you recommend? Implementation and analyses of collaborative filtering of Web resources for education. *Instructional Science, 31,* 229-316.

Resnick, L. B., Levine, J. M., & Teasley, S. D. (1991). *Perspectives on socially shared cognition.* Washington DC: American Psychological Association (APA).

Resnick, P., & Sami, R. The Influence Limiter: Provably Manipulation Resistant Recommender Systems. In *Proceedings of the 2007 ACM Conference on Recommender Systems (RecSys).* Minneapolis, USA: ACM Press.

Resnick, P., & Varian, H. R. (1997). Recommender systems. *Communications of the ACM, 40*(3), 56-58.

Resnick, P., Iacovou, N., Suchak, M., Bergstrom, P., & Riedl, J. (1994). Grouplens: An open architecture for collaborative filtering of netnews. In *Conference on Computer Supported Cooperative Work* (pp. 175–186). ACM.

Resnick, P., Iacovou, N., Suchak, M., Bergstrom, P., & Riedl, J. (1994). Grouplens: An Open Architecture for Collaborative Filtering Of Netnews. In *Proceedings of the 1994 ACM conference on Computer supported cooperative work.* Chapel Hill, North Carolina. ACM Press (p. 175-186).

Resnick, P., Iacovou, N., Suchak, M., Bergstrom, P., & Riedl, J. (1994). GroupLens: An Open Architecture for Collaborative Filtering of Netnews. *Proceedings of the Conference on Computer Supported Cooperative Work,* Chapel Hill, NC, 175-186.

Resnik, P. (1995). *Disambiguating noun groupings with respect to WordNet senses.* Chelmsford, MA: Sun Microsystems Laboratories.

Rich, E. (1978). User modeling via stereotypes. *Cognitive Science, 3,* 329–354.

Robertson, S. E. (1990). On term selection for query expansion. *Journal of Documentation,* 46(4):359–364.

Robertson, S. E., & Spärck Jones, K. (1976). Relevance weighting of search terms. *Journal of the American Society for Information Science,* 27(3), 129–146.

Robertson, S. E., Walker, S., Hancock-Beaulieu, M., Gull, A., & Lau, M. (1992). Okapi at TREC. In Harman, D., editor, *Proceedings of the First Text REtrieval Conference (TREC),* pages 21–30, Gaithersburg, MD. NIST, USA.

Rochio, J. J. (1971). Relevance feedback in information retrieval. *The Smart retrieval system- experiments in automatic document processing,* (pp. 313–323).

Rolland, P. Y. (2001). Adaptive User Modeling in a Content-Based Music Retrieval System. *Proc. of the International Conference on Music Information Retrieval (ISMIR) 2001.*

Rose, D., & Levinson D. (2004). Understanding User Goals in Web search. In *Proceedings of the International World Wide Web Conference 2004,* (pp 13–19), New York, USA.

Roseman, M., & Greenberg, S. (1996). Building real-time groupware with GroupKit, a groupware toolkit. *ACM Trans. Comput.-Hum. Interact.,* 3(1), 66–106.

Rouvoy, R. & Merle, P. (2006, July). Leverage Component-Oriented Programming with Attribute-Oriented Programming. Paper presented at the *11th International ECOOP Workshop on Component-Oriented Programming* (*WCOP'06*), Nantes, France. Retrieved January 2008, from http://research.microsoft.com/~cszypers/events/WCOP2006/rouvoy-wcop-06.pdf

Ruthven, I., & M. Lalmas. (2003). A survey on the use of relevance feedback for information access systems. *Knowledge Engineering Review, 18*(2), 95–145.

Salton, G. & Buckley, C. (1990). Improving Retrieval Performance by Relevance Feedback. *Journal of the American Society for Information Science, 41(4)*, 288–297.

Salton, G. (1971). *The SMART Retrieval System-Experiments in Automatic document Processing.* Prentice-Hall, Inc., Upper Saddle River, NJ, USA.

Salton, G. (1989). *Automatic text processing: The transformation, analysis and retrieval of information by computer.* Reading, MA: Addison-Wesley.

Salton, G., & Buckley, C. (1988). Term-weighting approaches in automatic text retrieval. *Information Processing & Management, 24*(5), 513-523. Retrieved May 22, 2008, from http://www.doc.ic.ac.uk/~jmag/classic/1988.Term-weighting%20approaches%20in%20automatic%20text%20retrieval.pdf

Salton, G., & McGill, M. (1983). *Introduction to Modern Information Retrieval.* McGraw-Hill Book Company.

Santos, E. Jr, Nguyen, H., Zhao, Q. & Pukinskis, E. (2003b). Empirical Evaluation of Adaptive User Modeling in a Medical Information Retrieval Application. In: *Proceedings of the ninth User Modeling Conference UM 2003*, (pp. 292–296). Johnstown. Pennsylvania.

Santos, E. Jr, Nguyen, H., Zhao, Q., & Wang, H. (2003). User Modelling for Intent Prediction in Information Analysis. In: *Proceedings of the 47th Annual Meeting for the Human Factors and Ergonomincs Society (HFES-03)*, (pp. 1034–1038).

Santos, E. Jr., & Dinh, H. T. (2008). Automatic Knowledge Validation for Bayesian Knowledge Bases. *Data and Knowledge Engineering, 64*, 218-241.

Santos, E. Jr., Brown, S. M., Lejter, M., Ngai, G., Bank, S., & Stytz, M. R. (1999). Dynamic User Model Construction with Bayesian Networks for Intelligent Information Queries. In: *Proceedings of the 12th International FLAIRS Conference.* pp. 3–7. Orlando. FL.

Santos, E. Jr., Nguyen, H., & Brown, M. S. (2001). Kavanah: An active user interface Information Retrieval Application. In: *Proceedings of 2nd Asia-Pacific Conference on Intelligent Agent Technology*, (pp. 412–423).

Santos, E. Jr., Santos, E. S., & Shimony, S., E. (2003). Implicitly Preserving Semantics During Incremental Knowledge Base Acquisition Under Uncertainty. *International Journal of Approximate Reasoning 33(1)*, 71-94.

Santos, E. Jr., Zhao, Q., Nguyen, H., & Wang, H. (2005). Impacts of User Modeling on Personalization of Information Retrieval: An evaluation with human intelligence analysts. In Weibelzahl, S., Paramythis, A., & Mastho, J. (Eds.). Proceedings of the Fourth Workshop on the Evaluation of Adaptive Systems, held in conjunction with the 10th International Conference on User Modeling (UM'05), (pp 19-26).

Saracevic, T. (1996). Relevance reconsidered. In: Ingwersen, P & Pors, P.O. (Eds.), *Proceedings of the Second International Conference on Conceptions of Library and Information Science: Integration in Perspective. Copenhagen: The Royal School of Librarianship*, (pp. 201–218).

Saracevic, T., Spink A., & Wu, M. (1997). Users and Intermediaries in Information Retrieval: What Are They Talking About? In *Proceedings of the 6th International Conference in User Modeling UM 97,* (pp. 43–54).

Sarwar, B. M., Karypis, G., Konstan, J. A., & Riedl, J. (2000). Analysis of recommendation algorithms for e-commerce. In *ACM Conference on Electronic Commerce* (pp. 158–167).

Sarwar, B. M., Karypis, G., Konstan, J., & Riedl, J. (2001). Item-based collaborative filtering recommendation algorithms. In *10th International World Wide Web Conference.*

Sarwar, B., Karypis, G., Konstan, J., & Riedl, J. (2001). Item-based collaborative filtering recommendation algorithms. In *Proceedings of the 10th International World Wide Web Conference (WWW10),* Hong Kong, China: ACM Press.

Sarwar, B., Karypis, G., Konstan, J., & Riedl, J. (2001). Item-Based Collaborative Filtering Recommendation Algorithms WWW10, May 15, 2001, Hong Kong.

Sarwar, B., Konstan, J., Borchers, A., Herlocker, J., Miller, B., & Riedl, J. (1998). Using Filtering Agents to Improve Prediction Quality in the GroupLens Research Collaborative Filtering System. *Proceedings of the 1998 Conference on Computer Supported Cooperative Work.* New Orleans, USA: ACM Press.

Sashima, A., Izumi, N., & Kurumatani, K. (2004). Bridging Coordination Gaps between Devices, Services, and Humans in Ubiquitous computing. *Workshop on Agents for Ubiquitous Computing (UbiAgents04)*. Retrieved January 2008, from http://www.ift.ulaval.ca/~mellouli/ubiagents04/

Schafer, B., Frankowski, D., Herlocker, J., & Sen, S. (2007). Collaborative Filtering Recommender Systems. In: Brusilovsky, P., Kobsa, A., Nejdl, W. (Eds*.), The Adaptive Web: Methods and Strategies of Web Personalization*. LNCS 4321. Springer

Schafer, J., Konstan, J., & Riedl, J. (2001) E-Commerce Recommendation Applications. In *Data Mining and Knowledge Discovery, 5*(1), 115-153.

Schmidt, A., & Kunzmann, C. (2006). Towards a Human Resource Development Ontology for Combining Competence Management and Technology-Enhanced Workplace Learning, In *Proceedings of OntoContent 2006* , LNCS, Springer

Schmidt, K. (2002). The problem with 'awareness': introductory remarks on 'Awareness in CSCW'. *Computer Supported Cooperative Work, 11*(*3-4*), 285-298.

Schütz, A. (1946). The well-informed citizen. An essay on the social distribution of knowledge. *Social Research, 13*(4), 463-478.

Sebastiani, F. (2002) Machine Learning in Automated Text Categorization. *ACM Computing Surveys, 34*(1), 1-47. Retrieved February 14, 2008, from http://dienst.isti.cnr.it/Dienst/UI/2.0/Describe/ercim.cnr.iei/1999-B4-31-12?tiposearch=cnr

Shafer, G. (1976). *A Mathematical Theory of Evidence*, Princeton University Press.

Shahabi, C., Banaei-Kashani, F., Chen Y.-S., & McLeod, D. (2001). Yoda: An Accurate and ScalableWeb-based Recommendation System. In *Proceedings of Sixth International*

Shany, G., Heckerman, D., & Barfman, R. (2005). An MDP-based recommender system. *Journal of Machine Learning Research 6*(9), 1265-1295.

Shardanand, U., & Maes, P. (1995). Social information filtering: Algorithms for automating "word of mouth". In *ACM Conference on Human Factors in Computing Systems, 1*, 210–217.

Shen, C., Vernier, F. D., Forlines, C., & Ringel, M. (2004). DiamondSpin: An extensible toolkit for around-the-table interaction. In *CHI '04: Proceedings of the SIGCHI conference on Human factors in computing systems*, pages 167–174, Vienna, Austria. ACM Press.

Sidler, G., Scott, A., & Wolf, H. (1997). Collaborative Browsing in the World Wide Web. In *Proceedings of the 8th Joint European Networking Conference*, Edinburgh, Scotland. Springer.

Simpson, E. (2007). Clustering Tags in Enterprise and Web Folksonomies. *HP Labs Technical Report HPL-2007-190.* Retrieved January 24, 2008, from http://library.hp.com/techpubs/2007/HPL-2007-190.html

Sinha, R. (2005). *A cognitive analysis of tagging (or how the lower cognitive cost of tagging makes it popular)*. Retrieved January 25, 2007, from http://www.rashmisinha.com/2005/09/a-cognitive-analysis-of-tagging

Sleator, D. D., & Temperley, D. (1993). Parsing English with a link grammar. In: *Proceedings of the Third International Workshop on Parsing Technologies*, (pp. 277–292).

Smeaton, A. F., Lee, H., Foley, C., & Mc Givney., S. (2006). Collaborative Video Searching on a Tabletop. *Multimedia Systems Journal, 12*(4):375–391.

Smeaton, A. F., Murphy, N., O'Connor, N., Marlow, S., Lee, H., Donald, K. M., Browne, P., & Ye., J. (2001). The Físchlár Digital Video System: A Digital Library of Broadcast TV Programmes. In *JCDL 2001 - ACM+IEEE Joint Conference on Digital Libraries*, pages 312–313, Roanoke, VA, USA.

Smyth, B., & Cotter, P. (2000). A personalised TV listings service for the digital TV age. *Knowledge-Based Systems, 13*, 53-59.

Smyth, B., & Cotter, P. (2000). A Personalized Television Listings Service. *Communications of the ACM, 43*(8).

Song, X., Tseng, L., Lin, C-Y., & Sun, M-T. (2005). ExpertiseNet: Relational and Evolutionary Expert Modeling, *LNCS 3538*, Springer

Soulier, E. (2004). Les communautés de pratique au cœur de l'organisation réelle des entreprises. *Systèmes d'Information et Management (SIM), 9*(1).

Soulier, E., Delalonde, C., & Petit, O. (2007, Du 28 au 31 août). *Subjectivation et singularisation dans la perspective de l'apprentissage situé et de l'acteur-réseau*. Paper presented at the Congrès international AREF 2007 (Actualité de la Recherche en Education et en Formation), Strasbourg.

Spärck Jones, K. (1997). Search term relevance weighting given little relevance information. *Readings in information retrieval* pages 329–338, Morgan Kaufmann Publishers Inc.

Speller, E. (2007). Collaborative tagging, folksonomies, distributed classification or ethnoclassification: a literature review. *Library Student Journal 2007, University of Buffalo*. Retrieved January 25, 2008, from http://informatics.buffalo.edu/org/lsj/articles/speller_2007_2_collaborative.pdf

Spink, A., & Losee, R. M. (1996). Feedback in information retrieval. In Williams, M., (Ed.), *Annual Review of Information Science and Technology, 31,* 33–78.

Srivastava, J., Cooley, R., Deshpande, M., & Tan, P.N. (2000). Web usage mining: discovery and applications of usage patterns from web data. *SIGKDD Explorations, 1*(2), 12–23.

Srivihok, A., & Sukonmanee, V. (2005). E-commerce intelligent agent: personalization travel support agent using Q-Learning. In Q. Li, & T. P. Liang (Eds.): *Proceedings of the 7th International Conference on Electronic Commerce* (pp. 287-292). Xi'an, China: ACM Press.

Stewart, J., Bederson, B. B., & Druin, A. (1999). Single display groupware: a model for co-present collaboration. In *CHI '99: Proceedings of the SIGCHI conference on Human factors in computing systems*, pages 286–293, Pittsburgh, Pennsylvania, USA. ACM Press.

Stojanovic, L., Stojanovic, N., & Volz, R. (2002). Migrating data-intensive Web sites into the semantic Web. *Proceedings of the 17th ACM Symposium on Applied Computing* (pp. 1100-1107).

Stutt, A., & Motta, E. (2004). Semantic learning Webs. *Journal of Interactive Media in Education,* (10).

Stützle, T., & Hoos, H. (2000) MAX-MIN Ant System. Journal of Future Generation Computer Systems, *16,* 889 – 914.

Suchman, L. A. (1987). Plans and situated actions - the problem of human-machine communication. Cambridge: Cambridge University Press.

Suchman, L. A. (1987). *Plans and Situated Actions – The Problem of Human-Machine Communciation.* Cambridge, UK: Cambridge University Press.

Sugiyama, K., Hatano, K., and Yoshikawa, M. (2004). Adaptive web search based on user profile constructed without any effort from users. In *Proceedings of the 13th International Conference on World Wide Web* (New York, NY, USA, May 17 - 20, 2004). WWW '04. ACM, New York, NY, 675-684.

Sutton, R. S., & Barto, A. G. (1998) *Reinforcement Learning: An Introduction,* Cambridge, MA, USA: MIT Press.

Taghipour, N., & Kardan, A. (2007, September). Enhancing a recommender system based on Q-Learning. In A. Hinneburg (Ed.), *LWA 2007: Lernen - Wissen - Adaption, Workshop Proceedings, Knowledge Discovery, Data Mining and Machine Learning Tack,* (pp. 21-28). Halle, Germany: Martin-Luther-University Publications.

Taghipour, N., & Kardan, A. (2008, March). A hybrid web recommender system based on Q-Learning. In R. L. Wainwright, & H. Haddad (Eds.), *Proceedings of the 2008 ACM Symposium on Applied Computing* (pp. 1164-1168). Fortaleza, Brazil: ACM Press.

Taghipour, N., Kardan, A., & Shiry Ghidary, S. (2007, October). Usage-based web recommendations: a reinforcement learning approach. In J. A. Konstan, J. Riedl, & B. Smyth (Eds.), *Proceedings of the First ACM Conference on Recommender Systems* (pp. 113-120). Minneapolis, MN, USA: ACM Press.

Takacs, G., Pilaszy, I., Nemeth, B., & Tikk, D. (2007). On the gravity recommendation system. In *KDD cup Workshop at SIGKDD.*

Tang, T., & McCalla, G. (2005). Smart recommendation for an evolving e-learning system: Architecture and experiment. *International Journal on E-Learning, 4*(1), 105-129.

Teevan, J., Alvarado, C., Ackerman, M. S., & Karger, D. R. (2004). *The perfect search engine is not enough: A study of orienteering behavior in directed search.* Paper presented at the SIGCHI Conference on Human Factors in Computing Systems (pp. 415-422). New York: ACM Press.

Tintarev, N., & Masthoff, J. (2007). Effective Explanantions of Recommendations: User-Centered Design. In *Proceedings of the 2007 ACM Conference on Recommender Systems (RecSys).* Minneapolis, USA: ACM Press.

Trichet, F., & Leclere, M. (2003). A Framework for building competency-based systems. In N. Zhong et al. (Eds.): *ISMIS 2003,* LNAI 2871, 633–639, Springer.

Tsiriga, V., & Virvou, M. (2003) Modelling the student to individualise tutoring in a web-based ICALL, *International Journal of Continuing Engineering Education and Life Long Learning,* Vol 13; Part 3/4, pp. 350-365, Switzerland, ISSN 1560-4624

Twidale, M. B., & Nichols, D. M. (1998). Designing interfaces to support collaboration in information retrieval. *Interacting with Computers. The Interdisciplinary Journal of Human-Computer Interaction, 10*(2), 177-193.

Typke, R., Wiering, F., & Veltkamp, R. C. (2005). A Survey of Music Information Retrieval Systems. *Proc. of the International Conference on Music Information Retrieval (ISMIR) 2005.*

Tzanetakis, G., & Cook, P. (2002). Musical genre classification of audio signals. *IEEE Transactions on Speech and Audio Processing, 10*(5), 293–302.

Uitdenbogerd, A., & van Schyndel, R. (2002). A review of factors affecting music recommender success. *Proc. of the International Conference on Music Information Retrieval (ISMIR).*

Ungar, L., & Foster, D. (1998). Clustering methods for collaborative filtering. In *Workshop on Recommendation Systems.* AAAI Press.

Van Damme, C., Hepp, M., & Siorpaes, K. (2007, June). *FolksOntology: An Integrated Approach for Turning Folksonomies into Ontologies.* Paper presented at the European Semantic Web Conference , Innsbruck, Austria. Retrieved February 15, 2008, from http://www.kde. cs.uni-kassel.de/ws/eswc2007/proc/ProceedingsSemnet07.pdf

Vanderwal, T. (2007). *Folksonomy Coinage and Definition.* Retrieved January 21, 2008, from http://www. vanderwal.net/folksonomy.html

Viappiani, P., Pu, P., & Faltings, B. (2007). Conversational Recommenders with Adaptive Suggestions. In *Proceedings of Recommender Systems (RecSys).* Minneapolis, USA: ACM Press

Vignoli, F., & Pauws, S. (2005). A Music Retrieval System Based on User-Driven Similarity and Its Evaluation. *Proc. of the International Conference on Music Information Retrieval (ISMIR).*

Vozalis, M., & Margaritis, K. G. (2004). Enhancing collaborative filtering with demographic data: The case of item-based filtering. In *4th International Conference on Intelligent Systems Design and Applications* (pp. 361–366).

Vygotsky, L. S. (1978). *Mind in society.* Cambridge MA: Harvard University Press.

Wang, J., de Vries, A. P., & Reinders, M. J. (2006). Unifying user-based and item-based collaborative filtering approaches by similarity fusion. In *29th International ACM SIGIR Conference on Research and Development in Information Retrieval* (pp. 501-508).

Wang, J., de Vries, A. P., & Reinders, M. J.T. (2006). A User-Item Relevance Model for Log-Based Collaborative Filtering. *ECIR 2006*, LNCS 3936, pp. 37–48.

Wasfi, A. M. (1999). Collecting User Access Patterns for Building User Profiles and Collaborative Filtering. In: *IUI '99: Proceedings of the 4th International Conference on Intelligent User Interfaces* (pp. 57-64).

Wasserman, S., & Faust, K. (1994). *Social Network Analysis.* Cambridge, UK: Cambridge University Press.

Watson, I. (1997). *Applying Case-Based Reasoning: Techniques for Enterprise Systems.* Morgan Kaufmann.

Weibelzahl, S. (2003). *Evaluation of Adaptive Systems.* Ph.D Dissertation. University of Trier, Germany.

Wenger, E. (1998). Communities of practice. Learning, meaning, and identity. Cambridge: University Press.

Whitehead, A. N. (1929/1995). *Procès et réalité. Essai de cosmologie.* Paris: Editions Gallimard.

Wilkinson, R. & Wu, M. (2004). Evaluation Experiments and Experience from Perspective of Interactive Information Retrieval. In *Adaptive Hypermedia 2004 - Workshop Proceedings -Part I. Eindhoven,* (pp 221-230), Eindhoven, the Netherlands.

Wilson, T. D. (1981). On user studies and information needs. *Journal of Documentation, 37(1),* 3–15.

Windows Live Messenger (2007). http://get.live.com/ messenger/overview.

Winter, W. de, & Rijke, M. de (2007, March). *Identifying Facets in Query-Biased Sets of Blog Posts.* Paper presented at the International Conference on Weblogs and Social Media, Boulder, Colorado. Retrieved February 17, 2008, from http://icwsm.org/papers/3--Winter-Rijke.pdf

Witten, I. H., & Frank, E. (2000). Weka. Machine Learning Algorithms in Java. In *Data Mining: Practical Machine Learning. Tools and Techniques with Java Implementations,* Morgan Kaufmann Publishers

Wood, C. C. (1993). *A cognitive dimensional analysis of idea sketches.* University of Sussex, Falmer, Brighton.

Wu, F., & Huberman, B. A. (2007). *Public Discourse in the Web Does Not Exhibit Group Polarization* (Technical Report). Palo Alto, CA: HP Labs Research.

Xu, Z., Mao, F. J., & Su, D. (2006). Towards the Semantic Web: Collaboration Tag Suggestions. *In Proceedings of the Collaborative Web Tagging Workshop, World Wide Web Conference (WWW 2006).*

Yahoo! (2005). Yahoo! Questions/réponses. Retrieved July 5th 2006, from http://fr.answers.yahoo.com/

Yahoo! My Web 2.0. (2006). My web 2.0. Retrieved March 12th 2006, from http://myweb2.search.yahoo.com/

Yao, K.-T., Neches, R., Ko, I.-Y., Eleish, R., & Abhinkar, S. (1999). Synchronous and Asynchronous Collaborative Information Space Analysis Tools. In *ICPP '99: Proceedings of the 1999 International Workshops on Parallel Processing*, page 74, Washington, DC, USA. IEEE Computer Society.

Yapriady, B., & Uitdenbogerd, A.L. (2005). Combining Demographic Data with Collaborative Filtering for Automatic Music Recommendation. *Knowledge-Based Intelligent Information and Engineering Systems, LNCS* Volume 3684/2005.

Yedda. (2007). *Yedda*. Retrieved February 9th 2007, from http://www.yedda.com/

Yee, K. P., Swearingen, K., & Hearst, M. (2003). Faceted Metadata for Image Search and Browsing. In *Proceedings of the Conference on Human Factors in Computing Systems* (pp. 401-408). New York: ACM Press. Retrieved January 25, 2008, from http://flamenco.berkeley.edu/papers/flamenco-chi03.pdf

Yeung, C. A., Gibbins, N., & Shadbolt, N. (2007). Tag Meaning Disambiguation through Analysis of Tripartite Structure of Folksonomies. In *Proceedings of the 2007 IEEE/WIC/ACM International Conferences on Web Intelligence and Intelligent Agent Technology - Workshops* (pp. 3-6). New York: ACM Press. Retrieved February 14, 2008, from http://eprints.ecs.soton.ac.uk/14762/1/tag_disambiguation.pdf

Yoshii, K., Goto, M., Komatani, K., Ogata, T., & Okuno, H.G. (2006). Hybrid Collaborative and Content-based Music Recommendation Using Probabilistic Model with Latent User Preferences. *Proc. of the International Conference on Music Information Retrieval (ISMIR).*

Yu, K., Schwaighofer, A., Tresp, V., Xu, X., & Kriegel, H. (2004). Probabilistic memory-based collaborative filtering. *IEEE Transactions on Knowledge and Data Engineering, 16*, 56–69.

Yu, K., Wen, Z., Xu, X., & Ester, M. (2001). Feature Weighting and Instance Selection for Collaborative Filtering. In *Proceedings of the 12th International Workshop on Database and Expert Systems Applications*. Munich, Germany: IEEE Press.

Yudelson, M., Gavrilova, T., & Brusilovsky, P. (2005). Towards User Modeling Meta-ontology. In L. Ardissono, P. Brna & A. Mitrovic (Ed.), *10th International Conference on User Modeling (UM 2005): Vol. 3538. Lecture Notes In Computer Science* (pp. 448-452). Springer-Verlag.

Zeballos, G. S. (1998). Tools for Efficient Collaborative Web Browsing. In *Proceedings of CSCW '98 workshop on Collaborative and co-operative information seeking in digital information environment.*

Zhang, B., & Seo, Y. (2001). Personalized web-document filtering using reinforcement learning. *Applied Artificial Intelligence, 15*(7), 665-685. Los Angels, CA, USA: ACM Press.

Zhang, Y., Callan, J., & Minka, T. (2002). Novelty and redundancy detection in adaptive filtering. In *ACM SIGIR '02.*

Ziegler, C. (2005). *Towards Decentralised Recommender Systems*. (PhD Thesis), Freiburg, Germany: Freiburg University, Department of Computer Science.

Ziegler, C.-N., McNee, S., Konstan, J., & Lausen, G. (2005). Improving recommendation lists through topic diversification. In *14th International World Wide Web Conference* (pp. 22–32).

Zukerman I., & Albrecht, D. (2001). Predictive statistical models for user modling. In A. Kobsa (Ed.), *User Modeling and User-Adapted Interaction Journal, 11*(1-2), 5-18. Kluwer Academic Publishers.

About the Contributors

Max Chevalier is an associate professor in computer science at the University Paul Sabatier of Toulouse III (France) since 2002. His research addresses user centered approaches in information systems like personalization, visual information retrieval interface, social computing. He conducts research on these topics within the Toulouse Computing Research Laboratory (IRIT - UMR 5505).

Christine Julien is an associate professor in computer science at the University Paul Sabatier of Toulouse III (France) since 1989 and carries out her research at the Toulouse Computing Research Laboratory (IRIT - UMR 5505). She initially worked in document engineering and particularly in structured documents and hypertext documents. Her current works are oriented on personalized information access on the web using social approaches.

Chantal Soulé-Dupuy received the PhD degree in computer science from the University of Toulouse 3 (France) in 1990. She is currently professor of computer science at the University of Toulouse 1 and serves as the head of the Department of Computer Science (since November 2003). Her recent research addresses information modeling and retrieval in digital libraries, personalized and social search. She conducts and supervises research on these topics within the Toulouse Computing Research Laboratory (IRIT - UMR 5505).

* * *

Berna Altinel received the BS degree in computer science and engineering from Yeditepe University, Istanbul, Turkey, in 2004. Her BS thesis topic was on natural language processing. During 2004, she was a teaching assistant at the computer laboratories at the same university. In 2004, she joined the Computer Engineering at Istanbul Technical University (ITU), Turkey as an MS student and received her MS degree in 2007. Her thesis topic was on hybrid music recommendation. She is currently working at a software company in Istanbul. Her current research interests are pattern recognition and music recommendation.

Yolande Berbers is associate professor in the Katholieke Universiteit Leuven's Department of Computer Science and a member of the DistriNet research group. Her research interests include software engineering for embedded software, ubiquitous computing, service architectures, middleware, real-time systems, component-oriented software development, distributed systems, environments for distributed and parallel applications, and mobile agents. She received her PhD in computer science from the Katholieke Universiteit Leuven. She's a member of the IEEE.

Mihaela Brut is lecturer at the Faculty of Computer Science from the "Al. I. Cuza" University of Iasi, Romania. She has a PhD in humanities since 2000, and now she is PhD student in computer science, working in personalized recommendations, multimedia indexing and semantic Web research areas. Her Web address: http://www.infoiasi.ro/~mihaela

Mark Butler has a first class Master of Engineering degree in computer science and electronic engineering, a PhD in computer science and is a senior member of the IEEE. He has worked as a researcher at Hewlett Packard Laboratories Bristol, Unilever Research Port Sunlight and has also lectured at the University of the West of England. His research interests include mobile devices, the Semantic Web, digital media, machine learning and large scale distributed systems.

Laurent Candillier conducted this research during a visiting post-doctorate at Orange Labs, Lannion. He investigated algorithms and metrics in the scope of collaborative recommenders systems for large scale data. He holds a PhD in informatics from the University of Lille, France. His main research interests are learning methods for supervised and unsupervised problems.

Angela Carrillo-Ramos, systems and computing engineer of the Universidad de los Andes, Bogota, Colombia (1996). Magister in systems and computing engineering of the Universidad de los Andes, Bogota, Colombia (1998). PhD in informatics of the Université Joseph Fourier, Grenoble, France (2007). Research Assistant of the Universidad de los Andes (1996-1997). Assistant professor of the Universidad de los Andes (1998-2003). Actually, she is associate professor and researcher of ISTAR and SIDRe teams of the Pontificia Universidad Javeriana, Bogota, Colombia. Her research work is focused on information systems acceded through mobile devices using software agents. Other research subjects are adaptation (personalization) of information in nomadic environments according to user preferences and context of use, and software engineering.

Zehra Cataltepe is an assistant professor at Computer Engineering Department, Istanbul Technical University. Her research interests are machine learning theory and applications, especially in bioinformatics, web/document mining, and music recognition and recommendation. She got her PhD degree from Caltech in computer science in 1998 and her BS degree from Bilk-ent University, Ankara, in 1992. She worked at Bell Labs as a postdoc and then at StreamCenter Inc. and Siemens Corporate Research as researcher after she got her PhD

Steve Cayzer is an expert technologist at Hewlett-Packard Laboratories where he has worked since 2000. Prior to HP he was a consultant with the IT systems integration company Logica. Steve holds a BSc in Physiology from Bristol University and a PhD in computational neurobiology from the University of Cambridge. His research interests cover information management, semantic web, web2.0, machine learning, biologically inspired computing and sustainable IT. He is also employed as a visiting lecturer at UWE and Bristol University where he delivers a number of modules in the artificial intelligence syllabus.

After his studies at the University of Central Florida, **Charles Delalonde** has completed his PhD in Orange R&D labs. His research seeks a deeper understanding of how social networks might improve information retrieval activities. His results have been patented by Orange, published in books, and presented in conferences. He is now a driving force behind Electricite de France's Social Computing and Web 2.0 research activities.

Françoise Fessant is currently a research engineer at Orange Labs, Lannion, France. She holds a PhD in signal processing from the University of Rennes, France. Her main research interests concern data mining and machine learning like self organizing map for exploratory data analysis.

Colum Foley is a postdoctoral researcher at the Centre for Digital Video Processing at Dublin City University. Colum has just recently completed his PhD dissertation under the supervision of Prof. Alan F. Smeaton. Colum's research interests are in synchronous collaborative information retrieval, and in particular in extending traditional information retrieval processes and algorithms in order to support multi-user search and retrieval.

Jérôme Gensel received his PhD in computer science in 1995 and an Accreditation to Supervise Research (Habilitation à Diriger des Recherches) in 2006 at the University Joseph Fourier (Grenoble, FRANCE). He is professor in Computer Science at the University Pierre Mendès France (Grenoble, France) since 2007 (he has been assistant professor in this University since 1996). Jérôme Gensel is member of the STEAMER research team at the Grenoble Computer Science Laboratory (LIG) since its creation in 2007. He has been member of the SIGMA research team at the Software, Systems and Networks Laboratory (LSR-IMAG) from 2001 to 2006, and researcher at INRIA Rhône-Alpes until 2001. His research interests include the representation of Spatio-Temporal Information, dynamic cartography techniques, Geographic Information Systems, Adaptability to Users, Ubiquitous Information Systems.

Kris Jack conducted this research during a visiting post-doctorate at Orange Labs, Lannion, France. He investigated how to personalise an information retrieval system using semantic data. He holds a PhD in computational linguistics from the University of Dundee, Scotland, with emphasis on the psycholinguistic modelling of child language acquisition. He is currently on post-doctorate research in the CEA, France, working on automatic semantic classification within huge volumes of linguistic data

Gareth Jones is senior lecturer in Computing and a Principal Investigator in the Centre for Digital Video Processing at Dublin City University. He holds B.Eng. and PhD degrees from the University of Bristol, U.K. He has previously held appointments at the University of Cambridge and the University of Exeter, U.K., and was as a Toshiba Fellow at Toshiba Corporation R&D Center in Kawasaki, Japan. His research focuses primarily on information retrieval, including multimedia, multilingual and context-aware retrieval applications. He has published more than 180 papers describing this work, including Best Paper Awards at ACM SIGIR and ACM Multimedia.

Christine Julien is an associate professor in computer science at the University Paul Sabatier of Toulouse III (France) since 1989 and carries out her research at the Toulouse Computing Research Laboratory (IRIT - UMR 5505). She initially worked in document engineering and particularly in structured documents and hypertext documents. Her current works are oriented on personalized information access on the web using social approaches.

Ahmad A. Kardan, PhD, DIC, received his BS in electrical engineering from Sharif University (1976-Iran), his MSc in digital systems from the Brunel University (1997-UK), and his PhD in computerized bioelectric engineering from Imperial College of Science and Technology (2001-UK). He is currently a faculty member of the Computer Engineering Department, Amirkabir University of Technology. He is head of information technology and also e-learning planning in the Ministry of Higher Education in Iran. He Founded The Virtual Education Center of Amirkabir University of Technology in 2002. He teaches graduate courses in computing and information technology with emphasis on advanced e-learning and distributed educational systems. He is involved in researches in intelligent tutoring systems (ITS), GRID learning, adaptive learning and learning styles, learner modeling, and applying data discovery in e-learning. Dr. Kardan has presented more than 60 papers at national and international conferences and has written papers for journals and edited books.

Hager Karoui is a new associate professor in ISMAI Institute in Kairouan (TUNISIA). He accomplished his Masters in Science (MSc) in artificial intelligence at University of Paris Dauphine (FRANCE) in 2003. After he did his PhD in the machine learning & applications (A³) research team of the Computer Science Laboratory of the Paris 13 University (LIPN) on December 2007. The topic of his thesis is *A Peer-to-Peer cooperative system for recommendation: Application on to the management and recommendation of bibliographical references.* His current research focuses on information retrieval, data mining, recommender systems, case-based reasoning and agent cooperation. He is particularly interested on assistant agents, community computation on distributed systems and automatic experience sharing.

Neal Lathia is a PhD student in the Department of Computer Science, University College London, United Kingdom, supervised by prof. Stephen Hailes and Dr. Licia Capra. His research focuses on the algorithm fuelling the online success of recommender systems: collaborative filtering, and how the paradigm of trust can be effectively used to both increase the algorithm's performance and evaluate how it functions over time. Neal can be contacted via email: n.lathia@cs.ucl.ac.uk

Frank Meyer is currently a research engineer at Orange Labs, Lannion, France. He received a Engineer Degree and a Master degree in computer science from the University of Montpellier, France. He works on data mining techniques including decision trees, k-nearest neighbours, supervised learning metrics and collaborative filtering with industrial applications, and holds 4 international patents on the data mining fields.

Elke Michlmayr holds a MSc and a PhD degree in computer science from Vienna University of Technology. From 2001 to 2003, she was with the Telecommunications Research Center Vienna, working on prototypes for location-based services for UMTS. From 2003 to 2007 she was a PhD student at the Women's Postgraduate College for Internet Technologies (WIT), doing research in peer-to-peer systems, social networks, and graph-based optimization algorithms. In early 2008 Elke joined Google's Mobile Group in London. The work described in this paper was partly carried out while Elke was an intern in the Semantic and Adaptive Systems Group, HP Labs Bristol.

Hien Nguyen is an assistant professor in the Department of Mathematical and Computer Sciences at the University of Wisconsin-Whitewater. She received her PhD in computer science from the University of Connecticut in 2005. Her research interests include user modeling, information retrieval, collaborative information retrieval, recommender systems, intent inferencing, and text summarization with a current focus on hybrid user model for improving a user's performance in information retrieval. Professional services and committee work include program committees for 2009 and 2008 FLAIRS Conference, 2007 and 2006 IEEE International Conference on Systems, Man, and Cybernetics (IEEE SMC 2007 and SMC 2006). She also is a member of User Modeling-User Adapted Interactions Journal Special Reviewers Board. She also serves as a reviewer for SMC (2008), User Modeling conference (2007), IEEE Transactions on Systems, Man, and Cybernetics, Part B, Information Processing and Management, and AAAI 2006 (Poster).

Since September 2008, **Manuele Kirsch Pinheiro** is associate professor in the Centre de Recherche en Informatique of the Université Paris 1 Panthéon-Sorbonne. Previously, she occupied a post-doctoral position on the Katholieke Universiteit Leuvens Department of Computer Science. She received her PhD in computer science form the Université Joseph Fourier Grenoble I (2006), and her Master degree from the Universidade Federal do Rio Grande do Sul, Porto Alegre, Brazil. Her research interests include ubiquitous computing, context-aware computing, adaptation (personalization), cooperative work (CSCW), group awareness and information systems.

Eugene Santos, Jr. is a professor of Engineering in the Thayer School of Engineering at Dartmouth College. He received his BS ('85) in mathematics and computer science from Youngstown State University, a MS ('86) in mathematics (specializing in numerical analysis) from Youngstown State University, as well as ScM ('88) and PhD ('92) degrees in computer science from Brown University. His areas of research interest include artificial intelligence, intent inferencing, information retrieval, automated reasoning, decision science, adversarial reasoning, user modeling, natural language processing, probabilistic reasoning, and knowledge engineering, verification and validation, protein folding, load balancing, virtual reality, and active user interfaces. He has served on many major conference program committees from intelligent agents to evolutionary computing. He is currently Editor-in-Chief for the *IEEE Transactions on Systems, Man, and Cybernetics* and an associate editor for the *International Journal of Image and Graphics*; and, is also on the editorial advisory boards for the *Journal of Intelligent Information Systems* and the System and Information Sciences Notes.

Florence Sedes is a full professor working at the Generalized Information Systems group at the Information Technology Research Institute IRIT of University Paul Sabatier (Toulouse - France) and she's the director of the "Information-Interaction-Intelligence GDR i3 group". Her research works are concentrated around adaptation within semi-structured documents in different applications.

Edwin Simpson is a researcher working in the Web Services and Systems Laboratory at HP labs, where he develops prototypes and carries out practical experiments with software. He obtained a first class masters in computer science from the University of Bristol, where he investigated social network analysis and how it may be applied to determine the strong and weak points of a community. More recently, Edwin has worked in the fields of Social Media and Recommender Systems, examining the application of Machine Learning techniques such as clustering to these areas in order to minimize the workload required for participation in the community.

Alan Smeaton is a professor of Computing at DCU and the director of the Centre for Digital Video Processing. His research work addresses analysis and content-based retrieval of all kinds of multimedia information and sensor-web technologies. Since 2001 he has coordinated the annual TRECVid activity, which benchmarks the effectiveness of video search and retrieval and coordinates submissions from almost 70 research groups worldwide.

Chantal Soulé-Dupuy received the PhD degree in computer science from the University of Toulouse 3 (France) in 1990. She is currently professor of computer science at the University of Toulouse 1 and serves as the head of the Department of Computer Science (since November 2003). Her recent research addresses information modeling and retrieval in digital libraries, personalized and social search. She conducts and supervises research on these topics within the Toulouse Computing Research Laboratory (IRIT - UMR 5505).

Eddie Soulier is associate professor in computer science in the University of Technology of Troyes. He belongs to Tech-CICO laboratory (Cooperative technology for innovation and organisational changes). Its PhD deals with storytelling technics for knowledge sharing in virtual communities in the field of consulting firms. His research focuses on management information system, storytelling for knowledge engineering, communities of practice, business process management and service engineering, and systems design in the computer supported cooperative work perspective.

Nima Taghipour is a research assistant in the AELT research group at the Department of Computer Engineering and Information Technology of Amirkabir University of Technology (Tehran Polytechnic). He received a master's diploma in information technology from Amirkabir University of Technology (2008-Iran) and a bachelor's in computer engineering from Shahid Beheshti University with his major in software engineering (2005-Iran). He has also been working as a system analyst and designer in various industrial projects. His research interests include machine learning, data mining, Web mining, information retrieval and recommendation systems. His master's thesis is titled, *A Hybrid Web Recommendation System Based on Web Mining*, with a focus on exploiting reinforcement learning techniques for web page recommendation, i.e. the personalized suggestion of relevant web pages.

Marlène Villanova-Oliver received her PhD in computer science at the Grenoble Institute of Technology in 2002. She is assistant professor in Computer Science at the University Pierre Mendès France (Grenoble, France) since 2003. She is member of the STEAMER research team at the Grenoble Computer Science Laboratory (LIG) since its creation in 2007. She has been member of the SIGMA research team at the Software, Systems and Networks Laboratory (LSR-IMAG) from 1999 to 2006. Her research interests include adaptability to users and context of use, web-based information systems, geographic information systems and representation of spatio-temporal information.

Corinne Zayani hold her PhD in computer science at Information Technology Research Institute IRIT of University Paul Sabatier (Toulouse - France) under the direction of prof. Florence Sedes. Currently she is lecturer in Tunis; her research works are treating user modeling and personalization.

Index